D0605751

Basic Conversational French

REPUBLIQUE FRANÇAISE
0,95
BOULOGNE SUR MER
POSTES
1967

REPUBLIQUE FRANÇAISE
POSTES
1,00
FRANÇOIS 1er PAR JEAN CLOUET

Basic Conversational French

Fourth Edition

JULIAN HARRIS **ANDRÉ LÉVÊQUE**

UNIVERSITY OF WISCONSIN

HOLT, RINEHART AND WINSTON

New York Toronto London

The *Student's Book* for **Basic Conversational French, Fourth Edition** is accompanied by the following Supplementary Materials:

Filmstrips: VOICI LA FRANCE!
(Four full color Filmstrips, Script-Booklet and one reel of Tape.)

Laboratory Manual.

Disc Recordings.

Magnetic Tape Recordings.

For further detailed information please write to the publisher.

Library of Congress Catalog Card Number: 68–18697

Printed in the United States of America

03-069695-X

0123 19 987654

Table of Contents

REFERENCE MATERIALS

Introduction

The present edition differs from the previous one in several ways:

(1) In response to numerous requests, we have written a Laboratory Manual and prepared ready-to-use tapes to accompany it. The taped lessons contain exercises in listening, in listening and repeating, in answering questions, in asking questions, various types of substitution and transformation exercises, and *Dictées.* (2) We have reworked extensively Grammar Units 7 (descriptive adjectives), 10 and 12 (personal pronouns, stressed and unstressed), 18 (relative pronouns), and 22 (the subjunctive), and we have clarified certain paragraphs of a number of others. (3) We have revised two of the Conversations (8 and 12) and made a few changes in several others. (4) We have increased the number of substitution exercises, frequently introducing "new" words whose meaning can be easily deduced from the context. (5) Beginning with Grammar Unit 13, we have included a series of paragraphs or stories in the present tense in French that are to be transformed to the past, future, conditional or pluperfect. This is a refinement of the transformation exercises of earlier editions and it is devised to give the students practice in using correctly the imperfect and the *passé composé*, and so on. (6) We have replaced practically all English-to-French exercises by all-French ones except a few review exercises designed to overcome "interference", e.g.: Dites en français: 1. What time is it? 2. How is the weather? 3. This is the first time . . ., and so on. (7) We have kept the *Thèmes;* for while some teachers do not like them, others find them invaluable. However, we have simplified those that proved to be somewhat "tricky". The *Thèmes* seem to be particularly helpful in overcoming the students' tendency to imagine that "I was" is always "J'étais" in French, and so on. (8) We have restudied the reference materials and made extensive revisions — particularly in the section entitled "How to get a good French accent". (9) Many details have been changed: John is called "Jean"; Roger and Marie and Roger and Mme Deschamps use the *tutoiement* (Jean et Roger still use *vous* if only for pedagogical reasons); prices have been changed; a few informal expressions (but not slang) have been introduced; *causeries* are suggested; and so on.

The basic philosophy of the book remains unchanged. We always take as our point of departure the following assumptions: that language is something you *do*, that the easiest and most natural way to learn a language is by using it, and that — at least for literate adults and adolescents — a systematic study of practical grammar is an invaluable aid. In constructing teaching materials, we have always proceeded from the known to the unknown, one step at a time, for we regard this procedure as absolutely basic in language teaching and language learning. Dialogs and grammar units are so arranged that students learn concrete examples before being introduced to abstract principles of grammar. For example, before they come to the first grammar unit, they have four units with dialogs and exercises that give them practice in answering and asking questions in French, in thinking in French about a few very simple matters, and in "reacting" in French to a few everyday situations. From the very beginning, they are building up the habit of hearing, understanding, and saying simple things in French.

The exercises of the first dialogs are nothing more than a series of devices to get the students to use correctly, intelligently, and with confidence the phrases of the dialogs. The first grammar unit presents systematically what they have already more or less learned about the forms and use of definite and indefinite articles. It is based entirely on examples that have appeared in the preceding dialogs. The exercises of this and other grammar units, like those in the units devoted to dialogs, should be done orally of course, and with books closed. They are frankly intended to drive home the principles of French grammar. Although we try to avoid an over-emphasis upon grammar, we are convinced that such material should be presented fully and with the greatest possible clarity; because if students are not given comprehensible explanations, they will make rules for themselves — phony rules, of course, since they are certainly not in a position to make tenable generalizations about French usage. We have not attempted to explain all the fine points of French grammar; but we have tried to explain without over-simplification whatever we *do* present, and we have emphasized points of syntax in which French is different from English — points which have been stumbling blocks for generations and generations of young Americans. Each grammar unit throughout the book is preceded by dialogs in which a few new forms and constructions are worked on orally and aurally preparatory to being considered from the point of view of grammar. Thus, instead of trying to learn the subtleties, say, of the use of the partitive by poring over abstract explanations, the students first learn a few concrete examples in easily remembered contexts, and, a few days later, come fore-armed to the complicated matter of the use of *du, de la, des*, and *pas de*. With rare exceptions, new vocabulary items are introduced in the dialogs so that the grammar lessons can be devoted exclusively to the business of understanding principles of grammar and learning how they work in practice. While the grammar lessons *look* long, it is surprising how quickly points of grammar can be assimilated when the students know in advance what the examples really mean: many of them know, *before* the lesson on the partitive, that you say: "Nous n'avons *pas de* café", but "Nous n'aimons *pas le* café".

A WORD ABOUT TIMING. We recommend that all exercises be done at a fairly rapid tempo. (1) It is much easier to avoid diphthongization of vowels and over-emphasis on consonants if a phrase is uttered quickly; (2) a class in which one student is allowed to ponder endlessly over a response that is obvious to other students becomes very tiresome; and (3) if students are given time to break each utterance up into words, to translate each word into English, to decide the proper response, and to translate this response into French, some of them will do so! Students of course have the habit of analyzing whatever they do not understand in English; but while it is appropriate to analyze difficult passages, it is bad practice, if not absurd, to go through a long rigmarole to explain things that are perfectly obvious to the students.

The exercises in which students merely repeat phrases present no difficulty in timing — since the instructor determines the rhythm. This exercise should set the pace for responses in subsequent exercises so that the answers to questions (*Répondez en français*) should be almost in the same rhythm. It should take only a *little more time* for students to respond to the command (*Dites-moi* or *Demandez-moi*) than it does to repeat a phrase. But this type of exercise calls for a little dramatization — at least until the students get the hang of it. At first it is necessary to reiterate the rubric for each question and to give a sample response. For example, we say "*Demandez* (point to the student) *à Monsieur Hughes* (point to an imaginary Mr. Hughes) *comment il va.*" Then we ask (looking at the imaginary Mr. Hughes) "*Comment allez-vous, monsieur?*" *Then* we repeat the command *without gestures:* "*Demandez à Monsieur Hughes comment il va.*" By this time the students catch on and are ready to do the exercise. This seems terribly roundabout at first because it is so much easier just to have the students repeat phrases. But the idea is not to get students to repeat phrases as many times as possible (the way they used to copy verb forms 50 times), but to get them to understand and use phrases intelligently, correctly, and with assurance. By understanding the "new word" *il y a* without having it explained, the students begin to develop the ability to sense what words *must* mean. And seeing what a word *must* mean in a specific context is vastly more instructive than memorizing one of its English equivalents. This kind of exercise calls their imagination into play, makes them swim beyond their depth for a moment, and helps to wean them from a sort of literal-mindedness that besets the path of beginning foreign language students.

Pattern Practice exercises also should be done with verve. The purpose of these exercises is to give students further practice in using and varying authentic patterns of the language. At first glance, some of them may look absurdly simple and "much too easy for serious students!" But, as we have often insisted, you learn a language by using it, not by talking about it and not by solving problems — at least not at this level. The exercises are easy — so easy that the student can do them correctly without worrying *how* to do them. And by doing good pattern practice exercises, students repeat over and over a pattern that they understand while concentrating upon remembering and repeating a variation of one element of the pattern. We find that this helps to drive the pattern home far better than mere repetition. We hold that learning a foreign language is not a matter of memorizing words, conjugations, rules, or even patterns of the language, but, rather, a matter of learning to understand and use them all intelligently and correctly. Listening and repeating until one can say phrases correctly and glibly looms large in this method at first. In fact, that is all a student can do at first. However, *at first* does not mean the first few days, weeks, or months, but *the first few minutes of the first class.* As soon as a student can understand and repeat a phrase correctly, he must move into the next stage of learning, and use the phrase correctly in response to a question or a statement. The third stage of mastery of a pattern is the point at which the student can recall and use it without outside stimulus. The fourth stage is the point at which the student can recall the basic pattern and use it with variations without outside stimulus.

We have constructed a great number of exercises that will give students practice in varying the subject of a sentence, or the verb, or the object, or the adjective modifiers, or the adverbial modifiers, and so on. At first they are so simple that beginners can do them quickly, correctly, and with confidence. The answers are implicit in the questions — and intentionally so. After a few weeks, the exercises become more subtle; but throughout the book, we have tried to construct exercises in such a way that students can scarcely avoid making correct responses. In reality, hearing and understanding in French what they are supposed to do is perhaps quite as instructive as giving the correct response. The experience of hearing a phrase and retaining it long enough to answer it is a necessary step towards remembering it for twenty-four hours or six weeks. In spite of the old saw, we find that instead of learning by making mistakes, beginning language students who cannot do exercises correctly build up dreadful inhibitions against foreign language study!

Each dialog is accompanied by an English translation whose functions are (1) to provide a means by which students can understand precisely and immediately what a given sentence means, and (2) to serve as a prompt-script from which they can practice saying the French sentences of the dialog at home. With this arrangement, it is possible to proceed without having them begin by studying definitions and memorizing lists of words; in fact, *on the first day* they begin to work at the stage which many classes reach only after long and tedious manipulation of more or less artificial sentences, word-lists, and abstract definitions. And what is more important, from the first day students begin to acquire mastery of authentic French word patterns — patterns that they will always find useful in speaking, reading, or writing in French.

WRITTEN WORK. We recommend that students begin to practice writing in French before the end of the first week. On the day they take up Conversation 2 audio-lingually, we ask them to write a *Dictée* from Conversation 1 (See Special Note on p. 6). Thereafter, for each new dialog, the students are expected to learn to write the phrases of the preceding one. In this way, they learn that the art of spelling is merely a means of recording a language (rather than the language itself).

QUIZZES. We find that a short weekly or at least a fortnightly quiz is an invaluable teaching device. From day to day, students should be encouraged to use the language orally as much as possible, and without worrying too much about mistakes; but it is necessary to keep a very careful check on the progress each student makes, and to keep each student informed as to the result of his work. The first quiz will necessarily consist only of a *Dictée*, a few questions asked orally in French that are to be answered in French, perhaps a series of sentences in French for which the students will be expected to give the English equivalent, and a question to test their ability to use the prepositions *à* and *de* with the definite article. All the material in the first quizzes will of course be taken from the dialogs. As the first semester progresses, and as the exercises become more and more varied, any of the types of questions found in the exercises can be used. For variety, true-false statements may be included, but it is very difficult to construct such questions that are not trite. The *Dictée* may occasionally be replaced by a simple anecdote that the students retell in their own words though, again, it is not always easy to find anecdotes that are simple enough to be comprehensible and at the same time capable of interesting the students. After a few grammar units have been studied, questions calling for a thorough mastery of points of grammar can be included, and after a reader has been begun, passages can be included for translation into English or as a basis for questions in French to be answered in French.

READING IN FRENCH. In the present edition, the eight prose sketches (*Lectures*) that deal with the subject matter of the dialogs (formerly grouped together in a sort of appendix) are placed in the text itself. Before we have the students read the first sketch (based on Conversations 1–5), we explain to them that reading is, essentially, understanding what is written or printed, and that reading the sketches in this book is little more than understanding the written form of a few phrases — slightly rearranged, of course — that they have been understanding and using orally for some time. To introduce a reading exercise, we make it a point to read a paragraph aloud while the students listen and read it silently. In a reading lesson, the books are of course always open. (How else could the students read?) We have tried to combine text, subject matter, and illustrations so that from the beginning students can have the experience of reading in French something that they can actually understand *in French*. The purpose of reading aloud to them and with them is (1) to give them the experience of reading by thought groups instead of word by word or syllable by syllable, (2) to show them from the beginning that they *can* read for meaning without constantly resorting to the vocabulary, and (3) to give them the pleasure(!) of hearing, seeing, and understanding French. A reading lesson should never lapse into a pronunciation exercise, or a grammar drill, or a "chasse aux mots", or, worst of all, a "word-calling" session; it should always be practice in trying to understand the meaning of the text in French.

We try to give students the experience of reading in French with understanding and pleasure, in the hope that they will not form the habit of trying to find a supposed English equivalent of every word in a passage before they attempt to understand what it is all about. If they are left to their own devices, however, they will go to any amount of trouble to avoid thinking — underlining "new" words, looking up the same words time after time, writing them down, memorizing English equivalents, and "overlearning" them. Meanwhile, instead of learning to read in French, they are building the habit of trying to "get by" without learning to read!

We recommend that after about three weeks, students be given short reading assignments once a week in a French reader, brief periods of practice in sight reading, and, eventually, a little outside reading. The reader best adapted to our method is, in our opinion, the Harris and Lévêque, *Basic French Reader*, revised, (published by Holt, Rinehart and Winston, Inc.). It goes without saying that students who ask and answer questions in French in connection with the dialogs and grammar units, can do the same in connection with easy texts of a French reader. Such exercises need not be used to the exclusion of brief translation exercises, but whenever one can be sure the students understand a passage in French, it is obviously good practice to ask them questions on it in French rather than to have them translate it into English.

We find that questionnaires such as those we have provided help students reach the point where they can understand the text in French without translating it into English. When a student cannot grasp the meaning of a question — and this will frequently happen, of course — there are several ways of helping him understand it: (1) Let him read the question. (2) Have him repeat the question in French before trying to answer it. (3) Answer the question in French and then ask the student to answer it. (4) Explain what the question means. (5) Tell him precisely where the answer may be found in the book. Only after a great deal of practice in listening to questions and finding the answers in the book can students be expected to prepare a reading lesson well enough to answer questions in French without referring to the book.

This may seem like a lot of trouble. And it certainly takes more effort (on the part of the instructor), at least at first, than it does to have students look up words, write them between the lines (or elsewhere) and "translate". But it is worth the trouble, because students learn more quickly to read a printed text if the emphasis is always upon understanding *meaning* instead of on learning words. Translating a word or phrase here and there can frequently give a clue to the meaning of a passage in the foreign language, but it is all but impossible to make a decent translation of a paragraph if you do not really know precisely what it means. (Cf. Introduction to our Basic French Reader.)

HOW WE GO ABOUT IT. We have been so often asked for a description of the way we teach the dialogs and grammar lessons, that although it may seem almost supererogatory, we have decided to explain here precisely how we proceed. We realize that there are many other ways of going about it and that some of them are undoubtedly better than ours. We also realize that excellent results can be had by strictly following the exercises as they are printed in the book. But here is the way we do it. (Cf. Teacher's Manual for our Basic Conversational French, 4th edition.)

At the first meeting of the class, we give the students a mimeographed schedule of assignments and quizzes for the semester. (We give 30-minute quizzes every two weeks and we cover 38 units in the first semester — that is, not quite three units per week, on the average, for sixteen weeks.) We explain very briefly the basic assumptions of the course and the procedures that are to be used, insisting especially on the importance (1) of listening with all possible attention to the way the instructor and the voices on the tapes utter each phrase, (2) of trying to understand the meaning of each French phrase each time it is repeated, and (3) of trying to reproduce each phrase precisely as the instructor and the voices on the tapes utter it — with proper intonation and, when appropriate, with gestures. We explain that the difficult part of French pronunciation is not *producing* the sounds but *hearing* them as they are! We point out also that a foreign language must be learned bit by bit and that trying to learn two weeks' work on the night before quizzes — as students do in certain courses — simply will not work.

After this brief introduction (five minutes at most), we explain that the first dialog takes place between John Hughes, a young American chemical engineer who is living in Paris, and the concierge, or caretaker-superintendent, of the apartment house in which he lives. Then we say, "The concierge says to John, Good morning, Sir, *Bonjour, monsieur*. *Bonjour, monsieur*. *Bonjour, monsieur*. Please listen with all possible concentration. Notice that the greeting contains four short, equally-stressed syllables. *Bonjour, monsieur*. Now repeat after me: *Bon-jour mon-sieur*." It takes a great many repetitions and much listening to get the students to utter this phrase correctly. In fact, this may be the most difficult and important step in their entire language-learning career! But the best time to teach French pronunciation is before students build up bad habits of pronunciation and phony notions about French accent. If they start off saying something like: bong-zhoor′, mon-shoor′, instead of really learning how to say it, they will find it vastly more difficult to learn to say it correctly later on.

After they can say *Bonjour, monsieur* in four short, equally-stressed syllables and without adding an *r* to *monsieur*, we introduce John's answer *Bonjour, madame*. While it takes six or seven minutes to teach them to say *Bonjour, monsieur*, it then takes only a minute or two to get them to say *Bonjour, madame* correctly — again in four short, equally-stressed syllables. But the accent-less rhythm of French phrases must be carefully practiced day after day so that the students will not slip into the habit of uttering French phrases with American rhythms. Detailed suggestions for this sort of practice will be found in the special section on "How to Get a Good French Accent" (page 361 ff.).

When the first two lines are more or less mastered, we say to the class: "*Dites-moi bonjour*" with an appropriate gesture at the word *moi*. Some of the students will understand at once and say "*Bonjour, monsieur*." We then repeat "*Dites-moi bonjour*" and all the students respond. In teaching the first class, we say "Repeat after me" a few times in English, but thereafter we give the direction in French. Translation or explanation of *Répétez* or *Répétez après moi* after the first day is quite unnecessary.

As soon as they can respond easily to *Dites-moi bonjour*, we point to an imaginary John Hughes and say "*Dites bonjour à Monsieur Hughes, Dites bonjour à la concierge*," and so on. We do this at a fairly quick tempo so the students will develop the habit of grasping meaning immediately.

After the initial greeting is more or less mastered, the next two lines are taken up in the same way. We say "The concierge says, Are you Mr. Hughes, *Êtes-vous Monsieur Hughes?*" and so on. But instead of seven or eight minutes, the second two lines can be introduced in three or four. As soon as they can say *Êtes-vous Monsieur Hughes?* we say "*Demandez-moi si je suis Monsieur Hughes,*" as above, and then, "*Demandez à ce monsieur* (point to an imaginary person) *s'il est Monsieur Hughes.*"

Each pair of lines takes less time than the preceding pair. After each pair of lines, we return to the beginning of the dialog and have the students say as much of it as they can — prompting whenever it is necessary. We work through the entire dialog in this way, but at an increasing tempo. This takes about 25–30 minutes.

We then use ten to twelve minutes in a variety of ways. Sometimes we have the students repeat the phrases of the dialog while looking at the French text, or again we tell them to look only at the English — for the first two or three weeks. We are not sure that there is any difference in the result, but we rather think it is a good idea to have the students see the French as soon as they have learned how it sounds so that they will begin to grasp the relationship between spelling and pronunciation. We find, moreover, that even when we tell them not to look at the French, many of the students do so anyway; and if they have no copy of the material used, they will write down in a phony phonetic spelling what they think they hear. This is infinitely worse than French orthography! Besides, there are always a certain number of visual-minded students who find it very upsetting to be told not to look at the French text. In any case, if students are constantly working with the tapes — listening, responding, recording, comparing their pronunciation with that of French voices — conventional French spelling will not be such a handicap as it was in the days when students were supposed to figure out from a lot of rules (and exceptions) about silent letters how each word *would be* pronounced. Sometimes (but not the first day) we have students run through a dialog while looking at the IPA transcription so that they will know how to consult a transcription whenever they wish to do so. Usually, we do as many of the exercises as we can; but whatever else we do on the first day, we always make it a point to work seriously on the French uvular **r** and the French **u** (see pp. 366–367).

Finally, we devote the last ten minutes or so of the hour to running rapidly through the dialog in a variety of ways: the teacher says the lines of the concierge and the students, those of John. Then we reverse the rôles. Next, one half of the class says the lines of the concierge and the others those of John. Then two of the more dynamic students run through the dialog alone.

As we remarked above, we are not at all sure that this way of doing it produces any better results in the long run than following the lesson precisely as it stands in the book; but we feel that the class may possibly get off to a faster start if the students are constantly being told (forced) to listen, to repeat, to answer, to ask, and so on. This change of pace is one way of getting them to practice a great deal without lapsing at any time into the stultifying business of absent-minded parroting. (We have never approved the practice of 50-minute periods of "mimicry-memorizing".)

As for the grammar units, we run through the explanation of one paragraph, have the students repeat the examples carefully and do the exercises based on that paragraph at once. Then we take up the rest of the lesson paragraph by paragraph.

In addition to the work in class, we recommend that students work on the exercises three or four hours a week in small sections with skilled teaching assistants or with tapes under the guidance of an experienced laboratory assistant. We believe it is better to begin to work on a dialog in class than to have students study it ahead of time. When they study a dialog *before* the class, they are sure to make all sorts of mistakes in pronunciation; but after a dialog has been thoroughly worked over in class, serious study at home or in the laboratory will greatly strengthen the correct impressions that have been planted.

ACKNOWLEDGMENTS. Although it would be impossible to mention by name all who have contributed to the improvement of successive versions of the Harris and Lévêque books, we would like to express again our deep indebtedness to Pierre Delattre and Madame Jeanne Varney Pleasants for suggestions concerning the pronunciation exercises and to our colleagues in this University — including hundreds of young and knowledgeable teaching assistants. Many of them have given us invaluable suggestions for clarifying details of pronunciation, usage, or presentation. Others have passed on to us teaching devices that they have found effective. Still others have tried out new kinds of exercises for us. We take this opportunity also of thanking the teachers from all over the country who have generously sent us their observations and impressions as well as their desiderata for new editions. Without their ideas, their interest and their encouragement, we might never have undertaken the present edition. We hope they will give us their reaction to it and especially that they will call our attention to its weaknesses so that they may eventually be corrected.

J. H.
A. L.

The University of Wisconsin
Madison, Wisconsin

Marseille

En France

Paris

Paris

JE REVIENS

Bourgogne

Marseille

Bretagne

Marseille

Vannes

Le Pont du Gard

BASIC CONVERSATIONAL FRENCH

PARIS: LA TOUR EIFFEL

Getting Acquainted

As John Hughes, a young American chemist, leaves his apartment on the Avenue de l'Observatoire in Paris, he speaks to the concierge of the building. (A concierge is the doorkeeper, janitress, and general caretaker of an apartment house or hotel.)

LA CONCIERGE – 1Bonjour, monsieur.	THE CONCIERGE – 1*Good morning, sir.*
JEAN HUGHES – 2Bonjour, madame.	JOHN HUGHES – 2*Good morning, (Madam).*
LA CONCIERGE – 3Êtes-vous M. Hughes?	THE CONCIERGE – 3*Are you Mr. Hughes?*
JEAN HUGHES – 4Oui, madame. Je suis Jean Hughes.	JOHN HUGHES – 4*Yes, (Madam) I am John Hughes.*
LA CONCIERGE – 5Comment allez-vous, monsieur?	THE CONCIERGE – 5*How do you do, sir?*
JOHN HUGHES – 6Bien, merci. 7Et vous-même?	JOHN HUGHES – 6*Well, thank you.* 7*And you (yourself)?*
LA CONCIERGE – 8Pas mal, merci.	THE CONCIERGE – 8*Not bad (thank you).*
JEAN HUGHES – 9Parlez-vous anglais?	JOHN HUGHES – 9*Do you speak English?*
LA CONCIERGE – 10Non, je ne parle pas anglais. 11Mais vous parlez français, n'est-ce pas?	THE CONCIERGE – 10*No, I don't speak English.* 11*But you speak French, don't you?*
JEAN HUGHES – 12Oui, madame, je parle un peu français.	JOHN HUGHES – 12*Yes, (Madam) I speak French a little.*
LA CONCIERGE – 13Voici une lettre pour vous.	THE CONCIERGE – 13*Here is a letter for you.*
JEAN HUGHES – 14Merci beaucoup.	JOHN HUGHES – 14*Thank you very much.*
LA CONCIERGE – 15A votre service, monsieur.	THE CONCIERGE – 15*You are welcome, (sir).**
JEAN HUGHES – 16Au revoir, madame.	JOHN HUGHES – 16*Good-bye, (Madam).*
LA CONCIERGE – 17Au revoir, monsieur.	THE CONCIERGE – 17*Good-bye, sir.*

* It is not necessary to say *you are welcome* in French, but various expressions are frequently used: **De rien, Il n'y a pas de quoi,** or **Je vous en prie.**

I. Exercices de rythme.*

A. QUATRE SYLLABES. *Repeat in four short, equally stressed syllables:*

1. Bonjour monsieur.
2. Bonjour madamɇ.
3. Merci monsieur.
4. Merci madamɇ.
5. Merci beaucoup.
6. Au rɇvoir monsieur.
7. Au rɇvoir madamɇ.

B. CINQ SYLLABES. *Repeat in five short, equally stressed syllables:*

(1)

1. Bonjour madɇmoisellɇ.
2. Merci madɇmoisellɇ.
3. Au rɇvoir madɇmoisellɇ.
4. A votre servicɇ.

(2)

1. Êtɇs-vous Monsieur Hughɇs?
2. Comment allez-vous?
3. Parlez-vous français?
4. Parlez-vous anglais?
5. Jɇ parlɇ un peu français.
6. Jɇ parlɇ un peu anglais.

C. SIX SYLLABES. *Repeat in six short, equally stressed syllables:*

1. Merci beaucoup monsieur.
2. Merci beaucoup madamɇ.
3. Je nɇ parle pas français.
4. Je nɇ parle pas anglais.
5. Mais vous parlez français.
6. Mais vous parlez anglais.

D. SEPT SYLLABES. *Repeat in seven short, equally stressed syllables:*

1. Vous parlez français n'est-cɇ pas?
2. Vous parlez anglais n'est-cɇ pas?
3. Jɇ parlɇ un peu français monsieur.
4. Jɇ parlɇ un peu français madamɇ.
5. Jɇ parlɇ un peu anglais monsieur.
6. Voici unɇ lettre pour vous.

E. HUIT SYLLABES. *Repeat in eight short equally stressed syllables:*

1. Je nɇ parle pas français monsieur.
2. Je nɇ parle pas français madamɇ.
3. Je nɇ parle pas anglais monsieur.
4. Je nɇ parle pas anglais madamɇ.

---

*In order to make the rhythm exercises perfectly clear, silent e's are printed ɇ and commas are omitted. For additional pronunciation exercises, see pp. 365–367.

II. *Donnez une réponse convenable à chacune des expressions suivantes* (Give a suitable response to each of the following expressions):

1. Bonjour, monsieur. [Bonjour, monsieur. *or*, Bonjour, madame. *or*, Bonjour, mademoiselle.]
2. Êtes-vous Monsieur Hughes? [Oui, madame. Je suis Jean Hughes.]
3. Comment allez-vous? [Bien, merci. Et vous-même?]
4. Parlez-vous anglais? [Non, je ne parle pas anglais.]
5. Vous parlez français, n'est-ce pas? [Oui, je parle un peu français.]
6. Voici une lettre pour vous. [Merci beaucoup.]
7. Merci beaucoup. [A votre service, monsieur.]
8. Au revoir, madame. [Au revoir, monsieur.]

III. *Dites en français* (Say in French):

1. Dites-moi bonjour. [Bonjour, monsieur. Bonjour, madame. Bonjour, mademoiselle.]
2. Dites bonjour à Monsieur Hughes. [Bonjour, monsieur.]
3. Dites bonjour à la concierge. [Bonjour, madame.]
4. Dites-moi au revoir. [Au revoir, monsieur. Au revoir, madame. Au revoir, mademoiselle.]
5. Dites au revoir à M. Hughes. [Au revoir, monsieur.]
6. Dites au revoir à la concierge. [Au revoir, madame.]
7. Dites-moi merci. [Merci, monsieur, madame, mademoiselle.]
8. Dites merci à M. Hughes. [Merci, monsieur.]
9. Dites merci à la concierge. [Merci, madame.]

IV. *Demandez en français* (Ask in French):

1. Demandez-moi si je suis M. Hughes. [Êtes-vous Monsieur Hughes?]
2. Demandez-moi si je parle français. [Parlez-vous français?]
3. Demandez à M. Hughes s'il parle français. [Parlez-vous français?]
4. Demandez à la concierge si elle parle anglais. [Parlez-vous anglais?]
5. Demandez-moi comment je vais. [Comment allez-vous, monsieur? *or*, Comment allez-vous, madame? *or*, Comment allez-vous, mademoiselle?]
6. Demandez à M. Hughes comment il va. [Comment allez-vous, monsieur?]
7. Demandez à la concierge comment elle va. [Comment allez-vous, madame?]

V. Dialogue.

Act out the scene between John Hughes and the concierge. Practice doing the scene until you are perfectly at home in both roles.

Special Note

The exercises of Conversation 2 will include a short dictation taken from Conversation 1. Before the next meeting of the class, you should learn to write all the sentences of the first dialog.

The easiest and most natural way to do this is to spell through a phrase while looking at it, pronounce it correctly, then write it down without looking at it, and finally check what you have written against the original. When you can write the first phrase correctly, continue the same exercise until you can write all the sentences of the first dialog.

The purpose of this exercise is to help you learn to write correctly in French. A brief dictation will be included in the exercises of each new dialog hereafter, and you should learn to write the sentences of the dialog that is indicated in the lesson.

A PARIS

A FONTAINEBLEAU

Asking for Directions

John Hughes is spending a few days visiting some of the interesting places in the Île-de-France (the region around Paris). He has just arrived at Chantilly where he plans to see the château, museum, racetrack, etc. He asks for information first in the railroad station and then on the street.

A la gare

JEAN – 1Pardon, monsieur. Où est le château, s'il vous plaît?

UN EMPLOYÉ – 2Tout droit, monsieur.

JEAN – 3Où est le musée?

L'EMPLOYÉ – 4Le musée est dans le château.

JEAN – 5Y a-t-il un restaurant près du château?

L'EMPLOYÉ – 6Oui, monsieur. Il y a un restaurant près du château.

JEAN – 7Merci beaucoup.

L'EMPLOYÉ – 8De rien, monsieur.

At the Station

JOHN – 1*Pardon me, sir. Please tell me where the château is.*

AN EMPLOYEE – 2*Straight ahead, sir.*

JOHN – 3*Where is the museum?*

THE EMPLOYEE – 4*The museum is in the château.*

JOHN – 5*Is there a restaurant near the château?*

THE EMPLOYEE – 6*Yes, sir. There is a restaurant near the château.*

JOHN – 7*Thank you very much.*

THE EMPLOYEE – 8*You are welcome, sir.*

PARIS: LA PLACE DE LA CONCORDE

Dans la rue

JEAN – 9*(A un passant)* Pardon, monsieur. Où est le bureau de poste?

LE PASSANT – 10La poste* est sur la place, là-bas, à gauche.

JEAN – 11Y a-t-il un bureau de tabac† près d'ici?

LE PASSANT – 12Mais oui, monsieur. Il y a un bureau de tabac dans la rue de la Paix.

JEAN – 13Où est la rue de la Paix?

LE PASSANT 14– A droite, monsieur.

JEAN – 15Merci beaucoup.

In the Street

JOHN – 9(To a passer-by) *Pardon me, sir. Where is the post office?*

THE PASSER-BY – 10*The post office is on the square, over there, to the left.*

JOHN – 11*Is there a tobacco shop near here?*

THE PASSER-BY – 12*Oh, yes, sir. There is a tobacco shop on (in) the Rue de la Paix.*

JOHN – 13*Where is the Rue de la Paix?*

THE PASSER-BY – 14*To the right, sir.*

JOHN – 15*Thank you very much.*

* Both **la poste** and **le bureau de poste** are commonly used.
† A **bureau de tabac** is a tobacco shop in which one can buy also stamps, stationery, newspapers, and in which there is usually a bar.

I. Exercices de rythme.*

A. QUATRE SYLLABES:

1. Où est lɇ château?
2. Où est lɇ musée?

B. CINQ SYLLABES:

1. Où est lɇ bureau dɇ poste?
2. Où est lɇ restaurant?

C. SIX SYLLABES:

1. Où est lɇ bureau dɇ tabac?
2. Où est la rue dɇ la Paix?
3. Y a-t-il un restaurant . . . ?
4. Il y a un restaurant . . .?

D. SEPT SYLLABES:

1. Où est lɇ château, s'il vous plaît?
2. Où est lɇ musée, s'il vous plaît?

II. Substitutions. *Répétez les phrases suivantes, en substituant les mots indiqués* (Repeat the following with the suggested substitutions):

1. Où est le château?

   le musée / le bureau de tabac / le bureau de poste / le restaurant

2. Le château est près d'ici.

   Le musée / Le bureau de tabac / La poste / Le restaurant

3. Le musée est près d'ici.

   là-bas, à droite / là-bas, à gauche / sur la place / près du château

4. Il y a un restaurant près du château.

   près d'ici / sur la place / dans la rue de la Paix / dans le château

5. Y a-t-il un restaurant près d'ici?

   près du château / dans le château / sur la place / dans la rue de la Paix

III. *Répondez en français, d'après le texte* (according to the dialog):

1. Où est le château, s'il vous plaît? **2.** Où est le musée? **3.** Où est la poste? **4.** Y a-t-il un restaurant près du château? **5.** Où est le bureau de poste? **6.** Y a-t-il un bureau de tabac près d'ici? **7.** Où est la rue de la Paix? **8.** Comment allez-vous? **9.** Parlez-vous français? **10.** Parlez-vous anglais?

---

* For additional pronunciation exercises, see pp. 368–369.

IV. *Demandez-moi:*

Ex.:—Demandez-moi où est le château.
—Où est le château, s'il vous plaît?

1. où est la gare. **2.** où est le bureau de poste. **3.** s'il y a un restaurant près d'ici. **4.** s'il y a un bureau de tabac près d'ici. **5.** s'il y a un restaurant près du château. **6.** s'il y a un musée dans le château. **7.** s'il y a un restaurant dans la rue de la Paix. **8.** s'il y a un bureau de tabac dans la rue de la Paix.

V. *Comptez en français de un à dix* (Count in French from 1 to 10):

1. un (1), deux (2), trois (3), quatre (4), cinq (5). **2.** six (6), sept (7), huit (8), neuf (9), dix (10). **3.** un franc, deux francs, trois francs. **4.** quatre francs, cinq francs, six francs. **5.** sept francs, huit francs, neuf francs, dix francs. **6.** un étudiant, deux étudiants, trois étudiants. **7.** quatre étudiants, cinq étudiants, six étudiants. **8.** sept étudiants, huit étudiants, neuf étudiants, dix étudiants.

VI. Dictée d'après la Conversation 1, p. 3.

VII. Conversations.

(1)

"Good morning, sir (*Mlle*), (*Madame*). Do you speak English?"
"No, sir, I do not speak English."
"Please tell me where the station is."
"Straight ahead, sir."
"Thank you very much."

(2)

You stop someone and ask for the location of a restaurant.

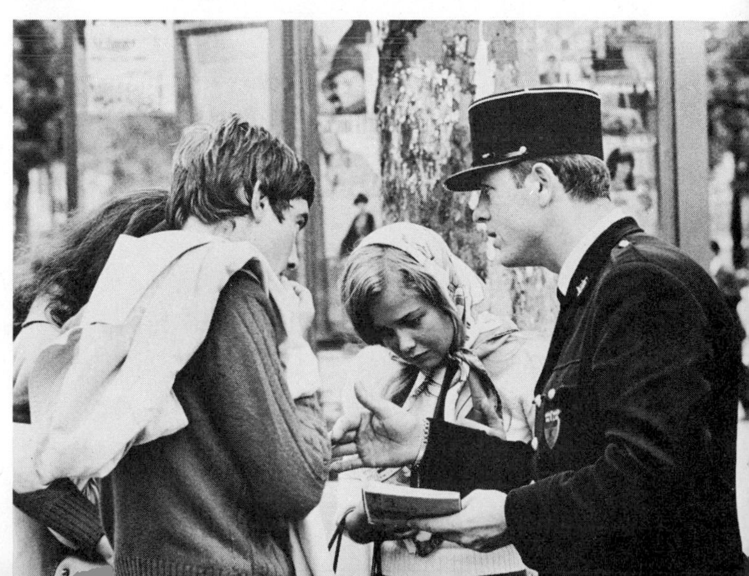

Getting a Hotel

Dans la rue

JEAN – [1]Pardon, où est l'hôtel du Cheval blanc?

UN AGENT DE POLICE – [2]Sur la place, monsieur.

JEAN – [3]Est-ce que c'est loin d'ici?

L'AGENT – [4]Non, ce n'est pas loin d'ici.

JEAN – [5]Est-ce que c'est un bon hôtel?

L'AGENT – [6]Oui, monsieur, c'est un très bon hôtel.

JEAN – [7]Est-ce que la cuisine est bonne?

L'AGENT – [8]Certainement, monsieur. La cuisine est excellente.

JEAN – [9]Y a-t-il un autre hôtel ici?

L'AGENT – [10]Oui, il y a un hôtel en face de l'église.

JEAN – [11]Merci beaucoup.

On the Street

JOHN – [1]*Pardon me, where is the White Horse Inn?*

A POLICEMAN – [2]*On the square, sir.*

JOHN – [3]*Is it far from here?*

THE POLICEMAN – [4]*No, it isn't far (from here).*

JOHN – [5]*Is it a good hotel?*

THE POLICEMAN – [6]*Yes, sir, it is a very good hotel.*

JOHN – [7]*Is the food (cuisine) good?*

THE POLICEMAN – [8]*Certainly, sir. The food is excellent.*

JOHN – [9]*Is there another hotel here?*

THE POLICEMAN – [10]*Yes, there is a hotel opposite the church.*

JOHN – [11]*Thank you very much.*

A l'hôtel du Cheval blanc	At the White Horse Inn
JEAN – 12 Quel est le prix des chambres?	JOHN – 12 *What is the price of rooms?*
L'HÔTELIER – 13 De quinze à vingt-cinq francs,* monsieur.	THE INNKEEPER – 13 *From fifteen to twenty-five francs, sir.*
JEAN – 14 Quel est le prix des repas?	JOHN – 14 *What is the price of meals?*
L'HÔTELIER – 15 Quatre francs pour le petit déjeuner, 16 dix francs pour le déjeuner, 17 et douze francs pour le dîner.	THE INNKEEPER 15 *Four francs for breakfast,* 16 *ten francs for lunch,* 17 *and twelve francs for dinner.*

* 1 franc is currently worth about 20 cents.

A PARIS

I. Substitutions. *Répétez les phrases suivantes, en substituant les mots indiqués:**

1. Est-ce que c'est <u>près d'ici</u>?
   près du château / près de la gare / loin de la gare / loin d'ici
2. Est-ce que <u>l'hôtel</u> est loin d'ici?
   l'hôtel du Cheval blanc / l'autre hôtel / la gare / le musée
3. <u>L'hôtel</u> n'est pas loin d'ici.
   Le musée / La poste / L'autre hôtel / La rue de la Paix
4. Y a-t-il un bon restaurant <u>près d'ici</u>?
   sur la place / près de la gare / près du musée / en face du musée
5. Il y a un hôtel <u>en face de l'église.</u>
   en face de la poste / près de la poste / en face du château / près du château

II. *Répondez en français:*

1. Où est l'hôtel du Cheval blanc? **2.** Est-ce que c'est loin d'ici? **3.** Est-ce que c'est un bon hôtel? **4.** Est-ce que la cuisine est bonne? **5.** Y a-t-il un autre hôtel ici? **6.** Quel est le prix des chambres?

* For pronunciation exercises, see p. 371.

III. *Demandez en français:*

1. où est l'hôtel du Cheval blanc. **2.** si c'est loin d'ici. **3.** si c'est un bon hôtel. **4.** si la cuisine est bonne. **5.** s'il y a un autre hôtel ici. **6.** le prix des chambres. **7.** le prix des repas.

IV. *Mettez les phrases suivantes à la forme interrogative en plaçant* **est-ce qu(e) . . . ?** *devant chacune d'elles* (Put the following sentences in the interrogative form by placing **est-ce qu(e) . . . ?** in front of each of them):

Ex.:—Il y a un bon hôtel près d'ici.
Est-ce qu'il y a un bon hôtel près d'ici?

1. L'hôtel du Cheval blanc est près d'ici. **2.** L'hôtel du Cheval blanc est loin d'ici. **3.** Il y a un bon restaurant près d'ici. **4.** Il y a un restaurant en face de l'église. **5.** Il y a un bureau de tabac dans la rue de la Paix. **6.** Il y a un bureau de tabac en face de la gare. **7.** Il y a un restaurant dans la gare. **8.** La cuisine de l'hôtel du Cheval blanc est bonne.

V. *Comptez en français de onze à vingt:*

1. onze (11), douze (12), treize (13). **2.** quatorze (14), quinze (15), seize (16). **3.** dix-sept (17), dix-huit (18), dix-neuf (19), vingt (20). **4.** onze étudiants, douze étudiants, treize étudiants, quatorze étudiants, quinze étudiants, seize étudiants, dix-sept étudiants, dix-huit étudiants, dix-neuf étudiants, vingt étudiants. **5.** *Donnez les nombres pairs de deux à vingt* (Give the even numbers from 2 to 20). **6.** *Donnez les nombres impairs* (odd numbers) *de un à dix-neuf.* **7.** Dites en français: 1 franc, 11 francs; 2 francs, 12 francs; 3 francs, 13 francs; 4 francs, 14 francs; 5 francs, 15 francs; 6 francs, 16 francs; 7 francs, 17 francs; 8 francs, 18 francs; 9 francs, 19 francs; 10 francs, 20 francs.

VI. Conversation.

"Is there another hotel here?"
"Yes, there is the Hotel Continental."
"Where is the Hotel Continental?"
"On the square, opposite the station."
"What is the price of board and room?"
"Twenty-five francs a day."

VII. Dictée d'après la Conversation 2, pp. 8-9.

0694 10097
PARIS-LYON
COMBS-la-VILLE
-QUINCY
EVRY-PETIT-BOU
**7.50
**3.50
N
0695 10097
PARIS-LYON
COMBS-la-VILLE
-QUINCY
EVRY-PETIT-BOURG
**7.50
**3.50
N
2
51C

Catching a Train

A l'hôtel

L'HÔTELIER – [1]Comment ça va,* monsieur?

JEAN – [2]Ça va bien, merci. [3]Quelle heure est-il?

L'HÔTELIER – [4]Il est onze heures.

JEAN – [5]Est-ce que le déjeuner est prêt?

L'HÔTELIER – [6]Non, monsieur, pas encore. [7]A quelle heure voulez-vous déjeuner?

JEAN – [8]A onze heures et quart, [9]ou à onze heures et demie.

L'HÔTELIER – [10]A quelle heure allez-vous à la gare?

JEAN – [11]Je vais à la gare à midi. [12]Le train pour Paris arrive à midi et quart, n'est-ce pas?

L'HÔTELIER – [13]Non, monsieur. Il arrive à deux heures moins le quart.

JEAN – [14]Alors, je vais déjeuner à midi, comme d'habitude. [15]Est-ce que le bureau de poste est ouvert cet après-midi?

L'HÔTELIER – [16]Oui, monsieur. [17]Il est ouvert de huit heures du matin à sept heures du soir.

At the Hotel

THE INNKEEPER – [1]*How are you, sir?*

JOHN – [2]*Fine, thanks.* [3]*What time is it?*

THE INNKEEPER – [4]*It is eleven o'clock.*

JOHN – [5]*Is lunch ready?*

THE INNKEEPER – [6]*No, sir, not yet.* [7]*At what time do you want to have lunch?*

JOHN – [9]*At a quarter past eleven,* [9]*or at half past eleven.*

THE INNKEEPER – [10]*At what time are you going to the station?*

JOHN – [11]*I am going to the station at noon. The train for Paris arrives at a quarter past twelve, doesn't it?*

THE INNKEEPER – [13]*No, sir. It comes at a quarter of two.*

JOHN – [14]*Then I am going to have lunch at noon, as usual.* [15]*Is the post office open this afternoon?*

THE INNKEEPER – [16]*Yes, sir.* [17]*It is open from eight o'clock in the morning to seven o'clock in the evening.*

---

* **Comment ça va?** is less formal than **comment allez-vous?**

I. Substitutions. *Répétez les phrases suivantes, en substituant les mots indiqués:*

1. Il est onze heures.

dix heures et demie / neuf heures et quart / huit heures moins le quart / midi

2. A quelle heure allez-vous à la gare?

à l'hôtel / au restaurant / au musée / à la poste

3. Je vais à la gare à midi.

à six heures / à dix heures et quart / à cinq heures et demie /à midi moins le quart

4. Le train pour Paris arrive à midi et quart, n'est-ce pas?

à une heure et quart / à deux heures et quart / à deux heures moins le quart / à cinq heures moins le quart

5. Est-ce que le bureau de poste est ouvert cet après-midi?

le musée / le château / le bureau de tabac

6. Il est ouvert de huit heures du matin à sept heures du soir.

neuf heures / dix heures / onze heures

7. Il est ouvert de six heures du matin à six heures du soir.

huit heures / neuf heures / dix heures / sept heures

8. Je vais au musée ce matin.

ce soir / cet après-midi / à midi et demi

II. Exercices d'application.

A. *Mettez les phrases suivantes à la forme interrogative en plaçant* **Est-ce qu(e) . . .** *devant chacune d'elles:*

1. Le déjeuner est prêt. **2.** Le bureau de poste est ouvert cet après-midi. **3.** Le dîner est prêt. **4.** Le musée est dans le château. **5.** Il y a un restaurant près du château. **6.** Il y a un bureau de tabac en face du château. **7.** Il y a un train pour Paris cet après-midi. **8.** Il y a un bon restaurant sur la place. **9.** Le train pour Paris arrive à midi et quart. **10.** Il y a un bureau de tabac dans la rue de la Paix.

B. *Mettez les phrases suivantes à la forme négative:*

Ex.:—Je parle français.
—Je ne parle pas français.

1. Je suis M. Hughes. **2.** Je parle anglais. **3.** Je vais à la gare. **4.** Je vais déjeuner à onze heures et demie. **5.** C'est loin d'ici. **6.** C'est un bon hôtel. **7.** Le déjeuner est prêt. **8.** Le dîner est prêt. **9.** Le bureau de poste est ouvert. **10.** Il est ouvert à huit heures.

III. *Répondez en français, d'après le texte:*

1. Comment ça va? **2.** Quelle heure est-il? **3.** Est-ce que le déjeuner est prêt? **4.** A quelle heure voulez-vous déjeuner? **5.** A quelle heure allez-vous à la gare? **6.** Le train pour Paris arrive à midi et quart, n'est-ce pas? **7.** Est-ce que le bureau de poste est ouvert cet après-midi? **8.** Est-il ouvert à midi? **9.** Est-ce qu'il est ouvert à six heures du soir? **10.** Est-ce que le train pour Paris arrive à midi et demi?

IV. *Demandez à quelqu'un* (Ask someone):

(1)

1. comment ça va. **2.** quelle heure il est. **3.** si le déjeuner est prêt. **4.** si le train pour Paris arrive à midi et quart. **5.** si le bureau de poste est ouvert cet après-midi. **6.** si le bureau de poste est loin d'ici. **7.** s'il y a un bureau de tabac près d'ici. **8.** s'il y a un train pour Paris cet après-midi.

(2)

1. s'il parle français. **2.** s'il parle anglais. **3.** comment ça va. **4.** comment il va. **5.** à quelle heure il va à la gare. **6.** s'il va au musée cet après-midi. **7.** à quelle heure il va déjeuner. **8.** à quelle heure il veut déjeuner. **9.** s'il veut déjeuner à midi. **10.** s'il veut déjeuner à midi et quart.

V. Conversation.

"How are you?"
"Fine. What time is it?"
"It is noon. Where are you going?"
"I am going to the station. Does the train for Paris arrive at 12:15?"
"Yes."
"Thank you very much."

VI. Dictée d'après la Conversation 3, pp. 12-13.

Articles and Prepositions *de* and *à*

1. *Masculine and feminine gender.*

In French, nouns fall into two classes, or, as they are traditionally called, *genders:* masculine and feminine. You have noticed that we say «Y a-t-il **un restaurant** près d'ici» but «Voici **une lettre** pour vous.» **Un restaurant** belongs to the masculine gender; **Une lettre** belongs to the feminine gender. While in English the question of gender is of little importance, it is very important in French because the form of articles and adjectives as well as pronouns must conform to the gender of the noun to which they refer. There is no dependable rule for finding the gender of nouns; it is true that the gender of nouns that denote persons normally corresponds to their sex, but the gender of those that denote animals, inanimate objects, ideas, etc., does not follow so simple a pattern.

The easiest and most effective way to learn the gender of a noun is to practice using the noun with its article in a phrase. Of course it would be a simple matter to learn each day a short list of detached words with their genders; but unfortunately words which are merely memorized are soon forgotten. On the other hand, it is relatively easy to remember words learned in context: the meaning of the sentence, its sounds, its rhythm — everything helps you recall all the parts of the sentence. Therefore, even in grammar exercises, we shall continue to work with complete phrases rather than with detached words.

2. *Indefinite article* **un, une** (*a, an*).

The masculine form **un** is used with masculine singular nouns; the feminine form **une,** with feminine singular nouns:

un restaurant	*a* restaurant
un bureau de tabac	*a* tobacco shop
un hôtel	*a* hotel
un bon hôtel	*a* good hotel
un autre hôtel	*an*other hotel

une lettre	*a* letter
une gare	*a* railroad station
une place	*a* public square
une rue	*a* street
une église	*a* church
une autre église	*an*other church

3. *Definite article* **le, la, l', les** (*the*).

A. Form **le**:

The form **le** (masculine singular) is used before nouns or adjectives that are masculine and singular if they begin with a consonant other than a mute **h***:

le bureau de tabac	*the* tobacco shop
le déjeuner	lunch, or *the* lunch
le restaurant	*the* restaurant
le bon restaurant	*the* good restaurant
le bon hôtel	*the* good hotel
le petit hôtel	*the* little hotel

B. Form **la**:

The form **la** (feminine singular) is used before nouns or adjectives that are feminine and singular if they begin with a consonant other than a mute **h**:

la gare	*the* railroad station
la rue	*the* street
la poste	*the* post office
la cuisine	*the* cooking
la bonne cuisine	good cooking
la chambre	*the* room

---

* Although all **h**'s in French are silent in everyday conversation, they fall into two groups traditionally known as mute **h**'s and aspirate **h**'s:

Before a word beginning with a mute **h,** linking and elision take place precisely as if the word began with a vowel. Ex.: **l'hôtel, les hôtels.**

Before a word beginning with an aspirate **h,** linking and elision do not take place. Ex.: **Le /héros** (*the hero*), **les /héros.**

In the vocabulary of this book, and in most dictionaries, words beginning with an aspirate **h** are marked with an asterisk.

For a discussion of linking, see pp. 369–370.

C. Form **l'**:

The form **l'** (masculine or feminine singular) is used before nouns or adjectives of either gender if they begin with a vowel or mute **h:**

l'agent de police *m.*	*the* policeman
l'hôtel *m.*	*the* hotel
l'autre hôtel	*the* other hotel
l'église *f.*	*the* church
l'autre église	*the* other church
l'autre restaurant *m.*	*the* other restaurant
l'autre gare *f.*	*the* other station

In order to explain the form **l',** it is usually said that the vowel of **le** or **la** is elided or that elision takes place. However, do not infer that this is an operation that *you* are supposed to perform: there is no point in imagining a vowel and then eliding it! Just say, think, and write **l'hôtel** and be done with it.

D. Form **les:**

The form **les** is used before any plural noun or adjective:

les restaurants	*the* restaurants
les autres restaurants	*the* other restaurants
les églises	*the* churches
les hôtels	*the* hotels
les bons restaurants	*the* good restaurants
les autres hôtels	*the* other hotels

(1) Note that the **s** of **les** is linked (and pronounced **z**) if the noun or adjective which follows begins with a vowel or mute **h.**

(2) In writing, the plural of French nouns is usually formed by adding "s" to the singular. This "s" is of course not pronounced.

In speaking, the plural of nouns is usually distinguished from the singular by the article used.

4. *Preposition* **de** (*of*, *from*).

A. **du**

When the preposition **de** is used with a noun before which the definite article **le** would normally stand, you say **du** — never *de le*.

le déjeuner	le prix **du** déjeuner	the price *of* lunch
le château	près **du** château	near *the* château
le musée	loin **du** musée	far *from the* museum

B. de la

When the preposition **de** is used with a noun before which the definite article **la** would normally stand, you say **de la**—just as you would expect.

la chambre	le prix **de la** chambre	the price *of the* room
la gare	près **de la** gare	near *the* station
la place	loin **de la** place	far *from the* square

C. de l'

When the preposition **de** is used with a noun before which the definite article **l'** would normally stand, you say **de l'**—as you would expect.

l'hôtel	la cuisine **de l'**hôtel	*the* hotel'*s* cooking
l'église	près **de l'**église	near *the* church
l'autre hôtel	près **de l'**autre hôtel	near *the* other hotel

D. des

When the preposition **de** is used with a noun before which the definite article **les** would normally stand, you say **des**—never *de les*.

les repas	le prix **des** repas	the price *of* meals
les chambres	le prix **des** chambres	the price *of* rooms
les hôtels	la cuisine **des** hôtels	*the* hotels' cooking

5. *Preposition* **à** (*to, at, in*).

A. au

When the preposition **à** is used with a noun before which the definite article **le** would normally stand, you say **au**—never *à le*.

le château	Je vais **au** château.	I am going *to the* château.
le restaurant	Je vais **au** restaurant.	I am going *to the* restaurant.
le musée	Je vais **au** musée.	I am going *to the* museum.

B. à la

When the preposition **à** is used with a noun before which the definite article **la** would normally stand, you say **à la**—as you would expect.

la gare	Je vais **à la** gare.	I am going *to the* station.
la poste	Je vais **à la** poste.	I am going *to the* postoffice.
la concierge	Je parle **à la** concierge.	I speak *to the* concierge.

C. à l'

When the preposition **à** is used with a noun before which the definite article **l'** would normally stand, you say **à l'** — as you would expect.

l'hôtel	Je vais **à l'**hôtel.	I am going *to the* hotel.
l'agent de police	Je parle **à l'**agent de police.	I speak *to the* policeman.
l'église	Je vais **à l'**église.	I am going *to* (*the*) church.

D. aux

When the preposition **à** is used with a noun before which the definite article **les** would normally stand, you say **aux** — never *à les.*

les bons restaurants	Je vais **aux** bons restaurants.	I go *to the* good restaurants.
les employés	Je parle **aux** employés.	I speak *to the* employees.
les étudiants	Je parle **aux** étudiants.	I speak *to the* students.

6. *Use of the definite article.*

The definite article is used much more commonly in French than in English. Specific cases of its use or omission will be studied later. But meanwhile, note that in French you say:

Quel est le prix **des** repas?	What is the price *of* meals?
Dix francs **pour le** déjeuner et douze francs **pour le** dîner.	Ten francs *for* lunch and twelve francs *for* dinner.
Je vais **à l'**église.	I am going *to* church.
Le déjeuner et **le** dîner.	Lunch and dinner.

I. Exercices d'application.

A. *Répétez en remplaçant l'article défini* **(le, la, l')** *par l'article indéfini* **(un, une):**

EX.:—le restaurant.
—un restaurant

1. le bureau de tabac, le musée, le déjeuner.
2. la gare, la place, la rue.
3. l'hôtel, l'agent de police, l'église.

B. *Répétez en remplaçant l'article défini* **(le, la, l')** *par* **au, à la,** *ou* **à l':**

EX.:—le déjeuner.
—au déjeuner.

1. le bureau de poste, le dîner, le passant.
2. la gare, la rue, la place.
3. l'hôtelier, l'employé, l'étudiant.

C. *Répétez en remplaçant l'article défini* **(le, la, l')** *par* **du, de la, de l':**

EX.:—le déjeuner
—du déjeuner

1. le bureau de poste, le dîner, le passant.
2. la gare, la rue, la place.
3. l'hôtelier, l'employé, l'étudiant.

D. *Donnez le pluriel des mots suivants:*

1. le dîner, le repas, le train.
2. la garc, la ruc, la placc.
3. l'employé, l'hôtelier, l'église.
4. l'autre hôtel, l'autre église, l'autre train.
5. le bon dîner, le bon restaurant, le petit restaurant.

E. *Répétez et remplacez l'article défini* **(les)** *par* **aux:**

EX.:—les employés.
—aux employés.

1. les restaurants, les bons restaurants, les repas.
2. les étudiants, les étudiantes (*f.*), les autres étudiants.

II. *Complétez les phrases suivantes, en employant les mots indiqués:*

1. Je vais (à) . . .

EX.:—(le) restaurant.
—Je vais au restaurant.

(le) musée / (le) château / (le) petit hôtel / (le) bureau de poste

2. Je parle (à) . . .

EX.:—(lcs) passants.
—Je parle aux passants.

(les) étudiants / (les) agents de police / (les) employés
(la) concierge / l'étudiante / l'hôtelier

3. L'autre hôtel est près (de) . . .

EX.:—(le) château.
—L'autre hôtel est près du château.

(le) musée / (le) bureau de poste / (le) bureau de tabac
(la) gare / (la) place / (la) rue de la Paix
l'église / l'autre gare / l'autre place.

III. *Répondez en français:*

1. A quelle heure allez-vous à la gare? **2.** A quelle heure allez-vous au théâtre? **3.** A quelle heure allez-vous à l'hôtel? **4.** A quelle heure allez-vous à l'église? **5.** A quelle heure allez-vous au restaurant? **6.** Y a-t-il une lettre pour moi? **7.** Est-ce que le déjeuner est prêt? **8.** Quel est le prix des chambres? **9.** Quel est le prix du dîner? **10.** Quel est le prix du déjeuner? **11.** Quel est le prix du petit déjeuner?

IV. *Demandez en français:*

1. s'il y a un restaurant près d'ici. **2.** si c'est un bon restaurant. **3.** si la cuisine est bonne. **4.** si l'hôtel du Cheval blanc est un bon hôtel. **5.** si c'est loin d'ici. **6.** le prix des chambres. **7.** le prix des repas. **8.** le prix du déjeuner. **9.** le prix du dîner. **10.** le prix du petit déjeuner.

V. *Dites en français:*

1. Where are you going to have lunch? **2.** At what time are you going to have lunch? **3.** At what time do you want to have lunch? **4.** Where do you want to have lunch? **5.** Is there a good restaurant on the square? **6.** Is there a good restaurant near the square? **7.** Is there a good restaurant on the Rue de la Paix? **8.** I am going to the restaurant. **9.** I am at the restaurant. **10.** I am going to have lunch at the restaurant. **11.** The cooking of the restaurant is excellent.

6me Arrt
RUE
DE L'ABBAYE
RUE
DE L'ÉCHAUDÉ
St GERMAIN
RESTAURANT
AU
VIEUX PARIS
RUE
DE
L'ABBAYE

CONVERSATION 5

Getting Identification Papers

A la préfecture de police*	At the Prefecture
L'EMPLOYÉ – 1 Comment vous appelez-vous, monsieur?	THE EMPLOYEE – 1 *What is your name, sir?*
JEAN – 2 Je m'appelle Jean Hughes.	JOHN – 2 *My name is John Hughes.*
L'EMPLOYÉ – 3 Quelle est votre nationalité?	THE EMPLOYEE – 3 *What is your nationality?*
JEAN – 4 Je suis Américain.	JOHN – 4 *I am an American.*
L'EMPLOYÉ – 5 Où êtes-vous né?	THE EMPLOYEE – 5 *Where were you born?*
JEAN – 6 Je suis né à Philadelphie.	JOHN – 6 *I was born in Philadelphia.*
L'EMPLOYÉ – 7 Quel âge avez-vous?	THE EMPLOYEE – 7 *How old are you?*
JEAN – 8 J'ai vingt et un ans.	JOHN – 8 *I am twenty-one.*
L'EMPLOYÉ – 9 Quelle est votre profession?	THE EMPLOYEE – 9 *What is your profession?*
JEAN – 10 Je suis ingénieur-chimiste.	JOHN – 10 *I am a chemical engineer.*
L'EMPLOYÉ – 11 Où demeurez-vous?	THE EMPLOYEE – 11 *Where do you live?*
JEAN – 12 Je demeure à Paris.	JOHN – 12 *I live in Paris.*

* Administrative offices of Prefect of Police (in Paris).

L'EMPLOYÉ – 13 Quelle est votre adresse à Paris?

JEAN – 14 Quinze, avenue de l'Observatoire.

L'EMPLOYÉ – 15 Où habitent vos parents?

JEAN – 16 Mon père habite à Philadelphie. 17 Je n'ai plus ma mère.

L'EMPLOYÉ – 18 Avez-vous des parents en France?

JEAN – 19 Non, je n'ai pas de parents en France.

L'EMPLOYÉ – 20 Voilà votre carte d'identité.

JEAN – 21 Merci, monsieur.

THE EMPLOYEE – 13 *What is your Paris address?*

JOHN – 14 *Fifteen Observatory Avenue.*

THE EMPLOYEE – 15 *Where do your parents live?*

JOHN – 16 *My father lives in Philadelphia.* 17 *My mother is no longer alive.*

THE EMPLOYEE – 18 *Have you any relatives in France?*

JOHN – 19 *No, I haven't any relatives in France.*

THE EMPLOYEE – 20 *Here is your identification card.*

JOHN – 21 *Thank you, sir.*

A PARIS

DANS UNE PETITE VILLE

I. Substitutions. *Répétez les phrases suivantes, en substituant les mots indiqués:*

1. Quelle est votre nationalité?

votre profession / votre adresse / la nationalité de Jean / la profession de Jean / l'adresse de Jean

2. Quel est le prix des repas?

du déjeuner / du dîner / du petit déjeuner / des chambres

3. J'ai vingt et un ans.

dix-huit / dix-sept / dix-neuf / vingt-deux

4. Je n'ai pas encore vingt et un ans.

vingt / dix-neuf / vingt-deux / vingt-cinq

5. Où habite votre père?

mère / sœur / frère / oncle

6. Mon père habite à Philadelphie.

Mon frère / Ma sœur / Mon oncle / Ma tante

II. *Répondez en français à chacune des questions suivantes, d'après le texte* (according to the text):

1. Comment vous appelez-vous? **2.** Quelle est votre nationalité? **3.** Où êtes-vous né? **4.** Quel âge avez-vous? **5.** Quelle est votre profession? **6.** Où demeurez-vous? **7.** Quelle est votre adresse? **8.** Où habitent vos parents? **9.** Avez-vous des parents en France?

III. *Répondez en français à chacune des questions personnelles suivantes:*

1. Comment vous appelez-vous? **2.** Quelle est votre nationalité? **3.** Où êtes-vous né(e)? **4.** Quel âge avez-vous? **5.** Quelle est votre profession? (étudiant, étudiante). **6.** Où demeurez-vous? **7.** Quelle est votre adresse? **8.** Où habitent vos parents? **9.** Avez-vous des parents en France?

IV. *Demandez à un autre étudiant* (*à une autre étudiante*):

1. comment il (elle) s'appelle. **2.** où il (elle) est né (née). **3.** quel âge il (elle) a. **4.** où il (elle) demeure. **5.** quelle est son (*his* or *her*) adresse. **6.** quelle est sa (*his* or *her*) nationalité. **7.** quelle est sa profession. **8.** s'il (si elle) a des parents en France. **9.** s'il (si elle) a des frères. **10.** s'il (si elle) a des sœurs. **11.** s'il (si elle) a des oncles. **12.** s'il (si elle) a des tantes. **13.** où habitent ses (*his* or *her*) parents. **14.** si ses parents demeurent près d'ici.

V. Nombres.

(1) *Répétez en français les nombres suivants:*

vingt et un (21), vingt-deux (22), vingt-trois (23), vingt-quatre (24), vingt-cinq (25), vingt-six (26), vingt-sept (27), vingt-huit (28), vingt-neuf (29), trente (30).

(2) *Comptez par cinq* (by fives) *de cinq à trente.*

(3) *Comptez par trois de trois à trente.*

(4) *Dites en français:* 1, 11, 21 2, 12, 22 3, 13, 23 4, 14, 24

VI. Dictée d'après la Conversation 4, p. 17.

VII. Conversation.

Inquiries about birthplace, age, family connections, etc. between students.

LA PLACE DE LA CONCORDE

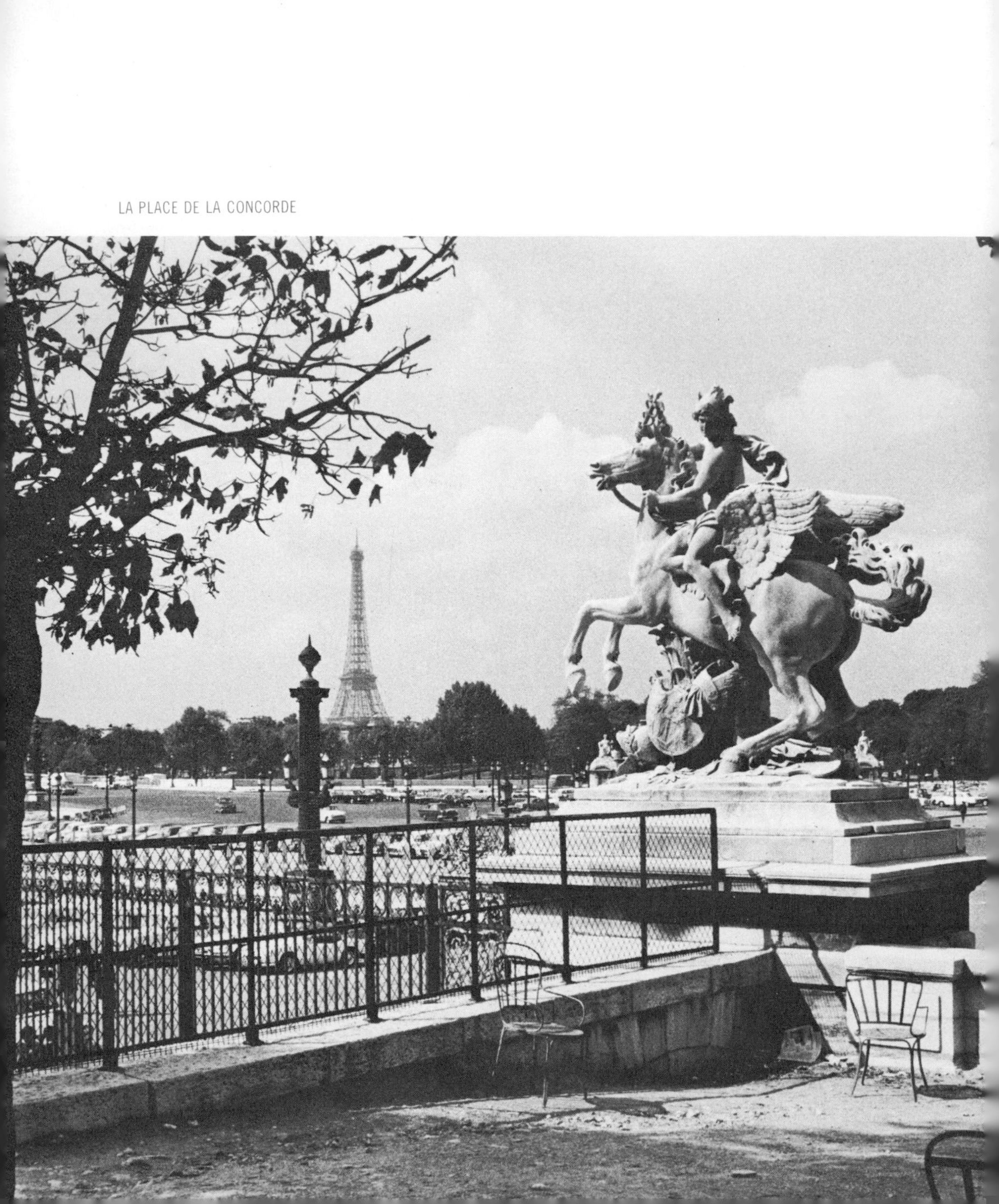

Arrivée à Paris

Jean Hughes, jeune ingénieur-chimiste américain, arrive à Paris pour travailler dans les laboratoires d'une compagnie américaine établie en France. Il va en taxi au numéro quinze, avenue de l'Observatoire, fait la connaissance de la concierge et s'installe dans sa nouvelle chambre. Il passe les premiers jours à voir les endroits célèbres de la capitale, l'île de la Cité, la place de la Concorde, les Champs-Élysées, Montmartre, etc. Tout est nouveau pour lui, et les premiers jours dans un pays étranger sont toujours difficiles, même s'ils sont très intéressants.

Habiter un pays où tout le monde parle français, même les enfants qui ne vont pas encore à l'école, est pour Jean une expérience nouvelle.

Un jour qu'il visite Notre-Dame, Jean va à la préfecture de police, voisine de la cathédrale, se procurer la carte d'identité obligatoire pour les étrangers qui habitent en France. Le commissaire lui demande son âge, sa profession, son adresse à Paris, le nom et l'adresse de ses parents. Avec sa carte d'identité dans sa poche, Jean a la satisfaction d'être en règle avec la police française.

Au cours de sa première visite au laboratoire, Jean fait la connaissance d'un jeune chimiste français, Roger Duplessis. Les deux jeunes chimistes sont bientôt de bons amis.

Un jour, Roger invite Jean à aller avec lui à Chantilly voir les célèbres courses de chevaux. Un autobus conduit les deux jeunes gens à la gare du Nord. Une heure plus tard, le train arrive à Chantilly.

Le château est situé près d'une rivière et le champ de courses est près du château. «C'est un endroit magnifique pour des courses de chevaux, pense Jean. Le beau château, les jardins, les chevaux, tout donne l'impression d'une autre époque et d'un autre monde». Jean remarque dans l'assistance des femmes très chics, qui attirent l'attention des spectateurs. «Ce sont des mannequins des grandes maisons de couture parisiennes, explique Roger. Les courses de chevaux sont un rendez-vous de la société élégante, et par conséquent un excellent endroit pour lancer les nouvelles modes.» Jean conclut qu'après tout l'élégance n'est pas encore morte.

QUESTIONS

1. Quelle est la nationalité de Jean Hughes? **2.** Quelle est sa profession? **3.** Pourquoi est-il à Paris? **4.** Où demeure Jean? **5.** Où habitent ses parents? **6.** Pourquoi est-ce que Jean va à la préfecture de police? **7.** Est-ce que la préfecture de police est loin de Notre-Dame? **8.** Qui est Roger Duplessis? **9.** Où est situé le château de Chantilly? **10.** Est-ce que le champ de courses est loin du château?

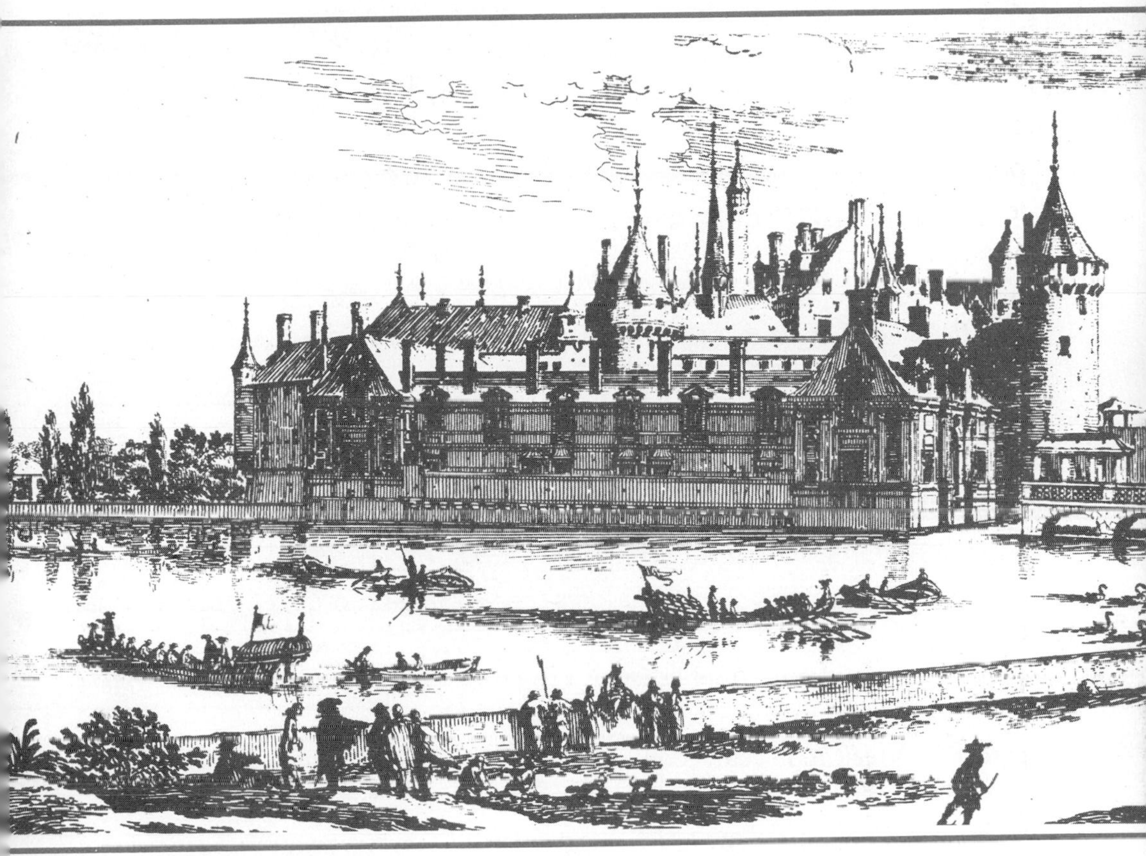

LE CHATEAU DE CHANTILLY

Having Lunch

John Hughes is going out to lunch with Roger Duplessis, a young French engineer who is employed in the research laboratory where John works.

JEAN – 1J'ai faim.

ROGER – 2Moi aussi.

JEAN – 3Allons déjeuner.

ROGER – 4Voici un restaurant. Entrons.

JEAN – 5Voilà une table libre. Asseyez-vous.

ROGER – 6Garçon, donnez-moi la carte, s'il vous plaît.

LE GARÇON – 7Voici, monsieur. Voulez-vous des *hors-d'œuvre?

ROGER – 8Oui, apportez-moi des hors-d'œuvre. 9(*à Jean*) Voulez-vous du vin blanc ou du vin rouge?

JEAN – 10Du vin rouge, s'il vous plaît.

ROGER – 11Qu'est-ce que vous voulez comme plat de viande?

JEAN – 12Un biftek aux pommes.†

JOHN – 1*I am hungry.*

ROGER – 2*So am I.*

JOHN – 3*Let's go have lunch.*

ROGER – 4*Here is a restaurant. Let's go in.*

JOHN – 5*Here is a (free) table. Sit down.*

ROGER – 6*Waiter, give me the menu, please.*

THE WAITER – 7*Here (it) is, sir. Do you want hors d'œuvres?*

ROGER – 8*Yes, bring me some hors d'œuvres.* 9*(to John) Do you want white wine or red wine?*

JOHN – 10*Red wine, please.*

ROGER – 11*What do you want for your meat course?*

JOHN – 12*Minute steak and French fried potatoes.*

---

* The **h** in **hors-d'œuvre** is aspirate (*See note, p. 21*).
Hors-d'œuvre, highly seasoned dishes (olives, radishes, anchovies, salami, etc.), usually served on a large tray at the beginning of a meal.

† The French word for *potatoes* is **pommes de terre.** But for *French fries* they say: **des pommes de terre frites, des pommes frites,** or **des frites!** Note also the expression: **Un biftek aux pommes.**

LE GARÇON – [13]Qu'est-ce que vous voulez comme dessert?	THE WAITER – [13]*What do you want for dessert?*
ROGER – [14]Qu'est-ce que vous avez?	ROGER – [14]*What have you?*
LE GARÇON – [15]Nous avons des pommes, des bananes, des poires et du raisin.	THE WAITER – [15]*We have apples, bananas, pears, and grapes.*
ROGER – [16]Apportez-moi une poire.	ROGER – [16]*Bring me a pear.*
LE GARÇON – [17]Voulez-vous du café?	THE WAITER – [17]*Do you want coffee?*
ROGER – [18]Oui, donnez-moi du café noir.	ROGER – [18]*Yes, give me some black coffee.*
LE GARÇON (*à Jean*) – [19]Et vous, monsieur?	THE WAITER (to John) – [19]*What about you, sir?*
JEAN – [20]Merci, je n'aime pas le café.	JOHN – [20]*No, thank you, I don't like coffee.*
ROGER (*au garçon*) – [21]Garçon, l'addition, s'il vous plaît.	ROGER (to the waiter) – [21]*Waiter, the bill, please.*
LE GARÇON – [22]Tout de suite, monsieur.	THE WAITER – [22]*Right away, sir.*

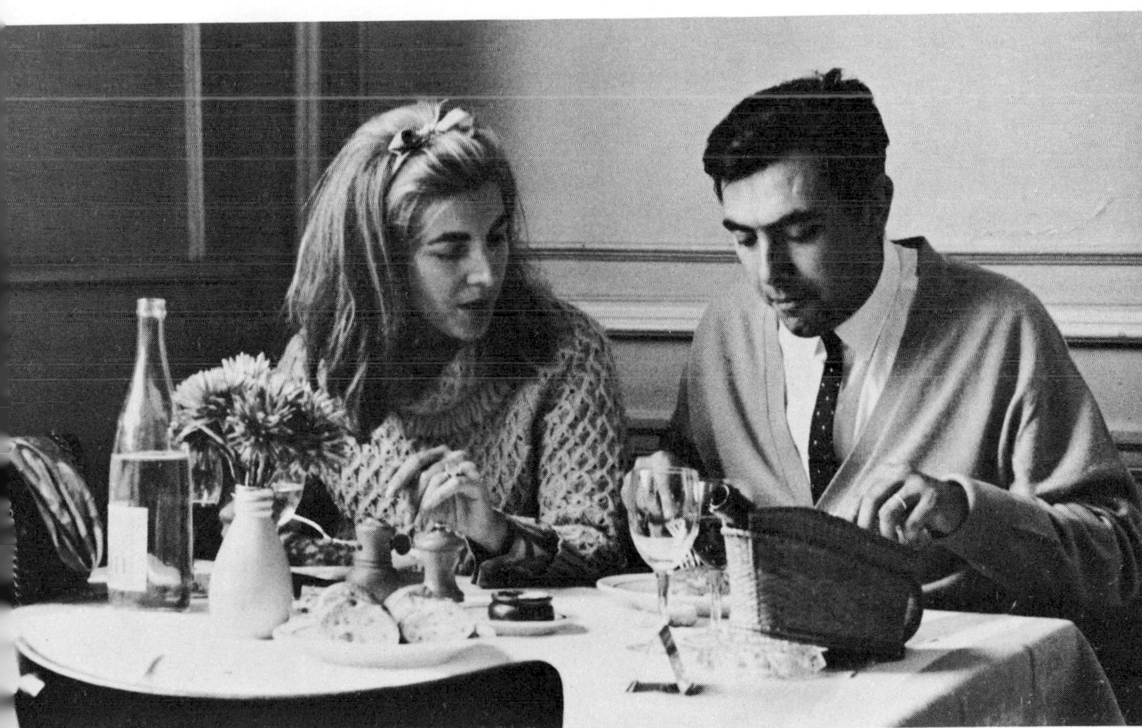

I. Substitutions. *Répétez les phrases suivantes, en substituant les mots indiqués:*

1. Allons déjeuner au restaurant.
   à l'hôtel / à l'hôtel du Cheval blanc / à l'autre hôtel / à l'autre restaurant
2. Voulez-vous des hors-d'œuvre?
   du vin blanc / du rosbif (*roast beef*) / des pommes frites / du café
3. Apportez-moi des hors-d'œuvre.
   du vin rouge / du café noir / un biftek aux pommes / une poire
4. Qu'est-ce que vous voulez comme plat de viande?
   comme dessert / comme hors-d'œuvre / comme vin / comme légumes (*vegetables*)
5. Est-ce que vous avez des pommes?
   des bananes / des poires / du raisin / des frites
6. Nous avons des pommes.
   des bananes / des poires / du raisin / des pommes de terre frites
7. Je n'aime pas le café.
   le café noir / le vin rouge / le lait (*milk*) / le chocolat
8. J'aime beaucoup les hors-d'œuvre.
   le rosbif / le poulet (*chicken*) / les gâteaux (*pastry*) / la soupe

A PARIS

II. *Répondez en français à chacune des questions suivantes:*

1. Quelle heure est-il? **2.** Avez-vous faim? **3.** A quelle heure allez-vous déjeuner? **4.** Y a-t-il un restaurant près d'ici? **5.** Où est le restaurant? **6.** Y a-t-il une table libre? **7.** Voulez-vous des hors-d'œuvre? **8.** Voulez-vous du vin blanc ou du vin rouge? **9.** Qu'est-ce que vous voulez comme plat de viande? **10.** Qu'est-ce que vous voulez comme dessert? **11.** Qu'est-ce que vous avez comme dessert? **12.** Voulez-vous du café noir? **13.** Aimez-vous le café? **14.** Aimez-vous les hors-d'œuvre? **15.** Aimez-vous les gâteaux?

III. *Dites à un autre étudiant* (*à une autre étudiante*):

1. qu'il est midi. **2.** que vous avez faim. **3.** qu'il y a un restaurant en face. **4.** que c'est un bon restaurant. **5.** d'entrer dans le restaurant. **6.** qu'il y a une table libre là-bas à droite. **7.** de s'asseoir (*to sit down*). **8.** de vous donner la carte. **9.** de vous apporter l'addition. **10.** de vous donner son adresse.

IV. *Demandez à quelqu'un* (someone):

1. s'il a faim. **2.** à quelle heure il va déjeuner. **3.** à quelle heure il va dîner. **4.** où il va déjeuner. **5.** où il va dîner. **6.** s'il veut (*if he wants*) des hors-d'œuvre. **7.** s'il veut du café.

V. Révision. *Dites en français:*

1. Right away. **2.** Please. **3.** Over there. **4.** To the right. **5.** To the left. **6.** Straight ahead. **7.** Not yet. **8.** Me too (So do I). **9.** Near the station. **10.** Across from the station. **11.** How old are you? **12.** What's your name? **13.** How are you? **14.** Where were you born? **15.** And (what about) you? **16.** Sit down. **17.** Let's go to lunch. **18.** Let's go in. **19.** What time is it? **20.** It's 7:00 A.M. **21.** It's 7:00 P.M. **22.** As usual. **23.** At 11:15. **24.** At 2:30. **25.** At a quarter of four.

VI. Dictée d'après la Conversation 5, pp. 28-29.

VII. Conversations.

(1)

Dans la rue:
Vous proposez à un ami (une amie) d'aller déjeuner (dîner).

(2)

Vous commandez un repas au restaurant.

Nouns Used in a Partitive Sense

7. *Explanations of nouns used in a partitive sense.*

—Voulez-vous **du café?**	Do you want *some coffee?*
—Voulez-vous **des pommes?**	Do you want *some apples?*
—Apportez-moi **des hors-d'œuvre.**	Bring me *some hors d'œuvres.*
—Avez-vous **des parents** en France?	Have you *any relatives* in France?

The nouns **café, pommes, hors-d'œuvre,** and **parents** are taken in a partitive sense; i.e., they refer to A PART OF the beverage, the fruit, the food, or the people in question.

In English the partitive sense is frequently expressed by the words *some* or *any*, but it is often implied rather than expressed. You can say: *Do you want some coffee? Do you want any coffee?* or *Do you want coffee?* In French, however, the only possible way to express the idea is **Voulez-vous du café?**

8. *The use of* du, de la, de l', des *in expressing the partitive.*

When nouns are used in a partitive sense in affirmative statements, commands, and questions, they are preceded by one of the special partitive forms, **du, de la, de l',** or **des.**

A. The form **du** is used with a masculine singular noun before which **le** would normally stand:

le café	Voulez-vous **du café?**	Do you want (*some*) *coffee?*
le café noir	Voulez-vous **du café noir?**	Do you want (*some*) *black coffee?*

B. **De la** is used with a feminine singular noun before which **la** would normally stand:

la crème	Donnez-moi **de la crème.**	Give me *some cream.*
la monnaie	Avez-vous **de la monnaie?**	Have you *any change?*

C. **De l'** is used with a masculine or feminine singular noun before which **l'** would normally stand:

l'argent (*m.*)	Avez-vous **de l'argent?**	Have you *any money?*
l'eau (*f.*)	Donnez-moi **de l'eau.**	Give me *some water.*

D. **Des** is used with masculine or feminine plural nouns:

les fruits (*m.*)	Avez-vous **des fruits?**	Have you *any fruit?*
les pommes (*f.*)	Nous avons **des pommes.**	We have *apples.*
les poires (*f.*)	Voulez-vous **des poires?**	Do you want *pears?*

9. *Use of* **de** *alone.*

A. **De** is used instead of **du, de la, de l', des,** when a noun in the partitive sense is the direct object of the negative form of a verb:

—Nous **n'avons pas de café.**	We don't have *any coffee.*
BUT: Nous avons **du café.**	We have (*some*) *coffee.*
—Nous **n'avons pas de crème.**	We have *no cream.*
BUT: Avez-vous **de la crème?**	Have you *any cream?*
—Je **n'**ai **pas de parents** en France.	I have *no relatives* in France.
BUT: Avez-vous **des parents** en France?	Have you *any relatives* in France?
—Il **n'**y a **pas d'eau** sur la table.	There is *no water* on the table.
BUT: Y a-t-il **de l'eau** sur la table?	Is there *any water* on the table?

B. **De** is used instead of **un, une,** when the noun is the direct object of the negative form of a verb:

—Je **n'**ai **pas de carte d'identité.**	I have *no identification card.*
BUT: J'ai **une carte d'identité.**	I have *an identification card.*
—Il **n'y a pas d'hôtel** près d'ici.	There is *no hotel* near here.
BUT: Y a-t-il **un hôtel** près d'ici?	Is there *a hotel* near here?

C. **De** is frequently used instead of **des,** when the noun is preceded by an adjective:

—Il y a **de bons restaurants** sur la place.	There are *good restaurants* on the square.
(BUT: Il y a **des restaurants** sur la place.)	There are *restaurants* on the square.
—Y a-t-il **d'autres hôtels** ici?	Are there *other hotels* here?
(BUT: Y a-t-il **des hôtels** ici?)	Are there *any hotels* here?

D. De alone is used after adverbs **beaucoup** *much*, **un peu** *a little*, and most expressions of quantity:

—Il y a **beaucoup de restaurants** sur la place.	There are *many restaurants* on the square.
—Voulez-vous **un peu de café?**	Do you want *a little coffee?*

10. *Remarks about when to use the partitive forms.*

(1) With verbs such as *want*, *have*, *eat*, *order*, *bring*, etc., you often use nouns in a partitive sense because you are likely to want, have, order, etc., only a part of the thing or things you are talking about.

(2) After **aimer** (*to like*), however, nouns are taken in a general (not partitive) sense, and therefore you use the definite article **le, la, l' les,** *whether the verb is affirmative or negative*) You say:

—J'aime **le café.**	I like *coffee.*
—J'aime **le café noir.**	I like *black coffee.*
—Je n'aime pas **le café.**	I don't like *coffee.*

If you say "I like *some* coffee", you are still not using the noun in a partitive sense because you like *all* the particular kind of coffee you are referring to. The partitive could not be used to express this phrase which means "I like certain kinds of coffee."

(3) Observe the sense in which the nouns are taken in the following sentences and try to see how the different meanings are expressed:

—Aimez-vous **les poires?**	Do you like *pears?* (in general)
—Voulez-vous **une poire?**	Do you want *a pear?*
—Voulez-vous **de la poire?**	Do you want *a part of the pear?*
—Voulez-vous **des poires?**	Do you want *some pears?*

I. Exercices d'application.

A. *Répétez en remplaçant l'article défini* **(le, la, l', les)** *par le partitif* **(du, de la, de l', des, de):**

1. le café. Donnez-moi du café, s'il vous plaît.
le café noir / le lait (*milk*) / le raisin / le chocolat

2. la crème. Donnez-moi de la crème.
la monnaie / la viande / la salade / la soupe

3. l'eau. Donnez-moi de l'eau.
l'argent / l'omelette / l'aspirine / l'eau minérale

4. les pommes. Donnez-moi des pommes.
les bananes / les poires / les hors-d'œuvre / les fruits

5. les pommes. Nous n'avons pas de pommes.
les bananes / les poires / les hors-d'œuvre / les fruits

B. *Dites au pluriel:*

EX.:—Avez-vous un frère? Avez-vous des frères?
une sœur / un oncle / une pomme / une poire

C. *Mettez à la forme négative:*

1. J'ai un frère. Je n'ai pas de frère.
une sœur / un oncle / une pomme / une poire

2. J'ai des frères. Je n'ai pas de frères.
des sœurs / des oncles / des pommes / des poires

3. Il y a un hôtel près d'ici. Il n'y a pas d'hôtel près d'ici.
un restaurant / des restaurants / un bureau de tabac / des bureaux de tabac

D. *Mettez chacune des phrases suivantes à la forme négative:*

EX.:—Il y a une table libre.
—Il n'y a pas de table libre.

1. Il y a des tables libres. **2.** Il y a une lettre pour vous. **3.** Il y a des lettres pour vous. **4.** Il y a de l'eau sur la table. **5.** Il y a du vin rouge sur la table. **6.** Il y a de la crème. **7.** Il y a des fruits. **8.** Il y a des hors-d'œuvre.

E. *Employez* **beaucoup,** *puis* **un peu,** *avec chacun des mots suivants:*

EX.:—le vin.
—beaucoup de vin, un peu de vin.
le lait / l'argent / le sucre / l'eau / la monnaie / la crème

F. *Répétez les deux phrases suivantes, en substituant les mots indiqués:*

EX.:—le lait.
—Avez-vous du lait? —Aimez-vous le lait?
le vin blanc / la viande / la crème / le café noir

EX.:—le lait.
—Je n'ai pas de lait. —Je n'aime pas le lait.
le vin blanc / la viande / la crème / le café noir

II. *Demandez en français:*

A. *Demandez à un autre étudiant (à une autre étudiante):*

1. s'il (si elle) a un frère. **2.** s'il (si elle) a des sœurs. **3.** s'il y a un hôtel ici. **4.** s'il y a un autre hôtel ici. **5.** s'il y a de bons hôtels ici.

B. *Imaginez que vous êtes dans un restaurant et demandez au garçon:*

1. s'il y a une table libre. **2.** s'il y a d'autres tables libres. **3.** s'il y a des poires. **4.** s'il y a du raisin. **5.** s'il y a des fruits.

III. *Dites en français:*

1. (*a*) Do you like coffee? (*b*) Have you any coffee? (*c*) I have no coffee. **2.** (*a*) Do you like grapes? (*b*) Have you any grapes? (*c*) I have no grapes. **3.** (*a*) Do you like pears? (*b*) Do you want some pears? (*c*) I have no pears. **4.** (*a*) Here are some apples. (*b*) Here are some good apples. (*c*) I like good apples. (*d*) Do you want some apples? **5.** (*a*) Do you want some water? (*b*) Give me some water. (*c*) There is no water on the table.

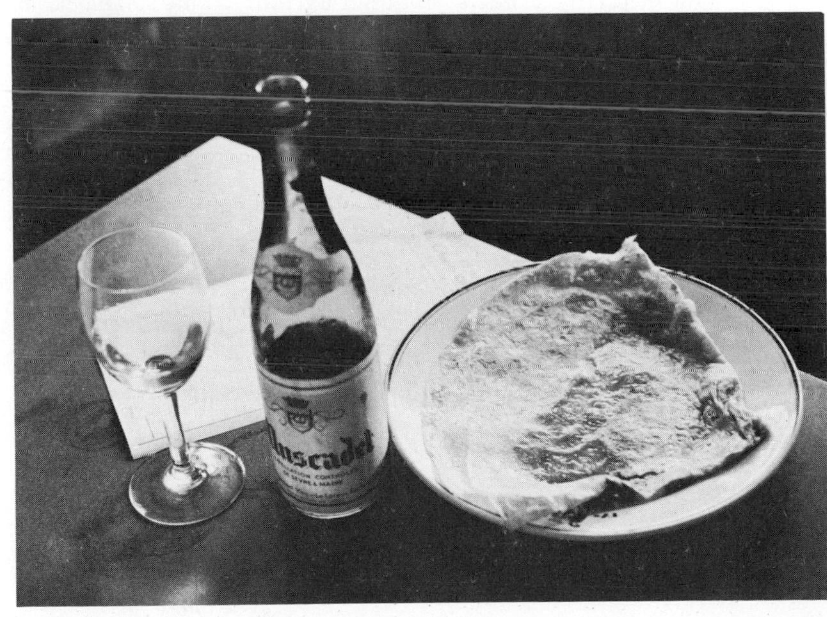

Making Plans

JEAN – 1 Quelle est la date aujourd'hui?

ROGER – 2 C'est aujourd'hui le trente septembre. 3 Quand allez-vous à Marseille?

JEAN – 4 Au mois d'octobre. 5 Voici mes projets pour l'année: 6 octobre et novembre à Marseille; 7 décembre, janvier et février à Paris; 8 mars et avril à Lyon; 9 mai, juin, juillet et août à Paris.

ROGER – 10 Est-ce que vous êtes libre la semaine prochaine?

JEAN – 11 Voyons . . . Quel jour sommes-nous aujourd'hui?

ROGER – 12 C'est aujourd'hui vendredi.

JEAN – 13 Je vais au laboratoire lundi, mardi, mercredi et jeudi. 14 Je suis libre vendredi, samedi et dimanche.

ROGER – 15 Voulez-vous venir à Rouen avec moi?

JEAN – 16 Volontiers. A quelle heure partez-vous?

ROGER – 17 Le train part à dix-sept heures.

JEAN – 18 C'est entendu. A jeudi après-midi.

JOHN – 1 *What's the date today?*

ROGER – 2 *Today is September 30.* 3 *When are you going to Marseilles?*

JOHN – 4 *In (the month of) October.* 5 *Here are my plans for the year:* 6 *October and November in Marseilles;* 7 *December, January, and February in Paris;* 8 *March and April in Lyons;* 9 *May, June, July and August in Paris.*

ROGER – 10 *Are you free next week?*

JOHN – 11 *Let's see . . . What's today?*

ROGER – 12 *Today is Friday.*

JOHN – 13 *I go to the laboratory Monday, Tuesday, Wednesday and Thursday.* 14 *I am free Friday, Saturday and Sunday.*

ROGER – 15 *Do you want to go (come) with me to Rouen?*

JOHN – 16 *Gladly. What time are you leaving?*

ROGER – 17 *The train leaves at five o'clock.*

JOHN – 18 *Agreed. See you Thursday afternoon.*

MARSEILLE

I. Substitutions. *Répétez les phrases suivantes, en substituant les mots indiqués:*

1. C'est aujourd'hui le 30 septembre.
le 30 octobre / le 30 novembre / le 30 décembre /
le 11 avril / le 11 mai / le 11 juin /
le premier* juillet / le premier août / le premier septembre

2. Je vais à Marseille au mois d'octobre.
de janvier / d'avril / de juin / d'août

3. Je vais à Lyon le 15 mars.
le 10 février / le 16 juin / le 13 juillet / le 14 mai

4. Est-ce que vous êtes libre la semaine prochaine?
lundi prochain / mardi prochain / mercredi prochain

5. C'est aujourd'hui jeudi.
vendredi / samedi / dimanche

6. Êtes-vous libre ce matin?
ce matin à onze heures / cet après-midi / cet après-midi à quatre heures / ce soir /
ce soir à dix heures

7. Je suis libre aujourd'hui à midi.
cet après-midi à trois heures / ce soir à six heures /
ce soir à neuf heures et demie

8. Le train part à dix-sept heures.
à dix-sept heures trente / à seize heures quinze / à douze heures vingt /à onze heures trente

II. *Répondez en français à chacune des questions suivantes, d'après le texte:*

1. Quelle est la date aujourd'hui? **2.** Quand allez-vous à Marseille? **3.** Quels jours allez-vous au laboratoire? **4.** Quels jours êtes-vous libre? **5.** Quel jour sommes-nous? **6.** Voulez-vous venir à Rouen avec moi? **7.** A quelle heure le train part-il? **8.** A quelle heure allez-vous à la gare?

III. *Répétez en français après le professeur:*

1. Premier (*m.*), première (*f.*) (*first*). **2.** deuxième (*second*). **3.** troisième (*third*). **4.** quatrième (*fourth*). **5.** cinquième (*fifth*). **6.** sixième (*sixth*). **7.** septième (*seventh*). **8.** huitième (*eighth*). **9.** neuvième (*ninth*). **10.** dixième (*tenth*). **11.** onzième (*eleventh*). **12.** douzième (*twelfth*).

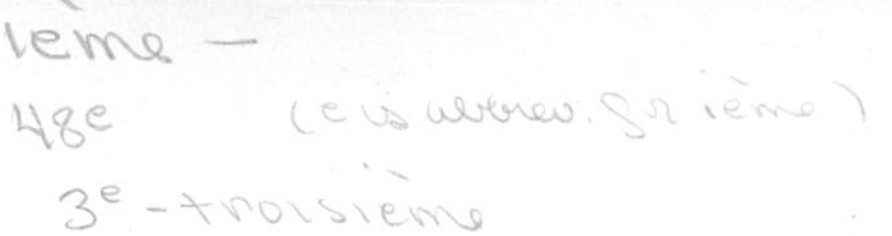

IV. *Répondez en français:*

EX.:—Quel est le premier mois de l'année?
—**Janvier est le premier mois de l'année.**

1. Quel est le deuxième mois de l'année? **2.** Quel est le troisième mois de l'année? **3.** Quel est le quatrième mois de l'année? **4.** Quel est le cinquième mois de l'année? **5.** Quel est le dixième mois de l'année? **6.** Quel est le onzième mois de l'année? **7.** Quel est le douzième mois de l'année? **8.** Quel est le dernier mois de l'année?

V. *Dites en anglais ce que vous suggère chacune des dates suivantes* (Say in English what each of the following dates suggests to you):

1. Le premier* avril. **2.** Le dernier jeudi de novembre. **3.** Le trente et un octobre. **4.** Le quatre juillet. **5.** le vingt-cinq décembre. **6.** Le vingt-deux février. **7.** Le vingt-neuf février.

VI. *Demandez à un autre étudiant* (*à une autre étudiante*):

1. quel jour nous sommes aujourd'hui. **2.** quelle heure il est. **3.** à quelle heure il (elle) déjeune. **4.** si le bureau de poste est ouvert à neuf heures. **5.** si le bureau de poste est ouvert cet après-midi. **6.** comment il (elle) s'appelle. **7.** quel âge il (elle) a. **8.** où il (elle) est né (née). **9.** où il (elle) habite. **10.** s'il (si elle) est libre dimanche. **11.** quand il (elle) va à Marseille. **12.** à quelle heure il (elle) part.

VII. Dictée d'après la Conversation 6, pp. 36-37.

VIII. Conversation.

Vous invitez un de vos amis (une de vos amies) (*a friend of yours*) à faire un voyage avec vous. Vous fixez un rendez-vous (*Decide upon a time and place to meet*).

* Note that the ordinal number is used for the first of the month, but that the cardinal numbers are used for the other days of the month.

3 Present Indicative of *être, avoir*; Regular Verbs, First Conjugation

11. *How to learn verb forms.*

The best way to learn *anything* is to associate the thing to be learned with something that you already know. In studying the present indicative of the verb **être,** for example, you should bear in mind the forms that you have already mastered and relate the unfamiliar forms to them.

If you make it a point to think what each form means each time you say it or hear it, you will have little difficulty in learning verb forms.

12. *Present indicative of* **être** (*to be*)*: irregular.*

—**Êtes-vous** Français?	*Are you* French?
—Non, **je ne suis pas** Français.	No, *I am not* French.
Je suis Américain.	*I am* an American.
—Quelle heure **est-il?**	What time *is it?*
—**Il est** dix heures.	*It is* ten o'clock.
—Où **sont** Roger et Jean?	*Where are* Roger and John?
—**Ils sont** à Paris.	*They are* in Paris.

The forms of the present indicative of **être** are:

AFFIRMATIVE		NEGATIVE
je suis	*I am*	je ne suis pas (*I am not*)
tu es	*you are*	tu n'es pas
il est	*he* or *it is*	il n'est pas
elle est	*she* or *it is*	elle n'est pas
on est	*one* or *one is*	on n'est pas
nous sommes	*we are*	nous ne sommes pas
vous êtes	*you are*	vous n'êtes pas
ils sont	*they are* (*m.* or *m.* and *f.*)	ils ne sont pas
elles sont	*they are* (*f.*)	elles ne sont pas

INTERROGATIVE

est-ce que je suis? (*am I?*)
es-tu?
est-il?
est-elle?
est-on?
sommes-nous?
êtes-vous?
sont-ils?
sont-elles?

(1) The **vous** form, the second person plural, is used in speaking either to one person or to more than one — as in English *you:*

Vous êtes Américain, n'est-ce pas?	*You are* an American, aren't you?
Vous êtes Américains, n'est-ce pas?	*You are* Americans, aren't you?

(2) The **tu** form, the second person singular, was formerly used only in speaking to members of one's family, to children, or to very intimate friends; but today it is used more and more commonly by young people in speaking to each other even when they are not close friends. The use of the **tu** form (called **le tutoiement**) will be introduced in oral practice exercises later on.

(3) **Il, elle, ils, elles** are used to refer to persons or things that have already been definitely identified in the context.

Jean et Roger ont faim. **Ils** vont déjeuner.
Voilà une pomme. **Elle** est rouge.

(4) **On** is an indefinite pronoun that is often used somewhat as we use *one, we, they*, or *people*. It is always used with the third person singular of verbs.

On est en retard.	*We* are late.
On va à l'hôtel.	*We* are going to the hotel.
A Paris, **on** dîne à 8 heures.	In Paris, *they* have dinner at 8 o'clock.
	In Paris, *people* dine at 8 o'clock.

(5) The form given for the first person singular of the interrogative is **Est-ce que je suis?** This form is given because the inverted form **suis-je** is hardly ever used except in literary style. **Est-ce que?** may of course be used with the other forms.

13. *Present indicative of* **avoir** (*to have*)*: irregular.*

—**Avez-vous** des frères?	*Have you* any brothers?
—Non, **je n'ai pas** de frères.	No, *I have no* brothers.
—Qu'est-ce que **vous avez** comme dessert?	What *do you have* for dessert?
—**Nous avons** des pommes et des poires.	*We have* apples and pears.

The forms of the present indicative of **avoir** are:

AFFIRMATIVE		NEGATIVE
j'ai	*I have*	je n'ai pas (*I have not*)
tu as	*you have*	tu n'as pas
il a	*he has*	il n'a pas
elle a	*she has*	elle n'a pas
on a	*one has*	on n'a pas
nous avons	*we have*	nous n'avons pas
vous avez	*you have*	vous n'avez pas
ils ont	*they have* (*m.*)	ils n'ont pas
elles ont	*they have* (*f.*)	elles n'ont pas

INTERROGATIVE

est-ce que j'ai? (*have I?*)
as-tu?
a-t-il?
a-t-elle?
a-t-on?
avons-nous?
avez-vous?
ont-ils?
ont-elles?

Note that in the inverted form of the third person singular, the subject pronoun (**il, elle, on**) is always preceded by the sound *t*. For verbs whose third person singular ends in a **t** (or **d**), it is simply a matter of linking the final consonant. Ex.: **Est-il?** For verbs whose third person does not end in a **t** (or **d**), a **t** is inserted between the verb and pronoun subject anyway.

14. *Present indicative of* **déjeuner** (*to lunch*): *first conjugation, regular.*

—A quelle heure **déjeunez-vous?**	At what time *do you have lunch?*
—**Je déjeune** à midi et quart.	*I have lunch* at a quarter past twelve.
—A quelle heure Roger **déjeune-t-il?**	At what time *does* Roger *have lunch?*
—**Il déjeune** à midi et demi.	*He lunches* at half past twelve.
—A quelle heure **déjeunent** vos parents?	At what time *do* your parents *have lunch?*
—**Ils déjeunent** à une heure.	*They lunch* at one o'clock.
—Ici **on** déjeune à midi.	*We* (or *people*) have lunch at noon here.
—A Paris, **on** déjeune à une heure.	In Paris, *they* (or *people*) have lunch at one o'clock.

The forms of the present indicative of **déjeuner** are:

AFFIRMATIVE	NEGATIVE	INTERROGATIVE
je déjeune	je ne déjeune pas	est-ce que je déjeune?
I have lunch	*I do not have lunch*	*Am I having lunch?*
I am having lunch	*I am not having lunch*	*Do I have lunch?*
tu déjeunes	tu ne déjeunes pas	déjeunes-tu?
il (elle) (on) déjeune	il (elle) (on) ne déjeune pas	déjeune-t-il (elle) (on)?
nous déjeunons	nous ne déjeunons pas	déjeunons-nous?
vous déjeunez	vous ne déjeunez pas	déjeunez-vous?
ils (elles) déjeunent	il (elles) ne déjeunent pas	déjeunent-ils (elles)?

(1) Note that the endings of the first, second, and third person singular and of the third person plural are all silent, and that the verb forms in **je déjeune, tu déjeunes, il déjeune,** and **ils déjeunent** are all pronounced alike.

(2) The present indicative of regular verbs of the first conjugation consists of a stem and endings: the stem may be found* by dropping the **-er** of the infinitive; the endings are **-e, -es, -e, -ons, -ez, -ent.**

(3) Verbs ending in **-ier (étudier,** *to study*) are of course conjugated like **déjeuner: J'étudie, tu étudies, il étudie, nous étudions, vous étudiez, ils étudient.**

(4) The first conjugation has by far the largest number of verbs. You have already met the following verbs of this conjugation: **parler, apporter, donner, dîner, entrer, demeurer, habiter, arriver, fermer, s'appeler,** as well as **demander,** and **compter.**

I. Exercices d'application.

A. *Répétez les phrases suivantes, en substituant les formes indiquées:*

1. Je suis au restaurant.

Il est / Il n'est pas / Êtes-vous? / John et Roger sont / Ils sont / Nous sommes

2. Il a des parents en France.

Elle a / A-t-elle . . . ? / Avez-vous . . . ? / Nous avons / A-t-il . . . ? / Ont-ils . . . ?

---

* For a few verbs in which the final vowel of the stem is an **e** (e.g. **acheter**), it is necessary to note that this **e** is silent in forms in which the ending is pronounced (**nous achetons, vous achetez**), and that it is pronounced like the **è** in **père** in the persons whose endings are silent (**j'achète, tu achètes, il achète,** and **ils achètent**). For **acheter,** this difference in pronunciation is indicated by writing **è** instead of **e.** In **appeler,** however, this difference in pronunciation of the final vowel of the stem is indicated by writing **ll** instead of **l** in the singular and in the third person plural: **appelle, appelles, appelle, appelons, appelez, appellent.** Ex.:—Comment vous **appelez**-vous? —Je m'**appelle** Jean Hughes.

B. *Mettez les phrases suivantes au pluriel:*

EX.:—Je suis Américain.
—**Nous sommes Américains.**

(*a*) **1.** Je suis étudiant. **2.** Je suis libre ce soir. **3.** Je ne suis pas libre ce soir. **4.** J'ai faim. **5.** Je n'ai pas faim. **6.** J'ai de la monnaie. **7.** Je n'ai pas de monnaie. **8.** J'ai une carte d'identité.

(*b*) **1.** Il est ingénieur-chimiste. **2.** Il n'est pas Américain. **3.** Où est-il? **4.** Il a faim. **5.** Elle a vingt et un ans. **6.** Il n'a pas de monnaie. **7.** Quel âge a-t-il? **8.** Elle est Américaine. **9.** Elle n'est pas Française.

(*c*) **1.** Je déjeune à midi. **2.** Je dîne à sept heures. **3.** Je demeure avenue de l'Observatoire. **4.** J'habite à Paris. **5.** J'arrive le 30 novembre. **6.** J'entre. **7.** Je parle un peu français. **8.** Je ne parle pas anglais. **9.** J'étudie le français. **10.** Je n'étudie pas l'anglais.

(*d*) **1.** Il habite à Paris. **2.** Il arrive le 29 novembre. **3.** Il parle anglais. **4.** Elle entre. **5.** Elle déjeune à l'hôtel. **6.** A quelle heure arrive-t-il? **7.** Où demeure-t-elle? **8.** Parle-t-il français? **9.** Il n'habite pas à Paris. **10.** N'habite-t-il pas à Paris? **11.** Étudie-t-il le français?

C. *Répondez affirmativement, puis négativement:*

EX.:—Êtes-vous Américain?
—**Je suis Américain. Je ne suis pas Américain.**

1. Êtes-vous étudiant? **2.** Êtes-vous libre dimanche? **3.** Est-ce que le déjeuner est prêt? **4.** Le bureau de poste est-il ouvert cet après-midi? **5.** Avez-vous faim? **6.** Sommes-nous Américains? **7.** Êtes-vous étudiants? (*Réponse au pluriel.*) **8.** Étudiez-vous le français?

II. *Répondez en français:*

1. A quelle heure dînez-vous? **2.** A quelle heure déjeunez-vous? **3.** Où demeurez-vous? **4.** Parlez-vous français? **5.** Comment vous appelez-vous? **6.** A quelle heure Roger déjeune-t-il? **7.** A quelle heure dîne-t-il? **8.** Où demeure-t-il? **9.** Parle-t-il français? **10.** A quelle heure déjeunez-vous? (*Réponse au pluriel*) **11.** A quelle heure dînez-vous (*Rép. au pl.*) **12.** Parlez-vous français? (*Rép. au pl.*) **13.** Où demeurez-vous? (*Rép. au pl.*) **14.** Où Jean et Roger demeurent-ils? **15.** Où dînent-ils? **16.** Est-ce qu'ils parlent français? **17.** Le garçon apporte-t-il des hors-d'œuvre? **18.** Qu'est-ce qu'il apporte comme plat de viande?

III. *Demandez à un autre étudiant (à une autre étudiante):*

1. s'il (si elle) est libre ce soir. **2.** s'il (si elle) est Français (Française)? **3.** s'il (si elle) est ingénieur-chimiste. **4.** où il (elle) est. **5.** quand il (elle) est libre. **6.** quelle est son adresse. **7.** quelle est sa nationalité. **8.** sa profession. **9.** la date. **10.** s'il (si elle) a faim. **11.** quel âge il (elle) a. **12.** s'il (si elle) a de la monnaie. **13.** s'il (si elle) a des frères. **14.** combien de frères il (elle) a. **15.** à quelle heure il (elle) déjeune aujourd'hui. **16.** à quelle heure il (elle) dîne d'habitude. **17.** où il (elle) demeure. **18.** à quelle heure il (elle) arrive. **19.** s'il (si elle) étudie le français.

A MARSEILLE

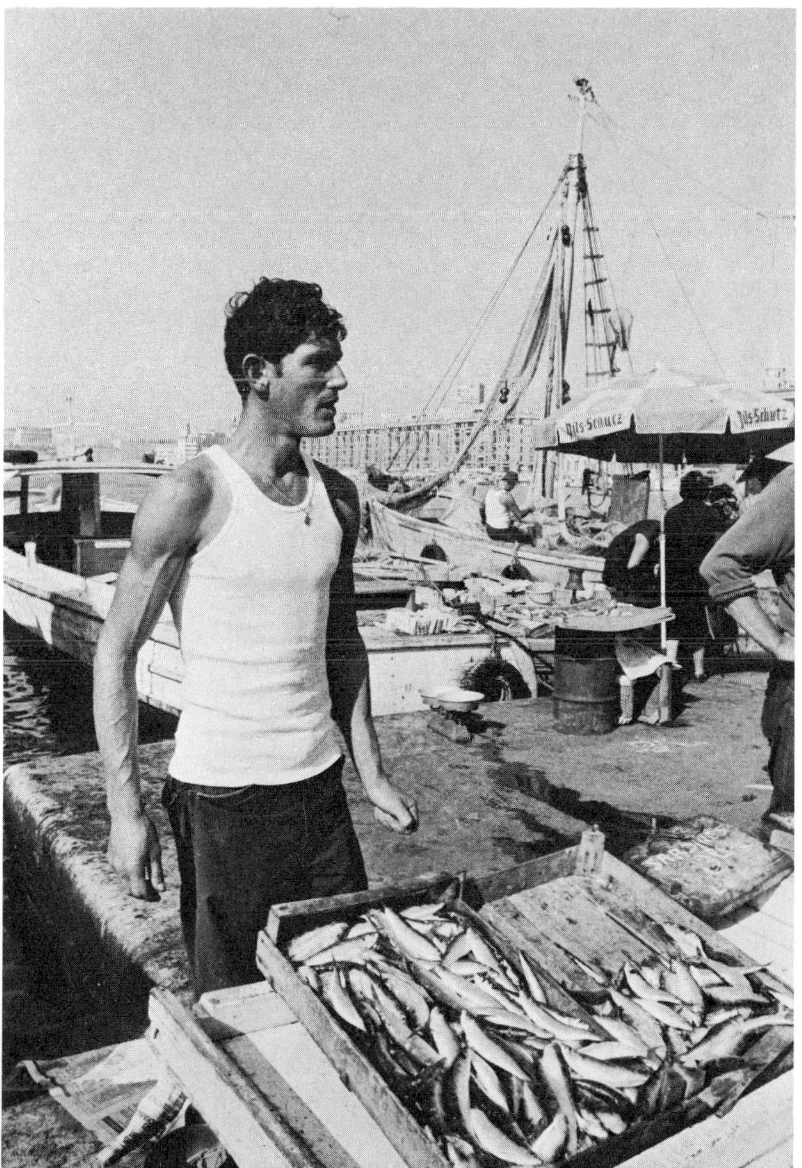

Buying a Paper

Dans la rue

ROGER – [1]Où allez-vous?

JEAN – [2]Je vais acheter un journal. [3]Où achète-t-on des journaux?*

ROGER – [4]On vend des journaux au bureau de tabac.

Au bureau de tabac

JEAN – [5]Avez-vous des journaux, madame?

MME COCHET – [6]Oui, monsieur. Les voilà.†

JEAN – [7]Donnez-moi *Le Figaro* s'il vous plaît.

MME COCHET – [8]Le voici, monsieur.

JEAN – [9]C'est combien?‡

MME COCHET – [10]C'est trente centimes.

JEAN – [11]Voilà un franc.

MME COCHET – [12]Voilà la monnaie: soixante-dix centimes.

JEAN – [13]Avez-vous des revues américaines?

MME COCHET – [14]Je regrette, monsieur. Nous n'avons pas de revues américaines. [15]Mais nous avons des romans policiers.

On the Street

ROGER – [1]*Where are you going?*

JOHN – [2]*I am going to buy a paper.* [3]*Where do you buy papers?*

ROGER – [4]*They sell papers at the tobacco shop.*

At the Tobacco Shop

JOHN – [5]*Do you have newspapers, madam?*

MME COCHET – [6]*Yes, sir. Here they are.*

JOHN – [7]*Give me Le Figaro, please.*

MME COCHET – [8]*Here it is, sir.*

JOHN – [9]*How much is it?*

MME COCHET – [10]*Thirty centimes.*

JOHN – [11]*Here is one franc.*

MME COCHET – [12]*Here's the change: seventy centimes.*

JOHN – [13]*Do you have any American magazines?*

MME COCHET – [14]*I'm sorry, sir. We have no American magazines.* [15]*But we have detective stories.*

---

* Although the plural of French nouns (and adjectives) is usually found by adding an **s** to the singular, most nouns ending in **-al** have the plural ending **-aux**: **journal — journaux, cheval — chevaux.**

† In spoken French, **voici** and **voilà** are practically interchangeable. **Voilà** is more frequently used.

‡ For questions by intonation, see Par. 20, page 81.

JEAN – [16]Je n'aime pas beaucoup les romans policiers. [17]Combien coûte cette petite carte de Paris?

MME COCHET – [18]Deux francs cinquante, monsieur. [19]C'est une carte très utile.

JEAN – [20]Bon. Voilà un billet de cinquante francs. [21]Avez-vous la monnaie de cinquante francs?

MME COCHET – [22]Je crois que oui. La voilà. [23]Est-ce que c'est tout, monsieur?

JEAN – [24]Oui, c'est tout pour aujourd'hui.

JOHN – [16]*I don't like detective stories very much.* [17]*How much does this little map of Paris cost?*

MME COCHET – [18]*Two francs fifty, sir.* [19]*It's a very useful map.*

JOHN – [20]*Okay. Here's a 50 franc bill.* [21]*Do you have change for 50 francs?*

MME COCHET – [22]*I think so. Here it is.* [13]*Is that all, sir?*

JOHN – [24]*Yes, that's all for today.*

I. Substitutions. *Répétez les phrases suivantes en substituant les mots indiqués:*

1. Je vais acheter un journal.
   des journaux / des romans policiers / des revues / une carte de Paris
2. Nous n'allons pas acheter de journal aujourd'hui.
   de journaux / de revues / de romans policiers / de carte de Paris
3. Où vend-on des journaux?
   des revues / des romans policiers / des cartes de Paris / du lait (*milk*)
4. Où achète-t-on des journaux?
   de la crème / du café / du vin / des romans policiers
5. Combien coûte cette petite carte de Paris?
   cette revue/ ce journal/ ce roman policier/ ce vin rouge

II. *Répétez les phrases suivantes en remplaçant le nom par le pronom* **le, la** *ou* **les:**

EX.:—Voilà *Le Figaro.*
—**Le voilà.**

1. Voilà la carte. **2.** Voilà l'addition. **3.** Voilà les journaux. **4.** Voilà les revues. **5.** Voilà votre carte d'identité. **6.** Voilà les hors-d'œuvre. **7.** Voilà mon adresse.

III. *Répondez en français:*

1. Où allez-vous? **2.** Où vend-on des journaux? **3.** Avez-vous des journaux? **4.** Avez-vous *Le Figaro?* **5.** Combien est-ce? **6.** Avez-vous des revues américaines? **7.** Avez-vous des romans policiers? **8.** Combien coûtent-ils? **9.** Avez-vous la monnaie de cinquante francs? **10.** Où Jean achète-t-il un journal? **11.** Quel journal achète-t-il? **12.** Où achète-t-on des journaux en France?

IV. *Répondez (1) affirmativement et puis (2) négativement à chacune des questions suivantes:*

1. Avez-vous des revues américaines? **2.** Aimez-vous les romans policiers? **3.** Aimez-vous le café? **4.** Avez-vous du café? **5.** Aimez-vous le vin rouge? **6.** Avez-vous du vin rouge? **7.** Avez-vous des frères? **8.** Avez-vous de la monnaie?

V. *Posez la question à laquelle répond chacune des phrases suivantes* (Ask the question to which each of the following sentences is the answer):

EX.:—C'est trente centimes.
—Combien est-ce?

1. C'est loin d'ici. **2.** C'est un bon hôtel. **3.** C'est tout. **4.** C'est deux francs cinquante. **5.** C'est à dix heures. **6.** Le train arrive à midi. **7.** J'étudie la chimie. **8.** Nous sommes étudiants.

VI. *Demandez à un autre étudiant (à une autre étudiante):*

1. où il (elle) va. **2.** pourquoi (*why*) il va au bureau de tabac. **3.** si on* vend des journaux au bureau de tabac. **4.** si l'on* vend des revues au bureau de tabac. **5.** quel journal il (elle) va acheter. **6.** combien coûte *Le Figaro*. **7.** s'il (si elle) a des revues américaines. **8.** s'il (si elle) aime les revues américaines. **9.** s'il (si elle) a des romans policiers. **10.** s'il (si elle) a la monnaie de cinquante francs. **11.** si c'est tout. **12.** où il achète le journal. **13.** quel journal il achète. **14.** où on achète des journaux en France.

VII. Dictée d'après la Conversation 7, p. 46.

VIII. Conversations.

(1)

"Do you have any pears?"
"I am sorry, sir. We have no pears. We have bananas and grapes."
"I don't like bananas. Bring me some grapes."

(2)

"Waiter, bring me the bill, please."
"Here it is, sir."
"How much is it?"
"Eight francs, sir."
"Have you the change for fifty francs?"
"I think so. Here it is."

* Careful speakers are likely to use **l'on** instead of **on** after the word **si** or **où**.

Numbers

15. *Cardinal numbers (one, two, three, etc.).**

1	un, une	**22**	vingt-deux	**73**	soixante-treize
2	deux	**23**	vingt-trois	**80**	quatre-vingts
3	trois	**30**	trente	**81**	quatre-vingt-un
4	quatre	**31**	trente et un	**82**	quatre-vingt-deux
5	cinq	**32**	trente-deux	**83**	quatre-vingt-trois
6	six	**33**	trente-trois	**90**	quatre-vingt-dix
7	sept	**40**	quarante	**91**	quatre-vingt-onze
8	huit	**41**	quarante et un	**92**	quatre-vingt-douze
9	neuf	**42**	quarante-deux	**100**	cent
10	dix	**43**	quarante-trois	**101**	cent un
11	onze	**50**	cinquante	**102**	cent deux
12	douze	**51**	cinquante et un	**103**	cent trois
13	treize	**52**	cinquante-deux	**200**	deux cents
14	quatorze	**53**	cinquante-trois	**300**	trois cents
15	quinze	**60**	soixante	**1000**	mille†
16	seize	**61**	soixante et un	**1100**	onze cents
17	dix-sept	**62**	soixante-deux	**1200**	douze cents
18	dix-huit	**63**	soixante-trois	**1300**	treize cents
19	dix-neuf	**70**	soixante-dix	**1400**	quatorze cents
20	vingt	**71**	soixante et onze	**1900**	dix-neuf cents
21	vingt et un	**72**	soixante-douze	**2000**	deux mille‡

2100	deux mille cent		
2110	deux mille cent dix	**100.000**	cent mille
20.000	vingt mille§	**1.000.000**	un million

* For phonetic transcription of numbers, see pp. 379–380.

† From 1100 to 1900 you may also say: **mille cent, mille deux cents,** etc., though **onze cents, douze cents,** etc., are somewhat more commonly used.

‡ Beginning with 2,000, you always count in thousands in French. In English you may say: *twenty-one hundred, twenty-two hundred,* etc., but in French you may say only: **deux mille cent, deux mille deux cents,** etc.

§ In French numbers, a period is used where we use a comma, and vice versa: ENGLISH: 12,000.85; FRENCH: 12.000,85.

(1) The French count by tens from 1 to 60 but by twenties from 61 to 100. The Celts, whose language was spoken in Gaul before the Roman conquest, counted by twenties. The Romans counted by tens. The French system of numbers is a combination of the two.

(2) **Et** is used only in the numbers 21, 31, 41, 51, 61, and 71.

(3) Pronunciation of final consonant of numbers:

(*a*) The final consonant of numbers is ordinarily silent when the word immediately following the number begins with a consonant. Ex.: **cinq francs: six pommes; huit lettres; dix poires; vingt francs,** etc. Note however that the final **t** is pronounced in **vingt-deux, vingt-trois,** etc.

(*b*) The final consonant of numbers is pronounced when the word immediately following the number begins with a vowel or a mute **h.** Ex.: **trois ans; cinq ans; six étudiants; sept heures; huit étudiants; cent ans,** etc. Note, however, that in **cent un** (101) the **t** is not pronounced.

(*c*) The final consonant of **cinq, six, sept, huit, neuf** and **dix** is pronounced when the numbers are used alone, in counting, or at the end of a phrase or sentence. Ex.: **Combien de frères avez-vous? —Cinq.**

16. *Ordinal numbers (first, second, third, etc.).*

—Lundi est **le premier** jour de la semaine.	Monday is *the first* day of the week.
—Quel est **le troisième** mois de l'année?	What is *the third* month of the year?
—C'est un étudiant de **deuxième** année.	He is a *second* year student.

premier, première	*first*	huitième	*eighth*
second, seconde; deuxième	*second*	neuvième	*ninth*
troisième	*third*	dixième	*tenth*
quatrième	*fourth*	onzième	*eleventh*
cinquième	*fifth*	douzième	*twelfth*
sixième	*sixth*	vingtième	*twentieth*
septième	*seventh*	vingt et unième	*twenty-first*

Note that the word **an** is used with cardinal numbers but that **année** is used with ordinals. Ex.: **trois ans** (*three years*); **la troisième année** (*the third year*).

17. *Dates.*

C'est aujourd'hui **le onze juin.**	Today is *the eleventh of June.*
Je vais à Marseille **le huit octobre.**	I am going to Marseilles *on October 8th.*
Louis XIV est mort **en 1715** (dix-sept cent quinze).	Louis XIV died *in 1715.*

(1) You always use the cardinal numbers for the days of the month except for the first of the month. Ex.: le **deux** mai, le **trois** mai, etc., but **le premier** mai.

(2) In English, we say: *seventeen fifteen, seventeen hundred fifteen,* or *seventeen hundred and fifteen.* In French, 1715 can be read in only two ways: **dix-sept cent quinze** or **mille sept cent quinze.** Do not omit the word **cent.**

(3) Note that **le** is not elided with **onze** or **huit**.

18. *Time of day.*

A. In conversation:

—Quelle heure est-il?	What time is it?
—Il est onze heures et quart.	It is quarter past eleven.
—Il est onze heures et demie.	It is half past eleven.
—Il est midi moins le quart.	It is a quarter to twelve.
—Il est midi. Il est minuit.	It is noon. It is midnight.
—Il est trois heures vingt-cinq.	It is twenty-five minutes past three.
—Il est quatre heures moins dix.	It is ten minutes to four.

(1) To express the quarter-hours, you say **et quart** (*quarter past*), **et demie** (*half past*), **moins le quart** (*quarter to*).

(2) To express minutes between the hour and the half hour following (*e.g. 4:00–4:30*), you say **quatre heures cinq** (*4:05*); **quatre heures dix** (*4:10*); **quatre heures vingt-cinq** (*4:25*).

But to express minutes between the half hour and the following hour (*e.g., 4:30–5:00*) you measure back from the next hour. Thus *4:35* is **cinq heures moins vingt-cinq;** *4:50* is **cinq heures moins dix.**

(3) To express A.M., you say **du matin;** for P.M., you say **de l'après-midi** (*in the afternoon*) or **du soir** (*in the evening*). Ex.: **Neuf heures du matin** (*9:00 A.M.*); **trois heures de l'après-midi** (*3:00 P.M.*); **onze heures du soir** (*11:00 P.M.*).

B. Official time (twenty-four hour system):

une heure trente (1 h. 30)	1:30 A.M.
treize heures trente (13 h. 30)	1:30 P. M.
six heures cinquante (6 h. 50)	6:50 A.M.
dix-huit heures cinquante (18 h. 50)	6:50 P. M.
zéro heure vingt (0 h. 20)	12:20 A.M.
douze heures vingt (12 h. 20)	12:20 P. M.

(1) The twenty-four hour system is used in all official announcements: railroads, banks, stores, theatres, offices, army, navy, etc.

(2) In this system, fractions of an hour are always expressed in terms of minutes after the hour.

I. Exercice sur les nombres.

1. Comptez par dix de dix à cent.

2. Comptez par cinq de cinquante à cent.

3. Dites en français: 21, 31, 41, 51, 61, 71, 81, 91, 101.

4. Dites en français: 1, 11; 2, 12, 22; 3, 13, 30; 4, 14, 40, 44; 5, 15, 50, 55; 6, 16, 60, 66, 76; 7, 17, 77; 8, 18, 80, 88, 98; 9, 19, 90, 99; 20, 24, 80, 84, 40, 24.

II. Substitutions.

A. *Répondez à chacune des questions suivantes en employant les nombres indiqués:*

1. Quel âge a-t-il? Il a dix ans.

neuf ans / huit ans / sept ans / six ans / cinq ans

2. Quel âge a-t-elle? Elle a dix-sept ans.

dix-huit ans / dix-neuf ans / vingt ans / vingt et un ans

3. Combien coûte ce livre? Il coûte dix francs.

neuf francs / huit francs / sept francs / six francs / cinq francs

4. Combien coûtent ces tomates? Elles coûtent deux francs le kilo.

deux francs cinquante / deux francs soixante-quinze / trois francs / trois francs soixante-quinze

5. Quelle heure est-il? Il est dix heures.

neuf heures / huit heures / sept heures / six heures / cinq heures

B. *Répétez la phrase suivante en substituant les mots indiqués:*

Lundi est le premier jour de la semaine.

mardi . . . deuxième / mercredi . . . troisième / jeudi . . . quatrième / vendredi . . . cinquième / samedi . . . sixième / dimanche . . . dernier

III. *Répondez en français par une phrase complète à chacune des questions suivantes:*

1. Combien de jours y a-t-il en mars? **2.** Combien de jours y a-t-il en février? **3.** Combien de jours y a-t-il en décembre? **4.** Combien de jours y a-t-il dans une année? **5.** Quel âge avez-vous? **6.** Quel âge a votre père? **7.** Quel âge a votre mère? **8.** Quel est le premier jour de la semaine? **9.** Quel est le troisième jour de la semaine? **10.** Quel est le troisième mois de l'année? **11.** Quel est le deuxième mois de l'année? **12.** Êtes-vous un étudiant de troisième année (une étudiante de troisième année)?

IV. *Lisez* (Read) *en français les heures suivantes d'après le système officiel et donnez l'équivalent anglais de chaque heure indiquée:*

1. 1 h. 10, 2 h. 27, 4 h. 55. **2.** 5 h. 33, 6 h. 05, 8 h. 31. **3.** 9 h. 37, 10 h. 45, 12 h. 10. **4.** 13 h. 08, 14 h. 22, 16 h. 50. **5.** 17 h. 50, 18 h. 55, 20 h. 39. **6.** 21 h. 39, 22 h. 13, 23 h. 14, 0 h. 45.

V. *Dites en français:*

1. May 10th, May 13th, May 21. **2.** June 5, Aug. 5, July 5. **3.** Dec. 31, March 31, Jan. 31. **4.** April 1, March 1, Aug. 1. **5.** Feb. 1, Feb. 11, Feb. 21.

VI. Exercice sur les nombres.

1. *Comptez en français:* onze cents, douze cents, etc. jusqu'à dix-neuf cents. **2.** *Lisez les dates suivantes en français:* (*a*) 1900, 1940, 1945, 1845, 1745. (*b*) 1645, 1545, 1515, 1615, 1715. (*c*) 1815, 1915, 1940, 1950, 1960, 1962, 1972.

Taking a History Quiz

Roger's fiancée, Marie Bonnier, is checking up on John's knowledge of French history.

MARIE – [1]Connaissez-vous* l'histoire de France?

JEAN – [2]Certainement. Je connais Jeanne d'Arc et Napoléon.

MARIE – [3]Qu'est-ce que vous savez de Jeanne d'Arc?

JEAN – [4]Je sais* qu'elle est née à Domrémy et qu'elle est morte à Rouen.

MARIE – [5]Savez-vous où est né Napoléon?

JEAN – [6]Il est né en Corse, au dix-huitième siècle.

MARIE – [7]Quelle est la date de la bataille de Waterloo?

JEAN – [8]Dix-huit cent quinze est la date de Waterloo. [9]Napoléon est mort six ans plus tard.

MARIE – [1]*Do you know the history of France?*

JOHN – [2]*Certainly. I know about Joan of Arc and Napoleon.*

MARIE – [3]*What do you know about Joan of Arc?*

JOHN – [4]*I know she was born in Domremy and that she died in Rouen.*

MARIE – [5]*Do you know where Napoleon was born?*

JOHN – [6]*He was born in Corsica in the 18th century.*

MARIE – [7]*What is the date of the battle of Waterloo?*

JOHN – [8]*1815 is the date of Waterloo.* [9]*Napoleon died six years later.*

---

* **Savoir** and **connaître** both mean "to know." **Savoir,** however, has a much broader use: it governs clauses introduced by **que, quand, quel, pourquoi, où, à quelle heure,** etc. When it has a noun or pronoun object, it is used to refer chiefly to dates, time, names, age, prices, etc.

Connaître always takes a noun or pronoun object and is used to refer to persons, places, books, fields of learning, works of art, etc. It does not govern clauses beginning with **que.**

MARIE – [10]En quelle année Louis XIV (quatorze) est-il mort?

JEAN – [11]Il est mort en dix-sept cent quinze.

MARIE – [12]Vous connaissez le quatorze juillet, n'est-ce pas?

JEAN – [13]Bien entendu. C'est le jour de la fête nationale en France.

MARIE – [14]Savez-vous pourquoi?

JEAN – [15]Parce que c'est le jour de la prise de la Bastille, [16]le quatorze juillet dix-sept cent quatre-vingt-neuf.

MARIE – [17]Je ne vais plus vous poser de questions. [18]Vous savez tout!

MARIE – [10]*In what year did Louis XIV die?*

JOHN – [11]*He died in 1715.*

MARIE – [12]*You know about July 14, don't you?*

JOHN – [13]*Certainly. It is the day of the French National Holiday.*

MARIE – [14]*Do you know why?*

JOHN – [15]*Because it is the day of the fall (taking) of the Bastille,* [16]*July 14th, 1789.*

MARIE – [17]*I am not going to ask you any more questions.* [18]*You know everything!*

I. Substitutions. *Répétez les phrases suivantes en substituant les mots indiqués:*

1. Connaissez-vous l'histoire de France?
la concierge / l'hôtel du Cheval blanc / le château de Chantilly / le 14 juillet

2. Je connais l'histoire de France.
la concierge / l'hôtel du Cheval blanc / le château de Chantilly / le 14 juillet

3. Savez-vous où est née Jeanne d'Arc?
quand elle est née / où est né Napoléon / quand est né Napoléon / quelle est la date de Waterloo / la date de la prise de la Bastille

4. Je ne sais pas la date de la prise de la Bastille.
où est née Jeanne d'Arc / en quelle année Louis XIV est mort / l'adresse de Jean Hughes / pourquoi il est à Paris

5. J'étudie l'histoire de France.
l'histoire des États-Unis / la chimie / la littérature anglaise / l'économie politique (*economics*)

II. *Répondez en français, d'après le texte, aux questions suivantes:*

1. Connaissez-vous l'histoire de France? **2.** Où Jeanne d'Arc est-elle née? **3.** Savez-vous où elle est morte? **4.** Savez-vous où est né Napoléon? **5.** Quelle est la date de la bataille de Waterloo? **6.** Quand Napoléon est-il mort? **7.** Savez-vous quand Louis XIV est mort? **8.** Connaissez-vous le 14 juillet? **9.** Pourquoi est-ce la fête nationale? **10.** Quelle est la date de la prise de la Bastille?

III. *Demandez à quelqu'un:*

1. s'il connaît l'histoire de France. **2.** s'il connaît Jeanne d'Arc. **3.** s'il sait où Jeanne d'Arc est morte. **4.** s'il sait quand Napoléon est mort. **5.** la date de la prise de la Bastille. **6.** la date de la bataille de Waterloo. **7.** s'il étudie l'histoire des États-Unis.

IV. *Répondez en français à chacune des questions suivantes:*

1. En quelle année êtes-vous né (née)? **2.** Quelle est la date aujourd'hui? **3.** Quel jour de la semaine est-ce aujourd'hui? **4.** Quel âge a votre père? **5.** En quelle année est-il né? **6.** En quel mois êtes-vous né (née)? **7.** Quelle est la date de votre anniversaire (*birthday*)? **8.** Étudiez-vous l'économie politique?

V. *Dites en français en employant le mot indiqué:*

1. **(le)** On May 19th. On July 15th. On September 3rd. On December 20.
2. **(en)** In 1890, In 1850. In 1790. In 1789. In 1689.
3. **(au)** In the 20th century. In the 19th century. In the 18th century. In the 17th century.

VI. *Lisez les dates suivantes:*

1. Le 30 septembre 1965. **2.** Le 1er juin 1945. **3.** Le 27 avril 1889. **4.** Le 1er janvier 1837. **5.** Le 31 août 1698. **6.** Le 17 mars 1950. **7.** Le 29 juillet 1930. **8.** Le 12 octobre 1492.

VII. Dictée d'après la Conversation 8, pp. 56-57.

VIII. Conversations.

(1)

"Do you know when George Washington was born?"
"Yes, he was born in 1732."
"Where was he born?"
"He was born in Virginia" **(en Virginie.)**
"When did he die?"
"He died in 1799."

(2)

"Do you know (the significance of) the 4th of July?"
"Yes, certainly. It is the day of the American National Holiday."
"Do you know why?"
"It is Independence Day **(le jour de la Déclaration de l'Indépendance américaine)**, July 4, 1776."

A Friend Is Getting Married

ROGER – [1]Vous connaissez Louise Bedel?

JEAN – [2]Non, je ne la connais pas.

ROGER – [3]Mais si.* Vous avez fait sa connaissance chez Marie samedi dernier.

JEAN – [4]Est-ce† une petite jeune fille brune?

ROGER. – [5]Mais non. C'est† une grande jeune fille blonde.

JEAN – [6]De quelle couleur sont ses yeux?

ROGER – [7]Elle a les yeux bleus, comme toutes les blondes.

JEAN – [8]Oh! vous parlez de la jeune fille habillée en bleu? [9]Elle a les cheveux blonds, les joues roses et les lèvres rouges, n'est-ce pas?

ROGER – [1]*Do you know Louise Bedel?*

JOHN – [2]*No, I don't know her.*

ROGER – [3]*Yes, you do. You met her (made her acquaintance) at Marie's last Saturday.*

JOHN – [4]*Is she a small brunette girl?*

ROGER – [5]*Oh, no. She's a tall blonde.*

JOHN – [6]*What color are her eyes?*

ROGER – [7]*She has blue eyes, like all blondes.*

JOHN – [8]*Oh! You are speaking of the girl dressed in blue?* [9]*She has blond hair, rosy cheeks, and red lips, hasn't she?*

---

* **Si** meaning *yes* is used only to contradict a negative statement.

† Observe that *He is* or *She is* is expressed in French by **C'est** when **est** is directly followed by the article **le, la, un,** or **une.**

ROGER – [10]Oui, c'est ça.

JEAN – [11]Eh bien?

ROGER – [12]Elle va se marier jeudi prochain.

JEAN – [13]Avec qui?

ROGER – [14]Avec Charles Dupont.

JEAN – [15]Je connais très bien Charles.

ROGER – [16]Qu'est-ce qu'il fait?

JEAN – [17]Il est ingénieur.*

ROGER – [18]Que pensez-vous de Charles?

JEAN – [19]Je pense qu'il a de la chance. [20]Sa fiancée est jolie et elle est très gentille.

ROGER – [10]*Yes, that's right.*

JOHN – [11]*Well?*

ROGER – [12]*She is going to be married next Thursday.*

JOHN – [13]*To whom?*

ROGER – [14]*To Charles Dupont.*

JOHN – [15]*I know Charles very well.*

ROGER – [16]*What does he do?*

JOHN – [17]*He is an engineer.*

ROGER – [18]*What do you think of Charles?*

JOHN – [19]*I think he is lucky.* [20]*His fiancée is pretty and she is very nice.*

---

* Note that *He is*, *She is* is usually expressed in French by **Il est, Elle est** when **est** is directly followed by an adjective standing alone or by an unmodified noun.

UN MARIAGE EN BRETAGNE

I. Substitutions. *Répétez les phrases suivantes en substituant les mots indiqués:*

1. Vous avez fait sa connaissance chez Marie samedi dernier.
chez ma sœur / chez Roger / au laboratoire / à Paris

2. C'est une petite jeune fille brune.
grande / gentille / jolie

3. Elle a les yeux bleus.
les yeux noirs / les yeux marron (*brown*) / les cheveux blonds / les cheveux noirs / les cheveux blancs / les lèvres rouges / les joues roses

4. Elle va se marier jeudi prochain.
la semaine prochaine / le mois prochain / au mois d'août / au mois de juin / le 16 avril / le 15 mars / le 29 février

5. Il est ingénieur.
agent de police / hôtelier / Américain / Français / chimiste / étudiant

6. C'est un ingénieur.
un agent de police / un hôtelier / un Américain / un Français / un chimiste / un étudiant

7. C'est un jeune ingénieur.
un jeune Américain / une jeune Américaine / un jeune Français / une jeune Française / un jeune étudiant / une jeune étudiante

8. Elle est habillée en bleu.
en rouge / en blanc / en noir / en rose

II. *Répondez en français à chacune des questions suivantes, d'après le texte:*

1. Connaissez-vous Louise Bedel? **2.** Où avez-vous fait sa connaissance? **3.** Quand avez-vous fait sa connaissance? **4.** Est-ce une grande jeune fille blonde? **5.** A-t-elle les yeux bleus? **6.** A-t-elle les joues roses? **7.** A-t-elle les lèvres rouges? **8.** Quand va-t-elle se marier? **9.** Avec qui va-t-elle se marier? **10.** Connaissez-vous Charles Dupont? **11.** Qu'est-ce qu'il fait? **12.** Que pensez-vous de Charles? **13.** Est-ce que sa fiancée est jolie? **14.** Est-elle gentille?

III. *Répondez en français à ces questions personnelles:*

1. Avez-vous les cheveux blonds? **2.** Avez-vous les yeux bleus? **3.** De quelle couleur sont vos yeux? **4.** Comment êtes-vous habillé(e)? **5.** Est-ce que votre voisine (*neighbor*) a les cheveux blonds? **6.** A-t-elle les yeux bleus?

IV. *Dites en français en employant l'expression indiquée.*

A. Il est, Elle est

1. ____ ingénieur. **2.** ____hôtelier. **3.** ____ agent de police. **4.** ____ grand. **5.** ____ grande. **6.** ____ gentille. **7.** ____ concierge. **8.** ____jolie. **9.** ____ Français. **10.** ____ Française. **11.** ____ Américaine. **12.** ____ très gentille.

B. C'est un, C'est une

1. ____ grande jeune fille blonde. **2.** ____ petite jeune fille blonde. **3.** ____ bon hôtel. **4.** ____ bon déjeuner. **5.** ____ petite jeune fille brune. **6.** ____ bon journal. **7.** ____ bonne pomme. **8.** ____ bonne poire. **9.** ____ grand restaurant. ____ bon petit restaurant.

C. Il est, Elle est, ou **C'est un, C'est une**

1. ____ petite jeune fille brune. **2.** ____ très gentille. **3.** ____ ingénieur (two ways). ____ ingénieur. **4.** ____ très bon ingénieur. **5.** ____ bon journal. **6.** ____ jolie. **7.** ____ Américain. **8.** ____ étudiant. **9.** ____ Américaine. **10.** ____ étudiante. **11.** ____ jeune Américain. **12.** ____ jeune Américaine.

V. Dictée d'après la Conversation 9, pp. 66-67.

VI. Conversations.

(1)

"Do you know Louise Bedel?"
"Yes, why?"
"She is going to get married next Wednesday."
"To whom?"
"To Charles Dupont."
"He is lucky."

(2)

"Do you know when Napoleon was born?"
"No, but I know the date of the battle of Waterloo."
"Well?"
"1815."

La cuisine française

Roger et Jean dînent ensemble dans un des grands restaurants de la capitale. Leur table est près d'une fenêtre, d'où ils ont une belle vue sur la Seine. Le garçon apporte la carte avec tout le sérieux d'un diplomate. Jean examine le menu avec curiosité.

—Je suis toujours surpris du talent des Français dans la présentation des plats, dit-il à son ami. Aux États-Unis, les noms des plats sont d'habitude purement descriptifs, sans aucun ornement. Ici, ils font venir l'eau à la bouche. Voici par exemple, dans la liste des plats de poisson, l'indication «Filets de sole Tante-Marie.» Quelle différence entre «Filets de sole Tante-Marie» et simplement *Fillet of Sole*! Un appel au sentiment familial, une allusion à la chère tante Marie, de son vivant si bonne cuisinière, et les filets de sole deviennent quelque chose de rare, d'unique. Les gens qui inventent de telles appellations sont certes d'excellents psychologues.

—Puisque vous parlez de l'art de présenter les plats, répond Roger, regardez dans les «Spécialités recommandées.» Il y a là un soufflé avec la description suivante: «Mariage forcé de la glace et du feu. Plat délicieux spécialement recommandé. (Commander vingt minutes à l'avance)» . . . Ce «mariage forcé de la glace et du feu» est une jolie invention. Cela fait penser aux quatre éléments, à l'hostilité traditionnelle de l'eau et du feu, aux volcans couverts de neige de l'Islande. Le plaisir qu'on a à manger ce soufflé est à la fois d'ordre corporel et d'ordre spirituel!

Le repas terminé, Jean et Roger quittent le restaurant, très satisfaits spirituellement et corporellement. Ils s'arrêtent un instant devant un kiosque à journaux. Jean remarque qu'il y a là des journaux et des revues de tous les grands pays du monde, journaux américains, anglais, allemands, russes, italiens. Plusieurs sont dans une langue qu'il ne peut pas même identifier. Après tout, pense-t-il, Paris est une ville si cosmopolite qu'il y a des gens pour les acheter, et pour les lire.

QUESTIONS

1. Où Jean et Roger dînent-ils ensemble? **2.** Où est leur table? **3.** Qu'est-ce que le garçon apporte à Jean et à Roger? **4.** Quel plat de poisson y a-t-il sur la carte? **5.** Quelle description la carte donne-t-elle du soufflé? **6.** Quand Jean et Roger quittent-ils le restaurant? **7.** Sont-ils satisfaits de leur dîner? **8.** Où s'arrêtent-ils un instant? **9.** Qu'est-ce que Jean remarque quand il est devant le kiosque à journaux? **10.** Est-ce qu'il peut identifier tous les journaux? **11.** Quels journaux peut-il identifier? **12.** Est-ce que Paris est une ville très cosmopolite?

PRÉPARATION D'UN SOUFFLÉ

EN PROVENCE : LA CAMARGUE

Word Order in Asking Questions

19. *Questions by inversion and with* **Est-ce que?**

A. When the subject of the verb is a personal pronoun:

—**Êtes-vous** libre dimanche? —**Est-ce que vous êtes** libre dimanche?	*Are you* free Sunday?
—**Connaissez-vous** Louise Bedel? —**Est-ce que vous connaissez** Louise Bedel?	*Do you know* Louise Bedel?

When the subject of the verb is a *personal pronoun*, you ask a question *either* by inverting the order of subject and verb *or* by using the expression **est-ce que** and normal order of subject and verb. Both patterns are commonly used in French.

If you use an interrogative word or expression such as **où?** (*where*), **quand?** (*when*), **combien?** (*how much*), **à quelle heure?** (*at what time*), etc., the interrogative word or expression comes first and is followed *either* (1) by inverted order of subject and verb *or* (2) by **est-ce que?** and normal order.

—Où **allez-vous?** —Où **est-ce que vous allez?**	Where *are you going?*
—A quelle heure **voulez-vous** déjeuner? —A quelle heure **est-ce que vous voulez** déjeuner?	At what time *do you want* to have lunch?

B. When the subject of the verb is a noun:

—Le déjeuner **est-il** prêt? —**Est-ce que** le déjeuner **est** prêt?	*Is* lunch ready?
—Le train **arrive-t-il** à cinq heures? —**Est-ce que** le train **arrive** à cinq heures?	*Does* the train *arrive* at five o'clock?

When the subject of the verb is a *noun*, you *either* express the noun-subject, the corresponding pronoun-subject and the verb in the following order: noun-subject, verb, pronoun-subject, *or* use **est-ce que?** and normal word order.

If you use an interrogative word or expression, such as **où, quand, combien?, à quelle heure?,** the interrogative word or expression comes first and is followed by either of the patterns described above.

—**Où** vos parents **demeurent-ils?** —**Où est-ce que** vos parents **demeurent?**	*Where do* your parents *live?*
—**A quelle heure** le train **arrive-t-il?** —**A quelle heure est-ce que** le train **arrive?**	*At what time does* the train *arrive?*

Note also that in questions introduced by an interrogative word or expression, it is very common to ask a question simply by inverting the order of the noun-subject and the verb, *if the noun-subject is final in the question.*

—Où **demeurent vos parents?**	Where *do your parents live?*
—A quelle heure **arrive l'avion?**	At what time *does the plane arrive?*

If the noun-subject would not be final, only the two patterns described above are possible.

—Où **votre père achète-t-il** son journal?
—Où **est-ce que votre père achète** son journal?

—Quand **votre père va-t-il** en France?
—Quand **est-ce que votre père va** en France?

20. *Questions with* **n'est-ce pas?** *and by intonation.*

A. N'est-ce pas?

—Vous connaissez Louise Bedel, **n'est-ce pas?**	You know Louise Bedel, *don't you?*
—Oui, je la connais.	Yes, I know her.
—Vous ne connaissez pas sa sœur, **n'est-ce pas?**	You don't know her sister, *do you?*
—Non, je ne la connais pas.	No, I don't know her.

You often ask a question by simply adding **n'est-ce pas** to a declarative statement — especially if you expect an answer that agrees with what you have said. **N'est-ce pas?** corresponds to a number of expressions in English, such as: *don't you think so?, don't I?, don't you?, will you not?, wouldn't you?, didn't you?,* etc.

B. By intonation.

As in English, one often asks questions by making a declarative statement with an interrogatory intonation.

—C'est tout?	*That's all?*
—C'est combien?	*How much is it?* (lit. *It's how much?*)
—Le train est à l'heure?	*The train is on time?*
—Le déjeuner est prêt?	*Lunch is ready?*

This way of asking questions may imply surprise on the part of the speaker:

—Il est à Paris?	*Is he in Paris?* or *Is he really in Paris?*
—C'est tout ce que vous avez?	*Is that all you have?*

21. *Negative questions.*

—**N'**avez-vous **pas** faim? —**Est-ce que** vous **n'**avez **pas** faim?	Are*n't* you hungry?
—Si, j'ai faim.	Yes (on the contrary), I *am* hungry.
—**Ne** voulez-vous **pas** de café? —**Est-ce que** vous **ne** voulez **pas** de café?	Do*n't* you want any coffee?
—**Si,** donnez-moi du café.	Yes (on the contrary), give me some coffee.

You ask a negative question by putting **ne** before the inverted form and **pas** after it.

Avez-vous? —**N'**avez-vous **pas?** —A-t-il? —**N'**a-t-il **pas?**

In answering a negative question, you say **Si** instead of **Oui**.

N'avez-vous **pas** faim? —**Si,** j'ai faim.

I. Substitutions. *Répétez les phrases suivantes en substituant les mots indiqués:*

1. L'avion est-il à l'heure?
parti / arrivé / en retard / en avance

2. A quelle heure l'avion part-il?
le train / l'autobus / l'autocar (*tourist bus*) / l'express de Paris

3. Où votre père achète-t-il son journal?
ses revues / ses cigares / son essence (*gasoline*) / ses billets

4. Ne voulez-vous pas de hors-d'œuvre? Si, donnez-moi des hors-d'œuvre.
pas de vin ... du vin / pas de poire ... une poire / pas de viande ... de la viande / pas de crème ... de la crème

5. N'y a-t-il pas de restaurant près d'ici? Si, il y a un restaurant là-bas.
pas d'hôtel ... un hôtel / pas de garage ... un garage / pas de bureau de tabac ... un bureau de tabac / pas de taxi ... un taxi

II. *Mettez chacune des phrases suivantes à la forme interrogative par inversion.*

EX.:—Vous êtes étudiant.
—**Êtes-vous étudiant?**

1. Vous êtes en France. **2.** Vous allez à la gare. **3.** Ils sont à Paris. **4.** Elles sont à Paris. **5.** Elles ont des frères. **6.** Il y a un restaurant près d'ici. **7.** C'est une grande jeune fille blonde. **8.** Elle va se marier. **9.** Elle va au théâtre. **10.** Le bureau de poste est sur la place. **11.** Le théâtre est près d'ici. **12.** Votre père dîne à sept heures.

III. *Demandez en français, en employant la forme interrogative par inversion:*

1. si l'hôtel Continental est sur la place. **2.** si c'est loin d'ici. **3.** si c'est un bon hôtel. **4.** si c'est un grand hôtel. **5.** s'il y a un autre hôtel près de la gare. **6.** s'il y a d'autres hôtels sur la place. **7.** si Jean est à Paris. **8.** si son père est ici. **9.** si Jean et Roger sont au laboratoire. **10.** si Jeanne d'Arc est née au quinzième siècle. **11.** où Napoléon est mort. **12.** quand Louise Bedel va se marier.

IV. *Posez la question à laquelle répond chacune des phrases suivantes en commençant par* **où?, quand?, combien?, quel?, comment?,** etc. (Ask the question to which each of the following sentences is the answer—beginning with **où?, quand?,** etc.)

EX.:—Je demeure à Paris.
—**Où demeurez-vous?**

1. Mes parents demeurent à Paris. **2.** Napoléon est mort en 1821. **3.** *Le Figaro* coûte 30 centimes. **4.** Il est trois heures. **5.** Le train arrive à six heures. **6.** C'est aujourd'hui jeudi. **7.** Mercredi est le troisième jour de la semaine. **8.** Je vais très bien. **9.** Le train part à huit heures. **10.** Elle va se marier jeudi prochain. **11.** Louis XIV est mort en 1715. **12.** François Premier est mort en 1547.

V. *Posez les questions suivantes par l'inversion du nom sujet:*

EX.:—Où Jeanne d'Arc est-elle née?
—Où est née Jeanne d'Arc?

1. Quand Jeanne d'Arc est-elle née? **2.** Dans quelle ville Jeanne d'Arc est-elle née? **3.** Où votre père demeure-t-il? **4.** Quel âge votre sœur a-t-elle? **5.** A quelle heure le train part-il? **6.** Comment votre mère va-t-elle? **7.** En quelle année Louis XIV est-il mort? **8.** En quelle année Jeanne d'Arc est-elle morte?

VI. *Mettez les questions suivantes à la forme négative.*

EX.:—Voulez-vous du vin?
—Ne voulez-vous pas de vin?

1. Voulez-vous du café? **2.** Voulez-vous des hors-d'œuvre? **3.** Avez-vous des journaux américains? **4.** Aimez-vous les romans policiers? **5.** Y a-t-il un hôtel dans la rue de la Paix? **6.** Y a-t-il des hôtels sur la place? **7.** Y a-t-il de bons restaurants près du château? **8.** Demeurez-vous à Paris? **9.** Roger demeure-t-il à Paris? **10.** Savez-vous quand Jeanne d'Arc est morte? **11.** Savez-vous quel jour nous sommes aujourd'hui? **12.** Savez-vous à quelle heure on dîne à Paris?

VII. Révision. *Dites en français:*

(*a*) **1.** What color are her eyes? **2.** What color is her hair? **3.** What time is it? **4.** What time does the train leave? **5.** What does he do? **6.** What is the price of *Le Figaro*? **7.** What do newspapers cost? **8.** What's the price of meals? **9.** What's the date? **10.** What's today? **11.** What year were you born (In what . . .)? **12.** How old is she?
(*b*) **1.** He is lucky. **2.** He is out of luck. **3.** You are lucky. **4.** You are out of luck. **5.** I am sorry. **6.** Agreed. **7.** A little later. **8.** An hour later. **9.** Two years later. **10.** Gladly. **11.** I think so (**Je crois que oui**). **12.** Where do they sell papers?

CONVERSATION 11

PARIS: DEVANT L'ÉGLISE DE SAINT-GERMAIN DES PRÈS

Taking a Walk

JEAN – [1]Voulez-vous faire* une promenade?

JOHN – [1]*Do you want to take a walk?*

MARIE – [2]Je veux bien. Quel temps fait-il?

MARIE – [2]*Sure (I am quite willing). How is the weather?*

JEAN – [3]Il fait beau. [4]Mais il fait du vent.

JOHN – [3]*The weather is fine.* [4]*But it is windy.*

MARIE – [5]Est-ce qu'il fait froid?

MARIE – [4]*Is it cold?*

JEAN – [6]Non, pas du tout. [7]Il ne fait ni trop chaud ni trop froid. [8]C'est un beau temps pour une promenade.

JOHN – [6]*No, not at all.* [7]*It is neither too hot nor too cold.* [8]*It is fine weather for a walk.*

MARIE – [9]Faut-il prendre un imperméable?

MARIE – [9]*Must one (Is it necessary to) take a raincoat?*

JEAN – [10]Ce n'est pas la peine. [11]Il ne va pas pleuvoir.

JOHN – [10]*It is not worth the trouble.* [11]*It is not going to rain.*

MARIE – [12]Êtes-vous sûr qu'il ne va pas pleuvoir?

MARIE – [12]*Are you sure it is not going to rain?*

JEAN – [13]Oui, regardez le soleil. [14]Pas un seul nuage dans le ciel bleu.

JOHN – [13]*Yes, look at the sunshine.* [14]*(There is) not a cloud in the blue sky.*

MARIE – [15]Bon. Je vous crois. J'ai confiance en vous.

MARIE – [14]*Okay, I believe you.* [15]*I have confidence in you.*

(Une heure plus tard)

(One hour later)

MARIE – [16]Il pleut; il pleut à verse. [17]Je suis mouillée jusqu'aux os. [18]C'est votre faute.

MARIE – [16]*It is raining; it is pouring.* [17]*I am wet to the skin (right to the bones).* [18]*It is your fault.*

JEAN – [19]Ma faute? Comment cela?

JOHN – [19]*My fault? How (can you say) that?*

MARIE – [20]Vous savez bien. Je n'ai plus confiance en vous.

MARIE – [20]*You know (very well). I no longer have confidence in you.*

---

* **Faire** (*to do, to make*) is used in a number of idiomatic expressions, such as **faire une promenade** (*to take a walk*) and in impersonal expressions describing the weather.

AU JARDIN DU LUXEMBOURG

I. **Substitutions.** *Répétez les phrases suivantes en substituant les mots indiqués:*

1. Il fait beau.

froid / chaud / du vent / très beau / très froid / très chaud / trop froid / trop chaud / trop de vent

2. Il ne fait pas froid.

pas très froid / pas trop froid / pas chaud / pas très chaud / pas trop chaud / pas de vent / pas beaucoup de vent / pas trop de vent

3. Êtes-vous sûr qu'il ne va pas pleuvoir?

faire froid / faire chaud / faire du vent / faire trop de vent

4. Ce n'est pas la peine de prendre un imperméable.

un parapluie (*umbrella*) / un pardessus (*man's overcoat*) / un manteau (*girl's coat*) / un pull-over (*sweater*)

II. *Répondez en français, d'après le texte, à chacune des questions suivantes:*

1. Voulez-vous faire une promenade? **2.** Quel temps fait-il? **3.** Est-ce qu'il fait froid? **4.** Fait-il chaud? **5.** Est-ce un beau temps pour une promenade? **6.** Faut-il prendre un imperméable? **7.** Est-ce la peine de prendre un imperméable? **8.** Ne va-t-il pas pleuvoir? **9.** De quelle couleur est le ciel? **10.** Êtes-vous sûr qu'il ne va pas pleuvoir? **11.** Avez-vous confiance en moi? **12.** [*Une heure plus tard*] Est-ce qu'il pleut maintenant (*now*)? **13.** Êtes-vous mouillé(e)? **14.** Est-ce ma faute?

III. *Répondez en français à chacune des questions suivantes:*

1. Quel temps fait-il aujourd'hui? **2.** Est-ce qu'il fait du vent? **3.** Est-ce qu'il pleut? **4.** Est-ce qu'il va pleuvoir? **5.** Quel temps fait-il au mois de juillet?

6. Quel temps fait-il au mois de décembre? **7.** Fait-il du vent au mois de mars? **8.** Fait-il très froid ici au mois de janvier? **9.** Y a-t-il des nuages dans le ciel, aujourd'hui?

IV. *Demandez à quelqu'un:*

1. s'il veut faire une promenade. **2.** quel temps il fait. **3.** s'il fait froid. **4.** s'il fait trop froid. **5.** s'il fait trop chaud. **6.** s'il fait du vent. **7.** si c'est un beau temps pour une promenade. **8.** s'il faut prendre un imperméable. **9.** si c'est la peine de prendre un imperméable. **10.** s'il est sûr qu'il ne va pas pleuvoir.

V. *Mettez les phrases suivantes à la forme négative en employant* **ne . . . pas,** *puis* **ne . . . plus.**

EX.:—J'ai confiance en vous.
—Je n'ai pas confiance en vous.
—Je n'ai plus confiance en vous.

1. J'ai faim. **2.** Nous avons des cigarettes. **3.** Il pleut. **4.** Il fait du vent. **5.** Il fait froid. **6.** Elle est étudiante. **7.** Elle a de la monnaie. **8.** C'est un bon hôtel. **9.** Il y a un restaurant dans le musée. **10.** Je déjeune au restaurant. **11.** Je sais où Jeanne d'Arc est née. **12.** Je vais vous poser des questions.

VI. *Combinez deux phrases en une seule, en employant* **ne . . . ni . . . ni.**

EX.:—Il ne fait pas chaud. Il ne fait pas froid.
—Il ne fait ni chaud ni froid.

1. Il ne fait pas trop chaud. Il ne fait pas trop froid. **2.** Elle n'est pas petite. Elle n'est pas grande. **3.** Elle n'est pas brune. Elle n'est pas blonde. **4.** Je ne parle pas français. Je ne parle pas anglais. **5.** Je n'ai pas de frères.* Je n'ai pas de sœurs. **6.** Nous n'avons pas de vin rouge. Nous n'avons pas de vin blanc. **7.** Nous n'avons pas de pommes. Nous n'avons pas de bananes. **8.** Il n'y a pas d'hôtel ici. Il n'y a pas de restaurant ici.

VII. Dictée d'après la Conversation 10, pp. 70-71

VIII. Conversation.

Un rendez-vous pour une promenade.

---

* With **ne . . . ni . . . ni,** nouns are used without a definite article and without the preposition **de.** Ex.: **Elle n'a ni frères ni sœurs.**

CONVERSATION 12

Which Season Do You Prefer?

ROGER – [1]Regardez la neige!

JEAN – [2]Tiens! C'est la première fois qu'il neige* cette année.

ROGER – [3]Je n'aime pas du tout l'hiver.

JEAN – [4]Pourquoi pas? [5]L'hiver a ses plaisirs. [6]On peut patiner, faire du ski, aller au théâtre, [7]ou bien jouer aux cartes, écouter des disques, regarder la télévision . . .

ROGER – [8]Oui, mais l'hiver dure trop longtemps.

ROGER – [1]*Look at the snow!*

JOHN – [2]*Well! It is the first time it has snowed this year.*

ROGER – [3]*I don't like winter at all.*

JOHN – [4]*Why not?* [5]*Winter has its pleasures.* [6]*You can skate, ski, go to the theatre,* [7]*or play cards, listen to records, look at television . . .*

ROGER – [8]*Yes, but winter lasts too long.*

---

* Note that in French, the present tense is used in this phrase although in English we normally use the present perfect to express the same idea.

JEAN – [9]Quelle saison préférez-vous, alors?

ROGER – [10]Je crois que je préfère l'été. [11]J'aime voir des feuilles sur les arbres, [12]et des fleurs dans les jardins.

JEAN – [13]Mais la campagne est aussi belle en automne qu'en été. [14]Surtout, il fait moins chaud.

ROGER – [15]Oui. L'automne commence bien, [16]mais il finit mal. [17]J'aime mieux le printemps.

JEAN – [18]Vous avez raison. [19]Tout le monde est content de voir venir le printemps.

JOHN – [9]*What season do you prefer, then?*

ROGER – [10]*I think I prefer summer.* [11]*I like to see leaves on the trees,* [12]*and flowers in the gardens.*

JOHN – [13]*But the country is as beautiful in in the fall as in the summer.* [14]*Above all, it is not so hot.*

ROGER – [15]*Yes. The fall begins well,* [16]*but it ends badly.* [17]*I like the spring better.*

JOHN – [18]*You are right.* [19]*Everyone is glad to see the spring come.*

I. Substitutions. *Répétez les phrases suivantes en substituant les mots indiqués:*

1. Je n'aime pas du tout l'hiver.
la neige / les bananes / le vent / le mois de février

2. Je n'aime pas du tout faire du ski.
jouer aux cartes / patiner / aller au théâtre / aller à la campagne

3. J'aime voir venir le printemps.
l'été / l'automne / l'hiver / le beau temps

4. On peut aller au théâtre en hiver.
au printemps / en été / en automne / au mois de janvier

5. On peut jouer aux cartes.
aux échecs (*chess*) / au tennis / du piano / de la guitare

6. La campagne est aussi belle en automne qu'en été.
Les fleurs sont aussi belles / Les feuilles sont aussi belles / Les arbres sont aussi beaux / Les jardins sont aussi beaux / Le ciel est aussi beau / Il fait aussi beau

II. *Répondez en français à chacune des questions suivantes:*

1. Quel temps fait-il? **2.** Est-ce la première fois qu'il neige cette année? **3.** Est-ce que Roger aime l'hiver? **4.** Qu'est-ce qu'on peut faire en hiver? **5.** Est-ce que l'hiver dure longtemps ici? **6.** Quelle saison préférez-vous? **7.** Pourquoi Roger préfère-t-il l'été? **8.** En quelle saison y a-t-il des fleurs dans les jardins? **9.** En quelle saison y a-t-il des feuilles sur les arbres? **10.** Y a-t-il des feuilles sur les arbres en hiver? **11.** Aimez-vous la campagne en automne? **12.** Est-ce que la campagne est belle en automne? **13.** Est-ce que la campagne est aussi belle en automne qu'en été? **14.** Est-ce qu'il fait moins chaud en automne qu'en été? **15.** Est-ce que l'automne commence bien? **16.** Est-ce que l'automne finit bien?

III. *Demandez à quelqu'un:*

1. quel temps il fait. **2.** s'il pleut. **3.** s'il neige. **4.** si c'est la première fois qu'il neige cette année. **5.** si Roger aime l'hiver. **6.** ce qu'on peut faire en hiver (*what one can do in winter*). **7.** si l'hiver dure trop longtemps ici. **8.** quelle saison il préfère. **9.** pourquoi Roger préfère l'été. **10.** si la campagne est belle en automne. **11.** s'il fait moins chaud en automne qu'en été. **12.** si tout le monde est content de voir venir le printemps. **13.** quand commence le printemps. **14.** quand finit le printemps.

IV. Dictée d'après la Conversation 11, p. 85.

V. Causerie.

Quelle est votre saison préférée? Pourquoi?

Interrogative, Demonstrative and Possessive Adjectives

22. *Interrogative adjectives.*

—**Quel** âge avez-vous?	How old are (*what* age have) you?
—**Quelle** heure est-il?	*What* time is it?
—**Quelle** est votre adresse?	*What* is your address?
—A **quelle** heure arrive le train?	At *what* time does the train come?
—**Quels** sont les mois de l'année?	*What* are the months of the year?

A. Forms.

The forms of the interrogative adjective are:

	SINGULAR	PLURAL
MASCULINE:	quel?	quels?
FEMININE:	quelle?	quelles?

B. Agreement.

Like all adjectives, they agree in gender and number with the noun which they modify.

C. Use.

Do not confuse **Quel? Quelle?** etc. (*What?*), with **Que? Qu'est-ce que?** (*What?*). As **quel? quelle?** etc., are forms of the interrogative *adjective*, they are used only to modify nouns. The noun modified may stand next to the adjective (**Quel âge . . . ? Quelle heure . . . ?**) or it may be separated from it by a form of the verb **être** (**Quelle est votre adresse?**). But **Que?** (**Qu'est-ce que?**) is a pronoun and can not of course modify a noun. Ex.: **Que** pensez-vous de Charles? or **Qu'est-ce que** vous pensez de Charles?

23. *Demonstrative adjectives.*

—Quel temps fait-il **ce** matin?	How is the weather *this* morning?
—Êtes-vous libre **cet** après-midi?	Are you free *this* afternoon?
—C'est la première fois qu'il neige **cette** année.	It is the first time it has snowed *this* year.
—Je n'aime pas **ces** fruits.	I don't like *this* fruit.

A. Forms.

The forms of the demonstrative adjective are:

	SINGULAR	PLURAL
MASCULINE:	ce, (cet)	ces
FEMININE:	cette	ces

B. Use.

Ce is used before masculine singular nouns or adjectives that begin with a consonant. **Cet** is used before those beginning with a vowel or mute *h*. Ex.: **Ce** matin. **Ce** soir. BUT: **Cet** après-midi. **Cet** hôtel.

The suffix **-là** is often added to the noun following a demonstrative adjective — especially with expressions of time. The difference between **ce matin** and **ce matin-là** is *this* morning and *that* morning. Compare: **cet été** and **cet été-là, cette année** and **cette année-là.**

The suffix **-ci** is seldom used with demonstrative adjectives except in expressions of time. Ex.: **Ces** jours-**ci** (*these* days, some time soon).

24. *Possessive adjectives.*

—Où habitent **vos** parents?	Where do *your* parents live?
—**Mes** parents habitent à Paris.	*My* parents live in Paris.
—Voulez-vous **mon** imperméable?	Do you want *my* raincoat?

A. Forms.

The forms of the possessive adjectives are:

SINGULAR		PLURAL	
MASCULINE	FEMININE	MASCULINE AND FEMININE	
mon	ma (mon)	mes	*my*
ton	ta (ton)	tes	*your*
son	sa (son)	ses	*his, her, its*
notre	notre	nos	*our*
votre	votre	vos	*your*
leur	leur	leurs	*their*

B. Agreement and use.

Possessive adjectives agree in gender and number with the noun they modify. Ex.:

—Roger parle de **son** père et de **sa** mère.	Roger speaks of *his* father and mother.
—Marie parle de **son** père et de **sa** mère.	Mary speaks of *her* father and mother.

Note especially the difference between the possessive adjective of the third person singular (**son, sa, ses**) and that of the third person plural (**leur, leurs**):

(1) In referring to one person, you would use the third person singular forms:

—Où demeure **son** père?	Where does *his* (*her*) father live?
—Où demeure **sa** mère?	Where does *his* (*her*) mother live?
—Où demeurent **ses** parents?	Where do *his* (*her*) parents live?

(2) In referring to two or more persons, you would use the third person plural forms:

—Où demeure **leur** père?	Where does *their* father live?
—Où demeure **leur** mère?	Where does *their* mother live?
—Où demeurent **leurs** parents?	Where do *their* parents live?

(3) The forms **ma, ta, sa,** are used before feminine singular nouns or adjectives beginning with a consonant, the **mon, ton, son** forms before those beginning with a vowel or mute **h.**

ma sœur, **ma** petite sœur	BUT: **mon** autre sœur
ma petite auto	BUT: **mon** auto
ma nouvelle adresse	BUT: **mon** adresse

I. *Demandez en français à quelqu'un:*

1. quelle heure il est. **2.** quel temps il fait. **3.** quel âge il a. **4.** quel jour nous sommes. **5.** quelle saison il préfère. **6.** à quelle heure il va déjeuner. **7.** à quelle heure le train arrive. **8.** à quelle gare le train arrive. **9.** à quel restaurant il déjeune d'habitude. **10.** en quelle saison il y a des fleurs dans les jardins. **11.** en quel mois nous sommes. **12.** en quelle année il est né. **13.** quelle est son adresse. **14.** sa nationalité. **15.** sa profession. **16.** la date de son anniversaire. **17.** quels sont les jours de la semaine. **18.** quels sont les mois de l'année. **19.** quel est le premier jour de la semaine. **20.** quel est le dernier mois de l'année.

II. Exercices d'application.

A. *Répétez chacun des mots suivants, en employant un adjectif démonstratif:*

(*a*) EX.:—le matin,
—**ce matin.**

1. le soir, le journal, les journaux, le château, le cheval, les chevaux, le jardin. **2.** l'été, l'hôtel, les hôtels, l'hôpital, les hôpitaux, l'arbre, les arbres, l'après-midi, l'hiver, l'automne. **3.** la fleur, les fleurs, la rue, la jeune fille, les jeunes filles, l'adresse, la semaine, l'année.

(*b*) EX.:—ce matin (this morning)
—**ce matin-là** (that morning)

1. ce soir. **2.** cet après-midi. **3.** cette nuit. **4.** cette semaine. **5.** cette année. **6.** cet hiver. **7.** cet été. **8.** aujourd'hui (ce jour-là).

B. *Répétez les phrases suivantes, en employant l'adjectif possessif:*

EX.:—le frère de Marie,
—**son frère;**
—le frère de Jean,
—**son frère.**

1. le père de Marie. **2.** le père de Roger. **3.** la mère de Roger. **4.** la mère de Marie. **5.** la sœur de Jean. **6.** la sœur de Marie. **7.** l'adresse de Marie. **8.** l'adresse de Roger. **9.** les parents de Jean. **10.** les parents de Marie. **11.** la fiancée de Charles. **12.** les yeux de Louise. **13.** les yeux de Charles. **14.** les cheveux de Louise. **15.** les parents de Roger et de Marie. **16.** les cousines de Roger et de Marie. **17.** la nationalité de Roger et de Marie. **18.** la profession de Jean et de Roger. **19.** les promenades de Roger et de Marie. **20.** les heures de laboratoire de Jean et de Roger.

C. *Dites au pluriel:*

EX.:—votre frère,
—**vos frères.**

1. mon cousin, ma cousine, mon journal. **2.** votre cousin, votre cousine, votre journal. **3.** notre cousin, notre cousine, notre journal.

III. *Répondez en français à chacune des questions suivantes, en employant l'adjectif possessif convenable:*

1. Où demeurent vos parents? **2.** Où habitent les parents de Jean? **3.** Où habite le père de Jean? **4.** Est-ce que Jean a toujours sa mère? **5.** Est-ce que les frères de Jean sont en Amérique? **6.** Est-ce que ses sœurs sont aussi en

Amérique? **7.** Comment s'appelle la fiancée de Charles Dupont? **8.** Comment s'appelle le fiancé de Louise Bedel? **9.** Savez-vous l'adresse de Charles Dupont? **10.** Savez-vous l'adresse de Louise Bedel?

IV. *En commençant votre question par* **Qu'est-ce que,** *demandez en français à quelqu'un:*

EX.:—ce qu'il a comme dessert.
—Qu'est-ce que vous avez comme dessert?

1. ce qu'il veut comme dessert. **2.** ce qu'il veut comme plat de viande. **3.** ce qu'il veut comme vin. **4.** ce qu'il a comme hors-d'œuvre. **5.** ce qu'il a comme fruits. **6.** ce qu'il pense de Charles. **7.** ce qu'il pense de Marie. **8.** ce qu'il sait de Jeanne d'Arc. **9.** ce qu'il sait du 14 juillet. **10.** ce qu'on peut faire en hiver. **11.** ce qu'on peut faire au printemps. **12.** ce qu'on peut faire quand il neige.

V. *Dites en français à quelqu'un:*

EX.:—de vous donner son adresse.
—Donnez-moi votre adresse.

1. de vous donner son imperméable. **2.** d'apporter son imperméable. **3.** de vous donner son parapluie. **4.** de vous donner son adresse. **5.** de vous donner l'adresse de ses parents. **6.** de vous donner ses romans policiers.

VI. Révision. *Dites en français:*

1. You are right. **2.** He is lucky. **3.** As usual. **4.** Not yet. **5.** Not at all. **6.** When is your cousin going to be married? **7.** Winter lasts too long. **8.** Have you (the) change for one hundred francs? **9.** This little map is very useful. **10.** What color are her eyes? **11.** In the nineteenth century. **12.** In 1793. **13.** In the month of December. **14.** In the month of August. **15.** What is the date of the French national holiday? **16.** Do you want some coffee? **17.** Don't you want some coffee? **18.** It is the first time it has snowed this year. **19.** The last time.

Errands

JEAN – [1]J'ai des courses à faire. [2]Je veux d'abord acheter du pain. [3]On vend du pain à l'épicerie, n'est-ce pas?

MARIE – [4]Non. Il faut aller à la boulangerie.

JEAN – [5]Ensuite, je veux acheter de la viande.

MARIE – [6]Quelle espèce de viande?

JEAN – [7]Du bœuf et du porc.

MARIE – [8]Pour le bœuf, allez à la boucherie. [9]Pour le porc, allez à la charcuterie.

JEAN – [10]Faut-il aller à deux magasins différents?

MARIE – [11]Oui. En France, les charcutiers vendent du porc. [12]Les bouchers vendent les autres espèces de viande.

JEAN – [13]Je veux acheter aussi du papier à lettres. [14]On vend du papier à lettres à la pharmacie, n'est-ce pas?

MARIE – [15]Non. Les pharmaciens ne vendent que des médicaments.

JOHN – [1]*I have some errands to do.* [2]*First I want to buy some bread.* [3]*They sell bread at the grocery store, don't they?*

MARIE – [4]*No. You have to go to the bakery.*

JOHN – [5]*Then I want to buy some meat.*

MARIE – [6]*What sort of meat?*

JOHN – [7]*Some beef and pork.*

MARIE – [8]*For beef, go to the butcher's.* [9]*For pork, go to the pork butcher's.*

JOHN – [10]*Must one go to two different stores?*

MARIE – [11]*Yes. In France, pork butchers sell pork.* [12]*Butchers sell the other kinds of meat.*

JOHN – [13]*I want also to buy some stationery.* [14]*They sell stationery at the drug store, don't they?*

MARIE – [15]*No. The pharmacists sell only medicines.*

JEAN – 16 Où faut-il aller, alors?

JOHN – 16 *Where must one go, then?*

MARIE – 17 Allez à la librairie ou au bureau de tabac.

MARIE – 17 *Go to the bookstore or the tobacco shop.*

JEAN – 18 Ainsi, les bouchers ne vendent pas de porc, les pharmaciens ne vendent que des médicaments, et on vend du papier à lettres dans les bureaux de tabac!

JOHN – 18 *Thus, the butchers don't sell pork, the pharmacists sell only medicines, and they sell stationery in the tobacco shops!*

MARIE – 19 Vous pouvez aller au Supermarché ou au Drugstore, si vous voulez.

MARIE – 19 *You can go to the Supermarket or to the Drugstore, if you want to.*

JEAN – 20 Oh non! J'aime bien causer avec les marchands.

JOHN – 20 *Oh no! I like to chat with the shopkeepers.*

UNE LIBRAIRIE

I. Substitutions. *Répétez les phrases suivantes en substituant les mots indiqués:*

1. Il faut aller à la boulangerie.
à l'épicerie / à la boucherie / à la charcuterie / à la pharmacie / à la librairie

2. Il faut aller chez le boulanger.
l'épicier / le boucher / le charcutier / le pharmacien / le libraire

3. Où faut-il aller pour acheter du pain?
du bœuf / du porc / des médicaments / du papier à lettres / un journal / des cigarettes

4. Qu'est-ce qu'on vend à la boulangerie?
à la boucherie / à la charcuterie / à la pharmacie / à la librairie / au bureau de tabac

5. J'aime bien causer avec les marchands.
causer avec mes amis / faire des courses / aller au théâtre / voir venir le printemps

6. Pour acheter du bœuf allez à la boucherie.
des livres . . . librairie / du beurre (*butter*) et du fromage (*cheese*) . . . crémerie / du sel et du poivre (*salt and pepper*) . . . épicerie / des fourchettes et des couteaux (*forks and knives*) . . . quincaillerie

II. *Répondez en français à chacune des questions suivantes:*

1. Avez-vous des courses à faire? **2.** Que voulez-vous acheter d'abord? **3.** Est-ce qu'on vend du pain à l'épicerie? **4.** Où faut-il aller pour acheter du pain? **5.** Qu'est-ce que vous voulez acheter ensuite? **6.** Quelle espèce de viande voulez-vous acheter? **7.** Où faut-il aller pour acheter du bœuf? **8.** Où est-ce qu'il faut aller pour acheter du porc? **9.** Est-ce que les charcutiers vendent du bœuf? **10.** Est-ce que les bouchers vendent du porc? **11.** Où est-ce qu'on vend du papier à lettres? **12.** Qu'est ce qu'on achète à la pharmacie? **13.** Qu'est-ce qu'on achète à la crémerie? **14.** Où est-ce qu'on achète des fourchettes et des couteaux?

III. *Demandez à quelqu'un:*

1. s'il a des courses à faire. **2.** où l'on vend du pain. **3.** si l'on vend du pain à l'épicerie. **4.** quelle espèce de viande il veut acheter. **5.** où il faut aller pour acheter du bœuf. **6.** où il faut aller pour acheter du porc. **7.** si le charcutier vend du bœuf. **8.** si le boucher vend du porc. **9.** s'il faut aller à deux magasins différents. **10.** si l'on vend du papier à lettres à la pharmacie. **11.** où il faut aller pour acheter du papier à lettres. **12.** ce qu'on vend à la boulangerie. **13.** ce qu'on vend à la crémerie. **14.** ce qu'on vend à la charcuterie. **15.** ce qu'on vend à la pharmacie en France. **16.** ce qu'on vend à la quincaillerie.

IV. *Répétez les phrases suivantes en employant* **ne . . . que . . .** (only, nothing but).

EX.:—Les pharmaciens vendent des médicaments.
—**Les pharmaciens ne vendent que des médicaments.**

1. Les charcutiers vendent du porc. **2.** Les bouchers vendent de la viande. **3.** Mme Cochet a des revues françaises. **4.** Jean aime les revues américaines. **5.** Jean a un billet de cent francs. **6.** Il y a un restaurant sur la place. **7.** J'ai des frères. **8.** J'ai une sœur.

V. Dictée d'après la Conversation 12, pp. 88-89.

VI. Conversations.

(1)

Vous voulez acheter un journal, du papier à lettres et de l'aspirine. Vous demandez à quelqu'un où l'on vend ces différents articles.

(2)

Vous voulez faire un pique-nique. Vous demandez à quelqu'un où l'on vend les provisions que vous voulez acheter.

UN PEINTRE PARISIEN

25. *Forms and agreement of adjectives.*

un **petit** garçon	a *little* boy
une **petite** fille	a *little* girl
deux **petits** garçons	two *little* boys
deux **petites** filles	two *little* girls

A. Agreement.

Adjectives agree in gender and number with the noun modified.

B. Forms.

When the masculine singular form of an adjective ends in a consonant, you can often find the feminine by adding an **e** to the masculine singular. In these adjectives, the final consonant, which is normally silent in the masculine form, is pronounced in the feminine forms.

Ex.: content — conten**te**, grand — gran**de**, français — françai**se**, vert — verte (*green*), brun — brune (*brown*).

When the masculine singular form of an adjective ends in an **e**, the masculine and feminine forms are identical:

Ex.: **jeune** (*young*), **jaune** (*yellow*), **rouge** (*red*), **mince** (*thin*), **pâle** (*pale*), **russe** (*Russian*), **maigre** (*thin, too thin*), etc.

You obtain the plural form of most descriptive adjectives by adding an **s** to the singular: Ex.: petit — petit**s** (*m.*), petite — petite**s** (*f.*). This **s** is pronounced only in linking.

A few adjectives have slightly irregular forms:

SINGULAR		PLURAL	
MASCULINE	FEMININE	MASCULINE	FEMININE
actif	active	actifs	actives (*active*)
neuf	neuve	neufs	neuves (*new*)
heureux	heureuse	heureux	heureuses (*happy*)
sérieux	sérieuse	sérieux	sérieuses (*serious*)
doux	douce	doux	douces (*gentle*)
gras	grasse	gras	grasses (*fat*)
blanc	blanche	blancs	blanches (*white*)
italien	italienne	italiens	italiennes (*Italian*)

26. *In English, adjectives precede the nouns they modify. In French, only a few adjectives normally precede.*

A. Adjectives that precede:

—Est-ce que c'est un **bon** hôtel?	Is it a *good* hotel?
—C'est un **grand jeune** homme.	He's a *tall* young man.
—C'est une **petite jeune** fille.	She's a *small* girl.
—C'est un **vieux** monsieur.	He's an *old* gentleman.

The following adjectives normally precede the noun they modify:

(1) Regular: **grand** (*tall*), **petit** (*small*), **mauvais** (*bad*), **joli** (*pretty*), **jeune** (*young*).

(2) Irregular:

beau (bel)	belle	beaux	belles (*beautiful*)
bon	bonne	bons	bonnes (*good*)
gros	grosse	gros	grosses (*large, bulky*)
long	longue	longs	longues (*long*)
vieux (vieil)	vieille	vieux	vieilles (*old*)
nouveau (nouvel)	nouvelle	nouveaux	nouvelles (*new*)

The masculine forms **bel, vieil,** and **nouvel** are used only before masculine words that begin with a vowel or mute **h: Un bel enfant, un vieil employé, un nouvel hôtel.**

B. Adjectives that normally follow the noun modified:

—Elle a les yeux **bleus.**	She has *blue* eyes.
—L'hôtel du Cheval **blanc.**	The *White* Horse Inn.
—Elle a les cheveux **blonds.**	She has *blond* hair.
—C'est un ingénieur **français.**	He is a *French* engineer.

—C'est un garçon **maigre** (*thin*), **adroit** (*skilful*), **maladroit** (*awkward*), **sérieux** (*serious*), **poli** (*polite*).
—Elle porte une robe **bleue, verte** (*green*), **noire, rouge.**
—C'est une jeune fille **mince** (*slender*), **heureuse, sérieuse, douce, active.**
—Son père est d'origine **allemande** (*German*), **russe, espagnole** (*Spanish*), **italienne** (*Italian*).

Note (1) that adjectives of nationality always follow and those of color practically always do;

(2) Most adjectives normally follow the noun modified but occasionally they are placed before the noun for stylistic effect, for special emphasis, or for a special meaning; but it is scarcely useful to try to distinguish between «C'est une jeune fille charmante» and «C'est une charmante jeune fille» or between «C'est un dîner excellent» and «C'est un excellent dîner».

27. *Comparative of adjectives: regular.*

A. Superiority is expressed by **plus . . . que***

John est **plus grand que** sa sœur.	John is *taller than* his sister.
Il fait **plus froid qu'**hier.	It is *colder than* yesterday.

B. Equality is expressed by **aussi . . . que**

Roger est **aussi intelligent que** John.	Roger is *as intelligent as* John.
La campagne est **aussi belle** en automne **qu'**au printemps.	The country is *as beautiful* in fall *as* in spring.

C. Inferiority is expressed by **moins . . . que**

Marie est **moins grande que** son frère.	Marie is *less tall than* her brother.
En automne, il fait **moins chaud qu'**en été.	In fall, it is *cooler* (*less hot*) *than* in summer.

28. *Superlative of adjectives: regular.*

A. le plus (la plus, les plus)

Marie est **la plus jolie** jeune fille de la classe.	Mary is *the prettiest* girl in the class.
Henri est l'étudiant **le plus intelligent.**	Henry is *the most intelligent* student.
Ce sont les étudiants **les plus gentils.**	They are *the nicest* students.

* It is necessary to distinguish between **plus . . . que,** which is used in comparisons, and **plus de** which is an expression of quantity. Ex.: Marie a **plus de dix** cousins. Marie has more than ten cousins.

B. le moins (la moins, les moins)

L'hiver est **la moins belle** saison de l'année.	Winter is *the least beautiful* season of the year.
C'est aussi **la moins agréable.**	It is also *the least agreeable.*

(1) To express the superlative degree of adjectives, you insert the appropriate definite article before the comparative form. The comparative and superlative of the adjective **grand** (*tall*) have the following forms:

COMPARATIVE		SUPERLATIVE	
plus (moins) grand	*taller* (*less tall*)	le plus (moins) grand	*the tallest* (*the least tall*)
plus grande		la plus grande	
plus grands		les plus grands	
plus grandes		les plus grandes	

(2) Superlative forms of adjectives normally stand in the same position in relation to the noun modified as their positive forms.

(*a*) ADJECTIVES WHICH PRECEDE:

le **petit** garçon	**le plus petit** garçon
la **jolie** jeune fille	**la plus jolie** jeune fille

(*b*) ADJECTIVES WHICH FOLLOW:

l'étudiant **intelligent**	l'étudiant **le plus intelligent**
la chambre **agréable**	la chambre **la plus agréable**

Note that when the superlative form of an adjective which follows the noun modified is used, the definite article is used twice — once before the noun, and once as a part of the superlative form of the adjective.

29. *Irregular comparative and superlative of adjective* **bon** *and adverb* **bien.**

A. Adjective **bon:**

—L'hôtel Continental est un **bon** hôtel.	The Continental is a *good* hotel.
—L'hôtel du Cheval blanc est **meilleur.**	The White Horse Inn is *better.*
—C'est **le meilleur** hôtel de la ville.	It is *the best* hotel in town.

The forms are:

bon (*good*)	meilleur (*better*)	le meilleur (*best*)
bonne	meilleure	la meilleure
bons	meilleurs	les meilleurs
bonnes	meilleures	les meilleures

B. Adverb **bien:**

On mange **bien** à l'hôtel Continental.	The food is *good* at the Continental. (You eat *well* at the Continental.)
On mange **mieux** chez Jacques.	The food is *better* at Jack's.
C'est là qu'on mange **le mieux.**	That is where the food is *best.*
Je vais **bien.**	I am *well.*
Je vais **mieux.**	I am *better.*
Je vais **le mieux** du monde.	I couldn't possibly be better.

The forms are: **bien** (*well*) **mieux** (*better*) **le mieux** (*best*).

Note that in English the comparative and superlative of the adjective *good* and the adverb *well* are identical. We say *good, better, best,* and *well, better, best;* consequently we do not have to know whether *best* is an adjective or an adverb in such sentences as: *Spring is the best season,* and *It is the season I like best.* But in French you have to know whether the adjective or the adverb is called for in order to choose the correct form.

Le printemps est **la meilleure** saison (*adj.*).
C'est la saison que j'aime **le mieux** (*adv.*).

I. Exercices d'application.

A. *Employez la forme convenable de l'adjectif indiqué avec chacun des mots suivants:*

1. Beau, bel, belle.

EX.:—un château.
—**C'est un beau château.**

une jeune fille / un arbre / un hôtel / une maison / un printemps / un été

2. Vieux, vieil, vieille.

EX..—une église.
—**C'est une vieille église.**

un restaurant / un arbre / un hôtel / une maison / une rue / un ami

3. Bon petit, bonne petite.

EX.:—un restaurant.
—C'est un bon petit restaurant.

un garçon / une fille / une jeune fille / un vin blanc / un hôtel / une librairie

B. *Mettez au pluriel:*

EX.:—C'est un joli château.
—Ce sont de jolis châteaux.

1. C'est une jolie jeune fille. **2.** C'est un vieil ami. **3.** C'est un bel enfant.
4. C'est une longue histoire. **5.** C'est un mauvais restaurant.

C. *Répétez les phrases suivantes en substituant les mots indiqués:*

1. Marie a une nouvelle robe blanche.
rouge / noire / bleue / rose / jaune

2. C'est un jeune homme maigre.
poli / sérieux / adroit / maladroit

3. C'est une petite jeune fille brune.
blonde / grasse / mince / gaie / douce

4. Il fait plus beau aujourd'hui qu'hier.
plus chaud / plus mauvais / plus froid / plus de vent / moins chaud / moins froid / moins de vent

5. Marie est plus grande que sa cousine.
jeune / jolie / intelligente / gentille / agréable

6. Louise est moins grande que sa cousine.
jolie / gentille / intelligente

7. C'est une vieille légende bretonne (*from Brittany*).
irlandaise / allemande / norvégienne / suédoise

D. *Répétez, en employant le superlatif et* **de la ville:**

EX.:—C'est un bon restaurant.
—C'est le meilleur restaurant de la ville.

C'est un bon hôtel / C'est une bonne boulangerie / C'est une belle place / C'est une longue rue / C'est un joli jardin.

E. *Répétez les phrases suivantes en substituant les mots indiqués:*

1. Aujourd'hui, je vais bien.

mal / très mal / mieux qu'hier / moins bien qu'hier / le mieux du monde

2. Ici, on mange bien.

mieux qu'à l'autre hôtel / beaucoup mieux qu'à l'autre hôtel /
moins bien qu'à l'autre hôtel / beaucoup moins bien qu'à l'autre hôtel

3. J'aime mieux les pommes que les bananes.

le printemps . . . l'hiver / les arbres . . . les fleurs / les blondes . . . les brunes /
le vin blanc . . . le vin rouge / le tabac américain. . . le tabac français

II. *Répondez en français à chacune des questions suivantes:*

1. De quelle couleur sont les feuilles (*f.*) en été? **2.** De quelle couleur sont-elles en automne? **3.** De quelle couleur est le ciel quand il fait beau? **4.** Est-ce que la campagne est blanche en hiver? **5.** Est-ce que la campagne est aussi belle au printemps qu'en automne? **6.** Est-ce qu'il fait plus froid aujourd'hui qu'hier (*yesterday*)? **7.** Est-ce qu'il fait plus chaud aujourd'hui qu'hier? **8.** Quel est le mois le plus chaud de l'année? **9.** Quelle est la plus belle saison de l'année? **10.** Quelle est la plus mauvaise saison? **11.** Quelle est la meilleure saison pour faire du ski? **12.** Est-ce qu'il fait moins chaud au mois d'octobre qu'au mois de juin? **13.** Aimez-vous mieux le printemps que l'été? **14.** Aimez-vous mieux les blondes que les brunes? **15.** Est-ce que Jean est aussi grand que sa sœur? **16.** Marie est-elle aussi intelligente que son frère?

III. *Dites en français:*

1. What do you think of *Le Figaro?* **2.** I like *Le Figaro* a lot. **3.** It's one of the best French newspapers. **4.** I like *Le Figaro* better than *Le Monde.* **5.** French papers are smaller than American papers, aren't they? **6.** Are they as good as American papers? **7.** Certainly. **8.** Then, give me *Le Figaro*, please.

IV. Causeries:

(1)

Description d'une personne que vous aimez.

(2)

Description d'une personne que vous n'aimez pas.

An Invitation

JEAN – [1]Je suis invité chez les Brown. [2]Les connaissez-vous?

ROGER – [3]Non, je ne les connais pas. [4]Est-ce qu'ils sont Américains?

JEAN – [5]M. Brown est Américain, mais sa femme est Française.

ROGER – [6]Quand M. Brown est-il venu en France?

JEAN – [7]Il est venu en France il y a cinq ou six ans.

ROGER – [8]Est-il venu directement* des États-Unis?

JEAN – [9]Non, je crois qu'il a passé deux ou trois ans en Angleterre.

ROGER – [10]Où demeure-t-il à Paris?

JEAN – [11]Il demeure près du Bois de Boulogne.†

ROGER – [12]Qu'est-ce qu'il fait?

JEAN – [13]Il est banquier. [14]Sa banque se trouve près de l'Opéra.‡

JOHN – [1]*I am invited to the Browns'.* [2]*Do you know them?*

ROGER – [3]*No, I do not know them.* [4]*Are they Americans?*

JOHN – [5]*Mr. Brown is American, but his wife is French.*

ROGER – [6]*When did Mr. Brown come to France?*

JOHN – [7]*He came to France five or six years ago.*

ROGER – [8]*Did he come directly from the United States?*

JOHN – [9]*No, I think he spent two or three years in England.*

ROGER – [10]*Where does he live in Paris?*

JOHN – [11]*He lives near the Bois de Boulogne.*

ROGER – [12]*What does he do?*

JOHN – [13]*He is a banker.* [14]*His bank is near the Opera.*

---

* Adverbs are often formed by adding **-ment** to the feminine of an adjective.

† The Bois de Boulogne is a large and beautiful park west of Paris.

‡ The Great Opera House, which dominates the Place de l'Opéra, the Grands Boulevards, and the Avenue de l'Opéra, is one of the landmarks of Paris.

PARIS: L'OPÉRA

ROGER – [15]Comment avez-vous fait sa connaissance?

JEAN – [16]C'est un vieil ami de mon père. [17]Il est venu souvent chez nous à Philadelphie.

ROGER – [18]Êtes-vous déjà allé chez les Brown?

JEAN – [19]Oui, je suis allé chez eux plusieurs fois. [20]Sa femme et lui ont été très aimables pour moi.

ROGER – [15]*How did you meet him?*

JOHN – [16]*He's an old friend of my father.* [17]*He often came to our house in Philadelphia.*

ROGER – [18]*Have you been (gone) to the Browns' before?*

JOHN – [19]*Yes, I have gone to their house several times.* [20]*His wife and he have been very nice to me.*

PARIS: A MONTMARTRE

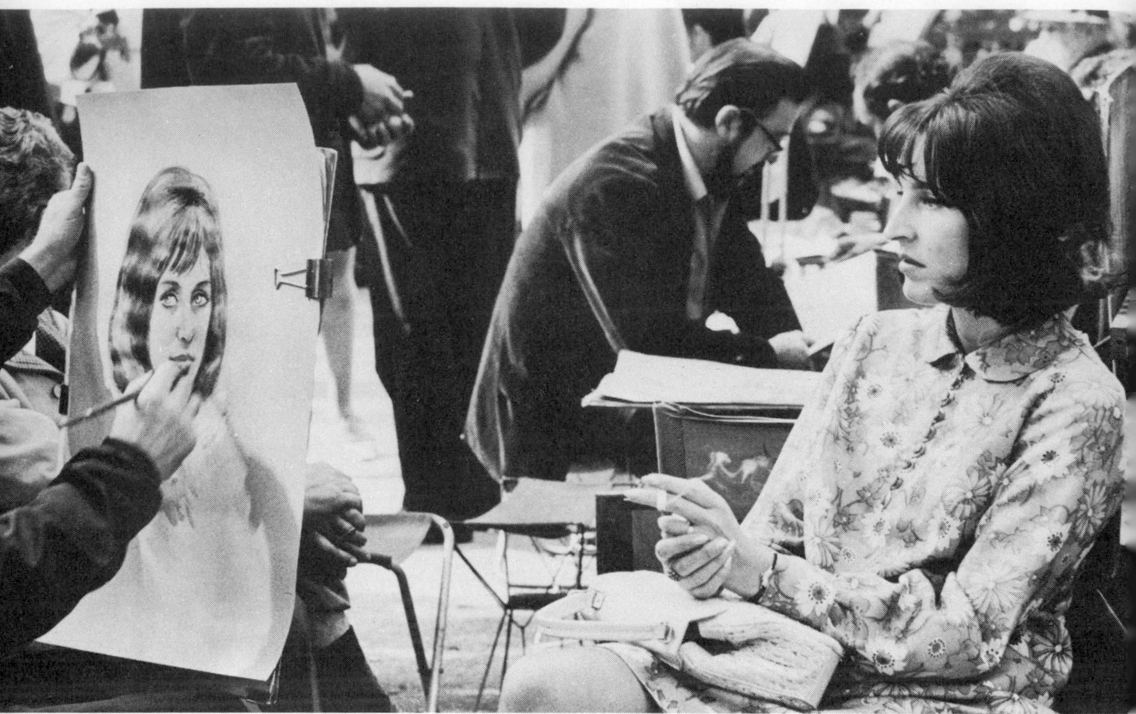

I. Substitutions. *Répétez les phrases suivantes en substituant les mots indiqués:*

1. Je suis invité chez les Brown.

chez eux / chez Marie / chez Roger / chez ma cousine

2. Il est venu en France il y a cinq ou six ans.

quatre ou cinq ans / deux ou trois ans / deux ou trois mois / deux ou trois semaines / cinq ou six semaines

3. Il a passé deux ou trois ans en Angleterre.

mois / semaines / jours / heures

4. Où se trouve sa banque?

sa maison / le Bois de Boulogne / l'Opéra / l'avenue de l'Observatoire

5. C'est un vieil ami de mon père.

grand / bon / nouvel / jeune

6. Je suis allé chez eux plusieurs fois.

deux fois / cinq ou six fois / la semaine dernière / dimanche dernier / au mois d'octobre

7. Sa femme et lui ont été aimables pour moi.

pour nous / pour eux / pour Jean / pour nos amis

8. Mon père est banquier.

agent de change (*investment broker*) / avocat (*lawyer*) / industriel (*manufacturer*) / négociant en vins (*wholesale wine merchant*) / fonctionnaire (*government employee*)

II. *Répondez en français à chacune des questions suivantes:*

1. Chez qui Jean est-il invité? **2.** Est-ce que Roger connaît les Brown? **3.** Est-ce que ce M. Brown est Américain? **4.** Est-ce que sa femme est Américaine? **5.** Quand M. Brown est-il venu en France? **6.** Est-il venu directement des États-Unis? **7.** Où les Brown demeurent-ils? **8.** Que fait M. Brown? **9.** Où se trouve sa banque? **10.** Comment Jean a-t-il fait sa connaissance? **11.** Où habite Jean? **12.** Est-ce que Jean est déjà allé chez les Brown? **13.** Est-ce que M. et Mme Brown ont été aimables pour Jean?

III. *Demandez à un autre étudiant (à une autre étudiante):*

1. chez qui Jean est invité. **2.** si Roger connaît les Brown. **3.** si M. Brown est Américain. **4.** quand M. Brown est venu en France. **5.** s'il est venu directement des États-Unis. **6.** où demeurent les Brown. **7.** ce que fait M. Brown. **8.** où se trouve sa banque. **9.** comment John a fait sa connaissance. **10.** où habite Jean. **11.** si Jean est allé chez les Brown. **12.** si M. et Mme Brown ont été aimables pour Jean.

IV. Révision. *Dites en français:*

1. How did you meet him? **2.** How did you meet her? **3.** Where did you meet him? **4.** Where did you meet her? **5.** When did you meet him? **6.** When did you meet her? **7.** How did you meet them? **8.** Where did you meet them? **9.** When did you meet them?

V. Dictée d'après la Conversation 13, pp. 96-97.

VI. Conversation.

Vous expliquez à un ami (une amie) pourquoi vous ne pouvez pas accepter son invitation à dîner.

The *Passé Composé*

30. *Meaning and formation of the* passé composé.

The **passé composé** (compound past) tense is used to indicate that the action or condition described by the verb took place in the past. It corresponds both to the English present perfect (*I have eaten lunch*) and the simple past (*I ate lunch*).

This tense is a combination of the past participle of a verb and the present indicative of an auxiliary verb. While in English the compound tenses of all verbs use the auxiliary verb *to have*, in French some verbs are conjugated with **avoir** and some with **être.** The first group is much more numerous than the second.

31. Passé composé *of verbs conjugated with auxiliary* avoir.

A. Passé composé of **être** (*to be*)*:* Irregular:

—**Avez-vous été** malade la semaine dernière?	*Were you* sick last week?
—Oui, **j'ai été** malade.	Yes, *I was* sick.

(1) The forms of the *passé composé* of **être** are:
J'ai été, *I was, I have been,* **tu as été, il (elle) a été, nous avons été, vous avez été, ils (elles) ont été.**

(2) This tense is composed of the present indicative of **avoir** and the past participle of **être,** i.e., **été.**

(3) For the negative of the *passé composé* of **être,** you use the negative form of the present indicative of **avoir** with the past participle **été.** Ex.: **Je n'ai pas été.**

(4) For the interrogative of this tense, you use the interrogative of the auxiliary with the past participle **été.** Ex.: **Avez-vous été?**

B. Passé composé of **avoir** (*to have*)*:* Irregular:

—**Avez-vous eu** le temps de déjeuner à midi?	*Did you have time* to lunch at noon?
—Non, **je n'ai pas eu** le temps de déjeuner.	No, *I didn't have* time to lunch.

(1) The forms of the **passé composé** of **avoir** are:
J'ai eu, *I had, I have had,* **tu as eu, il** (**elle**) **a eu, nous avons eu, vous avez eu, ils** (**elles**) **ont eu.**

(2) This tense is composed of the present indicative of **avoir** and the past participle of **avoir,** i.e., **eu.**

(3) For the negative and interrogative forms, you use the negative and interrogative forms of the auxiliary verb. Ex.: **Je n'ai pas eu. Avez-vous eu?**

C. Passé composé of déjeuner (*to lunch*): First Conjugation:

—**Avez-vous déjeuné** à midi?	*Did you lunch* at noon?
—Non, **j'ai déjeuné** à midi et demi.	No. *I lunched* at half past twelve.
—A quelle heure Roger **a-t-il dîné?**	What time *did* Roger *have dinner?*
—**Il a dîné** à six heures et quart.	*He had dinner* at a quarter past six.
—**Avez-vous acheté** un journal?	*Did you buy* a paper?
—Oui, **j'ai acheté** *Le Figaro.*	Yes, *I bought Le Figaro.*

(1) The forms of the **passé composé** of **déjeuner** are: **J'ai déjeuné,** *I had lunch, I have had lunch, I ate lunch, I have eaten lunch,* **tu as déjeuné, il** (**elle**) **a déjeuné, nous avons déjeuné, vous avez déjeuné, ils** (**elles**) **ont déjeuné.**

(2) This tense is composed of the present tense of the verb **avoir** and the past participle of **déjeuner,** i.e., **déjeuné.**

(3) You can always find the past participle of regular verbs of the first conjugation by substituting **-é** for the **-er** ending of the infinitive.

(4) For the negative and interrogative forms, you use the negative and interrogative of the auxiliary. Ex.: **Je n'ai pas déjeuné. Avez-vous déjeuné?**

The following regular verbs with which you are familiar will be used in the oral practice exercises: **dîner,** *to dine;* **acheter,** *to buy;* **parler,** *to speak;* **habiter, demeurer,** *to live in;* **apporter,** *to bring;* **commencer,** *to begin;* **donner,** *to give;* **jouer,** *to play;* **écouter,** *to listen to;* **regarder,** *to look at.*

32. Passé composé *of verbs conjugated with auxiliary* être.

—Quand **êtes-vous arrivé** à Paris?	When *did you get* to Paris?
—**Je suis arrivé** hier.	*I arrived* yesterday.
—Quand **M. Brown est-il venu** en France?	When *did Mr. Brown come* to France?
—**Il est venu** en France il y a deux ou trois ans.	*He came* to France two or three years ago.
—**Êtes-vous** déjà **allé** chez les Brown?	*Have you been* (*gone*) to the Browns' before?
—Oui, **je suis allé** chez eux plusieurs fois.	Yes, *I have been* to their house several times.

Aside from reflexive verbs (which will be studied later), the following verbs are the only common ones that are conjugated with **être:**

INFINITIVE	PAST PARTICIPLE
aller (*to go*)	allé
venir (*to come*)	venu
entrer (*to go in*)	entré
sortir (*to go out*)	sorti
partir (*to leave*)	parti
arriver (*to arrive*)	arrivé
rester (*to stay*)	resté
retourner (*to return*)	retourné
monter (*to go up*)	monté
descendre (*to go down*)	descendu
tomber (*to fall*)	tombé
naître (*to be born*)	né
devenir (*to become*)	devenu
mourir (*to die*)	mort

(1) Note also that **revenir,** *to come back;* **rentrer,** *to go back in, to go back home,* and other compounds of the verbs listed above are normally conjugated with **être.**

(2) The forms of the **passé composé** of **aller,** if the subject is masculine, are: **Je suis allé,** *I went, I have gone,* **tu es allé, il est allé, nous sommes allés, vous êtes allé(s), ils sont allés.**

(3) In compound tenses of the verbs listed above, the past participle agrees in gender and number with the subject of the verb. The feminine and plural forms of the participle follow the pattern of adjectives. Ex.: **Il est allé. —Elle est allée. —Ils sont allés. —Elles sont allées.**

I. Exercices d'application.

A. *Mettez les phrases suivantes à la forme négative:*

EX.:—J'ai dîné.
—Je n'ai pas dîné.

1. J'ai déjeuné à midi. **2.** Le garçon a apporté la carte. **3.** Il a parlé à Roger. **4.** Il a donné l'addition à Roger. **5.** Nous avons déjeuné. **6.** Nous avons parlé français. **7.** Nous avons habité à Paris. **8.** Nous avons été malades. **9.** Ils ont commencé à parler français. **10.** Ils ont passé trois ans en Angleterre. **11.** J'ai regardé la télévision. **12.** Il a apporté son imperméable. **13.** Je suis allé à la gare. **14.** Il a écouté. **15.** Il est arrivé hier. **16.** Nous sommes arrivés hier. **17.** Il est venu chez nous. **18.** Il est né en France. **19.** Nous sommes nés en France. **20.** Nous avons joué aux cartes.

B. *Mettez les phrases suivantes à la forme interrogative:*

EX.:—Roger a dîné.
—Roger a-t-il dîné?

1. Roger a déjeuné à midi. **2.** Roger a acheté un journal. **3.** Le garçon a apporté la carte. **4.** Le garçon a donné l'addition. **5.** Jean a parlé à la concierge. **6.** Jean et Roger ont dîné au restaurant. **7.** Jean est allé à la préfecture de police. **8.** Jean est déjà allé chez les Brown. **9.** M. Brown est venu des États-Unis. **10.** Jean est né à Philadelphie. **11.** Roger a regardé la télévision. **12.** Louis XIV est mort en 1715.

C. *Mettez les phrases suivantes au passé composé:*

EX.:—Je déjeune à midi.
—**J'ai déjeuné à midi.**

1. J'achète un journal. **2.** Nous parlons français. **3.** Il apporte la carte. **4.** Jean demande l'addition. **5.** Jean est malade. **6.** Il a le temps de déjeuner. **7.** Il va chez les Brown. **8.** Nous allons au bal. **9.** Il arrive à cinq heures. **10.** Le train part à six heures. **11.** Nous rentrons à cinq heures. **12.** Je dîne à sept heures. **13.** Nous jouons aux cartes. **14.** Nous écoutons des disques.

II. *Répondez en français à chacune des questions suivantes:*

1. A quelle heure avez-vous déjeuné? **2.** A quelle heure êtes-vous venu(e) à l'université? **3.** A quelle heure avez-vous dîné hier? **4.** A quelle heure êtes-vous entré(e) dans la classe de français? **5.** A quelle heure les autres étudiants sont-ils entrés dans la classe de français? **6.** Avez-vous acheté un journal aujourd'hui? **7.** Avez-vous commencé à parler français? **8.** Avez-vous regardé la télévision hier soir? **9.** Êtes-vous allé(e) à New York l'été dernier? **10.** Êtes-vous venu(e) à l'université hier? **11.** Avez-vous eu le temps de déjeuner? **12.** Avez-vous été malade hier? **13.** Les étudiants ont-ils commencé à parler français? **14.** Avez-vous joué aux cartes hier soir? **15.** A-t-il beaucoup neigé au mois de novembre?

III. *Répondez négativement:*

1. Avez-vous acheté un journal ce matin? **2.** Avez-vous passé deux ans en Angleterre? **3.** Avez-vous été malade l'été dernier? **4.** Êtes-vous allé(e) au laboratoire hier après-midi? **5.** Roger a-t-il regardé la télévision hier soir? **6.** Avez-vous apporté votre imperméable? **7.** Marie a-t-elle apporté son parapluie? **8.** Vos parents sont-ils allés en France? **9.** Êtes-vous sorti(e) hier soir? **10.** Êtes-vous rentré(e) à dix heures?

IV. *Demandez à quelqu'un:*

1. s'il a acheté un journal aujourd'hui. **2.** s'il est né à Chicago. **3.** s'il a donné son adresse à la concierge. **4.** s'il a eu le temps de déjeuner à midi. **5.** si son père est allé à Paris. **6.** où il est né. **7.** où son père est né. **8.** à quelle heure il a dîné hier soir. **9.** à quelle heure il a déjeuné aujourd'hui. **10.** quand Napoléon est mort. **11.** comment Jean a fait la connaissance des Brown. **12.** si Roger a joué aux cartes hier soir.

CONVERSATION 15

UN MAGASIN

Shopping

JEAN – [1]Où êtes-vous allée cet après-midi?

MARIE – [2]Je suis allée en ville.

JEAN – [3]Qu'est-ce que vous avez fait?

MARIE – [4]J'ai fait des courses.

JEAN – [5]Qu'est-ce que vous avez acheté?

MARIE – [6]Beaucoup de choses. [7]Je suis d'abord allée au Prisunic.

JEAN – [8]Qu'est-ce que c'est qu'un Prisunic?

MARIE – [9]C'est un magasin où l'on vend de tout, [10]à bon marché. [11]Ensuite, je suis allée chez la modiste.*

JEAN – [12]Quoi faire?

MARIE – [13]Acheter un chapeau.

JEAN – [14]Le chapeau que vous avez sur la tête?

MARIE – [15]Oui. Je l'ai payé très cher. Est-ce qu'il vous plaît?

JEAN – [16]Certainement. [17]Il est un peu drôle, [18]mais il vous va très bien.

MARIE – [19]J'ai marché tout l'après-midi. [20]Je suis un peu fatiguée.

JEAN – [21]Êtes-vous allée en ville à pied?

MARIE – [22]Oui, j'ai voulu profiter du beau temps. [23]En tout cas, cette promenade m'a fait beaucoup de bien.

JOHN – [1]*Where have you been this afternoon?*

MARIE – [2]*I went downtown.*

JOHN – [3]*What did you do?*

MARIE – [4]*I did some errands.*

JOHN – [5]*What did you buy?*

MARIE – [6]*Many things.* [7]*I went to the ten cent store first.*

JOHN – [8]*What is a Prisunic?*

MARIE – [9]*It is a store where they sell all sorts of things,* [10]*cheap.* [11]*Then I went to the milliner's.*

JOHN – [12]*What for?*

MARIE – [13]*To buy a hat.*

JOHN – [14]*The hat which you have on (your head)?*

MARIE – [15]*Yes. I paid plenty for it. Do you like it (does it please you)?*

JOHN – [16]*Certainly.* [17]*It is a little funny,* [18]*but it is very becoming.*

MARIE – [19]*I walked all the afternoon.* [20]*I I am a little tired.*

JOHN – [21]*Did you walk downtown?*

MARIE – [22]*Yes, I wanted to take advantage of the fine weather.* [23]*In any case, that walk did me a lot of good.*

---

* **Chez** means *at* (or *to*) *the house of, at* (or *to*) *the shop of* and is used only of persons. One says: **à la pharmacie,** but: **chez le pharmacien.**

I. Substitutions. *Répétez les phrases suivantes en substituant les mots indiqués:*

1. Qu'est-ce que c'est qu'un Prisunic?

un bureau de tabac / une modiste / une charcuterie / une épicerie / une librairie

2. Je suis allée chez la modiste.

la couturière (*dressmaker*) / le tailleur (*tailor*) / le cordonnier (*cobbler*) / l'antiquaire (*antique dealer*)

3. J'ai payé mon chapeau très cher.

trop cher / horriblement cher / cent francs / plus de cent francs

4. Est-ce que mon chapeau vous plaît?

mon nouveau chapeau / ma nouvelle robe / ce journal / ce magasin / mon papier à lettres

5. Est-ce que mon chapeau me va bien?

ma nouvelle robe / cette couleur / mon imperméable / mon nouvel imperméable / l'imperméable que j'ai acheté

6. Votre chapeau vous va très bien.

Votre nouvelle robe / Cette couleur / Votre manteau / Le rouge / Le bleu

7. En tout cas, cette promenade m'a fait beaucoup de bien.

le beau temps / le soleil / cet après-midi en ville / cette promenade à la campagne / ce médicament

II. *Répétez chacune des phrases suivantes en ajoutant* **et je suis un peu fatigué(e):**

1. J'ai marché tout l'après-midi . . . **2.** Je suis allé(e) chez la couturière . . . **3.** Je suis allé(e) en ville à pied . . . **4.** J'ai passé tout l'après-midi en ville . . . **5.** J'ai passé des heures en ville . . . **6.** Je suis allé(e) à plusieurs magasins différents . . .

III. *Répondez en français, d'après le texte, à chacune des questions suivantes:*

1. Où Marie est-elle allée cet après-midi? **2.** Qu'est-ce qu'elle a fait? **3.** Qu'est-ce qu'elle a acheté? **4.** Qu'est-ce que c'est qu'un Prisunic? **5.** Où Marie est-elle allée ensuite? **6.** Quoi faire? **7.** Qu'est-ce que Jean pense du chapeau de Marie? **8.** Est-ce qu'elle l'a payé cher? **9.** Pourquoi Marie est-elle fatiguée? **10.** Comment est-elle allée en ville? **11.** Pourquoi est-elle allée en ville à pied? **12.** Est-ce que cette promenade lui a fait du bien?

TRÉGUIER, PETITE VILLE BRETONNE

IV. *Demandez à quelqu'un:*

1. où il est allé cet après-midi. **2.** ce qu'il a fait en ville. **3.** ce qu'il a acheté. **4.** où il est allé ensuite. **5.** pourquoi il est allé au Prisunic. **6.** s'il a marché tout l'après-midi. **7.** s'il est allé en ville à pied. **8.** s'il a voulu profiter du beau temps.

V. *Répondez en français à chacune des questions suivantes:*

1. Qu'est-ce que c'est qu'une boulangerie? **2.** Qu'est-ce que c'est qu'une charcuterie? **3.** une boucherie? **4.** une pharmacie? **5.** un bureau de tabac? **6.** Qu'est-ce qu'on vend dans une boucherie? **7.** Qu'est-ce qu'on vend dans un Prisunic? **8.** Qu'est-ce qu'on achète chez la modiste? **9.** Où est-ce qu'on achète de la viande? **10.** des médicaments? **11.** du papier à lettres? **12.** des journaux?

VI. Dictée d'après la Conversation 14, pp. 108-109.

VII. Causerie.

Vous racontez (*tell*) comment vous avez passé l'après-midi.

Scènes parisiennes

Marie et Jean marchent ensemble dans le Jardin du Luxembourg. C'est un beau jardin près de l'Université, qui a été dessiné au dix-septième siècle et qui maintenant est très fréquenté par les étudiants.

Nous sommes à la fin de septembre. C'est le moment où l'été finit et où l'automne commence. Les feuilles des arbres sont déjà jaunes et la terre est couverte de feuilles mortes. Il y a un de ces légers brouillards si fréquents à Paris en automne, et l'humidité est assez pénétrante. Cependant l'automne parisien est d'ordinaire une saison charmante, juste assez triste pour être poétique.

Jean demande à Marie s'il fait froid à Paris pendant l'hiver.

AU JARDIN DU LUXEMBOURG.

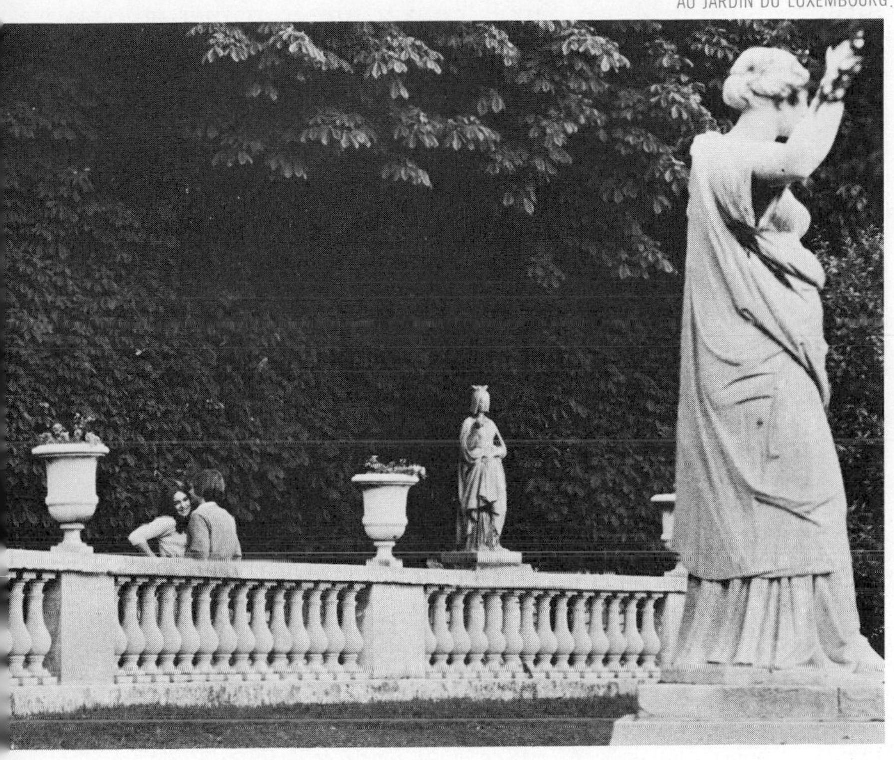

—Pas particulièrement, répond Marie. La température ne descend pas souvent au dessous de zéro degré centigrade et il neige rarement. Mais le ciel est souvent couvert et les pluies sont fréquentes, de sorte que l'hiver à Paris paraît plus froid qu'il ne l'est véritablement. Par contre, le printemps est une très jolie saison. Beaucoup des avenues parisiennes sont plantées de marronniers, et lorsqu'au printemps ces marronniers sont couverts de fleurs blanches et roses, c'est un spectacle magnifique.

Quittant le Jardin du Luxembourg, Jean et Marie descendent vers Saint-Germain-des-Prés. En face de la vieille église, Jean s'arrête un instant à la vitrine d'un libraire pour regarder les livres nouveaux.

—La plupart de ces livres ont une apparence bien austère, dit-il à Marie. Sur la couverture en papier jaune ou gris, il n'y a guère que le nom de l'auteur et le titre du livre. Aux États-Unis, il y a presque toujours sur la couverture de nos livres une image destinée à attirer l'attention, une jolie femme autant que possible . . .

—On achète un livre pour le lire et non pas pour la jolie femme sur la couverture, répond Marie. Les illustrations, même sur la couverture, sont réservées d'ordinaire aux livres de voyages et aux livres sur l'art, pour lesquels ces illustrations ont une espèce de valeur documentaire. Mais à quoi bon avoir une image sur la couverture d'un roman?

—Simplement parce que la figure ou la silhouette d'une jolie femme est toujours agréable à contempler, répond Jean.

QUESTIONS

1. Où se trouve le Jardin du Luxembourg? **2.** Quand a-t-il été dessiné? **3.** Par qui est-il fréquenté? **4.** Quand commence l'automne? **5.** Quel temps fait-il ce jour-là? **6.** Est-ce qu'il neige souvent à Paris pendant l'hiver? **7.** En quelle saison les marronniers sont-ils en fleurs? **8.** De quelle couleur sont les fleurs des marronniers? **9.** Où vont Jean et Marie lorsqu'ils quittent le Jardin du Luxembourg? **10.** Pourquoi Jean s'arrête-t-il un instant à la vitrine d'un libraire? **11.** Pourquoi dit-il que les livres français ont une apparence bien austère? **12.** Qu'est-ce qu'il y a souvent sur la couverture des livres aux États-Unis?

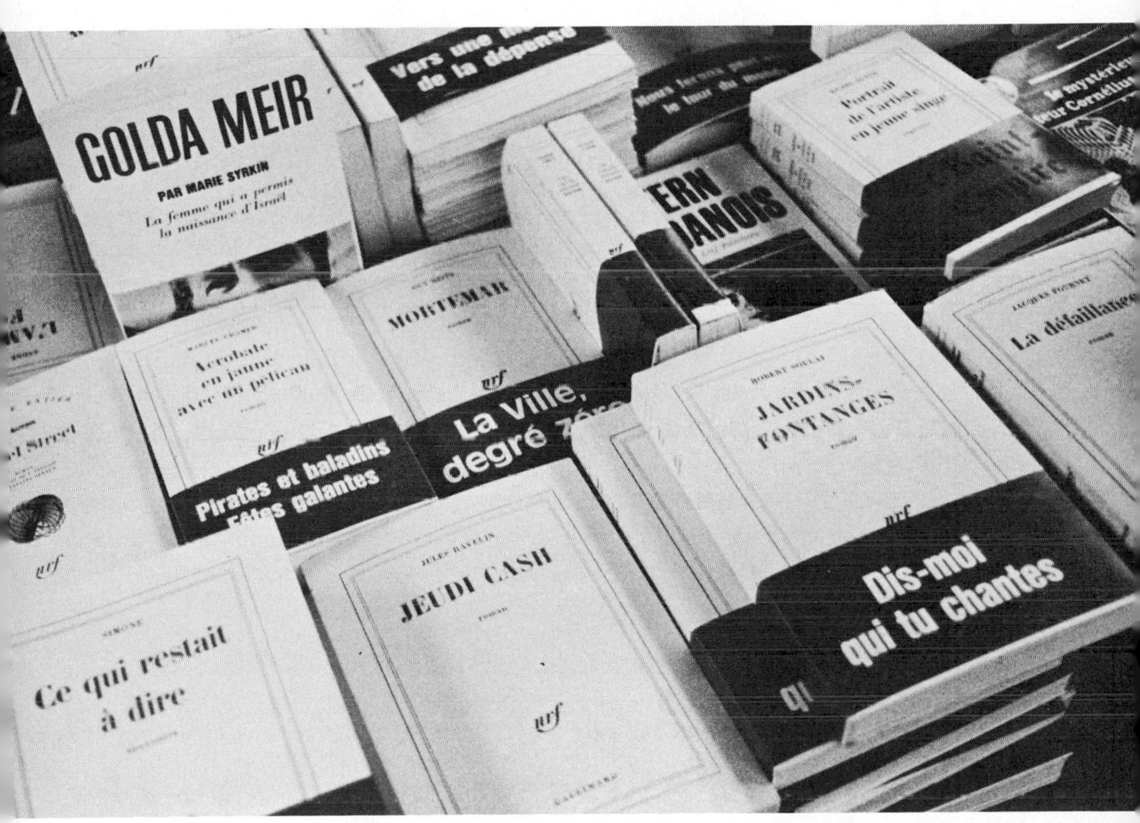

GOLDA MEIR
PAR MARIE SYRKIN
La femme qui a permis la naissance d'Israël
de la dépense
Portrait de l'artiste en jeune singe
MORTEMAR
Acrobate en jaune avec un pélican
La Ville,
Pirates et baladins
JARDINS-FONTANGES
JEUDI CASH
Ce qui restait à dire
Dis-moi qui tu chantes

9 Present Indicative and *Passé Composé* Second and Third Conjugations, and Reflexive Verbs

33. *Present indicative of* **finir** (*to finish*)*: second conjugation, regular.*

—A quelle heure **finissez-vous** votre travail?	At what time *do you finish* your work?
—**Je finis** vers cinq heures, mais les autres étudiants **finissent** d'habitude avant moi.	*I finish* around five o'clock, but the other students usually *finish* before I do.
—**J'obéis** à la loi.	*I obey* the law.

(1) The affirmative forms of the present indicative of **finir** are: **Je finis,** *I finish, I am finishing,* **tu finis, il (elle) finit, nous finissons, vous finissez, ils (elles) finissent.**

(2) The negative and interrogative forms follow the usual pattern. Ex.: **Il ne finit pas. Finit-il?**

(3) There are relatively few common verbs which belong to the second conjugation. **Choisir,** *to choose,* and **obéir à,** *to obey,* which are conjugated like **finir,** will be used in the oral practice exercises.

34. Passé composé *of* finir.

—A quelle heure **avez-vous fini** votre travail hier soir?	At what time *did you finish* your work last night?
—**J'ai fini** mon travail vers onze heures.	*I finished* my work at about eleven o'clock.

(1) The forms of the **passé composé** of **finir** are: **J'ai fini,** *I finished, I have finished,* **tu as fini, il a fini, nous avons fini, vous avez fini, ils ont fini.**

(2) For the negative and interrogative forms, you use the negative and interrogative of the auxiliary verb. Ex.: **Avez-vous fini? —Non, je n'ai pas fini.**

(3) The past participle of **finir** and other regular verbs of the second conjugation is found by substituting the ending **-i** for the infinitive ending **-ir.**

35. *Present indicative of* **répondre** (*to answer*): *third conjugation, regular.*

—**Répondez-vous** toujours aux lettres de vos amis? — *Do you* always *reply* to the letters of your friends?

—Oui, **je réponds** toujours à leurs lettres. — Yes, *I* always *answer* their letters.

(1) The affirmative forms of the present indicative of **répondre** are: **je réponds,** *I answer, I am answering,* **tu réponds, il répond, nous répondons, vous répondez, ils répondent.**

(2) The negative and interrogative forms follow the usual pattern. Note, however, that in **répond-il?** the **d** is linked and pronounced **t.**

(3) There are relatively few very common verbs which belong to the third conjugation. **Vendre,** *to sell,* and **entendre,** *to hear,* **attendre,** *to wait for,* **perdre,** *to lose,* which are conjugated like **répondre,** will be used in the oral practice exercises.

36. **Passé composé** *of* **répondre.**

—**Avez-vous répondu** à la demande de M. Duval? — *Have you answered* Mr. Duval's request?

—Oui, **j'ai répondu** à sa demande. — Yes, *I answered* his request.

(1) The forms of the **passé composé** of **répondre** are: **J'ai répondu,** *I answered, I have answered,* **tu as répondu, il a répondu, nous avons répondu, vous avez répondu, ils ont répondu.**

(2) The past participle of regular verbs of the third conjugation is found by substituting the ending **-u** for the infinitive ending **-re.**

37. *Present indicative of* **se dépêcher** (*to hurry*): *reflexive first conjugation, regular.*

—**Vous dépêchez-vous** pour arriver à l'heure à l'université? — *Do you hurry* to get to the University on time?

—Beaucoup d'étudiants **se dépêchent,** mais **je ne me dépêche pas.** — Many students *hurry,* but *I do not hurry.*

(1) A reflexive verb always has a pronoun object which refers to the subject of the verb. We have a few reflexive verbs in English (I hurt myself, you hurt yourself, etc.), but in French they are very common.

(2) The forms of the present indicative of **se dépêcher** are:

AFFIRMATIVE	NEGATIVE
Je me dépêche (*I hurry*)	Je ne me dépêche pas
Tu te dépêches	Tu ne te dépêches pas
Il se dépêche	Il ne se dépêche pas
Nous nous dépêchons	Nous ne nous dépêchons pas
Vous vous dépêchez	Vous ne vous dépêchez pas
Ils se dépêchent	Ils ne se dépêchent pas

INTERROGATIVE

Est-ce que je me dépêche?
Te dépêches-tu?
Se dépêche-t-il?
Nous dépêchons-nous?
Vous dépêchez-vous?
Se dépêchent-ils?

Note that in the affirmative forms both the pronoun subject (**il**) and the pronoun object (**se**) precede the verb. In the negative forms, **ne** follows the subject (**il**) and **pas** follows the verb — as you would expect. In the interrogative forms, the pronoun object (**se**) remains before the verb and the pronoun subject (**il**) follows the verbs according to the usual pattern.

(3) When the subject of a reflexive verb is a noun, it of course takes the place of the pronoun subject (**il, elle, on**); but the pronoun object (**se**) must always be expressed. Ex.: **Charles ne se dépêche pas. Charles se dépêche-t-il?**

(4) There are reflexive verbs in all conjugations, but in the oral practice exercises only the following ones will be used: **se coucher,** *to lie down, to go to bed;* **se lever,** *to get up, to rise;* **se réveiller,** *to wake up;* **se promener,** *to take a walk,* and **s'appeler,** *to be named.*

38. Passé composé *of* se dépêcher.

—**Vous êtes-vous dépêché** pour finir votre travail?	*Did you hurry* to finish your work?
—Oui, **je me suis dépêché.**	Yes, *I hurried.*

All reflexive verbs are conjugated with **être.** The easiest way to get the forms of the **passé composé** clearly in mind is to think of the auxiliary verb **être** as a reflexive verb (**je me suis**) and place the past participle (**dépêché**) after it.

(1) The forms of the **passé composé** of **se dépêcher** for MASCULINE subject* are:

* As the rule for agreement of the past participle in compound tenses of reflexive verbs is complicated (and of comparatively little importance for practical purposes), there is no point in trying to master it at this time. It will be explained in par. 74.

AFFIRMATIVE	INTERROGATIVE
Je me suis dépêché (*I hurried*)	Est-ce que je me suis dépêché?
Tu t'es dépêché	T'es-tu dépêché?
Il s'est dépêché	S'est-il dépêché?
Nous nous sommes dépêchés	Nous sommes-nous dépêchés?
Vous vous êtes dépêché(s)	Vous êtes-vous dépêché(s)?
Ils se sont dépêchés	Se sont-ils dépêchés?

NEGATIVE

Je ne me suis pas dépêché
Tu ne t'es pas dépêché
etc.

(2) If the subject is a noun, you follow the same word order as for the present tense (see par. 37). Of course the past participle comes at the end. Ex.: **Charles s'est dépêché. Charles ne s'est pas dépêché. Charles s'est-il dépêché?**

I. Exercices d'application.

A. *Répondez au singulier, puis au pluriel:*

EX.:—Finissez-vous?
—**Je finis. Nous finissons.**

1. Choisissez-vous? **2.** Obéissez-vous? **3.** Finit-il? **4.** Choisit-il? **5.** Obéit-il?

B. *Répétez, puis dites négativement:*

EX.:—Je finis.
—**Je finis. Je ne finis pas.**

1. Il finit. **2.** Il choisit. **3.** Il obéit. **4.** Nous finissons. **5.** Nous choisissons. **6.** Nous obéissons. **7.** Vous finissez. **8.** Vous choisissez. **9.** Vous obéissez. **10.** Ils finissent.

C. *Répondez au singulier, puis au pluriel:*

1. Répondez-vous? **2.** Vendez-vous? **3.** Entendez-vous? **4.** Attendez-vous? **5.** Répond-il? **6.** Vend-il? **7.** Entend-il? **8.** Perdez-vous votre temps?

D. *Répétez, puis dites négativement:*

1. Je réponds. **2.** Je vends. **3.** J'entends. **4.** J'attends. **5.** On vend. **6.** On entend. **7.** Nous répondons. **8.** Nous entendons. **9.** Vous répondez. **10.** Vous vendez. **11.** Vous entendez. **12.** Ils répondent. **13.** Ils entendent. **14.** Ils vendent. **15.** Il perd son temps.

E. *Mettez les phrases suivantes au passé composé:*

1. Je finis à cinq heures. **2.** J'obéis à la loi. **3.** Je choisis du papier à lettres. **4.** Nous obéissons à la loi. **5.** Nous répondons aux lettres. **6.** Je réponds au téléphone. **7.** Il répond à sa demande. **8.** Il vend son auto. **9.** Entendez-vous le téléphone? **10.** Répondez-vous au téléphone? **11.** Je ne vends pas de journaux. **12.** Ils n'obéissent pas. **13.** Je perds mon temps. **14.** J'attends l'avion.

F. *Répondez:*

EX.:—Vous dépêchez-vous?
—**Je me dépêche.**

1. Vous couchez-vous? **2.** Comment vous appelez-vous? **3.** Se dépêche-t-il? **4.** Se couche-t-il? **5.** Se lève-t-il? **6.** S'habille-t-il? **7.** Comment s'appelle-t-il?

G. *Répétez, puis dites négativement:*

EX.:—Je me dépêche.
—**Je me dépêche. Je ne me dépêche pas.**

1. Je me couche. **2.** Je me lève. **3.** Il se couche. **4.** Il se réveille. **5.** Elle se lève. **6.** Nous nous dépêchons. **7.** Nous nous levons. **8.** Nous nous couchons. **9.** Ils se lèvent (*pl.*). **10.** Il se dépêche. **11.** Je m'habille. **12.** Il s'habille.

H. *Mettez les phrases suivantes au passé composé:*

EX.:—Je me lève à sept heures.
—**Je me suis levé(e) à sept heures.**

1. Je me couche à minuit. **2.** Il se couche à minuit. **3.** Elle se réveille vers huit heures. **4.** Elle se lève. **5.** Elle se dépêche. **6.** Elle s'habille. **7.** Nous nous dépêchons. **8.** Nous nous habillons. **9.** Vous dépêchez-vous? **10.** Vous levez-vous? **11.** Vous couchez-vous? **12.** Se couchent-ils?

II. *Répondez en français à chacune des questions suivantes:*

(*a*) **1.** A quelle heure vous êtes-vous couché hier soir? **2.** A quelle heure vous êtes-vous levé ce matin? **3.** A quelle heure vous êtes-vous réveillé ce matin? **4.** A quelle heure avez-vous fini votre travail hier soir? **5.** A quelle heure êtes-vous venu à l'université? **6.** Vous êtes-vous dépêché pour arriver à l'heure à l'université?
(*b*) **1.** A quelle heure vous levez-vous le* dimanche? **2.** A quelle heure vous

* **Le dimanche** means *on Sunday* or *on Sundays*. This use of the definite article is explained in par. 113.

couchez-vous d'habitude? **3.** A quelle heure finissez-vous votre travail? **4.** Est-ce que vous obéissez à la loi? **5.** Répondez-vous aux lettres de vos amis? **6.** Est-ce qu'en France les pharmaciens vendent des journaux?

III. *Demandez à quelqu'un:*

1. comment il s'appelle. **2.** à quelle heure il se couche d'habitude. **3.** s'il se promène le dimanche. **4.** à quelle heure il se lève le dimanche. **5.** à quelle heure il se lève les autres jours de la semaine. **6.** comment s'appelle sa sœur. **7.** à quelle heure il s'est couché hier soir. **8.** s'il s'est promené dimanche. **9.** à quelle heure il s'est levé ce matin. **10.** ce qu'on vend dans un Prisunic. **11.** si en France les pharmaciens vendent des cigarettes. **12.** à quelle heure il finit d'habitude son travail.

A FOUGÈRES, EN BRETAGNE

Renting a Room

John and Roger have decided to take a room together and they find a room at 8, *rue du Docteur Roux in the* quinzième arrondissement.

JEAN – [1]Bonjour, madame. Avez-vous une chambre meublée à louer?

MME DUVAL – [2]Oui, monsieur. J'en ai une au premier.*

JEAN – [3]Est-ce que je peux la voir?

MME DUVAL – [4]Mais oui, monsieur. Par ici. [5]C'est la première porte à droite, en †haut de l'escalier. [6]Voulez-vous bien monter?

JEAN – [7]Volontiers.

MME DUVAL – [8]Voici la chambre. Comment la trouvez-vous?

JEAN – [9]Je la trouve vraiment très agréable.

MME DUVAL – [10]Et elle est très tranquille. [11]Il n'y a jamais de bruit dans le quartier.

JEAN – [12]Tant mieux, [13]car j'ai besoin de travailler le soir.

MME DUVAL – [14]Voici la salle de bains, avec eau chaude toute la journée. [15]Nous avons le chauffage central.

JEAN – [16]Quel est le loyer, s'il vous plaît?

MME DUVAL – [17]Trois cent cinquante francs par mois, monsieur.

JOHN – [1]*Good morning, Madam. Have you a furnished room for rent?*

MRS. DUVAL – [2]*Yes, sir. I have one (of them) on the second floor.*

JOHN – [3]*May I see it?*

MRS. DUVAL – [4]*Why of course, sir. This way.* [5]*It is the first door on the right at the top of the stairs.* [6]*Would you like to (will you please) go up?*

JOHN – [7]*Yes, I'll be glad to.*

MRS. DUVAL – [8]*Here is the room. How do you like it?*

JOHN – [9]*I think it is really very nice.*

MRS. DUVAL – [10]*And it is very quiet.* [11]*There is never any noise in this part of town.*

JOHN – [12]*So much the better,* [13]*for I have to (I need to) work in the evening.*

MRS. DUVAL – [14]*Here is the bathroom, with hot water all day.* [15]*We have central heating.*

JOHN – [16]*What is the rent, please?*

MRS. DUVAL – [17]*Three hundred and fifty francs a month, sir.*

---

* **Le premier (etage)** is one flight up from the ground floor.

† The **h** of the word **haut** is aspirate, therefore the **n** is not linked.

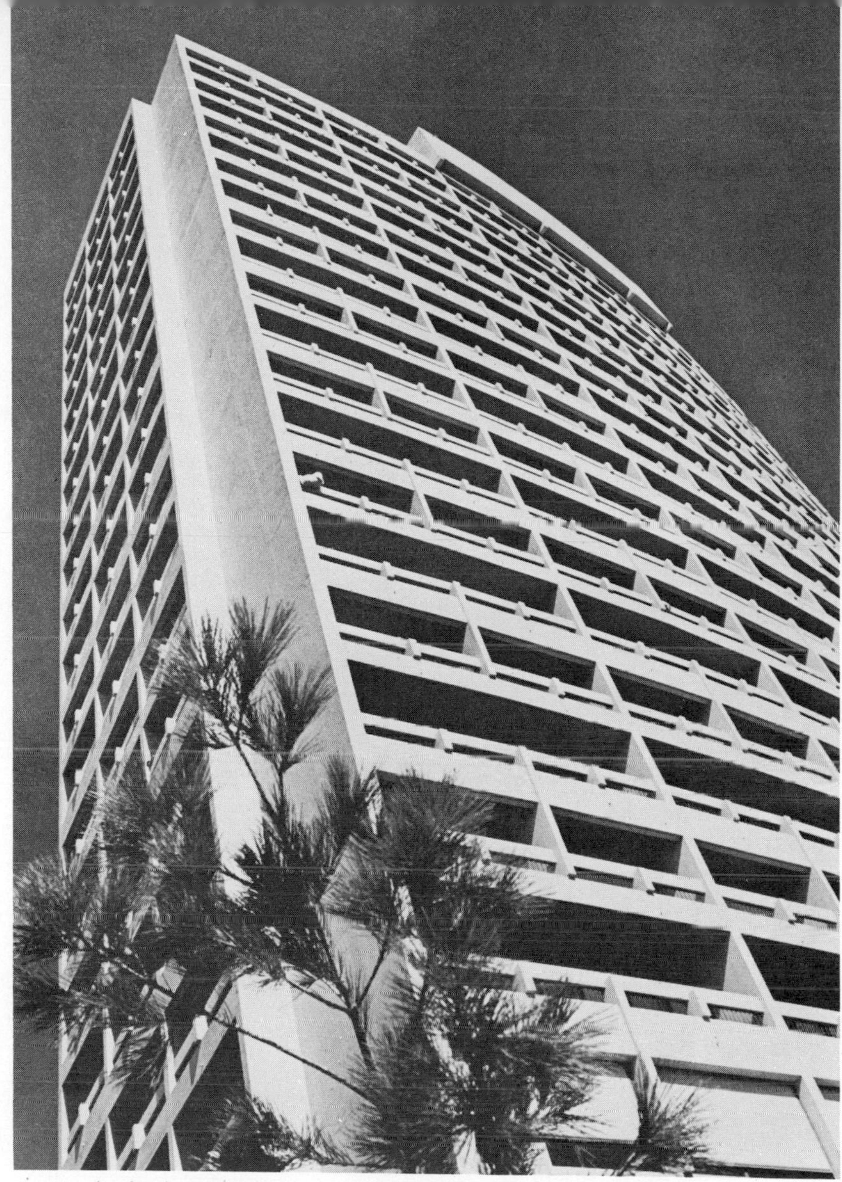

A MARSEILLE

JEAN – [18]Je crois que cette chambre me convient tout à fait. [19]Quand sera-t-elle prête?

MME DUVAL – [20]Est-ce que demain matin vous convient?

JEAN – [21]Oui, parfaitement.

MME DUVAL – [22]C'est entendu.

JEAN – [23]A demain, madame.

JOHN – [18]*I think that this room suits me perfectly.* [19]*When will it be ready?*

MRS. DUVAL – [20]*Does tomorrow morning suit you?*

JOHN – [21]*Yes, perfectly.*

MRS. DUVAL – [22]*All right.*

JOHN – [23]*See you tomorrow, Madam.*

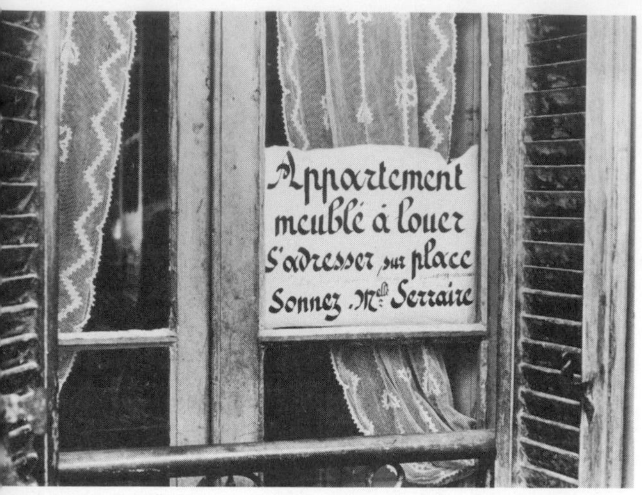

I. Substitutions. *Répétez les phrases suivantes en substituant les mots indiqués:*

1. Avez-vous une chambre à louer?
des chambres / un appartement / une maison / un piano

2. Avez-vous une maison à vendre?
des fleurs / une auto / un cheval / des meubles (*furniture*)

3. J'en ai une au premier.
deux / trois / quatre / plusieurs

4. Voulez-vous bien monter?
entrer / choisir / vous asseoir / vous dépêcher / répondre à cette question / rentrer à l'heure

5. Je crois que cette chambre me convient tout à fait.
cet appartement / cette maison / ce quartier / cette auto

6. J'ai besoin de travailler le soir.
toute la soirée / le matin / toute la matinée / la nuit / toute la nuit / le jour / toute la journée

II. *Répétez, en remplaçant le nom par* **le, la, les:**

EX.:—Comment trouvez-vous la chambre?
—Comment la trouvez-vous?

1. Comment trouvez-vous la maison? **2.** Comment trouvez-vous ma robe? **3.** Comment trouvez-vous le rosbif? **4.** Comment trouvez-vous ce raisin? **5.** Comment trouvez-vous mon chapeau? **6.** Comment trouvez-vous les hors-d'œuvre? **7.** Comment trouvez-vous ces poires?

III. *Répondez d'après le texte à chacune des questions suivantes:*

1. Avez-vous une chambre meublée à louer? **2.** Est-ce que je peux la voir? **3.** Comment trouvez-vous la chambre? **4.** Est-ce que la chambre est tranquille? **5.** Y a-t-il du bruit dans le quartier? **6.** Est-ce que Jean a besoin de travailler le soir? **7.** Y a-t-il une salle de bains? **8.** Y a-t-il de l'eau chaude toute la journée? **9.** Y a-t-il le chauffage central? **10.** Est-ce que cette chambre vous convient? **11.** Quel est le loyer? **12.** Quand la chambre sera-t-elle prête?

IV. *Demandez à quelqu'un:*

1. s'il a une chambre meublée à louer. **2.** si vous pouvez voir la chambre. **3.** si la chambre est au premier. **4.** où se trouve la porte de la chambre. **5.** comment il trouve la chambre. **6.** si la chambre est tranquille. **7.** s'il y a du bruit dans le quartier. **8.** quand la chambre sera prête. **9.** s'il y a le chauffage central.

V. *Répétez chacune des phrases suivantes en remplaçant* **ne . . . pas** *par* **ne . . . jamais.**

EX.:—Je n'ai pas d'argent.
—Je n'ai jamais d'argent.

1. Il n'y a pas de bruit dans le quartier. **2.** Ma tante n'est pas à l'heure. **3.** Ils ne sont pas à la maison. **4.** Je ne réponds pas aux lettres. **5.** Nous ne travaillons pas la nuit. **6.** Jean et Roger ne vont pas à la campagne. **7.** Ils ne répondent pas au téléphone. **8.** Je ne suis pas allé(e) en Angleterre. **9.** Il n'est pas venu me voir. **10.** Je ne me dépêche pas. **11.** Je ne me suis pas levé(e) avant sept heures. **12.** Je ne me suis pas couché(e) avant minuit.

VI. Dictée d'après la Conversation 15, p. 117.

VII. Dialogue.

Vous posez des questions au sujet d'une chambre que vous voulez louer.

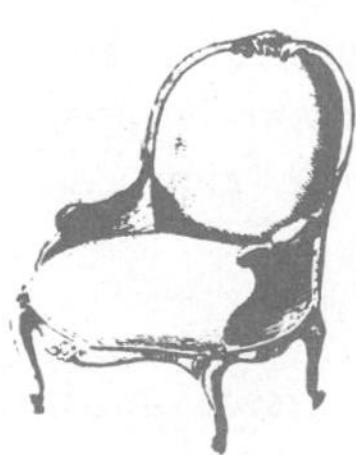

Unstressed Forms of Personal Pronouns

39. *Remark about the forms of personal pronouns.*

The French personal pronouns have two sets of forms: the unstressed forms, which are used only in conjunction with verbs (i.e., as subject or object of verbs), and the stressed forms, which will be studied later. The unstressed forms are sometimes called "conjunctive" pronouns and the stressed forms "disjunctive" pronouns.

40. *Unstressed forms of personal pronouns used as subjects of a verb.*

—**Je** vais à l'hôtel.	*I* am going to the hotel.
—**Il** est Américain.	*He* is an American.
—Qu'est-ce que **vous** voulez?	What do *you* want?

The subject forms are: **je, tu, il (elle, on), nous, vous, ils (elles).**

41. *Personal pronouns used as direct objects of a verb.*

—Allez-vous venir **me** voir?	Are you going to come to see *me?*
—Oui, je vais venir **vous** voir.	Yes, I am going to come to see *you.*
—Voici la chambre. Comment **la** trouvez-vous?	Here is the room. How do you like *it?*
—Je **la** trouve très agréable.	I think *it* is very nice.
—Aimez-vous les pommes?	Do you like apples?
—Oui, je **les** aime assez.	Yes, I like *them* all right.

A. Forms.

The direct object forms are: **me, te, le (la), nous, vous, les.**

B. Use and position.

(1) **Le, la,** and **les** refer either to persons or things. Ex.: Comment trouvez-vous **la chambre?** —Je **la** trouve très agréable. Comment trouvez-vous **Marie?** —Je **la** trouve très gentille.

(2) The direct object pronoun precedes the verb.* In compound tenses it precedes the auxiliary verb.

42. *Personal pronouns used as indirect objects of a verb — referring only to persons.*

—Avez-vous donné votre adresse à la concierge?	Did you give your address to the concierge?
—Oui, je **lui** ai donné mon adresse.	Yes, I have given *her* my address.
—Avez-vous parlé aux étudiants?	Did you speak to the students?
—Oui, je **leur** ai parlé.	Yes, I spoke *to them.*

Note that in «Je lui ai donné mon adresse», **lui** is the indirect object of **J'ai donné,** *I gave (it) to her;* in «Je leur ai parlé», **leur** is the indirect object of **J'ai parlé,** *I spoke to them.*

A. Forms.

The indirect object forms used to refer to persons are: **me, te, lui, nous, vous, leur.**

Note that **lui, leur,** replace either a masculine or feminine noun. Thus: «**Je lui ai donné mon adresse**» answers both the question «**Avez vous donné votre adresse à Charles?**» and the question «**Avez-vous donné votre adresse à Marie?**»

B. Position.

The personal pronoun object precedes the verb.†

If you have both a direct and an indirect object pronoun, they stand in the following order before the verb:

(1)	INDIRECT OBJECT		DIRECT OBJECT
	me		
	te		le
	se	*precede*	la
	nous		les
	vous		

* The only exception, that of affirmative imperative, will be studied in paragraph 52.

† Except affirmative imperatives.

Roger me montre le journal.	le
la revue.	Roger me la montre.
les romans.	les

(2)

DIRECT OBJECT		INDIRECT OBJECT
le		lui
la	*precede*	leur
les		

Roger donne le journal à Jean (Marie).	Roger le lui donne.
la revue	la lui
les livres	les lui

43. *Personal pronoun* **y** *used as indirect object of a verb — referring only to things.*

—Avez-vous répondu à la lettre?	Did you answer the letter?
—Oui, j'y ai répondu.	Yes, I answered (replied to) *it.*
—Avez-vous répondu aux lettres?	Did you answer the letters?
—Oui, j'y ai répondu.	Yes, I answered (replied to) *them.*

44. *Use of* **en** *as a partitive pronoun.*

A. To replace nouns in a partitive sense.

En is used here* as a pronoun object to replace nouns that are used in a partitive sense (**du pain, de la viande, des pommes**):

—Avez-vous du pain?	Have you any bread?
—Oui, j'**en** ai.	Yes, I have *some* (of it).
—Avez-vous acheté de la viande?	Have you bought any meat?
—Oui, j'**en** ai acheté.	Yes, I bought *some* (of it).
—Voici des pommes. **En** voulez-vous?	Here are some apples. Do you want *any* (of them)?

B. With expressions of quantity.

If you use expressions of quantity (**beaucoup, un peu, pas,** etc.) or numbers in such phrases, **en** must still be expressed:

* **En** used to replace a noun object of the preposition **de** will be studied in par. 52.

—Avez-vous une chambre à louer?	Have you a room for rent?
—Oui, j'**en** ai **une.**	Yes, I have *one* (of them).
—Avez-vous des cousins?	Have you any cousins?
—Oui, j'**en** ai **beaucoup.**	*Yes, I have a lot* (of them).
—Voici des pommes.	Here are some apples.
—**En** voulez-vous **une?**	Do you want *one* (of them)?

C. Position.

When there is another personal pronoun object of a verb, the pronoun **en** always comes last. Ex.: **Est-ce qu'il vous a donné des poires?** —Oui, il **m'en** a donné. —**Est-ce que vous avez donné des pommes à Charles?** —Oui, je **lui en** ai donné.

I. Exercices d'application. *Répétez en remplaçant les mots en italique* (in italics) *par un pronom personnel:*

A. le, la, les

1. Je trouve *la chambre* très agréable. **2.** J'aime bien *les revues françaises.* **3.** Je n'aime pas *les bananes.* **4.** Jean trouve *le chapeau de Marie* un peu drôle. **5.** Il connaît *Louise Bedel.* **6.** Il connaît très bien *les Brown.* **7.** Roger ne connaît pas *les Brown.* **8.** Comment avez-vous trouvé *la chambre?* **9.** J'ai trouvé *la chambre* agréable. **10.** Comment Jean et Roger ont-ils trouvé *le dîner?* **11.** Ils ont trouvé *le dîner* très bon. **12.** Le garçon apporte *la carte.*

B. en

1. J'ai *des fruits.* **2.** Je n'ai pas *de fruits.* **3.** Roger n'a pas *de frères.* **4.** Mme Cochet n'a pas *de revues américaines.* **5.** Elle a *des journaux français.* **6.** Jean n'a pas acheté *de romans policiers.* **7.** Avez-vous *des cousins?* **8.** A-t-il *des cousins?* **9.** Combien *de cousins* a-t-il? **10.** Il n'y a pas *de hors-d'œuvre.* **11.** Il n'y a plus *de hors-d'œuvre.*

C. en . . . une, plusieurs, *etc.*

1. J'ai *une chambre* au premier. **2.** J'ai acheté *un journal.* **3.** J'ai acheté *deux journaux.* **4.** J'ai acheté beaucoup *de fruits.* **5.** Je n'ai pas acheté beaucoup *de papier à lettres.* **6.** Il y a *une table* là-bas. **7.** Il y a *deux tables* par ici. **8.** Jean a mangé un peu *de viande.* **9.** Il a mangé un peu *de salade.* **10.** Il a mangé plusieurs *olives.* **11.** Roger a plusieurs *frères.* **12.** Marie a plusieurs *cousines.*

D. lui, leur

1. J'ai parlé *à la concierge*. **2.** J'ai parlé *à Jean*. **3.** Il n'obéit pas *à sa femme*. **4.** Elle n'obéit pas *à son mari* (*husband*). **5.** Jean a dit bonjour *à la concierge*. **6.** Il a dit au revoir *à Roger*. **7.** Il a dit au revoir *à ses cousins*. **8.** J'ai répondu *au professeur*. **9.** J'ai répondu *à mes parents*.

E. y

1. J'ai répondu *à la lettre*. **2.** Je n'ai pas répondu *à la lettre*. **3.** Je n'ai pas répondu *aux questions*. **4.** Je vais *à la gare*. **5.** Je suis allé *à la gare*. **6.** A quelle heure allez-vous *à la gare?* **7.** Quand allez-vous répondre *à cette lettre?* (y répondre). **8.** Je vais répondre *à cette lettre* demain matin.

II. Exercices d'application. *Compléments directs et indirects.*

A. *Répétez les phrases suivantes en substituant les mots indiqués et puis en remplaçant les noms par des pronoms personnels:*

EX.:—Il m'a donné le paquet.
—Il me l'a donné.

1. Il m'a donné le journal.
la carte / les fleurs / des fleurs / ma monnaie

2. Il nous a donné le journal.
la carte / les fleurs / des fleurs / notre monnaie

3. Vous a-t-il apporté le journal?
la carte / les fleurs / des fleurs / votre monnaie

B. *Répétez en remplaçant les noms par deux pronoms personnels:*

EX.:—J'ai donné le journal à mon père.
—Je le lui ai donné.

1. J'ai donné ma nouvelle adresse à la concierge. **2.** J'ai donné ma nouvelle adresse à mes amis. **3.** Il a apporté la carte à Jean et à Roger. **4.** Il a apporté des hors-d'œuvre à Jean et à Roger. **5.** J'ai donné les roses à ma mère. **6.** J'ai donné des roses à ma mère.

III. *Répondez en français en remplaçant les noms par les pronoms convenables:*

1. Connaissez-vous Louise Bedel? **2.** Connaissez-vous M. Brown? **3.** Connaissez-vous les Brown? **4.** Avez-vous apporté votre imperméable? **5.** Avez-vous des frères? **6.** Combien de frères avez-vous? **7.** Avez-vous acheté des journaux aujourd'hui? **8.** Y a-t-il des feuilles sur les arbres en été? **9.** Y a-t-il des feuilles sur les arbres en hiver? **10.** Avez-vous des parents en France? **11.** Est-ce que Jean a parlé au pharmacien? **12.** Est-ce que Jean a parlé à Mme Cochet? **13.** Est-ce que vous avez répondu à la concierge? **14.** Avez-vous répondu au télégramme? **15.** Jean a-t-il répondu aux questions de l'employé? **16.** Allez-vous au cinéma ce soir? **17.** Êtes-vous allé au cinéma hier soir? **18.** Avez-vous donné votre nom à l'agent de police? **19.** Avez-vous donné votre adresse à l'agent de police? **20.** Avez-vous donné vos papiers à l'agent de police? **21.** Avez-vous donné de l'argent à l'agent de police? **22.** Est-ce que votre père vous a donné de l'argent? **23.** Est-ce que le boulanger vous a donné votre monnaie? **24.** Vous a-t-il donné de la monnaie?

PATISSIER

CONVERSATION 17

Plans for the Afternoon

JEAN – [1]Où irez-vous cet après-midi?

MARIE – [2]J'irai en ville.

JEAN – [3]Qu'est-ce que vous ferez?

MARIE – [4]Je ferai des courses.

JEAN – [5]Qu'est-ce que vous achèterez?

MARIE – [6]J'achèterai un manteau et une robe.

JEAN – [7]Comment irez-vous en ville?

MARIE – [8]J'irai à pied, s'il fait beau.

JEAN – [9]Vous serez bientôt fatiguée. [10]Pourquoi ne prenez-vous pas l'autobus?

MARIE – [11]Je n'aime pas prendre l'autobus. [12]Il y a trop de monde.

JEAN – [13]Qu'est-ce que vous ferez s'il pleut?

MARIE – [14]S'il pleut, je prendrai un taxi.

JEAN – [15]A quelle heure rentrerez-vous?

MARIE – [16]Je rentrerai de bonne heure, avant cinq heures.

JEAN – [17]N'oubliez pas que nous allons tous les trois au cinéma ce soir.

MARIE – [18]Soyez tranquille. Je n'oublierai pas.

JOHN – [1]*Where are you going this afternoon?*

MARIE – [2]*I am going downtown.*

JOHN – [3]*What are you going to do?*

MARIE – [4]*I shall do some errands.*

JOHN – [5]*What are you going to buy?*

MARIE – [6]*I shall buy a coat* (*lady's coat*) *and a dress.*

JOHN – [7]*How will you go downtown?*

MARIE – [8]*I shall walk, if the weather is fine.*

JOHN – [9]*You will soon be tired.* [10]*Why don't you take the bus?*

MARIE – [11]*I don't like to take the bus.* [12]*There are too many people.*

JOHN – [13]*What will you do if it rains?*

MARIE – [14]*If it rains, I'll take a taxi.*

JOHN – [15]*What time will you get home?*

MARIE – [16]*I'll get back early, before five o'clock.*

JOHN – [17]*Don't forget that the three of us are going to the movies this evening.*

MARIE – [18]*Don't worry. I won't forget.*

JEAN – [19]A quelle heure Roger viendra-t-il vous chercher?

MARIE – [20]Il viendra me chercher à huit heures précises, dit-il. [21]Mais vous savez qu'il n'est pas toujours à l'heure. [22]Venez donc vers huit heures.

JEAN – [23]Entendu. A ce soir.

JOHN – [19]*What time will Roger come for you?*

MARIE – [20]*At eight o'clock sharp, he says.* [21]*But you know he is not always on time.* [22]*So come around eight o'clock.*

JOHN – [23]*Okay. See you this evening.*

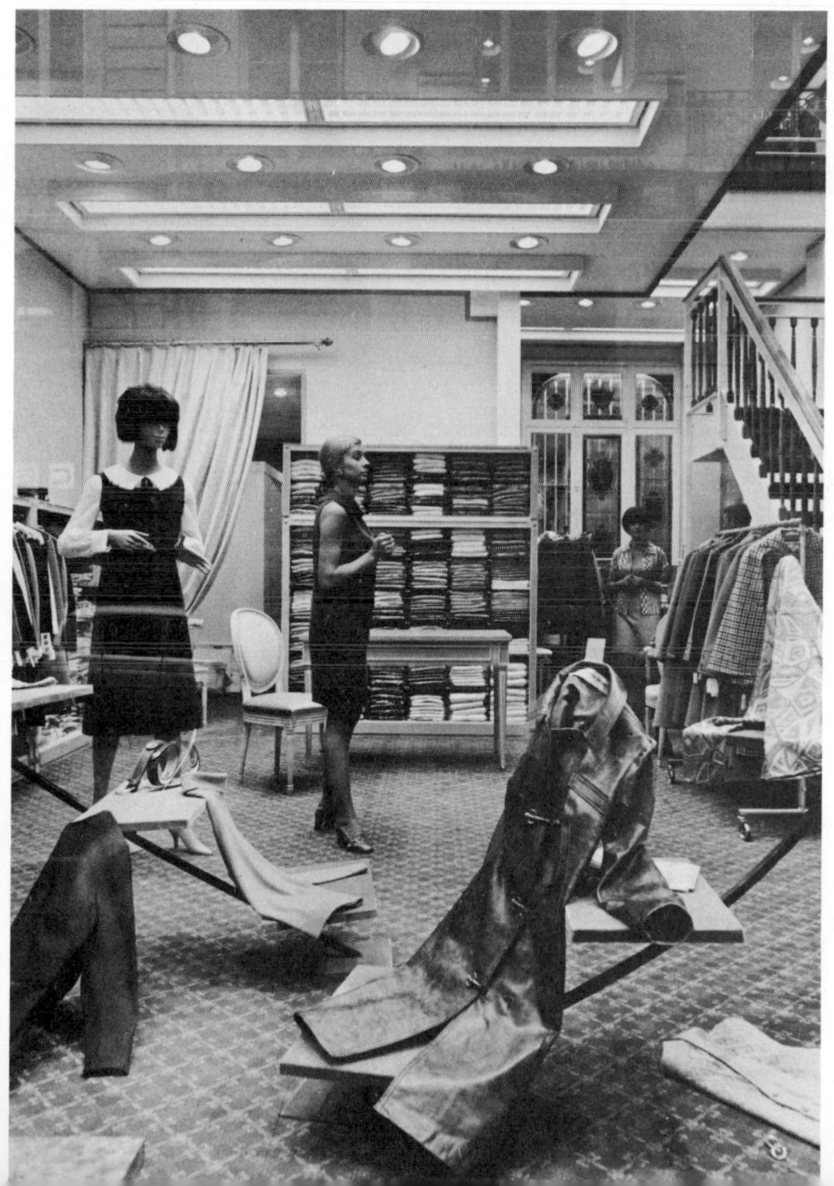

I. Substitutions. *Répétez les phrases suivantes en substituant les mots indiqués:*

1. Je rentrerai de bonne heure.

   à sept heures du soir / à quatre heures moins le quart / vers cinq heures et quart / vers minuit / à minuit

2. Il viendra me chercher.

   vous / le / la / nous / les

3. Je viendrai vous chercher à huit heures précises.

   à sept heures précises / à neuf heures précises / à cinq heures précises / à quatre heures précises

II. *Répétez en remplaçant les noms par les pronoms convenables:*

EX.:—Je viendrai chercher Jean.
—Je viendrai le chercher.

1. Je viendrai chercher Roger.

   Marie / Jean et Roger / Marie et Louise / les Brown

2. J'irai chercher les Brown.

   Louise Bedel / Charles Dupont / ma mère / mes cousines / mon imperméable

III. *Répondez en français, d'après le texte, à chacune des questions suivantes:*

1. Où irez-vous cet après-midi? **2.** Qu'est-ce que vous ferez? **3.** Qu'est-ce que vous achèterez? **4.** Comment irez-vous en ville? **5.** Pourquoi ne prenez-vous pas l'autobus? **6.** Qu'est-ce que vous ferez s'il pleut? **7.** A quelle heure rentrerez-vous? **8.** A quelle heure Roger viendra-t-il chercher Marie? **9.** Est-il toujours à l'heure?

IV. *Demandez à quelqu'un:*

1. où il ira cet après-midi. **2.** ce qu'il fera en ville. **3.** ce qu'il achètera. **4.** comment il ira en ville. **5.** ce qu'il fera s'il pleut. **6.** à quelle heure il rentrera. **7.** à quelle heure il (elle) finira son travail. **8.** à quelle heure il viendra vous chercher.

V. Révision. *Pronoms personnels. Répétez en remplaçant les noms par les pronoms convenables:*

EX.:—La concierge m'a donné la lettre.
—Elle me l'a donnée.

1. J'ai acheté le journal. **2.** Je l'ai donné à Jean. **3.** J'ai acheté les journaux.

4. J'ai acheté des journaux. **5.** J'ai acheté deux journaux. **6.** J'ai acheté un journal. **7.** Le marchand (*merchant*) m'a donné le journal. **8.** Le marchand vous a donné le journal. **9.** La concierge m'a donné la lettre. **10.** Elle vous a donné la lettre. **11.** Elle vous a donné les lettres. **12.** Elle vous a donné des lettres.

VI. Exercices d'application. *Verbes pronominaux.*

A. *Répétez les phrases suivantes en substituant les mots indiqués:*

1. Je vais me coucher.

me lever / m'habiller / me dépêcher / me promener

2. Il va se coucher.

se lever / s'habiller / se dépêcher / se promener

3. Nous allons nous coucher.

nous lever / nous habiller / nous dépêcher / nous promener

B. *Demandez en français à quelqu'un:*

1. comment il s'appelle. **2.** à quelle heure il s'est couché hier soir. **3.** à quelle heure il se couche d'habitude. **4.** à quelle heure il se lève d'habitude. **5.** à quelle heure il s'est levé ce matin. **6.** à quelle heure il s'habille le dimanche. **7.** à quelle heure il s'est habillé ce matin. **8.** s'il se dépêche le dimanche matin. **9.** s'il va se lever de bonne heure demain. **10.** s'il veut s'habiller pour aller en ville. **11.** si les étudiants se couchent de bonne heure le samedi soir.

VII. Dictée d'après la Conversation 16, pp. 130-131.

VIII. Dialogue.

Un rendez-vous pour samedi soir.

Future Tense and Imperative

45. *Formation of the future of regular verbs.*

—**Déjeunerez-vous** en ville?	*Will you have lunch* in town?
—Oui, **je déjeunerai** à l'hôtel du Cheval blanc.	Yes, *I shall have lunch* at the White Horse Inn.
—Quand **finirez-vous** votre travail?	When *will you finish* your work?
—**Je finirai** de bonne heure.	*I shall finish* early.
—**Je finirai** tard.	*I shall finish* late.
—**Je finirai** avant minuit.	*I'll finish* before midnight.
—**Je finirai** après minuit.	*I'll finish* after midnight.
—**Répondrez-vous** à sa lettre?	*Will you answer* his (her) letter?
—Oui, **je répondrai** bientôt à sa lettre.	Yes, *I shall answer* his (her) letter soon.
—**Vous dépêcherez-vous** de finir votre travail?	*Will you hurry* to finish your work?
—Oui, **je me dépêcherai.**	Yes, *I shall hurry.*

The forms of the future tense of regular verbs are:

FIRST CONJUGATION	SECOND CONJUGATION	THIRD CONJUGATION
je déjeunerai	je finirai	je répondrai
I shall have lunch	*I shall finish*	*I shall answer*
tu déjeuneras	tu finiras	tu répondras
il déjeunera	il finira	il répondra
nous déjeunerons	nous finirons	nous répondrons
vous déjeunerez	vous finirez	vous répondrez
ils déjeuneront	ils finiront	ils répondront

(1) The future tense of regular verbs may be found by adding the future endings **-ai, -as, -a, -ons, -ez, -ont** to the infinitive, except that in the case of verbs of the third conjugation (ending in **-re**) the final **e** is omitted.

(2) Reflexive verbs follow the usual pattern. Ex.: **Je me dépêcherai, tu te dépêcheras, il se dépêchera,** etc.

(3) Although the use of *shall* and *will* in English is somewhat delicate, the future tense in French simply denotes futurity. **Irez-vous** and **Voulez-vous aller . . .** are quite different in meaning; the former indicates futurity and the latter indicates willingness.

46. *Future tense of* être *and* avoir.

—Vos parents **seront** contents de vous voir.	Your parents *will be* glad to see you.
—**Je serai** content aussi de les voir.	*I'll be glad* to see them too.
—Est-ce que **j'aurai** le temps de déjeuner?	*Will I have* time to have lunch?

The forms of **être** and **avoir** are:

être	**avoir**
je serai (*I shall be*)	j'aurai (*I shall have*)
tu seras	tu auras
il sera	il aura
nous serons	nous aurons
vous serez	vous aurez
ils seront	ils auront

47. *Use of the future tense.*

—**Je ferai** des courses demain.	*I shall do* some errands tomorrow.
—S'il pleut, **je prendrai** un taxi.	If it rains, *I'll take* a taxi.

(1) Generally speaking, the future tense is used as in English. Note particularly that it is used in the result clause of conditional sentences which express what will happen if a given condition is fulfilled. Ex.: **Je prendrai un taxi** (*the result*), **s'il pleut** (*the condition*).

(2) As in English, (*a*) the present tense is frequently used for the future. Ex.: **Il part pour l'Europe la semaine prochaine.** (*b*) the present tense of **aller** with an infinitive is commonly used for the future. Ex.: **Il va faire des courses demain matin.**

(3) Contrary to English usage, however, the future tense is always used in temporal clauses introduced by **quand,** *when;* **lorsque**, *when*, etc., if the future time is implied. Ex.: Je déjeunerai **quand je rentrerai.** I shall have lunch, *when I get home*. **Lorsqu'il neigera,** je ferai du ski. *When it snows*, I shall go skiing.

48. *Formation and use of the imperative.*

A. Imperative of regular verbs:

—**Regardez** la neige!	*Look at* the snow!
—**Répondez** tout de suite à sa lettre.	*Reply* to his letter at once.
—J'ai faim. **Allons** déjeuner.	I'm hungry. *Let's go* to lunch.
—Voici un restaurant. **Entrons.**	Here's a restaurant. *Let's go in.*
—Garçon, **donnez-moi** la carte, s'il vous plaît.	Waiter, *give me* the menu, please.

(1) Forms of the imperative of regular verbs:

FIRST CONJUGATION		SECOND CONJUGATION	
regarde(s)*	*look* (**tu** form)	finis	*finish* (**tu** form)
regardons	*let's look*	finissons	*let's finish*
regardez	*look* (**vous** form)	finissez	*finish* (**vous** form)

THIRD CONJUGATION	
réponds	*answer* (**tu** form)
répondons	*let's answer*
répondez	*answer* (**vous** form)

(2) The imperative of regular verbs is the same as the second person singular* and the first and second person plural of the present indicative without the subject pronoun.

(3) The negative imperative is found by placing **ne** before the forms and **pas** after them: ne regarde pas, ne regardons pas, ne regardez pas.

B. Imperative of reflexive verbs:

—Dépêchez-vous!	*Hurry!*
—Asseyez-vous.	*Sit down.*

(1) Forms of the imperative of reflexive verbs:

AFFIRMATIVE	
dépêche-toi	*hurry* (**tu** form)
dépêchons-nous	*let's hurry*
dépêchez-vous	*hurry* (**vous** form)
NEGATIVE	
ne te dépêche pas	*don't hurry*
ne nous dépêchons pas	*let's not hurry*
ne vous dépêchez pas	*don't hurry*

(2) The reflexive object must always be expressed. With affirmative imperative, the object follows (dépêchez-**vous**); with negative imperative, the object precedes the verb (ne **vous** dépêchez pas).

C. Imperative of **être** and **avoir:**

(1) Forms of the imperative of **être** and **avoir:**

sois	*be* (**tu** form)	aie	*have* (**tu** form)
soyons	*let's be*	ayons	*let's have*
soyez	*be* (**vous** form)	ayez	*have* (**vous** form)

* The **tu** form of the imperative of the first conjugation has an **s** only when it is followed by **y** or **en.**

(2) The imperative of **être** and **avoir** is used primarily in set expressions such as:

—**Soyez tranquille.**	*Don't worry.*
—**Ayez la bonté de** vous asseoir.	*Please* (i.e., *Have the kindness to . . .*)

I. Exercices d'application.

A. *Mettez les formes suivantes au pluriel:*

EX. :—Je déjeunerai. **Nous déjeunerons.**

1. Je parlerai. **2.** Je rentrerai. **3.** Je me coucherai. **4.** Je finirai. **5.** J'obéirai. **6.** Je choisirai. **7.** Je répondrai. **8.** Je vendrai. **9.** J'entendrai. **10.** J'attendrai. **11.** J'irai. **12.** Je ferai. **13.** Je serai. **14.** Je prendrai. **15.** J'aurai.

B. *Mettez au pluriel:*

EX.:—Il parlera. **Ils parleront.**

1. Il dînera. **2.** Il rentrera. **3.** Il se couchera. **4.** Il se promènera. **5.** Il finira. **6.** Il achètera. **7.** Il donnera. **8.** Il partira. **9.** Il arrivera. **10.** Il prendra. **11.** Il aura. **12.** Il sera. **13.** Il regardera. **14.** Il fera. **15.** Il se lèvera.

C. *Mettez chacune des phrases suivantes au futur:*

1. Je prends un taxi. **2.** Il fait beau. **3.** Il fait des courses. **4.** Il a vingt et un ans. **5.** Il vend son auto. **6.** Il est ici. **7.** Nous avons faim. **8.** Il va en ville. **9.** Le train part à cinq heures. **10.** Je déjeune à la maison. **11.** Il y a de la neige en hiver. **12.** Y a-t-il beaucoup de monde? **13.** Avez-vous le temps d'aller au bureau de poste? **14.** A-t-il besoin de son auto? **15.** Est-il content de vous voir?

D. *Dites en français à quelqu'un:*

EX.:—de se lever. **Levez-vous.**
—de ne pas se lever. **Ne vous levez pas.**

1. d'entrer. **2.** de parler français. **3.** de regarder. **4.** de rentrer de bonne heure. **5.** d'aller à la charcuterie. **6.** de finir son travail. **7.** de se dépêcher. **8.** de se promener. **9.** de s'asseoir. **10.** de ne pas entrer. **11.** de ne pas aller au cinéma ce soir. **12.** de ne pas oublier votre rendez-vous. **13.** de ne pas se dépêcher. **14.** de ne pas vendre son auto.

II. Substitutions. *Répétez les phrases suivantes en substituant les mots indiqués:*

1. Je finirai de bonne heure.

   tard / avant minuit / après minuit / vers minuit

2. Quand je serai à la campagne (*in the country*), je me lèverai tard.

   je jouerai aux cartes / je jouerai du piano / j'écouterai des disques / je regarderai la télévision

3. Si vous êtes libre demain, nous irons au cinéma.

   nous irons à la campagne / nous déjeunerons ensemble / je viendrai vous voir / nous étudierons ensemble

4. Roger sera content quand vous arriverez.

   quand le printemps viendra / quand il fera chaud / quand vous serez ici / quand Marie rentrera

III. *Répondez en français à chacune des questions suivantes:*

(*a*) **1.** Qu'est-ce que Marie fera cet après-midi? **2.** Où ira-t-elle? **3.** Qu'est-ce qu'elle achètera? **4.** Comment ira-t-elle en ville? **5.** Qu'est-ce qu'elle fera s'il pleut? **6.** A quelle heure rentrera-t-elle? **7.** Qu'est-ce que Roger fera cet après-midi? **8.** A quelle heure finira-t-il son travail?

(*b*) **1.** Qu'est-ce que Marie fera s'il pleut? **2.** Qu'est-ce qu'elle fera si elle ne trouve pas de taxi? **3.** Qu'est-ce qu'elle fera quand elle rentrera? **4.** Qu'est-ce que vous ferez quand vous rentrerez ce soir? **5.** Où irez-vous cet après-midi s'il fait beau? **6.** Qu'est-ce que vous ferez cet hiver quand il neigera?

IV. *Répétez chacune des phrases suivantes en remplaçant* **quand** *par* **lorsque:**

1. Quand il neigera, je ferai du ski. **2.** Quand j'irai en ville, je ferai des courses. **3.** Je serai content quand l'été arrivera. **4.** Soyez prêt quand je viendrai vous chercher. **5.** Je serai prêt quand vous viendrez me chercher.

V. *Répétez en remplaçant* **si** *et le présent par* **quand** *et le futur:*

EX.:—. . . si je suis . . ., **quand je serai . . .**

1. S'il fait beau, je ferai une promenade. **2.** Si nous avons le temps, nous irons au cinéma. **3.** Si je suis libre, je viendrai vous voir. **4.** Si Jean vient me voir, je serai content. **5.** S'il y a de la neige, je ferai du ski. **6.** J'irai en France si j'ai de l'argent. **7.** Parlerez-vous français si vous allez en France? **8.** Il finira son travail s'il a le temps.

VI. Révision. *Dites en français:*

1. At first. **2.** Afterwards. **3.** In that case. **4.** The first time. **5.** Once. **6.** Once a (*par*) week. **7.** Several times. **8.** Several times a day. **9.** Several times a week. **10.** I haven't time. **11.** What time is it? **12.** How is the weather? **13.** A long time. **14.** Too long. **15.** Two years ago. **16.** In the evening. **17.** In the morning. **18.** All day long. **19.** All afternoon. **20.** Sunday. **21.** Next Sunday. **22.** Early. **23.** Late. **24.** Soon.

NOTE ON THE *Thèmes d'imitation*

The *Thèmes d'imitation* which will occur in some Grammar Units from now on, are little themes that are based upon one or more of the dialogs you have already studied. Their purpose is to give you additional practice in using authentic French word patterns. They are scarcely more difficult than the dialogs you have been doing orally; but they call for more conscious effort because they call into play a greater variety of expressions and make use of longer sentences.

The best way to turn out a good, correct, and idiomatic French *Thème* is to work through it orally, sentence by sentence, before putting pen to paper. When you cannot recall the right word or phrase, it is better to try to find it in a dialog than in the vocabulary; for if an expression is used in a dialog, you know precisely what it means and how it is used. When you *do* refer to the vocabulary, look for ways to express what you are trying to say. You cannot possibly produce a good *Thème* by merely "looking up" all the words and copying them down. YOU HAVE TO THINK THE THING THROUGH IN FRENCH.

When you have worked on a sentence orally until it sounds right to you, write it down, taking care to spell words correctly, to use the proper forms, etc. Then after you have written each sentence, reread it to be sure that it expresses the idea you set out to express.

VI. Thème d'imitation:

John Hughes is a young American chemical engineer. He lives in Paris. He has rented a room near the Observatory, in the Latin Quarter, in the house of (*chez*) an old lady, Mrs. Duval. She is seventy years old, she has white hair, and she is very nice to John, because she likes Americans. John is happy. He likes (**Il aime bien**) his room, and autumn in Paris is one of the most beautiful seasons of the year. The trees of the Avenue of the Observatory are very beautiful in the month of October. The month of November is usually less pleasant, because it is cold and it rains a good deal. But John forgets the bad weather and he thinks he is lucky to be (**d'être**) in Paris.

A Trip

Au guichet, à la gare de l'Est

At the Ticket Window of the Eastern Railway Station

JEAN – [1]Je voudrais un billet aller et retour pour Reims.

JOHN – [1]*I should like a round-trip ticket to Rheims.*

L'EMPLOYÉ – [2]Quelle classe, monsieur?

THE EMPLOYEE – [2]*Which class, sir?*

JEAN – [3]Seconde, s'il vous plaît. [4]Combien de temps ce billet est-il bon?

JOHN – [3]*Second, please.* [4]*How long is this ticket good?*

L'EMPLOYÉ – [5]Quinze jours,* monsieur.

THE EMPLOYEE – [5]*Two weeks, sir.*

JEAN – [6]Est-ce que je dois changer de train en route?

JOHN – [6]*Do I have to change trains on the way?*

L'EMPLOYÉ – [7]Oui, vous devez changer à Épernay.

THE EMPLOYEE – [7]*Yes, you have to change trains at Epernay.*

JEAN – [8]Combien de temps faut-il attendre la correspondance?

JOHN – [8]*How long do you have to wait for the connection?*

L'EMPLOYÉ – [9]Vous aurez à peu près une demi-heure à Épernay.

THE EMPLOYEE – [9]*You will have about half an hour at Epernay.*

* The French say **quinze jours** (15 days) for "two weeks" and **huit jours** for "a week."

A LA GARE

Sur le quai, à Épernay

JEAN – [10]Pardon, sur quelle voie le train de Reims arrive-t-il?

L'EMPLOYÉ – [11]Ici, monsieur, sur la première voie.

JEAN – [12]Le train est-il à l'heure?

L'EMPLOYÉ – [13]Oui, monsieur. En France, les trains ne sont jamais en retard.

JEAN – [14]Est-ce que j'aurai le temps d'aller au buffet?

L'EMPLOYÉ – [15]Vous pouvez essayer, mais dépêchez-vous. [16]Le train s'arrête seulement trois minutes. [17]Si vous manquez ce train, vous serez obligé de passer la nuit à Épernay.

On the Platform at Epernay

JOHN – [10]*Pardon me. On which track does the Rheims train come in?*

THE EMPLOYEE – [11]*Here, sir. On the first track.*

JOHN – [12]*Is the train on time?*

THE EMPLOYEE – [13]*Yes, sir. In France trains are never late.*

JOHN – [14]*Will I have time to go to the lunchroom.*

THE EMPLOYEE – [15]*You can try it, but hurry.* [16]*The train stops just three minutes.* [17]*If you miss this train, you will have to spend the night at Epernay.*

UN CHASSEUR

I. Substitutions. *Répétez les phrases suivantes en substituant les mots indiqués:*

1. Je voudrais un billet aller et retour pour Reims.
Lyon / Marseille / Bruxelles / Rome

2. Je voudrais bien aller voir M. Brown.
le voir / lui parler / leur parler / les voir

3. Est-ce que je dois changer de train?
d'avion/ de chambre/ d'hôtel/ de chemise (*shirt*)

4. Vous devez changer de train.
de gare / de chambre / d'hôtel / de robe / de souliers (*shoes*)

5. Le train est à l'heure.
juste à l'heure / en retard / en avance d'une ou deux minutes

II. *Répondez en français, d'après le texte, à chacune des questions suivantes:*

1. Où va Jean? **2.** Quelle espèce de billet veut-il? **3.** Quelle classe? **4.** Combien de temps son billet est-il bon? **5.** Est-ce qu'il doit changer de train en route? **6.** Combien de temps faut-il attendre la correspondance? **7.** Le train est-il en retard? **8.** Est-ce que Jean aura le temps d'aller au buffet? **9.** Qu'est-ce qu'il sera obligé de faire s'il manque la correspondance? **10.** Combien de temps le train s'arrête-t-il?

III. *Demandez à quelqu'un:*

1. un billet aller et retour pour Reims. **2.** combien de temps votre billet est bon. **3.** si vous devez changer de train en route. **4.** où vous devez changer de train. **5.** combien de temps il faut attendre la correspondance. **6.** sur quelle voie arrive le train de Reims. **7.** si le train est à l'heure. **8.** si le train est en retard. **9.** combien de temps le train s'arrête. **10.** s'il s'arrête dix minutes. **11.** si vous aurez le temps d'aller au buffet. **12.** ce que c'est que le buffet d'une gare.

IV. Exercices d'application.

A. *Posez la question à laquelle répond chacune des phrases suivantes, en commençant par* **combien de temps:**

EX.:—Il faut attendre vingt minutes.
—Combien de temps faut-il attendre?

1. Il faut travailler deux heures. **2.** Monsieur Brown a passé deux ans en Angleterre. **3.** Ce billet est bon quinze jours. **4.** Je serai ici deux jours. **5.** L'hiver dure longtemps. **6.** Il faut une demi-heure pour aller en ville. **7.** Il faut cinq minutes pour aller à la pharmacie.

B. *Répétez en remplaçant* **à** (at) *par* **vers** (at about):

1. Il arrive à cinq heures. **2.** Je déjeune à midi. **3.** Je me couche à onze heures. **4.** Je vais rentrer à six heures.

C. *Répétez en employant* **à peu près** (about) *devant le nombre indiqué:*

1. Vous aurez vingt minutes à Épernay. **2.** Il a passé dix ans en Angleterre. **3.** Il faut une heure pour dîner. **4.** Il est venu en France il y a cinq ans.

D. *Remplacez l'impératif par* **vous devez** *et l'infinitif:*

EX.:—Parlez français.
—Vous devez parler français.

1. Allez à la boulangerie. **2.** Finissez votre travail. **3.** Couchez-vous de bonne heure. **4.** Dépêchez-vous. **5.** Soyez à l'heure. **6.** Allez voir ce film. **7.** Commencez tout de suite . **8.** Travaillez davantage.

V. Dictée d'après la Conversation 17, pp. 140-141.

VI. Dialogue.

Vous demandez des renseignements (*information*) au guichet d'une gare.

At the Men's Furnishings Store

ROGER – [1]Combien coûtent ces mouchoirs?

LE VENDEUR – [2]Deux francs pièce.

ROGER – [3]Donnez-m'en une demi-douzaine, s'il vous plaît. [4]Combien coûte cette paire de gants?

LE VENDEUR – [5]Trente-cinq francs, monsieur.

ROGER – [6]Ces gants sont-ils de bonne qualité?

LE VENDEUR – [7]Certainement, monsieur. [8]Vous ne trouverez rien de meilleur.

ROBER – [9]En avez-vous d'autres?

LE VENDEUR – [10]Oui, monsieur. En voici des gris.

ROGER – [11]Bon. Donnez-les-moi. [12]Quel est le prix de ce pardessus?

LE VENDEUR – [13]Deux cent soixante-quinze francs, monsieur. [14]Voulez-vous l'essayer?

ROGER – [15]Volontiers.

LE VENDEUR – [16]Il vous va très bien. [17]Le voulez-vous?

ROGER – [18]Oui. Mettez-le dans un carton, s'il vous plaît.

ROGER – [1]*How much do these handkerchiefs cost?*

THE SALESMAN – [2]*Two francs each.*

ROGER – [3]*Give me a half dozen, please.* [4]*How much is this pair of gloves?*

THE SALESMAN – [5]*Thirty-five francs, sir.*

ROGER – [6]*Are these gloves of good quality?*

THE SALESMAN – [7]*Certainly, sir.* [8]*You won't find anything better.*

ROGER – [9]*Have you any others?*

THE SALESMAN – [10]*Yes, sir. Here are some gray ones.*

ROGER – [11]*All right. Give them to me.* [12]*What is the price of this topcoat?*

THE SALESMAN – [13]*Two hundred and seventy-five francs, sir.* [14]*Do you want to try it on?*

ROGER – [15]*Yes. I'll be glad to.*

THE SALESMAN – [16]*It looks very well on you.* [17]*Do you want it?*

ROGER – [18]*Yes, put it in a box (cardboard), please.*

LE VENDEUR – 19 Voulez-vous l'emporter tout de suite?

ROGER – 20 Non, je ne rentre pas chez moi maintenant.

LE VENDEUR – 21 Eh bien, je pourrai vous le faire envoyer cet après-midi.

ROGER – 22 Je n'ai pas d'argent sur moi . . .

LE VENDEUR – 23 Cela ne fait rien, monsieur. 24 Nous vous enverrons la facture.

THE SALESMAN – 19 *Do you want to take it with you?*

ROGER – 20 *No, I am not going home now.*

THE SALESMAN – 21 *Well, I can have it sent to you this afternoon.*

ROGER – 22 *I haven't any money on me . . .*

THE SALESMAN – 23 *That doesn't make any difference, sir.* 24 *We will send you the bill.*

DANS UN MAGASIN DE CONFECTION

I. Substitutions. *Répétez les phrases suivantes en substituant les mots indiqués:*

1. Ces gants sont-ils de bonne qualité?

Ces mouchoirs sont-ils / ces chemises (*shirts*) sont-elles / ces chaussettes (*socks*) sont-elles / ces cravates sont-elles / ces souliers (*shoes*) sont-ils

2. Quel est le prix de ce pardessus?

ce complet (*suit*) / ce veston (*coat, jacket*) / cette chemise / ce pantalon (*pair of pants*)

3. Vous ne trouverez rien de meilleur.

de plus joli / de meilleur marché / de plus beau / de plus élégant / de plus chaud

4. Je ne rentre pas chez moi maintenant.

tout de suite / à midi / pour déjeuner / après déjeuner / avant minuit

5. Je pourrai vous le faire envoyer cet après-midi.

bientôt / tout de suite / vers cinq heures / avant cinq heures / avant midi

6. Voilà de belles pommes. Donnez-m'en une.

une douzaine / deux / deux douzaines / une demi-douzaine / un kilo (*slightly over two pounds*)

II. *Répondez en français, d'après le texte:*

1. Combien coûtent ces mouchoirs? **2.** Combien de mouchoirs Roger achète-t-il? **3.** Combien coûte cette paire de gants? **4.** Ces gants sont-ils de bonne qualité? **5.** Est-ce que le vendeur en a d'autres? **6.** De quelle couleur sont-ils? **7.** Quel est le prix de ce pardessus? **8.** Est-ce que ce pardessus va bien à Roger? **9.** Où Roger dit-il de mettre le pardessus? **10.** Pourquoi ne l'emporte-t-il pas tout de suite? **11.** Quand le vendeur pourra-t-il envoyer le pardessus?

III. *Répondez en français:*

1. Irez-vous en ville cet après-midi? **2.** A quelle heure rentrerez-vous? **3.** Dînerez-vous en ville? **4.** Dînerez-vous quand vous rentrerez? **5.** Pourrez-vous m'acheter un journal? **6.** Irez-vous au cinéma si vous avez le temps? **7.** Pourrez-vous venir me chercher? **8.** A quelle heure viendrez-vous me chercher?

IV. *Répétez en remplaçant l'impératif par* **voulez-vous bien** *avec l'infinitif:*

EX.:—Donnez-moi la carte.
—Voulez-vous bien me donner la carte?

1. Entrez. **2.** Envoyez-moi la facture. **3.** Envoyez-la-moi. **4.** Essayez-le. **5.** Donnez-moi votre adresse. **6.** Donnez-la-moi. **7.** Donnez-lui votre adresse. **8.** Attendez deux minutes.

V. *Répétez les phrases suivantes en remplaçant le nom par le pronom convenable:*

EX.:—Avez-vous d'autres* gants?
—**En avez-vous d'autres?**

1. Avez-vous des gants gris?* **2.** Avez-vous des gants de meilleure qualité? **3.** Voici d'autres gants. **4.** Voilà de beaux mouchoirs. **5.** Voilà des mouchoirs de belle qualité. **6.** Mettez le pardessus dans un carton. **7.** Mettez la paire de gants dans le carton. **8.** Mettez les mouchoirs dans le carton. **9.** Voilà les gants. **10.** Voilà la paire de gants.

VI. *Répétez les phrases suivantes en remplaçant l'adjectif numéral par le nom et la préposition* **de:**

EX.:—Il y a **dix** personnes dans le restaurant.
—Il y a **une dizaine de** personnes dans le restaurant.

1. J'ai passé quinze jours à la campagne. **2.** Il y a vingt étudiants dans la classe. **3.** Il y a trente personnes dans l'autobus. **4.** Ces gants m'ont coûté cinquante francs. **5.** Il y a cent personnes dans cet avion. **6.** J'ai acheté douze tulipes.

VII. Dictée d'après la Conversation 18, pp. 150-151

VIII. Dialogue.

Vous achetez une douzaine d'oranges. Discutez le prix et la qualité des fruits.

---

* Note that with adjectives that precede nouns, you normally say **de** (Avez-vous **d'autres gants?** En avez-vous **d'autres?**); but with adjectives that follow nouns, you say **du, de la,** or **des** (Avez-vous **des gants gris?** En avez-vous **des gris?**).

MARSEILLE: LE PORT MODERNE

 Stressed Forms of Personal Pronouns

49. *Distinction between stressed forms and unstressed forms of personal pronouns.*

The stressed forms of personal pronouns differ from the unstressed forms in both form and usage. You have learned that the unstressed forms are ordinarily used as subject, direct object, and indirect object of verbs. The stressed forms are commonly used after prepositions and, in certain circumstances, with verbs.

50. *Stressed forms of personal pronouns.*

—Où allez-vous?	Where are you going?
—Je vais **chez moi.**	I am going *home.*
—Allez-vous chez M. Brown?	Are you going to Mr. Brown's?
—Oui, je vais **chez lui.**	Yes, I am going *to his house.*
—Êtes-vous déjà allé chez les Brown?	Have you been to the Browns' before?
—Oui, je suis déjà allé **chez eux.**	Yes, I have already been *to their house.*
—Êtes-vous allé au bal avec Marie?	Did you go to the dance with Mary?
—Oui, j'y suis allé **avec elle.**	Yes, I went *with her.*

The stressed forms of personal pronouns are: **moi, toi, lui (elle), nous, vous, eux (elles).**

Note carefully that the third person of *stressed* forms has different forms for masculine and feminine (**lui** and **elle, eux** and **elles**), whereas the third person of *unstressed* forms has only one form (**lui**) for the singular and one form (**leur**) for the plural.

51. *Use of the stressed forms of personal pronouns.*

A. As object of a preposition (**de, avec, sans, chez, pour,** etc.):

—Voulez-vous venir **avec moi?** Do you want to go along *with me?*
—Si Marie ne rentre pas, je déjeunerai **sans elle.** If Mary does not come back, I will have lunch *without her.*
—Connaissez-vous ses cousines? Do you know his (*or* her) cousins?
—Oui, je suis allé **chez elles** plusieurs fois. Yes, I have gone *to their house* several times.
—Avez-vous peur de votre père? Are you afraid of your father?
—Non, je n'ai pas peur **de lui.** No, I am not afraid *of him.*

The stressed forms are generally used only to refer to persons:

—Parlez-vous de **Charles?** —Oui, nous parlons de **lui.**
—Parlez-vous de **Marie?** —Oui, nous parlons d'**elle.**
—Avez-vous besoin de **moi?** —Non, je n'ai pas besoin de **vous.**

When speaking of things, instead of the prepositions **de** with a stressed form of the personal pronoun, you use the pronoun **en** (*of it, of them*).

—Parlez-vous **de votre voyage?** —Oui, nous **en** parlons.
—Avez-vous besoin **de gants?** —Oui, **j'en** ai besoin.
—Avez-vous peur **des examens?** —Non, je n'**en** ai pas peur.

B. After **c'est, ce sont** (whether expressed or understood):

—Qui est là? —C'est **moi**. (or **Moi.**) Who is there? It's *I.* (or *I.*)
—Qui a écrit cette lettre? Who wrote that letter?
—C'est **elle.** (or **Elle.**) It was *she.* (or *She did.*)
—Qui sont ces jeunes filles? Est-ce que ce sont vos cousines? Who are those girls? Are they your cousins?
—Oui, ce sont **elles.** —Yes, it is *they.*

C. To specify the persons indicated by a plural form of a personal pronoun:

—**Elle et moi,** nous sommes allés au cinéma ensemble. *She and I* (we) went to the movies together.
—**Lui et elle** sont allés en ville. *He and she* went downtown.

D. In addition to, or instead of, an unstressed form of personal pronouns, for emphasis:

—**Moi,** je ne sais pas. *I* don't know.
—**Moi,** je suis Américain. *I* am an American.
—**Lui** aussi est Américain. *He* too is an American.

52. *Use of personal pronouns with the imperative.*

A. With the affirmative imperative:

Personal pronoun objects follow the affirmative imperative:

—Mettez-**le** dans un carton. (dir. obj.)
—Donnez-**en** aussi à Roger. (dir. obj. partitive)
—Garçon, donnez-**moi** des hors-d'œuvre. (indir. obj.)

(1) For direct object you use the forms **le, la, les; en.** For indirect object the forms are: **moi (m'), toi (t'), lui, nous, vous, leur.**

(2) When you have both a direct and an indirect object pronoun, the indirect object comes last except when **en** is used.

(*a*)	Apportez-moi le journal.	Apportez-**le-moi.**
	Apportez-moi la carte.	Apportez-**la-moi.**
	Apportez-moi les hors-d'œuvre.	Apportez-**les-moi.**
	Donnez-lui le journal.	Donnez-**le-lui.**
	Donnez-nous le journal.	Donnez-**le-nous.**
	Donnez-leur le journal.	Donnez-**le-leur.**

(*b*)	Donnez-moi du café.	
	Donnez-moi de la crème.	} Donnez-**m'en.**
	Donnez-moi des hors-d'œuvre.	
	Donnez-lui du sucre.	Donnez-**lui-en.**
	etc.	

B. With the negative imperative:

With negative imperatives, the unstressed forms of personal pronouns are used and stand in the order of pronoun objects that is normal in declarative sentences (Par. 42).

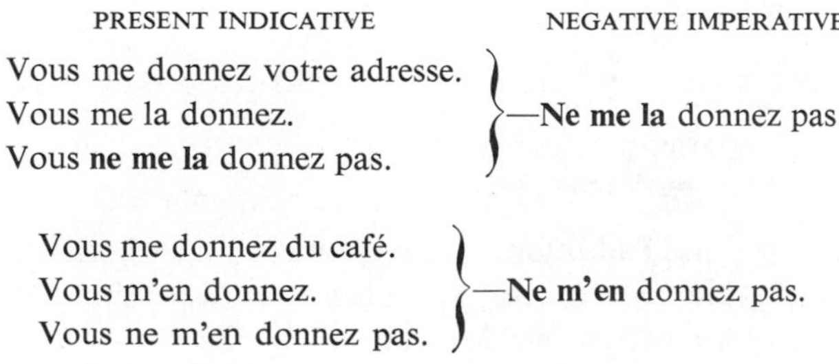

PRESENT INDICATIVE	NEGATIVE IMPERATIVE
Vous me donnez votre adresse.	
Vous me la donnez.	—**Ne me la** donnez pas.
Vous **ne me la** donnez pas.	
Vous me donnez du café.	
Vous m'en donnez.	—**Ne m'en** donnez pas.
Vous ne m'en donnez pas.	

I. Exercices d'application.

A. *Répétez en remplaçant les noms par les pronoms convenables:*

EX.:—Je suis allé chez les Brown.
—Je suis allé chez eux.

1. J'ai passé la journée chez mon oncle. **2.** J'ai passé la journée chez mes parents. **3.** Jean est allé au bal avec Marie. **4.** Il est allé au bal avec ses cousines. **5.** Je suis parti sans mon père. **6.** Je suis parti sans les jeunes filles.

B. *Répétez en remplaçant les noms par* **en** *ou* **y**:

1. Nous avons parlé de nos voyages. **2.** Nous avons parlé de notre promenade. **3.** Avez-vous répondu à sa lettre? **4.** Avez-vous répondu aux questions? **5.** Je n'ai pas peur des examens. **6.** Je n'ai pas peur de la neige.

II. *Répondez affirmativement en français à chacune des questions suivantes, en remplaçant les noms par les pronoms convenables:*

1. Êtes-vous déjà allé(e) chez M. Brown? **2.** Êtes-vous allé(e) au cinéma avec Marie? **3.** Êtes-vous déjà allé(e) chez Marie et chez Alice? **4.** Est-ce que vous avez déjeuné avec Roger? **5.** Avez-vous déjeuné avec votre ami? **6.** Êtes-vous allé(e) au bal samedi soir avec Marie? **7.** Êtes-vous parti(e) sans Marie? **8.** Avez-vous fait des courses pour votre mère? **9.** Avez-vous acheté des gants pour votre mère? **10.** Avez-vous confiance en votre père? **11.** Est-ce que Jean a loué une chambre chez Mme Duval?

III. *Répondez négativement, en employant le pronom convenable:*

1. Avez-vous besoin de moi? **2.** Avez-vous besoin de mon frère? **3.** Avez-vous besoin de mon auto? **4.** Est-ce que vous avez parlé de l'examen? **5.** Avez-vous parlé de votre travail? **6.** Avez-vous parlé de Jean et de Roger? **7.** Avez-vous peur de votre père? **8.** Avez-vous peur de vos parents? **9.** Avez-vous peur des trains? **10.** Avez-vous peur des agents de police? **11.** Avez-vous peur des taxis? **12.** Avez-vous confiance en moi? **13.** Est-ce que Marie a confiance en Jean? **14.** Est-ce que Jean a loué une chambre chez Mme Cochet?

IV. Exercices d'application. *Impératif.*

A. *Répétez en remplaçant les noms par les pronoms convenables:*

EX.:—Apportez-moi les fruits.
—Apportez-les-moi.

1. Apportez-moi l'addition. **2.** Apportez-moi les hors-d'œuvre. **3.** Apportez-nous le plat de viande. **4.** Apportez-nous du raisin. **5.** Apportez-moi de la crème. **6.** Apportez-nous des fruits.

B. *Mettez les phrases suivantes à la forme négative:*

EX.:—Donnez-moi la carte.
—**Ne me donnez pas la carte.**

1. Donnez-lui l'addition. **2.** Envoyez-lui la facture. **3.** Envoyez-lui de l'argent. **4.** Apportez-nous du café. **5.** Donnez-moi du café.

V. *Dites à quelqu'un:*

EX.:—de vous donner une paire de gants. **Donnez-moi une paire de gants.**
—de vous en donner une paire. **Donnez-m'en une paire.**

1. de vous donner une douzaine de mouchoirs. **2.** de vous en donner une douzaine. **3.** de vous apporter une pomme. **4.** de vous en apporter une. **5.** de vous en apporter une demi-douzaine. **6.** de vous donner un peu de café. **7.** de vous en donner un peu. **8.** de ne pas vous en donner beaucoup. **9.** de ne pas vous donner de crème. **10.** de ne pas vous en donner trop.

VI. Révision. *Dites en français:*

A. venir chercher

1. What time will you come for me? **2.** I am going to come for you at a quarter to one. **3.** What time did he come for you? **4.** He came for me at half past one.

B. aller chercher

1. We went for them yesterday. **2.** He went for her in a taxi. **3.** Have you your tickets? —Yes, we went for them yesterday. **4.** No, we will go for them tomorrow.

VII. Thème d'imitation:

Friday afternoon, John and Roger did some errands. They went into[1] a drugstore and John said to the druggist: "I would like some writing paper and some post cards." The pharmacist said to him: "If you need writing paper and post cards, sir, go to the bookstore or the tobacco shop. They do not sell medicines in tobacco shops, and I have neither[2] writing paper nor post cards." Roger thought[3] the incident[4] very funny;[5] but John thought it was less amusing.[6]

[1] **(entrer dans).** [2] Cf. **Il ne fait ni trop froid ni trop chaud.** [3] **a trouvé.** [4] **l'incident** (*m.*). [5] **drôle.** [6] **amusant.**

Going Downtown

A l'arrêt de l'autobus

ROGER – [1]Bonjour, Jean. Qu'est-ce que vous faites ici?

JEAN – [2]Vous voyez, j'attends l'autobus.

ROGER – [3]Est-ce que vous l'attendez* depuis longtemps?

JEAN – [4]Je l'attends depuis un quart d'heure.

ROGER – [5]Vraiment? Vous n'avez pas vu d'autobus depuis† un quart d'heure?

JEAN – [6]Si. Un autobus est venu.

ROGER – [7]Pourquoi ne l'avez-vous pas pris?

JEAN – [8]Je n'ai pas pu monter. [9]Il était complet.

ROGER – [10]Voici un autre autobus qui arrive.

JEAN – [11]Je vois des gens debout.

ROGER – [12]Ça ne fait rien. [13]Montons tout de même.

At the Bus Stop

ROGER – [1]*Good morning, John. What are are you doing here?*

JOHN – [2]*You see, I am waiting for the bus.*

ROGER – [3]*Have you been waiting for it long?*

JOHN – [4]*I have been waiting for it for a quarter of an hour.*

ROGER – [5]*Really? You haven't seen a bus for a quarter of an hour?*

JOHN – [6]*Yes, I have. A bus came.*

ROGER – [7]*Why didn't you take it?*

JOHN – [8]*I couldn't get on.* [9]*It was full.*

ROGER – [10]*Here comes another bus.*

JOHN – [11]*I see people standing.*

ROGER – [12]*That makes no difference.* [13]*Let's get on anyway.*

---

* When the present indicative of the verb is used with **depuis,** it indicates that the action began in the past and is still going on at the time the statement is made.

† When the **passé composé** is used with **depuis,** it indicates a simple past action.

Dans l'autobus

JEAN – [14]Il n'y a pas beaucoup de place . . .

ROGER – [15]Il y aura de la place plus loin, quand les gens commenceront à descendre.

JEAN – [16]Je l'espère. [17]Où descendez-vous?

ROGER – [18]Je descends à l'arrêt de la rue de la Paix. [19]Je vais chez le coiffeur.

JEAN – [20]Moi aussi. Si vous voulez, j'irai avec vous.

ROGER – [21]D'accord. Nous pourrons y aller ensemble.

On the Bus

JOHN – [14]*There is not much room . . .*

ROGER – [15]*There will be room further on, when people begin to get off.*

JOHN – [16]*I hope so.* [17]*Where are you getting off?*

ROGER – [18]*I am getting off at the Rue de la Paix.* [19]*I am going to the barber's.*

JOHN – [20]*So am I. I'll go with you, if you don't mind.*

ROGER – [21]*O.K. We can go there together.*

A L'ARRÊT DE L'AUTOBUS

I. Substitutions. *Répétez les phrases suivantes en substituant les mots indiqués:*

1. J'attends l'autobus depuis un quart d'heure.
Je suis ici / Il pleut / Marie parle / Nous sommes ici

2. Il y a un quart d'heure que j'attends l'autobus.
je suis ici / il pleut / Marie parle / nous sommes ici

3. Depuis combien de temps attendez-vous?
êtes-vous ici / fait-il froid / parlez-vous français / demeurez-vous ici

4. Depuis quand attendez-vous?
êtes-vous ici / fait-il froid / parlez-vous français / demeurez-vous ici

5. Je n'ai pas pu monter.
déjeuner à midi / arriver à l'heure / aller au buffet / y aller / venir vous chercher

6. Il n'y a pas beaucoup de place.
pas / pas encore / pas assez / plus

7. Je descends à l'arrêt de la rue de la Paix.
la rue de la Nation / la rue de la Gare / la rue de l'Hôpital / la rue de la Poste

II. *Répondez en français à chacune des questions suivantes, d'après le texte:*

(*a*) **1.** Bonjour. Qu'est-ce que vous faites ici? **2.** Est-ce que vous attendez l'autobus depuis longtemps? **3.** N'avez-vous pas vu d'autobus depuis un quart d'heure? **4.** Pourquoi n'avez-vous pas pris l'autobus? **5.** Y a-t-il des gens debout dans l'autobus? **6.** Quand y aura-t-il de la place dans l'autobus? **7.** Où descendez-vous? **8.** Où allez-vous?

(*b*) **1.** Où Jean attend-il l'autobus? **2.** L'attend-il depuis longtemps? **3.** Est-ce qu'un autobus est venu? **4.** Pourquoi Jean n'a-t-il pas pu monter? **5.** Y a-t-il beaucoup de gens dans l'autobus qui arrive? **6.** Où Roger va-t-il descendre? **7.** Où va-t-il?

III. *Demandez à quelqu'un:*

1. ce qu'il fait ici. **2.** s'il attend l'autobus depuis longtemps. **3.** s'il n'a pas vu d'autobus depuis un quart d'heure. **4.** pourquoi il n'a pas pris l'autobus. **5.** s'il y a des gens debout dans l'autobus. **6.** quand il y aura de la place dans l'autobus. **7.** où il descend. **8.** où il va.

IV. *Répétez chacune des phrases suivantes en ajoutant* **depuis longtemps:**

EX.:—Je n'ai pas vu d'autobus.
—Je n'ai pas vu d'autobus depuis longtemps.

1. Je n'ai pas vu mon père. **2.** Je ne suis pas allé(e) au cinéma. **3.** Jean n'est pas allé chez les Brown. **4.** Je n'ai pas pris l'autobus. **5.** Je n'ai pas fait de longue promenade. **6.** Nous n'avons pas écrit de lettres. **7.** Nous ne sommes pas sorti(e)s. **8.** Je ne suis pas allé(e) chez le coiffeur.

V. *Dites en français:*

A. depuis

1. I have been here for three months. **2.** I have been here for half an hour. **3.** I have been living here for a long time. **4.** I have been living here since the 20th of September. **5.** I have been speaking French since the 20th of September. **6.** I have been speaking French for three months. **7.** I have been studying French since the 20th of September. **8.** I have been studying French for three months.

B. temps, fois

1. How many times do you go to the movies per month? **2.** How long does winter last? **3.** How long are you going to work tonight? **4.** How long does the train stop? **5.** This is the first time it has snowed this year. **6.** This is the first time I have been skiing this year. **7.** This is the second time I have gone to the movies this week.

VI. Révision.

Répondez en français à chacune des questions suivantes, en remplaçant les mots en italique par l'adverbe **y** (there):

EX.:—Allez-vous *à la gare?*
—**Oui, j'y vais.**

1. Allez-vous *chez le coiffeur?* **2.** Allez-vous *au bureau de tabac?* **3.** Allez-vous *à la banque* ce matin? **4.** Allez-vous *au cinéma* demain soir? **5.** Roger va-t-il *chez le coiffeur?* **6.** Marie va-t-elle *chez la modiste?* **7.** Avez-vous besoin d'aller *chez le coiffeur?* **8.** Avez-vous besoin d'aller *à la banque?* **9.** Jean et Roger sont-ils montés *dans l'autobus?* **10.** Jean et Roger sont-ils allés *en ville* ensemble? **11.** Irez-vous *au cinéma* ce soir? ANSWER: Oui, j'irai. (**Y** is omitted before the future of **aller.**)

VII. Dictée d'après la Conversation 19, pp. 154-155.

VIII. Dialogue.

En attendant l'autobus.

110 PA

				211 DIRECT 2e cl.	21 EXPRESS 1re 2e cl.	23 EXPRESS 1re 2e cl.	213 DIRECT 2e cl.	215 DIREC 2e c
					◆	🍷		■
...	...	...	...	...	8 30	13 10	...	...
...	...	...	...	...	10 1	14 50	...	...
...	...	...	...	...	10 9	14 58	...	...
...	...	...	...	...	11 30	16 19	┐	...
...	...	...	...	6 3	11 38		16 29	17 3
...	...	...	...	6 20	11 55	...	16n45	17 4
...	...	...	...	6 21	11 57	...		17 5
...	...	...	...	7 19	12 45	...	...	18 4
...	...	...	...		12 55	...	...	18 5
...	...	...	...	...	13 11	...	...	19
...	...	...	...	...	13 25	...	...	
...	...	...	...	...	14 9	...	...	...

◆ Trains

22 et 25 ✕ Paris-Mézières-Charleville et *vice versa*.

Voyage à Reims

Jean et Roger ont décidé de profiter des derniers beaux jours de l'automne pour faire un petit voyage en province. Ils n'ont pas l'intention d'aller très loin, car ils ne disposent que de deux ou trois jours. Finalement, leur choix s'arrête sur Reims. Jean n'a jamais vu la cathédrale de Reims, et Reims est juste à la distance convenable.

Roger consulte l'horaire des chemins de fer.

—Tout s'arrange admirablement, dit-il à Jean. Nous n'aurons pas besoin d'aller à Épernay et d'y attendre la correspondance. La ligne Mézières-Charleville passe par Reims. Si nous prenons l'express qui quitte Paris à 8h. 30, nous arriverons à notre destination à 10h. Et l'horaire du

…ZIÈRES-CHARLEVILLE ↔ LUXEMBOURG **110**

…on électrique Mézières-Charleville — Luxembourg.

	270	20	22	202	204	24	218						
	2ᵉ cl.	EXPRESS 1re 2e cl.	EXPRESS 1re 2e cl.	DIRECT 1re 2e cl.	DIRECT 1re 2e cl.	EXPRESS 1re 2e cl.	DIRECT 2e cl.						
			◆	■	🍸	◆							
D PARIS-Est … A	...	8 52	13 44	...	19 13	22 38	...	...	...	...	...	...	...
A REIMS … D	...	7 21	12 13	...	17 31	21 7	...	...	...	...	...	...	...
D REIMS … A	...	7 13	12 5	...	17 23	20 58	...	...	...	...	...	...	...
A MÉZIÈRES-CHARLEVILLE … D	...	6 7	10 56	...	16 14	19 44	...	...	...	...	...	...	...
D MÉZIÈRES-CHARLEVILLE … A	5 40	↗	10 48	16 06	↗	19 34	22 42	...	...	...	...	...	...
A SEDAN … D	5 10	...	10 30	15 48	...	19 16	22 12	...	...	...	...	...	...
D SEDAN … A	...	...	10 28	...	...	19 14	22 10	...	...	...	...	...	...
A LONGUYON … D	...	...	9 39	...	...	18 25	21 13	...	...	...	...	...	...
D LONGUYON … A	...	...	9 34	...	...	18 17	21 1	...	...	...	...	...	...
A LONGWY … D	...	...	9 20	...	...	18 3	20 37	...	...	...	...	...	...
D LONGWY … A	...	...	9 »	...	...	17 51	...	...	...	...	...	...	...
A LUXEMBOURG … D	...	...	8 8	...	...	17 7	...	...	...	...	...	...	...

✕ Paris-Longwy et *vice versa*.

■ Les samedis, arrivée à Sedan : 16 h 59.

retour est tout aussi commode. En quittant Reims à 21h. 7, nous serons à Paris à 22h. 38, assez tôt pour avoir une bonne nuit de sommeil et être frais et dispos pour le travail de lundi.

Le lendemain matin, nos deux amis prennent le train à la gare de l'Est. Le compartiment où ils s'installent est très confortable. L'express roule à toute vitesse. Au delà des maisons grises de la capitale, il traverse la banlieue parisienne, avec ses jardins potagers et ses jolies maisons de pierre blanche, puis l'agréable et paisible campagne de l'Île-de-France, avec ses champs fertiles, ses arbres verts et ses petits villages aux toits rouges groupés autour de leur vieux clocher. Dans le voisinage de Reims, les vignes couvrent le flanc des collines.

C'est la saison des vendanges, et partout au milieu des vignes, hommes et femmes sont en train de cueillir les lourdes grappes de raisin.

—Savez-vous que le vin de champagne est en grande partie fabriqué avec du raisin rouge? dit Roger. Pour avoir un vin blanc, il suffit de laisser fermenter le jus du raisin sans la peau. C'est elle qui contient les pigments.

Tout de suite après leur arrivée à Reims, Jean et Roger vont voir la cathédrale. Jean est très impressionné. Malheureusement, une partie de la façade est cachée par des échafaudages.

—Je n'ai jamais encore vu une seule cathédrale sans échafaudages, remarque Roger. On est toujours en train de travailler quelque part, de réparer quelque chose, et ici encore plus qu'ailleurs. A la fin de la première guerre mondiale, la pauvre cathédrale de Reims, brûlée, mutilée, était presque en ruines. A travers d'énormes trous dans la voûte, on pouvait voir le ciel. Même maintenant, bien des statues, bien des sculptures portent encore des traces de ces mauvais jours. Et malgré tout, la vieille cathédrale des rois de France est toujours debout.

Le lendemain, les deux jeunes gens visitent les vastes caves souterraines d'une des maisons de champagne. Un guide leur explique comment on prépare le vin de champagne, comment les bouteilles sont laissées un certain temps dans une certaine position, puis placées dans une autre. Jean ne savait pas que la préparation du champagne était une opération si longue et si compliquée.

Leur visite terminée, Jean et Roger dînent dans un des bons restaurants de la ville. Puis ils vont prendre le train qui les ramènera à Paris.

QUESTIONS

1. Pourquoi Jean et Roger n'ont-ils pas l'intention de faire un long voyage? **2.** Comment iront-ils à Reims? **3.** A quelle heure quitteront-ils Paris? **4.** A quelle gare vont-ils le lendemain? **5.** Qu'est-ce qu'il y a dans la banlieue parisienne? **6.** Où se trouvent les vignes de Champagne? **7.** Pourquoi y a-t-il beaucoup d'hommes et de femmes au milieu des vignes? **8.** Est-ce que le vin de champagne est toujours fabriqué avec des raisins blancs? **9.** Qu'est-ce qu'il y a sur la façade de la cathédrale de Reims? **10.** Pourquoi y a-t-il souvent des échafaudages sur les cathédrales? **11.** Est-ce que la cathédrale de Reims a beaucoup souffert de la première guerre mondiale? **12.** Est-ce que la préparation du vin de champagne est une opération simple?

REIMS: L'ANGE AU SOURIRE

ÉCOLE DE VILLAGE (EN PROVENCE)

Talking Over School Days

JEAN – [1]A quelle école alliez-vous, quand vous aviez douze ans?

ROGER – [2]J'allais au collège,* c'est-à-dire à l'école secondaire.

JEAN – [3]Où habitiez-vous à ce moment-là?

ROGER – [4]J'habitais une petite ville des Alpes.

JEAN – [5]C'est une région très pittoresque, n'est-ce pas?

ROGER – [6]Oui, mais cette ville a bien changé depuis. [7]On y a construit des usines de produits chimiques. [8]Le progrès, vous savez . . .

JEAN – [9]Qu'est-ce que vous faisiez à l'école?

ROGER – [10]Je travaillais huit heures par jour.

JEAN – [11]Quoi?

ROGER – [12]J'y allais tous les matins à huit heures, et j'en sortais à quatre heures de l'après-midi.

JEAN – [13]Est-ce qu'il y avait beaucoup d'élèves dans cette école?

ROGER – [14]Non. Il n'y avait guère plus de deux cents élèves.†

JEAN – [15]Je crois qu'on travaillait trop dans cette école.

ROGER – [16]Je ne suis pas tout à fait de votre avis, Jean. [17]Je crois que cette école m'a fait beaucoup de bien.

JOHN – [1]*To what school did you go, when you were twelve years old?*

ROGER – [2]*I went to the "college," that is to say, to the secondary school.*

JOHN – [3]*Where did you live at that time?*

ROGER – [4]*I was living in a little city in the Alps.*

JOHN – [5]*That's a very picturesque region, isn't it?*

ROGER – [6]*Yes, but that city has changed a great deal since.* [7]*They have built chemical factories there.* [8]*Progress, you know . . .*

JOHN – [9]*What did you do at school?*

ROGER – [10]*I worked eight hours per day.*

JOHN – [11]*What?*

ROGER – [12]*I went (there) every morning at eight o'clock, and I got out at four o'clock in the afternoon.*

JOHN – [13]*Were there many pupils in that school?*

ROGER – [14]*No. There were hardly more than two hundred pupils.*

JOHN – [15]*I think that they worked too hard in that school.*

ROGER – [16]*I don't quite agree with you, John.* [17]*I think that school did me a great deal of good.*

---

* The secondary schools in France are called **Lycées** if they are entirely supported by the State, and **Collèges** if they are supported by a municipality, a church, etc.

† Note that with numbers you say **plus de** (*more than*), **moins de** (*less than*).

I. Substitutions. *Répétez les phrases suivantes en substituant les mots indiqués:*

1. A quelle école alliez-vous quand vous aviez douze ans?
dix ans / quinze ans / huit ans / seize ans

2. Où habitiez-vous à ce moment-là?
l'année dernière / il y a deux ans / quand vous aviez cinq ans / quand vous étiez en France

3. On y a construit des usines.
de grandes usines / de nouvelles usines / des usines de produits chimiques / des usines d'automobiles

4. Il n'y avait guère plus de deux cents élèves.
cent cinquante / deux cent cinquante / trois cents / cinq cents

5. Il n'y avait guère moins de mille élèves.
deux mille / trois mille / cinq mille / cinq cents

II. *Répétez les phrases suivantes en remplaçant le complément par* **y:**

EX.:—J'allais à l'école tous les matins.
—**J'y allais tous les matins.**

1. J'allais à l'école tous les jours. **2.** J'allais à la pharmacie tous les soirs. **3.** J'allais à la campagne tous les ans. **4.** J'allais au cinéma tous les samedis. **5.** J'allais en ville tous les huit jours. **6.** J'allais chez le coiffeur tous les quinze jours.

III. *Répondez en français à chacune des questions suivantes, d'après le texte:*

1. A quelle école alliez-vous quand vous aviez douze ans? **2.** Où habitiez-vous à ce moment-là? **3.** Est-ce que la région des Alpes est très pittoresque? **4.** Pourquoi la ville a-t-elle changé depuis ce moment-là? **5.** Qu'est-ce que vous faisiez à l'école? **6.** A quelle heure y alliez-vous? **7.** A quelle heure en sortiez-vous? **8.** Alliez-vous à l'école à pied? **9.** Alliez-vous à l'école tous les matins? **10.** Y avait-il beaucoup d'élèves dans cette école? **11.** Est-ce que Jean croit qu'on travaillait trop dans cette école? **12.** Est-ce que Roger est de son avis?

IV. *Demandez à quelqu'un:*

1. à quelle école il allait quand il avait douze ans. **2.** où il habitait à ce moment-là. **3.** à quelle heure il allait à l'école. **4.** combien d'heures par jour il passait à l'école. **5.** à quelle heure il en sortait. **6.** s'il allait à l'école à pied. **7.** si l'école était près de la maison. **8.** s'il allait à l'école tous les jours. **9.** s'il y avait beaucoup d'élèves dans cette école. **10.** si Jean croit qu'on travaillait trop dans cette école. **11.** s'il est de l'avis de Roger.

V. *Répondez en français à chacune des questions personnelles suivantes:*

1. A quelle école alliez-vous quand vous aviez quatorze ans? **2.** Comment s'appelait cette école? **3.** Combien d'élèves y avait-il dans cette école? **4.** Est-ce que vous aimiez bien cette école? **5.** Est-ce que vous aviez beaucoup de travail dans cette école? **6.** Est-ce que l'école était loin de chez vous?

VI. *Dites en français:*

1. Five or six years ago, Roger lived in Chambéry. **2.** He lives in Paris now. **3.** He has been living in Paris for several years. **4.** He came to Paris five or six years ago. **5.** He spent two years in England. **6.** He thinks the little school in Chambéry did him a lot of good. **7.** I used to go to school every morning at eight. **8.** I used to go to school every day. **9.** I used to work every evening. **10.** I used to go to Paris every year.

VII. Dictée d'après la Conversation 20, pp. 164-165.

VIII. Dialogue.

Vous parlez de l'école où vous alliez quand vous aviez quinze ans.

The Imperfect Tense

53. *Remark about the imperfect tense.*

Generally speaking, the French imperfect tense expresses habitual actions in the past (**A quelle école alliez-vous . . .**) or a state of affairs in the past (**quand vous aviez douze ans?**).

In order to distinguish clearly between the use of the imperfect and the **passé composé,** you could say that the **passé composé** expresses WHAT HAPPENED and that the imperfect describes the CIRCUMSTANCES OR STATE OF AFFAIRS at the time. Examples:

Dimanche dernier, j'ai fait une promenade (*what happened*). Il faisait beau (*state of the weather*) et j'avais l'intention (*state of mind*) de faire le tour du lac. Mais j'ai rencontré Marie (*what happened*) qui m'a dit (*what happened*) qu'il y avait un excellent film (*state of affairs at the local movie house*) au Rivoli . . . Nous y sommes allés ensemble (*what happened*). Le film était en effet très amusant (*state of affairs as to the particular film*). Nous avons passé un excellent après-midi (*what happened*).

54. *Imperfect of regular verbs.*

—Où **déjeuniez-vous** quand **vous étiez** à Paris?	Where *did you use to have lunch* when *you were* in Paris?
—A quelle heure **finissiez-vous** d'habitude votre travail?	What time *did you* usually *finish* your work?
—**Je finissais** vers six heures.	*I used to finish* around six.
—Jean est entré pendant que **je répondais** à sa lettre.	John came in as *I was answering* his letter.
—**Nous nous dépêchions** tous les matins pour prendre l'autobus de sept heures.	*We used to hurry* every morning in order to get the seven-o'clock bus.

A. The forms of the imperfect tense are:

FIRST CONJUGATION	SECOND CONJUGATION	THIRD CONJUGATION
je déjeunais *I was having lunch, I used to have lunch, etc.*	je finissais *I was finishing, I used to finish, etc.*	je répondais *I was answering, I used to answer, etc.*
tu déjeunais	tu finissais	tu répondais
il déjeunait	il finissait	il répondait
nous déjeunions	nous finissions	nous répondions
vous déjeuniez	vous finissiez	vous répondiez
ils déjeunaient	ils finissaient	ils répondaient

B. The imperfect tense is formed as follows:

(1) The imperfect stem is the same as that of the first person plural of the present indicative.

EXAMPLES: **déjeunons, déjeun-; finissons, finiss-; répondons, répond-.**

(2) The endings are: **-ais, -ais, -ait, -ions, -iez, -aient.** Thus, if you know the present indicative, you can always figure out the imperfect. For example:

PRESENT: **Nous déjeunons, nous finissons, nous répondons.**
IMPERFECT: **Nous déjeunions, nous finissions, nous répondions.**

Note that the three persons of the singular and the third person plural of the imperfect are pronounced alike, except in linking.

C. Reflexive verbs follow the usual pattern.

EXAMPLES: **Je me dépêchais, tu te dépêchais,** etc.

55. *Imperfect of* être *and* avoir.

The forms of the imperfect of **être** and **avoir** are:

être		**avoir**	
j'étais *I was*	nous étions	j'avais *I had, I used to have,* etc.	nous avions
tu étais	vous étiez	tu avais	vous aviez
il était	ils étaient	il avait	ils avaient

56. *The commonest uses of the imperfect.*

A. To describe a habitual action in the past (English *used to*):

—**J'allais** à l'école à sept heures du matin.	*I used to go* to school at seven o'clock in the morning.
—**Je me levais** à six heures.	*I used to get up* at six o'clock.

B. To describe what was going on when an action took place (English progressive past):

—**J'allais** en ville quand je l'ai rencontré.	*I was going* downtown when I met him.
—**Il pleuvait** quand j'ai quitté la maison.	*It was raining* when I left home.
—**Il faisait beau** quand je suis rentré(e).	*It was fine weather* when I got home.

Note that in these examples, **je l'ai rencontré, j'ai quitté la maison** and **je suis rentré(e)** are simple past actions, which are expressed by the **passé composé. J'allais en ville, il pleuvait** and **il faisait beau** describe what was going on when the specific action took place.

C. To describe a situation that existed in the past:

—L'école **n'était pas** loin de la maison.	The school *was not* far from my house.
—**Il n'y avait pas** beaucoup d'élèves dans cette école.	*There were not* many pupils in that school.
—Franklin **vivait** au dix-huitième siècle.	Franklin *lived* in the eighteenth century.

D. To describe the way a person felt, looked, etc., in the past, especially with the verbs **croire,** *to believe, to think;* **penser,** *to think;* **espérer,** *to hope*, and with many expressions containing **être** or **avoir (être content, avoir froid,** etc.):

—**Je croyais** que **vous étiez** malade.	*I thought* that *you were* sick.
—**J'espérais** vous voir au bal samedi soir.	*I was hoping* to see you at the dance Saturday evening.
—**J'étais** content de voir venir le printemps.	*I was* glad to see spring come.

E. With **depuis** and an expression of time, to report an action that had been going on for a specified period when another action took place.

—Jean **attendait** l'autobus **depuis un quart d'heure** quand Roger est arrivé.	John *had been waiting* for the bus *for a quarter of an hour* when Roger arrived.
—Il **neigeait depuis une demi-heure** quand je me suis levé.	It *had been snowing for a half hour* when I got up.

I. Exercices d'application.

A. *Répondez au singulier, puis au pluriel:*

EX.:—Déjeuniez-vous?
—Je déjeunais. —Nous déjeunions.

1. Parliez-vous? **2.** Habitiez-vous? **3.** Finissiez-vous? **4.** Obéissiez-vous? **5.** Répondiez-vous? **6.** Attendiez-vous? **7.** Étiez-vous? **8.** Aviez-vous? **9.** Vous couchiez-vous? **10.** Vous leviez-vous? **11.** Vous dépêchiez-vous?

B. *Répondez au singulier, puis au pluriel:*

EX.:—Parlait-il?
—Il parlait. —Ils parlaient.

1. Dînait-il? **2.** Habitait-il? **3.** Allait-il? **4.** Obéissait-elle? **5.** Entrait-elle? **6.** Attendait-elle? **7.** Se couchait-il? **8.** S'habillait-il? **9.** Avait-il? **10.** Était-elle?

C. *Mettez les phrases suivantes à l'imparfait:*

EX.:—Je parle.
Je parlais.

1. Je demeure à Paris. **2.** Je me lève à sept heures et demie. **3.** Il a dix-huit ans. **4.** Je finis à six heures. **5.** Combien d'élèves y a-t-il? **6.** Je ne suis pas de votre avis. **7.** Il attend l'autobus. **8.** Il attend l'autobus depuis un quart d'heure. **9.** Qu'est-ce que vous faites? **10.** Il ne travaille pas. **11.** Ils perdent leur temps. **12.** Ils jouent aux cartes. **13.** Ils étudient tous les soirs. **14.** Ils vont à l'école.

D. *Répétez les phrases suivantes en ajoutant les mots* **depuis un quart d'heure.**

EX.:—J'attendais l'autobus quand vous êtes arrivé.
—J'attendais l'autobus depuis un quart d'heure quand vous êtes arrivé.

1. J'étais à la maison quand vous avez téléphoné. **2.** Je travaillais quand vous êtes arrivé(e). **3.** Il neigeait quand je me suis couché(e). **4.** Il pleuvait quand je suis rentré(e). **5.** Le train était en gare quand je suis arrivé(e).

II. *Répondez en français:*

1. A quelle heure avez-vous quitté la maison ce matin? **2.** Est-ce qu'il pleuvait quand vous avez quitté la maison? **3.** Est-ce qu'il faisait beau quand vous vous êtes levé(e)? **4.** Quel temps faisait-il quand vous êtes arrivé(e) à l'université? **5.** Est-ce qu'il a neigé hier? **6.** Est-ce qu'il neigeait quand vous êtes rentré(e) hier soir? **7.** Êtes-vous allé(e) au cinéma hier? **8.** Est-ce que le film était bon?

9. Y avait-il beaucoup de monde au cinéma? **10.** Aviez-vous faim quand vous êtes rentré(e)? **11.** A quelle heure vous êtes-vous couché(e) hier soir? **12.** Étiez-vous fatigué(e) quand vous vous êtes couché(e)?

III. *Demandez à quelqu'un:*

1. s'il connaît l'histoire des États-Unis. **2.** s'il sait quand vivait Franklin. **3.** où demeurait Franklin. **4.** ce que faisait Franklin. **5.** si Franklin est allé en France. **6.** si Franklin parlait français. **7.** combien de temps Franklin est resté en France. **8.** où Franklin est allé quand il était en France. **9.** si La Fayette vivait à ce moment-là. **10.** si Louis XVI était roi (*king*) de France à ce moment-là. **11.** si Marie-Antoinette était reine (*queen*) de France.

IV. *Mettez le paragraphe suivant au passé en remplaçant le présent de l'indicatif par le* **passé composé** *ou* **l'imparfait,** *selon le cas.*

Ce matin, comme d'habitude, Henri quitte la maison à huit heures pour aller à l'école. Comme il pleut à ce moment-là, sa mère lui dit de prendre son imperméable et de se dépêcher car il est presque huit heures. Comme l'école n'est pas loin de la maison, Henri décide qu'il n'a pas besoin de se dépêcher. En passant devant une boulangerie, il remarque de beaux croissants et s'arrête. Il cherche dans sa poche et trouve qu'il a juste assez d'argent pour en acheter un. Il l'achète, le mange tranquillement et arrive à l'école juste à l'heure.

V. Thème d'imitation:

Last week, John and Roger took a trip[1] to Rheims. They took the train at the Eastern Railroad Station, and arrived at Rheims two hours later. John was hungry, and he went to the lunchroom of the station. After lunch they went through[2] the cathedral.[3] Then they saw the cellars[4] where champagne was made.[5] There were many bottles,[6] thousands[7] of bottles. They returned to Paris, very happy about[8] their trip.

[1] **faire un voyage.** [2] *to go through,* **visiter.** [3] *the cathedral,* **la cathédrale.** [4] *the cellar,* **la cave.** [5] *Lit.* one made the wine of Champagne. [6] *the bottle,* **la bouteille.** [7] **des milliers de.** [8] *happy about,* **content de.**

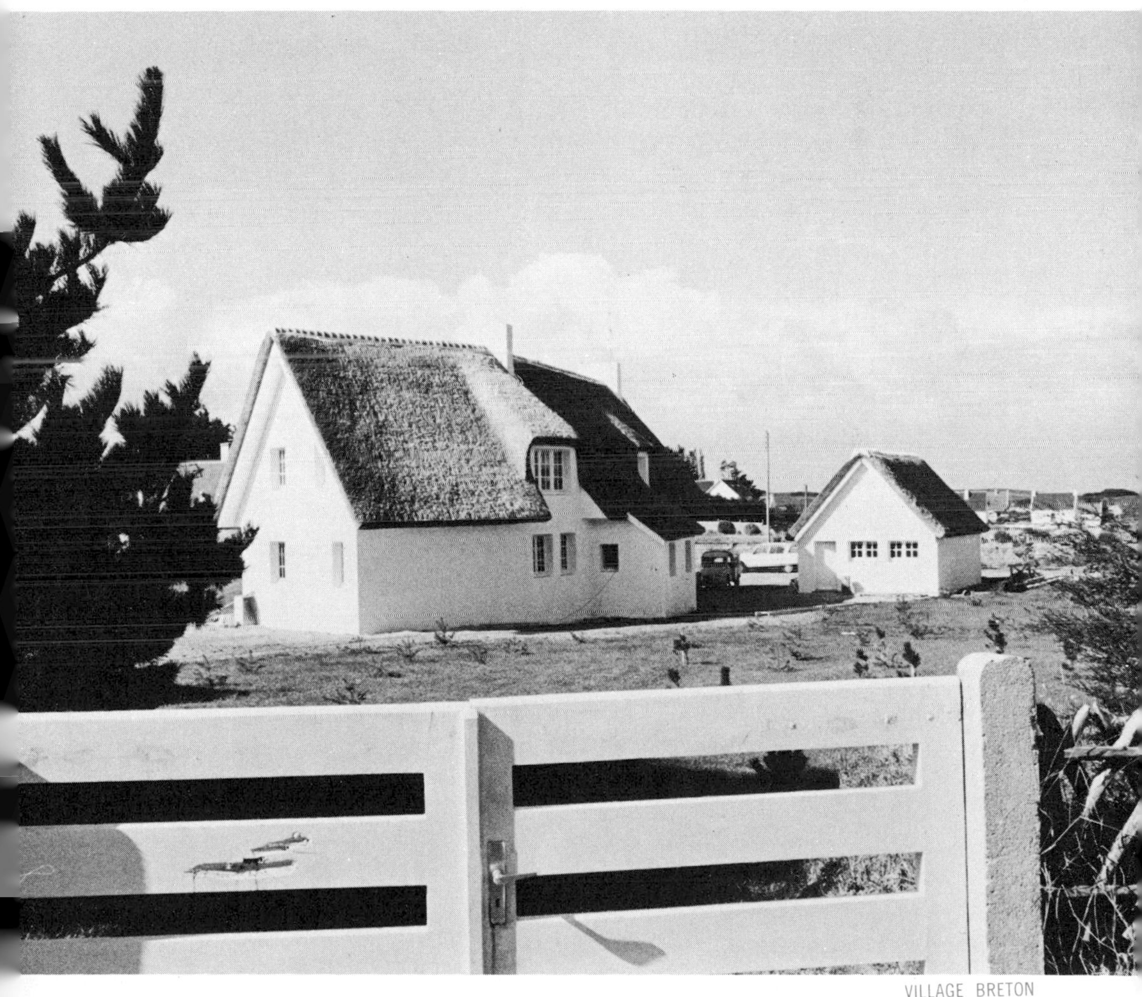

VILLAGE BRETON

PARIS

A Long Walk in the Snow

JEAN – [1]Bonjour, Marie. [2]Je ne vous ai pas vue au bal* samedi dernier. [3]J'espérais pourtant vous y voir.

MARIE – [4]Je suis restée à la maison ce soir-là. [5]Je ne me sentais pas très bien, [6]et je me suis couchée de bonne heure.

JEAN – [7]J'espère que cela n'était rien.

MARIE – [8]Je l'espérais aussi. [9]Mais le lendemain je toussais, et [10]j'avais mal à la gorge.

JEAN – [11]Avez-vous fait venir le médecin?

MARIE – [12]Non. C'était tout simplement un rhume.

JEAN – [13]J'espère que ce n'était pas grave.

MARIE – [14]Non. Je suis restée au lit deux jours. [15]Maintenant, je vais beaucoup mieux.

JEAN – [16]Mais comment avez-vous attrapé cela?

MARIE – [17]Vendredi, Roger et moi avons fait une longue promenade. [18]Il faisait beau, mais assez froid. [19]Nous avons marché dans la neige jusqu'à la nuit. [20]J'avais froid quand je suis rentrée.

JEAN – [21]Vous ferez bien de vous reposer. [22]Soignez-vous bien.

MARIE – [23]Oh! Je n'en mourrai pas!

JOHN – [1]*Hello, Marie.* [2]*I did not see you at the dance last Saturday.* [3]*I was hoping (however) to see you there.*

MARIE – [4]*I stayed at home that evening.* [5]*I didn't feel very well,* [6]*so I went to bed early.*

JOHN – [7]*I hope it was not anything serious.*

MARIE – [8]*I hoped so too.* [9]*But the next day I was coughing and* [10]*I had a sore throat.*

JOHN – [11]*Did you send for the doctor?*

MARIE – [12]*No. It was just a cold.*

JOHN – [13]*I hope that it was not serious.*

MARIE – [14]*No. I stayed in bed for two days.* [15]*Now I am much better.*

JOHN – [16]*But how did you catch it (that)?*

MARIE – [17]*Friday, Roger and I took a long walk.* [18]*It was fine weather, but pretty cold.* [19]*We walked in the snow until night-fall.* [20]*I was cold when I got home.*

JOHN – [21]*You'd better get a good rest (You will do well to rest.)* [22]*Take good care of yourself.*

MARIE – [23]*Oh! I won't die of it!*

---

* **un bal** is a large dance. A small informal dance is **une sauterie.**

I. Substitutions. *Répétez les phrases suivantes en substituant les mots indiqués:*

1. Je suis resté(e) à la maison parce que je ne me sentais pas très bien.
   Je ne suis pas allé(e) au bal / Je me suis couché(e) de bonne heure / J'ai fait venir le médecin / Je suis resté(e) au lit deux jours / Je suis resté(e) au lit plusieurs jours

2. Je ne suis pas sorti(e) hier soir parce que je ne me sentais pas très bien.
   j'étais fatigué(e) / je toussais / j'avais mal à la gorge / je voulais me reposer/ il faisait trop froid

3. J'avais froid quand je suis rentré(e).
   chaud / faim / soif (*thirst*) / un rhume

4. Mais le lendemain j'avais mal à la gorge.
   à la tête / aux yeux / aux dents (*teeth*) / à l'estomac (*stomach*)

5. Vous ferez bien de vous reposer.
   vous coucher de bonne heure / rester au lit / ne pas sortir / ne pas aller à la sauterie / vous soigner

II. *Répondez en français à chacune des questions suivantes:*

1. Est-ce que Jean a vu Marie au bal samedi soir? **2.** Est-ce qu'il espérait l'y voir? **3.** Pourquoi Marie est-elle restée à la maison ce soir-là? **4.** Est-ce qu'elle se sentait bien? **5.** Est-ce qu'elle s'est couchée tard ce soir-là? **6.** Pourquoi s'est-elle couchée de bonne heure? **7.** Est-ce qu'elle toussait le lendemain? **8.** Avait-elle mal à la gorge? **9.** A-t-elle fait venir le médecin? **10.** Est-ce qu'elle était très malade? **11.** Combien de temps est-elle restée au lit? **12.** Est-ce qu'elle va mieux maintenant? **13.** Avec qui a-t-elle fait une promenade vendredi? **14.** Quel temps faisait-il ce jour-là? **15.** Qu'est-ce que Marie et Roger ont fait jusqu'à la nuit? **16.** Est-ce que Marie fera bien de se soigner? **17.** Qu'est-ce qu'il faut faire quand on est fatigué?

III. *Demandez en français:*

1. si Marie était au bal samedi soir. **2.** pourquoi Marie n'y était pas. **3.** si Jean espérait l'y voir. **4.** pourquoi Marie s'est couchée de bonne heure ce soir-là. **5.** si Marie avait mal à la gorge quand elle s'est couchée. **6.** pourquoi Marie n'a pas fait venir le médecin. **7.** si Marie est restée longtemps au lit. **8.** comment Marie a attrapé un rhume. **9.** si Marie va mieux maintenant. **10.** si elle tousse toujours (*still*). **11.** si Marie fera bien de se reposer. **12.** ce qu'il faut faire quand on a un rhume.

IV. *Dites en français:*

A. avoir froid, avoir chaud, etc.

1. She was cold. **2.** I am cold. **3.** Are you cold? **4.** Are you warm? **5.** I was warm. **6.** I was hungry. **7.** Were you hungry? **8.** Was he hungry? **9.** He had a sore throat. **10.** Did you have a sore throat? **11.** No, I had a headache. **12.** I haven't a headache. **13.** I have a cold. **14.** She has a cold. **15.** She had a cold yesterday.

B. jusqu'à

1. We walked in the snow until nightfall. **2.** I am wet to the bones. **3.** I worked until midnight. **4.** I will go with you as far as the square. **5.** I will go with you that far (**jusque-là**). **6.** I will stay at home until five o'clock. **7.** I will rest until noon.

V. *Mettez le paragraphe suivant au passé en remplaçant le présent de l'indicatif pas le* **passé composé** *ou* **l'imparfait,** *selon le cas:*

Un jour Roger et Marie font une longue promenade. Ils marchent dans la neige jusqu'à la nuit. Quand Marie rentre chez elle, elle a froid et elle ne se sent pas très bien. Elle décide que ce n'est rien. Mais comme il fait froid, elle reste à la maison et se couche de bonne heure. Le lendemain, elle tousse et elle a mal à la gorge. Elle fait venir le médecin qui lui dit de rester au lit et lui recommande de boire beaucoup d'eau.

Quelques jours plus tard, elle rencontre Jean qui lui demande comment elle va. «Mal, répond Marie, mais beaucoup mieux que la semaine dernière».

VI. Dictée d'après la Conversation 21, p. 173.

VII. Causerie.

Vous racontez une visite à un jardin zoologique. Vous avez vu des singes (*monkeys*), des ours [uRs] (*bears,*) des lions, des hippopotames, des serpents, des oiseaux de toutes les couleurs, etc.

Où est ma cravate?

ROBER – [1]Serez-vous bientôt prêt, Jean?

JEAN – [2]Oui, tout à l'heure. [3]Je cherche ma cravate rouge, mais je ne sais pas où je l'ai mise.*

ROGER – [4]Je peux vous prêter une des miennes.

JEAN – [5]Non, merci. Je n'aime pas les vôtres.

ROGER – [6]Que voulez-vous dire? Que je n'ai pas de goût, n'est-ce pas?

JEAN – [7]Je ne dis pas cela. Je veux dire seulement que j'aime mieux mes cravates que les vôtres.

ROGER – [9]Eh bien, cherchez-les, puisque vous les aimez tant!

JEAN – [10]Est-ce que je peux porter une cravate verte avec un complet bleu?

ROGER – [11]Cela m'est égal . . . [12]Mais avez-vous regardé dans votre tiroir?

JEAN – [13]Oui, j'ai cherché partout.

ROGER – [1]*Will you soon be ready, John?*

JOHN – [2]*Yes, in a moment.* [3]*I am looking for my red tie, but I don't know where I put it.*

ROGER – [4]*I can lend you one of mine.*

JOHN – [5]*No, thank you. I don't like yours.*

ROGER – [6]*What do you mean? That I have poor taste, I suppose!*

JOHN – [7]*I am not saying that.* [8]*I just mean that I like my ties better than yours.*

ROGER – [9]*Well, look for them, since you like them so much!*

JOHN – [10]*Can I wear a green tie with a blue suit?*

ROGER – [11]*It's all right with me . . .* [12]*But have you looked in your drawer?*

JOHN – [13]*Yes, I have looked everywhere.*

* For the agreement of the past participle, see pp. 234–236.

ROGER – [14]Je vais regarder dans le mien. [15]Tiens! Cette cravate rouge n'est pas à moi. [16]Est-ce qu'elle est à vous, par hasard?

ROGER – [14]*I am going to look in mine.* [15]*Well! This red tie is not mine.* [16]*Is it yours, by chance?*

JEAN – [17]Mais oui, c'est une de mes cravates. [18]Pourquoi était-elle avec les vôtres?

JOHN – [17]*Why yes, it's one of my ties.* [18]*Why was it with yours?*

ROGER – [19]Je n'en sais rien. [20]Peut-être que la bonne admire tant vos cravates, qu'elle a essayé de m'en donner une!

ROGER – [19]*I have no idea.* [20]*Perhaps the maid admires your ties so much that she tried to give me one of them!*

AUX GALERIES LAFAYETTE

ÉTUDIANTS PARISIENS

I. Substitutions. *Répétez les phrases suivantes en substituant les mots indiqués:*

1. Je cherche ma cravate rouge.
   jaune / bleue / noire / grise / blanche
2. Je veux dire seulement que j'aime mieux mes cravates que les vôtres.
   mes gants / mes cigarettes / mes mouchoirs / mes complets / mes robes
3. Est-ce qu'on peut porter une cravate verte avec un complet bleu?
   une cravate rouge . . . un complet gris / un chapeau rouge . . . une robe grise / des gants jaunes . . . une robe verte / des gants blancs . . . un manteau noir
4. Peut-être que la bonne admire tant vos cravates qu'elle a essayé de m'en donner une.
   vos mouchoirs . . . un / vos robes . . . une / vos chapeaux . . . un / vos gants . . . une paire
5. J'aime mieux mes cravates que les vôtres.
   autant (*as well*) / presque autant / moins / beaucoup mieux
6. C'est une de mes cravates.
   un de mes livres / une de mes cousines / un de mes amis (*a friend of mine*)* / une de mes amies

* Note that while in English we say *a friend of mine*, *a cousin of mine*, etc., in French one says **un de mes amis** (lit. *one of my friends*).

II. *Répondez en français à chacune des questions suivantes:*

1. Quand Jean sera-t-il prêt? **2.** Où a-t-il mis sa cravate rouge? **3.** Est-ce que Roger veut bien lui prêter une cravate? **4.** Est-ce que Jean aime bien les cravates de Roger? **5.** Est-ce que Jean a cherché partout? **6.** A-t-il regardé dans son tiroir? **7.** Est-ce que sa cravate rouge y est? **8.** Où Roger va-t-il regarder? **9.** Qu'est-ce qu'il trouve dans son tiroir? **10.** Est-ce que la cravate qu'il trouve est à lui? **11.** Est-ce que Jean sait pourquoi sa cravate est dans le tiroir de Roger?

III. *Demandez à quelqu'un:*

1. s'il sera bientôt prêt. **2.** s'il veut bien vous prêter des gants. **3.** ce que cherche Jean. **4.** si l'on peut porter une cravate jaune avec un complet noir. **5.** si Jean a regardé dans son tiroir. **6.** si Jean a cherché partout. **7.** ce que Roger trouve dans son tiroir. **8.** si c'est la cravate que cherchait Jean. **9.** de quelle couleur est cette cravate. **10.** qui a mis cette cravate dans ce tiroir.

IV. Révision. *Dites en français:*

A. beaucoup, tant, trop

1. John has many ties. **2.** He has too many of them. **3.** Have you many (of them)? **4.** No, I haven't many. **5.** I am very fond of ties. **6.** John likes ties so much he buys too many.

B. chercher, regarder

1. I am looking for my gloves. **2.** Have you looked in your drawer? **3.** Yes, they are not there. **4.** Have you looked in mine? **5.** Yes, I have looked in yours, too. **6.** I have looked everywhere.

C. vouloir dire, aimer mieux

1. Do you mean I have poor taste? **2.** Do you mean she has no taste? **3.** What do you mean? **4.** I mean I do not like her hats. **5.** I mean I like my ties better than yours. **6.** I mean I like my gloves better than yours. **7.** I like red ties better than green ones.

V. Dictée d'après la Conversation 22, p. 183.

VI. Dialogue.

Vous demandez à un camarade de vous prêter son imperméable. Il en a besoin et il offre de vous prêter son parapluie.

Possessive Pronouns

57. *Remark on possessive adjectives and possessive pronouns.*

Possessive adjectives and possessive pronouns differ both in form and use. You have learned that possessive adjectives (**mon, ton, son,** etc.) are used TO MODIFY NOUNS. These words correspond to English forms *my*, *your*, *her*, etc.

Possessive pronouns are used AS EQUIVALENT OF NOUNS MODIFIED BY A POSSESSIVE ADJECTIVE. They correspond to the English forms *mine*, *yours*, *his*, *hers*, etc. Ex.: **My** (*adj.*) father is a doctor. **Mine** (*pron.*) is an engineer.

58. *Forms and use of possessive pronouns.*

—Voici mon adresse.	Here is my address.
—Donnez-moi **la vôtre.**	Give me *yours.*
—J'ai mes gants. Où sont **les vôtres?**	I have my gloves. Where are *yours?*
—**Les miens** sont dans ma poche.	*Mine* are in my pocket.
—Est-ce que Marie a **les siens?**	Does Marie have *hers?*
—Roger a apporté son imperméable.	Roger brought his raincoat.
—Marie a laissé **le sien** à la maison.	Marie left *hers* at home.

The forms of the possessive pronouns are:

SINGULAR		PLURAL		
MASCULINE	FEMININE	MASCULINE	FEMININE	
le mien	la mienne	les miens	les miennes	(*mine*)
le tien	la tienne	les tiens	les tiennes	(*yours*)
le sien	la sienne	les siens	les siennes	(*his, hers, its*)
le nôtre	la nôtre	les nôtres	les nôtres	(*ours*)
le vôtre	la vôtre	les vôtres	les vôtres	(*yours*)
le leur	la leur	les leurs	les leurs	(*theirs*)

They agree in gender and number with the things possessed. Ex.: In answer to the question: —Avez-vous **vos gants?,** either John or Mary could answer: —Oui, j'ai **les miens.**

59. *Possessive pronouns with prepositions* **à** *or* **de.**

—J'ai écrit à mes parents.	I have written to my parents.
—Avez-vous écrit **aux vôtres?**	Have you written to *yours?*
—J'ai besoin de mon imperméable, et Marie a besoin **du sien.**	I need my raincoat and Mary needs *hers.*

When used with the preposition **à** or **de** the forms are:

du mien, de la mienne, des miens, des miennes, etc.
au mien, à la mienne, aux miens, aux miennes, etc.

60. *Use of* **être à** (*to belong to*) *to express possession.*

—Ces gants **ne sont pas à moi.**	These gloves *are not mine* (lit.: to me).
—**Sont-ils à vous?**	*Are they yours* (lit.: to you)?
—Non. Je crois **qu'ils sont à Charles.**	No. I think *they are Charles'* (lit.: to Charles).

Note (1) that *mine, yours, his*, etc., are rendered in French by the possessive pronouns when they are used as subject or object of a verb or when they are object of a preposition other than **à** in the expression **être à.** Ex.: **Les miens** sont dans ma poche. Où avez-vous acheté **les vôtres?** Avez-vous besoin **des vôtres?**
(2) After the verb **être,** *mine, yours, his,* etc., are normally rendered by the preposition **à** followed by the forms **moi, toi, lui, elle,** etc., or a noun. EX.: Ces gants sont **à moi.** Cette auto est **à mon père.**

I. *Répétez les phrases suivantes en remplaçant le nom par le pronom possessif:*

EX.:—J'ai mon imperméable.
—**J'ai le mien.**

(*a*) **1.** J'ai ma cravate. **2.** J'ai mon chapeau. **3.** J'ai mon journal. **4.** J'ai mes gants. **5.** J'ai ma voiture. **6.** Roger a son imperméable. **7.** Il a sa cravate. **8.** Il a son chapeau. **9.** Il a son tabac. **10.** Il a ses gants. **11.** Il a ses cigarettes.
(*b*) **1.** Je peux vous prêter mon pardessus. **2.** Je peux vous prêter mon auto. **3.** Je peux vous prêter mes skis. **4.** Je peux vous prêter une de mes cravates. **5.** Je peux vous prêter une de mes paires de gants.
(*c*) **1.** Où avez-vous acheté votre journal? **2.** Où avez-vous acheté votre papier à lettres? **3.** Où avez-vous acheté votre cravate? **4.** Où avez-vous acheté vos cigarettes? **5.** Où avez-vous acheté vos mouchoirs?
(*d*) **1.** J'ai besoin de mes gants. **2.** Roger a besoin de ses gants. **3.** Marie a besoin de ses gants. **4.** Nous avons besoin de nos gants. **5.** Avez-vous besoin de vos gants?

II. *Dites en français:*

(*a*) With preposition **à:**

1. Are these gloves yours? **2.** Is this book his? **3.** This magazine belongs to me. **4.** This umbrella is not mine. **5.** These newspapers are Charles'. **6.** This hat belongs to Marie. **7.** This hat is hers. **8.** That car is my mother's.

(*b*) With preposition **à** or **possessive pronoun:**

(une auto) **1.** Is this automobile yours? **2.** No, it belongs to Charles. **3.** Where is yours? **4.** Mine is over there. **5.** What color is yours? **6.** Mine is black. **7.** His is yellow. **8.** Hers is white. **9.** Ours is blue. **10.** Theirs is red. **11.** Yours is blue, isn't it?

(*c*) With preposition **de:**

1. It is one of my gloves. **2.** It's one of my books. **3.** It's one of my ties. **4.** He's one of my professors. **5.** He's one of my cousins. **6.** She's one of my cousins. **7.** He's a friend of mine. **8.** She's a cousin of mine.

III. *Répondez à chacune des questions suivantes, en remplaçant le nom par le pronom possessif:*

EX.:—Roger a-t-il son imperméable?
—**Oui, il a le sien.**

1. Marie a-t-elle son imperméable? **2.** Marie a-t-elle ses gants? **3.** Avez-vous vos gants? **4.** Avez-vous besoin de vos gants? **5.** Roger a-t-il besoin de ses gants? **6.** Jean et Roger ont-ils besoin de leurs gants? **7.** Où avez-vous acheté votre journal? **8.** Où Jean et Roger ont-ils acheté leurs journaux? **9.** Où avez-vous acheté vos cigarettes? **10.** Où Jean a-t-il acheté ses cigarettes? **11.** Où Marie a-t-elle acheté ses cigarettes? **12.** Est-ce que votre chambre vous plaît?

IV. Révision des dialogues, pp. 150-151 et pp. 154-155.

1. Quelle espèce de billet Jean demande-t-il pour aller à Reims? **2.** En quelle classe voyage-t-il? **3.** Combien de temps son billet est-il bon? **4.** Est-ce que le train qu'il prend va directement à Reims? **5.** A quelle ville doit-il changer de train? **6.** Combien de temps doit-il attendre la correspondance? **7.** Est-ce que son train est à l'heure? **8.** Qu'est-ce qu'il veut faire avant l'arrivée du train? **9.** Qu'est-ce qui arrivera s'il manque son train? **10.** De combien de mouchoirs Roger a-t-il besoin? **11.** Quel est le prix de la paire de gants qu'il veut acheter? **12.** De quelle couleur sont les gants qu'il achète? **13.** Est-ce que le pardessus qu'il essaie lui va bien? **14.** Pourquoi n'emporte-t-il pas ses achats? **15.** Pourquoi ne paye-t-il pas tout de suite ses achats? **16.** Quand les payera-t-il?

V. Thème d'imitation:

Yesterday John did not feel very well. He took a long walk, and he was cold and (he was) wet when he got home. Roger said to him: "Go to bed. I am going to send for the doctor. It is probably (*sans doute*) not very serious, but you never can tell[1] . . ." The doctor came a half-hour later. He was an elderly gentleman,[2] dressed in black and very friendly. He took John's temperature (*la température*), looked at his throat and said to him: "You have a little fever,[3] but it is not serious. Stay in bed until tomorrow and rest. You will not die of it." Today, John is much better. He is going to get up tomorrow morning and go to his laboratory as usual.

---

[1] on ne sait jamais. [2] C'était un monsieur d'un certain âge. [3] un peu de fièvre.

CONVERSATION 24

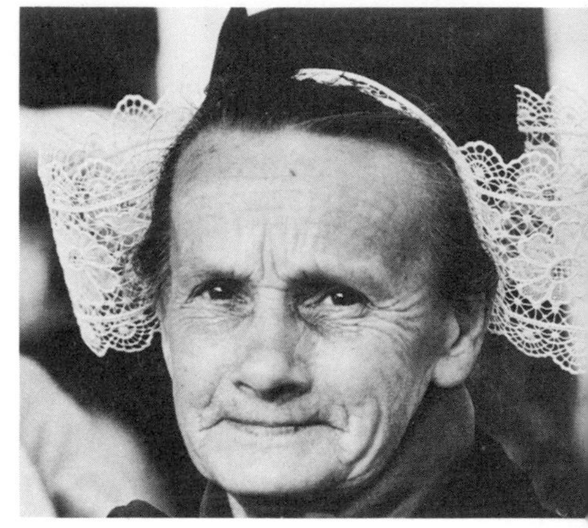

Retour de vacances

JEAN – [1]Tiens, bonsoir, Marie! Vous êtes de retour? [2]Je suis content de vous revoir. [3]Avez-vous passé de bonnes vacances de Noël en Bretagne?

MARIE – [4]Oui, excellentes, merci; mais trop courtes, comme toutes les vacances.

JEAN – [5]Quand êtes-vous revenue?

MARIE – [6]Hier soir à onze heures.

JEAN – [7]Avez-vous fait bon voyage?

MARIE – [8]Oh! ne m'en parlez pas! [9]A Rennes, l'express de Paris était bondé. [10]J'ai à peine pu trouver une place. [11]Et puis, les gens fumaient, [12]et il faisait horriblement chaud dans le compartiment.

JEAN – [13]Vous n'avez pas de chance!

MARIE – [14]J'ai dîné au wagon restaurant. [15]C'est la seule partie du voyage qui était supportable.

JOHN – [1]*Well, good evening, Marie! Are you back?* [2]*I am glad to see you again.* [3]*Did you have a good Christmas vacation in Brittany?*

MARIE – [4]*Yes, excellent, thank you; but too short, like all vacations.*

JOHN – [5]*When did you get back?*

MARIE – [6]*Last night at 11 o'clock.*

JOHN – [7]*Did you have a good trip?*

MARIE – [8]*Oh! Don't even mention it!* [9]*At Rennes the Paris express was crowded.* [10]*I could scarcely find a seat.* [11]*And then, people were smoking,* [12]*and it was terrifically hot in the compartment.*

JOHN – [13]*Tough luck!*

MARIE – [14]*I had dinner in the diner.* [15]*That's the only part of the trip that was bearable.*

JEAN – [16]Aimez-vous dîner au wagon-restaurant?

MARIE – [17]Assez. C'est une façon de passer une demi-heure.

JEAN – [18]Qu'est-ce que vous avez fait le jour de Noël?

MARIE – [19]Ce qu'on fait partout ce jour-là. [20]Nous sommes allés à la messe de minuit. [21]Nous avons fait le réveillon* chez les Kerguélen. [22]Je me suis bien amusée.

JOHN – [16]*Do you like to dine in the diner?*

MARIE – [17]*Pretty well. It's a way of spending half an hour.*

JOHN – [18]*What did you do on Christmas Day?*

MARIE – [19]*What one does everywhere on that day.* [20]*We went to midnight mass.* [21]*We had a réveillon at the Kerguélens'.* [22]*I had a good time.*

* Repas fait au milieu de la nuit, surtout la nuit de Noël. La pièce de résistance est d'ordinaire une oie (*goose*), une dinde (*turkey*), ou un jambon (*ham*).

LA CÔTE BRETONNE

TRÉGASTEL, PORT DE PÊCHE EN BRETAGNE

I. Substitutions. *Répétez les phrases suivantes en substituant les mots indiqués:*

1. Je suis revenu(e) hier soir à onze heures.

   hier soir à huit heures et demie / hier matin / hier après-midi / avant-hier (*day before yesterday*) / la semaine dernière

2. Je suis de retour depuis hier soir à onze heures.

   hier soir à huit heures et demie / hier matin / hier après-midi / avant-hier / la semaine dernière

3. J'ai à peine pu trouver une place.

   trouver un taxi / monter dans l'autobus / aller en ville / marcher

4. Je me suis bien amusé(e) le jour de Noël.

   la veille de Noël / le lendemain de Noël / le jour de l'An (*New Year's Day*) / pendant les vacances

5. C'est une façon de passer une demi-heure.

   de passer la soirée / de passer le temps / de tuer le temps (*to kill time*) / de se distraire (*to relax and have a good time*)

II. *Répondez en français à chacune des questions suivantes:*

1. Où Marie a-t-elle passé les vacances de Noël? **2.** A-t-elle passé de bonnes vacances? **3.** Est-ce qu'elle a trouvé les vacances trop courtes? **4.** Quand est-elle revenue? **5.** A-t-elle fait bon voyage? **6.** Y avait-il beaucoup de monde dans l'express de Paris? **7.** A-t-elle pu facilement (*easily*) trouver une place?

8. Est-ce qu'il faisait chaud dans le compartiment? **9.** Est-ce que les gens fumaient? **10.** Pourquoi Marie aime-t-elle dîner au wagon-restaurant? **11.** Qu'est-ce qu'elle a fait le jour de Noël? **12.** A quelle heure est-elle allée à la messe? **13.** Chez qui est-elle allée faire le réveillon? **14.** Est-ce que Marie s'est bien amusée le jour de Noël?

III. *Demandez à quelqu'un:*

1. si Marie a passé de bonnes vacances. **2.** où Marie a passé les vacances de Noël. **3.** quand Marie est revenue. **4.** si elle a trouvé les vacances trop courtes. **5.** si elle a fait bon voyage. **6.** s'il y avait beaucoup de monde dans l'express de Paris. **7.** si elle a pu facilement trouver une place. **8.** s'il faisait chaud dans le compartiment. **9.** si les gens fumaient. **10.** pourquoi elle aime dîner au wagon-restaurant. **11.** ce qu'elle a fait le jour de Noël. **12.** si elle est allée à la messe de minuit. **13.** chez qui elle est allée faire le réveillon. **14.** si elle s'est bien amusée le jour de Noël.

IV. *Répétez en remplaçant le passé composé par le passé composé de* **pouvoir** *et l'infinitif:*

EX.:—Il n'a pas déjeuné ce matin.
—Il n'a pas pu déjeuner ce matin.

1. Il n'a pas fait ses courses. **2.** Il n'a pas travaillé hier soir. **3.** Il n'a pas été à l'heure. **4.** Il n'a pas trouvé de place. **5.** Il ne s'est pas levé de bonne heure. **6.** Il ne s'est pas couché avant minuit.

V. *Répondez affirmativement aux questions suivantes en remplaçant les noms par les pronoms convenables:*

1. Avez-vous écrit à vos parents hier? **2.** Êtes-vous allé(e) au cinéma samedi dernier? **3.** Avez-vous parlé du film à votre frère? **4.** Est-ce que Roger vous a parlé du film? **5.** Est-ce que Marie vous a parlé de ses vacances? **6.** Est-ce qu'elle a pu trouver une place dans le train? **7.** Êtes-vous allé(e) au cinéma avec Roger? **8.** Êtes-vous allé(e) au cinéma avec Roger et Jean? **9.** Êtes-vous allé(e) au cinéma avec Marie? **10.** Avez-vous parlé de Charles? **11.** Avez-vous parlé de Marie? **12.** Marie s'est-elle bien amusée chez les Kerguélen?

VI. Dictée d'après la Conversation 23, pp. 186-187.

VIII. Causerie.

Ce que vous avez fait pendant les vacances.

CONVERSATION 25

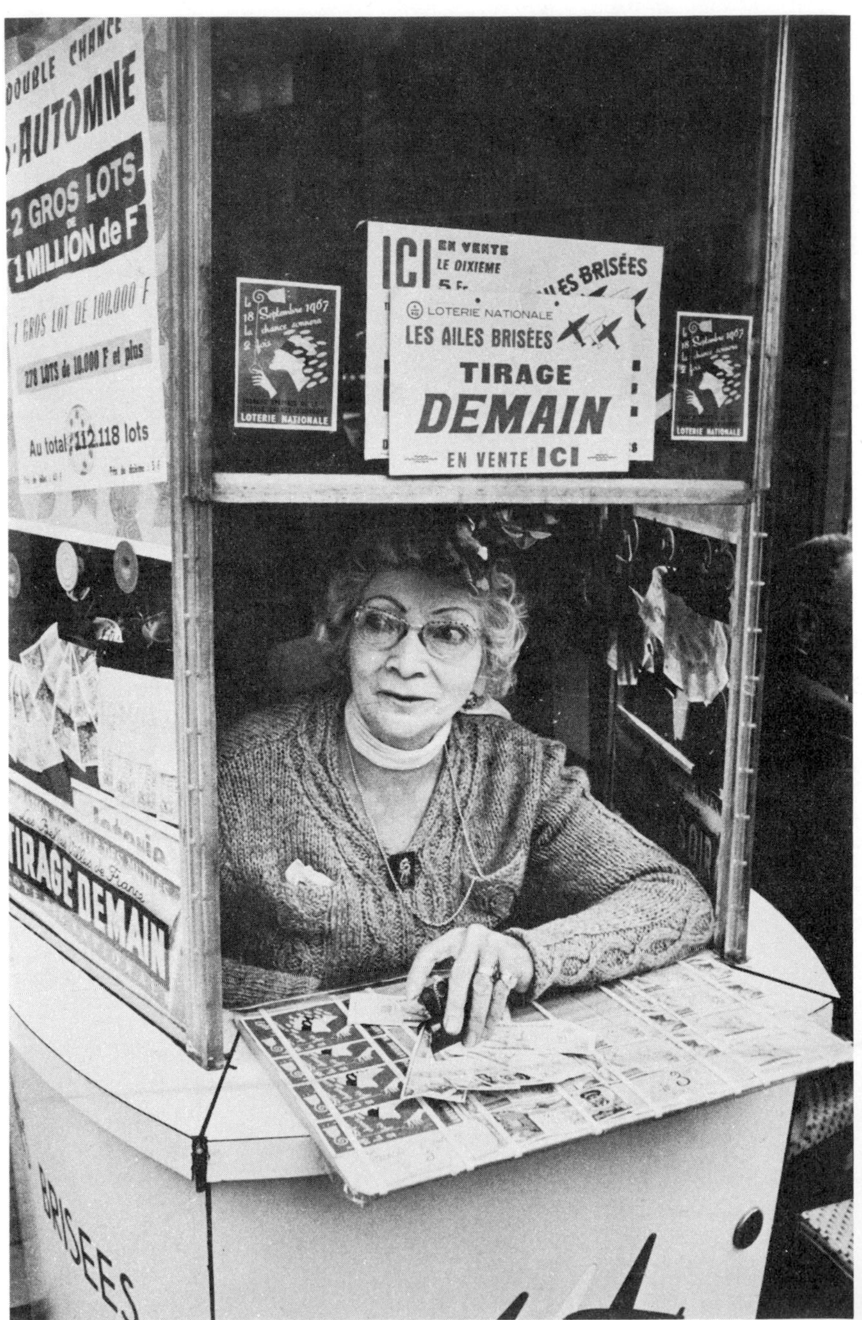

LA LOTERIE NATIONALE

9 Si j'étais riche

JEAN – [1]Qu'est-ce que vous feriez si vous étiez riche, Roger?

ROGER – [2]Je ne sais pas.

JEAN – [3]Ne voudriez-vous pas voyager?

ROGER – [4]Si. Je voudrais visiter plusieurs pays étrangers.

JEAN – [5]Où iriez-vous?

ROGER – [6]J'irais en Italie visiter Florence et Rome, [7]aux États-Unis voir les gratte-ciel, [8]et en Afrique voir ce qui se passe là-bas.

JEAN – [9]Est-ce que c'est tout?

ROGER – [10]Non. J'achèterais une grosse voiture, [11]et j'irais m'amuser au bord de la mer.

JEAN – [12]J'espère que vous ne serez jamais riche, Roger.

ROGER – [13]Pourquoi dites-vous cela?

JEAN – [14]Parce que vous seriez malheureux. [15]Vous ne sauriez pas dépenser votre argent.

ROGER – [16]Vous avez peut-être raison. [17]Je voudrais seulement être riche de temps en temps.

JEAN – [18]J'ai une idée, Roger!

ROGER – [19]Laquelle?

JEAN – [20]Vous n'avez qu'à chercher un millionnaire qui pense comme vous. [21]Vous pourriez changer de rôle [22]tous les six mois, par exemple!

JOHN – [1]*What would you do if you were rich, Roger?*

ROGER – [2]*I don't know.*

JOHN – [3]*Wouldn't you like to travel?*

ROGER – [4]*Yes. I'd like to visit several foreign countries.*

JOHN – [5]*Where would you go?*

ROGER – [6]*I'd go to Italy to visit Florence and Rome,* [7]*to the United States to see the skyscrapers,* [8]*and to Africa to see what's happening there.*

JOHN – [9]*Is that all?*

ROGER – [10]*No. I would buy a big car,* [11]*and I would go to the seashore to have a good time.*

JOHN – [12]*I hope you will never be rich, Roger.*

ROGER – [13]*Why do you say that?*

JOHN – [14]*Because you would be unhappy.* [15]*You would not know how to spend your money.*

ROGER – [16]*You are perhaps right.* [17]*I'd like to be rich only from time to time.*

JOHN – [18]*I have an idea, Roger!*

ROGER – [19]*What is it?*

JOHN – [20]*You need only look for a millionaire who thinks as you do.* [21]*You could change places* [22]*every six months, for example!*

I. Substitutions. *Répétez les phrases suivantes en substituant les mots indiqués:*

1. Qu'est-ce que vous feriez si vous étiez riche?
   si vous étiez millionnaire / si vous étiez en France / si vous n'aviez pas d'argent / si vous aviez mal à la gorge
2. J'irais voir Florence.
   visiter / passer quelque temps à / passer quinze jours à / visiter les musées de
3. Si j'étais riche j'irais en Italie.
   aux États-Unis / à l'étranger (*abroad*) / à la plage / m'amuser au bord de la mer
4. Vous pourriez changer de rôle.
   de train / d'autobus / de robe / de chapeau / d'hôtel
5. Vous n'avez qu'à chercher un millionnaire.
   trouver un millionnaire / acheter une grosse voiture / aller au bord de la mer / aller à la plage
6. Je voudrais aller en Italie et en Suisse.
   en Angleterre et en Écosse (*Scotland*) / en Turquie et en Grèce / à Florence et à Rome / à Madrid et à Lisbonne
7. Savez-vous ce qui se passe en Afrique?
   Je ne sais pas / Voudriez-vous savoir / Ne voudriez-vous pas savoir / Je voudrais bien savoir

II. *Répondez en français à chacune des questions suivantes:*

1. Êtes-vous allé(e) au bord de la mer l'été dernier? **2.** Est-ce que vous voudriez voyager en Europe? **3.** Avez-vous déjà visité des pays étrangers? **4.** Êtes-vous jamais allé(e) en France? **5.** Êtes-vous déjà allé(e) en Angleterre? **6.** Voudriez-vous aller en Russie? **7.** Voudriez-vous aller en Belgique? **8.** Quelles villes européennes voudriez-vous visiter? **9.** Voudriez-vous passer quelques semaines à Paris? **10.** Iriez-vous à Versailles si vous étiez en France? **11.** Seriez-vous malheureux (malheureuse) si vous étiez riche? **12.** Aimez-vous dépenser de l'argent?

III. *Demandez à quelqu'un:*

1. ce qu'il ferait s'il était riche. **2.** s'il ne voudrait pas voyager. **3.** s'il voudrait visiter des pays étrangers. **4.** où il irait. **5.** s'il voudrait aller en Italie. **6.** pourquoi il voudrait y aller. **7.** pourquoi il voudrait aller en Afrique. **8.** s'il achèterait une automobile. **9.** où il irait s'amuser. **10.** s'il saurait dépenser son argent. **11.** ce qu'il ferait s'il était millionnaire.

IV. Révision. *Répétez les phrases suivantes en remplaçant* **appartenir** (*to belong to*) *par l'expression* **être à:**

A. 1. Ces gants m'appartiennent. **2.** Ces gants ne m'appartiennent pas. **3.** Ces gants vous appartiennent-ils? **4.** Ces gants ne vous appartiennent-ils pas? **5.** Ils appartiennent à Charles. **6.** Ils lui appartiennent. **7.** Ils appartiennent à Marie. **8.** Ils ne lui appartiennent pas.

B. *Remplacez l'adjectif possessif et le nom par le pronom possessif dans les phrases suivantes:*

1. Mes gants sont à la maison. **2.** Ce sont mes gants. **3.** J'ai perdu mon parapluie. **4.** J'ai laissé mon parapluie à la maison. **5.** Marie a étudié sa leçon. **6.** Charles n'a pas étudié sa leçon. **7.** J'ai écrit à mes parents; avez-vous écrit à vos parents? **8.** Quand avez-vous reçu un chèque de vos parents?

V. Dictée d'après la Conversation 24, pp. 194-195.

VI. Causerie.

Votre idée d'une vie heureuse (six à huit phrases).

CHATEAU DE SULLY, EN BOURGOGNE

EN BRETAGNE

En province

Marie et Roger sont de retour à Paris, à la fin des vacances de Noël. Marie est allée passer ses vacances en Bretagne, où elle a de la famille, et Roger est allé revoir la petite ville des Alpes où il est né. Le lendemain de leur retour, Jean demande à ses amis leurs impressions.

—J'adore la Bretagne, dit Marie. Mon oncle et ma tante habitent à Saint-Malo, dans la partie de la ville encore entourée de vieilles fortifications. Avant la deuxième guerre mondiale, leur maison était une de ces grandes et belles demeures construites par les marchands d'autrefois, au temps où Saint-Malo était une ville prospère, enrichie par son commerce et par ses corsaires. Comme plus de la moitié des maisons de la ville, elle a été brûlée en 1944. Depuis, ces maisons ont été reconstruites, presque telles qu'elles étaient autrefois. C'est ainsi que la vieille cité garde, même maintenant, son ancien charme un peu triste.

—Vraiment, je ne sais pas si je choisirais la Bretagne pour y passer mes vacances de Noël, remarque Jean. Il y a des endroits plus gais.

—En réalité, continue Marie, mes vacances m'ont beaucoup plu. Nous avons fait le réveillon chez des amis, les Kerguélen, qui ont un vieux château à quelque distance de Saint-Malo, près du Mont-Saint-Michel. Quand vous irez au Mont-Saint-Michel, n'oubliez pas d'aller jusqu'à Saint-Malo. Vous ne regretterez rien.

—Entendu, répond Jean. Et vous, Roger, racontez-nous un peu ce que vous avez fait pendant vos vacances dans les Alpes.

—J'avais quitté ma ville natale lorsque j'étais enfant, et je n'y étais jamais retourné. Je ne m'attendais pas aux changements que j'y ai trouvés. On était en train de démolir l'école où j'allais lorsque j'avais douze ans pour installer à cet endroit les bureaux d'une compagnie d'électricité qui exploite l'énergie d'un grand barrage construit dans le voisinage. Cela m'a fait quelque chose de voir disparaître mon ancienne école. Comme le temps passe!

—Que voulez-vous, Roger, c'est la vie!, répond Jean. Marie a vu la France d'autrefois, celle de la Bretagne et des vieux châteaux, et vous, vous avez vu la France d'aujourd'hui, celle des barrages et des grandes usines.

QUESTIONS

1. Où Marie est-elle allée passer les vacances de Noël? **2.** Quels parents a-t-elle en Bretagne? **3.** Dans quelle partie de Saint-Malo son oncle et sa tante habitent-ils? **4.** Quand Saint-Malo était-elle une ville très prospère? **5.** Qu'est-ce qui faisait à ce moment-là la prospérité de la ville? **6.** Qu'est-ce que Marie pense de ses vacances? **7.** Où Marie dit-elle à Jean d'aller quand il ira au Mont-Saint-Michel? **8.** Qu'est-ce que Roger à fait pendant ses vacances de Noël? **9.** Est-ce qu'il s'attendait aux changements qu'il a trouvés dans sa ville natale? **10.** Qu'est-ce qu'on était en train de faire à ce moment-là? **11.** Pourquoi démolissait-on son ancienne école? **12.** Est-ce que ça lui a fait quelque chose de voir disparaître son ancienne école?

DANS LES ALPES: CHAMONIX

The Conditional

61. *Conditional of regular verbs.*

—**Je déjeunerais** à la maison, si j'avais le temps de rentrer.	*I would lunch* at home, if I had time to go home.
—**Je finirais** plus tôt, si je commençais plus tôt.	*I would finish* sooner, if I began sooner.
—**Je répondrais à** sa lettre, si j'avais son adresse.	*I would answer* his letter, if I had his address.
—**Je me dépêcherais,** si j'étais à votre place.	*I would hurry*, if I were in your place.

The forms of the conditional of regular verbs are:

FIRST CONJUGATION	SECOND CONJUGATION	THIRD CONJUGATION
je déjeunerais	je finirais	je répondrais
I would (should) lunch*	*I would (should*) finish*	*I would (should*) answer*
tu déjeunerais	tu finirais	tu répondrais
il déjeunerait	il finirait	il répondrait
nous déjeunerions	nous finirions	nous répondrions
vous déjeuneriez	vous finiriez	vous répondriez
ils déjeuneraient	ils finiraient	ils répondraient

The forms of the conditional of regular verbs may be found by adding the endings **-ais, -ais, -ait, -ions, -iez, -aient** to the infinitive, except that in the case of verbs of the third conjugation (ending in **-re**) the final **e** of the infinitive is omitted. As the endings are the same as those of the imperfect indicative, you should be able to learn the forms of the conditional at a glance.

* Very careful speakers are likely to say *I should*, *you would*, etc., although most people say *I would*, *you would*, etc. Whatever pattern you happen to follow in English, you say **je finirais, tu finirais,** etc., in French. There is no alternative.

Note that the three forms of the singular and the third person plural are all pronounced alike except for linking.

The conditional of reflexive verbs follows the usual pattern: **Je me dépêcherais, tu te dépêcherais,** etc.

62. *Conditional of* **être** *and* **avoir.**

—**Vous seriez** malheureux, si vous étiez riche.	*You would be* unhappy, if you were rich.
—**J'aurais** le temps, si je me levais de bonne heure.	*I would have time*, if I got up early.

The forms of the conditional of **être** and **avoir** are:

être	**avoir**
je serais *I would (should) be*	j'aurais *I would (should) have*
tu serais	tu aurais
il serait	il aurait
nous serions	nous aurions
vous seriez	vous auriez
ils seraient	ils auraient

63. *Commonest uses of the conditional.*

(1) The conditional is used in the result clause of certain conditional sentences:

—**Je répondrais** à sa lettre, si j'avais son adresse.	*I would answer* his letter, if I had his address.
—**Je travaillerais** davantage, si j'étais à votre place.	*I would work* more, if I were in your place.

In conditional sentences which describe *what would happen* if a certain condition were fulfilled, the conditional is used in the result clause (**Je répondrais à sa lettre**) and the imperfect is used in the if-clause **(si j'avais son adresse).**

Note the difference between this conditional sentence and those you have seen (see par. 47), which describe *what will happen* if a certain condition is fulfilled. Ex.: **Je prendrai un taxi** (*fut.*) **s'il pleut** (*present*).

(2) The conditional is often used even though the if-clause is omitted. Ex.: **Vous ne sauriez pas** dépenser votre argent. *You would not know* how to spend your money (i.e., if you were rich).

—A votre place, **je travaillerais** davantage.	(If I were) in your place, *I would work* harder.

(3) To express future action in indirect discourse which depends upon a verb in a past tense:

—Il a dit qu'**il irait** en Italie.	He said *he would go* to Italy.
—Elle a dit qu'**elle ferait** des courses.	She said *she would do* some errands.

Note that this use of the conditional is parallel to English usage. If someone said: *I shall go to Italy*, you could report it by a direct quotation (direct discourse), or by an indirect quotation (indirect discourse). For example:

DIRECT: He said, "*I shall go to Italy.*" Il a dit: «**J'irai** en Italie.»
INDIRECT: He said *he would go* to Italy. Il a dit qu'**il irait** en Italie.

64. *Remark about English* should *and* would.

While it is generally bad practice to think of French words and phrases in terms of their supposed English equivalents, it is particularly dangerous in the case of *should* and *would*. While these words are indeed used to form a conditional in English, they have other very common meanings which have nothing whatever to do with the conditional.

(1) *Should* denoting obligation (meaning "ought to"): To express in French "I should go to the library" (i.e., I ought to go to the library), you use a form of the verb **devoir.** This verb will be studied later. Meanwhile, remember that the conditional forms themselves carry no suggestion of obligation.

(2) *Would* denoting habitual action (meaning "used to"): You have seen in paragraph 56 that habitual action in the past is expressed in French by the imperfect indicative. Ex.:

—**Il allait** au cinéma tous les soirs après le dîner.	*He would go* (used to go) to the movies every evening after dinner.

I. Exercices d'application.

A. *Répétez, en remplaçant le futur par le conditionnel:*

1. Je lui parlerai. **2.** J'irai en ville. **3.** Je n'aurai pas le temps. **4.** Achèterez-vous ces gants? **5.** Déjeunerez-vous en ville? **6.** Lui répondrez-vous? **7.** Il se dépêchera. **8.** Vous dépêcherez-vous? **9.** Ils commenceront tout de suite. **10.** A quelle heure finiront-ils? **11.** Y aura-t-il de la place? **12.** Qu'est-ce que vous achèterez?

B. *Répétez, en remplaçant le présent par le conditionnel:*

1. J'achète le journal. **2.** Je me lève de bonne heure. **3.** Il obéit à la loi. **4.** Il est à l'heure. **5.** Vous avez le temps. **6.** Nous n'avons pas le temps. **7.** Ils vont en Italie. **8.** Ils font du ski. **9.** Que faites-vous? **10.** Je ne sais pas. **11.** Ne voulez-vous pas aller à Versailles? **12.** Pouvez-vous m'envoyer son adresse?

C. *Répétez les phrases suivantes, en remplaçant le présent et le futur par l'imparfait et le conditionnel:*

EX.:—Si je commence plus tôt, je finirai plus tôt.
—Si je commençais plus tôt, je finirais plus tôt.

1. Si j'ai le temps de rentrer, je déjeunerai à la maison. **2.** S'il fait beau, j'irai en ville. **3.** Si mon père m'envoie un chèque, j'achèterai un manteau. **4.** Nous monterons s'il y a de la place. **5.** S'il neige, je prendrai un taxi. **6.** Si je me couche de bonne heure, je me lèverai de bonne heure. **7.** Si Roger ne finit pas son travail, il ne sera pas content.

D. *Mettez les phrases suivantes au conditionnel en remplaçant* **quand** *par* **si**.

EX.:—Quand j'aurai le temps, j'irai voir ce film.
Si j'avais le temps, j'irais voir ce film.

1. Quand Marie aura de l'argent, elle achètera un manteau. **2.** Il y aura de la place quand les gens descendront. **3.** Roger me téléphonera quand il sera de retour. **4.** Quand il fera beau, nous ferons une promenade ensemble. **5.** Quand mon père m'enverra un chèque, je vous inviterai à dîner. **6.** Je passerai quelque temps à Venise quand je serai en Italie.

E. *Mettez les phrases suivantes à la forme indirecte.*

EX.:—Il a dit: J'irai en Italie.
—Il a dit qu'il irait en Italie.

1. Il a dit: Je rentrerai à midi. **2.** Je lui ai dit: Je ferai des courses cet après-midi. **3.** Je lui ai dit: Je me coucherai de bonne heure. **4.** Il m'a dit: Je me dépêcherai. **5.** Ils nous ont dit: Nous serons à l'heure.

II. *Exercice sur le conditionnel et sur l'imparfait. Dites en français:*

1. (*a*) I would be. (*b*) I was. (*c*) If I were . . . **2.** (*a*) He would have. (*b*) He had. (*c*) If he had . . . **3.** (*a*) We would have lunch. (*b*) We were having lunch. (*c*) If we were having lunch . . . **4.** (*a*) You would finish. (*b*) You were finishing. (*c*) If you finished . . . **5.** (*a*) They would answer. (*b*) They were answering. (*c*) If they answered . . . **6.** (*a*) I would go. (*b*) I was going. (*c*) If I were going . . .

III. *Demandez à quelqu'un:*

1. s'il déjeunerait à la maison, s'il avait le temps de rentrer. **2.** s'il achèterait une grosse auto, s'il était riche. **3.** s'il saurait dépenser son argent, s'il était millionnaire. **4.** s'il ferait une promenade, s'il faisait beau. **5.** ce qu'il ferait, s'il avait faim. **6.** ce qu'il ferait, s'il était fatigué. **7.** ce qu'il ferait, s'il était malade. **8.** ce qu'il achèterait, si son père lui envoyait un chèque de cinquante dollars. **9.** s'il serait heureux de passer quelques semaines à Paris, s'il avait le temps.

IV. *Dites en français:*

1. You are right. **2.** I hope it will snow. **3.** I hoped it would snow. **4.** Will you go skiing if it snows? **5.** Will you go skiing when it snows? **6.** Would you go skiing if it snowed? **7.** He said he would go skiing if it snowed. **8.** He always goes skiing when there is enough snow (**assez de neige**). **9.** He always went skiing when there was enough snow.

V. Révision des dialogues, pp. 164-165 et p. 173.

1. Qu'est-ce que Jean fait à l'arrêt de l'autobus? **2.** Depuis combien de temps attend-il l'autobus? **3.** Est-ce qu'il y avait beaucoup de monde dans l'autobus qui est arrivé? **4.** Y a-t-il des gens debout dans l'autobus qui arrive? **5.** Est-ce qu'il y a de la place dans l'autobus? **6.** Est-ce que Jean et Roger sont montés tout de même? **7.** Quand est-ce qu'il y aura de la place? **8.** Pourquoi Roger descend-il à l'arrêt de la rue de la Paix? **9.** Où Roger habitait-il quand il avait douze ans? **10.** A quelle école allait-il? **11.** Dans quelle région se trouve la ville où il habitait? **12.** A quelle heure partait-il pour l'école? **13.** A quelle heure en sortait-il? **14.** Y avait-il beaucoup d'élèves dans cette école? **15.** Croyez-vous que les élèves de cette école travaillaient trop?

VI. Thème d'imitation:

Today is Christmas Day. After Midnight Mass, John and Roger went to the Christmas-Eve Party[1] at the Browns. On the table there was a beautiful turkey. John likes turkey very much. He thought[2] that turkey (was) delicious.[3] There was lots of wine, red and white.

John and Roger got home at five o'clock in the morning! When John woke up, he said to Roger: "Santa Claus[4] brought me a good headache.[5] But that doesn't make any difference. I had a very good time. The Browns are very nice and their turkey was excellent, wasn't it?

---

[1] *to go to the Christmas-Eve party,* **aller faire le réveillon.** [2] use **passé composé** because it describes John's reaction. [3] *delicious,* **délicieux** *m.*, **délicieuse** *f.* [4] *Santa Claus,* **le Pere Noël.** [5] **un bon mal de tête.**

CI
ORGANISATION
IVAN LE TERRIBLE
SERGE PROKOFIEV
J.C. BACH
ANDRE CAMPRA
3018
Trouvères et Troubadours
Minnesänger et Meistersinger
vous connaissez
raimon
jacques bertin
PLAYPHONE
PHILIPS
ligne extra-plate
ouverture secrétaire
haute musicalité

A Versailles

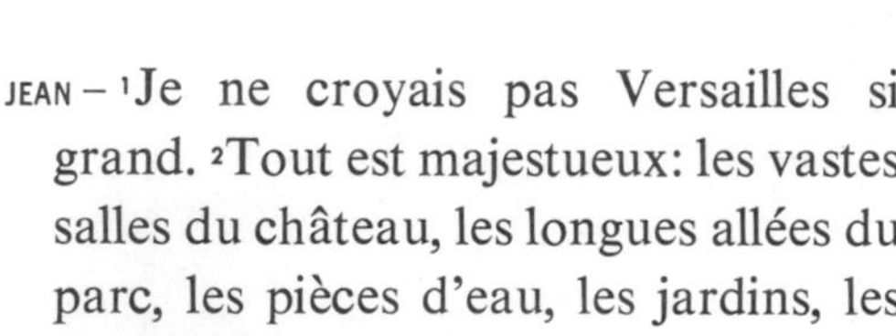

JEAN – [1]Je ne croyais pas Versailles si grand. [2]Tout est majestueux: les vastes salles du château, les longues allées du parc, les pièces d'eau, les jardins, les fontaines . . .

JOHN – [1]*I did not think Versailles was so large.* [2]*Everything is majestic: the enormous rooms of the château, the long walks of the park, the ornamental pools, the gardens, the fountains . . .*

ROGER – [3]Louis XIV aimait la splendeur. [4]Maintenant, comprenez-vous pourquoi on l'appelait le Grand Roi?

ROGER – [3]*Louis XIV went in for magnificence.* [4]*Now do you understand why they called him the Great King?*

JEAN – [5]Oui, je comprends.

JOHN – [5]*Yes, I understand.*

ROGER – [6]«Noblesse oblige,» vous savez.

ROGER – [6]*"Noblesse oblige",* you know.*

JEAN – [7]Je sais que Louis XIV a fait construire Versailles. [8]Mais qui est-ce qui l'a construit pour lui?

JOHN – [7]*I know that Louis XIV had Versailles built.* [8]*But who built it for him?*

ROGER – [9]Un des architectes était Mansart.

ROGER – [9]*Mansard was one of the architects.*

JEAN – [10]J'ai entendu parler de lui. [11]Nous avons en anglais le mot «mansard».

JOHN – [10]*I have heard of him.* [11]*We have the word "mansard" in English.*

ROGER – [12]Tiens! Qu'est-ce que cela veut dire?

ROGER – [12]*Really! What does that mean?*

JEAN – [13]Je crois que c'est une espèce de toit.

JOHN – [13]*I think it is a sort of roof.*

ROGER – [14]Le mot «mansarde» existe aussi en français.

ROGER – [14]*We also have the word "mansarde" in French.*

JEAN – [15]Qu'est-ce que c'est qu'une «mansarde»?

JOHN – [15]*What is a "mansarde"?*

---

* Nobility imposes obligations (i.e. it is up to persons of high birth, rank, or position to live up to their position in every way).

ROGER – [16]C'est d'ordinaire une chambre sous le toit. [17]C'est là qu'on met les vieux meubles, les chaises cassées, les tapis usés, et cætera. [18]Le sort est parfois ironique.

JEAN – [19]Qu'est-ce qui vous fait dire cela?

ROGER – [20]Mansart a passé sa vie à construire des palais, [21] et son nom est resté à une humble chambre.

ROGER – [16]*It is usually a room under the roof (i.e. a garret room).* [17]*That's where we put pieces of old furniture, broken chairs, worn-out carpets, etc.* [18]*Fate is sometimes ironical.*

JOHN – [19]*What makes you say that?*

ROGER – [20]*Mansard spent his life building palaces,* [21]*and (yet) his name has been given to an humble room.*

I. Substitutions. *Répétez les phrases suivantes en substituant les mots indiqués:*

1. Je ne croyais pas Versailles si grand.

   les jardins si beaux / les salles si vastes / les allées si longues / les allées si larges (*wide*) / Mansart si bon architecte

2. Remarquez cette fontaine.

   ce plafond (*ceiling*) / cette tapisserie magnifique / ce fauteuil doré (*gilded armchair*) / ce portrait de Marie-Antoinette

3. Louis XIV a fait construire Versailles.

   une belle chapelle / de beaux châteaux / plusieurs palais / de beaux monuments

4. Nous avons fait construire une maison.

   J'ai / Ma sœur a / Mes parents ont / Avez-vous / Votre père a-t-il

5. J'ai entendu parler de lui.

   de Mansart / des Brown / d'eux / de Jeanne d'Arc / d'elle

6. Il a passé sa vie à construire des palais.

   l'après-midi à faire des courses / la soirée à travailler / le week-end à faire du ski / trois jours à se reposer / l'été à visiter l'Italie

II. *Répondez à chacune des questions suivantes en remplaçant le nom par le pronom convenable.*

EX.:—Avez-vous entendu parler de Mansart?
—Oui, j'ai entendu parler de lui.
—Avez-vous entendu parler de Versailles?
—Oui, j'en ai entendu parler.

1. Avez-vous entendu parler de Louis XIV?

   des Brown / de Napoléon / de Jeanne d'Arc / des rois de France

2. Avez-vous entendu parler du château de Versailles?

   des fontaines de Versailles / du parc de Versailles / de la chapelle de Versailles / des tapisseries de Versailles

III. *Répondez à chacune des questions suivantes:*

1. De quel château parlent Jean et Roger? **2.** Est-ce que Jean croyait que Versailles était si grand? **3.** Qu'est-ce qu'on trouve dans le château? **4.** Qu'est-ce qu'il y a dans le parc? **5.** Comment appelait-on Louis XIV? **6.** Est-ce qu'il aimait la splendeur? **7.** Comprenez-vous la phrase «Noblesse oblige»? **8.** Qui a fait construire Versailles? **9.** Qui est-ce qui a construit le château pour Louis XIV? **10.** Avez-vous entendu parler de Mansart? **11.** Avez-vous entendu parler des allées du parc? **12.** Avez-vous entendu parler des fontaines de Versailles? **13.** Connaissez-vous le mot anglais «mansard»? **14.** Qu'est-ce que cela veut dire? **15.** Est-ce que le mot *mansarde* existe aussi en français? **16.** Qu'est-ce que c'est qu'une mansarde? **17.** Qu'est-ce qu'on met dans les mansardes? **18.** Qu'est-ce que Mansart a fait pendant sa vie? **19.** A quoi son nom est-il resté?

IV. *Demandez à quelqu'un:*

1. s'il y a beaucoup de fontaines à Versailles. **2.** comment on appelait Louis XIV. **3.** ce que veut dire «Noblesse oblige». **4.** qui a fait construire le château de Versailles. **5.** qui a construit le château. **6.** s'il a entendu parler de Mansart. **7.** s'il connaît le mot anglais «mansard». **8.** si le mot «mansarde» existe aussi en français. **9.** ce que veut dire le mot anglais «mansard». **10.** où l'on met les vieux meubles. **11.** ce qu'on met dans les mansardes. **12.** si le sort est parfois ironique. **13.** comment Mansart a passé sa vie. **14.** à quoi son nom est resté.

V. Révision. *Verbes pronominaux. Demandez à quelqu'un:*

1. comment il s'appelle. **2.** s'il se lève tard pendant les vacances. **3.** à quelle heure il se lève pendant les vacances. **4.** à quelle heure il s'est levé ce matin. **5.** à quelle heure il s'est couché hier soir. **6.** s'il s'est bien reposé dimanche dernier. **7.** comment s'appelle son professeur de français. **8.** s'il s'est bien amusé samedi soir.

VI. Dictée d'après la Conversation 25, p. 199.

VII. Causerie.

Une visite à Versailles.

Qu'est-ce que tu as?

ROGER – [1]Qu'est-ce que tu as*, Marie?

MARIE – [2]Je n'ai rien du tout, je t'assure.

ROGER – [3]Mais si, tu as quelque chose. [4]Tu as l'air triste. [5]A quoi penses-tu?

MARIE – [6]Je pense à Jeanne. La connais-tu?

ROGER – [7]Non, je ne crois pas. Qui est-ce?

MARIE – [8]C'est une de mes cousines.

ROGER – [9]Tu as tant de cousines! [10]Laquelle de tes cousines est-ce?

MARIE – [11]C'est ma cousine qui demeure à Reims.

ROGER – [12]Oh oui! tu m'as déjà parlé d'elle. [13]Qu'est-ce qui lui est arrivé?

MARIE – [14]J'ai reçu hier une lettre de ma tante Ernestine. [15]Elle m'écrit que Jeanne va se marier jeudi prochain.

ROGER – [16]Quoi? Est-ce que cette nouvelle te rend triste? Tu es jalouse?

MARIE – [17]Non, je ne suis ni triste ni jalouse.

ROGER – [1]*What is the matter with you, Marie?*

MARIE – [2]*Nothing is the matter, really.*

ROGER – [3]*Yes there is. Something is wrong.* [4]*You look very sad.* [5]*What are you thinking about?*

MARIE – [6]*I am thinking of Jeanne. Do you know her?*

ROGER – [7]*No, I don't think so. Who is she?*

MARIE – [8]*She's a cousin of mine.*

ROGER – [9]*You have so many cousins!* [10]*Which of your cousins is she?*

MARIE – [11]*She's my cousin who lives in Rheims.*

ROGER – [12]*Oh yes! You have already spoken to me about her.* [13]*What has happened to her?*

MARIE – [14]*I had a letter from my aunt Ernestine yesterday.* [15]*She writes me that Jeanne is going to get married next Thursday.*

ROGER – [16]*What? Does that news make you sad? Are you jealous?*

MARIE – [17]*No. I am neither sad nor jealous.*

---

* For note on use of **tutoiement** see par. 12, (2).

ROGER – 18 Qu'est-ce qui t'ennuie, alors?

MARIE – 19 Je ne pourrai pas aller à son mariage.

ROGER – 20 C'est dommage, en effet. 21 Avec qui ta cousine se marie-t-elle?

MARIE – 22 Avec un jeune homme que je connaissais quand il avait dix ans. 23 Comme le temps passe!

ROGER – 18 *What is bothering you then?*

MARIE – 19 *I cannot go to her wedding.*

ROGER – 20 *It is indeed too bad.* 21 *To whom is your cousin getting married?*

MARIE – 22 *To a young man I knew when he was ten years old.* 23 *How time flies!*

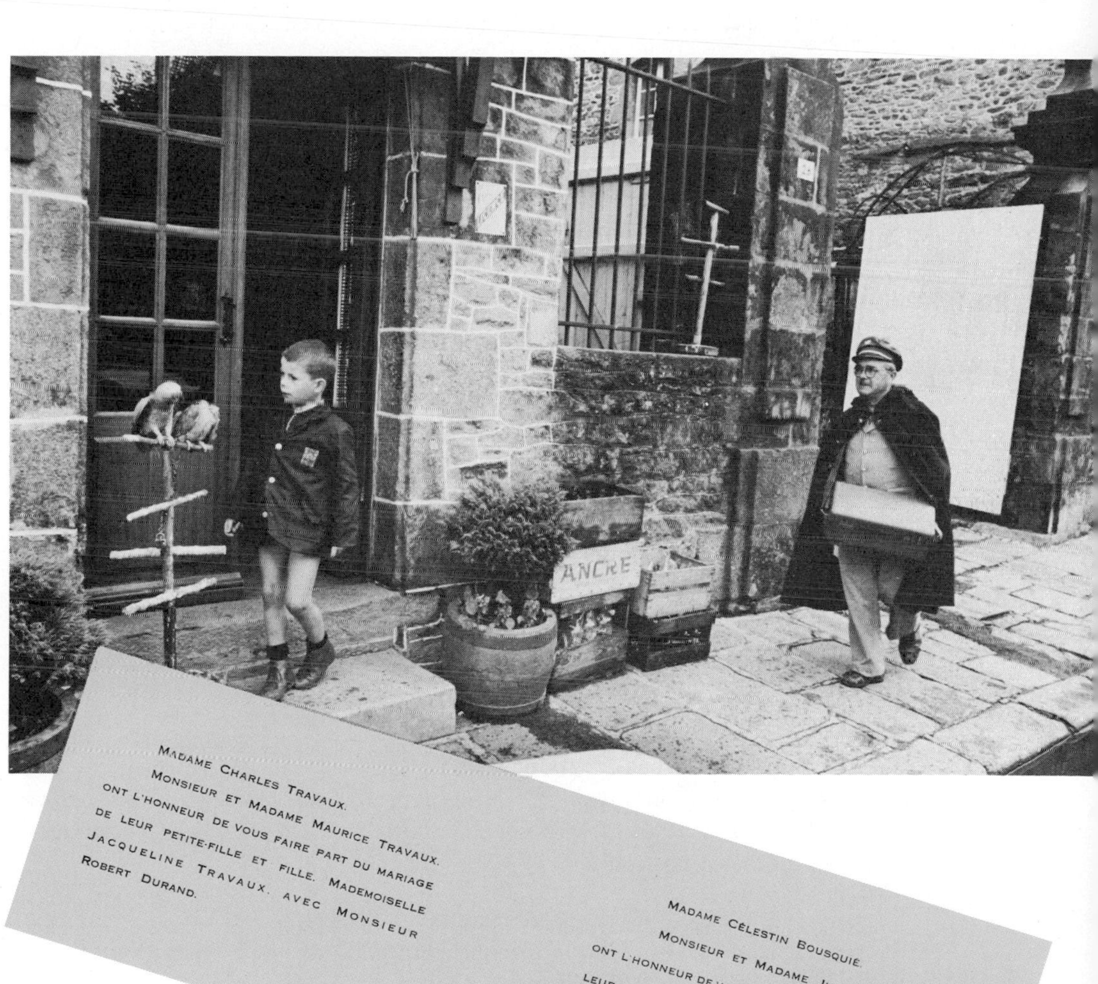

I. Substitutions. *Répétez les phrases suivantes en substituant les mots indiqués:*

1. Il a l'air triste.
fatigué / content / jeune / agréable / gentil / intelligent

2. Tu as l'air d'avoir chaud.
froid / faim / soif (*thirsty*) / quelque chose / très chaud

3. Est-ce que cette nouvelle te rend triste?
te rend malheureuse / t'ennuie / te fait plaisir

4. Je le connaissais quand il avait dix ans.
il était jeune / j'allais au collège / j'étais étudiant / j'habitais dans les Alpes

5. Qu'est-ce qui te rend triste?
le / la / les / vous

6. A quelle heure vas-tu partir?
sortir / rentrer / dîner / te coucher

II. *Répondez affirmativement, puis négativement à chacune des questions suivantes:*

EX.:—Avez-vous acheté quelque chose?
—**Oui, j'ai acheté quelque chose.**
—**Non, je n'ai rien acheté.**

1. Avez-vous reçu quelque chose? **2.** Avez-vous trouvé quelque chose? **3.** Avez-vous entendu quelque chose? **4.** Avez-vous envoyé quelque chose? **5.** Avez-vous fait quelque chose? **6.** Avez-vous quelque chose à faire? **7.** Avez-vous quelque chose?

III. *Remplacez le nom par le pronom convenable dans les phrases suivantes:*

A. penser à*

EX.:—Je pense à Jeanne. **Je pense à elle.**
—Je pense à mes examens. **J'y pense.**

1. Je pense à mes parents. **2.** Je pense à mon examen. **3.** Roger pense à son père. **4.** Il pense à son travail. **5.** Nous pensons à nos amis. **6.** Nous pensons à votre demande. **7.** Pensez-vous à cette lettre? **8.** Pensez-vous à votre mère? **9.** Il faut penser à vos examens.

* It is important to distinguish between **penser à** and **penser de.** While both are translated "to think of" in English, **penser à** means *to think of* a person or a thing, and **penser de** means *to think something about* a person or a thing, i.e. to hold an opinion.
Penser à. When the object of **penser à** is a personal pronoun which refers to a person or persons, the stressed form of the personal pronoun is used: Pensez-vous **à Marie?** Oui, je pense **à elle.** When the object of **penser à** is a pronoun referring to things, the form **y** is used: Pensez-vous **à vos examens?** Oui, j'y pense.

B. penser de*

EX.:—Que pensez-vous **de Jeanne?** Que pensez-vous **d'elle?**
—Que pensez-vous **de ce journal?** Qu'**en** pensez-vous?

1. Que pensez-vous de Louis XIV? **2.** Que pensez-vous de Versailles? **3.** Qu'est-ce que Jean pense de Versailles? **4.** Que pense-t-il de son auto? **5.** Que pensez-vous de ce film? **6.** Que pensez-vous de mes cousins? **7.** Que pensez-vous de mon chapeau? **8.** Que pensez-vous des Brown?

IV. *Répondez en français à chacune des questions suivantes:*

1. Qu'est-ce que Marie a? **2.** A-t-elle l'air triste? **3.** A quoi pense-t-elle? **4.** Est-ce que Roger connaît Jeanne? **5.** Qui est Jeanne? **6.** Est-ce que Marie a déjà parlé d'elle à Roger? **7.** De qui Marie a-t-elle reçu une lettre hier? **8.** Qu'est-ce que sa tante Ernestine lui dit dans sa lettre? **9.** Est-ce que cette nouvelle la rend triste? **10.** Est-ce que Marie est jalouse? **11.** Qu'est-ce qui l'ennuie? **12.** Avec qui sa cousine se marie-t-elle? **13.** Quel âge avait le fiancé de Jeanne quand Marie le connaissait?

V. *Demandez à quelqu'un en employant le* **tutoiement:**

1. ce qu'il a. **2.** s'il a quelque chose. **3.** pourquoi il a l'air triste. **4.** à quoi il pense. **5.** s'il connaît Jeanne. **6.** s'il a des cousines. **7.** de qui il parle. **8.** s'il a reçu une lettre de sa tante hier. **9.** s'il a reçu des nouvelles de ses parents. **10.** pourquoi il est triste. **11.** s'il est déjà allé en Europe. **12.** à qui il pense.

VI. *Répétez les phrases suivantes et posez la question qui correspond à chacune d'elles:*

EX.:—Tu as l'air triste.
—Tu as l'air triste. **Qu'est-ce que tu as?**

1. Vous avez l'air triste. **2.** Il a l'air triste. **3.** Elle a l'air triste. **4.** Ils ont l'air triste. **5.** Ils avaient l'air fâché (*angry*). **6.** Il avait l'air fâché. **7.** Elle avait l'air fâché. **8.** Elles avaient l'air fâché.

VII. Dictée d'après la Conversation 26, pp. 212-213.

VIII. Conversation.

Vous avez reçu une invitation à un mariage.

---

* **Penser de.** When the object of **penser de** is a personal pronoun which refers to a person or persons, the stressed form of the personal pronoun is used: Qu'est-ce que vous pensez **d'elle?** Je pense beaucoup de bien **d'elle.** When the object of **penser de** is a personal pronoun referring to things, the form **en** is used: Qu'est-ce que vous pensez **de ce livre?** Qu'est-ce que vous **en** pensez?

A MARSEILLE

Interrogative Pronouns

65. *Interrogative pronouns referring to persons.*

A. Subject forms: **qui?** or **qui est-ce qui?** (*who?*):

—**Qui** a dit cela?	*Who* said that?
OR	
—**Qui est-ce qui** a dit cela?	

B. Object forms: **qui?** and **qui est-ce que?** (*whom?*):

—**Qui** avez-vous vu?	*Whom* did you see?
OR	
—**Qui est-ce que** vous avez vu?	
—**A qui** avez-vous parlé?	*To whom* did you speak?
OR	
—**A qui est-ce que** vous avez parlé?	
—**Avec qui** ta cousine se marie-t-elle?	*To whom* is your cousin getting married?
OR	
—**Avec qui est-ce que** ta cousine se marie?	
—**De qui** parlez-vous?	*About whom* are you talking?
OR	
—**De qui est-ce que** vous parlez?	

Note that when **Qui?** is used as object of a verb or preposition, you invert the order of subject and verb. With **Qui est-ce qui?** or **Qui est-ce que?** you use normal word order.

C. à qui? (*whose?*):

—**A qui** sont ces gants?	*Whose* gloves are these?
—**A qui** est ce chapeau?	*Whose* hat is this?

Note that **à qui?** is the interrogative form corresponding to **à moi, à vous,** etc., which you have seen in paragraph 60.

66. *Interrogative pronouns referring to things, etc. (i.e., not persons).*

A. Subject form: **qu'est-ce qui?** (*What?*):

—**Qu'est-ce qui** se passe?	*What* is happening?
—**Qu'est-ce qui** lui est arrivé?	*What* happened to him (*or* to her)?

The short form **que?** is also used as subject in such phrases as **Que** se passe-**t-il?** and **Qu'**arrive-**t-il?**

B. Direct object form: **que?** and **qu'est-ce que?** (*what?*):

—**Que** vous a-t-il dit? OR —**Qu'est-ce qu'**il vous a dit?	*What* did he say to you?
—**Que** lui avez-vous répondu? OR —**Qu'est-ce que** vous lui avez répondu?	*What* did you reply to him?
—**Qu'**avez-vous? OR —**Qu'est-ce que** vous avez?	*What* is the matter with you?

C. Object of a preposition: **quoi?** (*what?*):

—**A quoi** pensez-vous? OR —**A quoi est-ce que** vous pensez?	*What* are you thinking *of?*
—**De quoi** parlez-vous? OR —**De quoi est-ce que** vous parlez?	*What* are you talking *about?*
—**De quoi** avez-vous besoin? OR —**De quoi est-ce que** vous avez besoin?	*What* do you need?

Since the verb **penser à** means *to think of*, you naturally say: **A quoi pensez-vous?** (Cf. note on p. 218.)

67. **Qu'est-ce que c'est que . . . ?** (*What is . . . ?*)

—**Qu'est-ce que c'est qu'**un Prisunic?	*What is* a "Prisunic"?
—**Qu'est-ce que c'est que** cela?	*What is* that?

You use **Qu'est-ce que c'est que . . . ?** to ask for a description or a definition.

68. *Interrogative pronoun* **lequel? laquelle? lesquels? lesquelles?** (*which? which one? which ones?*) (persons or things.)

A. Subject or object:

—**Laquelle** de tes cousines va se marier?	*Which one* of your cousins is getting married?
—Voici des livres. **Lesquels** voulez-vous?	Here are some books. *Which ones* do you want?

(1) **Lequel? laquelle?**, etc., are used to distinguish between two or more persons or things within a group. Ex.: *Who* are those people? **Qui** sont ces gens? BUT: *Which one* is Mr. Duval? **Lequel** est M. Duval?

(2) These forms agree in gender and number with the nouns to which they refer.

B. With prepositions **à** or **de:**

—Voici deux livres. **Duquel** avez-vous besoin?	Here are two books. *Which one* do you need?
—**A laquelle** de tes cousines as-tu écrit?	*To which one* of your cousins did you write?

In combination with prepositions **à** and **de** the forms of **lequel?**, etc., are:

auquel? à laquelle? auxquels? auxquelles?
duquel? de laquelle? desquels? desquelles?

I. Exercices d'application.

A. *Posez la question à laquelle répond chacune des phrases suivantes en remplaçant le sujet par* **Qui?** *puis par* **Qui est-ce qui?**

EX.:—Mon père a dit cela.
—**Qui a dit cela? Qui est-ce qui a dit cela?**

1. Roger est allé au bal. **2.** La bonne a sa cravate. **3.** Mansart a construit ce château. **4.** Jean a acheté ce journal. **5.** Je suis allé à la gare. **6.** Elle est venue chez eux. **7.** Roger veut du café. **8.** Je connais Louise Bedel. **9.** Je sais la date de la prise de la Bastille.

B. *Posez la question à laquelle répond chacune des phrases suivantes en remplaçant le complément par* **Qui?** *puis par* **Qui est-ce que?**

EX.:—J'ai vu Marie.
—**Qui avez-vous vu? Qui est-ce que vous avez vu?**

1. J'ai rencontré Marie. **2.** J'ai parlé à Marie. **3.** Je suis sorti avec elle. **4.** J'ai écrit à M. Brown. **5.** Roger a écrit à ses parents. **6.** Il a acheté des fleurs pour Marie. **7.** Il est allé au bal avec elle. **8.** Il a envoyé chercher le médecin. **9.** Nous avons envoyé des gants à ma mère.

C. *Posez la question à laquelle répond chacune des phrases suivantes en employant* **A qui . . . ?**

EX.:—Ces gants sont à moi.
—A qui sont ces gants?

1. Ce pardessus est à Charles. **2.** Ces mouchoirs sont à moi. **3.** Cette auto est à mon père. **4.** Cet imperméable est à mon frère. **5.** Cette cravate est à lui.

D. *Posez la question à laquelle répond chacune des phrases suivantes en remplaçant le sujet par* **Qu'est-ce qui?**

EX.:—Le vent fait ce bruit.
—Qu'est-ce qui fait ce bruit?

1. Mon auto fait ce bruit. **2.** Cette nouvelle me rend triste. **3.** Cette nouvelle m'ennuie. **4.** La neige me rend triste. **5.** Rien ne m'ennuie. **6.** Rien ne me plaît. **7.** Rien ne se passe. **8.** Quelque chose de terrible est arrivé. **9.** Rien ne lui est arrivé. **10.** Ce mauvais café m'a rendu malade.

E. *Posez la question à laquelle répond chacune des phrases suivantes en remplaçant le complément par* **Qu'est-ce que?** *puis par* **Que?**

EX.:—J'ai fait des courses.
—Qu'est-ce que vous avez fait? Qu'avez-vous fait?

1. J'ai acheté des bonbons. **2.** Il a dit bonjour. **3.** Il a apporté des hors-d'œuvre. **4.** Elle n'a rien dit. **5.** Je n'ai rien du tout. **6.** Nous avons fait une promenade cet après-midi. **7.** J'ai mangé une pomme. **8.** J'ai choisi une belle cravate.

F. *Posez la question à laquelle répond chacune des phrases suivantes en remplaçant le complément par* **quoi?**

EX.:—Je pense à l'examen.
—A quoi pensez-vous?

1. Je pense à mes examens. **2.** J'ai besoin de papier à lettres. **3.** J'ai besoin d'un journal. **4.** J'ai besoin d'argent. **5.** Nous parlons de notre voyage. **6.** Je commencerai par des hors-d'œuvre. **7.** Je finirai par des fruits. **8.** Je pense à l'été prochain.

G. *Posez la question à laquelle répond chacune des phrases suivantes en remplaçant le nom par* **lequel? laquelle?** *etc.*

EX.:—Voilà plusieurs jeunes filles. Jeanne est la plus grande.
—**Laquelle est la plus grande?**

1. Marie est la plus jolie. **2.** Alice est la plus intelligente. **3.** Hélène et Marguerite sont blondes. **4.** Je préfère Marie. **5.** J'ai parlé de Louise. **6.** Je pense à Louise.

II. *Demandez à quelqu'un:*

1. qui a construit le château de Versailles. **2.** pour qui le château a été construit **3.** ce que c'est qu'un château. **4.** laquelle des villes de France est la plus grande. **5.** de qui Marie a reçu une lettre hier. **6.** à qui pense Marie. **7.** ce qui ennuie Marie. **8.** ce que la tante de Marie a dit dans sa lettre. **9.** lesquelles des villes d'Italie Roger aimerait visiter. **10.** ce que Roger voudrait voir aux États-Unis.

III. Révision des dialogues, (p. 183 et pp. 186-187).

1. Pourquoi Marie n'est-elle pas allée au bal samedi dernier? **2.** Comment se sentait-elle ce soir-là? **3.** Est-ce qu'elle était très malade? **4.** A-t-elle fait venir le médecin? **5.** Comment va-t-elle maintenant? **6.** Est-ce qu'il faisait très froid le jour où elle a fait une longue promenade? **7.** Avait-elle froid en rentrant? **8.** Est-ce qu'elle fera bien de se reposer? **9.** Pourquoi Jean n'est-il pas prêt à sortir? **10.** Pourquoi Jean n'accepte-t-il pas la cravate de Roger? **11.** Est-ce qu'on pourrait porter une cravate verte avec un complet bleu? **12.** Est-ce que Jean a cherché dans son tiroir? **13.** Où Roger trouve-t-il la cravate de Jean? **14.** Pourquoi la bonne a-t-elle mis la cravate de Jean avec celles de Roger?

IV. Thème d'imitation:

Louis XIV is doubtless the most famous (*célèbre*) of the kings of France. He was born in 1638 and he died in 1715. He had an enormous château built at Versailles. For (*pendant*) more than forty years the best artists (*artistes*) of the seventeenth century worked at Versailles. The magnificent rooms of the château, the long walks of the park, the beautiful gardens, everything gives an impression of splendor. Louis XIV had the sun as an emblem (*comme emblème*). It is at Versailles that one understands why they called him the Sun-King (*le Roi-Soleil*).

Un accident

Au commissariat de police

LE COMMISSAIRE DE POLICE – [1]Vous êtes bien M. Jean Hughes, ingénieur-chimiste, [2]demeurant huit, rue du Docteur Roux?

JEAN – [3]Oui, monsieur le commissaire.

LE COMMISSAIRE DE POLICE – [4]Hier après-midi, vous avez été témoin de l'accident [5]au cours duquel le docteur Lambert a été blessé?

JEAN – [6]Oui, monsieur le commissaire.

LE COMMISSAIRE DE POLICE – [7]Où étiez-vous au moment où l'auto du docteur, [8]qui suivait la rue de Vaugirard, [9]est entrée en collision avec un camion [10]venant de l'avenue Pasteur?

JEAN – [11]J'étais devant l'Institut Pasteur.*

LE COMMISSAIRE DE POLICE – [12]Comment l'accident a-t-il eu lieu?

JEAN – [13]La chaussée était très glissante, [14]car il avait plu. [15]Le docteur Lambert, dont l'auto allait très vite, [16]n'a pas pu s'arrêter à temps.

LE COMMISSAIRE DE POLICE – [17]A quelle vitesse le camion allait-il [10]quand l'accident a eu lieu?

JEAN – [19]A environ 30 kilomètres à l'heure.

LE COMMISSAIRE DE POLICE – [20]Je vous remercie, monsieur. [21]Ce que vous venez de dire [22]est d'accord avec les renseignements que nous avons déjà.

At the Police Station

THE COMMISSAIRE DE POLICE – [1]*You are indeed Mr. John Hughes, a chemical engineer,* [2]*who lives at 8 rue du Dr. Roux?*

JOHN – [3]*Yes, sir.*

THE COMMISSAIRE DE POLICE – [4]*Yesterday afternoon you were a witness of the accident* [5]*in the course of which Dr. Lambert was hurt?*

JOHN – [6]*Yes, sir.*

THE COMMISSAIRE DE POLICE – [7]*Where were you at the moment when the doctor's car,* [8]*which was going along Vaugirard Street,* [9]*collided with a truck* [10]*that was coming from Pasteur Avenue?*

JOHN – [11]*I was in front of the Pasteur Institute.*

THE COMMISSAIRE DE POLICE – [12]*How did the accident take place?*

JOHN – [13]*The street was very slippery,* [14]*for it had been raining.* [15]*Dr. Lambert, whose car was going very fast,* [16]*couldn't stop in time.*

THE COMMISSAIRE DE POLICE – [17]*How fast was the truck going* [18]*when the accident took place?*

JOHN – [19]*About 30 kilometers per hour.*

THE COMMISSAIRE DE POLICE – [20]*I thank you, sir.* [21]*What you have just said* [22]*agrees with the information we already have.*

---

* The Institut Pasteur, founded by the great Pasteur, consists of a hospital, a museum, and a research institute for biological chemistry.

I. Substitutions. *Répétez les phrases suivantes en substituant les mots indiqués:*

1. Le docteur Lambert a été blessé.
   Un passant / Un médecin / Un agent de police / Un vieux monsieur
2. . . . l'accident au cours duquel le docteur Lambert a été blessé.
   un passant / un médecin / un agent de police / un vieux monsieur
3. Vous avez été témoin de l'accident au cours duquel le docteur Lambert a été blessé.
   un passant / un médecin / un agent de police / un vieux monsieur
4. Le docteur Lambert, dont l'auto allait très vite, n'a pas pu s'arrêter à temps.
   assez vite / trop vite / beaucoup trop vite / à trente kilomètres à l'heure
5. Où étiez-vous au moment où l'accident a eu lieu?
   la collision / l'incident / la bataille / la querelle / la dispute
6. Où étiez-vous au moment de l'accident?
   la collision / l'incident / la bataille / la querelle / la dispute
7. Ce que vous venez de dire . . .
   faire / acheter / manger / répondre / chercher / regarder

II. *Répondez en français à chacune des questions suivantes:*

1. A qui Jean parle-t-il? **2.** Où la conversation a-t-elle lieu? **3.** Que fait Jean Hughes? **4.** Où demeure-t-il? **5.** De quoi a-t-il été témoin? **6.** Quand l'accident a-t-il eu lieu? **7.** Qui a été blessé au cours de l'accident? **8.** Quelle rue suivait l'auto du docteur Lambert? **9.** D'où venait le camion? **10.** Où était Jean au moment de l'accident? **11.** Pourquoi la chaussée était-elle glissante? **12.** Pourquoi le docteur Lambert n'a-t-il pas pu s'arrêter à temps? **13.** A quelle vitesse le camion allait-il quand l'accident a eu lieu? **14.** Est-ce que le commissaire a déjà parlé à des témoins de l'accident? **15.** Qu'est-ce que le commissaire a dit à Jean en le remerciant? **16.** Avez-vous jamais été témoin d'un accident d'auto?

III. *Demandez à quelqu'un:*

1. à qui parle Jean Hughes. **2.** pourquoi le commissaire a fait venir Jean Hughes. **3.** l'adresse de Jean. **4.** sa profession. **5.** de quoi il a été témoin. **6.** où l'accident a eu lieu. **7.** quand l'accident a eu lieu. **8.** pourquoi l'accident a eu lieu. **9.** comment l'accident a eu lieu. **10.** s'il avait plu avant l'accident. **11.** pourquoi la chaussée était glissante. **12.** à quelle vitesse allait le camion au moment de l'accident.

IV. *Répétez, en remplaçant le passé composé par* **Je viens de** (I have just) *avec l'infinitif.*

EX.:—J'ai déjeuné.
—Je viens de déjeuner.

1. J'ai acheté un journal. **2.** J'ai trouvé ma cravate. **3.** J'ai fini ma lettre. **4.** Je suis allé(e) à la pharmacie. **5.** Je me suis levé(e). **6.** Je me suis habillé(e). **7.** J'ai été témoin de l'accident.

V. Révision. *Dites en français:*

A. qu'est-ce que? (object form)

1. What's the matter with you? **2.** What's the matter with him? **3.** What's the matter with her? **4.** What's the matter with them? **5.** What was the matter with them? **6.** What was the matter with him?

B. qu'est-ce qui? (subject form)

1. What happened to her? **2.** What happened to him? **3.** What happened to them? **4.** What happened to you? **5.** What happened to Marie? **6.** What happened? **7.** What's bothering you? **8.** What's bothering her? **9.** What's bothering them?

VI. Dictée d'après la Conversation 27, pp. 216-217.

VII. Causerie.

Vous parlez d'un accident dont vous avez été témoin.

LE PEINTRE ET SON MODÈLE

The *Passé Simple* and the Pluperfect, Future Perfect and Conditional Perfect

69. *Meaning and use of the* passé simple.

The names **passé simple** (*simple past*) and **passé composé** (*compound past*) are used to distinguish two tenses which, generally speaking, have the same meaning: both tenses are used to express simple past actions.

You have seen that the **passé composé** is commonly used in conversation. The **passé simple** is used only in literary narrative style and in rather formal speech. Even then, only the third person (singular and plural) is ordinarily used today.

EXAMPLE OF THE USE OF THE PASSÉ SIMPLE

A cette époque, il y **eut** une épidémie dans le pays des Troglodytes. Un médecin habile **arriva** du pays voisin et **donna** ses remèdes. Quand il **demanda** à ses clients de lui payer ses services, il ne **trouva** que des refus.

At that time an epidemic broke out in the land of the Troglodytes. A skillful doctor *arrived* from the neighboring country and *gave* his remedies. When he *asked* his patients to pay him for his services he *received* only refusals.

Le médecin **retourna** dans son pays et il y **arriva** très fatigué. Il **apprit** bientôt après que la même maladie ravageait de nouveau le pays des Troglodytes. Ils **allèrent** à lui tout de suite lui demander de revenir avec ses remèdes.

The doctor *returned* to his own country and he *arrived* there very tired. He *learned* soon afterwards that the same disease was again ravaging the land of the Troglodytes. They *went* to him immediately to ask him to come back with his remedies.

Le médecin **refusa.** Les Troglodytes **moururent** et **furent** victimes de leurs propres injustices.

The doctor *refused.* The Troglodytes *died* and they *were* victims of their own injustice.

70. *Forms of the* **passé simple.**

A. Regular verbs:

FIRST CONJUGATION	SECOND CONJUGATION	THIRD CONJUGATION
je déjeunai	je finis	je répondis
I lunched	*I finished*	*I answered*
tu déjeunas	tu finis	tu répondis
il déjeuna	il finit	il répondit
nous déjeunâmes	nous finîmes	nous répondîmes
vous déjeunâtes	vous finîtes	vous répondîtes
ils déjeunèrent	ils finirent	ils répondirent

B. Être and **avoir:**

être	**avoir**
je fus	j'eus
I was	*I had*
tu fus	tu eus
il fut	il eut
nous fûmes	nous eûmes
vous fûtes	vous eûtes
ils furent	ils eurent

(The **passé simple**, which is primarily used in writing, will be used here only for aural practice and will appear only in exercise I, A.)

71. *Pluperfect* **(plus-que-parfait)** *of regular verbs and of* **avoir** *and* **être.**

—**J'avais** déjà **accepté** l'invitation de Robert, quand j'ai reçu la vôtre.
I had already *accepted* Robert's invitation when I received yours.

—La chaussée était très glissante, car **il avait plu.**
The surface of the street was very slippery, for *it had been raining*.

—**Il était** déjà **parti,** quand je lui ai téléphoné.
He had already *left*, when I telephoned him.

The forms of the pluperfect indicative are:

J'avais déjeuné, etc. *I had lunched,* etc.
J'avais fini, etc. *I had finished,* etc.
J'avais répondu, etc. *I had answered,* etc.
J'avais été, etc. *I had been,* etc.
J'avais eu, etc. *I had had,* etc.
J'étais arrivé(e), etc. *I had arrived,* etc.
Je m'étais levé(e), etc. *I had got up,* etc.

(1) The pluperfect is formed like the **passé composé** except that the imperfect of the auxiliary is used.

(2) As in English, the pluperfect tense expresses an action that had already taken place when another past action took place. When the first action immediately precedes the second, the pluperfect is usually replaced by the imperfect of **venir** followed by **de** and an infinitive. Ex.: Je **venais d'**accepter l'invitation de Robert, quand j'ai reçu la vôtre.

72. *Future perfect tense* (futur antérieur).

—**J'aurai fini** mon travail quand il arrivera.	*I shall have finished* my work when he arrives.

The future perfect is formed like the other compound tenses except that the future of the auxiliary verb is used.

J'aurai déjeuné, etc.	*I shall have lunched*, etc.
Je serai arrivé(e), etc.	*I shall have arrived*, etc.

As in English, the future perfect tense is used to express an action that will take place in the future before another future action takes place. In sentences in which you use a future perfect in one clause, the verb in the other clause is always in the future tense (cf. paragraph 17). Ex.: **Je serai parti** quand elle **recevra** ma lettre. *I shall have left* when she gets my letter (*will receive*).

73. *The conditional perfect* (conditionnel passé).

—Si nous avions eu le temps, **nous serions allés** au bal.	If we had had time, *we would have gone* to the dance.
—**Je serais** volontiers **allé** avec lui, si je n'avais pas eu mal à la tête.	*I would have* gladly *gone* with him if I hadn't had a headache.

The conditional perfect is formed like the other compound tenses except that the conditional of the auxiliary verb is used.

J'aurais déjeuné, etc.	*I would have lunched*, etc.
J'aurais répondu, etc.	*I would have answered*, etc.
Je serais arrivé(e), etc.	*I would have arrived*, etc.
Je me serais levé(e), etc.	*I would have got up*, etc.

It is most commonly used in conditional sentences in which the verb in the if-clause is in the pluperfect. It expresses an action which would have taken place, if another action had taken place (cf. paragraph 63).

74. *Agreement of the past participle* in compound tenses.*

A. Verbs conjugated with **avoir:**

—J'ai **planté** des fleurs dans mon jardin.	I have *planted* flowers in my garden.
—Les fleurs que j'ai **plantées** n'ont pas **poussé**.	The flowers I *planted* did not *grow*.

When a verb is conjugated with **avoir,** the participle agrees in gender and number with a preceding direct object. If the direct object follows the participle, or if the verb has no direct object, there is of course no agreement and the masculine singular form of the participle is used.

Thus in **J'ai planté des fleurs,** there is no agreement because the direct object follows the participle.

In **Les fleurs que j'ai plantées n'ont pas poussé,** the participle **plantées** is feminine plural because the direct object **que,** which precedes the verb, refers to **les fleurs,** which is feminine plural. In the same sentence, **poussé** has no direct object and therefore cannot agree.

B. Verbs conjugated with **être** (not including reflexives):

—**Jean** est **allé** en ville.	John *went* downtown.
—**Marie** est **allée** en ville.	Marie *went* downtown.
—**Ils** sont **arrivés** à dix heures.	They (*masc.*) *arrived* at ten o'clock.
—**Elles** sont **arrivées** à neuf heures.	They (*fem.*) *arrived* at nine o'clock.

Except for reflexive verbs, when a verb is conjugated with **être,** the past participle agrees in gender and number with the subject of the verb. **Vous** may of course be masculine or feminine, singular or plural. Ex.: **Marie, êtes-vous allée** au cinéma? **Henri, êtes-vous allé** au cinéma? **Êtes-vous allés** au cinéma ensemble?

C. Reflexive verbs:

—Roger s'est **levé** à sept heures.	Roger *got* up at seven o'clock.
—Marie s'est **levée** à neuf heures.	Marie *got* up at nine o'clock.

Although reflexive verbs are conjugated with **être,** their past participles agree as if they were conjugated with **avoir,** i.e. they agree with a preceding direct object. In the preceding examples, **se** is the preceding direct object in each case. In the first example, it refers to Roger and the agreement is masculine. In the second it refers to Marie and the agreement is feminine.

* The agreement of the past participle is purely a matter of spelling in most cases but while it is of comparatively little importance in spoken French, it should be carefully observed in writing.

I. Exercices d'application.

A. *Indiquez le temps de chacune des formes suivantes:*

EX.:—Il arriva: **passé simple.** Il arrivera: **futur.** Il arrive: **présent.**

1. Il entra. **2.** Il se leva. **3.** Il se lèvera. **4.** Il répondit. **5.** Il répond. **6.** Il répondra. **7.** Il acheta. **8.** Ils achètent. **9.** Ils achetèrent. **10.** Ils choisissent. **11.** Ils choisirent. **12.** Ils entrèrent. **13.** Ils entreront. **14.** Il eut. **15.** Il vendit. **16.** Ils finirent. **17.** Ils furent. **18.** Ils auront. **19.** Ils eurent. **20.** Il ne fut pas.

B. *Mettez les phrases suivantes au plus-que-parfait:*

EX.:—Il a plu.
—Il avait plu.

1. J'ai répondu à sa lettre. **2.** Il a fini son dîner. **3.** Nous avons fait nos courses. **4.** Le train est déjà parti. **5.** Nous sommes allés en ville. **6.** Je me suis couché de bonne heure. **7.** Ils sont arrivés en retard. **8.** J'ai toujours obéi à la loi. **9.** J'ai acheté une auto. **10.** A-t-il neigé?

C. *Répétez les phrases suivantes en substituant les mots indiqués:*

1. J'avais fini mon travail quand vous avez téléphoné.

Je m'étais couché(e) / J'étais sorti(e) / Je n'avais pas fini mon travail / Je n'avais pas encore dîné / Je n'avais pas reçu votre lettre

2. Je venais de finir mon travail quand vous avez téléphoné.

Je venais de me coucher / Je venais de rentrer / Il venait de partir / Nous venions de dîner

3. Il aurait fait des courses s'il avait eu le temps.

Il serait allé en ville / Il aurait répondu à cette lettre / Il aurait fait une promenade / Il se serait bien amusé à Paris

D. *Employez le plus-que-parfait et le conditionnel passé dans les phrases suivantes:*

EX.:—Si j'avais de l'argent, j'irais en Italie.
—Si j'avais eu de l'argent, je serais allé(e) en Italie.

1. S'il faisait beau, j'irais en ville. **2.** S'il pleuvait, je prendrais un taxi. **3.** Si j'avais des courses à faire, je prendrais mon auto. **4.** Je répondrais à sa lettre, si j'avais son adresse. **5.** Elle irait au bal, si elle n'avait pas mal à la gorge. **6.** Si nous manquions notre train, nous passerions la nuit à Épernay.

E. *Répétez la phrase suivante en substituant les mots indiqués:*

J'aurai fini mon travail quand vous arriverez.

quand vous serez prêt / quand Marie sera prête / quand vous viendrez me chercher / quand Jean viendra me chercher

II. *Répondez en français à chacune des questions suivantes:*

1. Si vous aviez eu le temps, est-ce que vous seriez allé au cinéma hier soir? **2.** Est-ce que la chaussée aurait été glissante s'il n'avait pas plu? **3.** Étiez-vous parti ce matin quand il a commencé à pleuvoir? **4.** Est-ce que vous aviez fini votre travail hier soir quand je vous ai téléphoné? **5.** Est-ce que vous aurez fini votre travail à cinq heures et demie? **6.** Est-ce que vous aurez fini votre travail quand votre frère arrivera?

III. Révision. *Répondez en français à chacune des phrases suivantes:*

1. A quelle heure avez-vous déjeuné? **2.** A quelle heure dînerez-vous ce soir? **3.** A quelle heure dîneriez-vous si vous alliez en ville? **4.** A quelle heure dînez-vous le dimanche? **5.** A quelle heure dîniez-vous pendant les vacances? **6.** Est-ce que vous vous couchez de bonne heure le dimanche? **7.** Est-ce que vous vous couchez plus tard en été qu'en hiver? **8.** Vous êtes-vous levé(e) de bonne heure ce matin? **9.** Vous êtes-vous couché(e) tard hier soir? **10.** Est-ce que vous vous couchiez tard pendant les vacances? **11.** Est-ce que vous vous coucherez tard ce soir? **12.** Est-ce que vous vous coucheriez tard si vous aviez un examen demain?

IV. *Mettez le passage suivant au passé, en employant* **l'imparfait** *ou* **le passé composé** *selon le cas:*

Un jour qu'il suit la rue de Vaugirard, Jean entend tout à coup un bruit métallique et violent. Il se retourne et voit deux hommes, l'un dans un camion l'autre au volant d'une automobile, qui discutent avec véhémence. Lequel des deux est responsable de l'accident? Jean n'en sait rien, mais à en juger par leur indignation, ils ont tous les deux raison. Heureusement, un agent de police arrive et sa présence ramène le calme entre les antagonistes.

Deux jours plus tard, Jean reçoit une lettre qui le prie de se présenter au commissariat de police du XVe arrondissement. Quand il arrive à l'heure indiquée, le commissaire lui pose toute sorte de questions auxquelles Jean répond de son mieux.

V. Révision des dialogues, pp. 194-195 et p. 199.

1. Où Marie est-elle allée passer ses vacances de Noël? **2.** Comment est-elle revenue de Bretagne? **3.** Y avait-il beaucoup de monde dans l'express de Paris? **4.** Comment dit-on en français "You are lucky"? **5.** Comment dit-on en français "You are out of luck"? **6.** Chez qui Marie a-t-elle fait le réveillon?

7. Est-ce qu'elle s'est bien amusée pendant les vacances? **8.** Qu'est-ce que vous feriez si vous étiez riche? **9.** Quels pays voudriez-vous visiter? **10.** Qu'est-ce que vous achèteriez si vous alliez en France? **11.** Voudriez-vous changer de rôle tous les six mois avec un millionnaire? **12.** Savez-vous ce qui se passe en Europe?

VI. Thème d'imitation:

Two days ago, in front of the Pasteur Institute, John witnessed an accident in the course of which Dr. Lambert was hurt. Dr. Lambert's car collided with a truck. When the truck-driver (*le chauffeur du camion*) saw the doctor's car, he tried to stop, but too late . . . At the noise of the accident, some passers-by came to see what was happening. A little later, a policeman arrived and they took (*on a conduit*) Dr. Lambert to the hospital.

That afternoon, John went to the police station. The police commissioner asked him (*poser*) all sorts of questions which (*auxquelles*) he answered the best he could (*de son mieux*).

Chez l'horloger

L'HORLOGER* – [1]Qu'est-ce qu'il y a, monsieur?	THE JEWELER – [1]*What can I do for you, sir?*
JEAN – [2]Je voudrais faire réparer cette montre. [3]Je l'ai laissée tomber hier, [4]et elle ne marche plus.	JOHN – [2]*I'd like to have this watch repaired.* [3]*I dropped it yesterday,* [4]*and now it won't run.*
L'HORLOGER – [5]Où avez-vous acheté cette montre-là?	THE JEWELER – [5]*Where did you buy that watch?*
JEAN – [6]Je l'ai achetée en Amérique.	JOHN – [6]*I bought it in America.*
L'HORLOGER – [7]Je m'en doutais. [8]Je n'ai jamais vu une montre comme ça.	THE JEWELER – [7]*I rather thought so.* [8]*I have never seen a watch like that.*
JEAN – [9]Est-ce que vous pourrez la réparer tout de même?	JOHN – [9]*Can you repair it anyway?*
L'HORLOGER – [10]Je crois.	THE JEWELER – [10]*I think so.*
JEAN – [11]De quoi s'agit-il?	JOHN – [11]*What's wrong with it? (lit. Of what is it a question?)*
L'HORLOGER – [12]Il s'agit d'une réparation simple. [13]Mais je serai obligé de faire venir un ressort.	THE JEWELER – [12]*It is a question of a simple repair job.* [13]*But I'll have to send for a spring.*
JEAN – [14]Pouvez-vous me dire quand ma montre sera prête?	JOHN – [14]*Can you tell me when my watch will be ready?*

* Un horloger est une personne qui fait, répare, vend des horloges, des pendules et des montres.

L'HORLOGER – [15]Voyons . . . Je vais commander aujourd'hui le ressort dont j'ai besoin. [16]Je le recevrai sans doute vers le milieu de la semaine prochaine.

THE JEWELER – [15]*Let's see . . . Today I'll order the spring I need.* [16]*I'll probably get it toward the middle of next week.*

JEAN – [17]Je voudrais bien avoir ma montre le plus tôt possible.

JOHN – [17]*I'd certainly like to have my watch as soon as possible.*

L'HORLOGER – [18]Revenez d'aujourd'hui en quinze.

THE JEWELER – [18]*Come back two weeks from today.*

JEAN – [19]Bon. J'attendrai jusque-là.

JOHN – [19]*Okay. I'll wait till then.*

I. Substitutions. *Répétez les phrases suivantes en substituant les mots indiqués:*

1. Je voudrais faire réparer cette montre.

cette auto / cette pendule / ce tapis / cette chaise cassée / le toit de ma maison

2. Il s'agit d'une réparation simple.

d'une vieille maison / d'un vieux toit / d'une montre qui ne marche plus / d'une auto qui ne marche plus

3. Il s'agissait (*It was a question of*) d'une réparation difficile.

d'une montre américaine / d'un ressort cassé / d'un ami de mon père / tout simplement d'un rhume

4. Il s'agit de réparer cette montre.

de construire une maison / de faire des courses / de trouver ma cravate / de s'arrêter à temps

5. De quoi s'agit-il?

De quelle réparation / De quelle espèce de réparation / De quelle cousine de Marie / De qui

6. Je voudrais bien avoir ma montre le plus tôt possible.

d'aujourd'hui en quinze / d'aujourd'hui en huit / de vendredi en huit / lundi prochain / vers le milieu de la semaine prochaine

7. Je vais commander aujourd'hui le ressort dont j'ai besoin.

les livres / les chaises / les meubles / le tapis / les journaux

II. *Répondez en français à chacune des questions suivantes:*

1. Pourquoi Jean va-t-il chez l'horloger? **2.** Qu'est-ce que c'est qu'un horloger? **3.** Est-ce que la montre de Jean marche toujours (*still*)? **4.** Pourquoi ne marche-t-elle plus? **5.** Où Jean a-t-il acheté sa montre? **6.** Est-ce que l'horloger a déjà vu une montre comme ça? **7.** Est-ce qu'il pourra la réparer tout de même? **8.** De quoi s'agit-il? **9.** Qu'est-ce que l'horloger sera obligé de faire venir? **10.** Pourquoi sera-t-il obligé de faire venir un ressort? **11.** Est-ce que l'horloger peut dire à Jean quand sa montre sera prête? **12.** Quand va-t-il commander le ressort dont il a besoin? **13.** Quand pense-t-il le recevoir? **14.** Quand dit-il à Jean de revenir? **15.** Est-ce que Jean sera obligé d'attendre longtemps? **16.** Quand Jean reviendra-t-il chez l'horloger? **17.** Quand voudrait-il bien avoir sa montre?

III. *Demandez en français à quelqu'un:*

1. s'il a jamais laissé tomber sa montre. **2 .** si sa montre s'est arrêtée. **3.** si une montre peut marcher sans ressort. **4.** ce qui fait marcher une montre. **5.** ce qui se passe quand le ressort d'une montre est cassé. **6.** si l'horloger peut réparer la montre de John. **7.** de quoi il s'agit. **8.** s'il s'agit d'une réparation difficile. **9.** ce que l'horloger va commander. **10.** de quoi il aura besoin. **11.** quand il recevra le ressort.

IV. *Répondez en français:*

1. Avez-vous fait réparer votre montre? **2.** Avez-vous fait réparer votre auto? **3.** Marie a-t-elle fait venir le médecin? **4.** L'horloger a-t-il fait venir un ressort? **5.** Allez-vous faire venir un taxi? **6.** Allez-vous faire construire une maison? **7.** Qui a fait construire Versailles? **8.** Où Jean fera-t-il réparer sa montre?

V. *Mettez le passage suivant au passé en employant* **l'imparfait, le passé composé** *ou* **le conditionnel** *selon le cas:*

Un jour Jean laisse tomber sa montre. Il est très inquiet, car c'est une bonne petite montre que sa mère lui a donnée pour son anniversaire. Quand il la ramasse, la montre ne marche plus. De plus en plus inquiet, il va chez l'horloger et lui explique ce qui s'est passé. L'horloger ouvre la montre, prend sa loupe, et regarde l'intérieur. Il trouve que le ressort est cassé. Il demande à Jean où il a acheté sa montre, car il n'a jamais vu de montre comme ça. Jean dit que c'est une montre américaine et lui demande s'il pourra la réparer tout de même. L'horloger dit qu'il commandera aujourd'hui même le ressort dont il a besoin, qu'il le recevra dans quelques jours et que Jean pourra revenir d'aujourd'hui en quinze.

VI. Dictée d'après la Conversation 28, p. 227.

VII. Conversation.

You have broken your glasses (**lunettes,** *f.*). You need new lenses (**verres,** *m.*). You want your glasses repaired as soon as possible. You can't see without glasses, etc. The oculist (**l'oculiste**) answers that he is very busy (**très occupé**), he has many customers (**clients,** *m.*), but that you can come back Saturday afternoon at 5:00.

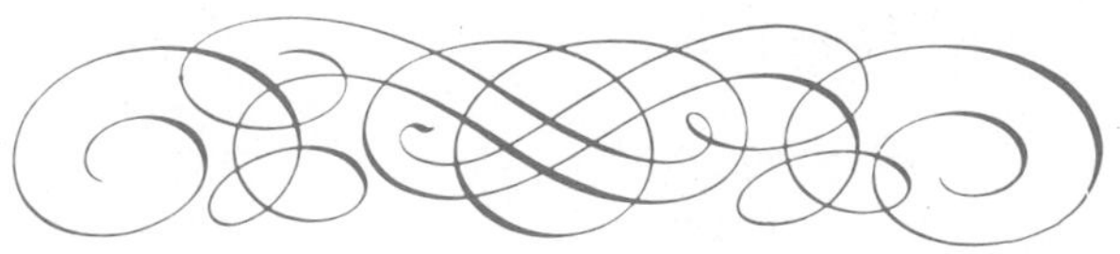

Relative Pronouns

75. *The relative pronoun* **qui.**

The relative pronoun **qui** (*who, which, that*) is used as the *subject of a verb* and may refer to persons or things. (Cf. the interrogative form **Qui?** which refers only to persons.)

—C'est ma cousine **qui** demeure à Reims.	She's my cousin *who* lives in Rheims.
—Voici un autre autobus **qui** arrive.	Here comes another bus.

The relative pronoun **qui** is also used as *object of prepositions*, but in this case it may refer only to persons.

—Le docteur Lambert, **à qui** j'ai parlé, est un bon médecin.	Dr. Lambert, *to whom* I spoke, is a good doctor.
—La dame **chez qui** je demeure a des chambres à louer.	The lady *at whose house* I live has rooms to rent.

76. *The relative pronoun* **que.**

The relative pronoun **que** (*whom, which*) is used as the *direct object* of a verb and may refer to either persons or things:

—C'est un jeune homme **que** je connaissais quand j'avais dix ans.	He's a young man I used to know when I was ten.
—Voici la cravate **que** je cherchais.	Here's the tie I was looking for.

In English the object form of the relative pronoun is practically always omitted: we say *He's a boy I used to know*, rather than *He's a boy whom I used to know;* but in French the relative pronoun must always be expressed in relative clauses.

77. *The relative pronoun* **dont.**

Dont (*whose, of whom, of which, about whom*, etc.) is equivalent to a relative pronoun preceded by the preposition **de.** It may refer to persons or things and is used only after an expressed antecedent.

—Le docteur Lambert, **dont** l'auto allait très vite, n'a pas pu s'arrêter à temps.	Dr. Lambert, *whose* car was going very fast, could not stop in time.
—Je vais commander aujourd'hui le ressort **dont** j'ai besoin.	I am going to order today the spring *which* I need (*of which* I have need).

78. *Relative pronouns* lequel, laquelle, lesquels, lesquelles (*which*):

To refer to *things*, **lequel,** etc., is the relative pronoun you use after prepositions such as: **à, avec, dans, pour, sans,** etc. When used with preposition **à** and **de,** the forms are **auquel, duquel,** etc.

—L'auto **dans laquelle** il était est entrée en collision avec un camion.	The car *in which* he was collided with a truck.
—La lettre, **à laquelle** j'ai déjà répondu, est sur mon bureau.	The letter, *to which* I have already replied, is on my desk.
—Les vacances **auxquelles** je pense seront, hélas, trop courtes.	The vacation I am thinking about will, alas, be too short.

(1) The forms **duquel, de laquelle,** etc., are rarely used since **dont** is the equivalent of a relative pronoun with preposition **de.** However, with the prepositional expressions **à côté (de), près (de), autour (de), au cours (de), au-dessus (de),** etc., the forms **duquel,** etc., must be used. **Dont** cannot be used with these expressions. Ex.: l'accident **au cours duquel . . .** ; la maison **près de laquelle . . .**

(2) Note that in clauses indicating time or place, **où** is ordinarily used instead of **auquel, dans lequel, etc.** Thus it corresponds to English *when* as well as *where.* Ex.: La ville **où** je suis né. The city *in which* (*where*) I was born. L'année **où** je suis né. The year *in which* (*when*) I was born.

79. *Use of* ce qui, ce que (*what, that which*).

A. Subject form **ce qui:**

—J'irais en Afrique voir **ce qui** se passe là-bas.	I'd go to Africa to see *what* is going on there.
—Savez-vous **ce qui** se passe en Afrique?	Do you know *what* is going on in Africa?

Ce qui is the relative pronoun which corresponds to the interrogative pronoun **Qu'est-ce qui?** Ex.: **Qu'est-ce qui** se passe en Afrique? (*interrogative*) —Je ne sais pas **ce qui** se passe en Afrique. (*relative*)

Note that the entire clause **ce qui se passe en Afrique** is the direct object of **voir** and of **Savez-vous. Ce qui** is the subject of **se passe.**

B. Object form **ce que:**

—**Ce que** vous venez de me dire est très vrai.	*What* you have just told me is quite true.
—**Ce qu'**il dit est absurde.	*What* he says is absurd.

Ce que is the relative pronoun which corresponds to the interrogative form **Qu'est-ce que?** Ex.: —**Qu'est-ce que** vous avez dit? (*interrog.*) Je n'ai pas entendu **ce que** vous avez dit. (*relative*) Note that the clause **Ce qu'il dit** is the subject of **est;** but that **ce qu'** is the object of **dit.**

I. Exercices d'application.

A. *Répétez les phrases suivantes en employant* **Voilà . . . qui . . . :**

EX.:—Un autobus arrive.
—**Voilà un autobus qui arrive.**

1. Ma cousine demeure à Reims. **2.** Mon ami va se marier. **3.** Un taxi s'arrête. **4.** Un avion passe. **5.** Le printemps arrive. **6.** Les feuilles tombent. **7.** Le vent se lève. **8.** Les enfants s'amusent.

B. *Répétez les phrases suivantes en employant* **Voilà le (la, les) . . . que . . . :**

EX.:—J'ai acheté des gants.
—**Voilà les gants que j'ai achetés.**

1. J'ai acheté des cigarettes. **2.** J'ai planté des fleurs. **3.** J'ai reçu une lettre. **4.** Je cherchais ma cravate. **5.** Nous avons trouvé de l'argent. **6.** Nous avons commandé un ressort. **7.** Il a fait réparer cette montre. **8.** Il m'a donné cette adresse.

C. *Répétez les phrases suivantes en employant* **Voilà le (la, les) . . . dont . . . :**

EX.:—J'ai besoin de papier à lettres.
—**Voilà le papier à lettres dont j'ai besoin.**

1. J'ai besoin de gants. **2.** J'ai besoin d'argent. **3.** Il a besoin de monnaie. **4.** Il a besoin d'un ressort. **5.** Je vous ai parlé de cette jeune fille. **6.** Il vous a parlé de ce musée. **7.** J'ai entendu parler de ce château. **8.** Il s'agit de ce journal. **9.** Il s'agissait de cette montre.

D. *Répétez en employant* **Voilà le (la, les) . . . (à, pour, avec, chez) qui . . . :**

EX.:—Je suis allé(e) au cinéma avec cette jeune fille.
—**Voilà la jeune fille avec qui je suis allé(e) au cinéma.**

1. J'ai parlé à cet agent de police. **2.** J'ai envoyé des fleurs à cette jeune fille. **3.** J'ai donné le journal à cet étudiant. **4.** J'ai demandé des renseignements à cet agent de police. **5.** Je suis allé(e) au bal avec ce jeune homme. **6.** J'ai fait une promenade avec ce petit garçon. **7.** Je demeure chez cette dame. **8.** J'ai acheté des bonbons pour ces enfants.

E. *Répétez en employant* **Voilà le (la, les) . . . (à, dans, pour, sur) lequel (laquelle, lesquels, lesquelles) . . . :**

EX.:—Il était dans cette auto.
—Voilà l'auto dans laquelle il était.

1. Il était dans ce taxi. **2.** J'ai répondu à cette lettre. **3.** Nous avons répondu à ces questions. **4.** Je pensais à ce restaurant. **5.** J'ai acheté un ressort pour cette montre. **6.** J'ai commandé un tapis pour cette chambre. **7.** J'ai posé mes lunettes sur cette table. **8.** J'ai mis mes cigarettes sur cette chaise.

II. *Répondez à chacune des questions suivantes en commençant par* **Je ne sais pas ce qui . . . :**

EX.:—Qu'est-ce qui se passe?
—Je ne sais pas ce qui se passe.

1. Qu'est-ce qui s'est passé? **2.** Qu'est-ce qui arrive? **3.** Qu'est-ce qui est arrivé? **4.** Qu'est-ce qui lui est arrivé? **5.** Qu'est-ce qui ennuie Marie? **6.** Qu'est-ce qui l'ennuie? **7.** Qu'est-ce qui la rend triste? **8.** Qu'est-ce qui l'a rendue malade?

III. *Répondez à chacune des questions suivantes en commençant par* **Je ne sais pas ce qu(e) . . . :**

EX.:—Qu'est-ce qu'il a dit?
—Je ne sais pas ce qu'il a dit.

1. Qu'est-ce qu'il a acheté? **2.** Qu'est-ce qu'il a fait? **3.** Qu'est-ce que vous ferez ce soir? **4.** Qu'est-ce que l'horloger a commandé? **5.** Qu'est-ce qu'il a reçu? **6.** Qu'est-ce que vous feriez si vous étiez riche? **7.** Qu'est-ce que c'est qu'un Prisunic? **8.** Qu'est-ce que c'est qu'une charcuterie? **9.** Que veut dire «Noblesse oblige»? **10.** Que veut dire le mot «mansarde»?

IV. *Répondez en français à chacune des questions suivantes:*

1. Comment s'appelle la dame chez qui Jean demeure? **2.** Est-ce que la chambre que Jean a louée est agréable? **3.** Croyez-vous tout ce que disent (*say*) les journaux? **4.** Savez-vous avec qui Charles ira en vacances? **5.** Avez-vous entendu ce que je vous ai dit? **6.** Quel est le nom de la ville où vous habitez? **7.** Y avait-il beaucoup de monde à l'endroit où vous êtes monté dans l'autobus? **8.** Quel temps faisait-il le jour où l'accident a eu lieu? **9.** D'où venait le camion? **10.** Avez-vous été témoin de l'accident dont nous avons parlé?

V. Thème d'imitation:

Yesterday, Roger told John that there was a good film at the Cinéma Marignan. He asked him if he wanted to go to see it. It was an American film which John had already seen in the United States. But he gladly accepted Roger's invitation. John thought (*croyait*) that the film was in English. He was very much surprised (*Il a été très surpris*) when he heard Hollywood actors and actresses talking (*parler*) French perfectly (*parfaitement*) and with the best accent.

Au Bon Marché*

LA VENDEUSE – [1]Qu'est-ce que vous désirez, mademoiselle?

MARIE – [2]Je voudrais une écharpe.

LA VENDEUSE – [3]Choisissez, mademoiselle. Nous avons un excellent choix.

MARIE – [4]Une de mes amies en a une que j'aime beaucoup. [5]Elle l'a achetée ici, je crois.

LA VENDEUSE – [6]De quelle couleur est celle de votre amie?

MARIE – [7]C'est une écharpe de soie blanche.

LA VENDEUSE – [8]Que pensez-vous de cette écharpe-ci, mademoiselle?

MARIE – [9]Combien est-ce?

LA VENDEUSE – [10]Trente francs.

MARIE – [11]Et celle-là?

LA VENDEUSE – [12]Quarante francs.

MARIE – [13]C'est un peu cher. [14]Avez-vous quelque chose de meilleur marché?

LA VENDEUSE – [15]Mais oui, mademoiselle. Celle-ci ne coûte que vingt-cinq francs.

MARIE – [16]Je crois que j'aime mieux celle que vous m'avez montrée tout à l'heure.

THE SALESGIRL – [1]*Something for you, (Mademoiselle)?*

MARY – [2]*I'd like a scarf.*

THE SALESGIRL – [3]*Choose, (Mademoiselle). We have an excellent selection.*

MARY – [4]*A friend of mine has one which I like very much.* [5]*She bought it here, I think.*

THE SALESGIRL – [6]*What color is your friend's?*

MARY – [7]*It's a white silk scarf.*

THE SALESGIRL – [8]*What do you think of this scarf, (Mademoiselle)?*

MARY – [9]*How much is it?*

THE SALESGIRL – [10]*Thirty francs.*

MARY – [11]*And that one?*

THE SALESGIRL – [12]*Forty francs.*

MARY – [13]*It's rather expensive.* [14]*Have you something cheaper?*

THE SALESGIRL – [15]*Oh yes, (Mademoiselle). This one costs only twenty-five francs.*

MARY – [16]*I think I prefer the one which you showed me a moment ago.*

* Well-known department store in Paris.

LA VENDEUSE – 17 Laquelle, mademoiselle?

MARIE – 18 Celle-ci. Voulez-vous bien la mettre dans une boîte?

LA VENDEUSE – 19 Volontiers. Désirez-vous autre chose, mademoiselle?

MARIE – 20 Je voudrais aussi des mouchoirs.

LA VENDEUSE – 21 Aimez-vous ceux-ci?

MARIE – 22 Quel en est le prix?

LA VENDEUSE – 23 Deux francs cinquante pièce.

MARIE – 24 J'en prendrai une demi-douzaine.

LA VENDEUSE – 25 Voulez-vous bien passer à la caisse, mademoiselle? 26 Vous y trouverez vos achats.

THE SALESGIRL – 17 *Which one, (Mademoiselle)?*

MARY – 18 *This one. Will you please put it in a box?*

THE SALESGIRL – 19 *Certainly. Do you wish something else, (Mademoiselle)?*

MARY – 20 *I'd also like some handkerchiefs.*

THE SALESGIRL – 21 *Do you like these?*

MARY – 22 *What is the price of them?*

THE SALESGIRL – 23 *Two francs fifty apiece.*

MARY – 24 *I'll take half a dozen of them.*

THE SALESGIRL – 25 *Will you please pay the cashier (go to the cashier's window), (Mademoiselle)?* 26 *You will find your purchases there.*

DANS UN MAGASIN

I. Substitutions. *Répétez les phrases suivantes en substituant les mots indiqués:*

1. Que pensez-vous de cette écharpe-ci?
   celle-ci / celle-là / ces mouchoirs / ceux-ci / ceux-là
2. Avez-vous quelque chose de meilleur marché?
   de meilleure qualité / d'autre / de moins cher / de plus clair (*light color*) / de plus foncé (*dark*)
3. Nous n'avons rien de meilleur marché.
   de meilleure qualité / d'autre / de moins cher / de plus clair / de plus foncé
4. Cette écharpe-ci est meilleur marché que celle-là.
   moins chère / plus chère / plus originale / plus jolie / de meilleure qualité

II. *Répondez à chacune des questions suivantes, d'après le texte:*

1. A qui parle Marie? **2.** Qu'est-ce que c'est qu'une vendeuse? **3.** Dans quel magasin la conversation a-t-elle lieu? **4.** Qu'est-ce que Marie veut acheter? **5.** Y a-t-il beaucoup d'écharpes dans ce magasin? **6.** Où l'amie de Marie a-t-elle acheté la sienne? **7.** De quelle couleur est cette écharpe? **8.** Combien d'écharpes la vendeuse montre-t-elle à Marie? **9.** Quel est le prix de l'écharpe que la vendeuse lui montre? **10.** Est-ce que la vendeuse a quelque chose de meilleur marché? **11.** Quelle écharpe Marie achète-t-elle? **12.** Est-ce que Marie achète autre chose? **13.** Combien de mouchoirs prend-elle? **14.** Où la vendeuse lui dit-elle d'aller pour payer ses achats? **15.** Qu'est-ce qu'elle trouvera à la caisse?

III. *Répondez à chacune des questions suivantes, affirmativement, puis négativement en employant* **rien . . . d'autre:**

EX.:—Avez-vous acheté autre chose?
—**Oui, nous avons acheté autre chose.**
—**Non, nous n'avons rien acheté d'autre.**

1. Avez-vous trouvé autre chose? **2.** Marie a-t-elle trouvé autre chose? **3.** Avez-vous vu autre chose? **4.** Marie a-t-elle vu autre chose? **5.** Avez-vous cherché autre chose? **6.** Avez-vous autre chose?

IV. Révision. *Dites en français:*

A. il s'agit de

1. It's a matter of a simple repair. **2.** It's a question of a white silk scarf. **3.** What's up (of what is it a question)? **4.** It's just a question of giving your address to the postman **(au facteur).**

B. rendre

5. Does that make you sad? **6.** That letter made me happy. **7.** That long walk in the snow made me sick. **8.** The postman brought me a letter which made me sad.

C. venir de

9. What you have just said is true. **10.** Marie has just arrived from Brittany. **11.** I have just finished my work. **12.** The postman has just brought me a letter.

D. de quelle couleur

13. What color is your scarf? **14.** What color are your gloves? **15.** What color is her car? **16.** I don't know what color it is.

V. Dictée d'après la Conversation 29, pp. 238-239.

VI. Révision des dialogues, pp. 212-213 et pp. 216-217.

1. Où se trouve Versailles? **2.** Qu'est-ce qu'il y a de célèbre à Versailles? **3.** Qui est-ce qui a fait construire le château de Versailles? **4.** Quand le château a-t-il été construit? **5.** Avez-vous entendu parler de la Galerie des Glaces (*Hall of Mirrors*)? **6.** Comprenez-vous la phrase «Noblesse oblige»? **7.** Qui était Mansart? **8.** Qu'est-ce que c'est qu'une mansarde? **9.** Qu'est-ce qu'on met dans les mansardes? **10.** Qui est-ce qui a dessiné les jardins de Versailles? **11.** Avez-vous entendu parler des pièces d'eau et des fontaines de Versailles? **12.** Pourquoi Marie a-t-elle l'air triste? **13.** Qu'est-ce qu'elle a? **14.** A qui pense-t-elle? **15.** Comment sait-elle que sa cousine va se marier? **16.** Est-ce que sa cousine Jeanne va bientôt se marier? **17.** Avec qui doit-elle se marier? **18.** Est-ce que la nouvelle du mariage la rend triste? **19.** Qu'est-ce qui l'ennuie? **20.** Est-ce qu'elle voudrait bien aller au mariage de Jeanne?

VII. Conversations.

(1)

Conversation avec une vendeuse au sujet d'une écharpe — le prix, la couleur, si l'écharpe vous va bien, etc.

(2)

Conversation avec un vendeur au sujet d'une paire de chaussures (*a pair of shoes*) — le prix, la pointure (*size*). Vous pouvez dire que les chaussures sont trop étroites (*narrow*), trop longues, trop courtes, qu'elles vous font mal aux pieds (*hurt your feet*), etc.

A VERSAILLES: LE GRAND TRIANON

Versailles

Un bel après-midi de mai, Jean et Roger ont décidé d'aller visiter le château de Versailles. Jean connaissait l'histoire de l'ancienne résidence royale, dont il avait vu des photographies. Mais il faut aller à Versailles pour se rendre compte de ce qu'est vraiment le palais de Louis XIV. L'ensemble est si vaste que la photographie ordinaire ne peut en donner qu'une vue fragmentaire — une pièce d'eau, une allée dans le parc, un coin du palais ou d'un des Trianons. Si la photographie aérienne peut donner une vue d'ensemble, elle ne donne ni échelle, ni perspective, ni détails. Jean ne s'attendait pas à trouver des vues si lointaines et si habilement ménagées.

A ce moment de l'année, les touristes, encore peu nombreux, semblaient perdus dans l'immensité des jardins et du parc, parmi les statues impassibles des dieux et des déesses. A l'intérieur du palais, Jean trouva la décoration des grandes galeries un peu lourde, un peu trop somptueuse, avec tous ces guerriers musclés et cuirassés, ces armes, ces plumes, ces chevaux impétueux. Cela ne l'empêcha pas d'être fort impressionné. On peut ne pas aimer Versailles, le trouver trop froid et trop majestueux. Personne ne peut nier que c'est une étonnante œuvre d'art.

Le lendemain matin, de retour à Paris, Jean va chez un horloger faire réparer sa montre. Arrivé au coin d'une rue, il entend tout à coup un grand bruit métallique. Une auto vient d'entrer en collision avec un camion. Le chauffeur descend de son camion sain et sauf. L'automobiliste a eu moins de chance: il est sans connaissance au volant de son auto. Aussitôt les passants s'assemblent à l'endroit où l'accident a eu lieu, et plusieurs d'entre eux s'occupent de la victime. Deux agents arrivent. L'un d'eux s'approche de Jean et tire un petit carnet de sa poche.

—C'est toujours à moi que ces choses arrivent, se dit Jean. Vingt personnes au moins ont été témoins de l'accident, et je suis celui que l'agent choisit pour avoir des renseignements!

Néanmoins, Jean donne volontiers tous les détails qu'il peut donner. Après avoir indiqué son nom et son adresse, il donne sa version de l'accident. Il lui a semblé que l'automobiliste allait trop vite, car il avait plu et la chaussée était fort glissante.

—Je vous remercie, monsieur, dit l'agent de police en remettant son petit carnet dans sa poche. Le commissaire de police du XVe arrondissement vous enverra une convocation s'il a besoin de renseignements supplémentaires.

—Zut alors! pense Jean. Maintenant, je vais être obligé d'aller au commissariat de police du XVe arrondissement! Quelle barbe!

UN AGENT DE POLICE

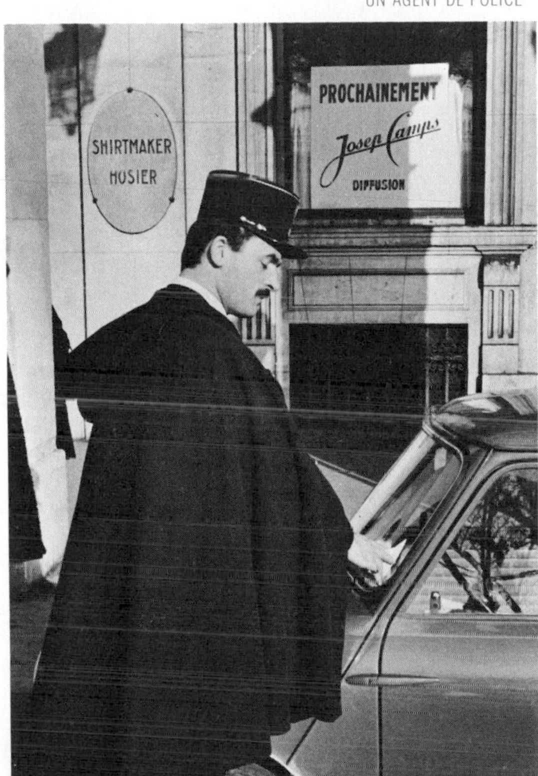

QUESTIONS

1. Est-ce que Jean avait entendu parler du château de Versailles? **2.** Est-ce qu'il avait vu des photographies du château? **3.** Y avait-il beaucoup de touristes le jour où il est allé à Versailles? **4.** Qu'est-ce qu'il a pensé de la décoration des galeries? **5.** Est-ce que cela l'a empêché d'être impressionné? **6.** Qu'est-ce que Jean a fait le lendemain matin? **7.** Qu'est-ce qui s'est passé quand il est arrivé au coin d'une rue? **8.** Est-ce que le chauffeur du camion a été blessé au cours de l'accident? **9.** Comment a-t-on trouvé l'automobiliste après l'accident? **10.** Qui s'est occupé de la victime? **11.** Qu'est-ce que l'agent de police a demandé à Jean? **12.** Qu'est-ce que Jean pense de ce qui lui est arrivé?

GRAMMAR UNIT 19

Demonstrative Pronouns

80. *Forms and uses of* **celui-ci** (*this one*), **celui-là** (*that one*), *etc.*

—Nous avons de jolies écharpes.	We have pretty scarves.
—Que pensez-vous de **celle-ci?**	What do you think of *this one?*
—Combien est-ce?	How much is it?
—Vingt francs.	Twenty francs.
—Et **celle-là?**	And *that one?*

The forms of **celui-ci,** *etc.*, are:

SINGULAR		PLURAL	
celui-ci (*m.*)	*this one*	ceux-ci (*m.*)	*these*
celle-ci (*f.*)		celles-ci (*f.*)	
celui-là (*m.*)	*that one*	ceux-là (*m.*)	*those*
celle-là (*f.*)		celles-là (*f.*)	

You use **celui-ci, celui-là,** etc., to distinguish between persons or things within a group. They agree in gender and number with the word to which they refer. In speaking of handkerchiefs (*mouchoirs, m.*) you say: Que pensez-vous de **celui-ci** (*sing.*), **ceux-ci** (*pl.*)?

81. *Use of* **celui, celle** (*the one*)*;* **ceux, celles** (*the ones*).

These forms, as opposed to the forms **celui-ci,** etc., are always modified by a relative clause or a prepositional phrase.

A. Modified by a relative clause:

—J'ai plusieurs cousins. **Celui qui** habite à Paris s'appelle Lambert.	I have several cousins. *The one* who lives in Paris is named Lambert.
—**Ceux qui** habitent à Tours s'appellent Dupuy.	*The ones* who live in Tours are named Dupuy.

Celui que vous connaissez arrive ce soir.	*The one* you know arrives this evening.
—**Celui à qui** j'ai écrit est architecte.	*The one* I wrote to is an architect.
—**Celui dont** je vous ai parlé hier va se marier.	*The one* I mentioned (*of whom* I spoke to you) yesterday is going to get married.

The commonest combinations of **celui,** etc., with relative pronouns are:

(*masculine singular*) celui qui, celui que, celui dont, celui auquel, etc.

(*feminine singular*) celle qui, celle que, celle dont, celle à laquelle, etc.

(*masculine plural*) ceux qui, ceux que, ceux dont, ceux auxquels, etc.

(*feminine plural*) celles qui, celles que, celles dont, celles auxquelles, etc.

B. Modified by a prepositional phrase beginning with **de:**

—Une de mes amies a une jolie écharpe.	One of my friends has a pretty scarf.
—De quelle couleur est **celle de votre amie?**	What color is *your friend's?*
—Je n'aime pas ce chapeau.	I don't like that hat.
—**Celui de Marie** est plus joli.	*Mary's* is prettier.

(1) In English we say: *My book and my friend's*. In French you say: **Mon livre et celui de mon ami** (*that of my friend*).

(2) Note that **l'un** (*the one*) is not a demonstrative pronoun and cannot be used in place of **celui, celle,** etc. Although in English we say: *The one I bought*, you must say: **Celui** (or **celle**) **que j'ai acheté(e).**

82. *Use of* ceci (*this*) *and* cela, ça* (*that*).

Unlike the other demonstrative pronouns, **ceci** and **cela** are used to refer to something that has not been specifically named. They never refer to persons. They are used:

A. To refer to an idea, a statement, or a situation:

—**Ça (cela)** m'est égal.	*That* (or *It*) is all the same to me.
—Est-ce que **ça (cela)** vous rend triste?	Does *that* make you sad?
—Pourquoi dites-vous **ça (cela)?**	Why do you say *that?*
—**Ceci** est très important.	*This* is very important.

* **Cela** and **ça** have the same use and meaning, but **cela** is more formal.

B. To refer to objects which have not been specifically named:

—Qu'est-ce que c'est que **ça** (**cela**)?	What is *that?*
—J'ai acheté **ceci** pour mon frère et **cela** pour ma sœur.	I bought *this* for my brother and *that* for my sister.

I. Exercices d'application.

Répétez les phrases suivantes, en remplaçant le nom par le pronom démonstratif.

A. EX.:—Envoyez-moi cette écharpe-ci.
—Envoyez-moi celle-ci.

1. Envoyez-moi ce chapeau-là. **2.** Envoyez-moi ces mouchoirs-ci. **3.** Envoyez-moi cette photo-ci. **4.** Envoyez-moi ces photos-là. **5.** Envoyez-moi ces gants-là. **6.** Envoyez-moi ce livre-ci.

B. EX.:—J'ai acheté ces gants à Paris.
—J'ai acheté ceux-ci (ou **ceux-là**) **à Paris.**

1. J'ai acheté cette robe à Paris. **2.** J'ai acheté cette auto à Paris. **3.** J'ai acheté ce chapeau à Paris. **4.** J'ai acheté ces cravates à Paris. **5.** J'ai acheté ce pardessus à Paris. **6.** J'ai acheté ces montres à Paris.

C. EX.:—Ma cousine qui demeure à Reims s'appelle Duval.
—Celle qui demeure à Reims s'appelle Duval.

1. Mes cousines qui demeurent à Paris s'appellent Dupuy. **2.** Mes cousins qui demeurent à Lyon s'appellent Dupont. **3.** Mon cousin qui demeure à Philadelphie s'appelle Hughes. **4.** Mon cousin dont nous parlions habite à Rome. **5.** Ma cousine que vous avez vue au bal est gentille. **6.** Mon cousin dont vous avez fait la connaissance hier est ici. **7.** Ma cousine à qui j'ai écrit hier va se marier. **8.** Voilà le livre dont j'ai besoin.

D. EX.:—Voilà le livre de Jean.
—Voilà celui de Jean.

1. Voilà les livres de Jean. **2.** Voilà les livres de Marie. **3.** Voilà la cravate de Roger. **4.** Voilà l'auto de mon frère. **5.** Voilà le journal de mon père. **6.** Voilà la plume de ma tante.

II. *Dites en français:*

EX.:—My book and my friend's.
—Mon livre et celui de mon ami.

1. My watch and my friend's. **2.** My gloves and my friend's. **3.** Her scarf and her friend's. **4.** My scarf and Marie's. **5.** My car and my brother's. **6.** Our parents and our friend's. **7.** Our parents and our friends' (*plural*).

III. *Répondez en français, en employant un pronom démonstratif:*

EX.:—Voilà deux écharpes. Laquelle préférez-vous?
—Je préfère celle-ci.

1. Voilà deux mouchoirs. Lequel préférez-vous? **2.** Voilà des cartes postales. Lesquelles allez-vous acheter? **3.** Cette jeune fille-ci est-elle aussi grande que cette jeune fille-là? **4.** Est-ce que ce livre-ci est aussi gros que ce livre-là? **5.** Est-ce que le château de Chantilly est aussi grand que le château de Versailles? (Non . . .) **6.** Est-ce que les tragédies de Marlowe sont aussi belles que les tragédies de Shakespeare? (Non . . .) **7.** Aimez-vous mieux les romans (*novels*) de Dumas que les romans de Balzac? **8.** Préférez-vous la musique de Debussy ou la musique de Berlioz?

IV. *Répétez chacune des phrases suivantes en remplaçant le nom par le pronom démonstratif convenable:*

1. Pourriez-vous m'envoyer cette écharpe-ci ce soir? **2.** Les photos que j'ai prises hier ne sont pas très bonnes. **3.** J'ai acheté le livre dont je vous ai parlé. **4.** Comment trouvez-vous l'auto de M. Duval? **5.** Les gants que j'ai achetés hier sont très chauds. **6.** Donnez-moi ce livre-ci et gardez (*keep*) ce livre-là.

V. *Dites en français en employant* **ceci, cela (ça):**

1. What's that? **2.** It (that) makes no difference. (It's all the same to me.) **3.** It makes me sad. **4.** Who told you that? **5.** Why do you say that? **6.** This is very important. **7.** Where did you buy that? **8.** I bought this for you. **9.** I can have that sent to you this afternoon.

VI. Révision des dialogues, p. 227 et pp. 238-239.

1. Pourquoi le commissaire de police a-t-il fait venir Jean Hughes? **2.** De quel accident a-t-il été témoin? **3.** Pourquoi l'accident a-t-il eu lieu? **4.** Est-ce qu'il avait plu ce jour-là? **5.** Où était Jean au moment de l'accident? **6.** Est-ce que le camion allait vite au moment de l'accident? **7.** A quelle vitesse allait-il? **8.** Est-ce que le commissaire de police avait déjà parlé à d'autres témoins de l'accident? **9.** Qu'est-ce que c'est qu'un horloger? **10.** Pourquoi Jean porte-t-il sa montre chez l'horloger? **11.** Pourquoi sa montre ne marche-t-elle plus? **12.** Pourquoi l'horloger se doute-t-il que Jean a acheté sa montre en Amérique? **13.** Quand l'horloger va-t-il commander le ressort dont il a besoin? **14.** Quand est-ce qu'il espère recevoir (*to receive*) le ressort? **15.** Quand dit-il à Jean de revenir? **16.** Pourquoi Jean voudrait-il bien avoir sa montre le plus tôt possible?

VII. Thème d'imitation:

John and Roger spent the afternoon in the Jardin du Luxembourg, near the University. There were many students there with their girl friends,[1] many children with their nurses,[2] and many Parisians who had come there to look at the people, the sky, the flowers, and the trees.

John was looking at an elderly gentleman dressed in black who was giving bread to the birds.[3] He had birds on his[4] head, on his shoulders,[5] on his hands,[6] everywhere. Suddenly[7] an old lady came and said to John: "Sir, will you please[8] pay me for your chair?[9] It's ten centimes." Roger told John that in France in the public parks,[10] you (*on*) rent a chair for the afternoon. "After all, you rent a room for a week or for a month", said John to himself.[11] "Why not rent[12] a chair for an afternoon?" And he gave the old lady the ten centimes she was asking for.

---

[1] *girl friend*, **une amie.** [2] *nurse*, **la bonne.** [3] *bird*, **l'oiseau — les oiseaux** (*m.*). [4] Cf. **Le chapeau que vous avez sur la tête?** [5] *shoulder*, **une épaule.** [6] *hand*, **la main.** [7] *suddenly*, **tout à coup.** [8] **Voulez-vous bien.** [9] *pay me for your chair*, **me payer votre chaise.** [10] **dans les jardins publics.** [11] **s'est dit Jean.** Note that in French, after a direct quotation the subject of the verb *said*, *answered*, *asked*, etc., always follows the verb. Ex.: **a dit Roger, a-t-il dit, a demandé Marie, a répondu Roger,** etc. [12] *Why not rent*, **Pourquoi ne pas louer.**

Excursion à la campagne

ROGER – [1]Il y a presque deux heures que nous avons quitté Melun.

ROGER – [1]*We left Melun almost two hours ago.*

JEAN – [2]Je commence à avoir mal aux jambes. [3]Je n'ai pas l'habitude d'aller à bicyclette.

JOHN – [2]*My legs are beginning to hurt.* [3]*I am not used to bicycling.*

ROGER – [4]Je crois que nous avons pris la mauvaise route.

ROGER – [4]*I think we took the wrong road.*

JEAN – [5]J'en ai peur.

JOHN – [5]*I'm afraid so.*

ROGER – [6]Voilà un homme qui travaille dans son champ. [7]Il pourra nous donner des renseignements.

ROGER – [6]*There's a man working his field.* [7]*He can give us information.*

ROGER (*à l'homme*) – [8]Est-ce que nous sommes loin de Fontainebleau?*

ROGER (to the man) – [8]*Are we far from Fontainebleau?*

L'HOMME – [9]Mais oui, mon pauvre monsieur. [10]Je suis fâché de vous apprendre [11]que vous vous êtes trompé de route.

THE MAN – [9]*You certainly are, sir.* [10]*I am sorry to tell you* [11]*that you took the wrong road.*

---

* Fontainebleau, célèbre pour son château de la Renaissance et sa belle forêt, est à une cinquantaine de kilomètres au sud-est de Paris.

CHATEAU DE FONTAINEBLEAU

ROGER – [12]Quelle route faut-il prendre, alors?

L'HOMME – [13]Vous voyez ce village, là-bas? [14]C'est Barbizon.* Allez-y. [15]A la sortie du village, prenez le premier chemin à gauche. [16]Il vous mènera à Fontainebleau.

ROGER – [17]A quelle distance est-ce d'ici?

L'HOMME – [18]C'est à sept ou huit kilomètres.

ROGER – [19]Zut alors! Par cette chaleur, ce n'est pas drôle! [20]La prochaine fois, nous prendrons ma voiture.

L'HOMME – [21]Si vous avez chaud et si vous avez soif, [22]vous pourrez vous arrêter à Barbizon. [23]C'est ma femme qui tient le petit café [24]juste en face de l'église.

ROGER – [12]*Which road must we take then?*

THE MAN – [13]*You see that village over there?* [14]*It's Barbizon. Go to it.* [15]*As you leave the village, take the first road on the left.* [16]*It will take you to Fontainebleau.*

ROGER – [17]*How far is it from here?*

THE MAN – [18]*It's seven or eight kilometers.*

ROGER – [19]*Well, confound it! In such hot weather, that's not funny!* [20]*Next time we'll use my car.*

THE MAN – [21]*If you are hot and if you are thirsty,* [22]*you can stop at Barbizon.* [23]*My wife runs the pub* [24]*right across the street from the church.*

---

* Barbizon est un village près de Fontainebleau. Au XIXème siècle, ce village a été la résidence favorite de plusieurs peintres célèbres, entre autres Corot et Millet.

I. Substitutions. *Répétez les phrases suivantes en substituant les mots indiqués:*

1. Il y a presque deux heures que* nous avons quitté Melun.

nous avons quitté la maison / nous sommes arrivé(e)s / je suis parti(e) / Jean et Roger sont partis

2. Voilà presque deux heures que nous avons quitté Melun.

nous avons quitté la maison / nous sommes arrivé(e)s / je suis parti(e) / Jean et Roger sont partis

3. Je commence à avoir mal aux jambes.

à la tête / aux yeux / aux dents (*teeth*) / aux pieds / à la gorge

4. Je n'ai pas l'habitude d'aller à bicyclette.

de marcher / de travailler le soir / de me lever de bonne heure / de me coucher tard

5. Je suis fâché de vous apprendre que vous vous êtes trompé(s) de route.

que vous êtes sur la mauvaise route / que vous n'êtes pas sur la bonne route / que vous avez pris la mauvaise route / que Fontainebleau est à 7 ou 8 kilomètres d'ici

6. A la sortie, prenez le premier chemin à gauche.

le premier chemin à droite / la première route à gauche / la première rue à droite / la grande avenue à gauche

II. *Répondez en français à chacune des questions suivantes:*

1. Où vont Roger et Jean? **2.** Comment voyagent-ils? **3.** Combien de temps y a-t-il qu'ils ont quitté Melun? **4.** Est-ce que Jean est fatigué? **5.** Pourquoi a-t-il mal aux jambes? **6.** Est-ce qu'ils sont sur la bonne route? **7.** A qui Roger demande-t-il des renseignements? **8.** Qu'est-ce qu'il demande à l'homme qui travaille dans son champ? **9.** Est-ce qu'ils sont près d'un village? **10.** Comment s'appelle ce village? **11.** Quelle route l'homme leur dit-il de prendre à la sortie du village? **12.** Où cette route les mènera-t-elle? **13.** A quelle distance de Barbizon est Fontainebleau? **14.** Pourquoi Roger dit-il que ce n'est pas drôle? **15.** Que feront Jean et Roger la prochaine fois? **16.** Où pourront-ils s'arrêter s'ils ont chaud?

---

* **Il y a . . . que, voilà . . . que** as expressions of time: When **il y a . . . que, voilà . . . que** are used with a **passé composé,** they mean *ago*. Ex.: **Il y a deux heures que nous avons quitté Melun. Voilà deux heures que nous avons quitté Melun.**

When used with a present indicative, **il y a . . . que, voilà . . . que** indicate that the action began in the past and is still going on at the time the statement is made. They have practically the same meaning as **depuis.**

—Depuis combien de temps attendez-vous l'autobus?
OR
—Combien de temps y a-t-il que vous attendez l'autobus?

—Je l'attends depuis un quart d'heure.
OR
—Voilà un quart d'heure que je l'attends.

III. *Demandez à quelqu'un:*

1. s'il y a longtemps que Jean et Roger ont quitté Melun. **2.** pourquoi Jean commence à avoir mal aux jambes. **3.** ce que fait l'homme à qui Roger demande des renseignements. **4.** pourquoi Roger demande des renseignements. **5.** ce que Roger demande. **6.** si Jean et Roger sont sur la mauvaise route. **7.** quel chemin il faut prendre à la sortie de Barbizon. **8.** à quelle distance est Fontainebleau de Barbizon. **9.** quel temps il fait ce jour-là. **10.** ce que Jean et Roger feront la prochaine fois.

IV. *Dites en français, en employant* **se tromper:**

1. You took the wrong road (you were mistaken about the road). **2.** You were mistaken. **3.** I was mistaken. **4.** He was mistaken. **5.** He is mistaken. **6.** I think he is mistaken. **7.** I think you are mistaken.

V. *Mettez les paragraphes suivants au passé en employant* **l'imparfait, le passé composé,** *ou* **le plus-que-parfait** *selon le cas:*

Roger et Jean décident un jour d'aller voir des cousins de Roger qui habitent à la campagne, dans le voisinage de Fontainebleau. Le lendemain, ils se lèvent de bonne heure et vont par le train jusqu'à Melun. Là, ils louent des bicyclettes et continuent leur voyage. C'est une belle journée de printemps, le ciel est bleu, le soleil brille. Tout à coup Roger annonce qu'ils ont sans doute pris la mauvaise route. «Où sommes-nous? » demande-t-il à Jean. Jean répond non sans raison qu'il est en France depuis quelques mois, qu'il n'est jamais allé voir les Deschamps, et que si Roger ne sait pas où il est, lui, Jean, le sait encore moins que lui . . . Un homme qui travaille dans son champ et à qui Roger demande des renseignements, finit par les mettre sur la bonne route. L'homme ajoute qu'il fait chaud, que la route est encore longue.

Il leur conseille donc de s'arrêter au petit café du village, d'autant plus que c'est sa femme qui le tient. Même si le conseil est quelque peu intéressé, les deux amis en profitent volontiers.

VI. *Répondez en français à chacune des questions suivantes:*

A. quitter, partir de

1. A quelle heure avez-vous quitté la maison ce matin? **2.** A quelle heure êtes-vous parti de la maison ce matin? **3.** Êtes-vous parti sans déjeuner? **4.** Avez-vous quitté la maison sans déjeuner? **5.** Y a-t-il longtemps que Jean et Roger ont quitté Melun? **6.** Y a-t-il longtemps qu'ils sont partis de Melun?

B. combien de temps y a-t-il que . . . ? depuis quand?

7. Combien de temps y a-t-il que vous attendez l'autobus? **8.** Combien de temps y a-t-il que vous étudiez le français? **9.** Combien de temps y a-t-il que vous êtes à l'Université? **10.** Depuis quand êtes-vous à l'Université? **11.** Depuis quand étudiez-vous le français?

VII. Dictée d'après la Conversation 30, pp. 246-247

VIII. Conversation.

Vous vous êtes égaré(e) (*lost*) dans la forêt de Fontainebleau. Vous demandez le chemin de Barbizon à un peintre qui travaille dans la forêt.

Irregular Verbs in *-er* and in *-ir*

83. *Remarks about irregular verbs.*

The easiest and quickest way to learn irregular verbs is to examine their forms carefully, note which forms are irregular, and practice using them in exercises such as those suggested below. It is perhaps useful to note:

A. PRESENT INDICATIVE:

The only tense of irregular verbs that is practically always irregular is the present indicative.

(1) STEM: Instead of having one stem throughout the tense like **parler** (PARL-,)—irregular verbs generally have two stems, one for the first and second person plural and another for the other persons. Sometimes this difference is very striking (**je vais, nous allons**) and sometimes it is scarcely noticeable (**je connais, nous connaissons**).

(2) ENDINGS: Practically all irregular verbs have the present indicative endings **-s, -s, -t, -ons, -ez, -ent,** but a few have **-e, -es, -e** in the singular.

B. FUTURE:

Very few irregular verbs have an irregular future (and conditional). Those that *are* irregular are irregular only as to the stem: **aller**—**j'irai, envoyer**—**j'enverrai,** etc.

C. IMPERFECT:

Except for **être,** the imperfect always follows the pattern of regular verbs; i.e., the endings, which are always the same, are used with the stem of the first person plural of the present indicative: **nous allons**—**nous allions, nous envoyons**—**nous envoyions.** (see paragraph 54).

D. PAST PARTICIPLE:

The past participle of irregular verbs follows several different patterns. Those following the same pattern are grouped together in this book.

84. *Irregular verbs ending in* **-er.**

There are only two irregular verbs in this group: **aller,** *to go*, and **envoyer,** *to send.* **Renvoyer,** *to send back, to send away*, is of course conjugated like **envoyer.**

85. **Aller** (*to go*).

—Où **allez-vous** ce soir?	Where *are you going* this evening?
—**Je vais** au cinéma.	*I am going* to the movies.
—Où **êtes-vous allé(e)** l'été dernier?	Where *did you go* last summer?
—**Je suis allé(e)** à la campagne.	*I went* to the country.
—Comment **irez-vous** en ville?	How *will you go* downtown?
—**J'irai** à pied.	*I shall* walk.

PRÉSENT: Je vais, tu vas, il va, nous allons, vous allez, ils vont.
IMPARFAIT: J'allais.
PASSÉ COMPOSÉ: Je suis allé(e).
FUTUR: J'irai.

86. *Special uses of* **aller** (*to go*), *and* **s'en aller** (*to leave, to go away*).

—**Je vais** chercher mon pardessus.	*I am going* to get my overcoat.
—A quelle heure **allez-vous** à la gare?	At what time *are you going* to the station?
—**J'y vais** à cinq heures.	*I am going* (*there*) at five o'clock.
—Quand partez-vous?	When are you leaving?
—**Je m'en vais** demain soir.	*I am leaving* tomorrow evening.

Note that **s'en aller** and **partir** have practically the same meaning and use except that **s'en aller** is rarely used in compound tenses. It is conjugated like **aller** except that it is reflexive: **Je m'en vais, il s'en va,** etc.

87. **Envoyer** (*to send*).

—**Envoyez-vous** des cartes postales à vos amis quand vous voyagez?	*Do you send* post cards to your friends when you travel?
—Oui, **j'en envoie** quelquefois.	Yes, *I send* some occasionally.
—**J'ai envoyé** hier des fleurs à ma grand-mère.	*I sent* some flowers to my grandmother yesterday.
—**Nous** vous **enverrons** la facture.	*We shall send* you the bill.
—**J'ai envoyé** chercher le journal.	*I sent* for the paper.
—Je pourrai vous **le faire envoyer** cet après-midi.	I can *have it sent* to you this afternoon.

PRÉSENT: J'envoie, tu envoies, il envoie, nous envoyons, vous envoyez, ils envoient.
IMPARFAIT: J'envoyais, etc.
PASSÉ COMPOSÉ: J'ai envoyé, etc.
FUTUR: J'enverrai, etc.

88. *First group of irregular verbs in* **-ir: partir, sortir, sentir, servir, dormir,** *etc.*

The characteristics of this group are that they all have two stems in the present indicative: **par- part-, sor- sort-, sen- sent-,** etc., and a past participle ending in **-i** — which is to say that they are scarcely irregular at all.

A. Partir (*to leave*):

—Quand **partez-vous?**	When *are you leaving?*
Mon train **part** à neuf heures.	My train *leaves* at nine o'clock.
—**Je partirai** de la maison à huit heures et demie.	*I shall leave* the house at 8:30.

PRÉSENT: Je pars, tu pars, il part, nous partons, vous partez, ils partent.
IMPARFAIT: Je partais. PASSÉ COMPOSÉ: Je suis parti(e). FUTUR: Je partirai.

B. Sortir (*to go out*) (intransitive)

—**Est-ce que vous sortez** souvent le soir?	*Do you go out* often in the evening?
—Oui, **je sors** assez souvent.	Yes, *I go out* rather often.

PRÉSENT: Je sors, tu sors, il sort, nous sortons, vous sortez, ils sortent.
IMPARFAIT: Je sortais. PASSÉ COMPOSÉ: Je suis sorti(e). FUTUR: Je sortirai.

C. Sentir (*to smell*); se sentir (*to feel*):

—**Sentez-vous** ces roses?	*Do you smell* those roses?
—Oui, **elles sentent** très bon.	Yes, *they smell* very good.
—**Je ne me sens pas** très bien.	*I don't feel* very well.

PRÉSENT: Je sens, tu sens, il sent, nous sentons, vous sentez, ils sentent.
IMPARFAIT: Je sentais. PASSÉ COMPOSÉ: J'ai senti. FUTUR: Je sentirai.

D. Servir (*to serve*); se servir de (*to use, to help oneself*):

—**Vous êtes-vous servi de** votre auto hier soir?	*Did you use* your car last night?
—Voici les hors-d'œuvre. **Servez-vous.**	Here are the hors d'œuvres. *Help yourself.*

PRÉSENT: Je sers, tu sers, il sert, nous servons, vous servez, ils servent.
IMPARFAIT: Je servais. PASSÉ COMPOSÉ: J'ai servi. FUTUR: Je servirai.

E. dormir (*to sleep*); **s'endormir** (*to fall asleep*):

—**Avez-vous** bien **dormi** cette nuit?	*Did you sleep* well last night?
—Oui, **je me suis endormi**(e) à dix heures, et **j'ai dormi** toute la nuit.	Yes, *I went to sleep* at ten o'clock, and *I slept* all night.

PRÉSENT: Je dors, tu dors, il dort, nous dormons, vous dormez, ils dorment.
IMPARFAIT: Je dormais. PASSÉ COMPOSÉ: J'ai dormi. FUTUR: Je dormirai.

Compounds of these verbs follow the same pattern of conjugation. Ex.: **sentir** — **consentir** (*to consent*).

89. *Second group of irregular verbs in* **-ir: venir, tenir.**

The characteristics of this group are that they have two stems for the present indicative (**viens-venons**), an irregular future (**viendrai**), and a past participle in **-u** (**venu**).

A. venir (*to come*):

—D'où **venez-vous?**	Where have you been? (From where *do you come*)?
—**Je viens** de la gare.	I've been to the station. (*I come* from the station).
—**Il est venu** nous chercher en auto.	*He came* for us in his car.
—**Nous viendrons** vous voir à cinq heures.	*We shall come* to see you at 5:00.

PRÉSENT: Je viens, tu viens, il vient, nous venons, vous venez, ils viennent.
IMPARFAIT: Je venais. PASSÉ COMPOSÉ: Je suis venu(e). FUTUR: Je viendrai.

B. venir de + infinitive = (*to have just*) + past participle:

—Ce que **vous venez de dire** est vrai.	What *you have just said* is true.
—Le docteur **vient d'arriver.**	The doctor *has just come.*
—Je **venais d'arriver** quand vous avez téléphoné.	I *had just arrived* when you telephoned.

The present tense of **venir** followed by **de** and an infinitive expresses immediate past action: **Je viens d'arriver** has the same meaning as **Je suis arrivé il y a un instant.**

The imperfect of **venir** followed by **de** and an infinitive expresses immediate *past* action *in the past:* **Je venais d'arriver quand vous avez téléphoné** has the same meaning as **J'étais arrivé un instant plus tôt quand vous avez téléphoné.**

C. tenir (*to hold, to keep*):

—C'est ma femme qui **tient** le petit café.	My wife *runs* the pub.
—**Tenez** la porte ouverte, s'il vous plaît.	*Hold* the door open, please.

PRÉSENT: Je tiens, tu tiens, il tient, nous tenons, vous tenez, ils tiennent.
IMPARFAIT: Je tenais. PASSÉ COMPOSÉ: J'ai tenu. FUTUR: Je tiendrai.

Revenir, *to come back;* **devenir,** *to become;* **se souvenir (de),** *to remember,* **prévenir,** *to warn;* **appartenir (à),** *to belong to*, and other compounds are conjugated like **venir.**

90. *Third group of irregular verbs in* **-ir: ouvrir** (*to open*), *etc.*

The characteristics of this group are that the past participle ends in **-ert** and that the endings of the singular of the present indicative are **-e, -es, -e.**

—A quelle heure le bureau de poste **ouvre-t-il?**	What time *does* the post office *open?*
—**Il ouvre** à neuf heures du matin.	*It opens* at 9:00 A.M.
—Qui **a ouvert** la fenêtre?	Who *opened* the window?

PRÉSENT: J'ouvre, tu ouvres, il ouvre, nous ouvrons, vous ouvrez, ils ouvrent.
IMPARFAIT: J'ouvrais. PASSÉ COMPOSÉ: J'ai ouvert. FUTUR: J'ouvrirai.

Offrir, *to offer;* **souffrir,** *to suffer;* **couvrir,** *to cover;* and compounds of **ouvrir** and **couvrir** are conjugated according to the same pattern.

I. Exercices d'application.

A. *Mettez les formes suivantes au singulier.*

EX.:—Nous allons: **Je vais.**
—Ils vont: **Il va.**

1. Nous envoyons. **2.** Nous partons. **3.** Elles sortent. **4.** Nous ouvrons. **5.** Nous dormons. **6.** Nous venons. **7.** Ils viennent. **8.** Nous tenons. **9.** Nous devenons. **10.** Nous souffrons. **11.** Ils dorment. **12.** Nous nous en allons. **13.** Ils s'endorment. **14.** Nous nous endormons. **15.** Nous nous souvenons. **16.** Elles se souviennent. **17.** Nous nous sentons. **18.** Elles se sentent.

B. *Mettez les formes suivantes au futur.*

EX.:—Je vais.
—**J'irai.**

1. Il va. **2.** Ils vont. **3.** J'envoie. **4.** Ils envoient. **5.** Envoie-t-il? **6.** Nous partons. **7.** Je m'endors. **8.** Il ouvre. **9.** Nous venons. **10.** Vous venez. **11.** Il devient. **12.** J'offre. **13.** Je m'en vais. **14.** Je me souviens.

C. *Mettez les formes suivantes au passé composé.*

EX.:—Nous allons.
—Nous sommes allé(e)s.

1. Il va. **2.** Il envoie. **3.** Il dort. **4.** Il s'endort. **5.** Je sens. **6.** Il part. **7.** Elle sort. **8.** Je viens. **9.** Il devient. **10.** Il ouvre. **11.** Nous ouvrons. **12.** Il souffre. **13.** J'offre. **14.** Ouvre-t-il? **15.** Dort-il?

D. *Répétez les phrases suivantes en substituant les mots indiqués:*

1. Je vais chercher des cigarettes (*I am going to get . . .*).
les billets / le journal / les journaux / un agent de police / mon ami

2. J'enverrai chercher le médecin (*I'll send for . . .*).
les billets / les journaux / des cigarettes / un agent de police / mon ami

II. *Répondez affirmativement:*

1. Allez-vous dîner à la maison ce soir? **2.** Envoyez-vous des cartes postales à vos amis quand vous voyagez? **3.** Est-ce que vous sortez souvent le soir? **4.** Êtes-vous sorti(e) hier soir? **5.** Avez-vous bien dormi cette nuit? **6.** Vous êtes-vous endormi(e) de bonne heure? **7.** Envoyez-vous des fleurs à vos parents pour leur anniversaire (*birthday*)? **8.** Partez-vous aujourd'hui pour le week-end? **9.** Venez-vous à l'université à pied? **10.** Viendrez-vous me voir dimanche?

III. **A.** *Remplacez le passé composé par le présent de* **venir de** *et l'infinitif:*

EX.:—J'ai fini (il y a un instant).
—Je viens de finir.

1. Le train est parti. **2.** Il s'est endormi. **3.** Elle est sortie. **4.** Elles sont sorties. **5.** J'ai ouvert la fenêtre. **6.** J'ai envoyé chercher le journal. **7.** Il est revenu. **8.** Il m'a offert son auto.

B. *Remplacez le plus-que-parfait par l'imparfait de* **venir de** *et l'infinitif:*

EX.:—J'avais fini (un instant plus tôt).
—Je venais de finir.

1. Le train était parti. **2.** Il s'était endormi. **3.** Elle était sortie. **4.** Elles étaient sorties. **5.** J'avais ouvert la fenêtre. **6.** J'avais envoyé chercher le journal. **7.** Il était revenu. **8.** Il m'avait offert son auto.

IV. *Dites en français:*

A. sortir (de)

1. The doctor has gone out. **2.** He went out five minutes ago. **3.** He goes out every morning. **4.** He used to go out at night (*le soir ou la nuit*). **5.** You can't go out in winter. **6.** If you go out, bring me a sandwich. **7.** The train was pulling out of the station when I arrived. **8.** Go out! **9.** Don't go out.

B. partir (de)

1. What time does the train leave Rheims? **2.** It left five minutes ago. **3.** It just left. **4.** I left early. **5.** I shall leave tomorrow. **6.** Are you going away for the week end? **7.** When are you leaving? **8.** Leave! **9.** Don't leave.

C. se servir (de)

1. Are you using your car this afternoon? **2.** I am using my bicycle. **3.** John used the bus. **4.** He used to use his bicycle when he was twelve. **5.** Do you want to use my car? **6.** Use my car. **7.** Don't use my car. **8.** Help yourself.

V. Révision du dialogue, pp. 246-247.

1. Pourquoi Marie va-t-elle au Bon Marché? **2.** Est-ce qu'elle achète une écharpe comme celle de son amie? **3.** De quelle couleur est l'écharpe de son amie? **4.** Est-ce que les premières écharpes qu'on lui montre sont trop chères? **5.** Est-ce que la vendeuse a quelque chose de meilleur marché? **6.** Après avoir choisi une écharpe, est-ce que Marie veut acheter autre chose? **7.** Est-ce que Marie paye la vendeuse? **8.** Où trouvera-t-elle ses achats?

VI. Thème d'imitation:

In the United States, children ride bicycles; then when they are seventeen or eighteen years old, most young Americans drive (*conduisent*) a car. But in Europe, there are still (*encore*) many people who ride bicycles. The distances are not too great, the roads are excellent, and if you choose country roads[1] where there are not too many cars, it is very pleasant to travel by bicycle. You[2] see many interesting things in the villages, you can stop where you wish and when you wish. Of course you[3] have to have good legs! But with a little practice,[4] you can do fifty or seventy-five kilometers without needing to send for the doctor . . .

---

[1] *country road* **le chemin.** [2] Use **vous** in this passage. To repeat **on** so many times would sound awkward. [3] Use **il faut** + infinitive. [4] *practice*, **l'habitude** (*f.*).

Arrivée à la ferme des Deschamps

ROGER – [1]Bonjour, ma cousine.

MME DESCHAMPS – [2]Tiens! bonjour, Roger. [3]Quelle bonne surprise!

ROGER – [4]Je te présente Jean Hughes. [5]C'est mon meilleur ami.

MME DESCHAMPS – [6]Enchantée,* monsieur. [7]Roger m'a souvent parlé de vous.

JEAN – [8]Nous avons décidé de profiter du beau temps pour venir vous voir.

MME DESCHAMPS – [9]C'est une excellente idée. [10]Avez-vous fait bon voyage?

ROGER – [11]Oui. Mais nous sommes assez fatigués.

MME DESCHAMPS – [12]Asseyez-vous et reposez-vous. [13]Voulez-vous prendre quelque chose?

ROGER – [14]Je prendrai de la bière, si tu en as.

MME DESCHAMPS – [15]Et vous, monsieur?

JEAN – [16]Je boirais volontiers un verre d'eau fraîche.

MME DESCHAMPS – [17]Ne préférez-vous pas autre chose?

ROGER – [1]*Hello, cousin!*

MRS. DESCHAMPS – [2]*Well! Hello, Roger.* [3]*What a pleasant surprise!*

ROGER – [4]*May I introduce John Hughes?* [5]*He's my best friend.*

MRS. DESCHAMPS – [6]*I am happy to meet you, sir.* [7]*Roger has often spoken of you.*

JOHN – [8]*We decided to take advantage of the fine weather to come to see you.*

MRS. DESCHAMPS – [9]*It's an excellent idea.* [10]*Did you have a good trip?*

ROGER – [11]*Yes. But we are rather tired.*

MRS. DESCHAMPS – [12]*Sit down and rest.* [13]*Will you have something to eat or drink?*

ROGER – [14]*I'll have some beer, if you have some.*

MRS. DESCHAMPS – [15]*And what about you, sir?*

JOHN – [16]*I'd be glad to drink a glass of cold water.*

MRS. DESCHAMPS – [17]*Wouldn't you rather have something else?*

---

* On dit aussi **Je suis enchanté** (ou **heureux**) **de faire votre connaissance,** mais **Enchanté(e), monsieur** (**madame**) est une formule plus courante.

JEAN – [18]Merci, madame. [19]Il n'y a rien de meilleur qu'un verre d'eau fraîche quand il fait chaud.

MME DESCHAMPS – [20]J'espère bien que vous allez passer quelques jours avec nous.

JEAN – [21]Nous ne voulons pas vous déranger. [22]Nous avons l'intention de repartir ce soir.

MME DESCHAMPS – [23]Vous n'êtes pas pressés. [24]Restez quelques jours ici. [25]C'est le moment de la moisson. [26]Si vous voulez, vous pourrez nous aider.

JOHN – [18]*No, thank you.* [19]*There is nothing better than a glass of cool water when it is hot.*

MRS. DESCHAMPS – [20]*I certainly hope you are going to spend a few days with us.*

JOHN – [21]*We don't want to put you out (inconvenience you).* [22]*We are intending to go back this evening.*

MRS. DESCHAMPS – [23]*You are not in a hurry.* [14]*Stay here a few days.* [25]*It's harvest time.* [26]*If you want to, you can help us.*

A LA CAMPAGNE

I. Exercices d'application. *Répétez les phrases suivantes en substituant les mots indiqués:*

1. Nous avons décidé de profiter du beau temps pour venir vous voir.

   aller à la campagne / faire une excursion / faire une promenade à bicyclette / jouer au tennis

2. Nous avons l'intention de repartir ce soir.

   partir demain soir / quitter Fontainebleau demain / rester quelques jours ici / nous reposer aujourd'hui

3. C'est le moment de la moisson.

   de partir / de vous lever / de nous en aller / de rentrer

4. Je boirais volontiers de la bière.

   du vin / de l'eau / du lait / un jus de fruit

5. Il n'y a rien de meilleur qu'un verre d'eau fraîche.

   qu'un verre de lait frais / qu'un jus de fruit / qu'une tasse de café / qu'une bouteille de bière

II. *Répondez en français à chacune des questions suivantes:*

1. Où Jean et Roger viennent-ils d'arriver? **2.** Qui est Madame Deschamps? **3.** Est-ce qu'elle attendait l'arrivée de Jean et Roger? **4.** Est-ce qu'elle a déjà fait la connaissance de Jean? **5.** Est-ce que Roger a parlé de Jean à sa cousine? **6.** Pourquoi Jean et Roger ont-ils décidé de venir voir les Deschamps? **7.** Est-ce que leur voyage à bicyclette les a fatigués? **8.** Que veut dire «prendre quelque chose»? **9.** Que prend Roger? **10.** Et Jean? **11.** Quand Jean et Roger ont-ils l'intention de repartir? **12.** Est-ce qu'ils ont peur de déranger les Deschamps? **13.** Est-ce qu'ils sont pressés? **14.** Qu'est-ce que leur dit Madame Deschamps pour les faire rester?

III. *Répondez en français à chacune des phrases impératives suivantes:*

1. Présentez un étudiant (une étudiante) à un autre (à une autre). **2.** Dites à un autre étudiant qu'on vous a souvent parlé de lui. **3.** Demandez à un autre étudiant s'il a fait bon voyage. **4.** Dites-lui de s'asseoir. **5.** Dites-lui de se reposer. **6.** Demandez-lui s'il veut prendre quelque chose. **7.** Demandez-lui ce qu'il veut prendre. **8.** Demandez-lui s'il ne préfère pas autre chose. **9.** Dites-lui que vous prendrez un verre d'eau fraîche.

IV. *Mettez chacune des phrases suivantes au temps passé convenable.*

Il est presque quatre heures de l'après-midi quand Jean et Roger arrivent à la ferme des Deschamps. Roger présente son ami à sa cousine, qui dit à Jean que Roger lui a souvent parlé de lui et qu'elle est heureuse de faire sa connaissance. Elle invite les deux jeunes gens à se reposer un peu, car ils sont sans doute fatigués. Puis elle leur demande s'ils désirent prendre quelque chose. Roger répond à sa cousine qu'il prendra volontiers de la bière, si elle en a. Mme Deschamps offre aussi de la bière à Jean. Mais ce dernier la remercie, en lui disant que par cette chaleur, il n'y a rien de plus rafraîchissant qu'un bon verre d'eau fraîche. Il boit son eau, Roger sa bière, et, en attendant le retour de M. Deschamps, ils causent avec Mme Deschamps des travaux de la ferme et des occupations du ménage (*housekeeping*).

V. Dictée d'après la Conversation 31, pp. 260-261.

VI. Conversation.

Vous faites une promenade à bicyclette et vous vous arrêtez dans une ferme pour demander un verre d'eau.

Dans la forêt de Fontainebleau

ROGER – [1]Je vois des champignons au bord de la route. [2]Il doit y en avoir beaucoup dans le bois. [3]Si nous en rapportions quelques-uns à la maison?

JEAN – [4]Est-ce que vous connaissez les champignons?

ROGER – [5]Plus ou moins. [6]Ramassez seulement ceux-ci. [7]Ils sont très faciles à reconnaître. [8]Le dessus est brun et le dessous est jaune. [9]On ne peut pas se tromper.

JEAN – [10]Bon. Mais je ne sais pas où les mettre.

ROGER (*Lui tendant un sac*) – [11]Tenez, mettez-les là-dedans.

JEAN – [12]Est-ce que celui-ci est bon?

ROGER – [13]Oui.

JEAN – [14]Et celui-là?

ROGER – [15]Excellent.

ROGER – [1]*I see some mushrooms on the side of the road.* [2]*There must be lots of them in the woods.* [3]*Suppose we take a few of them back home (How about taking a few of them home)?*

JOHN – [4]*Do you know mushrooms?*

ROGER – [5]*More or less.* [6]*Just pick these.* [7]*They are very easy to recognize.* [8]*The upper surface is brown and the under side is yellow.* [9]*You can't go wrong.*

JOHN – [10]*O.K. But I do not know where to put them.*

ROGER (Handing him a bag) – [11]*Here, put them in this.*

JOHN – [12]*Is this one good?*

ROGER – [13]*Yes.*

JOHN – [14]*And that one?*

ROGER – [15]*Excellent.*

JEAN – [16]Oh! J'en vois beaucoup au pied de cet arbre.

ROGER – [17]Faites attention! [18]Est-ce que vous voulez empoisonner toute la famille?

JEAN – [19]Mais ces champignons ressemblent à ceux que vous m'avez montrés.

ROGER – [20]Les mauvais champignons ressemblent beaucoup aux bons.

JEAN – [21]Vous auriez dû me dire ça plus tôt.

ROGER – [22]J'ai eu tort de ne pas vous prévenir. [23]En tout cas, il vaut mieux laisser ceux dont on n'est pas sûr . . .

JOHN – [16]*Oh! I see lots of them at the foot of this tree.*

ROGER – [17]*Watch out!* [18]*Do you want to poison the entire family?*

JOHN – [19]*Well, these mushrooms look like those you showed me.*

ROGER – [20]*The poisonous mushrooms look very much like the good ones.*

JOHN – [21]*You should have told me so sooner.*

ROGER – [22]*I was wrong not to warn you.* [23]*In any case, it is better to leave those you are not sure of . . .*

DANS LA FORÊT DE FONTAINEBLEAU

I. Substitutions. *Répétez les phrases suivantes en substituant les mots indiqués:*

1. Je vois des champignons au bord de la route.
   le long de la route / à côté de la route / de l'autre côté de la route / tout près de la route
2. J'en vois beaucoup au pied de cet arbre.
   devant / derrière (*behind*) / sous / près de
3. Si nous en rapportions quelques-uns à la maison?
   à ma cousine / à nos cousins / dans ce sac / sur nos bicyclettes
4. J'ai eu tort de ne pas vous prévenir.
   de ne pas vous dire au revoir / de ne pas faire mes courses / de ne pas travailler hier soir / de ne pas écrire à mon père
5. Vous avez eu tort de ramasser de mauvais champignons.
   de dépenser tout votre argent / de sortir hier soir / de dormir tout l'après-midi / de vous coucher si tard
6. Vous auriez dû (*should have*) me dire ça plus tôt.
   me prévenir / venir me voir / revenir / rentrer / commencer à travailler

II. *Répondez en français à chacune des questions suivantes:*

1. Qu'est-ce que Roger voit au bord de la route? **2.** Qu'est-ce qu'il propose de faire? **3.** Est-ce que Roger connaît les champignons? **4.** Est-ce que Roger dit à Jean de ramasser tous les champignons? **5.** Pourquoi ces champignons-là sont-ils faciles à reconnaître? **6.** De quelle couleur est le dessus des champignons dont il s'agit? **7.** De quelle couleur est le dessous des champignons dont il s'agit? **8.** Qu'est-ce que Roger dit à Jean en lui tendant un sac? **9.** Qu'est-ce que Jean trouve au pied d'un arbre? **10.** Est-ce qu'il en voit beaucoup? **11.** Pourquoi Roger lui dit-il de faire attention? **12.** Est-ce que Jean veut empoisonner toute la famille? **13.** Alors, pourquoi a-t-il ramassé de mauvais champignons? **14.** Qu'est-ce que Roger aurait dû lui dire plus tôt? **15.** Est-ce qu'il a eu raison de ne pas lui dire cela plus tôt? **16.** Est-ce qu'il vaut mieux laisser les champignons dont on n'est pas sûr?

III. *Demandez à quelqu'un:*

1. s'il connaît les champignons. **2.** s'il va quelquefois ramasser des champignons à la campagne. **3.** ce que Roger voit au bord de la route. **4.** si les bons champignons sont difficiles à reconnaître. **5.** si on peut ramasser tous les champignons qu'on trouve. **6.** de quelle couleur est le dessus des champignons dont parle Roger. **7.** pourquoi il faut faire attention en ramassant des champignons. **8.** si les mauvais champignons ressemblent beaucoup aux bons. **9.** s'il est dangereux de ramasser des champignons qu'on ne connaît pas.

IV. Exercices d'application.

A. *Remplacez* **il y a** *par* **il doit y avoir** (there must be) *dans chacune des phrases suivantes.*

EX.:—Il y a des champignons dans le bois.
—Il doit y avoir des champignons dans le bois.

1. Il y a beaucoup de champignons dans le bois. **2.** Il y en a beaucoup dans le bois. **3.** Il y en a quelques-uns dans le bois. **4.** Il y a un train cet après-midi. **5.** Il y en a un cet après-midi. **6.** Il y en a plusieurs cet après-midi.

B. *Répétez, en remplaçant l'impératif par* **si nous** *avec l'imparfait.*

EX.:—Rapportons des champignons à la maison.
—Si nous rapportions des champignons à la maison?

1. Ramassons des champignons. **2.** Ramassons des fraises des bois (*wild strawberries*). **3.** Allons à la campagne pour le week-end. **4.** Allons chercher des fleurs sauvages. **5.** Partons ce soir. **6.** Quittons la maison de bonne heure.

C. *Répondez négativement aux questions suivantes:*

1. Ressemblez-vous à votre père? **2.** Les enfants ressemblent-ils toujours à leurs parents? **3.** Est-ce que votre frère vous ressemble? **4.** Est-ce que votre sœur vous ressemble? **5.** Est-ce que les jumeaux (*twins*) se ressemblent toujours? **6.** Est-ce que les mauvais champignons ressemblent toujours aux bons?

V. *Exercice sur* **dessus, dessous,** *etc.*

Le dessus (*upper surface*) and **le dessous** (*lower surface*) are of course nouns. Note the adverbs that correspond to these words: **là-dessus** (*on that, thereon*), **là-dessous** (*under that, under there*). Compare also: **là-haut** (*up there*), **là-dedans** (*in there*), **là-bas** (*over there, down there*).

Répétez les phrases suivantes en substituant les mots indiqués:

1. Mettez-les dans ce sac.
là-dedans / sur cette table / là-dessus / dans cette casserole (*sauce pan*) / là-dedans

2. J'ai laissé le panier (*basket*) au premier.
là-haut / sur la table / là-dessus / sous la table / là-dessous

VI. Dictée d'après la Conversation 32, pp. 272-273.

VII. Conversation.

Au cours d'une promenade dans une forêt, vous parlez avec un ami de ce que vous voyez.

Irregular Verbs in -re

91. *First group: past participle in* **-u.**

A. connaître (*to know, to be acquainted with*):

—**Connaissez-vous** Roger Duplessis?	*Do you know* Roger Duplessis?
—Oui, **je** le **connais** un peu.	Yes, *I know* him slightly.
—Où l'**avez-vous connu?**	Where *did you know* him?
—**Je** l'**ai connu** à Paris.	*I knew* him in Paris.

PRÉSENT: Je connais, tu connais, il connaît, nous connaissons, vous connaissez, ils connaissent.
IMPARFAIT: Je connaissais. PASSÉ COMPOSÉ: J'ai connu. FUTUR: Je connaîtrai.

B. croire (*to believe*):

—**Croyez-vous** ce que disent les journaux?	*Do you believe* what the papers say?
—**Je ne crois pas** tout ce qu'ils disent.	*I do not believe* all they say.
—**Je n'ai pas cru** ce qu'il m'a dit.	*I did not believe* what he told me.

PRÉSENT: Je crois, tu crois, il croit, nous croyons, vous croyez, ils croient.
IMPARFAIT: Je croyais. PASSÉ COMPOSÉ: J'ai cru. FUTUR: Je croirai.

C. boire (*to drink*):

—**Buvez-vous** du café?	*Do you drink* coffee?
—Non, **je** ne **bois** que du lait.	No, *I drink* only milk.
—Qu'est-ce que Jean **a bu?**	What *did* John *drink?*
—**Il a bu** de l'eau fraîche.	*He drank* some cold water.

PRÉSENT: Je bois, tu bois, il boit, nous buvons, vous buvez, ils boivent.
IMPARFAIT: Je buvais. PASSÉ COMPOSÉ: J'ai bu. FUTUR: Je boirai.

D. lire (*to read*):

—**Lisez-vous** *la Nouvelle Revue Française?*	*Do you read* the NRF?
—Oui, **je** la **lis** quelquefois.	Yes, *I read* it sometimes.
—**Avez-vous lu** des romans de Balzac?	*Have you read* any novels of Balzac?
—Oui, **j'en ai lu** deux ou trois.	Yes, *I have read* two or three of them.

PRÉSENT: Je lis, tu lis, il lit, nous lisons, vous lisez, ils lisent.
IMPARFAIT: Je lisais. PASSÉ COMPOSÉ: J'ai lu. FUTUR: Je lirai.

92. *Second group: past participle in* **-i, -is,** *or* **-it.**

A. dire (*to say, to tell*):

—Qu'est-ce que **vous dites?**	What's that (What *do you say*)?
—**Je dis** que je ne crois pas ce que le marchand m'**a dit.**	*I say* I don't believe what the storekeeper *told me.*

PRÉSENT: Je dis, tu dis, il dit, nous disons, vous dites, ils disent.
IMPARFAIT: Je disais. PASSÉ COMPOSÉ: J'ai dit. FUTUR: Je dirai.

B. écrire (*to write*):

—**Écrivez-vous** souvent à votre mère?	*Do you write* to your mother often?
—**Je** lui **écris** tous les huit jours.	*I write* her every week.
—**Je** lui **ai écrit** dimanche.	*I wrote* her Sunday.

PRÉSENT: J'écris, tu écris, il écrit, nous écrivons, vous écrivez, ils écrivent.
IMPARFAIT: J'écrivais. PASSÉ COMPOSÉ: J'ai écrit. FUTUR: J'écrirai.

C. suivre (*to follow, to take a course*):

—**Suivez-vous** les conseils de vos parents?	*Do you follow* the advice of your parents?
—Oui, **je** les **suis** toujours.	Yes, *I* always *follow* it (them).
—**Avez-vous suivi** un cours d'histoire?	*Did you take* a history course?
—Oui, **j'en ai suivi** plusieurs.	Yes, *I took* several of them.

PRÉSENT: Je suis, tu suis, il suit, nous suivons, vous suivez, ils suivent.
IMPARFAIT: Je suivais. PASSÉ COMPOSÉ: J'ai suivi. FUTUR: Je suivrai.

D. prendre (*to take*):

—Est-ce que **vous prenez** l'autobus?	*Are you taking* the bus?
—Non, **je prends** l'avion.	No, *I am taking* the plane.
—**J'ai** déjà **pris** mon billet.	*I have* already *gotten* (taken) my ticket.
—**Prenez-vous** du sucre?	*Do you take* sugar?
—Non, **je prends** un peu de crème.	No, *I take* a little cream.

PRÉSENT: Je prends, tu prends, il prend, nous prenons, vous prenez, ils prennent.
IMPARFAIT: Je prenais. PASSÉ COMPOSÉ: J'ai pris. FUTUR: Je prendrai.

E. (1) **mettre** (*to put, to put on*):

—Où **mettez-vous** votre argent?	Where *do you put* your money?
—**Je** le **mets** dans mon porte-monnaie.	*I put* it in my pocketbook.
—Je ne sais pas où **j'ai mis** ma cravate.	I do not know where *I put* my tie.
—Marie **a mis** sa nouvelle robe.	Marie *put on* her new dress.

(2) **se mettre à** (*to begin*):

—**Nous nous sommes mis à** travailler à une heure et demie.	*We started* to work at 1:30.
Il **se met à** pleuvoir.	It *is beginning* to rain.

PRÉSENT: Je mets, tu mets, il met, nous mettons, vous mettez, ils mettent.
IMPARFAIT: Je mettais. PASSÉ COMPOSÉ: J'ai mis. FUTUR: Je mettrai.

93. Faire (*to do, to make*), etc.

A. Normal uses of **faire:**

—Qu'est-ce que **vous faites** (pres.) ce soir?	What *are you doing* tonight?
—Je ne sais pas ce que **je ferai** (fut.).	I don't know what *I shall do.*
—Je n'ai rien à **faire.**	I have nothing *to do.*
—Cela ne **fait** rien.	That *makes* no difference.

B. Special uses of **faire:**

(1) Impersonal:

Il fait beau.	*It's* fine weather.
Il fait bon (jour, nuit, etc.).	*It's* pleasant (light, dark, etc.).

(2) **faire** + an infinitive = *to have* + past participle:

—Qui **a fait construire** ce château?	Who *had* this château *built?*
—**J'ai fait réparer** ma montre.	*I had* my watch *repaired.*

PRÉSENT: Je fais, tu fais, il fait, nous faisons, vous faites, ils font.
IMPARFAIT: Je faisais. PASSÉ COMPOSÉ: J'ai fait. FUTUR: Je ferai.

94. Plaindre (*to pity*); se plaindre (*to complain*).

—De quoi **vous plaignez-vous?**	What *are you complaining* about?
—**Je ne me plains pas.**	*I am not complaining.*

PRÉSENT: Je plains, tu plains, il plaint, nous plaignons, vous plaignez, ils plaignent.
IMPARFAIT: Je plaignais, etc. PASSÉ COMPOSÉ: J'ai plaint, etc. FUTUR: Je plaindrai, etc.

Craindre, *to fear,* is conjugated like **plaindre.** Ex.: Qu'est-ce que **vous craignez? Je** ne **crains** rien.

A few verbs ending in **-eindre** and **-oindre** are conjugated like **plaindre** except that the vowel **e** and **o** of the ending remains **e** and **o** respectively: **atteindre,** *to reach, to attain;* **éteindre,** *to extinguish;* **peindre,** *to paint;* **rejoindre,** *to meet, to catch up with;* etc.

—**Éteignez** le feu.	*Put out* the fire.
—Je vous **rejoins** tout de suite.	*I'll be with* you right away.

I. Exercices d'application.

A. *Répondez affirmativement:*

EX.:—Connaissez-vous?
—**Je connais.**

1. Croyez-vous? **2.** Lisez-vous? **3.** Connaissez-vous? **4.** Buvez-vous? **5.** Dites-vous? **6.** Écrivez-vous? **7.** Suivez-vous? **8.** Prenez-vous? **9.** Mettez-vous? **10.** Faites-vous? **11.** Plaignez-vous? **12.** Vous plaignez-vous? **13.** Craignez-vous? **14.** Peignez-vous? **15.** Rejoignez-vous?

B. *Mettez les phrases suivantes au passé composé:*

EX.: —Je suis un cours de chimie.
—**J'ai suivi un cours de chimie.**

1. Je ne bois pas de café. **2.** Je ne prends pas de crème. **3.** Je ne crois pas ce qu'il m'a dit. **4.** Nous ne lisons pas le journal. **5.** Qu'est-ce que vous lui dites? **6.** Nous ne disons rien. **7.** A qui écrivez-vous? **8.** Que faites-vous? **9.** Qu'est-ce que vous craignez? **10.** Où rejoignez-vous vos amis? **11.** Il suit mes conseils.

C. *Mettez les phrases suivantes à l'imparfait en commençant par* **A ce moment-là:**

EX.:—Je ne connais pas Paris.
—**A ce moment-là, je ne connaissais pas Paris.**

1. Je crois tout ce qu'on me dit. **2.** Je ne bois pas de vin. **3.** Je ne lis pas le journal. **4.** Il n'écrit pas beaucoup. **5.** Il suit les conseils de ses parents. **6.** Il ne prend pas de café. **7.** Il fait du ski. **8.** Il se plaint tout le temps.

D. *Répétez en remplaçant* **commencer** *par* **se mettre à:**

EX. —Je commence à travailler à huit heures.
—Je me mets à travailler à huit heures.

1. A quelle heure commencez-vous à travailler? **2.** Il a commencé à lire. **3.** Nous avons commencé à écrire des lettres. **4.** Il a commencé à pleuvoir. **5.** J'ai commencé à acheter de vieux livres. **6.** Ils ont commencé à ramasser des champignons.

II. *Demandez à quelqu'un:*

EX.:—s'il prend du sucre dans son café.
—Prenez-vous du sucre dans votre café?

1. s'il connaît Versailles. **2.** s'il croit qu'il va pleuvoir. **3.** s'il boit du lait. **4.** s'il lit beaucoup de romans. **5.** ce qu'il dit. **6.** s'il écrit beaucoup de lettres. **7.** quels cours il suit. **8.** ce qu'il prend comme dessert. **9.** où il met son argent. **10.** s'il se plaint. **11.** s'il craint la pluie. **12.** ce qu'il fait le dimanche. **13.** quel temps il faisait hier. **14.** à quelle heure il fait nuit en hiver. **15.** où Roger a fait réparer sa montre. **16.** ce qu'on fait réparer dans un garage.

III. *Employez* **faire** *avec l'infinitive dans les phrases suivantes:*

EX.:—J'ai réparé ma voiture.
—J'ai fait réparer ma voiture.

1. Il a construit ce château. **2.** Il a peint sa maison. **3.** Elle a fait sa robe. **4.** Mme Deschamps a arrosé son jardin. **5.** Elle a nettoyé (*cleaned*) la maison. **6.** Elle lui a dit de venir la voir. **7.** Il m'a dit qu'il était malade. **8.** Il s'est réveillé à six heures.

IV. *Dites en français:*

1. I took the train at Épernay. **2.** I got my ticket in Paris. **3.** I took a chemistry course last year. **4.** I took (followed) his advice. **5.** I had some coffee at noon. **6.** She put on her new dress. **7.** He put on his hat. **8.** They started to work early. **9.** They will start to work tomorrow. **10.** Have you read what they wrote? **11.** Do you believe what they said? **12.** What are you doing this evening? **13.** I have nothing to do. **14.** I have something to do. **15.** I have a great deal to do.

V. Révision des dialogues, pp. 260-261 et pp. 272-273.

1. Comment Jean et Roger vont-ils à la campagne? **2.** Pourquoi craignent-ils d'avoir pris la mauvaise route? **3.** Qu'est-ce que Roger demande à l'homme qui travaille dans son champ? **4.** Où cet homme leur dit-il d'aller? **5.** Quel chemin doivent-ils prendre à la sortie de Barbizon? **6.** A quelle distance est Barbizon de Fontainebleau? **7.** Savez-vous ce que c'est qu'un kilomètre? **8.** Savez-vous combien il y a de mètres dans un kilomètre? **9.** Pourquoi Roger a-t-il chaud? **10.** Pourquoi Jean a-t-il mal aux jambes? **11.** A qui Roger présente-t-il Jean? **12.** Qu'est-ce que vous diriez pour présenter quelqu'un? **13.** Qu'est-ce que vous dites quand on vous présente quelqu'un? **14.** Qu'est-ce que Mme Deschamps demande à Jean et à Roger? **15.** Est-ce que Jean boit de la bière? **16.** Qu'est-ce qu'il prend? **17.** Pourquoi Jean et Roger ont-ils l'intention de repartir le même soir? **18.** Est-ce qu'ils sont pressés? **19.** Pourquoi les Deschamps avaient-ils besoin d'aide à ce moment-là? **20.** Avez-vous jamais travaillé dans une ferme au moment de la moisson?

VI. Thème d'imitation:

As[1] they were bicycling in the Fontainebleau Forest, Roger saw some mushrooms on the side of the road. "I'm crazy about[2] mushrooms", said he to John. "Let's pick some. I'll give them to my cousin, and we'll eat them this evening." "Eat all the mushrooms you wish," answered John. "*I* shall not eat any." "Why?" asked Roger. "There is no danger[3] when you just pick the mushrooms you know." "Do you think (so)?"[4] said John. "In America, my father knew a professor of botany[5] who had spent his life studying[6] mushrooms. Do you know how the poor man died? He died of mushroom poisoning[7] . . ."

Roger picked mushrooms all the same; but that evening he didn't have much appetite.

---

1 *as*, **comme.** 2 *to be crazy about*, **adorer.** 3 *danger*, **le danger.** 4 **Vous croyez?** 5 *botany*, **la botanique.** 6 **à étudier.** 7 *lit.* poisoned by mushrooms.

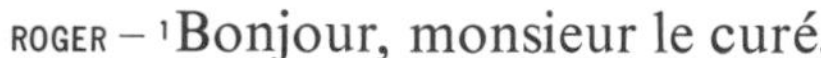

A l'église du village

ROGER – [1]Bonjour, monsieur le curé.

LE CURÉ – [2]Bonjour, mes amis. [3]Entrez donc. [4]J'étais en train de travailler dans mon jardin quand vous avez sonné.

JEAN – [5]Nous nous excusons de vous déranger quand vous êtes occupé.

LE CURÉ – [6]Vous ne me dérangez pas du tout. [7]Je viens de tailler mes rosiers, [8]et je suis à votre disposition.

ROGER – [9]Nous avons entendu dire que vous avez une très belle église, [10]et nous avons envie de la visiter.

LE CURÉ – [11]Je me ferai un plaisir de vous accompagner dans votre visite. [12]Je crains pourtant que vous ne* soyez un peu déçus. [13]Bien qu'elle soit classée «monument historique», [14]c'est une simple église de village.

JEAN – [15]J'ai lu quelque part que votre église date du douzième siècle.

ROGER – [1]*Good morning, sir.*

LE CURÉ – [2]*Good morning, my friends.* [3]*Do come in.* [4]*I was busy working in my garden, when you rang.*

JOHN – [5]*We apologize for bothering you when you are busy.*

LE CURÉ – [6]*You aren't bothering me at all.* [7]*I have just trimmed my rosebushes,* [8]*and I am at your service.*

ROGER – [9]*We have heard that you have a very beautiful church,* [10]*and we are eager to go through it.*

LE CURÉ – [11]*I shall take pleasure in showing you through it.* [12]*I'm afraid, however, that you'll be a little disappointed.* [13]*Although it is classified as a "historical monument,"* [14]*it's a simple village church.*

JOHN – [15]*I have read somewhere that your church dates from the XIIth century.*

* When a subordinate clause depends upon **craindre** or **avoir peur** used affirmatively, the subordinate clause is introduced by **que . . . ne** instead of **que** alone. This pleonastic **ne,** as it is called, is meaningless and is frequently omitted in conversation.

LE CURÉ – [16]Une partie seulement de l'édifice actuel date de l'époque romane.* [17]L'église a été brûlée en 1392. [18]Elle a été en partie reconstruite au siècle suivant.

LE CURÉ – [16]*Just a part of the present building dates from the romanesque period.* [17]*The church was burned in 1392.* [18]*It was partly rebuilt in the following century.*

ROGER – [19]J'ai entendu parler des vitraux de votre église. [20]On dit qu'ils sont très vieux.

ROGER – [19]*I have heard of the stained-glass windows of your church.* [20]*They say they are very old.*

LE CURÉ – [21]Je ne crois pas qu'il y ait plus de deux ou trois vitraux vraiment anciens. [22]La plupart d'entre eux† sont relativement modernes . . . [23]Voulez-vous bien entrer par cette porte? [24]L'intérieur de l'église est un peu sombre, [25]mais vos yeux s'habitueront vite à l'obscurité.

LE CURÉ – [21]*I don't believe there are more than two or three of the stained-glass windows which are really old.* [22]*Most of them are relatively modern . . .* [23]*Will you come in through this door?* [24]*The inside is a little dark,* [25]*but your eyes will quickly get used to the darkness.*

---

* Les plus vieilles églises françaises datent de l'époque romane, c'est-à-dire des dixième au douzième siècle. L'architecture de cette époque est caractérisée par l'emploi fréquent de l'arc en demi-cercle. Les murs très épais n'ont que de rares fenêtres, ce qui explique l'obscurité de l'intérieur de ces églises.

† Note that you say **la plupart d'entre eux,** not *la plupart d'eux*. The same is true for **beaucoup, quelques-uns, plusieurs.**

UN VILLAGE DE BOURGOGNE

I. Substitutions. *Répétez les phrases suivantes en substituant les mots indiqués:*

1. J'étais en train de travailler dans mon jardin quand vous avez sonné.
   tailler mes rosiers / lire le journal / réparer mon auto / écrire des lettres
2. Nous nous excusons de vous déranger.
   de ne pas être à l'heure / d'être en retard / d'être en avance (*ahead of time*) / d'avoir oublié notre rendez-vous
3. Nous avons entendu dire que vous avez une très belle église.
   les Brown sont de retour / Louise Bedel va se marier / elle va habiter dans notre quartier / l'église a été construite au douzième siècle
4. J'ai entendu parler des vitraux de votre église.
   des fontaines de Versailles / de Mansart / de lui / de Jeanne d'Arc / d'elle

II. *Répondez en français à chacune des questions suivantes:*

1. Qu'est-ce que Roger a dit quand le curé a ouvert la porte? **2.** Que faisait le curé quand Roger a sonné? **3.** De quoi Jean s'excuse-t-il? **4.** Qu'est-ce que le curé répond? **5.** Que vient-il de faire dans son jardin? **6.** Qu'est-ce que Roger a entendu dire à propos de l'église? **7.** Pourquoi Jean et Roger sont-ils venus voir le curé? **8.** Qu'est-ce que le curé offre de faire? **9.** Pourquoi le curé dit-il: «Je crains que vous ne soyez un peu déçus?» **10.** Est-ce que cette église est classée «monument historique»? **11.** Où Roger a-t-il lu que l'église date de l'époque romane? **12.** En quelle année l'église a-t-elle été brûlée? **13.** Quand a-t-elle été reconstruite? **14.** Est-ce que Roger a entendu parler des vitraux de l'église? **15.** Qu'est-ce qu'il a entendu dire à leur sujet? **16.** Est-ce que la plupart des vitraux de l'église sont anciens? **17.** Est-ce que la plupart d'entre eux sont modernes? **18.** Est-ce que l'intérieur de l'église est sombre? **19.** Est-ce que les yeux de Jean et de Roger s'habitueront vite à l'obscurité?

III. *Répétez les phrases suivantes, en remplaçant le nom par le pronom personnel:*

EX.:—La plupart des vitraux sont relativement modernes.
—La plupart **d'entre eux** sont relativement modernes.

1. Quelques-uns des vitraux sont relativement modernes. **2.** Plusieurs des vitraux sont relativement modernes. **3.** La plupart des statues (*f.*) sont relativement modernes. **4.** Quelques-unes des statues sont relativement modernes. **5.** Plusieurs des statues sont relativement modernes.

IV. *Répétez les phrases suivantes en employant l'expression indiquée:*

A. Je crains que . . . ne

1. Je crois que vous serez un peu déçu. **2.** Je crois que vous serez un peu fatigué. **3.** Je crois que vous serez un peu en retard. **4.** Je crois que vous serez en avance.

B. Bien qu'elle soit

1. Même si elle est classée monument historique, c'est une simple église de village. **2.** Même si elle est fatiguée, elle ira au bal ce soir. **3.** Même si elle est occupée, elle sera heureuse de vous voir. **4.** Même si elle est en retard, elle ne se dépêche pas.

V. *Dites en français, en employant les expressions indiquées:*

A. avoir envie de

1. We are eager to visit your church. **2.** I'm anxious to see the stained-glass windows. **3.** Are you interested in seeing Florence and Rome? **4.** Yes, I feel like taking a trip. **5.** I felt like working in my garden.

B. s'habituer à

1. Your eyes will quickly get used to the darkness. **2.** Your eyes will quickly get used to it (y). **3.** I am not used to riding a bicycle, but I shall get used to it. **4.** I am not used to drinking black coffee, but I shall get used to it.

VI. Révision de l'impératif. *Dites à quelqu'un:*

1. d'entrer. **2.** de ne pas entrer. **3.** de s'asseoir. **4.** de ne pas s'asseoir. **5.** de se dépêcher. **6.** de ne pas se dépêcher. **7.** de ne pas se déranger. **8.** de vous excuser. **9.** de prendre l'autobus. **10.** de faire attention. **11.** de faire venir le médecin. **12.** de ne pas croire tout ce que disent les journaux. **13.** de s'en aller. **14.** de ne pas partir.

VII. Dictée d'après la Conversation 33, pp. 276-277.

VIII. Conversation.

Vous demandez des renseignements à un guide au sujet d'un château de la Renaissance que vous voulez visiter (date de construction, nom de l'architecte, jours et heures de visite, etc.).

CONVERSATION 35

Au jardin

MME DESCHAMPS – [1]Il faut que j'aille au jardin cueillir des fleurs.

ROGER – [2]Veux-tu que nous t'aidions?

MME DESCHAMPS – [3]Oui, mais fais attention de bien fermer la porte derrière toi. [4]Je ne veux pas que les poules puissent entrer. [5]Elles mangent à peu près toute ma salade.

ROGER – [6]Quelles fleurs vas-tu cueillir?

MME DESCHAMPS – [7]J'ai besoin de roses et d'œillets. [8]J'en ferai un bouquet pour la salle à manger.

ROGER – [9]Tu as un très beau jardin.

MME DESCHAMPS – [10]Je devrais m'en occuper davantage, [11]mais je n'ai pas le temps.

JEAN – [12]Est-ce que vous avez du maïs?

MME DESCHAMPS – [13]Non, je n'en ai pas. [14]D'ailleurs, l'été est trop frais [15]pour que le maïs puisse mûrir ici.

JEAN – [16]Je m'en doutais un peu.

ROGER – [17]Regardez ces pois, ces *haricots verts et ces choux. [18]Ils poussent à merveille.

MME DESCHAMPS – [19]Oui, mais il n'a guère plu cette année. [20]Une bonne pluie ferait du bien à mes légumes.

ROGER – [21]Veux-tu que nous les arrosions?

MME DESCHAMPS – [22]Je crois qu'il vaut mieux attendre [23]jusqu'à ce qu'il fasse moins chaud . . .

MRS. DESCHAMPS – [1]*I must go to the garden to pick some flowers.*

ROGER – [2]*Do you want us to help you?*

MRS. DESCHAMPS – [3]*Yes, but be careful to close the garden gate (properly) behind you.* [4]*I don't want the hens to be able to get in.* [5]*They eat practically all my salad greens.*

ROGER – [6]*What flowers are you going to pick?*

MRS. DESCHAMPS – [7]*I need roses and carnations.* [8]*I'll make a bouquet of them for the dining room.*

ROGER – [9]*You have a very fine garden.*

MRS. DESCHAMPS – [10]*I ought to take care of it better (more),* [11]*but I haven't the time.*

JOHN – [12]*Have you got any corn?*

MRS. DESCHAMPS – [13]*No, I haven't any.* [14]*Anyway, the summer is too cool* [15]*for corn to mature here.*

JOHN – [16]*I rather thought so.*

ROGER – [17]*Look at those peas, green beans, and cabbages.* [18]*They certainly are growing.*

MRS. DESCHAMPS – [19]*Yes; but it hasn't rained much this year.* [20]*A good rain would do a good deal for my vegetables.*

ROGER – [21]*Do you want us to water them?*

MRS. DESCHAMPS – [22]*I think it's better to wait* [23]*till it's cooler . . .*

* The **h** of **haricots** is aspirate.

I. Substitutions. *Répétez les phrases suivantes en substituant les mots indiqués:*

1. Fais attention de bien fermer la porte.

   de ne pas laisser la porte ouverte / de ne pas laisser entrer les poules / de ne pas être en retard / de ne pas manquer ton avion (*plane*)

2. J'ai besoin de roses et d'œillets.

   de papier à lettres et d'enveloppes / d'une nouvelle auto / de cigarettes / d'argent / de monnaie

3. Je devrais m'en occuper davantage, mais je n'ai pas le temps.

   me reposer / m'amuser / travailler / dormir

4. Je crois qu'il vaut mieux attendre jusqu' à la nuit.

   à demain / à six heures / à la semaine prochaine / à l'été prochain / à dimanche

5. Je crois qu'il vaut mieux attendre jusqu'à ce qu'il fasse moins chaud.

   plus chaud / moins froid / plus froid / beau

II. *Répondez en français à chacune des questions suivantes:*

1. Pourquoi faut-il que Mme Deschamps aille au jardin? **2.** Est-ce qu'elle veut que Jean et Roger l'aident? **3.** Pourquoi faut-il qu'ils fassent attention de bien fermer la porte du jardin? **4.** Pourquoi Mme Deschamps ne veut-elle pas que les poules puissent entrer dans son jardin? **5.** Quelles fleurs veut-elle cueillir? **6.** Qu'est-ce qu'elle fera de ces fleurs? **7.** Comment Roger trouve-t-il le jardin de Mme Deschamps? **8.** Est-ce que Mme Deschamps devrait s'occuper davantage de son jardin? **9.** Pourquoi ne peut-elle pas s'en occuper davantage? **10.** Est-ce que Mme Deschamps a du maïs dans son jardin? **11.** Pourquoi le maïs ne peut-il pas mûrir dans le Nord de la France? **12.** Quels légumes y a-t-il dans le jardin? **13.** Est-ce qu'ils poussent bien? **14.** Est-ce qu'il a beaucoup plu cette année-là? **15.** Pourquoi Mme Deschamps voudrait-elle une bonne pluie? **16.** Qu'est-ce que Roger propose de faire? **17.** Est-ce que Mme Deschamps croit qu'il faut arroser tout de suite? **18.** Jusqu'à quand dit-elle d'attendre? **19.** Savez-vous vous occuper d'un jardin? **20.** Qu'est-ce qu'il faut faire s'il ne pleut pas? **21.** Est-ce qu'il vaut mieux arroser le matin ou le soir? **22.** Est-ce qu'on peut avoir un beau jardin si on ne s'en occupe pas?

III. *Demandez à quelqu'un en employant, quand il convient,* **la forme familière:**

1. s'il doit aller au jardin cueillir des fleurs. **2.** s'il veut bien fermer la porte. **3.** s'il veut bien vous aider. **4.** quelles fleurs Mme Deschamps veut cueillir. **5.** s'il sait s'occuper d'un jardin. **6.** s'il vaut mieux arroser les légumes quand il fait chaud ou quand il fait frais.

IV. Exercices d'application.

A. *Répétez les phrases suivantes en remplaçant* **Je vais** *par* **Il faut que j'aille:**

1. Je vais au jardin cueillir des fleurs. **2.** Je vais à la gare. **3.** Je vais au restaurant. **4.** Je vais en ville faire des courses. **5.** Je vais voir ce film. **6.** Je vais à la banque toucher un chèque. **7.** Je vais au bureau de tabac chercher un journal. **8.** Je vais mettre une lettre à la poste (*mail a letter*). **9.** Je vais à la maison pour le week-end.

B. *Répétez les phrases suivantes en remplaçant* **ne . . . pas** *par* **ne . . . guère:**

1. Il n'a pas plu cette année. **2.** Je n'ai pas travaillé aujourd'hui. **3.** Je n'ai pas dormi la nuit dernière. **4.** Il n'a pas neigé cet hiver. **5.** Je ne me suis pas amusé cet hiver. **6.** Je ne me suis pas reposé pendant le week-end. **7.** Je n'ai pas l'habitude d'aller à bicyclette. **8.** Je n'ai pas le temps de m'occuper de mon jardin.

V. Dictée d'après la Conversation 34, pp. 286-287.

VI. Conversation.

Un ami vient vous voir et vous l'invitez à voir votre jardin. Il y a dans votre jardin des choux (*m.*), des tomates (*f.*), des asperges (*f.*) (*asparagus*), des pommes de terre (*f.*), de la laitue (*lettuce*), des pivoines (*f.*) (*peonies*), des marguerites (*f.*) (*daisies*), des violettes (*f.*) et des pensées (*f.*) (*pansies*).

SAINTS BRETONS

A la campagne

Ce matin, Jean et Roger ont quitté Paris de bonne heure pour aller voir des cousins de Roger, les Deschamps, qui habitent dans un petit village près de Fontainebleau. Ils ont pris le train jusqu'à Melun. Là, ils ont descendu leurs bicyclettes du fourgon, pour faire à bicyclette le reste du voyage. A dix heures du matin, ils sont en train de pédaler le long d'une jolie route, heureux de l'ombre des arbres qui la bordent, car la journée est chaude et le soleil haut dans le ciel.

—Voilà une auberge qui a l'air sympathique, dit Jean à Roger au moment où ils traversent la place d'un village. Si nous nous arrêtions pour prendre quelque chose, un bon verre de bière bien fraîche par exemple? Je meurs de soif et j'ai un peu mal aux jambes, car je n'ai pas l'habitude d'aller à bicyclette.

—Ne voulez-vous pas attendre jusqu'à ce que nous soyons arrivés chez mes cousins? répond Roger. Nous

serons à leur ferme dans un quart d'heure. Si vous buvez maintenant un verre de bière, vous aurez encore plus chaud qu'auparavant et vos jambes vous abandonneront tout à fait.

—Eh bien, répond Jean avec résignation, j'attendrai jusque-là.

Un quart d'heure plus tard, nos deux amis arrivent à la grille de la ferme. Mme Deschamps, qui les voit arriver, vient à leur rencontre. Les présentations faites, elle conduit les visiteurs dans la vaste cuisine, qui depuis les temps les plus anciens est la salle familiale des fermes françaises. Jean remarque la haute cheminée et les vieux ustensiles de cuivre accrochés au mur. On les distingue à peine dans la demi-obscurité, car Mme Deschamps tient les volets fermés à cause de la chaleur.

—Vous allez prendre quelque chose, n'est-ce pas? leur dit-elle. Par cette chaleur, vous devez en avoir besoin.

Jean boit enfin son verre de bière.

—Il faut que j'aille au jardin chercher des légumes et cueillir des fleurs, dit Mme Deschamps aux jeunes gens lorsqu'ils sont un peu reposés de leur fatigue. Voulez-vous m'accompagner?

Comme beaucoup de jardins en France, le jardin des Deschamps est entouré de murs et ces murs sont couverts d'espaliers d'où pendent des poires magnifiques. Le jardin lui-même est divisé en carrés séparés les uns des autres par de petites allées.

—Cette symétrie, ces arbres taillés en espalier, ces fleurs, ces allées de sable, tout cela me rappelle un peu Versailles, dit en riant Jean à Mme Deschamps.

—Après tout, pourquoi ne pas joindre l'utile à l'agréable? répond-elle.

On se partage le travail. Tandis que Mme Deschamps cueille des roses et des œillets, Jean cueille des haricots verts et Roger choisit quelques pieds de salade.

Puis tout le monde revient à la maison attendre le retour de M. Deschamps. Il est avec son tracteur dans un champ près du village et il a promis de revenir à midi et quart ou à midi et demi, au plus tard.

QUESTIONS

1. Qui sont les Deschamps? **2.** Comment Jean et Roger sont-ils allés à Melun? **3.** Comment font-ils le reste du voyage? **4.** Qu'est-ce que Jean propose à Roger de faire au moment où ils traversent la place d'un village? **5.** Pourquoi voudrait-il boire un verre de bière bien fraîche? **6.** Pourquoi Roger lui dit-il d'attendre jusqu'à ce qu'ils soient arrivés à la ferme? **7.** Qui vient à leur rencontre? **8.** Où Mme Deschamps conduit-elle ses visiteurs? **9.** Pourquoi tient-elle fermés les volets de la cuisine? **10.** Pourquoi faut-il que Mme Deschamps aille à son jardin? **11.** Qu'est-ce qu'il y a sur les murs du jardin? **12.** A quelle heure M. Deschamps a-t-il promis de revenir?

The Subjunctive

95. *Present subjunctive of* **être** *and* **avoir,** *and of regular verbs.*

A. être:

que je sois, que tu sois, qu'il soit, que nous soyons, que vous soyez, qu'ils soient.

B. avoir:

que j'aie, que tu aies, qu'il ait, que nous ayons, que vous ayez, qu'ils aient.

C. Regular verbs:

donner: que je donne, que tu donnes, qu'il donne, que nous donnions, que vous donniez, qu'ils donnent.

finir: que je finisse, que tu finisses, qu'il finisse, que nous finissions, que vous finissiez, qu'ils finissent.

répondre: que je réponde, que tu répondes, qu'il réponde, que nous répondions, que vous répondiez, qu'ils répondent.

(1) The endings of the present subjunctive of all verbs (except **être** and **avoir**) are: **-e, -es, -e, -ions, -iez, -ent.**

(2) The stem of the present subjunctive of regular verbs is the same as that of the first person plural of the present indicative. EX.: PRES. IND. **Nous finissons.** PRES. SUBJ. **je finisse,** etc.

96. *Commonest use of the present subjunctive.*

A. —Il faut que **je donne** mon adresse à la concierge.	I must give my address to the concierge.
—Il faut qui **je finisse** mon travail.	I must finish my work.
—Il faut que **je réponde** à cette lettre.	I must answer this letter.
—Il faut que **je sois** à la gare à 4 heures.	I must be at the station at 4:00 o'clock.
—Il vaut mieux que **vous finissiez** votre travail.	It's better for you to finish (*that you finish*) your work.

The subjunctive is used in subordinate clauses introduced by **que** and depending upon **falloir (il faut)** and **valoir mieux (il vaut mieux).** Note, however, that if the dependent verb has no expressed subject, the infinitive is normally used instead of the subjunctive. Ex.:

—Il faut **travailler** d'avantage. (*inf.*)	It is necessary to work harder.
—Il faut que **vous travailliez** d'avantage. (*subj.*)	You must work harder.
—Il vaut mieux **partir** tout de suite. (*inf.*)	It is better to leave right away.
—Il vaut mieux que **vous partiez** tout de suite. (*subj.*)	It is better for you to leave (*that you leave*) right away.

B.

—Voulez-vous que nous **vous aidions?**	Do you want us to help you?
—J'aime mieux qu'**il attende** jusqu'à ce soir.	I prefer that he wait until this evening.
—Je regrette que **vous ayez** mal à la tête.	I'm sorry you have a headache.
—J'ai peur que **vous** ne **soyez** un peu déçu.	I'm afraid you will be a little disappointed.
—Je doute qu'**il vienne** ce soir.	I doubt that he will come this evening.
—Je suis content que **vous ayez répondu** à cette lettre.	I am glad you have answered that letter.
—Je suis content que **vous soyez arrivé.**	I am glad you have arrived.

The subjunctive is used in subordinate clauses introduced by **que** and depending upon certain verbs that express *wishing*, *wanting*, *desiring; joy, sorrow, happiness, regret, doubt, fear;* etc. Among the verbs of this group that take the subjunctive, the following are the ones most frequently used: **vouloir, désirer, souhaiter** (*to wish*)*;* **aimer mieux, préférer; douter** (*to doubt*), **craindre** (*to fear*)*;* **être content, être heureux, regretter, avoir peur,** etc. In the above examples, the subject of the verb of the dependent clause is different from that of the main clause. Note that when the main verb and the subordinate verb have the same subject, the infinitive is used instead of the subjunctive.

(*Subjunctive*):	
—**Je** regrette que **vous** soyez en retard.	*I'm* sorry that *you* are late.
(*Infinitive*):	
—Je regrette d'être en retard.	*I'm* sorry that *I'm* late.
	I'm sorry to be late.
(*Subjunctive*):	
—**J'**aime mieux qu'**il** attende jusqu'à ce soir.	*I* prefer that *he* wait until this evening.
(*Infinitive*):	
—Il aime mieux attendre jusqu'à ce soir.	He prefers to wait until this evening.

C. —Croyez-vous qu'il **y ait** de la place dans l'autobus? — Do you think *there will be* room in the bus?

—Je ne pense pas que **vous soyez** en retard. — I don't think *you'll be* late.

Croire, penser, and **espérer** do *not* always take the subjunctive. For these verbs and others that express *belief* (**être sûr, il me semble,** etc.), it is necessary to observe:

(1) the indicative is always used in clauses depending upon affirmative forms: (**Je crois qu'il y aura de la place. J'espère que vous viendrez**);

(2) either the indicative or the subjunctive may be used in clauses depending upon interrogative or negative forms. In such clauses, the subjunctive is supposed to express a greater degree of uncertainty. However, the difference between **Croyez-vous qu'il y aura de la place?** (*indicative*) and **Croyez-vous qu'il y ait de la place?** (*subjunctive*) is scarcely perceptible.

In conversation most people simply use the indicative after all forms of **croire, penser** and **espérer.**

D. —Bien qu'**elle soit classée** monument historique . . . — Although *it is classed* as a historical monument . . .

—Je vais attendre jusqu'à ce qu'**il ait répondu** à ma lettre. — I am going to wait until *he has answered* my letter.

The subjunctive must be used in clauses introduced by certain conjunctive expressions of which the following are the most frequently used: **à moins que,** *unless;* **avant que,** *before;* **bien que,** *although;* **jusqu'à ce que,** *until;* **pour que,** *so that;* **de peur que,** *for fear that;* etc.

E. —C'est le meilleur roman que **j'aie lu.** — That's the best novel *I've read.*

—Henri est le seul étudiant qui **soit** absent. — Henry is the only student who *is* absent.

The subjunctive is used in relative clauses whose antecedent is modified by a superlative or by the word **seul.**

97. *Present subjunctive of the commonest irregular verbs.*

—Il faut que **j'aille** à un de mes champs. — I must *go* to one of my fields.

—Je ne veux pas que les poules **puissent** entrer. — I don't want the hens *to be able* to get in.

—Il vaut mieux attendre jusqu'à ce qu'**il fasse** moins chaud. — It's better to wait until *it is* cooler.

—Je ne crois pas qu'**il sache** mon adresse. — I don't think *he knows* my address.

A. The commonest irregular verbs whose present subjunctive has two stems are:

aller: aille, ailles, aille, **allions, alliez,** aillent.
boire: boive, boives, boive, **buvions, buviez,** boivent
croire: croie, croies, croie, **croyions, croyiez,** croient
envoyer: envoie, envoies, envoie, **envoyions, envoyiez,** envoient
prendre: prenne, prennes, prenne, **prenions, preniez,** prennent
recevoir: reçoive, reçoives, reçoive, **recevions, receviez,** reçoivent
tenir: tienne, tiennes, tienne, **tenions, teniez,** tiennent
venir: vienne, viennes, vienne, **venions, veniez,** viennent
voir: voie, voies, voie, **voyions, voyiez,** voient
vouloir: veuille, veuilles, veuille, **voulions, vouliez,** veuillent

B. The commonest irregular verbs whose present subjunctive has a single irregular stem:

faire: fasse, fasses, fasse, fassions, fassiez, fassent
pouvoir: puisse, etc.
savoir: sache, etc.

C. The commonest irregular verbs whose present subjunctive follows the pattern of regular verbs and can be found from the first person plural of the present indicative (see paragraph 95) are: **connaître, dire, dormir, écrire, lire, mettre, partir, plaindre, sentir, servir, sortir, suivre.**

98. *Formation and use of the* **passé composé*** *of the subjunctive.*

A. Formation:

The **passé composé** of the subjunctive is composed of the present subjunctive of the auxiliary verb and the past participle of the verb. Ex.:

être: j'aie été, tu aies été, il ait été, nous ayons été, vous ayez été, ils aient été.
avoir: j'aie eu, tu aies eu, etc.
donner: j'aie donné, tu aies donné, etc.
arriver: je sois arrivé(e), tu sois arrivé(e), etc.

* As the imperfect and pluperfect subjunctive are purely literary tenses, they will appear only in the verb tables in the Appendix.

B. Use:

Generally speaking, the **passé composé** of the subjunctive is used like the present subjunctive except that it expresses actions that have already taken place. Ex.:

Je regrette que l'accident **ait eu** lieu. I am sorry the accident *took* place.
Nous sommes contents qu'il **soit arrivé.** We are glad he *has arrived.*
Je ne crois pas que vous **ayez lu** ce roman. I don't think you *have read* this novel.

I. *Dites en français chacune des phrases suivantes, en employant* **il faut que:**

1. Je donne mon adresse à la concierge. **2.** Vous donnez votre adresse à la concierge. **3.** Je finis mon travail à onze heures. **4.** Nous finissons notre travail à minuit. **5.** Je réponds à la lettre de mon cousin. **6.** Vous répondez à la lettre de votre cousin. **7.** Je suis toujours à l'heure. **8.** Il est toujours à l'heure. **9.** Nous sommes toujours à l'heure. **10.** Vous vous couchez de bonne heure. **11.** Je vais à la bibliothèque. **12.** Je vais chercher un journal. **13.** Je fais mon travail. **14.** Nous faisons notre travail. **15.** J'écris à ma mère. **16.** Je prends le train à quatre heures. **17.** Il part aujourd'hui. **18.** Je mets la lettre à la poste. **19.** Vous venez me voir. **20.** Nous savons l'heure de son arrivée. **21.** Vous dites ce que vous pensez. **22.** Il ouvre la fenêtre.

II. *Dites en français chacune des phrases suivantes, en employant l'expression indiquée:*

A. Il vaut mieux que:

1. Nous parlons français. **2.** Vous finissez votre travail avant de vous coucher. **3.** Nous attendons l'arrivée du train. **4.** Vous buvez un verre d'eau fraîche. **5.** Il prend une tasse de café. **6.** Il se sert de mon auto. **7.** Vous dormez jusqu'à huit heures. **8.** Je suis les conseils de mes parents. **9.** Nous sommes toujours à l'heure.

B. Voulez-vous que:

1. Nous arrosons le jardin. **2.** Nous vous envoyons la facture. **3.** Nous rentrons de bonne heure. **4.** Nous prenons nos billets aujourd'hui. **5.** Je viendrai vous voir dimanche. **6.** Je tiens la porte ouverte.

C. J'aime mieux que:

1. Vous parlez français. **2.** Nous ne parlons pas anglais. **3.** Vous choisissez votre écharpe. **4.** Vous commencez tout de suite. **5.** Vous n'êtes pas en retard.

D. J'ai peur que . . . ne (or **ne . . . pas**):

1. Vous serez un peu déçu. **2.** Il n'y aura pas de place dans l'autobus. **3.** Il est malade. **4.** Il fera froid demain. **5.** Il boit trop de café. **6.** Il ne croit pas ce que je lui dis. **7.** Nous avons suivi la mauvaise route. **8.** Nous sommes en retard.

E. Je regrette que:

1. Vous avez mal à la tête. **2.** Votre mère est malade. **3.** Vous n'êtes pas venu me voir. **4.** Il ne m'a pas écrit. **5.** L'accident a eu lieu. **6.** Vous avez répondu à cette lettre. **7.** Il n'a pas pu s'arrêter à temps.

F. Je ne crois pas que:

1. Il peut aller en ville. **2.** Il a lu tous les romans de Balzac. **3.** Il est allé voir le Panthéon. **4.** Il sait le grec (*Greek*). **5.** Vous pouvez finir aujourd'hui. **6.** Il recevra ma dépêche (*telegram*) avant six heures.

III. *Répétez les phrases suivantes en remplaçant l'infinitif par* **qu'il** *et le subjonctif:*

EX.:—Je regrette d'être en retard.
—Je regrette qu'il soit en retard.

1. Il faut être toujours à l'heure. **2.** Il faut venir me voir. **3.** Il vaut mieux aller à l'hôpital. **4.** Je veux savoir ce qui se passe. **5.** J'aime mieux boire du lait. **6.** J'ai peur de ne pas avoir le temps. **7.** Je ne crois pas pouvoir finir aujourd'hui. **8.** Je suis content d'être arrivé. **9.** Je suis content d'avoir vu Versailles. **10.** Je ne veux pas faire cela.

IV. *Dites en français:*

1. She's (**C'est**) the prettiest girl I know. **2.** That's (**C'est**) the most beautiful château I have seen. **3.** The most interesting novel I have read is *Les Trois Mousquetaires*. **4.** It's the best novel I have read. **5.** It's the only French novel I know. **6.** That's the only advice I can give you.

V. Révision du dialogue, pp. 276-277.

1. Où Jean a-t-il vu des champignons? **2.** Est-ce que Roger connaît les champignons? **3.** Est-ce que les mauvais champignons ressemblent aux bons? **4.** Est-ce qu'il vaut mieux laisser ceux dont on n'est pas sûr? **5.** Est-ce qu'on risque de s'empoisonner si on mange des champignons des bois? **6.** Que feriez-vous si vous trouviez des fraises des bois? **7.** Est-ce que vous cueillez des fleurs sauvages (*wild*) quand vous en trouvez dans les bois? **8.** En quelle saison trouve-t-on le plus de fleurs sauvages?

VI. Thème d'imitation:

Mrs. Deschamps said to Roger and John "Do you want to come to the garden with me? I have to pick some green beans. It is already six o'clock. If I do not hurry, dinner will never be ready by[1] seven o'clock and my husband[2] will not be happy." Roger opened the garden gate. "What a[3] fine garden (you have), cousin! How do you find the time to take care of it, with all the work of the harvest?" "I get up every morning at five o'clock to water my garden . . . Be careful to close the gate behind you, Roger. If you leave it open, the hens get into the garden. Look at that one over there! She is busy[4] eating my salad greens! Let's chase her out.[5] I am no longer young and I do not like to chase hens." Roger shooed the hen out. Then he began[6] to pick green beans so that[7] dinner would be ready on time and so that Mr. Deschamps would be happy.

[1] i.e. at seven o'clock. [2] *husband*, **le mari.** [3] After **quel** the noun is used without an article. [4] **en train de.** [5] *chase*, *chase out*, *shoo out*, **chasser.** [6] **se mettre à.** [7] **pour que.**

PLEUMEUR-BODOU (EN BRETAGNE): STATI
DE TÉLÉCOMMUNICATIONS SPATIALES

Une partie de pêche

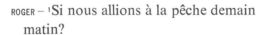

ROGER – 1Si nous allions à la pêche demain matin?

ROGER – 1*How about going fishing tomorrow morning?*

JEAN – 2A quoi bon? Nous n'attraperons rien.

JOHN – 2*What's the use? We won't catch anything.*

ROGER – 3Je n'y vais pas pour attraper quelque chose.

ROGER – 3*I don't go to catch something.*

JEAN – 4Pourquoi y allez-vous alors?

JOHN – 4*Why do you go then?*

ROGER – 5J'y vais parce que j'aime être 6au bord de l'eau, à l'ombre des grands arbres. 7Êtes-vous jamais allé à la pêche le matin de bonne heure?

ROGER – 5*I go because I like to be* 6*beside the water, in the shade of the tall trees.* 7*Have you ever gone fishing in the early morning?*

JEAN – 8Oui, j'y suis allé quelquefois.

JOHN – 8*Yes, I've gone occasionally.*

ROGER – 9N'aimez-vous pas être en plein air?

ROGER – 9*Don't you like to be in the open air?*

JEAN – 10Si. Mais je ne prends jamais de poissons.

JOHN – 10*Yes. But I never catch any fish.*

ROGER – 11Moi non plus, mais cela ne fait rien. 12Si l'on en prend, tant mieux, 13si l'on n'en prend pas, tant pis.

ROGER – 11*Neither do I, but that makes no difference.* 12*If you catch some, so much the better,* 13*if you don't catch any, too bad* (*so much the worse*).

JEAN – 14Où voulez-vous aller?

JOHN – 14*Where shall we go?*

ROGER – 15Je connais un endroit sous le vieux pont, 16de l'autre côté de la rivière, 17où il y a des poissons gros comme ça!

ROGER – 15*I know a place under the old bridge* 16*on the other side of the creek,* 17*where there are fish as large as that!* (gesture)

JEAN – [18]Ceux que vous manquez?

ROGER – [19]Ne vous moquez pas de moi . . .

JEAN – [20]A quelle heure voulez-vous partir?

ROGER – [21]De bonne heure. Il faudra que nous nous levions à 4 heures du matin.

JEAN – [22]Mais il ne fait pas encore jour à cette heure-là!

ROGER – [23]Justement! Nous verrons le soleil se lever sur la rivière. [24]De quoi vous plaignez-vous?

JEAN – [25]Je ne me plains pas. [26]Mais j'aime mieux dormir dans mon lit que dormir sur l'herbe — si les poissons ne mordent pas.

JOHN – [18]*The ones which get away?*

ROGER – [19]*Do not make fun of me . . .*

JOHN – [20]*What time do you want to leave?*

ROGER – [21]*Early. We'll have to get up at 4:00 A.M.*

JOHN – [22]*But it isn't yet daylight at that time!*

ROGER – [23]*Precisely! We shall see the sun rise over the creek.* [24]*What are you complaining about?*

JOHN – [25]*I'm not complaining.* [26]*But I'd rather sleep in my bed than sleep on the grass — if the fish don't bite.*

I. Substitutions. *Répétez les phrases suivantes en substituant les mots indiqués:*

1. Je n'y vais pas pour attraper quelque chose.

   prendre des poissons / voir le soleil se lever / manquer des poissons / manquer les gros poissons

2. J'y vais parce que j'aime être au bord de l'eau.

   à l'ombre des grands arbres / en plein air / à la campagne / au bord de la rivière

3. Si l'on en prend, tant mieux, si l'on n'en prend pas, tant pis.

   attrape / voit / a pour le dîner / rapporte à la maison

4. Il faudra que nous nous levions de bonne heure.

   nous nous couchions / nous quittions la maison / nous nous mettions en route / nous nous mettions à pêcher

5. Si les poissons ne mordent pas, nous pourrons dormir sur l'herbe.

   faire un somme (*take a nap*) / nager (*swim*) dans la rivière / regarder couler (*to flow*) l'eau / prendre un bain de soleil

6. J'aime regarder couler l'eau.

   entendre couler l'eau / écouter couler l'eau / entendre chanter les oiseaux / écouter chanter les oiseaux

II. *Répondez en français:*

1. Où Roger propose-t-il d'aller demain matin? **2.** Est-ce que Jean espère attraper quelque chose? **3.** Est-ce que Roger va à la pêche pour attraper quelque chose? **4.** Alors, pourquoi y va-t-il? **5.** Est-ce que Jean est jamais allé à la pêche le matin de bonne heure? **6.** A-t-il l'habitude de prendre beaucoup de poissons? **7.** Et Roger? **8.** Est-ce que Roger est content quand il prend des poissons? **9.** Est-ce qu'il est mécontent (*unhappy*) quand il n'en prend pas? **10.** Est-ce qu'il connaît un endroit où il y a de gros poissons? **11.** Où se trouve cet endroit? **12.** A quelle heure faudra-t-il qu'ils se lèvent? **13.** Est-ce qu'il fait déjà jour à cette heure-là? **14.** Pourquoi Roger veut-il partir de si bonne heure? **15.** Que fera Jean si les poissons ne mordent pas? **16.** Croyez-vous toujours ce que disent les pêcheurs?

III. *Demandez à quelqu'un:*

1. s'il aime voir le soleil se lever sur la rivière. **2.** s'il aime voir le soleil se coucher sur le lac. **3.** s'il a jamais attrapé des poissons. **4.** s'il connaît un endroit où il y a de gros poissons. **5.** s'il croit tout ce que disent les pêcheurs. **6.** à quelle heure il part quand il va à la pêche. **7.** de quoi il se plaint. **8.** s'il fait jour à quatre heures du matin. **9.** à quelle heure il fait jour au mois de mai. **10.** s'il vaut mieux pêcher le matin ou le soir.

IV. *Répétez chacune des phrases suivantes en remplaçant les mots en italique par l'adverbe* **y:**

EX.:—Êtes-vous allé *à la pêche?*
—Y êtes-vous allé?

1. Êtes-vous allé *à la pêche* ce matin? **2.** Allez-vous souvent *à la pêche?* **3.** Êtes-vous jamais allé *à la pêche?* **4.** N'êtes-vous jamais allé *à la pêche?* **5.** Voulez-vous aller *en ville* cet après-midi? **6.** Voulez-vous que j'aille *en ville* avec vous? **7.** Croyez-vous que les Brown soient allés *en Angleterre* cet été? **8.** Sont-ils jamais allés *au bord de la mer?* **9.** Ne sont-ils pas allés *au bord de la mer?* **10.** Ne sont-ils jamais allés *au bord de la mer?* **11.** Allons *à la pêche.* **12.** N'allez pas *au cinéma* ce soir.

V. *Répondez négativement en employant* **ne . . . jamais:**

1. Avez-vous jamais vu Versailles? **2.** Avez-vous jamais lu *Les Trois Mousquetaires?* **3.** Avez-vous jamais été à l'hôpital? **4.** Avez-vous jamais entendu parler des vitraux de Chartres? **5.** Êtes-vous jamais allé à Marseille? **6.** Vous êtes-vous jamais occupé d'un jardin?

VI. *Dites en français:*

1. That makes no difference. **2.** What's the use? **3.** It's too bad. **4.** You are lucky. **5.** Don't make fun of me. **6.** The ones that get away (that you miss)? **7.** A fish *that big* got away (I missed a fish *that big.*) **8.** I never catch any fish. **9.** Neither do I. **10.** Neither does he. **11.** Neither do they. **12.** Precisely.

VII. Dictée d'après la Conversation 35, p. 291.

VIII. Conversation.

Vous parlez d'une partie de pêche que vous avez faite ou d'un week-end que vous avez passé à la campagne.

Arrivée à la gare de Lyon

MARIE – [1]Bonjour, Jean. Bonjour, Roger. Je suis heureuse que vous soyez de retour.

JEAN – [2]Nous aussi, nous sommes enchantés de vous revoir, Marie. [3]Vous nous avez manqué beaucoup, vous savez.

MARIE – [4]Flatteur!

ROGER – [5]C'est gentil de ta part d'être venue nous attendre à la gare.

MARIE – [6]Je me demande si vous vous rendez compte que j'ai fait pour vous un grand sacrifice. [7]Je devais jouer au tennis ce matin. [8]Mais quand j'ai appris que vous deviez revenir aujourd'hui, j'ai décidé de venir vous attendre ici.

ROGER – [9]Quand as-tu reçu ma dépêche?

MARIE – [10]Il y a à peu près une heure. [11]Mais tu aurais dû me dire l'heure exacte de ton arrivée.

ROGER – [12]Nous ne la savions pas nous-mêmes. [13]Nous n'étions pas sûrs d'attraper le train de huit heures et demie.

MARIE – [14]Jean, votre concierge m'a téléphoné qu'un câble pour vous est arrivé ce matin.

MARY – [1]*Hello, John. Hello, Roger. I am glad that you are back.*

JOHN – [2]*We are delighted to see you again too, Mary.* [3]*We have missed you very much, you know.*

MARY – [4]*Flatterer!*

ROGER – [5]*It's nice of you to have come to meet us at the station.*

MARY – [6]*I wonder if you realize that I made a great sacrifice for you.* [7]*I was to play tennis this morning.* [8]*But when I found out that you were to come back today, I decided to come to meet you here.*

ROGER – [9]*When did you get my wire?*

MARY – [10]*About an hour ago.* [11]*But you should have told me the exact time of your arrival.*

ROGER – [12]*We didn't know it ourselves.* [13]*We were not sure of catching the eight-thirty train.*

MARY – [14]*John, your concierge telephoned me that a cable came for you this morning.*

LA TOUR EIFFEL

JEAN – [15]Oh! Je sais ce que c'est. [16]Hélène Frazer doit arriver ces jours-ci. [17]Elle m'indique sans doute le jour de son arrivée.

MARIE – [18]Tiens, tiens! Qui est cette Hélène?

JEAN – [19]C'est une jeune Américaine de mes amies qui est actuellement à Londres. [20]Elle m'a demandé de lui servir de guide à Paris.

JOHN – [15]*Oh! I know what it is.* [16]*Helen Frazer is to arrive some time soon.* [17]*She's doubtless telling me the date of her arrival.*

MARY – [18]*Aha! Who is this Helen?*

JOHN – [19]*She is a friend of mine, an American girl who is in London at present.* [20]*She asked me to act as guide for her in Paris.*

I. Substitutions. *Répétez les phrases suivantes en substituant les mots indiqués:*

1. Marie m'a manqué beaucoup. (*I missed Marie very much.*)
   Elle / Il / Mon chien (*dog*) / Ma famille
2. J'ai manqué à ma mère. (*My mother missed me.*)
   à mon père / à ma famille / à mes amis / à mon chien
3. C'est gentil de votre part d'être venu(e) nous attendre à la gare.
   de nous inviter à dîner / de nous avoir invités à dîner / de m'avoir envoyé des fleurs / d'être venu(e) nous chercher
4. C'est gentil de sa part (*of him, of her*) de venir nous voir.
   de nous prêter son appartement / de nous offrir ce tableau / de vous donner sa place / de nous accompagner
5. Je sais ce que c'est.
   Je me demande / Savez-vous / Ne savez-vous pas / Je ne sais pas / Ils ne savent pas
6. C'est une jeune Américaine de mes amies.
   une Américaine / une / une jeune fille / une étudiante

II. *Répondez en français à chacune des questions suivantes:*

1. A quelle gare Jean et Roger arrivent-ils? **2.** Qui est venu les attendre à la gare? **3.** Comment Marie savait-elle qu'ils allaient arriver ce matin-là? **4.** Savait-elle l'heure exacte de leur arrivée? **5.** Quand a-t-elle reçu leur dépêche? **6.** Pourquoi Jean et Roger n'ont-ils pas indiqué l'heure exacte de leur arrivée? **7.** Qu'est-ce que Marie devait faire ce matin-là? **8.** Qu'est-ce qu'elle a décidé de faire quand elle a reçu leur télégramme? **9.** Est-ce que Jean et Roger se rendent compte du sacrifice qu'elle a fait? **10.** Étaient-ils sûrs d'attraper le train de huit heures et demie? **11.** Comment Marie a-t-elle appris qu'il y a un câble pour Jean? **12.** Quand ce câble est-il arrivé? **13.** Est-ce que Jean sait ce que c'est? **14.** Quand Hélène doit-elle arriver? **15.** Qu'est-ce que dit Marie quand elle entend parler d'Hélène? **16.** D'où vient Hélène? **17.** Qu'est-ce qu'elle a demandé à Jean? **18.** Où est-elle actuellement?

III. Exercices d'application.

A. *Répétez en remplaçant la forme négative du passé composé par* **Je devais** (I was supposed to) *et l'infinitif:*

EX.:—Je n'ai pas joué au tennis ce matin.
—Je devais jouer au tennis ce matin.

1. Je ne suis pas allé(e) au bal. **2.** Je n'ai pas travaillé hier soir. **3.** Je n'ai pas vu ce film. **4.** Je ne suis pas rentré(e) à midi. **5.** Je ne me suis pas levé(e) de bonne heure. **6.** Je ne suis pas parti(e) hier soir.

B. *Répétez en remplaçant la forme négative du passé composé par* **Vous auriez dû** (You should have) *et l'infinitif:*

EX.:—Vous ne m'avez pas dit l'heure exacte de votre arrivée.
—Vous auriez dû me dire l'heure exacte de votre arrivée.

1. Vous ne m'avez pas donné votre adresse. **2.** Vous ne m'avez pas téléphoné. **3.** Vous ne m'avez pas prévenu. **4.** Vous n'avez pas écrit à votre mère. **5.** Vous ne m'avez pas indiqué le jour de votre arrivée. **6.** Vous n'êtes pas parti hier soir.

IV. *Dites en français en employant* **se rendre compte (que)**:

1. I wonder if you realize that I made a great sacrifice for you. **2.** Do you realize that the church is very old? **3.** Do you realize that the stained-glass windows are very beautiful? **4.** Do you realize that I am very tired? **5.** Do you realize that I was supposed to play tennis this morning? **6.** Do you realize that it is midnight?

V. Dictée d'après la Conversation 36, pp. 306-307.

VI. Narration.

Racontez ce que vous avez fait au cours d'un séjour dans une ferme. Dans cette ferme il y avait des vaches (*f.*) (*cows*), des cochons (*m.*) (*pigs*), des bœufs (*m.*) (*oxen*), des chèvres (*goats*), des moutons (*m.*) (*sheep*), des oies (*f.*) (*geese*), un âne (*a donkey*). Dans les champs, dont le sol (*soil*) était très fertile, il y avait du blé (*wheat*), du foin (*hay*), de l'avoine (*f.*) (*oats*), des betteraves à sucre (*sugar beets*), etc.

Irregular Verbs in *-oir*

99. *Remarks about verbs in* **-oir.**

The characteristics of this group are that they have two stems in the present indicative (**pouvoir: peu-pouv-**), an irregular future (**je pourrai**), and a past participle in **-u** (except **s'asseoir**).

As **devoir** corresponds to English *must, should, ought, have to, was to, should have, ought to have*, and so on(!), it is necessary to study with the greatest attention the use and meaning of the different tenses of this verb. **Pouvoir** and **vouloir** are also very tricky for English speaking students.

100. Devoir.*

A. Présent:

The present tense is used to express:

(1) probability:

—**Il doit** être chez lui en ce moment.	*He must* be (*probably is*) at home now.
—**Il doit** y avoir un train vers 8 heures.	*There must* be a train around 8:00.

(2) an action that one expects to fulfill:

—Quand est-ce que **vous devez** être de retour?	When *are you supposed to* be back?
—**Je dois** être de retour demain.	*I am supposed to* be back tomorrow.

(3) necessity:

—**Vous devez** changer de train à Épernay.	*You have to* change trains at Epernay.

B. Imparfait:

The imperfect is most commonly used to express an action that was expected to take place but which did not necessarily take place:

—**Je devais** jouer au tennis ce matin, mais j'ai décidé de venir vous attendre à la gare.	*I was to* (*was supposed to*) play tennis this morning but I decided to come to meet you at the station.

* **Devoir** is also used as a transitive verb meaning *to owe*. Ex.: Vous me devez mille francs.

C. Passé composé:

The **passé composé** is most commonly used to express probability (past):

—Où est votre livre? — Where is your book?
—Je ne sais pas. **J'ai dû** le laisser dans l'autobus. — I don't know. *I must have* left it in the bus.

D. Conditionnel:

(1) The conditional is used to express the speaker's judgment as to the desirability or propriety of a present or future action:

—**Vous devriez** travailler davantage. — *You should* work harder.
—**Vous ne devriez pas** faire cela. — *You ought not* to do that.

(2) The conditional perfect is used to express the desirability or propriety of a past action:

—**Vous n'auriez pas dû** faire cela. — *You ought not to have* done that.
—**Vous auriez dû** me dire l'heure exacte de votre arrivée. — *You should have* told me the exact time of your arrival.

PRÉSENT: Je dois, tu dois, il doit, nous devons, vous devez, ils doivent.
IMPARFAIT: Je devais, etc. PASSÉ COMPOSÉ: J'ai dû, etc. FUTUR: Je devrai, etc.
CONDITIONNEL: je devrais, etc.

101. Pouvoir (*to be able*).

PRÉSENT: *may, can*
—Est-ce que **je peux** voir la chambre? — *May I* see the room? OR *Can I* see the room?
—Oui, **vous pouvez** la voir. — Yes, *you may* see it.

PASSÉ COMPOSÉ: *could, was able to*
—**Je n'ai pas pu** trouver une place dans l'autobus. — *I couldn't* find a seat in the bus.

FUTUR: *may, can*
—**Vous pourrez** revenir dans huit jours. — *You may* come back in a week.

CONDITIONNEL: *could, might*
—**Vous pourriez** changer de rôle avec un millionnaire. — *You could* change places with a millionaire.

PRÉSENT: Je peux, tu peux, il peut, nous pouvons, vous pouvez, ils peuvent. *I may; I can; I am able.*

IMPARFAIT: Je pouvais, etc. *I was able, I could.* PASSÉ COMPOSÉ: J'ai pu, etc. *I have been able, I could.*

FUTUR: Je pourrai, etc. *I shall be able, I can, I may.* CONDITIONNEL: Je pourrais, etc. *I could, I might.*

102. Vouloir (*to want*).

PRÉSENT: *want*

—**Voulez-vous** essayer ce chapeau?	*Do you want* to try on this hat?
—Roger **veut** aller à la pêche.	Roger *wants* to go fishing.
—Jean **ne veut pas** y aller.	John *refuses* to go.

IMPARFAIT: *wanted*

—**Je voulais** faire une promenade hier, mais il a plu toute la journée.	*I wanted to* (but didn't necessarily act on my desire) take a walk, but it rained all day.

PASSÉ COMPOSÉ: *wanted, decided*

—**J'ai voulu** profiter du beau temps.	*I decided* to take advantage of the fine weather (and did so).
—Marie **n'a pas voulu** sortir.	Marie *refused* to go out.

CONDITIONNEL: *would like, want*

—**Je voudrais** un billet aller et retour pour Reims.	*I would like* a round-trip ticket to Rheims.
—**Je voudrais** partir le plus tôt possible.	*I would like* to leave as soon as possible.

PRÉSENT: Je veux, tu veux, il veut, nous voulons, vous voulez, ils veulent. *I want; I will* (i.e. *I insist*).

IMPARFAIT: Je voulais, etc. *I wanted, I intended.* PASSÉ COMPOSÉ: J'ai voulu, etc. *I wanted, I decided.*

FUTUR: Je voudrai, etc. *I shall want*, etc. CONDITIONNEL: Je voudrais, etc. *I would like, I want.*

103. *Expressions with* vouloir.

A. vouloir bien (*to be willing*):

—**Je veux bien.**	*I am willing.*
—**Voulez-vous bien** payer la caissière?	*Will you please* pay the cashier?
—**Voulez-vous bien** monter?	*Will you please* go up?
—**Je voudrais bien** avoir ma montre le plus tôt possible.	*I would like* to have my watch as soon as possible.

B. vouloir dire (*to mean*):

—Que **voulez-vous dire?**	What *do you mean?*
—Que **veut dire** «déçu»?	What *does* "déçu" *mean?*

104. (1) Falloir (*to have to, must*), *etc.: impersonal.*

—**Il faut que** j'aille en ville faire des courses.	*I must* go downtown to do some errands.
—**Il a fallu que** nous attendions la correspondance.	*We had to* wait for the connection.
—**Il faudra que** nous nous levions de bonne heure.	*We shall have to* get up early.
—**Il ne faut pas** faire cela.	*You must not* do that.

(2) Falloir (*it takes*), *etc.*

—**Il faut** une heure pour aller de Paris à Versailles.	*It takes* an hour to go from Paris to Versailles.
—**Il a fallu plus** de 300 ans pour construire le Louvre.	*It took more than* 300 years to build the Louvre.

PRÉSENT: Il faut (*must*). IMPARFAIT: Il fallait (*had to, should have*). PASSÉ COMPOSÉ: Il a fallu (*had to*). FUTUR: Il faudra (*will have to*).

105. Valoir* mieux (*to be better*): *impersonal.*

—**Il vaut mieux** laisser ceux dont vous n'êtes pas sûr.	*It is better* to leave the ones about which you are not sure.
—**Il vaudrait mieux** faire venir le médecin.	*It would be better* to send for the doctor.

PRÉSENT: Il vaut mieux (*It is better*). IMPARFAIT: Il valait mieux. PASSÉ COMPOSÉ: Il a mieux valu. FUTUR: Il vaudra mieux.

106. Pleuvoir (*to rain*): *impersonal.*

—**S'il pleut,** je prendrai un taxi.	*If it rains,* I'll take a taxi.
—**Il pleuvait** quand j'ai quitté la maison.	*It was raining* when I left the house.
—**Il a plu** cette nuit.	*It rained* last night.

PRÉSENT: Il pleut. *It rains, it is raining.* IMPARFAIT: Il pleuvait. *It was raining.* PASSÉ COMPOSÉ: Il a plu. *It rained.* FUTUR: Il pleuvra. *It will rain.*

---

* **Valoir** is also used as a transitive verb meaning *to be worth.* Ex.: Cette montre **vaut** mille francs.

107. Voir (*to see*).

—**Vous voyez** ce village là-bas?	*You see* that village over yonder?
—**Je vois** des champignons au bord de la route.	*I see* some mushrooms on the side of the road.
—Il y a longtemps que **je ne** vous **ai pas vu.**	*I haven't seen* you in a long time.
—**Je vois venir** le facteur.	*I see* the postman *coming*.

PRÉSENT: Je vois, tu vois, il voit, nous voyons, vous voyez, ils voient. *I see*, etc. IMPARFAIT: Je voyais, etc. *I saw*, etc. PASSÉ COMPOSÉ: J'ai vu, etc. *I saw*, *I have seen*, etc. FUTUR: Je verrai, etc. *I shall see*, *I'll see*, etc.

108. Savoir (*to know, to know how*).

—**Savez-vous** quand vivait Jeanne d'Arc?	*Do you know* when Joan of Arc lived?
—**Je sais** qu'elle est morte en 1431.	*I know* that she died in 1431.
—Je vous le dirai aussitôt que **je** le **saurai.**	I shall tell you as soon as *I find out*.
—**Vous ne sauriez pas** dépenser votre argent.	*You wouldn't know how* to spend your money.
—**Savez-vous** conduire une auto?	*Do you know how* to drive a car?

PRÉSENT: Je sais, tu sais, il sait, nous savons, vous savez, ils savent. *I know*, etc. IMPARFAIT: Je savais, etc. *I knew*, etc. PASSÉ COMPOSÉ: J'ai su, etc. *I knew*, *I found out*, etc. FUTUR: Je saurai, etc. *I shall know how*, *I shall find out*.

I. Exercices d'application.

A. *Répondez affirmativement:*

1. Pouvez-vous? **2.** Pourriez-vous? **3.** Avez-vous pu? **4.** Voudriez-vous? **5.** A-t-il voulu? **6.** Devez-vous? **7.** Deviez-vous? **8.** Devriez-vous? **9.** Auriez-vous dû? **10.** Voyez-vous? **11.** Savez-vous? **12.** Saviez-vous?

B. *Remplacez le présent par le passé composé:*

1. Je peux. **2.** Nous pouvons. **3.** Je veux. **4.** Nous voulons. **5.** Je dois. **6.** Nous devons. **7.** Il vaut mieux. **8.** Il faut. **9.** Vous voulez. **10.** Vous voyez. **11.** Vous ne savez pas. **12.** Vous pouvez.

C. *Remplacez l'imparfait par le conditionnel:*

1. Je voulais. **2.** Il voulait bien. **3.** Je ne pouvais pas. **4.** Il fallait. **5.** Il pleuvait. **6.** Je savais. **7.** Il savait. **8.** Il voyait.

II. Emploi du verb **devoir**

A. *Répétez en remplaçant le présent du verbe et* **sans doute** *par le présent de* **devoir** *et l'infinitif.*

EX.:—Il est sans doute chez lui en ce moment.
—Il doit être chez lui en ce moment.

1. Il arrive sans doute ce soir. **2.** La poste est sans doute ouverte en ce moment. **3.** Nous avons sans doute le temps d'aller au buffet. **4.** Ils sont sans doute en vacances. **5.** Il y a sans doute des champignons dans le bois. **6.** Il y a sans doute un train vers 8 heures.

B. *Répétez en remplaçant le passé composé du verbe et* **sans doute** *par le passé composé de* **devoir** *et l'infinitif.*

EX.:—J'ai sans doute laissé mon livre dans l'autobus.
—J'ai dû laisser mon livre dans l'autobus.

1. Elle a sans doute attrapé un rhume. **2.** Nous avons sans doute pris la mauvaise route. **3.** J'ai sans doute laissé mon portefeuille (*wallet*) à la maison. **4.** Ils ont sans doute manqué leur train. **5.** Il a sans doute plu cette nuit. **6.** Elle a sans doute reçu* un chèque de son père. **7.** Vous avez sans doute entendu parler de lui.

C. *Répétez en remplaçant* **Je crois** *et le présent de* **devoir** *par le conditionnel de* **devoir.**

EX.:—Je crois que vous devez répondre à cette lettre.
—Vous devriez répondre à cette lettre.

1. Je crois que vous devez travailler davantage. **2.** Je crois que vous ne devez pas sortir ce soir. **3.** Je crois qu'elle doit s'occuper davantage de son jardin. **4.** Je crois que nous devons partir de bonne heure. **5.** Je crois que nous devons nous mettre en route tout de suite. **6.** Je crois qu'elle doit partir plus tôt.

---

* For the forms of **recevoir** (*to receive*) see p. 431

D. *Répétez en remplaçant le conditionnel de* **devoir** *et* **aujourd'hui** *par le conditionnel passé de* **devoir** *et* **hier.**

EX.:—Vous devriez répondre à cette lettre aujourd'hui.
—**Vous auriez dû répondre à cette lettre hier.**

1. Vous devriez travailler aujourd'hui. **2.** Vous ne devriez pas sortir aujourd'hui. **3.** Il devrait rester à la maison aujourd'hui. **4.** Nous devrions partir aujourd'hui. **5.** Ils devraient se mettre en route aujourd'hui. **6.** Vous ne devriez pas boire tant de café aujourd'hui.

III. *Répondez en français:*

1. Savez-vous conduire une auto? **2.** Savez-vous jouer au tennis? **3.** Si vous étiez riche, sauriez-vous dépenser votre argent? **4.** Avez-vous lu le journal d'aujourd'hui? **5.** Quand est-ce que vous verrez Paris? **6.** Quand est-ce que vous reverrez vos parents? **7.** Est-ce que vous recevez souvent des nouvelles de vos amis? **8.** Est-ce que vous avez jamais reçu des cartes postales de Paris? **9.** Est-ce que vous devez aller à la campagne pour le week-end? **10.** Qu'est-ce que Marie devait faire le jour où elle a reçu la dépêche de Roger? **11.** Comment a-t-elle appris que ses amis devaient revenir ce jour-là? **12.** Qu'est-ce que Roger aurait dû lui dire dans sa dépêche?

IV. *Dites en français:*

1. May I see the room? **2.** Could you tell me the time? **3.** I could send it to you. **4.** I could not (*passé composé*) find it. **5.** I'd like to see you. **6.** I want (would like) some handkerchiefs. **7.** I am willing. **8.** Let's see. **9.** I should work harder. **10.** You should go to spend a few days in the country. **11.** I must have left my book in the bus. **12.** They ought to have sent the telegram sooner.

V. Révision du dialogue, pp. 286-287.

1. Qu'est-ce que le curé était en train de faire quand Roger a sonné? **2.** De quoi Jean s'excuse-t-il? **3.** Pourquoi Jean a-t-il envie de visiter l'église? **4.** Qu'est-ce que le curé venait de faire? **5.** Pourquoi le curé craint-il qu'ils ne soient un peu déçus? **6.** A quelle époque l'église a-t-elle été construite? **7.** Est-ce que Roger a entendu parler des vitraux de l'église? **8.** Est-ce que la plupart d'entre eux sont anciens? **9.** Combien y a-t-il de vitraux vraiment anciens? **10.** Pourquoi l'intérieur des églises romanes est-il d'ordinaire sombre?

VI. Thème d'imitation:

"I must tell you what happened to me last Saturday, John. That day I went fishing near the old bridge on the other side of the creek. You know the place, don't you? . . . Suddenly, I felt a fish on the end of my line.[1] I was going to take him out[2] of the water, when a fish *that big*, which was following mine, opened its enormous mouth,[3] took my fish, and went away with it."[4] "You ought to put that in the paper," said John. "You caught the big fish, didn't you?" "No," Roger replied, "he broke my line." "That's really too bad," said John. "It's the sad story of the big fish that gets away."[5] "Don't make fun of me," answered Roger. "Big fish are much harder to catch than little ones, because they are larger. People[6] do not believe fishermen. They say: 'Oh! that's a fish story!'[7] Believe me, those who say that do not know what they are saying."

---

[1] *on the end of my line*, **au bout de ma ligne.** [2] *take out*, **sortir.** (**Sortir** is used either as a transitive or intransitive verb). [3] *its enormous mouth*, **une bouche énorme.** [4] Omit *it*. Never mind if your sentence ends with **avec.** In such phrases, **avec** is regarded by grammarians as an adverb. [5] *lit.*: that one misses. [6] *people*, **les gens.** [7] *lit.*: a story of fishermen.

VILLAGE ET CHATEAU EN BOURGOGNE

AIX-EN-PROVENCE

A la terrasse d'un café

JEAN – 1 Asseyons-nous à la terrasse de ce café. 2 Nous pourrons voir passer les gens.

HÉLÈNE – 3 Quel est ce monument là-bas, au bout de la rue?

JOHN – 1 *Let's sit down in this sidewalk café.* 2 *We can see the people go by.*

HELEN – 3 *What is that monument over there at the end of the street?*

JEAN – [4]Vous devriez le reconnaître. C'est le Panthéon.

HÉLÈNE – [5]Oh! je me rappelle maintenant. [6]C'est l'endroit où l'on enterre les grands hommes, n'est-ce pas?

JEAN – [7]Oui, quelques-uns d'entre eux. [8]On trouve là notamment les tombeaux de Voltaire et de Victor Hugo.

HÉLÈNE – [9]Pourquoi appelle-t-on cette partie de Paris le Quartier latin?

JEAN – [10]Parce que c'est le quartier de l'université, et que le latin était autrefois la langue de l'université.

HÉLÈNE – [11]Où est donc la Sorbonne?

JEAN – [12]A deux pas d'ici. [13]Nous irons tout à l'heure, si vous voulez.

HÉLÈNE – [14]Pourquoi appelle-t-on l'université de Paris la Sorbonne? [15]J'ai lu l'explication quelque part, mais je ne m'en souviens plus.

JEAN – [16]C'est qu'au temps de saint Louis,* un certain Robert de Sorbon a fondé un collège pour les étudiants de théologie. [17]Ce collège, appelé la Sorbonne, est devenu la Faculté des Lettres.

HÉLÈNE – [18]Tous ces étudiants ont l'air sérieux et préoccupé . . .

JEAN – [19]Il y a de quoi. [20]Ils sont en train de passer leurs examens et les examens en France ne sont pas faciles.

JOHN – [4]*You ought to recognize it. It's the Pantheon.*

HELEN – [5]*Oh! now, I remember.* [6]*It's the place where they bury the great men, isn't it?*

JOHN – [7]*Yes, some of them.* [8]*In particular, there are the tombs of Voltaire and Victor Hugo.*

HELEN – [9]*Why do they call this part of Paris the Latin Quarter?*

JOHN – [10]*Because it is the quarter of the University, and that Latin was formerly the language of the University.*

HELEN – [11]*Well, where is the Sorbonne?*

JOHN – [12]*Just a few steps from here.* [13]*We'll go there after a while if you wish.*

HELEN – [14]*Why do they call the University of Paris the Sorbonne?* [15]*I read the explanation somewhere, but I don't remember it (any longer).*

JOHN – [16]*It's that in the time of Saint Louis, a man named Robert de Sorbon founded a college for theology students.* [17]*This college, called the Sorbonne, has become the Faculty of Letters.*

HELEN – [18]*All these students look serious and worried . . .*

JOHN – [19]*There is reason for it.* [20]*They are busy taking their examinations, and in France examinations are not easy.*

* Saint Louis (Louis IX), roi de France de 1226 à 1270. Il a fondé un hôpital pour trois cents chevaliers devenus aveugles au cours des croisades, d'où le nom de Quinze-Vingts donné à cet hôpital, qui existe toujours à Paris. On lui doit aussi la construction de la Sainte-Chapelle, un des plus élégants monuments de l'art gothique. La ville de Saint-Louis aux États-Unis a été nommée d'après lui.

LE PANTHÉON

I. Substitutions. *Répétez les phrases en substituant les mots indiqués:*

1. Nous pourrons voir passer les gens.

voir venir l'avion / voir arriver le train / regarder passer les gens / entendre parler le Président

2. La Sorbonne a été fondée au temps de saint Louis.

au treizième siècle / au cours du treizième siècle / au moment des croisades / en 1253

3. Je ne me souviens plus de lui.

d'eux / d'elle / de Louise / de cette explication

4. Je me rappelle son nom.

son adresse / son numéro de téléphone / la date de son anniversaire / le jour de son mariage

II. *Répondez en français à chacune des questions suivantes:*

1. Où sont assis Jean et Hélène? **2.** Dans quel quartier se trouve la terrasse où ils sont assis? **3.** Quel monument voit-on de la terrasse de ce café? **4.** Qu'est-ce que c'est que le Panthéon? **5.** Connaissez-vous des hommes célèbres qui sont enterrés au Panthéon? **6.** Pourquoi appelle-t-on cette partie-là de Paris le Quartier latin? **7.** Saviez-vous qu'autrefois tous les étudiants de l'université parlaient latin? **8.** En quelle langue les professeurs faisaient-ils leurs conférences (*lectures*)? **9.** Qui a fondé la Sorbonne? **10.** Quand vivait Robert de Sorbon? **11.** Qu'est-ce que c'était autrefois que la Sorbonne? **12.** Qu'est-ce que c'est maintenant que la Sorbonne? **13.** Où Hélène a-t-elle lu l'explication du nom «Sorbonne»? **14.** Est-ce qu'elle se souvient de cette explication? **15.** Pourquoi les étudiants ont-ils l'air sérieux et préoccupé? **16.** Est-ce qu'il y a un Panthéon en Amérique? **17.** Où est-ce qu'on enterre les grands hommes aux États-Unis? **18.** Où est enterré George Washington? **19.** Où est enterré Victor Hugo? **20.** Croyez-vous que ce soit une bonne idée d'enterrer les grands hommes dans un monument comme le Panthéon? **21.** Vous souvenez-vous de la date de la mort de Louis XIV?

III. *Demandez à quelqu'un:*

1. ce que c'est que ce monument là-bas au bout de la rue. **2.** quelle langue on parlait autrefois dans les universités. **3.** ce qu'est devenu le collège fondé par Robert de Sorbon. **4.** dans quel siècle la Sorbonne a été fondée. **5.** s'il savait pourquoi on appelle l'Université de Paris «la Sorbonne».

IV. Exercices d'application.

A. *Répétez les phrases suivantes, en remplaçant* **être** *par* **avoir l'air:**

EX.:—Il est préoccupé.
—Il a l'air préoccupé.

1. Vous êtes préoccupé. **2.** Elle est fatiguée.* **3.** Ils sont heureux. **4.** Tous ces étudiants sont sérieux et préoccupés. **5.** Cette jeune fille est triste. **6.** Les Brown sont très gentils.

B. *Répétez les phrases suivantes, en remplaçant* **avoir** *par* **avoir l'air d'avoir:**

EX.:—Il a faim.
—Il a l'air d'avoir faim.

1. Il a froid. **2.** Vous avez chaud. **3.** Jean a soif. **4.** Il a mal à la tête. **5.** Il a un rhume. **6.** Les Brown ont beaucoup d'argent.

* Either: Elle a l'air **fatigué** or **fatiguée** may be used.

V. *Dites en français:*

A. il y a de quoi

1. There is a good reason. **2.** There is reason to be worried. **3.** There is no reason to be worried. **4.** There is no reason to thank me. **5.** You are welcome (**Il n'y a pas de quoi**).

B. au temps de . . . , au . . . , en . . .

1. In the time of Louis XIV. **2.** In the seventeenth century. **3.** In 1657. **4.** In the time of François Premier. **5.** In the sixteenth century. **6.** In 1525. **7.** In the time of Saint Louis. **8.** In the thirteenth century. **9.** In 1253.

C. se rappeler, se souvenir de*

(1) *Employez* **se rappeler** *dans chacune des phrases suivantes:*

1. I read the explanation somewhere, but I don't remember it. **2.** I saw that explanation somewhere, but I don't remember it. **3.** I used to know his address, but I don't remember it. **4.** Do you remember it? **5.** I do not remember it any longer.

(2) *Employez* **se souvenir de** *dans chacune des phrases précédentes.*

VI. Rèvision. *Mettez les phrases suivantes au futur:*

1. Jean va au cinéma ce soir. **2.** Hélène vient cet après-midi. **3.** Elle s'en va la semaine prochaine. **4.** Elle fait des courses demain matin. **5.** Je vous envoie vos achats cet après-midi. **6.** Je peux vous envoyer la facture plus tard. **7.** Vous aurez vos achats quand vous voulez. **8.** Il faut payer la facture un de ses jours. **9.** Elle doit passer à la caisse pour payer ses achats. **10.** Elle a vu la tour Eiffel. **11.** Il a plu cet après-midi. **12.** Elle ne sait pas dépenser son argent. **13.** Il vaut mieux rentrer plus tôt. **14.** Elle se souvient avec plaisir de son séjour à Paris.

VII. Dictée d'après la Conversation 37, pp. 310-311.

* While **se souvenir de** and **se rappeler** both mean *to remember*, they are not quite interchangeable: **se rappeler** takes a direct object and is used primarily to refer to things rather than to persons. **Se souvenir de** refers to either persons or things:

Je me souviens de mon grand-père.	Je me souviens de lui.
Je me souviens de ses conseils.	Je m'en souviens.
Je me rappelle ses conseils.	Je me les rappelle.

LA SEINE ET NOTRE-DAME DE PARIS

Le long des quais

HÉLÈNE – [1]Que regardent ces gens-là, le long de la Seine?

JEAN – [2]Ils examinent les étalages des bouquinistes.

HÉLÈNE – [3]Que vendent ces bouquinistes?

JEAN – [4]Toutes sortes de choses. [5]Les uns vendent de vieilles estampes, d'autres des timbres-poste, d'autres de vieilles pièces de monnaie, mais la plupart d'entre eux font le commerce des livres d'occasion.

HÉLÈNE – [6]Mon frère m'a demandé de lui envoyer des timbres. [7]Traversons la rue. [8]Nous pourrons jeter un coup d'œil sur les étalages.

JEAN – [9]Savez-vous quels timbres votre frère veut se procurer?

HÉLÈNE – [10]Oui, j'ai dans mon sac une liste qu'il a dressée.

HÉLÈNE *(au bouquiniste)* – [11]Avez-vous les timbres indiqués sur cette liste?

LE BOUQUINISTE – [12]Voyons un peu . . . Martinique, 1886; Second Empire, 1853; Sénégal, 1903; etc. [13]Oui, mademoiselle. Je crois les avoir tous, sauf les timbres du Second Empire, série 1853. [14]Il ne m'en reste aucun.

HELEN – [1]*What are those people looking at along the Seine?*

JOHN – [2]*They are examining the displays of the old-book dealers.*

HELEN – [3]*What do those old-book dealers sell?*

JOHN – [4]*All sorts of things.* [5]*Some sell old prints, others postage stamps, others old coins, but most of them deal in second-hand books.*

HELEN – [6]*My brother asked me to send him some stamps.* [7]*Let's cross the street.* [8]*We can take a look at the displays.*

JOHN – [9]*Do you know what stamps your brother wants to get?*

HELEN – [10]*Yes. I have in my bag a list which he drew up.*

HELEN – [11]*Have you the stamps noted on this list?*

LE BOUQUINISTE – [12]*Let's take a look . . . Martinique, 1886; Second Empire, 1853; Senegal, 1903; etc.* [13]*Yes, Mademoiselle, I think I have them all, except the 1853 series of the Second Empire.* [14]*I haven't a one of them left.*

HÉLÈNE – [15]Tant pis.

LE BOUQUINISTE – [16]Voulez-vous consulter cet album? [17]Vous y trouverez peut-être certains timbres qui vous intéressent.

HÉLÈNE – [18]Je ne connais pas grand-chose aux timbres-poste.

JEAN – [19]Vous n'avez qu'à choisir les plus jolis!

HÉLÈNE – [20]Oh non! Il y a quelque temps, j'ai envoyé plusieurs timbres à mon frère. [21]J'avais choisi les plus jolis. [22]Mais il avait déjà la plupart d'entre eux, et il m'a dit que mon choix ne valait* rien.

HELEN – [15]*Too bad.*

LE BOUQUINISTE – [16]*Do you want to look at this album?* [17]*You will perhaps find in it certain stamps that interest you.*

HELEN – [18]*I don't know much about postage stamps.*

JOHN – [19]*All you have to do is to choose the prettiest (ones).*

HELEN – [20]*Oh no! Some time ago, I sent several stamps to my brother.* [21]*I had chosen the prettiest.* [22]*But he already had most of them and he told me my selection was no good (was worth nothing).*

* From **valoir,** used here as transitive verb meaning *to be worth.*

I. Substitutions. *Répétez les phrases suivantes, en substituant les mots indiqués:*

1. Nous pourrons jeter un coup d'œil sur les étalages.
   sur les journaux / sur les revues (*magazines*) / sur les estampes / sur les livres d'occasion
2. La plupart d'entre eux font le commerce des livres.
   Beaucoup / Plusieurs / Quelques-uns / Peu (*only a few*)
3. Savez-vous quels timbres votre frère veut se procurer?
   quelles estampes / quelles photos / quels vieux livres / quelles pièces de monnaie
4. Il ne m'en reste aucun.
   pas / pas beaucoup / plus / plus du tout / guère / qu'un / que deux
5. Vous n'avez qu'à choisir les plus jolis.
   traverser la rue / consulter cet album / téléphoner à vos parents / appeler un taxi / suivre cette rue

II. *Répondez en français à chacune des questions suivantes:*

1. Où sont les étalages des bouquinistes? **2.** Que vendent les bouquinistes? **3.** Où iriez-vous si vous vouliez acheter des livres d'occasion? **4.** Qui est-ce qui a demandé à Hélène de lui envoyer des timbres? **5.** Pourquoi Hélène propose-t-elle de traverser la rue? **6.** Comment sait-elle quels timbres son frère veut se procurer? **7.** Où a-t-elle mis la liste qu'il lui a envoyée? **8.** Connaissez-vous quelques-uns des timbres qu'il voudrait se procurer? **9.** Est-ce que le bouquiniste a tous les timbres qu'Hélène voudrait acheter? **10.** Est-ce qu'il lui reste des timbres du Second Empire, série 1853? **11.** Qu'est-ce que c'est qu'un album? **12.** Pourquoi Hélène ne sait-elle pas quels timbres choisir dans l'album? **13.** Quels timbres Jean lui dit-il de choisir? **14.** Pourquoi ne suit-elle pas son conseil? **15.** Est-ce que vous collectionnez les timbres-poste? **16.** Est-ce que vous collectionnez autre chose? **17.** Est-ce que tous les vieux timbres valent quelque chose?

III. *Demandez à quelqu'un:*

1. ce que vendent la plupart des bouquinistes. **2.** où l'on vend des timbres-poste. **3.** s'il connaît des gens qui font collection de vieilles estampes. **4.** s'il reste au marchand des timbres du Second Empire. **5.** si Hélène sait quels timbres son frère veut se procurer. **6.** si Hélène s'est déjà procuré des timbres pour son frère. **7.** ce qu'on met dans un album. **8.** ce qu'Hélène a envoyé à son frère il y a quelque temps. **9.** s'il a déjà entendu parler des bouquinistes de Paris.

IV. Exercices d'application.

A. *Répétez les phrases suivantes en employant l'infinitif:*

EX.:—Je crois que je les ai tous.
—Je crois les avoir tous.

1. Je crois que je les connais tous. **2.** Je crois que je sais son adresse. **3.** Je crois que je peux venir vous chercher. **4.** Je ne crois pas que je puisse partir aujourd'hui. **5.** Je ne crois pas que je sache son adresse. **6.** Je ne crois pas que j'irai en ville cet après-midi.

B. *Répétez en remplaçant* **rien** *par* **pas . . . grand-chose:**

EX.:—Il ne m'a rien dit.
—Il ne m'a pas dit grand-chose.

1. Il ne me reste rien. **2.** Je n'ai rien trouvé. **3.** Il n'a rien à faire. **4.** Je ne connais rien aux timbres. **5.** Nous ne connaissons rien à l'art gothique. **6.** Nous n'avons rien fait.

C. *Employez* **la plupart** *dans chacune des expressions suivantes:*

EX.:—Beaucoup de bouquinistes.
—La plupart des bouquinistes.

1. Beaucoup de gens. **2.** Beaucoup d'entre eux. **3.** Beaucoup d'églises gothiques. **4.** Beaucoup d'entre elles. **5.** Quelques-uns des timbres. **6.** Quelques-uns d'entre eux. **7.** Plusieurs des estampes. **8.** Plusieurs d'entre elles.

V. *Dites en français:*

A. valoir

1. My choice was no good. **2.** Most stamps are worthless. **3.** Most old books are worthless. **4.** This old book is worthless. **5.** This old book is not worth much. **6.** That old book is worth 500 francs. **7.** It is better not to buy it.

B. il (me) reste

1. I haven't a one of them left. **2.** I have several (of them) left. **3.** I have one left. **4.** I have two Martinique stamps left. **5.** Have you any Second Empire stamps left? **6.** How many of them do you have left?

C. le long de

1. Along the quais. **2.** Along the Seine. **3.** Along the street. **4.** Along the roads. **5.** Along the Grands Boulevards.

VI. Dictée d'après la Conversation 38, pp. 322-323.

VII. Conversation.

Vous voyez à la devanture (*shop window*) d'un magasin où l'on vend des objets d'art, une série de gravures (*engravings*) représentant des coins du vieux Paris. Vous demandez des renseignements sur l'auteur de ces gravures, la date, etc., et vous discutez du prix avec le marchand.

Indefinite Adjectives and Pronouns; Use of Articles and Prepositions Summarized

109. *Indefinite adjectives and pronouns.*

The word "indefinite" when applied to adjectives and pronouns means that the adjective or pronoun concerned does not define or determine the person or thing to which it refers. The corresponding indefinite adjectives and pronouns in English are: *each, every, several, all, no, such, same,* etc.

110. *Commonest indefinite adjectives and pronouns that have the same form:*

ADJECTIVES	PRONOUNS
—Avez-vous **tous** ces timbres?	Oui, je crois les avoir **tous.**
—J'ai envoyé **plusieurs** timbres à mon frère.	Je lui en ai envoyé **plusieurs.**
—Il ne me reste **aucun** timbre du Second Empire.	Il ne m'en reste **aucun.**
—Avez-vous **d'autres** journaux?	Non, je n'en ai pas **d'autres.**

The forms of these adjectives and pronouns are:

tout, toute, tous, toutes: *all, every*
plusieurs: *several*
aucun, aucune: Adj. *no, not a;* Pron. *none, not a one*
autre, autres: Adj. *other;* Pron. *another one, others*
même, mêmes: Adj. *same;* Pron. *same one, same ones*

(1) When **aucun** is used with a verb, the verb must be preceded by **ne.** Note, however, that **pas** is not used with **aucun.**

(2) When **tous** is used as a pronoun, the final **s** is pronounced.

111. *Commonest indefinite adjectives and pronouns whose corresponding forms are different:*

ADJECTIVES	PRONOUNS
Chaque timbre vaut 10 francs.	**Chacun** de ces timbres vaut 10 francs.
Si nous rapportions **quelques** champignons?	Si nous en rapportions **quelques-uns?**
J'ai passé **quelque** temps à Lyon.	Est-ce que **quelqu'un** est venu?

(1) The corresponding forms of these adjectives and pronouns are:

ADJECTIVE: chaque, *each*
PRONOUN: chacun, chacune, *each, each one*
ADJECTIVE: quelque, quelques, *some, a few*
PRONOUN: quelqu'un, quelques-uns, quelques-unes, *someone, somebody; some, a few*

(2) They of course agree in gender and number with the noun to which they refer; but **quelqu'un** in the singular is usually thought of as neither masculine nor feminine.

(3) When **quelque chose** or **rien** is followed by an adjective, the adjective is preceded by **de** and has the masculine form. Ex: **quelque chose de bon,** *something good;* **rien d'intéressant,** *nothing interesting.*

(4) It is curious to note that while **quelque** is an *adjective* and **chose** is a *noun*, when they are used together (**quelque chose**) they form a *pronoun!*

112. *Indefinite pronouns that have no corresponding indefinite adjective:*

—Est-ce qu'**on** est venu me voir?	Did *anyone* come to see me?
—Non, **personne n'**est venu vous voir.	No, *no one* came to see you.
—Avez-vous trouvé **quelque chose** d'intéressant?	Did you find *anything* interesting?
—Non, je **n'**ai **rien** trouvé d'intéressant.	No, I didn't find *anything* interesting.
—Oui, j'ai trouvé **quelque chose** d'intéressant.	Yes, I found *something* interesting.
—Avez-vous **quelque chose** à faire?	Have you *anything* to do?
—Non, je **n'**ai **rien** à faire. **Rien** du tout.	No, I have *nothing* to do. *Nothing* at all.
—Est-ce que les magasins sont ouverts ce soir?	Are the stores open this evening?
—Pas tous. **Les uns** sont ouverts, **les autres** sont fermés.	Not all. *Some* are open, *the others* are closed.

—**Les uns** vendent de vieilles estampes, **d'autres** des timbres-poste, **d'autres** des livres d'occasion.	*Some* sell old prints, *others* stamps, *others* old books.
—Avez-vous ces deux timbres?	Do you have these two stamps?
—Non, je **n'ai** ni **l'un** ni **l'autre.**	No, I don't have *either of them.*

(1) The forms of these pronouns are:

l'un, l'une, les uns, les unes, *the one, the ones*
on, *one, they, people, someone, anybody,* etc.
personne, *no one, nobody*

Note that **l'un, l'une,** etc., are always used in opposition to **l'autre,** etc. For **celui qui,** *the one who,* see pp. 254–255.

(2) When **rien** or **personne** is used with a verb, the verb is preceded by **ne. Pas** is not used with **rien** or **personne.**

(3) In giving a negative answer to a question in which the subject is **on** or **quelqu'un,** you say **personne;** if the subject is **quelque chose,** the answer is **rien.**

113. *Use of definite article in French contrary to English usage.*

A. With nouns which indicate profession or official function:

—**Le docteur Lambert** n'a pas pu s'arrêter à temps.	*Doctor Lambert* couldn't stop in time.
—Bonjour, **monsieur le curé.**	Good morning, *sir* (*to a priest*).

B. With parts of the body, when the person concerned is clearly identified by the context:

—Elle a **les yeux bleus.**	She has *blue eyes.*
—Je commence à avoir mal **aux jambes.**	*My legs* are beginning to hurt.
—Le chapeau que vous avez **sur la tête.**	The hat you have *on your head.*
—Je me suis lavé **les mains.**	I washed *my hands.*

C. With the names of the days of the week, to indicate habitual occurrence:

—Je vais à la pêche **le samedi.**	I *usually* go fishing *on Saturday.*
BUT: Je vais à la pêche samedi.	I am going fishing Saturday (i.e. next Saturday).

D. In the expressions **le matin, l'après-midi, le soir, la nuit,** meaning *in the:*

—Je me lève **le matin** de bonne heure.	I get up early *in the morning.*
—Je vais au laboratoire **l'après-midi.**	I go to the laboratory *in the afternoon.*

E. With expressions of measure in specifying the price:

—Les œufs coûtent trois francs **la douzaine.**	Eggs cost three francs *a dozen.*
—Le lait coûte soixante centimes **le litre.**	Milk costs sixty centimes *a liter.*
—Ce tabac coûte un franc cinquante **le paquet.**	This tobacco costs one franc fifty *a package.*
—Cette étoffe coûte cinq francs **le mètre.**	This material costs five francs *per meter.*
—Le beurre coûte quatre francs cinquante **la livre.**	Butter costs four francs fifty *per pound.*

Note that you say **deux francs pièce,** *two francs apiece* or *each;* and that with the expressions of time, you use **par** when the price is being specified. Ex.: **—Quel est le loyer? —Cent cinquante francs par mois.**

F. With nouns taken in a general sense:

L'homme est mortel.	*Man* is mortal.
Vive **la liberté!**	Hurrah for *liberty!*
La vie est chère.	*Living* is high.
La viande est chère.	*Meat* is expensive.
Je n'aime pas **le café**.	I don't like *coffee.*

114. *Omission of indefinite article in French contrary to English usage.*

A. When a noun, especially a proper name, is followed by a second noun which is added to explain the first one, the second noun ordinarily has no article:

—Vous êtes bien M. Jean Hughes, ingénieur-chimiste?	Are you (indeed) Mr. John Hughes, *a* chemical engineer?
—C'est le Louvre, ancien palais royal.	It is the Louvre, *a* former royal palace.

B. When a noun (or personal pronoun) referring to a person is followed by the verb **être** and a noun indicating profession or nationality, the latter is used without an article:

—Il est Américain, mais sa femme est Française.	He is *an* American, but his wife is French.
—M. Brown est banquier.	Mr. Brown is *a* banker.

Do not forget that a noun following **c'est** always has a modifier. Ex.: **C'est un** banquier. **C'est un** Américain. **C'est ma** bicyclette.

115. *Use of prepositions and definite articles with geographical names.*

A. With names of continents and countries that are feminine:

—J'irais **en** Suisse et **en** Belgique.	I would go *to* Switzerland and *to* Belgium.
—J'irais **en** Amérique et **en** Afrique.	I would go *to* America and *to* Africa.
—Les olives viennent **de** France, **d'**Espagne et **d'**Afrique.	Olives come *from* France, Spain and Africa.

With the name of a continent or a country that is feminine, you use **en** without an article to express *to* or *in*, and **de** without an article to express *from:* **en** France, **de** France. If the geographical name has a modifier (l'Amérique **du Sud**), careful speakers often use **dans** WITH THE ARTICLE to express *to* or *in* and **de** WITH THE ARTICLE to express *from* but **en** and **de** (without the article) are also used:

—Ces oranges viennent **de l'**Afrique du Nord *or* **d'**Afrique du Nord.	These oranges come *from* North Africa.
—Un de mes oncles habite **dans l'**Amérique du Sud *or* **en** Amérique du Sud.	One of my uncles lives *in* South America.

B. With names of countries that are masculine:

—Il demeure **au** Canada.	He lives *in* Canada.
—Il vient **du** Mexique.	He comes *from* Mexico.
—J'irais **aux** États-Unis voir les gratte-ciel.	I would go *to the* United States to see the skyscrapers.

You always use the article in combination with **à** or **de** with the names of countries that are masculine.

C. With names of cities:

—Il demeure **à** Clermont-Ferrand.	He lives *in* Clermont-Ferrand.
—Je suis né **à** Rouen.	I was born *in* Rouen.
—Mon père vient **de** Paris.	My father comes *from* Paris.
—Êtes-vous allé **à** Versailles?	Have you been *to* Versailles?

You never use an article with the name of a city except with **Le Havre** and a few other cities in which the article is a part of the name. Ex.: —Connaissez-vous **Le Havre?** Êtes-vous allé à **La Nouvelle-Orléans?**

I. Substitutions. *Répétez les phrases suivantes, en substituant les mots indiqués:*

1. Je ne vais pas souvent en ville le samedi, mais j'irai samedi prochain.
l'après-midi . . . cet après-midi / le matin . . . ce matin / le soir . . . ce soir / le vendredi . . . vendredi

2. Je ne vais pas souvent en ville le samedi, mais j'y suis allé samedi dernier.
le matin . . . hier matin / l'après-midi . . . hier après-midi / le soir . . . hier soir / le vendredi soir . . . vendredi soir

3. Elle doit passer quelques jours à Londres.
Paris / Rome / (Le) Havre / (Le) Mans

4. Elle est actuellement en Angleterre.
(la) Normandie / (l') Italie / (l') Europe / (la) Suisse / (le) Canada / (les) États-Unis / (le) Mexique / (le) Japon

5. Elle revient ces jours-ci d'Angleterre.
Bretagne / Italie / Allemagne / Rome / Paris / Amsterdam / (le) Canada / (les) États-Unis / (le) Mexique / (Le) Havre

II. Exercices d'application.

A. *Répondez affirmativement à chacune des questions suivantes, en employant le pronom indéfini convenable:*

EX.:—Est-ce qu'il reste au marchand des timbres du Second Empire?
—Oui, il lui en reste quelques-uns.

1. Est-ce qu'Hélène a envoyé plusieurs timbres à son frère? **2.** Est-ce que le marchand a tous les timbres qu'Hélène voudrait acheter? **3.** A-t-il d'autres timbres? **4.** Avez-vous trouvé toutes les estampes que vous vouliez acheter? **5.** Avez-vous vu quelques-unes des estampes de Daumier? **6.** Est-ce qu'il reste au marchand des timbres de la Martinique?

B. *Répondez négativement à chacune des questions suivantes, en employant le pronom indéfini convenable:*

EX.:—Avez-vous acheté quelque chose au Bon Marché?
—Non, je n'ai rien acheté au Bon Marché.

1. Est-ce qu'il vous reste des timbres du Second Empire? **2.** Est-ce que le marchand a tous les timbres qu'Hélène voudrait acheter? **3.** Est-ce qu'il a d'autres timbres à vendre? **4.** Avez-vous vu quelqu'un devant la maison? **5.** Est-ce que quelqu'un a téléphoné? **6.** Avez-vous quelque chose à faire ce soir? **7.** Avez-vous trouvé quelque chose d'intéressant?

C. *Répondez négativement, en employant* **ni l'un ni l'autre:**

1. Avez-vous ces deux timbres? **2.** Voulez-vous du thé ou du café? **3.** Avez-vous acheté du pain ou de la viande? **4.** Avez-vous un frère ou une sœur? **5.** Avez-vous choisi un fruit ou une pâtisserie (*French pastry*)?

III. *Dites en français:*

A. tout

1. All the stamps. **2.** Every day. **3.** Every week. **4.** Every Thursday.

B. fois

1. Sometimes. **2.** Each time. **3.** Several times. **4.** Once. **5.** Twice.

C. quelque chose, rien

1. Something. **2.** Something good. **3.** Something better. **4.** Something else (**quelque chose d'autre, autre chose**). **5.** Nothing. **6.** Nothing interesting. **7.** Nothing else. **8.** Nothing important.

D. le, la

1. Eggs cost 3 francs a dozen. **2.** Sugar costs 25 centimes per pound. **3.** Potatoes cost 25 centimes per kilo. **4.** Milk costs 50 centimes a litre. **5.** Good wine costs 10 francs per bottle. **6.** This material costs 5 francs per meter.

IV. Révision des dialogues, p. 291 et pp. 306-307.

1. Pourquoi Madame Deschamps veut-elle aller au jardin? **2.** Qu'est-ce que Roger offre de faire? **3.** Pourquoi Madame Deschamps lui dit-elle de bien fermer la porte? **4.** Qu'est-ce qu'elle fera des fleurs qu'elle va cueillir? **5.** Pourquoi ne s'occupe-t-elle pas davantage de son jardin? **6.** Pourquoi n'y a-t-il pas de maïs dans son jardin? **7.** Est-ce qu'il a beaucoup plu cette année-là? **8.** Pourquoi ne veut-elle pas que Jean arrose le jardin tout de suite? **9.** A quel moment de la journée vaut-il mieux arroser un jardin? **10.** Quand Roger veut-il aller à la pêche? **11.** Pourquoi Jean ne veut-il pas y aller? **12.** Est-ce que Roger prend d'habitude beaucoup de poissons? **13.** Où se trouve l'endroit où il y a de gros poissons? **14.** Pourquoi Jean se moque-t-il de Roger? **15.** A quelle heure faudra-t-il qu'ils se lèvent? **16.** Aimez-vous mieux la pêche ou la chasse (*hunting*)? **17.** En quelle saison la chasse est-elle ouverte?

V. Thème d'imitation:

Along the Seine, especially near the Île de la Cité, are[1] the displays of the old-book dealers. Those dealers in old books are ordinarily elderly people. Each of them has one or two boxes[2] which he opens in the morning and closes in the evening. Nearly all of them buy and sell secondhand books. A hundred years ago, you could buy rare books for almost nothing. But things have changed a great deal since. Rare books are becoming rarer and rarer[3] and the dealers in old books know the value of what they sell. However, you still find things worth buying[4] in their displays, which are[5] a part of the Parisian landscape[6] like Notre-Dame or the Eiffel Tower.

---

1 Use **se trouver.** 2 *box*, **la boîte.** 3 *rarer and rarer*, **de plus en plus rares.** 4 *worth buying*, **intéressant** 5 *to be a part of*, **faire partie de.** 6 *landscape*, **le paysage.**

L'ÉTALAGE D'UN BOUQUINISTE

Aux Tuileries

JEAN – [1]Maintenant entrons dans le jardin des Tuileries.* [2]Que pensez-vous de ce coin de Paris?

HÉLÈNE – [3]Je suis étonnée de trouver tant d'espace au cœur même de la ville. [4]Je n'avais pas la moindre idée de l'étendue de la place de la Concorde.† [5]Mais, dites-moi, quel est ce grand bâtiment devant nous?

JEAN – [6]C'est le Louvre, ancien palais royal.‡

HÉLÈNE – [7]Est-ce que c'est là qu'est le musée du Louvre?

JEAN – [8]Oui; le musée occupe la plus grande partie de l'édifice. [9]Il possède d'immenses collections.

JOHN – [1]*Now, let's go into the Tuileries Gardens.* [2]*What do you think of this section of Paris?*

HELEN – [3]*I am astonished to find so much (open) space in the very heart of the city.* [4]*I didn't have the slightest idea of the size of the Place de la Concorde.* [5]*But, tell me, what is this great building in front of us?*

JOHN – [6]*It's the Louvre, a former royal palace.*

HELEN – [7]*Is that where the Louvre Museum is?*

JOHN – [8]*Yes, the museum occupies most of the building.* [9]*It has immense collections.*

---

* Jardin d'un ancien palais habité par Napoléon et détruit par le feu en 1871.

† La vaste place de la Concorde, dont le centre est occupé par un obélisque, est entourée de statues monumentales symbolisant les principales villes de France.

‡ La construction du Louvre actuel, commencée au XVIème siècle, n'a été terminée que vers la fin du XIXème siècle.

HÉLÈNE – [10]Et voilà l'Arc de triomphe. [11]D'après les photographies que j'ai vues, je le croyais plus grand.

JEAN – [12]C'est l'Arc de triomphe du Carrousel que vous voyez là. [13]L'autre, celui de l'Étoile,* est au bout de l'avenue des Champs-Élysées.† [14]Si vous vous retournez, vous pourrez l'apercevoir là-bas . . .

HÉLÈNE – [15]Regardez cette petite fille qui pleure, Jean. [16]Le vent a emmené son bateau à voile au milieu du bassin. [17]Est-ce que vous pouvez l'aider?

JEAN – [18]J'aurais beau faire. [19]Le bateau est trop loin pour que je puisse l'atteindre. [20]Le vent finira sans doute par le ramener au bord.

HÉLÈNE – [21]J'ai envie de cueillir une de ces fleurs comme souvenir de notre promenade.

JEAN – [22]Gardez-vous-en bien. [23]Si un agent de police vous voyait, il pourrait bien vous faire un procès-verbal!

HELEN – [10]*And there is the Arch of Triumph.* [11]*From the photographs I have seen, I thought it was larger.*

JOHN – [12]*That's the Arch of Triumph of the Carrousel that you see there.* [13]*The other one, that of the Étoile, is at the end of the Champs-Elysées.* [14]*If you turn around, you can see (get a glimpse of) it over there . . .*

HELEN – [15]*Look at this little girl who is crying, John.* [16]*The wind has carried her sailboat to the middle of the pool.* [17]*Can you help her?*

JOHN – [18]*Whatever I would do would be in vain.* [19]*The boat is too far for me to be able to reach it.* [20]*The wind will finally bring it back to the edge, no doubt.*

HELEN – [21]*I wish I could pick one of those flowers as a souvenir of our walk.*

JOHN – [22]*Don't do anything of the kind.* [23]*If a policeman should see you, he might very well give you a ticket!*

---

* Arc de triomphe, dédié aux armées de Napoléon 1er. Il doit son nom aux douze avenues qui rayonnent autour de la place, formant une étoile dont il occupe le centre.

† Belle avenue qui va de la place de la Concorde à la place de l'Étoile.

I. Substitutions. *Répétez les phrases suivantes, en substituant les mots indiques.*

1. Je n'avais pas la moindre idée de l'étendue de la place de la Concorde.

Je n'avais pas idée / Je n'avais aucune idée / Je ne me rendais pas compte / Je ne me rendais pas du tout compte

2. D'après les photos que j'ai vues, je le croyais plus grand.

D'après les cartes postales que j'ai vues / D'après ce que j'ai lu / D'après ce qu'on m'a dit / D'après ce que j'ai entendu dire

3. Le vent a emmené son bateau à voile au milieu du bassin

au beau milieu du bassin / de l'autre côté du bassin / loin du bord / près de l'autre bord

4. Le vent finira sans doute par le ramener au bord.

près du bord / de notre côté / près de nous / de ce côté

II. *Répétez en employant* **finir par** *avec l'infinitif:*

EX.:—J'irai en Europe.
—**Je finirai par aller en Europe.**

1. Je trouverai mon porte-monnaie. **2.** Elle ira en France. **3.** Vos yeux s'habitueront à l'obscurité. **4.** Il a répondu à ma lettre. **5.** J'ai trouvé le timbre que je cherchais. **6.** La jeune fille que j'attendais est venue. **7.** J'ai trouvé un taxi. **8.** L'autobus est arrivé. **9.** Je me suis souvenu de son adresse.

III. *Répondez en français à chacune des questions suivantes:*

1. Où Jean et Hélène entrent-ils? **2.** Qu'est-ce que c'est que le jardin des Tuileries? **3.** De quoi Hélène est-elle étonnée? **4.** Est-ce qu'elle croyait que la place de la Concorde était aussi vaste? **5.** Quel est le grand bâtiment qu'elle voit devant elle? **6.** Qu'est-ce que c'est que le Louvre? **7.** Où se trouve le musée du Louvre? **8.** Est-ce que le musée occupe tout l'édifice? **9.** Qu'est-ce que le musée possède? **10.** Combien y a-t-il d'arcs de triomphe à Paris? **11.** Qui les a fait construire? (Napoléon.) **12.** Où se trouve l'Arc de triomphe de l'Étoile? **13.** Pourquoi la petite fille pleure-t-elle? **14.** Qu'est-ce qu'Hélène demande à Jean de faire? **15.** Qu'est-ce que Jean répond? **16.** Pourquoi ne peut-il pas atteindre le petit bateau? **17.** Comment le bateau reviendra-t-il au bord? **18.** Pourquoi Hélène a-t-elle envie de cueillir une fleur? **19.** Pourquoi Jean lui dit-il de ne pas le faire?

IV. *Répondez en français à chacune des questions suivantes:*

1. Avez-vous jamais entendu parler du Louvre? **2.** Avez-vous jamais entendu parler du jardin des Tuileries? **3.** Avez-vous vu des photographies de l'Arc de triomphe de l'Étoile? **4.** Connaissez-vous quelques tableaux (*pictures*) qui sont au Louvre? **5.** Y a-t-il des arcs de triomphe en Amérique? **6.** Est-ce que vous avez jamais cueilli des fleurs dans un jardin public? **7.** Est-ce qu'un agent de police vous a jamais fait un procès-verbal? **8.** Êtes-vous jamais allé dans un bateau à voile?

V. *Dites en français:*

A. avoir beau faire, avoir beau essayer

1. Whatever I would do would be in vain. **2.** Whatever we would do would be in vain. **3.** Whatever you would do would be in vain. **4.** Whatever I did was in vain. **5.** Whatever we did was in vain. **6.** Whatever you did was in vain. **7.** Whatever I do will be in vain. **8.** Whatever we do will be in vain. **9.** Whatever you do will be in vain. **10.** It will be no use for me to try. **11.** It will be no use for him to try. **12.** It will be no use for her to try.

B. Emploi ou omission de l'article

1. What is that large building in front of us? It's the Louvre, a former royal palace. **2.** What is that book you have in your hand **(à la main)**? It's *Le Père Goriot*, a novel of Balzac. **3.** Who's the gentleman with whom you were talking? It's Mr. Lejeune, a former cabinet minister (**ministre**). **4.** It's Mr. Bedel, a former professor at the Sorbonne.

VI. Dictée d'après la Conversation 39, p.. 328-329.

VII. *Mettez le passage suivant au passé en employant* **le passé composé, l'imparfait, le conditionnel** *selon le cas:*

Un jour qu'ils se promènent dans le jardin des Tuileries, Hélène et Jean voient près du bassin une petite fille qui pleure. Hélène s'approche d'elle et lui demande ce qu'elle a. La petite fille répond que le vent a emmené son bateau à voile au milieu du bassin et qu'elle ne peut pas l'atteindre. Jean lui dit de ne pas pleurer, que son bateau n'est pas perdu, que le vent finira sûrement par le ramener au bord. Quelques minutes plus tard, la petite fille court de l'autre côté du bassin. Aux pleurs qui coulent de ses yeux succède un sourire de bonheur.

VIII. Conversation.

"Have you been to the Louvre?"
"Yes. I have just visited a part of the museum."
"Which part?"
"The picture galleries (**Les galeries de peinture**)."
"Did you see the Mona Lisa (**la Joconde**)?"
"Yes. I looked for it everywhere. But it was no use looking. I couldn't find it. I finally asked the guard (**le gardien**) . . ."
"What do you think of it?"
"It's doubtless a very fine picture. But I don't know much about pictures."

RUE DE RIVOLI ET LE LOUVRE

A Notre-Dame

JEAN – [1]Nous sommes maintenant dans l'île de la Cité.*

HÉLÈNE – [2]Est-ce qu'on n'appelle pas aussi cette île l'Île-de-France?

JEAN – [3]J'ai peur que vous ne confondiez vos îles, Hélène. [4]L'Île-de-France est la région autour de Paris. [5]L'île de la Cité est une île au milieu de la Seine.

HÉLÈNE – [6]Je reconnais, à droite, les tours de Notre-Dame. [7]Si nous visitions Notre-Dame?

JEAN – [8]Mais oui. Traversons la place et entrons dans la cathédrale.

HÉLÈNE – [9]Attendez que je prenne une photo.

JOHN – [1]*We are now on the Island of the City.*

HELEN – [2]*Don't they also call this island the Island of France?*

JOHN – [3]*I am afraid you are confusing your islands, Helen.* [4]*The Île-de-France is the region around Paris.* [5]*The Île de la Cité is an island in the middle of the Seine.*

HELEN – [6]*I recognize on the right the towers of Notre-Dame.* [7]*Suppose we visit Notre-Dame.*

JOHN – [8]*Certainly. Let's cross the square and go into the cathedral.*

HELEN – [9]*Wait for me to take a picture.*

* Le mot **Cité** est employé à Paris, comme à Londres, pour désigner la partie la plus ancienne et la plus centrale de la ville. Dans l'expression **l'île de la Cité** le mot **île** s'écrit avec **"î,"** tandis qu'on écrit l'**Île-de-France,** qui est un nom propre, avec un Î majuscule.

Dans Notre-Dame

HÉLÈNE – [10]Comme l'intérieur est vaste et silencieux! [11]On ose à peine parler, même à voix basse. [12]Je voudrais bien assister à une messe à Notre-Dame.

JEAN – [13]Si vous voulez, nous reviendrons dimanche prochain. [14]Vous pourrez entendre les grandes orgues.

HÉLÈNE – [15]Est-ce qu'on peut monter en *haut des tours?

JEAN – [16]Rien de plus facile. [17]Cet escalier en colimaçon nous y conduira. [18]En arrivant en haut, vous pourrez prendre d'autres photos.

In Notre-Dame

HELEN – [10]*How large and silent the interior is!* [11]*You hardly dare speak, even in a low voice.* [12]*I would like to go to a service at Notre-Dame.*

JOHN – [13]*If you want to, we will come back next Sunday.* [14]*You will be able to hear the great organ.*

HELEN – [15]*Can you go up to the top of the towers?*

JOHN – [16]*Nothing is easier.* [17]*This spiral staircase will take us up there.* [18]*When we get up to the top, you can take some more pictures.*

En haut d'une des tours de Notre-Dame

HÉLÈNE – [19]Je suis essoufflée . . . [20]Mais quel panorama! On voit Paris tout entier.

JEAN – [21]Devant vous, vous avez la Sainte-Chapelle, le Louvre et les Champs-Élysées; sur la rive gauche, le Quartier latin et la Sorbonne; et sur la rive droite, les grands boulevards et Montmartre.

HÉLÈNE – [22]J'ai hâte de visiter les quartiers de Paris que je ne connais pas encore.

At the top of one of the towers of Notre-Dame

HELEN – [19]*I am out of breath . . .* [20]*But what a panorama! You can see all Paris.*

JOHN – [21]*In front of you, you have the Sainte-Chapelle, the Louvre and the Champs Elysées; on the left bank, the Latin Quarter and the Sorbonne; and on the right bank, the Grands Boulevards and Montmartre.*

HELEN – [22]*I am very eager to visit the parts of Paris with which I am not yet acquainted.*

* Aspirate **h.**

I. Substitutions. *Répétez les phrases suivantes, en substituant les mots indiqués:*

1. Je voudrais bien assister à une messe à Notre-Dame.

   à une représentation à la Comédie-Française / à un concert à la salle Pleyel / à une conférence à la Sorbonne / aux courses à Chantilly

2. Ils ont assisté à une représentation à l'Opéra.

   au match de football / au mariage de Louise / à la cérémonie / à la messe de minuit

(Note that **assister à** means *to go to* or *to attend* a specific event or performance but that you don't use **assister à** with places, schools, etc.)

3. Je voudrais bien aller à Notre-Dame.

   à la Comédie-Française / à l'Opéra / à la Sorbonne / au cinéma

4. Mon oncle est allé à l'école en France.

   au lycée Henri Quatre / à l'université de Rennes / à la Sorbonne / au Collège de France

II. *Répondez en français à chacune des questions suivantes:*

1. Où sont Jean et Hélène maintenant? **2.** Qu'est-ce que c'est que l'Île-de-France? **3.** Où se trouve l'île de la Cité? **4.** Que confond Hélène? **5.** Qu'est-ce qu'elle voit à droite? **6.** Qu'est-ce qu'elle propose de faire? **7.** Qu'est-ce qu'Hélène veut faire avant d'entrer dans la cathédrale? **8.** Comment trouve-t-elle l'intérieur de la cathédrale? **9.** A quoi Hélène voudrait-elle assister? **10.** Quand Jean propose-t-il de revenir? **11.** Pourquoi propose-t-il de revenir ce jour-là? **12.** Est-ce qu'on peut monter en haut des tours de Notre-Dame? **13.** Comment y monte-t-on? **14.** Qu'est-ce qu'Hélène pourra faire en arrivant en haut? **15.** Comment se sent-elle en arrivant en haut? **16.** Qu'est-ce qu'on voit du haut des tours de Notre-Dame? **17.** Qu'est-ce qu'on voit sur la rive gauche? **18.** Qu'est-ce qu'on voit sur la rive droite? **19.** Qu'est-ce qu'Hélène a hâte de visiter? **20.** Quels quartiers de Paris a-t-elle déjà visités?

III. *Demandez à quelqu'un:*

1. s'il voudrait assister à une messe à Notre-Dame. **2.** s'il voudrait voir la place de la Concorde. **3.** s'il voudrait voir l'Arc de triomphe. **4.** s'il voudrait visiter le musée du Louvre. **5.** s'il sait conduire une auto. **6.** s'il aime bien conduire une auto. **7.** s'il voudrait conduire une auto à Paris.

IV. Exercices d'application.

A. *Répétez les phrases suivantes, en remplaçant* **craindre que (ne)** *par*

(1) **Avoir peur que (ne)** (See footnote on page 286).

1. Je crains que vous ne confondiez vos îles. **2.** Je crains que vous ne soyez en retard. **3.** Je crains que vous ne soyez pas à l'heure. **4.** Nous craignons que vous ne soyez un peu déçus. **5.** Nous craignons que vous ne soyez pas contents.

(2) **avoir peur de:**

1. Je crains la pluie. **2.** Il craint le froid. **3.** Elle ne craint rien. **4.** Qu'est-ce que vous craignez? (De quoi . . .) **5.** Je crains d'être en retard. **6.** Je crains de ne pas arriver à l'heure. **7.** Vous craignez tout.

B. *Répétez les phrases suivantes, en employant* **attendez que** *et le subjonctif*:

EX.:—Je vais prendre une photo.
Attendez que je prenne une photo.

1. Je vais acheter des cigarettes. **2.** Je vais jeter un coup d'œil sur le journal. **3.** Je vais finir cette histoire. **4.** Je vais boire mon café. **5.** Je vais finir mon travail. **6.** Je vais ouvrir la fenêtre.

C. *Répétez en remplaçant* **avoir envie** (to feel like) *par* **avoir hâte** (to be eager to):

1. J'ai envie de visiter les quartiers de Paris que je ne connais pas encore. **2.** J'ai envie d'aller à la campagne. **3.** J'ai envie de partir en vacances. **4.** Nous avons envie de déjeuner. **5.** Nous avons envie de voir la Sainte-Chapelle. **6.** Nous avons envie d'assister à une représentation à la Comédie-Française.

V. *Dites en français:*

1. There are many factories around Paris. **2.** There used to be a château in the middle of the Garden of the Tuileries. **3.** There is an Egyptian Obelisk (**un obélisque égyptien**) in the middle of the Place de la Concorde. **4.** Have you ever been up (**monter**) to the top of the towers of Notre-Dame? **5.** I would like to go up to the top of the Eiffel Tower. **6.** From the top of the towers of Notre-Dame, you can see all of Paris.

VI. Dictée d'après la Conversation 40, pp. 341-342.

VII. Conversation.

Vous montez avec un ami (une amie) en haut d'un gratte-ciel de New York. Vous prenez l'ascenseur (*elevator*). Arrivé(e) en haut, vous attirez l'attention de votre ami(e) sur le port, les grands bateaux, le musée Métropolitain, le Parc Central, etc.

AUX GRANDS HOMMES LA PATRIE RECONNAISSANTE

De retour à Paris

—Si nous visitions le Panthéon? dit un jour Jean à Roger. Je n'y suis jamais allé.

Les deux jeunes gens se dirigent donc vers le Panthéon. A quelque distance, ils s'arrêtent un instant pour regarder la façade de l'édifice.

—Vous voyez là-haut la Patrie entre la Liberté et l'Histoire en train de distribuer des prix aux grands hommes, explique Roger. Lisez l'inscription: AUX GRANDS HOMMES LA PATRIE RECONNAISSANTE.

Tout en montant l'escalier, Roger lui dit un mot de l'histoire du Panthéon. C'est une ancienne église du dix-huitième siècle que la Révolution a transformée en temple destiné à servir de lieu de sépulture à ses grands hommes. La Révolution y a mis Voltaire et Rousseau. On y a enterré ensuite des hommes politiques ou des écrivains plus ou moins continuateurs de la tradition révolutionnaire, Hugo et Zola par exemple.

A l'intérieur, un guide explique aux visiteurs les peintures murales qui représentent des scènes de la vie de sainte Geneviève. C'était une jeune fille qui vivait il y a quinze cents ans et qui, selon la légende, a sauvé Paris d'Attila et de ses Huns.

—Elle est devenue la patronne de la ville, continue le guide. En son honneur, on appelait autrefois le quartier de l'université la Montagne Sainte-Geneviève.

—Voilà une montagne facilement accessible, dit Jean à son ami. Le boulevard Saint-Michel vous mène tout droit au sommet.

—Rappelez-vous qu'une partie du vignoble champenois est sur des collines appelées la Montagne-de-Reims. Il y a montagnes et montagnes, des grandes et des petites . . .

—Après tout, Mount Vernon n'est qu'une simple colline.

Le guide conduit ensuite les visiteurs dans la galerie souterraine où se trouvent les tombeaux. D'une voix monotone, il récite des phrases apprises par cœur. Arrivé devant le tombeau de Jean-Jacques Rousseau, il explique que «par la porte entr'ouverte du tombeau sort une main tenant une torche allumée». Symbolisme assez lugubre, pense Jean, mais fort clair.

Après leur visite, les deux jeunes gens descendent le boulevard Saint-Michel jusqu'à la Seine. Arrivés en vue de Notre-Dame, ils tournent à gauche. Les rues le long de la Seine dominent le fleuve, et c'est sur le parapet du fleuve, à l'ombre des arbres, que les bouquinistes ont installé leurs boîtes. Jean s'étonne un peu du choix de cet endroit.

—Vous avez peut-être vu de vieilles estampes représentant le Pont-Neuf tel qu'il était il y a trois siècles, avec des boutiques de chaque côté, explique Roger. Le pont était toute la journée couvert de monde et c'était naturellement un excellent endroit pour le commerce des livres, des modes, etc. Chassés du pont, les commerçants se sont installés au bord du fleuve.

Tout en marchant, Jean jette un coup d'œil sur les étalages. Il voit là toute sorte de choses, livres anciens et modernes, timbres-poste et vieilles pièces de monnaie pour les collectionneurs. Dans une boutique du quai Malaquais, il achète une paire de vieux pistolets — «pour ma chambre en Amérique», explique-t-il à Roger. Il met l'un des pistolets dans la poche droite, l'autre dans la poche gauche de son pardessus.

—Attention! lui dit en riant son ami. Si un agent de police vous voyait, il pourrait bien vous faire un procès-verbal: Vous avez sur vous des armes prohibées!

Les deux amis continuent leur promenade, traversent la Seine, la place de la Concorde et finissent l'après-midi à la terrasse d'un café sur les Grands Boulevards.

QUESTIONS

1. Quelle est l'inscription sur la façade du Panthéon? **2.** Connaissez-vous des grands hommes qui sont enterrés au Panthéon? **3.** Que représentent les peintures murales à l'intérieur du Panthéon? **4.** Quand vivait sainte Geneviève? **5.** Pourquoi est-elle devenue la patronne de Paris? **6.** Où le guide conduit-il les visiteurs? **7.** Où les bouquinistes ont-ils installé leurs boîtes? **8.** Qu'est-ce qu'il y avait autrefois de chaque côté du Pont-Neuf? **9.** Qu'est-ce que Jean achète dans une boutique du quai Malaquais? **10.** Où met-il les pistolets qu'il achète? **11.** Pourquoi Roger lui dit-il de faire attention? **12.** Comment les deux amis finissent-ils l'après-midi?

PARIS: L'ÎLE SAINT-LOUIS

Use of Infinitives and Present Participles

116. *Verbs that may take infinitives.*

A. Verbs and verbal expressions followed by the preposition **de** that may take infinitives:

—**Permettez-moi de** vous présenter mon ami Jean Hughes.	*Allow me to* introduce my friend John Hughes.
—**Vous serez obligé de** passer la nuit à Épernay.	*You will be obliged to* spend the night at Épernay.
—**Je regrette d'**être en retard.	*I am sorry to* be late.
—**Nous avons décidé de** profiter du beau temps.	*We decided to* take advantage of the fine weather.
—**J'ai demandé** à mon père **de** m'envoyer un chèque.	*I asked* my father *to* send me a check.
—**Il** m'**a dit de** ne pas l'attendre.	*He told* me *not to* wait for him.
—**Il** m'**a conseillé** de me reposer.	*He advised* me to rest.

(1) The commonest verbs followed by **de** that may take infinitives are: **conseiller de, décider de, se dépêcher de, dire de, essayer de, être obligé de, permettre de, refuser de,** etc., and such expressions as **avoir besoin de, avoir l'habitude de, être en train de,** etc.

(2) You have seen that some of these verbs may govern a subordinate clause. Ex.: —**Il m'a dit qu'il reviendrait. Je regrette qu'il soit venu.**

B. Verbs followed by the preposition **à** that may take infinitives:

—**Il a commencé à** pleuvoir.	*It began to* rain.
—**Il s'est mis à** pleuvoir.	*It began to* rain.
—**Avez-vous appris à** parler français?	*Have you learned to* speak French?
—**Nous avons continué à** marcher.	*We kept on* walking.
—**Vous n'avez qu'à** traverser la rue.	*You have only to* cross the street.

The commonest verbs followed by the preposition **à** that may take infinitives are: **aider à,** *to help;* **apprendre à,** *to learn;* **commencer à; réussir à,** *to succeed;* **inviter à,** *to invite;* **se mettre à,** *to begin;* **avoir à,** *to have to,* etc.

C. Verbs that may take infinitives without a preposition:

—**Je vais faire** des courses cet après-midi.	*I am going to do* some errands this afternoon.
—**Pouvez-vous** me **donner** votre adresse?	*Can you give* me your address?
—**Savez-vous jouer** au bridge?*	*Do you know* how *to play* bridge?
—**Savez-vous jouer** de la guitare?	*Do you know* how *to play* the guitar?
—**Je dois partir** par le train de sept heures.	*I am to leave* by the seven o'clock train.
—**Voulez-vous faire** une promenade avec moi?	*Do you want to take* a walk with me?
—**Faut-il changer** de train en route?	*Must one change* trains on the way?

The commonest verbs that may take an infinitive without a preposition are: **aller; devoir; faire; falloir (il faut,** etc.); **oser,** *to dare;* **pouvoir; savoir; venir; vouloir.**

117. *Forms of the verb used after prepositions.*

A. Present infinitive after prepositions **par, pour, sans,** and expressions such as **avant de:**

—Il m'a envoyé une dépêche **avant de partir.**	He sent me a wire *before leaving.*
—Il est parti **sans dire** au revoir.	He left *without saying* good-bye.
—Le vent finira **par** le **ramener** au bord.	The wind will finally *bring* it *back* to the edge.
—Nous ne l'attendrons pas **pour déjeuner.**	We will not wait with lunch for him (We will not wait for him *to have lunch*).
—**Pour arriver** à l'heure, j'ai quitté la maison à sept heures.	*So as to arrive* on time, I left home at seven o'clock.
—Il faut manger **pour vivre . . .**	You must eat *to live . . .*

Pour is generally used with an infinitive to express the idea *so as to* or *in order to;* but when it is used after **aller** with an infinitive, it has the meaning *for the express purpose of.* Ex.:

—Je vais en ville **faire** des courses.	I am going downtown *to do* some errands.
—Je vais en ville **pour faire** des courses.	I am going downtown *for the express purpose of doing* some errands.

* Note that playing games is **jouer à** but playing a musical instrument is **jouer de.**

B. Perfect infinitive after **après:**

—**Après avoir visité** Versailles, nous sommes allés à Fontainebleau.	*After visiting* (*having visited*) Versailles, we went to Fontainebleau.
—**Après être allé** en Normandie, Jean est allé en Bretagne.	*After going* (*having gone*) to Normandy, John went to Brittany.

C. Present participle after **en:**

—**En partant** à cinq heures, vous serez chez vous à sept heures.	*By leaving* at five o'clock, you will be home at seven.
—**En arrivant** en haut, vous pourrez prendre d'autres photos.	*On arriving* at the top, you can take some more pictures.

The present participle of verbs may be found by adding the ending **-ant** to the stem of the first person plural of the present indicative, except for the verbs **avoir, être,** and **savoir** whose present participles are, respectively, **ayant, étant,** and **sachant.**

I. Substitutions. *Répétez les phrases suivantes en substituant les mots indiqués:*

1. Il a décidé de partir ce soir.

a refusé / a été obligé / a regretté / m'a demandé / m'a dit

2. Elle a besoin de faire des courses.

a l'habitude / est en train / est contente / a envie

3. Nous avons commencé à parler français.

continué / réussi / appris

4. Savez-vous jouer au bridge?

du piano / au tennis / de la clarinette / aux cartes / de la harpe

II. Exercices d'application.

A. *Répétez les phrases suivantes, en remplaçant le passé composé, et le mot* **puis** *par le passé de l'infinitif avec* **après:**

EX.:—Nous avons visité Versailles, puis nous sommes allés à Fontainebleau.
—**Après avoir visité Versailles, nous sommes allés à Fontainebleau.**

1. Elle a visité l'Angleterre, puis elle est allée en France. **2.** Elle est allée à Rouen, puis elle est allée à Paris. **3.** Elle a déjeuné, puis elle a jeté un coup d'œil sur le journal. **4.** Il a regardé les étalages des bouquinistes, puis il a acheté des timbres. **5.** Il s'est couché, puis il s'est endormi tout de suite.

B. *Employez le participe présent dans chacune des phrases suivantes:*

EX.:—Si vous partez à cinq heures, vous serez chez vous à sept heures.
—**En partant à cinq heures, vous serez chez vous à sept heures.**

1. Si nous partons maintenant, nous arriverons à l'heure. **2.** Quand nous irons au Panthéon, nous verrons le Quartier latin. **3.** Quand je regardais les étalages des bouquinistes, j'ai trouvé une belle estampe. **4.** Quand nous irons à l'île de la Cité, nous traverserons le Pont-Neuf.* **5.** Quand nous traverserons le Pont-Neuf, nous jetterons un coup d'œil sur la Seine. **6.** Quand vous arriverez en haut de la tour, vous pourrez prendre d'autres photos.

III. *Répondez en français:*

1. Vous êtes-vous dépêché(e) de déjeuner ce matin? **2.** Avez-vous regretté de ne pas vous être levé(e) plus tôt? **3.** Avez-vous l'habitude de vous dépêcher le matin? **4.** Qu'est-ce que vous avez à faire cet après-midi? **5.** Prenez-vous l'autobus pour rentrer chez vous? **6.** Est-ce que vous attendez qu'il fasse chaud pour aller nager (*to swim*)? **7.** Avez-vous l'intention d'aller en France un de ces jours? **8.** Est-ce qu'Hélène a réussi à trouver les timbres qu'elle cherchait? **9.** Seriez-vous content(e) de passer quelques jours dans une ferme? **10.** Quels quartiers de Paris Hélène a-t-elle vus avant de visiter Notre-Dame?

IV. Révision. *Dites en français:*

(*a*) **1.** I am glad to know it. **2.** I am glad you know it. **3.** I am sorry to leave. **4.** I am sorry he has left. **5.** Helen wants to go the Louvre. **6.** She wants me to go with her. **7.** I shall wait for you until noon. **8.** I shall wait for you until you come.† **9.** I am sending him a wire to announce my arrival. **10.** I am sending him a wire so he will know I am coming.

(*b*) **1.** He finally sent me his address. **2.** We finally decided to stay at home. **3.** I finally found the Mona Lisa (**la Joconde**). **4.** He left without leaving his address. **5.** That goes without saying. **6.** "One must eat to live, not (**et non pas**) live to eat." **7.** He told me to wait for him. **8.** He told me not to wait for him. **9.** He told me to hurry. **10.** He told me not to hurry. **11.** He told me not to bother. **12.** I took a taxi so as not to be late. **13.** He asked me not to leave before seeing him. **14.** I told you not to pick those mushrooms.

* Le Pont-Neuf (*The New Bridge*) est le plus célèbre des ponts de Paris. Bien qu'il ait été construit au commencement du dix-septième siècle, on l'appelle toujours le Pont-Neuf.

† Use **jusqu'à ce que** and subjunctive.

V. Révision des dialogues, pp. 310-311 et pp. 322-323.

1. Qui est venu attendre Jean et Roger à la gare? **2.** Est-ce que Marie leur a manqué? **3.** Qu'est-ce que Marie devait faire le jour de leur arrivée? **4.** Comment a-t-elle appris qu'ils devaient arriver? **5.** Qu'est-ce qu'ils auraient dû lui dire dans leur dépêche? **6.** Pourquoi ne lui ont-ils pas dit l'heure exacte de leur arrivée? **7.** Est-ce qu'ils se rendent compte du sacrifice qu'elle a fait? **8.** Comment Jean a-t-il appris qu'Hélène Frazer devait arriver ces jours-ci? **9.** Dans quel quartier se trouve le Panthéon? **10.** Connaissez-vous quelques-uns des livres de Victor Hugo? **11.** Est-ce que la Sorbonne est loin du Panthéon? **12.** A quelle époque saint Louis était-il roi de France? **13.** Quand Robert de Sorbon a-t-il fondé son collège? **14.** Est-ce que vous vous rappelez le nom de l'hôpital fondé à Paris par saint Louis? **15.** De quel style d'architecture est la Sainte-Chapelle? **16.** Connaissez-vous d'autres monuments en France qui datent de l'époque gothique?

REFERENCE MATERIALS

Table of Sounds of the French Language

As Represented by Symbols of the International Phonetic Alphabet

		Bi-labial	*Labio-dental*	*Dental and Alveolar*	*Palato-alveolar*	*Palatal*	*Velar*	*Uvular*
CONSONANTS	*Plosive*	p b		t d			k g	
	Nasal	m		n		ɲ		
	Resonants			l				ʀ
	Fricative		f v	s z	ʃ ʒ			
	Semi-vowels	w ɥ				j (ɥ)	(w)	
VOWELS	*Close*					*Front Central Back* i y u		
	Half-close					e ø ə o õ		
	Half-open					ɛ ɛ̃ œ œ̃ ɔ		
	Open					a ɑ ɑ̃		

I. Introduction

In this section, and in the vocabulary, we indicate the pronunciation of French words by symbols of the International Phonetic Alphabet. It looks confusing at first: indeed, when you see that **Bonjour, monsieur,** for example, is pronounced [bõʒuʀ məsjø] you may think that the transcription is worse than the French spelling! But at least you can see clearly and immediately that the **n** of **bon** is not sounded, that **mon** is not pronounced **mŏn,** that **sieur** is not pronounced **shur,** and so on. With a little practice, you will find that the transcriptions are invaluable for pronunciation exercises. If you refer to the Key whenever you do not understand what a symbol indicates, you will quickly learn what each of the 36 symbols represents. In the Key, we use only French words to illustrate the sounds that the symbols represent instead of trying to explain the sounds of French in terms of English. The reason for this is (1) it is misleading, if not downright false, to say that any French sound is the same as any English sound, and (2) the easiest and most direct way of knowing what a given symbol represents is to hear it in a familiar word or phrase. (The key can be found on p. 364.)

You don't need to memorize the symbols before you begin using them — any more than you would memorize all the diacritical marks in an English dictionary before looking up a word. And you don't need to write in phonetic symbols any more than you need to be able to write diacritical marks in English — at least not at first.

II. Transcriptions and Exercises

A. THE FIRST STEP

The first step in getting a good French accent is to *hear* how French phrases really sound. If you listen carefully to your instructor and the voices on the tapes, you will quickly realize that the rhythm and intonation of French phrases are entirely different from English. In saying "Where is the restaurant?" for example, most of us would put strong accents on *where* and on the syllable *rest-*, and we would enunciate the vowels quite clearly; but we would pronounce the rest of the syllables of the phrase with so little stress that the vowels *e*, *au*, and *a* would all sound very much alike. A French person who is not familiar with our system of accented and unaccented syllables, however, would say something like: "Wear eez zee res-tau-rant?" in six syllables of equal length. You are so used to hearing certain syllables stressed and others unstressed, that you would *think* the Frenchman is merely accenting the wrong syllables. But that is not what he is doing: he is really giving each syllable equal stress as he would in speaking French — where there are no accented syllables and, consequently, no unaccented ones. To make things even worse, he is using French sounds because in French there is no *wh* (as in *where*), no ĭ (as in *is*), and no *th* (as in *the*). Moreover the French "R" is entirely different from ours.

Once you accept the idea that French people really give equal stress to each pronounced syllable, you can quickly catch the rhythm of simple French phrases and you are ready to do the first rhythm exercises. Don't worry about the individual sounds for the moment. It will be much easier to learn them after you catch the rhythm of a few complete phrases.

B. A NOTE ON FRENCH INTONATION

French intonation differs from English intonation in at least three ways. The following sentences, based on the vocabulary of Conversation 5, will roughly illustrate all three differences. (The intonations given below are free from word emphasis.)

Mon père // habite / à Philadelphie.

Mais la sœur / de mon père // est en France.

My father // lives / in Philadelphia.

But my father's / sister // is in France.

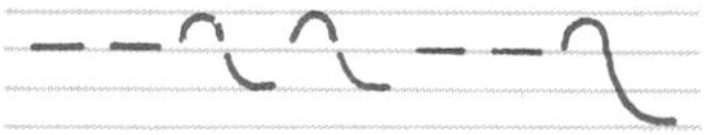

First difference. To express continuation, to indicate that a statement is not finished, French sense-groups, such as **Mon père, habite, Mais la sœur, de mon père,** *rise* to the last syllable: **. . . père, . . . -bite, . . . sœur, . . . père:** whereas English sense-groups, such as *My father, lives, But my father's, sister,* tend to *fall after the stressed syllable: . . . father, . . . lives, . . . father's, . . . sister.*

Second difference. To express finality, to indicate that a sentence is ending, French intonation falls continuously, starting with the very *first* syllable of the last sense-group: **. . . Philadelphie, . . . est en France;** whereas English intonation falls only *after* the last stressed syllable of the last sense-group: **. . . Philadelphia,** or after the beginning of the last stressed syllable: **. . . France.**

Note 1. The contrast between continuation and finality is well marked in French since continuation is rising and finality falling. In English, both continuation and finality are falling — the difference is only a matter of degree: finality falls lower than continuation.

Third difference. In the rising curves of continuation, French makes a clear distinction between the high rise of *major* continuation, as in **Mon père, de mon père,** and the moderate rise of *minor* continuation, as in **habite, Mais la sœur.** English does not make this distinction, or does not stress it to the same extent as French. Between the falling curves of *father* and *lives*, of *father's* and *sister*, no significant difference is made.

Note 2. The continuity of the fall, for finality, and of the rise, for continuation, applies to all the other types of falling or rising intonations in French. For instance, falling questions, such as:

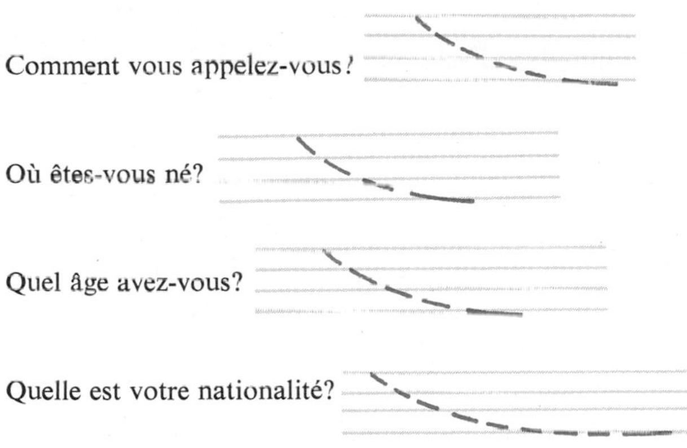
Comment vous appelez-vous?
Où êtes-vous né?
Quel âge avez-vous?
Quelle est votre nationalité?

always begin to fall at the very first syllable.

In English, such questions tend to fall only after the last syllable:

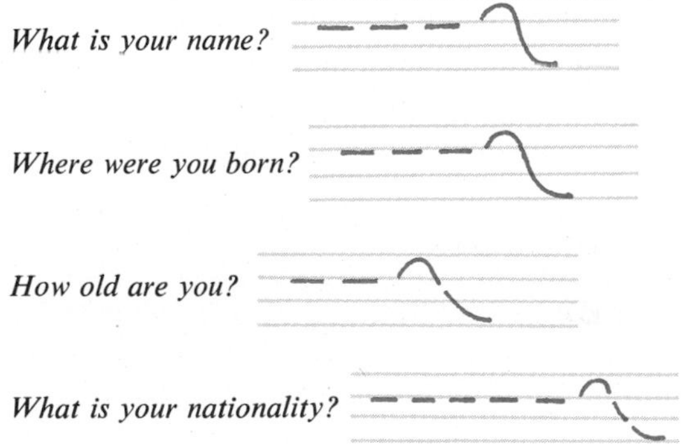
What is your name?
Where were you born?
How old are you?
What is your nationality?

Similarly, rising questions, such as:

Avez-vous des parents?

rise continuously, from the first to the last syllable.

In English, rising questions, such as:

Have you any relatives?

tend to rise only after the last stressed syllable.

C. KEY TO PHONETIC ALPHABET

CONSONANTS

[p] *as in* **p**arlez-vous?
[b] *as in* **b**onjour
[t] *as in* **t**out droit
[d] *as in* **d**e rien
[k] *as in* **c**omment?
[g] *as in* la **g**are
[m] *as in* **m**onsieur
[n] *as in* u**n**e ba**n**a**n**e
[ɲ] *as in* à la campa**gn**e
[l] *as in* **l**e château
[ʀ] *as in* bonjou**r**
[f] *as in* en **f**ace
[v] *as in* au re**v**oir
[s] *as in* **s**'il vous plaît
[z] *as in* mu**s**ée
[ʃ] *as in* à gau**ch**e
[ʒ] *as in* **j**e vais

VOWELS

[i] *as in* voic**i**
[y] *as in* s**u**r la place
[e] *as in* all**e**z-vous?
[ø] *as in* un p**eu**
[ə] *as in* d**e** rien
[ɛ] *as in* **ê**tes-vous?
[ɛ̃] *as in* v**in**
[œ] *as in* onze h**eu**res
[œ̃] *as in* **un** restaurant
[a] *as in* **à** l**a** g**a**re
[ɑ] *as in* là-b**a**s
[ɑ̃] *as in* **en** Fr**an**ce
[ɔ] *as in* le bureau de p**o**ste
[o] *as in* l'h**ô**tel
[õ] *as in* b**on**jour
[u] *as in* bonj**ou**r

SEMI-VOWELS

[w] *as in* **ou**i [j] *as in* b**i**en [ɥ] *as in* h**u**it

D. THE TRANSCRIPTION AND THE TAPES

In the phonetic transcription, we have tried to follow the normal usage of conservative people from the region around Paris. For example, we distinguish between the back "a" [ɑ] (as in **pas**) and the front "a" [a] (as in **la table**) even though many people are failing, more and more, to make this distinction. And we use the open "e" [ɛ] in **est, -ais, -ait, -aient, -et,** although there is a strong tendency to pronounce the "e" in **est** like the "é" in **été.**

We have tried to have the voices on the tapes follow patterns of intonation, pronunciation, and linking fairly consistently; but it should be observed that no one is absolutely consistent and that it is perfectly natural to utter a phrase one way one time and another the next. We have preferred natural variation rather than perfect consistency, since we aim to teach the normal speech of educated Parisians rather than an artificial language that no one speaks.

CONVERSATION 1

IPA Transcription of Dialog

1. bõʒuʀ, məsjø. **2.** bõʒuʀ, madam. **3.** ɛtvu məsjø yg? **4.** wi, madam, ʒəsɥi ʒɑ̃ yg. **5.** kɔmɑ̃talevu, məsjø? **6.** bjɛ̃, mɛʀsi. evu mɛm? **7.** pɑmal, mɛʀsi. **8.** paʀlevu ɑ̃glɛ? **9.** nõ, ʒən paʀlə pɑ(z)ɑ̃glɛ. **10** mɛ vu paʀle fʀɑ̃sɛ, nɛspa? **11.** wi, madam, ʒpaʀl œ̃pø fʀɑ̃sɛ. **12.** vwasi yn lɛtʀə puʀ vu. **13.** mɛʀsi boku. **14.** a vɔtʀə sɛʀvis, məsjø. **15.** ɔʀvwaʀ, madam. **16.** ɔʀvwaʀ, məsjø.

I. Exercices de rhythme (Rhythm exercises):

The first exercise contains phrases of four syllables. You first listen to the instructor or the voices on the tape. Then you establish the rhythm for yourself by tapping four sharp, even taps on the table or repeating four times a syllable such as *toc, toc, toc, toc.* Then you repeat the phrases several times in the same rhythm without accenting any syllable and without slighting any syllable.

A. *Repeat in four short, equally stressed syllables:*

1. Bonjour monsieur (madam~~e~~). [bõ ʒuʀ mə sjø (ma dam).]
2. Merci monsieur (madam~~e~~). [mɛʀ si mə sjø.]
3. Au r~~e~~voir monsieur (madam~~e~~). [ɔʀ vwaʀ mə sjø.]

B. *Repeat in five short, equally stressed syllables:*

(*a*)	**1.** Bonjour mad∉moisell∉.	[bõ ʒuʀ mad mwa zɛl.]
	2. Merci mad∉moisell∉.	[mɛʀ si mad mwa zɛl.]
	3. A votre servic∉.	[a vɔtʀə sɛʀvis.]
	4. Au r∉voir mad∉moisell∉.	[ɔʀvwaʀ mad mwa zɛl.]
(*b*)	**1.** Êtes-vous Monsieur Hughes?	[ɛt vu mə sjø yg?]
	2. Comment allez-vous?	[kɔ mɑ̃ ta le vu?]
	3. Parlez-vous français?	[paʀ le vu fʀɑ̃ sɛ?]
	4. Parlez-vous anglais?	[paʀ le vu ɑ̃ glɛ̃?]
	5. J∉ parl∉ un peu français.	[ʒpaʀl œ̃ pø fʀɑ̃ sɛ.]
	6. J∉ parl∉ un peu anglais.	[ʒpaʀl œ̃ pø ɑ̃ glɛ.]

C. *Repeat in six short, equally stressed syllables:*

1. Merci beaucoup monsieur.	[mɛʀ si bo ku mə sjø.]
2. Merci beaucoup madam∉.	[mɛʀ si bo ku ma dam.]
3. Mais vous parlez français.	[mɛ vu paʀ le fʀɑ̃ sɛ.]
4. Mais vous parlez anglais.	[mɛ vu paʀ le ɑ̃ glɛ.]

D. *Repeat in seven short, equally stressed syllables:*

1. Vous parlez français n'est-c∉ pas?	[vu paʀ le fʀɑ̃ sɛ nɛs pɑ?]
2. Vous parlez anglais n'est-c∉ pas?	[vu paʀ le ɑ̃ glɛ nɛs pɑ?]
3. J∉ parl∉ un peu français monsieur.	[ʒpaʀl œ̃ pø fʀɑ̃ sɛ mə sjø.]
4. J∉ parl∉ un peu français madam∉.	[ʒpaʀl œ̃ pø fʀɑ̃ sɛ ma dam.]
5. J∉ parl∉ un peu anglais monsieur.	[ʒpaʀl œ̃ pø ɑ̃ glɛ mə sjø.]
6. J∉ parl∉ un peu anglais madam∉.	[ʒpaʀl œ̃ pø ɑ̃ glɛ̃ ma dam.]
7. Voici un∉ lettre pour vous.	[vwa si yn lɛtʀə puʀ vu.]

E. *Repeat in eight short equally stressed syllables:*

1. Je n∉ parle pas français monsieur.	[ʒən paʀlə pɑ fʀɑ̃ sɛ mə sjø.]
2. Je n∉ parle pas français madam∉.	[ʒən paʀlə pɑ fʀɑ̃ sɛ ma dam.]
3. Je n∉ parle pas anglais monsieur.	[ʒən paʀlə pɑ ɑ̃ glɛ mə sjø.]
4. Je n∉ parle pas anglais madam∉.	[ʒən paʀlə pɑ ɑ̃ glɛ ma dam.]

II. Pronunciation exercises.

A. *French uvular "R".*

Your natural reaction to the letter "r" is to turn the tip of your tongue up as you do in pronouncing an **r** in English; but if you turn the tip of your tongue up, you will simply . . . produce an English **r**! So in learning the French uvular "ʀ", you first put the tip of your tongue against your lower front teeth and *hold it there firmly*. Then you pronounce the English words *Ah!* and *agog*, noting that the "g" is pronounced in the back of your mouth by raising the back of your tongue until it touches your palate. Next you move your tongue a little farther back than the position in which you pronounce this [g] and pronounce very lightly each of the following French words: **art** [aʀ], **rat** [ʀa], **gare** [gaʀ], **rare** [ʀaʀ]. Repeat this series a dozen times, keeping the tip of your tongue down, using as little breath as possible, and pronouncing the "ʀ" as lightly as you can. Avoid gargling the "ʀ"! Many French people pronounce it so lightly that Americans can scarcely hear it at all.

Now repeat three times each of the following words and expressions — giving equal stress to each syllable and producing the uvular "ʀ" with care:

1. Une lettre [yn lɛtʀə]. **2.** Voilà une lettre pour vous [vwa la yn lɛtʀə puʀ vu]. **3.** Bonjour [bõ ʒuʀ]. **4.** Au revoir [ɔʀ vwaʀ]. **5.** Merci [mɛʀ si]. **6.** A votre service [a vɔtʀə sɛʀvis]. **7.** Parlez-vous français? [paʀ le vu fʀɑ̃ sɛ?]. **8.** Je parle un peu français [ʒpaʀl œ̃ pø fʀɑ̃ sɛ].

Repeat this exercise several times each day until you can produce the [ʀ] lightly, elegantly, and unselfconsciously. Never under any circumstances substitute an American **r** or a Spanish **r** for the uvular "ʀ". If you pronounce French words and phrases wrong even *a few times*, it makes it much more difficult to get a good French accent.

B. *Exercise on the French* "u". (*Represented by the symbol* [y]).

When you see the letter "u" you will naturally put your tongue in position to say "oo" as in English; but if you put your tongue in that position, you will just say "oo." So in learning to pronounce the French [y], the first step is to put your tongue in the position to say "ee" in English or [i] in French *and keep it there.*

Now you say: **Voici, i, i, i** several times, keeping the vowel [i] short.

Next you say [i] several times and round your lips while repeating the sound [i]. If you do this, you will produce a proper French [y].

Now repeat several times: [i], [y], [i], [y] very crisply and without moving your tongue.

Now say: Voici une lettre pour vous [vwa si yn lɛ tʀə puʀ vu] several times.

If you still have trouble producing the French [y], you put your hands at the corners of your mouth, say **i, i, i, i,** while moving your lips forward and backwards so that you can't help saying [i] [y], [i] [y].

Repeat this exercise daily until you can produce this sound easily. Always think of the sound [i] as in **voici** and avoid thinking of [u] as in **vous.**

CONVERSATION 2

IPA Transcription of Dialog

a la gaʀ

1. paʀdõ məsjø. u ɛ lʃɑto, silvuplɛ? **2.** (œ̃nɑ̃plwaje) tudʀwɑ, məsjø. **3.** u ɛ lmyze? **4.** lmy ze ɛ dɑ̃ lʃɑto. **5.** jatil œ̃ʀɛstɔʀɑ̃ pʀɛ dy ʃɑto? **6.** wi, məsjø. ilja œ̃ ʀɛstɔʀɑ̃ pʀɛ dy ʃɑto. **7.** mɛʀsi boku. **8.** dəʀjɛ̃, məsjø.

dɑ̃ la ʀy

9. (a œ̃pɑsɑ̃) paʀdõ, məsjø. u ɛl byʀod pɔst? **10.** la pɔst ɛ syʀ la plas, la bɑ, a goʃ. **11.** jati lœ̃ byʀod taba pʀɛdisi? **12.** mɛ wi, məsjø. ilja œ̃ byʀod taba dɑ̃ laʀy dla pɛ? **13.** uɛ laʀy dla pɛ? **14.** a dʀwat, məsjø. **15.** mɛʀsi boku.

I. Exercices de rhythme.

A. *Répétez en quatre syllabes:*

1. Où est l~~e~~ château?	[u ɛ lʃɑ to?]
2. Où est l~~e~~ musée?	[u ɛ lmyze?]
3. Il n'y a pas d~~e~~ quoi.	[il nja pɑd kwa.]

B. *Répétez en cinq syllabes:*

1. Où est l~~e~~ bureau d~~e~~ post~~e~~?	[u ɛ lby ʀod pɔst?]
2. Où est l~~e~~ restaurant?	[u ɛ lʀɛs tɔ ʀɑ̃?]
3. Dans la rue d~~e~~ la Paix.	[dɑ̃ la ʀy dla pɛ.]
4. Sur la plac~~e~~, monsieur.	[syʀ la plas mə sjø.]

C. *Répétez en six syllabes:*

1. Où est l~~e~~ bureau d~~e~~ tabac?	[u ɛ lby ʀod ta ba?]
2. Où est la rue d~~e~~ la Paix?	[u ɛ la ʀy dla pɛ?]
3. Y a-t-il un restaurant . . .?	[ja ti lœ̃ ʀɛs tɔ ʀɑ̃ . . . ?]
4. Il y a un restaurant . . .	[i lja œ̃ ʀɛs tɔ ʀɑ̃ . . .]
5. Il n'y a pas d~~e~~ quoi, monsieur.	[il nja pɑd kwa mə sjø.]

II. Exercices de prononciation.

A. *Exercise on* **e** [e] *as in* **allez-vous** *and* **eu** [ø] *as in* **un peu.**

1. *Say* [e] as in allez; **e, e, e.** Keep the vowel short and clear.

Répétez: (1) Comment allez-vous? (2) un employ**é.** (3) le mus**ée.** (4) **et** vous? (5) un **é**tudiant.

2. *Say* [e], [e], [e]. Keep repeating this sound, holding the tip of your tongue against your lower front teeth and rounding your lips until you produce the sound [ø] as in **un peu.**

Répétez: [e], [e], [e]; [ø], [ø], [ø]. (1) un p**eu.** (2) monsi**eur.** (3) d**eux.**

B. *Review exercises on* [R] *and* [y] *from Conversation 1.*

III. Note on linking:

When a final consonant that is normally silent is pronounced with the initial vowel sound of the following word, linking (*liaison*) is said to take place: you say, of course, **les/Français** (without linking) but **les‿Américains** (with linking). It is important to note at once that linking does not take place before all words that begin with a vowel sound, but only between words that are naturally grouped together — such as the subject of a sentence and its modifiers or the verb and personal pronouns immediately associated with it.

Nevertheless, linking is very tricky: while in certain cases it *must* be made and in others it would be a dreadful mistake to make it, there are many cases where linking is correct in formal speaking and inappropriate in everyday, friendly conversation. In the transcriptions of the dialogs, we have tried to indicate the way the dialogs would be spoken in a friendly, natural, and correct conversation. Here are a few additional suggestions for those who are interested:

A. *Linking does take place:*

NOUNS: between articles and nouns, between articles and adjectives that precede nouns, and between nouns and the adjectives that precede them:

les‿étudiants, les bons‿étudiants, des‿étudiants, deux‿étudiants,
un‿autre étudiant, mes‿étudiants, mon‿étudiant.

PRONOUNS: between personal pronouns (including **y** and **en**) and verbs, and between pronouns:

ils‿ont, ont‿ils? vous‿êtes, vous‿allez. Je les‿ai achetés.
Nous‿en‿avons. Donnez - nous‿en. Allez‿-y.

PREPOSITIONS: between preposition and object:

dans‿un mois, en‿Italie, en‿hiver, sans‿effort, chez‿eux.

ADVERBS: between certain adverbs (the short ones) and adjectives:

très‿agréable, plus‿amusant, moins‿utile, bien‿aimable.

B. *Linking does not normally take place:*

NOUNS: between nouns and adjectives that follow them:

un étudiant /américain, des revues /américaines.

VERBS: between noun subject and verb:

Le temps /arrive. Ce Français /habite à Paris. Paris /est une belle ville.
Mes parents /aiment les sports.

C. *Linking is impossible:*

(*a*) before the word **huit** (tous les /huit jours); before the word **oui** (mais /oui, il a dit /oui); after the word **et** (Jean /et /Hélène); in the number **cent /un.** You do not link **les /onze** or **dans /onze.**

(*b*) before nouns beginning with aspirate "h":

des /hors-d'œuvre, en /haut de l'escalier

D. *Linking is optional in innumerable cases.*

However, optional linkings are generally to be avoided except in formal conversation, in singing, and in reading poetry. For example, we do not recommend that the following optional linkings after verbs be made in everyday conversation:

Je vais /à la gare. Je suis /à la maison. Vous parlez /anglais.
Je ne parle pas /anglais. Vous avez /un frère.

Even if you prefer to make such linkings after the verb, you should avoid linking after the inverted form between a personal pronoun and prepositions, nouns, or articles:

Allez-vous /à la gare? Parlez-vous /anglais? Avez-vous /un frère?

Such linkings would sound bookish or affected to many French people today. You will notice that on the tapes, the French voices are not consistent in their use of linking: one will make a *liaison* in a phrase and another will fail to make it in the same phrase. This is as it *should* be, because this is what you hear in France all the time. (For a detailed treatment of optional linking, see three articles of Pierre Delattre in the *French Review*, XXX (1956), pp. 48–54; XXIX (1955), pp. 42–49; XXI (1947), pp. 148–157.)

CONVERSATION 3

IPA Transcription of Dialog

dɑ̃laʀy

1. paʀdɔ̃, uɛ lotɛl dyʃvalblɑ̃? **2.** syʀlaplas, məsjø. **3.** ɛskəsɛ lwɛ̃disi? **4.** nɔ̃, snɛpɑ lwɛ̃disi. **5.** ɛskəsɛtœ̃ bɔnotɛl? **6.** wi, məsjø, sɛtœ̃ tʀɛ bɔnotɛl. **7.** ɛskə la kɥizin ɛ bɔn? **8.** sɛrtɛnmɑ̃, məsjø. la kɥizin ɛtɛksɛlɑ̃t. **9.** jatil œ̃notʀotɛl isi? **10.** wi, ilja œ̃notɛl ɑ̃ fas də legliz. **11.** mɛʀsi boku.

a lotɛl dyʃvalblɑ̃

12. kɛ lɛ lpʀi de ʃɑ̃bʀ? **13.** də kɛ̃ za vɛ̃t sɛ̃ fʀɑ̃, mə sjø. **14.** kɛ lɛ lpʀi deʀpa? **15.** katʀə fʀɑ̃ puʀ ləpti dejœne. **16.** di fʀɑ̃ puʀlə dejœne. **17.** e duz fʀɑ̃ puʀlə dine.

I. Exercice de rhythme:

Répétez en six syllabes:

1. Est-cȩ que c'est près d'ici? [ɛs kə sɛ pʀɛ di si?]
2. Est-cȩ que c'est loin d'ici? [ɛs kə sɛ lwɛ̃ di si?]
3. Est-cȩ que c'est près dȩ la garȩ? [ɛs kə sɛ pʀɛ dla gaʀ?]
4. Est-cȩ que c'est loin dȩ la garȩ? [ɛs kə sɛ lwɛ̃ dla gaʀ?]
5. Est-cȩ que c'est sur la placȩ? [ɛs kə sɛ syʀ la plas?]

II. Exercices de prononciation:

A. *Exercise on the mute* **e**:

Répétez en deux syllabes:

Lȩ musée	[lmy ze]
Lȩ château	[lʃɑ to]

Répétez en trois syllabes:

Lȩ bureau dȩ poste.	[lby ʀod pɔst]
Lȩ prix des rȩpas	[lpʀi de ʀpa]

Répétez en cinq syllabes:

Quel est lȩ prix des rȩpas?	[kɛ lɛ lpʀi de ʀpa?]
Jȩ parlȩ un peu français.	[ʒpaʀ lœ̃ pø fʀɑ̃ sɛ.]

B. *Exercise on French* "**ui**" (*Represented by the symbols* [ɥi]).

When you see the letters **ui,** you will probably want to put your lips in position to pronounce a [w] as in English words *suite*, *cuirass*, etc. So you must consciously avoid advancing your lips; because if you advance your lips as if to say [w], it will be difficult not to say [w].

To pronounce the French [ɥi], you first repeat several times:

[i] [y], [i] [y].

Then you say, several times:

[y] [i], [y] [i]

without pausing between the two sounds and without pronouncing a [w].

Then you pronounce the two sounds in one syllable several times and you will get a proper [ɥi]. This sound is very close to the sound (yē) that is often heard in English phrases such as "Are you eating?" which, when pronounced rapidly, sounds something like (yeeting?).

Now repeat each of the following, taking care not to insert a [w] after the "s":

Je suis Monsieur Hughes.	[ʒə sɥi mə sjø yg.]
Je ne̸ suis pas Monsieur Hughes.	[ʒən sɥi pɑ mə sjø yg.]
Je suis Américain.	[ʒə sɥi(z) a me ʀi kɛ̃.]
Je ne̸ suis pas Américain.	[ʒən sɥi pɑ a me ʀi kɛ̃.]

CONVERSATION 4

IPA Transcription of Dialog

alotɛl

1. kɔmɑ̃ sa va, məsjø? **2.** sa va bjɛ̃, mɛʀsi. **3.** kɛ lœ ʀɛ til? **4.** ilɛ õzœʀ. **5.** ɛskəldeʒœne ɛ pʀɛ? **6.** nõ, məsjø, pɑzɑ̃kɔʀ. **7.** a kɛl œʀ vulevu deʒœne? **8.** a õzœʀ e kaʀ. **9.** u a õzœʀ edmi. **10.** a kɛlœʀalevu a la gaʀ? **11.** ʒvɛa la gaʀ a midi. **12.** lə tʀɛ̃ puʀ paʀi aʀiv a midi e kaʀ, nɛspɑ? **13.** nõ, məsjø. ilaʀiv a døzœʀ mwɛ̃lkaʀ. **14.** alɔʀ, ʒvɛ deʒœne a midi, kɔm dabityd. **15.** ɛskəl byʀod pɔst ɛtuvɛʀ sɛtapʀɛmidi? **16.** wi, məsjø. **17.** ilɛtuvɛʀ də ɥitœʀ dy matɛ̃ a sɛtœʀ dy swaʀ.

I. Exercice de rhythme:

A. *Répétez en sept syllabes:*

Est-ce̸ que le̸ déjeuner est prêt?	[ɛs kə lde ʒœ ne ɛ pʀɛ?]
Je̸ vais à la gare à midi.	[ʒvɛ a la ga ʀa mi di.]
Je̸ vais déjeuner à midi.	[ʒvɛ de ʒœ ne a mi di.]

B. *Répétez en huit syllabes:*

Est-cǿ que lǿ bureau dǿ postǿ est ouvert? [ɛs kə lby ʀod pɔst ɛ tu vɛʀ?]

C. *Répétez en onze syllabes:*

Est-cǿ que lǿ bureau dǿ postǿ est ouvert ce matin? [ɛs kə lby ʀod pɔst ɛ tu vɛʀ sə matɛ̃?]

II. Exercice de prononciation: [ɛ] **(quelle)** and [œ] **(heure)**

A. *Répétez:*

Quelle heure est-il?

B. *Dites:*

Quelle, [ɛ], [ɛ], [ɛ]. Keep the vowel short and free from the following "l".

C. *Répétez:*

1. Cet après-midi. **2.** N'est-ce pas? **3.** Sept. **4.** Prêt. **5.** Près d'ici.

D. *Dites:*

Quelle heure . . . ? [œ], [œ], [œ].

E. *Répétez:*

1. Quelle heure est-il? [kɛ lœʀ ɛ til?] **2.** Neuf heures [nœ vœʀ]. **3.** Neuf [nœf]. **4.** Lǿ déjeuner [lde ʒœ ne]. **5.** Jǿ vais déjeuner [ʒvɛ de ʒœ ne].

GRAMMAR UNIT 1

III. Exercise on the French [t]

The first step in learning to pronounce the French [t] is to *hear* (1) that at the beginning of a word it is produced with much less flow of air than the corresponding English sound and (2) that in other positions it is completely articulated. Compare English *tent* and French **tente:** in *tent*, the first "t" is produced with a puff of air and the second one is hardly articulated at all; in **tente,** the first "t" is pronounced without the puff of air and the second is clearly articulated.

Next, note that the English "t" is produced with the tip of the tongue against the alveolar (the ridge behind the front teeth) but that the French "t" is produced with the tip of the tongue against the front teeth and the upper surface of the tongue against the alveolar.

Now hold your hand (or a strip of paper) in front of your mouth and say the following pairs of words, moving the tip of your tongue back for each English word and forward for each French word. Use as little breath as possible for the French words. (*a*) tobacco, **le tabac.** (*b*) tea, **le thè.** (*c*) two, **tout.** (*d*) toot, **toute.** (*e*) toe, **-teau.** Repeat this exercise until you can say the French words without feeling a puff of air on your hand (or seeing the paper move).

Finally, repeat each of the following, pronouncing the "t" with as little breath as possible:

1. une lettre. **2.** le restaurant. **3.** les hôtels. **4.** le petit hôtel. **5.** le petit déjeuner. **6.** le château. **7.** près du château. **8.** tout droit. **9.** à droite. **10.** il est ouvert. **11.** huit heures du matin. **12.** Comment allez-vous?

CONVERSATION 5

IPA Transcription of Dialog

a la pʀefɛktyʀd pɔlis

1. kɔmɑ̃ vuzaplevu, məsjø? **2.** ʒmapɛl ʒɑ̃ yg. **3.** kɛ lɛ vɔtʀə nasjɔnalite? **4.** ʒsɥizameʀikɛ̃. **5.** u ɛt vu ne? **6.** ʒsɥi ne a filadɛlfi. **7.** kɛl ɑʒ avevu? **8.** ʒe vɛ̃teœ̃nɑ̃. **9.** kɛ lɛ vɔtʀə pʀɔfɛsjõ? **10.** ʒsɥizɛ̃ʒenjœʀ ʃimist. **11.** udmœʀevu? **12.** ʒədmœʀ a paʀi. **13.** kɛ lɛ vɔtʀ adʀɛs a paʀi? **14.** kɛ̃z, avnyd lɔpsɛʀvatwaʀ. **15.** u abit vo paʀɑ̃? **16.** mõ pɛʀ abit a filadɛlfi. **17.** ʒne ply ma mɛʀ.. **18.** avevu de paʀɑ̃ ɑ̃ fʀɑ̃s? **19.** nõ, ʒnepɑd paʀɑ̃ ɑ̃ fʀɑ̃s. **20.** vwa la vɔtʀə kaʀtə didɑ̃tite. **21.** mɛʀsi, məsjø.

Exercise on the French [l] **l'hôtel**

The French "l", like the French "t" is produced with the tip of the tongue against the front teeth.

Compare English *eel* (ēŭl) in two syllables and French **il** [il] in one syllable.

Now pronounce English *eel* and French **il** several times, moving the tongue forward for the French word each time and giving the French word a very brief, light utterance.

Now pronounce the following with the tongue against the front teeth for all the *t's* and *l's:*

1. l'hôtel. **2.** la lettre. **3.** Pas mal. **4.** la place. **5.** l'hôtel Continental. **6.** l'hôtel du Cheval blanc. **7.** Quelle heure est-il? **8.** Comment s'appelle-t-il? **9.** Comment s'appelle-t-elle? **10.** Quel âge a-t-il? **11.** Quel âge a-t-elle?

CONVERSATION 6

IPA Transcription of Dialog

1. ʒe fɛ̃. **2.** mwa osi. **3.** alõ deʒœne. **4.** vwasi œ̃ ʀɛstɔʀɑ̃. ɑ̃tʀõ. **5.** vwala yn tablə libʀ. asɛjevu. **6.** gaʀsõ, dɔne mwa la kaʀt, silvuplɛ. **7.** vwasi, məsjø. vulevu de ɔʀdœvʀ? **8.** wi, apɔʀte mwa de ɔʀdœvʀ. **9.** vulevu dy vɛ̃ blɑ̃ u dy vɛ̃ ʀuʒ? **10.** dy vɛ̃ ʀuʒ, silvuplɛ. **11.** kɛskə vuvule kɔm pladvjɑ̃d? **12.** œ̃ biftɛk o pɔm. **13.** kɛskə vuvule kɔm desɛʀ? **14.** kɛskə vuzave? **15.** nuzavõ de pɔm, de banan, de pwaʀ e dy ʀɛzɛ̃. **16.** apɔʀte mwa yn pwaʀ. **17.** vulevu dy kafe? **18.** wi, dɔnemwa dykafenwaʀ. **19.** evu, məsjø? **20.** mɛʀsi, ʒənɛmpal kafe. **21.** gaʀsõ, ladisjõ, silvuplɛ. **22.** tutsɥit, məsjø.

Exercise on the front [a] (**la gare**), and the back [ɑ] (**pas**).

A. *Répétez:*

la gare, [a], [a], [a].

B. *Répétez:*

1. la carte. **2.** la table. **3.** la banane. **4.** la poire. **5.** à la gare. **6.** quatre heures et quart. **7.** le café noir.

C. *Répétez:*

n'est-ce pas? [ɑ], [ɑ], [ɑ].

D. *Répétez:*

1. trois. **2.** là-bas [la bɑ]. **3.** le château. **4.** pas encore. **5.** tout droit. **6.** Quel âge avez-vous?

GRAMMAR UNIT 2

I. Exercices de rhythme:

Répétez:

A. QUATRE SYLLABES.

J'ai du café.	[ʒe dy ka fe.]
Je̸ n'ai pas de̸ café.	[ʒne pɑd ka fe.]
J'ai de̸ la monnaie.	[ʒed la mɔ nɛ.]
Je̸ n'ai pas de̸ monnaie.	[ʒne pɑd mɔ nɛ.]

B. SIX SYLLABES.

J'ai des parents en France.	[ʒe de pa ʀɑ̃ ɑ̃ fʀɑ̃s.]
Je̸ n'ai pas de̸ parents en France.	[ʒne pɑd pa ʀɑ̃ ɑ̃ fʀɑ̃s.]

C. HUIT SYLLABES.

J'ai une̸ carte d'identité.	[ʒe yn ka ʀtə di dɑ̃ ti te.]
Je̸ n'ai pas de̸ carte d'identité.	[ʒne pɑd ka ʀtə di dɑ̃ ti te.]

II. Exercices de prononciation sur [ɔ] (**la pomme**) et [o] (**l'hôtel**).

A. *Répétez:* la pomme [ɔ], [ɔ], [ɔ].

Répétez:

1. un rest**au**rant. **2.** le bureau de p**o**ste. **3.** c**o**mme d'habitude. **4.** v**o**tre pr**o**fession. **5.** v**o**tre nati**o**nalité. **6.** l'**o**bservatoire. **7.** la m**o**nnaie. **8.** **o**ct**o**bre. **9.** pas enc**o**re. **10.** al**o**rs. **11.** h**o**rs-d'œuvre.

Note that the **o**'s in **octobre** are both [ɔ] [ɔk tɔbʀ], that they are not pronounced like either of the **o**'s in English *October*. The nearest English equivalent is the short **u** in Eng. *duck*.

B. *Répétez:*

l'hôtel, [o], [o], [o]. Keep the vowel short and clear.

Répétez:

1. b**eau**coup. **2.** l'**au**tre. **3.** le chât**eau.** **4.** le bur**eau.** **5.** l'h**ô**tel. **6.** v**o**s parents. **7.** **au**jourd'hui. **8.** de l'**eau.** **9.** l'h**ô**telier.

CONVERSATION 7

IPA Transcription of Dialog

1. kɛlɛladat oʒuʀdɥi? **2.** sɛtoʒuʀdɥi lə tʀɑ̃t sɛptɑ̃bʀ. **3.** kɑ̃(t)alevu amaʀsɛj? **4.** o mwɑdɔktɔbʀ. **5.** vwasi mɛ pʀɔʒɛ puʀ lane: **6.** ɔktɔbʀ e nɔvɑ̃bʀ amaʀsɛj; **7.** desɑ̃bʀ, ʒɑ̃vje e fevʀije apaʀi; **8.** maʀs e avʀil a ljõ; **9.** mɛ, ʒɥɛ̃, ʒɥijɛ, e u apaʀi . . . **10.** ɛskə vuzɛt libʀə lasmɛn pʀɔʃɛn? **11.** vwajõ . . . kɛl ʒuʀ sɔm nu oʒuʀdɥi? **12.** sɛtoʒuʀdɥi vɑ̃dʀədi. **13.** ʒvɛ olabɔʀatwaʀ lœ̃di, maʀdi, mɛʀkʀədi e ʒødi. **14.** ʒsɥi libʀə vɑ̃dʀədi, samdi e dimɑ̃ʃ. **15.** vulevuvniʀ a ʀwɑ̃ avɛkmwa? **16.** vɔlõtje. a kɛlœʀ paʀtevu? **17.** lə tʀɛ̃ paʀ a dissɛtœʀ. **18.** sɛtɑ̃tɑ̃dy. a ʒødi apʀɛmidi.

Exercise on the French mute "e" as in **le cheval.**

A. *Repeat:*

le cheval [lə ʃval], [ə], [ə], [ə].
Note that the [ə] is produced with the tip of the tongue against the lower front teeth and the lips slightly rounded.

B. *Now repeat the following expressions with a mute "e":*

1. le cheval [lə ʃval]. **2.** le repas [ləʀ pɑ]. **3.** le petit déjeuner [lə pti de ʒœ ne]. **4.** Je ne parle pas français [ʒən paʀlə pɑ fʀɑ̃ sɛ]. **5.** De rien, monsieur [də ʀjɛ̃ mə sjø]. **6.** est-ce que [ɛskə].

C. *Repeat the following phrases and note that these mute "e's" are entirely silent.*

1. *Répétez en quatre syllabes:*

Où est l~~e~~ château?	[u ɛ lʃɑ to?]
Où est l~~e~~ musée?	[u ɛ lmy ze?]
La rue d~~e~~ la Paix.	[la ʀy dla pɛ.]
J~~e~~ vais à la gare.	[ʒvɛ a la gaʀ.]
J~~e~~ n'aim~~e~~ pas l~~e~~ café.	[ʒnɛm pɑ lka fe.]
L~~e~~ bureau d~~e~~ tabac.	[lby ʀod ta ba.]
J~~e~~ m'appell~~e~~ Jean Hughes.	[ʒma pɛ lʒɑ̃ yg.]

2. *Répétez en cinq syllabes:*

Où est l~~e~~ bureau d~~e~~ poste?	[u ɛ lby ʀod pɔst?]
J~~e~~ parl~~e~~ un peu français.	[ʒpaʀ lœ̃ pø fʀɑ̃ sɛ.]
J~~e~~ déjeun~~e~~ à midi.	[ʒde ʒœ na mi di.]
J~~e~~ dîn~~e~~ au restaurant.	[ʒdi no ʀɛs tɔ ʀɑ̃.]
L'hôtel du Ch~~e~~val blanc.	[lo tɛl dy ʃval blɑ̃.]

NOTE. Don't imagine it is difficult to pronounce French words such as **Je déjeune, Je m'appelle, Je n'aime pas,** *etc.*, without sounding the mute e's. You produce these — and more difficult — combinations in English all the time without thinking about it. You have no trouble saying something like: "Zydad back" for "Is your dad back?" or "Dymother come" for "Did your mother come?" or "Zyname Percy?" for "Is your name Percy?" and so on. And don't imagine it is sloppy French pronunciation! This follows the very best usage. It would sound schoolteacherish to say «**Le bureau de tabac**» in six syllables.

GRAMMAR UNIT 3

Nasal Vowels

As English is very rich in nasal vowels, the only difficulty the French nasal vowels present is that they must be sounded without actually pronouncing the consonant **n** — except, of course, in linking.

I. Exercice sur [ɛ̃] (**ingénieur**).

Répétez:

1. Très **bien** [ɛ], [ɛ̃]. **2. bien.** [ɛ̃], [ɛ̃], [ɛ̃]. **3.** lo**in.** **4.** de **rien.** **5. cinq** heures mo**ins** le quart. **6. vingt-cinq.** **7.** Améric**ain.**

II. Exercice sur [ɑ̃] (**parents**).

Répétez:

1. Des par**ents** **en** Fr**an**ce. [ɑ̃], [ɑ̃], [ɑ̃]. **2. cent** fr**an**cs. **3. cent ans.** **4.** le restaur**ant.** **5.** du vin bl**an**c. **6.** un plat de vi**an**de. **7.** l'**an**glais. **8. en**t**en**du.

III. Exercice sur [õ] (**non**).

Répétez:

1. Pard**on**! [õ], [õ], [õ]. **2.** b**on**jour. **3.** à **on**ze heures. **4.** all**ons**. **5.** entr**ons**. **6.** votre professi**on.** **7.** le garç**on.** **8.** un b**on** dîner. **9.** nous av**ons**. **10.** ils **ont**.

IV. Exercice sur [œ̃] (**un restaurant**).

Répétez:

1. **un** restaurant [œ̃]. [œ̃], [œ̃]. **2.** **un** musée. **3.** **un** agent de police. **4.** l**un**di. **5.** **un** an.

Note that many French people usually substitute [ɛ̃] for [œ̃] so that **un** rhymes with **vin.** We do not recommend that students follow this practice but that they be prepared to understand words like [ɛ̃fʀɑ̃] (**un franc**) or [lɛ̃di] (**lundi**) when they hear them.

CONVERSATION 8

IPA Transcription of Dialog

dɑ̃ la ʀy

1. ualevu? **2.** ʒvɛ aʃte œ̃ʒuʀnal. **3.** u aʃɛttõ deʒuʀno? **4.** õ vɑ̃deʒuʀno obyʀodtaba. **5.** avevudeʒuʀno, madam? **6.** wi məsjø. le vwala. **7.** dɔnemwa lfigaʀo silvuplɛ. **8.** ləvwasi, məsjø. **9.** sɛ kõbjɛ̃? **10.** sɛ tʀɑ̃t sɑ̃tim. **11.** vwala œ̃fʀɑ̃. **12.** vwala lamɔnɛ: swasɑ̃tdi sɑ̃tim. **13.** avevu deʀvy ameʀikɛn? **14.** ʒəʀgʀɛt, məsjø nu navõ pɑd ʀavyameʀikɛn. **15.** mɛ nuzavõ de ʀɔmɑ̃pɔlisje. **16.** ʒnɛmpɑ boku le ʀɔmɑ̃pɔlisje. **17.** kõbjɛ̃ kut sɛt pətit kaʀtə də paʀi? **18.** dœfʀɑ̃sɛ̃kɑ̃t, məsjø. **19.** bõ. ʒvɛ la pʀɑ̃dʀ. **20.** sɛ tynkaʀtə trɛzytil, məsjø. **21.** bõ vwala œ̃ bijɛd sɛ̃kɑ̃tfʀɑ̃. **22.** avevu la mɔnɛdsɛ̃kɑ̃tfʀɑ̃? **23.** ʒkʀwakwi. lavwala. **24.** ɛskə sɛ tu, mə sjø? **25.** wi, sɛ tu puʀoʒuʀdɥi.

Exercise on [ʃ] as in **le château** and [ʒ] as in **le déjeuner.**

These sounds are so much like those we produce in the words *sh*allow and ple*asu*re, that most students never bother to pronounce them as the French do. But if the tip of the tongue is turned up — as in English, it is very difficult to pronounce correctly such words as **je, juin, chercher,** etc.

Repeat the following words, trying hard to keep the tip of the tongue DOWN:

A. [ʃ] **1.** chercher. **2.** le château. **3.** la chambre. **4.** la chaise. **5.** je cherche.

B. [ʒ] **1.** le déjeuner. **2.** je déjeune. **3.** jeudi. **4.** le huit juin. **5.** je sais (*slowly*) [ʒə sɛ]. **6.** je sais (*quickly*) [ʒsɛ]. **7.** je suis (*slowly*) [ʒə sɥi]. **8.** je suis (*quickly*) [ʒsɥi]. **9.** Je suis ingénieur-chimiste. **10.** le quatorze juillet. **11.** Jeudi, je déjeune avec Jeanne. **12.** Je vais acheter un journal. **13.** Je crois que oui.

GRAMMAR UNIT 4

Cardinal Numbers

DATES, NUMBERS, COUNTING

A. In dates, street numbers, telephone numbers, in counting, etc., the cardinal numbers are pronounced as follows:

1. œ̃
2. dø
3. tʀwɑ
4. katʀ
5. sɛ̃k
6. sis
7. sɛt
8. ɥit
9. nœf
10. dis

11. õz
12. duz
13. tʀɛz
14. katɔʀz
15. kɛ̃z
16. sɛz
17. dissɛt
18. dizɥit
19. diznœf
20. vɛ̃

21. vɛ̃teœ̃
22. vɛ̃tdø
23. vɛ̃ttʀwɑ
24. vɛ̃tkatʀ
25. vɛ̃tsɛ̃k
26. vɛ̃tsis
27. vɛ̃tsɛt
28. vɛ̃tɥit
29. vɛ̃tnœf

30. tʀɑ̃t **31.** tʀɑ̃teœ̃ **32.** tʀɑ̃tdø, etc.
40. kaʀɑ̃t **41.** kaʀɑ̃teœ̃ **42.** kaʀɑ̃tdø, etc.
50. sɛ̃kɑ̃t **51.** sɛ̃kɑ̃teœ̃ **52.** sɛ̃kɑ̃tdø, etc.
60. swasɑ̃t **61.** swasɑ̃teœ̃ **62.** swasɑ̃tdø, etc.
70. swasɑ̃tdis **71.** swasɑ̃teõz **72.** swasɑ̃tduz, etc.

80. katʀəvɛ̃ **81.** katʀəvɛ̃œ̃, etc.
90. katʀəvɛ̃dis **91.** katʀəvɛ̃õz, etc.
100. sɑ̃ **101.** sɑ̃ œ̃ **102.** sɑ̃ dø, etc.
500. sɛ̃sɑ̃ **501.** sɛ̃sɑ̃ œ̃, etc.
600. sisɑ̃ **601.** sisɑ̃ œ̃, etc.
700. sɛtsɑ̃ **701.** sɛtsɑ̃ œ̃, etc.
800. ɥisɑ̃ **801.** ɥisɑ̃ œ̃, etc.
900. nœfsɑ̃ **901.** nœfsɑ̃ œ̃

1000. mil, **1001.** mil œ̃, etc.
1100. õzsɑ̃ *or* milsɑ̃
1200. duzsɑ̃ *or* mildøsɑ̃
1300. trɛzsɑ̃ *or* miltʀwɑsɑ̃, etc.
2000. dø mil
2100. dømil sɑ̃
2200. dømildøsɑ̃
2300. dømiltʀwɑsɑ̃, etc.

5000. sɛ̃mil
6000. simil
7000. sɛtmil
8000. ɥimil
9000. nœfmil
10.000. dimil
500.000. sɛ̃sɑ̃mil
1.000.000. œ̃miljõ

B. When cardinal numbers are used purely as adjectives and are immediately followed by the nouns they modify,

(1) their final consonants are linked to a word beginning with a vowel:

1.	un enfant	œ̃nɑ̃fɑ̃
2.	deux enfants	døzɑ̃fɑ̃
3.	trois enfants	trwɑzɑ̃fɑ̃
5.	cinq enfants	sɛ̃kɑ̃fɑ̃
6.	six enfants	sizɑ̃fɑ̃
7.	sept enfants	sɛtɑ̃fɑ̃
8.	huit enfants	ɥitɑ̃fɑ̃
9.	neuf* enfants	nœfɑ̃fɑ̃
10.	dix enfants	dizɑ̃fɑ̃

(2) the final consonant of 2, 3, 5, 6, 8, 10, is silent before a word beginning with a consonant:

2.	deux francs	døfʀɑ̃
3.	trois francs	tʀwɑfʀɑ̃
5.	cinq francs	sɛ̃fʀɑ̃
6.	six francs	sifʀɑ̃
8.	huit francs	ɥifʀɑ̃
10.	dix francs	difʀɑ̃

(3) The pronunciation of the final consonant of 7 and 9 before a word beginning with a consonant is optional but most people pronounce it:

7.	sept francs	sɛtfʀɑ̃	*or*	sɛfʀɑ̃
	dix-sept francs	dissɛtfʀɑ̃		dissɛfʀɑ̃
9.	neuf francs	nœffʀɑ̃		nœfʀɑ̃
	dix-neuf francs	diznœffʀɑ̃		diznœfʀɑ̃

CONVERSATION 9

IPA Transcription of Dialog

1. kɔnɛsevu listwaʀ də fʀɑ̃s? **2.** sɛʀtɛnmɑ̃. ʒkɔnɛ ʒɑndaʀk e napɔleõ. **3.** kɛskə vusaved ʒɑndaʀk? **4.** ʒsɛ kɛlene a dõremi e kɛlɛmɔʀt a ʀwɑ̃. **5.** savevu u ɛ ne napɔleõ? **6.** ilɛ ne ɑ̃ kɔʀs, o dizɥitjɛm sjɛkl. **7.** kɛlɛladat dəlabataj də vatɛʀlo? **8.** dizɥisɑ̃kɛ̃z ɛ ladat də la bataj dəvatɛʀlo. **9.** napɔleõ ɛmɔʀ sizɑ̃ plytaʀ. **10.** ɑ̃ kɛlane lwi katɔʀz ɛtilmɔʀ? **11.** il ɛmɔʀ ɑ̃ dissɛtsɑ̃kɛ̃z. **12.** vu kɔnɛsel katɔʀz ʒɥijɛ, nɛspɑ? **13.** bjɛ̃nɑ̃tɑ̃dy. sɛl ʒuʀd la fɛt nasjɔnal ɑ̃fʀɑ̃s. **14.** savevu puʀkwa? **15.** paʀskə sɛl ʒuʀd la pʀiz dəla bastij, **16.** lə katɔʀz ʒɥijɛ, dissɛtsɑ̃ katʀəvɛ̃nœf. **17.** ʒən vɛ ply vu pozed kɛstjõ. **18.** vusavetu!

Exercises on [s], [z], [d], [n].

As for French [t] and [l], the tip of the tongue should be against or near the front teeth to pronounce [s], [z], [d], and [n], and less breath is used than in pronouncing the equivalent consonants in English.

* Note, however, that in **neuf ans** and **neuf heures,** the **f** is pronounced **v.**

With the tip of your tongue against or near the front teeth, repeat each of the following:

A. [s] and [z]:

1. Est-ce tout [ɛs tu]? **2.** Vous savez tout. **3.** Des cigarettes. **4.** Six cents. **5.** Seize cents. **6.** dix-sept [dis sɛt]. **7.** Ils sont [il sõ]. **8.** Ils ont [il zõ].

B. [d] and [n]:

1. des bananes. **2.** la date. **3.** la date de la fête nationale. **4.** bien entendu. **5.** Suzanne n'aime pas les bananes. **6.** la date de la bataille de Waterloo.

CONVERSATION 10

IPA Transcription of Dialog

1. vukɔnɛse lwiz bədɛl? **2.** nõ, ʒən la kɔnɛpɑ. **3.** mɛ si. vuzave fɛ sa kɔnɛsɑ̃s ʃemaʀi samdi dɛʀnje. **4.** ɛs yn pətit ʒœnfij bʀyn? **5.** mɛ nõ. sɛtyn gʀɑ̃d ʒœnfij blõd. **6.** də kɛl kulœʀ sõ sezjø? **7.** ɛl a lezjøblø, kɔm tut leblõd. **8.** o! vupaʀlɛd la ʒœnfij abije ɑ̃ blø? **9.** ɛla leʃvø blõ, leʒu ʀoz e le lɛvʀə ʀuʒ, nɛspɑ? **10.** wi, sɛsa. **11.** e bjɛ̃? **12.** ɛl vasmaʀje ʒødɪ pʀɔʃɛ. **13.** avɛk ki? **14.** avɛk ʃaʀldypõ. **15.** ʒkɔnɛ tʀɛbjɛ̃ ʃaʀl. **16.** kɛskilfɛ? **17.** ilɛtɛ̃ʒɛnjœʀ. **18.** kə pɑ̃sevud ʃaʀl? **19.** ʒpɑ̃s kiladlaʃɑ̃s. **20.** safjɑ̃se ɛʒɔli e ɛlɛ tʀɛ ʒɑ̃tij.

Note that **Louise** is pronounced [lwiz] in one syllable. COMPARE: **oui** [wi]. *Repeat also:* **Louis quatorze** [lwi ka tɔʀz] in three syllables; **Louisiane** [lwi zjan] in two syllables.

CONVERSATION 11

IPA Transcription of Dialog

1. vulevu fɛʀ ynpʀɔmnad? **2.** ʒvø bjɛ̃. kɛltɑ̃fɛtil? **3.** ilfɛbo. **4.** mɛilfɛ dyvɑ̃. **5.** ɛskilfɛfʀwɑ? **6.** nõ, pɑdytu. **7.** ilnəfɛ nitʀoʃo nitʀofʀwɑ. **8.** sɛtœ̃botɑ̃ puʀ ynpʀɔmnad. **9.** fotil pʀɑ̃dʀ œ̃nɛ̃pɛʀmeabl? **10.** snɛ pɑ lapɛn. **11.** il nə vapɑ plœvwaʀ. **12.** ɛtvusyʀ kilnəvapɑ plœvwaʀ? **13.** wi. ʀ(ə)gaʀdel sɔlɛj. **14.** pazœ̃sœl nɥaʒ dɑ̃lsjɛl blø. **15.** bõ ʒvukʀwa. ʒekõfjɑ̃s ɑ̃vu.

(ynœʀ plytaʀ)

16. il plø; il plø(t)avɛʀs. **17.** ʒsɥi muje ʒyskozo. **18.** sɛ vɔtʀə fot. **19.** ma fot? kɔmɑ̃ sla? **20.** vusavebjɛ̃. ʒne ply kõfjɑ̃s ɑ̃vu.

Exercise on [u] (**vous**) and [y] (**sûr**).

A. *Repeat each of the following words and phrases, making it a point to sound the* [u] *clearly — without sounding an* **i** *or* **e** *before the* [u] *or* [ŭ] *after it.*

1. Bonjour. **2.** beaucoup. **3.** Voulez-vous faire une promenade? **4.** douze. **5.** C'est tout.

B. Note that the jaws are close together and the lips are rounded for both [u] (**tout**) and [y] (**du**): the difference between the two sounds is made by putting the tongue forward in the mouth for [y] and dropping it back for [u].

Repeat slowly and carefully: [u] [y], [u] [y], *several times, putting your tongue forward for* [y] *and retracting it for the* [u].

Repeat the following with great care several times:

1. [y] [u]. **2.** du tout. **3.** [ɑ] [y] [u]. **4.** pas du tout. **5.** Êtes-vous sûr? **6.** Je n'ai plus confiance en vous. **7.** le musée du Louvre.

CONVERSATION 12

IPA Transcription of Dialog

1. ʀgaʀde lanɛʒ! **2.** tjɛ̃! sɛ lapʀəmjɛʀfwa kilnɛʒ sɛtane. **3.** ʒnɛm pɑdytu livɛʀ. **4.** puʀkwapɑ? **5.** livɛʀa sɛ pleziʀ, **6.** õ pø patine, fɛʀ dy ski, ale oteɑtʀ, **7.** u bjɛ̃ ʒwe o kaʀt, ekute dɛ disk, r(ə) gaʀde la televizjõ. **8.** wi, mɛ livɛʀ dyʀ tʀo lõtɑ̃. **9.** kɛl sɛzõ pʀefeʀevu, alɔʀ? **10.** ʒkʀwa kəʒ pʀefɛʀ lete. **11.** ʒɛm vwaʀ de fœj syʀ lezaʀbʀ, **12.** e deflœʀ dɑ̃leʒaʀdɛ̃. **13.** mɛ la kɑ̃paɲ ɛtosi bɛl ɑ̃notɔn kɑ̃nete. **14.** syʀtu ilfɛ mwɛ̃ʃo. **15.** wi. lotɔn kɔmɑ̃s bjɛ̃, **16.** mɛ il finimal. **17.** ʒɛm mjøl pʀɛ̃tɑ̃. **18.** vuzave ʀɛzõ. **19.** tulmõd ɛ kõtɑ̃d vwar vəniʀ lə pʀɛ̃tɑ̃.

Exercise on [p], [f], [k].

These consonants are much like their English equivalents except that they are pronounced with noticeably less breath.

Pronounce each of the following with as little breath as possible:

A. [p]: **1.** le papier. **2.** on peut. **3.** on ne peut pas. **4.** Et puis, on peut patiner. **5.** On peut patiner un peu. **6.** un peu plus tard.

B. [f]: **1.** des fleurs. **2.** faire du ski. **3.** je préfère. **4.** des feuilles. **5.** la première fois.

C. [k]: **1.** Quelle heure est-il? **2.** la campagne. **3.** le café. **4.** Quelle est votre profession? **5.** Quand allez-vous à Caen [kɑ̃]? **6.** Quand allez-vous à Cannes [kan]?

CONVERSATION 13

IPA Transcription of Dialog

1. ʒedekuʀsafɛʀ. **2.** ʒvødabɔʀ aʃte dypɛ̃. **3.** õvɑ̃dypɛ̃ alepisʀi, nɛspɑ? **4.** nõ. ilfotale ala bulɑ̃ʒʀi. **5.** ɑ̃sɥit, ʒvø(z)aʃted lavjɑ̃d. **6.** kɛlɛspɛs dəvjɑ̃d? **7.** dybœf e dypɔʀ. **8.** puʀ ləbœf, ale(z)ala buʃʀi. **9.** puʀ ləpɔʀ, ale(z)ala ʃaʀkytʀi. **10.** fotil ale a dø magazɛ̃ difeʀɑ̃? **11.** wi. ɑ̃fʀɑ̃s, leʃaʀkytje vɑ̃d dypɔʀ. **12.** lebuʃe vɑ̃d lezotʀəzɛspɛs dəvjɑ̃d. **13.** ʒvø(z)aʃte osi dypapje alɛtʀ. **14.** ɔ̃vɑ̃ dypapjealɛtʀ alafaʀmasi, nɛspɑ? **15.** nɔ̃. lefaʀmasjɛ̃n vɑ̃d kədemedikamɑ̃. **16.** u fotilale alɔʀ? **17.** ale(z)ala libʀɛʀi u o byʀodtaba. **18.** ɛ̃si, lebuʃen vɑ̃d pɑdpɔʀ, lefaʀmasjɛ̃n vɑ̃d kə demedikamɑ̃, e ɔ̃vɑ̃ dypapjealɛtʀ dɑ̃lebyʀodtaba! **19.** vu pu ve(z)a le o sypɛʀ maʀʃe u o dʀœg stɔʀ, si vu vule. **20.** o nɔ̃! ʒɛm bjɛ̃ koze avɛk le maʀʃɑ̃.

CONVERSATION 14

IPA Transcription of Dialog

1. ʒsɥizɛ̃vite ʃe le bʀun. **2.** le kənɛsevu? **3.** nɔ̃, ʒən le kənɛpɑ. **4.** eskilsɔ̃tameʀikɛ̃? **5.** məsjø bʀun ɛtameʀikɛ̃, mɛ safam ɛfʀɑ̃sɛz. **6.** kɑ̃ məsjø bʀun ɛtilvəny ɑ̃fʀɑ̃s? **7.** ilɛvny ɑ̃fʀɑ̃s ilja sɛ̃kusizɑ̃. **8.** ɛtil vəny diʀɛktəmɑ̃ dezetazyni? **9.** nɔ̃, ʒkʀwa kilapase dø(z)utʀwɑzɑ̃ ɑ̃nɑ̃glətɛʀ. **10.** udmœrtilapaʀi? **11.** ildəmœʀ pʀɛ dy bwɑdbulɔɲ. **12.** kɛskilfɛ? **13.** ilɛbɑ̃kje. **14.** sabɑ̃k sətʀuv pʀɛdlɔpeʀa. **15.** kɔmɑ̃ avevufɛ sakɔnɛsɑ̃s? **16.** sɛtœ̃ vjɛjamid mɔ̃pɛʀ. **17.** ilɛvny suvɑ̃ ʃɛnu afiladɛlfi. **18.** ɛtvudeʒa ale ʃelebʀun? **19.** wi, ʒsɥizale ʃezø plyzjœʀfwa. **20.** safam ɛlɥi ɔ̃tete tʀɛzɛmablə puʀ mwa.

NOTE: French people who know English would be likely to pronounce *Brown* [braun], but others would say [brun] just as they pronounce the English word *clown* [klun].

CONVERSATION 15

IPA Transcription of Dialog

1. uɛtvuzale sɛtapʀɛmidi? **2.** ʒsɥizale ɑ̃vil. **3.** kɛskə vuzavefɛ? **4.** ʒefɛde kuʀs. **5.** kɛskəvuzave(z) aʃte? **6.** bokud ʃoz. **7.** ʒsɥi dabɔʀ ale o pʀizynik. **8.** kɛskəsɛ kœ̃pʀizynik? **9.** sɛtœ̃magazɛ̃ ulɔ̃vɑ̃ dətu, **10.** a bɔ̃ marʃe. **11.** ɑ̃sɥit, ʒsɥizale ʃelamɔdist. **12.** kwafɛʀ? **13.** aʃte œ̃ ʃapo. **14.** ləʃapok(ə) vuzave syʀlatɛt? **15.** wi. ʒle pɛje tʀɛʃɛʀ. ɛskilvuplɛ? **16.** sɛʀtɛnmɑ̃. **17.** ilɛtœ̃pødʀol, **18.** mɛ ilvuvatʀɛbjɛ̃. **19.** ʒemaʀʃe tulapʀɛmidi. **20.** ʒsɥi(z) œ̃pøfatige. **21.** ɛtvuzale ɑ̃vil apje? **22.** wi, ʒevuly pʀɔfite dybotɑ̃. **23.** ɑ̃tuka, sɛtpʀɔmnad mafɛ bokudbjɛ̃.

CONVERSATION 16

IPA Transcription of Dialog

1. bɔ̃ʒuʀ, madam. avevuynʃɑ̃bʀə mœble alwe? **2.** wi, məsjø. ʒɑ̃neyn opʀəmje. **3.** ɛskəʒpø lavwaʀ? **4.** mɛwi, məsjø. paʀisi. **5.** sɛlapʀəmjɛʀpɔʀtadʀwat ɑ̃ odlɛskalje. **6.** vulevu bjɛ̃ mɔ̃te? **7.** vɔlɔ̃tje. **8.** vwasi la ʃɑ̃bʀ. kɔmɑ̃ latruvevu? **9.** ʒlatʀuv vʀɛmɑ̃ tʀɛzagʀeabl. **10.** e ɛlɛ tʀɛtʀɑ̃kil. **11.** ilnja ʒamɛdbʀɥi dɑ̃lkaʀtje. **12.** tɑ̃mjø, **13.** kaʀ ʒebəzwɛ̃d tʀavajelswaʀ. **14.** vwasi lasaldəbɛ̃, avɛk oʃod tutlaʒuʀne. **15.** nuzavɔ̃lʃofaʒ sɑ̃tʀal. **16.** kɛlɛ l(ə) lwaje, silvuplɛ? **17.** tʀwɑsɑ̃ sɛ̃kɑ̃t fʀɑ̃ paʀmwɑ, məsjø. **18.** ʒkʀwaksɛtʃɑ̃bʀə m(ə) kɔ̃vjɛ̃ tutafɛ. **19.** kɑ̃sʀatɛl pʀɛt? **20.** ɛskədmɛ̃ matɛ̃ vukɔ̃vjɛ̃? **21.** wi, paʀfɛtmɑ̃. **22.** sɛtɑ̃tɑ̃dy. **23.** admɛ̃, madam.

CONVERSATION 17

IPA Transcription of Dialog

1. u iʀevu sɛtapʀɛmidi? **2.** ʒiʀe ɑ̃vil. **3.** kɛskəvufʀe? **4.** ʒ(ə)fʀe dekuʀs. **5.** kɛskəvuzaʃɛtʀe? **6.** ʒaʃɛtʀe œ̃ mɑ̃to e ynʀɔb. **7.** kɔmɑ̃iʀevu ɑ̃vil? **8.** ʒiʀe apje, silfɛbo. **9.** vusʀe bjɛ̃to fatige. **10.** puʀkwan pʀənevupɑ lotɔbys? **11.** ʒnɛmpɑ pʀɑ̃dʀə lotɔbys. **12.** ilja tʀɔdmɔ̃d. **13.** kɛskəvufʀe silplø? **14.** silplø, ʒpʀɑ̃dʀeœ̃taksi. **15.** akɛlœʀ ʀɑ̃tʀəʀevu? **16.** ʒ(ə)ʀɑ̃tʀəʀed bɔnœʀ, avɑ̃ sɛ̃k œʀ. **17.** nublijepɑk(ə)nuzalɔ̃ tuletʀwɑ osinema səswaʀ. **18.** swajetʀɑ̃kil. ʒnubliʀepɑ. **19.** akɛlœʀ ʀɔʒevjɛ̃dʀatil vuʃɛʀʃe. **20.** ilvjɛ̃dʀamʃɛʀʃe a ɥitœʀpʀesiz, ditil. **21.** mɛ vu save kilnɛpɑ tuʒuʀalœʀ. **22.** vənedɔ̃k vɛʀɥitœʀ. **23.** ɑ̃tɑ̃dy. asəswaʀ.

If you can produce a French uvular [ʀ] easily and naturally before and after all the vowels you do not need to do the following exercise. But if you are still having a little trouble with it, this is the point beyond which you should no longer postpone mastering it.

A. *Review the exercise on* [ʀ] *from the first pronunciation exercise on pp.* 366–367.

B. *Repeat carefully each of the following:*

1. le rat, l'art, la gare, rare, une orange.
2. près, très, rester, l'air, la guerre.
3. répéter, je ferai, je serai, rentrer, je rentrerai.
4. Paris, Américain, j'écrirai, j'irai, je rirai (*I shall laugh*).
5. l'heure, l'aurore, l'horreur, des roses, la route.
6. la rue, le fruit, le bruit, on construit, je crois, j'ai cru.
7. (*a*) A quelle heure finirez-vous votre travail?
(*b*) Je rentrerai de bonne heure.
(*c*) Je n'oublierai pas notre rendez-vous.

CONVERSATION 18

IPA Transcription of Dialog

o giʃɛ, a la gaʀ də lɛst

1. ʒvudʀɛ œ̃ bijɛ ale ɛʀtuʀ puʀ ʀɛ̃s. **2.** kɛl klɑs, məsjø? **3.** s(ə)gɔ̃d, silvuplɛ.

4. kõbjɛ̃dtɑ̃sbijɛ etilbõ? **5.** kɛ̃z ʒuʀ, məsjø. **6.** ɛskəʒdwa ʃɑ̃ʒedtʀɛ̃ ɑ̃ʀut? **7.** wi, vudve ʃɑ̃ʒe a epɛʀnɛ. **8.** kõbjɛ̃dtɑ̃ fotilatɑ̃dʀə lakɔʀɛspõdɑ̃s? **9.** vuzɔʀe apøpʀɛ yn dəmi œ̃ʀ a epɛʀnɛ.

syʀ ləke a epɛʀnɛ

10. paʀdõ. syʀ kɛl vwa lətʀɛ̃dʀɛ̃s aʀivtil? **11.** isi, məsjø, syʀ la pʀəmjɛʀ vwa. **12.** l(ə)tʀɛ̃ ɛtilalœʀ? **13.** wi məsjø. ɑ̃ fʀɑ̃s, letʀɛ̃nsõʒamɛ ɑ̃ʀtaʀ. **14.** ɛskə ʒɔʀeltɑ̃ dale obyfɛ? **15.** vupuve(z)esɛje, mɛ depeʃevu. **16.** l(ə)tʀɛ̃ saʀɛt sœlmɑ̃ tʀwɑ minyt. **17.** sivumɑ̃kestʀɛ̃, vusʀezɔbliʒed pɑselanɥi a epɛʀnɛ.

CONVERSATION 19

IPA Transcription of Dialog

1. kõbjɛ̃ kut sɛmuʃwaʀ? **2.** (ləvɑ̃dœʀ) dø fʀɑ̃ pjes, məsjø. **3.** dɔnemɑ̃ yn dəmiduzɛn, silvuplɛ. **4.** kõbjɛ̃ kut sɛt pɛʀ də gɑ? **5.** tʀɑ̃t sɛ̃ fʀɑ̃, məsjø. **6.** segɑ̃sõtil dəbɔnkalite? **7.** sɛʀtɛnmɑ̃, məsjø. **8.** vun tʀuvʀe ʀjɛ̃d mɛjœʀ. **9.** ɑ̃navevu dotʀ? **10.** wi, məsjø. ɑ̃vwasidegʀi. **11.** bõ. dɔnelemwa. **12.** kɛlɛl pʀid sə paʀdəsy? **13.** dø sɑ̃ swasɑ̃t kɛ̃z fʀɑ̃, məsjø. **14.** vulevu lesɛje? **15.** vɔlõtje. **16.** ilvuvatʀɛbjɛ̃. **17.** ləvulevu? **18.** wi. mɛtelə dɑ̃zœ̃kaʀtõ, silvuplɛ. **19.** vulevu lɑ̃pɔʀte tutsɥit? **20.** nõ, ʒən ʀɑ̃tʀəpɑ ʃemwa mɛ̃tnɑ̃. **21.** e bjɛ̃, ʒpuʀe vulfɛʀɑ̃vwaje sɛtapʀɛmidi. **22.** ʒnepɑdaʀʒɑ̃ syʀmwa . . . **23.** slanfɛʀjɛ̃, məsjø. **24.** nuvuzɑ̃vɛʀõ lafaktyʀ.

CONVERSATION 20

IPA Transcription of Dialog

a laʀɛd lotɔbys

1. bõʒuʀ ʒɑ̃. kɛskəvufɛtisi? **2.** vuvwaje, ʒatɑ̃ lotɔbys. **3.** ɛskɔ vu latɑ̃dedpɥi lõtɑ̃? **4.** ʒlatɑ̃dpɥi(z)œ̃kaʀ dœʀ. **5.** vʀɛmɑ̃? vunavepɑvy dotɔbys dəpɥi(z) œ̃kaʀdœʀ? **6.** si. œ̃notɔbys ɛvny. **7.** puʀkwan lavevupɑ pʀi? **8.** ʒnepɑ pymõte. **9.** ilete kõplɛ. **10.** vwasi œ̃notʀ otɔbys ki aʀiv. **11.** ʒvwa de ʒɑ̃dbu. **12.** sanfɛʀjɛ̃. **13.** mõtõ tudmɛm.

dɑ̃ lotɔbys

14. ilnjapɑ bokudplas . . . **15.** iljɔʀadlaplas ply lwɛ̃, kɑ̃ leʒɑ̃ kɔmɑ̃sʀõa desɑ̃dʀ. **16.** ʒlɛspɛʀ. **17.** u desɑ̃devu? **18.** ʒdesɑ̃ a laʀɛd laʀydlapɛ. **19.** ʒvɛʃelkwafœʀ. **20.** mwa osi. sivuvule, ʒiʀeavɛkvu. **21.** dakɔʀ. nupuʀõziale ɑ̃sɑ̃bl.

CONVERSATION 21

IPA Transcription of Dialog

1. a kɛlekɔl aljevu, kɑ̃ vuzavje duzɑ̃? **2.** ʒalɛ(z)okɔlɛʒ, sɛtadiʀ a lekɔlsəgõdɛʀ. **3.** u abitjevu asmɔmɑ̃la? **4.** ʒabitɛzyn pətitvil dezalp. **5.** sɛtyn ʀeʒjõ tʀɛ pitɔʀɛsk, nɛspɑ? **6.** wi, mɛ sɛtvil a bjɛ̃ ʃɑ̃ʒed(ə)pɥi. **7.** ɔ̃ni a kɔ̃stʀɥi dezyzin də pʀɔdɥi ʃimik. **8.** l(ə) pʀɔgʀɛ, vusave . . . **9.** kɛskəvufəzje(z) alekɔl? **10.** ʒtʀavajɛ ɥitœʀ paʀ ʒuʀ. **11.** kwa? **12.** ʒi alɛ tulematɛ̃ a ɥitœʀ, e ʒɑ̃ sɔʀtɛ a katʀœʀ dəlapʀɛmidi. **13.** ɛskiljavɛ bokudelɛv dɑ̃sɛtekɔl? **14.** nɔ̃. ilnjavɛgɛʀ plyd(ə)dø sɑ̃zelɛv. **15.** ʒkʀwakɔ̃tʀavajɛtʀo dɑ̃sɛtekɔl. **16.** ʒənsɥipɑ tutafɛdvɔtʀavi, ʒɑ̃. **17.** ʒkʀwaksɛtekɔl mafɛbokudbjɛ̃.

CONVERSATION 22

IPA Transcription of Dialog

1. bɔ̃ʒuʀ, maʀi. **2.** ʒənvuzepɑvy obal samdidɛʀnje. **3.** ʒɛspeʀɛ puʀtɑ̃ vuzi vwaʀ. **4.** ʒsɥi ʀɛste alamɛzɔ̃ səswaʀla. **5.** ʒənmə sɑ̃tɛpɑ tʀɛbjɛ̃, **6.** e ʒəmsɥi kuʃedbɔnœʀ. **7.** ʒɛspɛʀ kə sla netɛʀjɛ̃. **8.** ʒ(ə)lɛspeʀɛ osi. **9.** mɛl(ə) lɑ̃dmɛ̃ ʒtusɛ, **10.** e ʒavɛ malalagɔʀʒ. **11.** avevufɛvniʀl(ə) mɛtsɛ̃? **12.** nɔ̃. setɛ tusɛ̃pləmɑ̃ œʀym. **13.** ʒɛspɛʀ kəsnetɛpɑ gʀav. **14.** nɔ̃. ʒsɥi ʀɛsteoli døʒuʀ. **15.** mɛ̃tnɑ̃ ʒvɛbokumjø. **16.** mɛ kɔmɑ̃ avevu(z)atʀape sla? **17.** vɑ̃dʀədi, ʀɔʒe e mwa avɔ̃fɛ ynlɔ̃g pʀɔmnad. **18.** ilfəzɛbo, mɛ ase fʀwɑ. **19.** nuzavɔ̃maʀʃe dɑ̃lanɛʒ ʒyskalanɥi. **20.** ʒavɛfʀwɑ kɑ̃ʒsɥi ʀɑ̃tʀe. **21.** vufʀe bjɛ̃d vuʀpoze. **22.** swaɲevu bjɛ̃. **23.** o! ʒnɑ̃muʀʀepɑ.

CONVERSATION 23

IPA Transcription of Dialog

u ɛ makʀavat?

1. sʀevu bjɛ̃topʀɛ, ʒɑ̃? **2.** wi, tutalœʀ. **3.** ʒ(ə) ʃɛʀʃ ma kʀavat ʀuʒ, mɛ ʒənsɛpɑ u ʒle miz. **4.** ʒpø vupʀɛte yndemjɛn. **5.** nɔ̃, mɛʀsi. ʒnɛmpɑ levotʀ. **6.** kəvulevudiʀ? kəʒnepɑdgu, nɛspɑ? **7.** ʒəndipɑsla. **8.** ʒvødiʀ sœlmɑ̃ kʒɛm mjø mekʀavat kəlevotʀ. **9.** e bjɛ̃, ʃɛʀʃele, pɥiskə vulezɛmetɑ̃. **10.** ɛskəʒpø pɔʀte ynkʀavat vɛʀt avɛk œ̃ kɔ̃plɛblø? **11.** slamɛtegal . . . **12.** mɛ avevuʀgaʀde dɑ̃ vɔtʀətiʀwaʀ? **13.** wi, ʒeʃɛʀʃe paʀtu. **14.** ʒveʀgaʀde dɑ̃lmjɛ̃. **15.** tjɛ̃ sɛtkʀavatʀuʒ nɛpɑzamwa. **16.** ɛskɛlɛtavu, paʀazaʀ? **17.** mɛwi, sɛtyndəme kʀavat. **18.** puʀkwa etɛtɛl avɛklevotʀ? **19.** ʒnɑ̃sɛʀjɛ̃. **20.** pøtɛtʀək labɔn admiʀtɑ̃ vokʀavat, kɛlaesɛjed mɑ̃dɔne yn!

CONVERSATION 24

IPA Transcription of Dialog

ʀətuʀ də vakɑ̃s

1. tjɛ̃, bɔ̃swaʀ, maʀi! vuzɛt dəʀtuʀ? **2.** ʒsɥi kɔ̃tɑ̃d vuʀvwaʀ. **3.** avevupasedbɔnvakɑ̃s dənɔel ɑ̃bʀətaɲ? **4.** wi, ɛksɛlɑ̃t, mɛʀsi; mɛ tʀokuʀt, kɔm tutlevakɑ̃s. **5.** kɑ̃ɛtvu ʀəvny? **6.** jɛʀswaʀ aɔ̃zœʀ. **7.** avevu fɛbɔ̃vwajaʒ? **8.** o! nə mɑ̃ paʀlepɑ! **9.** a ʀɛn, lɛkspʀɛsdəpaʀi etɛbɔ̃de. **10.** ʒe apɛn pytʀuve ynplas. **11.** e pɥi, leʒɑ̃fymɛ, **12.** e ilfəzɛ(t)ɔʀibləmɑ̃ ʃo dɑ̃lkɔ̃paʀtimɑ̃. **13.** vunave pɑdʃɑ̃s. **14.** ʒedine ovagɔ̃ ʀɛstɔʀɑ̃. **15.** sɛ la sœlpaʀti dyvwajaʒ kietɛ sypɔʀtabl.

16. ɛmevu dine ovagõ ʀɛstɔʀɑ̃? **17.** ase. sɛtynfasõd pɑse yndəmiœʀ. **18.** kɛskəvuzavefɛ l(ə)ʒuʀ dənɔɛl? **19.** skõfɛ paʀtu səʒuʀla. **20.** nusɔmzale alamɛsdəminɥi. **21.** nuzavõfɛlʀevɛjõ ʃe le kɛʀgelɛn. **22.** ʒəmsɥi bjɛ̃namyze.

CONVERSATION 25

IPA Transcription of Dialog

si ʒetɛ ʀiʃ

1. kɛskəvufəʀje sivuzetjeʀiʃ, ʀɔʒe? **2.** ʒənsɛpɑ. **3.** nə vudʀijevupɑ vwajaʒe? **4.** si, ʒvudʀɛ vizite plyzjœʀ pei(z)etʀɑ̃ʒe. **5.** u iʀjevu? **6.** ʒiʀɛ(z)ɑ̃nitali, vizite flɔʀɑ̃s e ʀɔm, **7.** ozetazyni, vwaʀ legʀatsjɛl, **8.** e ɑ̃nafʀik vwaʀ skispɑs labɑ. **9.** ɛskəsɛtu? **10.** nõ. ʒaʃɛtʀɛyn gʀos vwatyʀ, **11.** e ʒiʀɛ mamyze obɔʀdlamɛʀ. **12.** ʒɛspɛʀ kəvunsʀeʒamɛʀiʃ, ʀɔʒe. **13.** puʀkwa ditvu sla? **14.** paʀskə vusəʀje malœʀø. **15.** vunsɔʀjepɑ depɑ̃se vɔtʀaʀʒɑ̃. **16.** vuzave pøtɛtʀə ʀɛzõ. **17.** ʒvudʀɛ sœlmɑ̃ ɛtʀəʀiʃ də tɑ̃zɑ̃tɑ̃. **18.** ʒe ynide, ʀɔʒe. **19.** lakɛl? **20.** vunaveka ʃɛʀʃe œ̃ miljɔnɛʀ kipɑ̃s kɔmvu. **21.** vupuʀje ʃɑ̃ʒedʀol **22.** tulesimwa, paʀɛgzɑ̃pl!

CONVERSATION 26

IPA Transcription of Dialog

a vɛʀsɑj

1. ʒənkʀwajɛpɑ vɛʀsɑj si gʀɑ̃. **2.** tut ɛ maʒɛstɥø: lɛ vastə saldyʃɑto, le lõgzale dypaʀk, le pjɛsdo, leʒaʀdɛ̃, lefõtɛn . . . **3.** lwikatɔʀz ɛmɛ lasplɑ̃dœʀ. **4.** mɛ̃tnɑ̃, kõpʀənevu puʀkwa õ laplɛ l(ə) gʀɑ̃ ʀwa? **5.** wi, ʒkõpʀɑ̃. **6.** nɔblɛs ɔbliʒ, vusave. **7.** ʒsɛk(ə) lwikatɔʀz a fɛkõstʀɥiʀ vɛʀsɑj. **8.** mɛ kiɛski lakõstʀɥi puʀ lɥi? **9.** œ̃ dezaʀʃitɛkt etɛ mɑ̃saʀ. **10.** ʒe ɑ̃tɑ̃dy paʀledlɥi. **11.** nuzavõ(z) ɑ̃nɑ̃glɛlmo «mænsard». **12.** tjɛ̃! kɛskəsla vødiʀ? **13.** ʒkʀwak(ə)sɛt ynɛspɛs datwɑ. **14.** l(ɔ)mo «mɑ̃saʀd» ɛgzistosi ɑ̃fʀɑ̃sɛ. **15.** kɛskəsɛ kynmɑ̃saʀd? **16.** sɛdɔʀdinɛʀ ynʃɑ̃bʀ(ə) sultwa. **17.** sɛlakõmɛ levjømœbl, leʃɛzkɑse, letapiyze, ɛtsetɛʀa. **18.** ləsɔʀ ɛpaʀfwa iʀɔnik. **19.** kɛski vufɛdiʀ sla? **20.** mɑ̃saʀ apasesavi akõstʀɥiʀdepalɛ, **21.** e sõnõ ɛʀɛste aynœ̃bləʃɑ̃bʀ.

CONVERSATION 27

IPA Transcription of Dialog

kɛskətya?

1. kɛskətya, maʀi? **2.** ʒneʀjɛ̃ dytu, ʒtasyʀ. **3.** mɛsi, tyakɛlkəʃoz. **4.** tya lɛʀtʀist. **5.** akwa pɑ̃sty? **6.** ʒpɑ̃s aʒɑn. lakɔnɛty? **7.** nõ. ʒənkʀwapɑ. ki ɛs? **8.** sɛtyndəmekuzin. **9.** tya tɑ̃dkuzin. **10.** lakɛldətekuzin ɛs? **11.** sɛ makuzin kidmœʀaʀɛ̃s. **12.** o wi! tymadeʒa parledɛl. **13.** kɛski lɥi ɛtaʀive? **14.** ʒeʀsy jɛr ynlɛtʀə dəmatɑ̃t ɛʀnɛstin. **15.** ɛlmekʀi k(ə)ʒɑn vasmaʀje ʒødipʀɔʃɛ̃. **16.** kwa? ɛskə sɛtnuvɛltəʀɑ̃ tʀist? tyɛʒaluz? **17.** nõ, ʒən sɥi nitʀist niʒaluz. **18.** kɛski-tɑ̃nɥi, alɔʀ? **19.** ʒənpuʀepɑzale asɔ̃maʀjaʒ. **20.** sɛdɔmaʒ, ɑ̃nefɛ. **21.** avɛk ki takuzin s(ə)maʀitɛl? **22.** avɛk œ̃ʒœnɔm kəʒkɔnɛsɛ kɑ̃tilavɛdizɑ̃. **23.** kɔm lətɑ̃pɑs!

CONVERSATION 28

IPA Transcription of Dialog

œ̃naksidɑ̃

o kɔmisaʀjadpɔlis

1. (lkɔmisɛʀ d(ə) pɔlis) vuzɛt bjɛ̃ məsjø ʒɑ̃ yg, ɛ̃ʒenjœʀʃimist, **2.** dəmœʀɑ̃ ɥit ʀydydɔktœʀ ʀu? **3.** wi, məsjølkɔmisɛʀ. **4.** jɛʀapʀɛmidi, vuzavezete temwɛ̃dlaksidɑ̃ **5.** okuʀdykɛl lədɔktœʀ lɑ̃bɛʀ aeteblɛse? **6.** wi, məsjø lkɔmisɛʀ. **7.** u etjevu omɔmɑ̃ u loto dydɔktœʀ, **8.** ki sɥivɛ laʀydvoʒiʀaʀ, **9.** ɛtɑ̃tʀe ɑ̃kɔlizjɔ̃ avɛkœ̃ kamjɔ̃ **10.** vənɑ̃dlavny pastœʀ? **11.** ʒetɛdvɑ̃ lɛ̃stity pastœʀ. **12.** kɔmɑ̃ laksidɑ̃ atilyljø? **13.** laʃose etɛ tʀɛglisɑ̃t, **14.** kaʀ ilavɛply. **15.** lədɔktœʀlɑ̃bɛʀ, dɔ̃lotoalɛ tʀɛvit, **16.** napɑpy saʀɛte atɑ̃. **17.** akɛlvitɛs ləkamjɔ̃ alɛtil **18.** kɑ̃ laksidɑ̃ ayljø? **19.** a ɑ̃viʀɔ̃ tʀɑ̃t kilɔmɛtʀalœʀ. **20.** ʒvuʀmɛʀsi, məsjø. **21.** skəvuvneddiʀ **22.** ɛdakɔʀ avɛk leʀɑ̃sɛɲmɑ̃k nuzavɔ̃ deʒa.

CONVERSATION 29

IPA Transcription of Dialog

ʃe lɔʀlɔʒe

1. kɛskilja, məsjø? **2.** ʒvudʀɛ fɛʀ ʀepaʀe sɛt mɔ̃tʀ. **3.** ʒle lɛsetɔ̃be jɛʀ, **4.** e ɛlnəmarʃə ply. **5.** u avevuzaʃtesɛtmɔ̃tʀəla? **6.** ʒleaʃte ɑ̃nameʀik. **7.** ʒmɑ̃dute **8.** ʒne ʒamɛ vy ynmɔ̃tʀ kɔmsa. **9.** ɛskəvupuʀe laʀepaʀe tud mɛm? **10.** ʒkʀwa. **11.** dəkwa saʒitil? **12.** ilsaʒi dynʀepaʀɑsjɔ̃ sɛ̃pl. **13.** mɛ ʒəsʀe ɔbliʒe fɛʀvəniʀ œ̃ʀsɔʀ. **14.** puvevumdiʀ kɑ̃ mamɔ̃tʀəsʀapʀɛt? **15.** vwajɔ̃ . . . ʒvɛkɔmɑ̃de oʒuʀdɥi ləʀsɔʀ dɔ̃ʒebəzwɛ̃. **16.** ʒəlʀəsəvʀe sɑ̃dut vɛʀ ləmiljødlasmɛnpʀɔʃɛn. **17.** ʒvudʀɛ bjɛ̃avwaʀ mamɔ̃tʀ lə plyto pɔsibl. **18.** ʀəvne doʒuʀdɥi ɑ̃ kɛ̃z. **19.** bɔ̃. ʒatɑ̃dʀe ʒyskə la.

CONVERSATION 30

IPA Transcription of Dialog

o bɔ̃maʀʃe

1. (lavɑ̃døz) kɛskəvudezire, madmwazɛl? **2.** ʒvudʀɛ(z)yneʃaʀp. **3.** ʃwazise, madmwazɛl. nuzavɔ̃(z)œnɛksɛlɑ̃ ʃwa. **4.** yndəmezami ɑ̃nayn kəʒɛmboku. **5.** ɛl la aʃte isi, ʒ(ə)kʀwa. **6.** də kɛl kulœʀ ɛ sɛldəvɔtʀami? **7.** sɛtyneʃaʀp dəswablɑ̃ʃ. **8.** kəpɑ̃sevud sɛteʃaʀpəsi, madmwazɛl? **9.** kɔ̃bjɛ̃ɛs? **10.** tʀɑ̃t fʀɑ̃. **11.** e sɛl la? **12.** kaʀɑ̃t fʀɑ̃. **13.** sɛtœ̃pøʃɛʀ. **14.** avevu kɛlkəʃoz dəmɛjœRmaRʃe? **15.** mɛwi, madmwazɛl. sɛlsi nəkutkə vɛ̃tsɛ̃ fRɑ̃. **16.** ʒkRwak(ə) ʒɛm mjø sɛlkə vumavemõtRe tutalœR. **17.** lakɛl, madmwazɛl? **18.** sɛlsi. vulevu bjɛ̃ lamɛtR dɑ̃zynbwat? **19.** vɔlõtje. deziRevu otRəʃoz, madmwazɛl? **20.** ʒvudRɛ(z)osi demuʃwaR. **21.** ɛmevu søsi? **22.** kɛlɑ̃nɛlpRi? **23.** dø fRɑ̃ sɛ̃kɑ̃t pjɛs. **24.** ʒɑ̃pRɑ̃dRe yndəmiduzɛn **25.** vulevubjɛ̃ pasealakɛs, madmwazel? **26.** vuzytRuvRe vozaʃa.

CONVERSATION 31

IPA Transcription of Dialog

ɛ̃kɛskyRsjɔ̃ ala kɑ̃paɲ

1. ilja pRɛskədøzœR kənuzavõkite məlœ̃. **2.** ʒkɔmɑ̃s a avwaR maloʒɑ̃b. **3.** ʒnepɑ labityd dale abisiklɛt. **4.** ʒkRwak(ə)nuzavõpRi lamɔvɛzRut. **5.** ʒɑ̃ne pœR. **6.** vwala œ̃nɔm kitRavaj dɑ̃sõʃɑ̃. **7.** ilpuRa nudɔne deRɑ̃sɛɲmɑ̃. **8.** (alɔm) ɛskə nu sɔm lwɛ̃dfõtɛnblo? **9.** mɛwi, mõpovR məsjø. **10.** ʒsɥifaʃed vuzapRɑ̃dR **11.** kə vuvuzɛt trõpe dRut. **12.** kɛlRut fotil pRɑ̃dR, alɔR? **13.** vuvwajes vilaʒ, labɑ? **14.** sɛ baRbizõ. alezi. **15.** alasɔRti, pRənel pRəmje ʃmɛ̃ agɔʃ. **16.** il vu mɛnRa afõtɛnblo. **17.** a kɛldistɑ̃s ɛsdisi? **18.** sɛtasɛt u ɥi kilɔmɛtR. **19.** zytalɔR! paRsɛtʃalœR, snɛpɑdRɔl! **20.** lapRɔʃɛnfwa, nu pRɑ̃dRõmavwatyR. **21.** sivuzaveʃo e sivuzaveswaf, **22.** vupuRe vuzaRɛte a baRbizõ. **23.** sɛmafam ki tjɛ̃ ləpti cafe **24.** ʒyst ɑ̃fas dəlegliz.

CONVERSATION 32

IPA Transcription of Dialog

aRive ala fɛRm dedeʃɑ̃

1. bõʒuR, makuzin. **2.** tjɛ̃! bõʒuR, Rɔʒe. **3.** kɛl bɔnsyRpRiz! **4.** ʒtəpRezɑ̃t ʒɑ̃ yg. **5.** sɛ mõ mɛjœR ami. **6.** ɑ̃ʃɑ̃te. məsjø. **7.** Rɔʒe masuvɑ̃ paRledvu. **8.** nuzavõdesided pRɔfite dybotɑ̃ puR vəniRvuvwaR. **9.** sɛtynɛksɛlɑ̃tide. **10.** avevu fɛbõvwajaʒ? **11.** wi. mɛ nusɔmzasefatige. **12.** asɛjevu eRpozevu. **13.** vulevu pRɑ̃dRə kɛlkəʃoz? **14.** ʒpRɑ̃dRed labjɛR, si ty ɑ̃na. **15.** evu, məsjø? **16.** ʒbwaRɛ vɔlõtje œ̃vɛR dofRɛʃ. **17.** n(ə) pReféRevupɑotRəʃoz? **18.** mɛRsi, madam. **19.** ilnjaRjɛ̃dmɛjœR kœ̃vɛRdofRɛʃ kɑ̃tilfɛ ʃo. **20.** ʒɛspɛR bjɛ̃k(ə) vuzale pɑse kɛlkəʒuR avɛknu. **21.** nunvulõpɑ vudeRɑ̃ʒe. **22.** nuzavõ lɛ̃tɑ̃sjõ dəRpaRtiR səswaR. **23.** vunɛtpɑ pRɛse. **24.** Rɛste kəlkəʒuR(z)isi. **25.** sɛlmɔmɑ̃d lamwasõ. **26.** sivuvule, vupuRe nuzɛde.

CONVERSATION 33

IPA Transcription of Dialog

dɑ̃ lafɔRɛd fõtɛnblo

1. ʒvwa deʃɑ̃piɲõ obɔRdlaRut. **2.** il dwatjɑ̃navwaR boku dɑ̃l bwa. **3.** si nuzɑ̃rapɔRtjõ kɛlkəzœ̃ alamɛzõ? **4.** ɛskəvukɔnɛse leʃɑ̃piɲõ? **5.** plyz u mwɛ̃.

6. ʀamɑse sœlmɑ̃ søsi. **7.** ilsõ tʀɛfasil aʀkɔnɛtʀ. **8.** lədsy ɛ bʀœ̃ e lədsu ɛ ʒon. **9.** õnpøpɑstʀõpe. **10.** bõ. mɛ ʒənsɛpɑ u lemɛtʀ. **11.** təne, mɛtele ladədɑ̃. **12.** ɛskə səlɥisi ɛbõ? **13.** wi. **14.** e səlɥila? **15.** ɛksɛlɑ̃. **16.** o! ʒɑ̃vwaboku opjedsɛtaʀbʀ. **17.** fɛt(z)atɑ̃sjõ! **18.** ɛskəvuvule(z)ɑ̃pwazɔne tutlafamij? **19.** mɛ seʃɑ̃piɲõ ʀəsɑ̃bl a søkvumave mõtʀe. **20.** lemɔvɛ ʃɑ̃piɲõ ʀəsɑ̃bl(ə) boku obõ. **21.** vuzɔʀjedym diʀsa plyto. **22.** ʒe y tɔʀ dən pɑ vu pʀevniʀ. **23.** ɑ̃tukɑ, ilvomjø lɛse sø dõtõnɛpɑsyʀ.

CONVERSATION 34

IPA Transcription of Dialog

a legliz dyvilaʒ

1. bõʒuʀ, məsjølkyʀe. **2.** bõʒuʀ, mezami. **3.** ɑ̃tʀedõ(k). **4.** ʒetezɑ̃tʀɛ̃d tʀavaje dɑ̃mõʒaʀdɛ̃ kɑ̃vuzavesɔne. **5.** nunuzɛkskyzõd vudeʀɑ̃ʒe kɑ̃vuzɛt(z)-ɔkype. **6.** vun mədeʀɑ̃ʒe pɑdytu. **7.** ʒvjɛ̃d taje meʀozje, **8.** eʒsɥiza vɔtʀə dispozisjõ. **9.** nuzavõzɑ̃tɑ̃dydiʀ kəvuzave yn tʀɛbɛlegliz, **10.** e nuzavõɑ̃vid lavizite. **11.** ʒəmfʀe œ̃plɛzir dəvuzakõpaɲe dɑ̃vɔtʀ(ə)visit. **12.** ʒkʀɛ̃ puʀtɑ̃k vunswaje œ̃pødesy. **13.** bjɛ̃kɛl swaklɑse mɔnymɑ̃istɔrik, **14.** sɛtyn sɛ̃plegliz dəvilaʒ. **15.** ʒely kɛlkəpaʀ kəvɔtʀegliz datdyduzjɛmsjɛkl. **16.** ynpaʀti sœlmɑ̃ dəledifisaktɥɛl dat də lepɔkʀɔman. **17.** legliz aetebʀyle ɑ̃tʀɛzsɑ̃katʀəvɛ̃duz. **18.** ɛl aete ɑ̃paʀti ʀkõstʀɥit osjɛkləsɥivɑ̃. **19.** ʒeɑ̃tɑ̃dy paʀle devitʀo dvɔtʀegliz. **20.** õdi kilsõ tʀɛvjø. **21.** ʒənkʀwapɑ kiljɛplyd dø(z)utʀwɑvitʀo vʀɛmɑ̃ ɑ̃sjɛ̃. **22.** laplypaʀdɑ̃tʀø sõ ʀ(ə)lativmɑ̃ mɔdɛʀn. **23.** vulevubjɛ̃ ɑ̃tʀe paʀsɛtpɔʀt? **24.** lɛ̃teʀjœʀ d(ə)legliz ɛtœ̃pøsõbʀ, **25.** mɛ vozjø sabityʀõvit alɔpskyʀite.

CONVERSATION 35

IPA Transcription of Dialog

o ʒaʀdɛ̃

1. ilfok(ə)ʒajoʒaʀdɛ̃ kœjiʀdeflœʀ. **2.** vøtykənutɛdjõ? **3.** wi, mɛfɛ atɑ̃sjõd bjɛ̃fɛʀmelapɔʀt dɛʀjɛʀtwa. **4.** ʒənvøpɑk lepul pɥisɑ̃tʀe. **5.** ɛlmɑ̃ʒapøpʀɛ tutmasalad. **6.** kɛlflœʀ vatykœjiʀ? **7.** ʒe bəzwɛ̃ dʀoz e dœjɛ. **8.** ʒɑ̃fʀe œ̃bukɛ puʀ lasalamɑ̃ʒe. **9.** tya œ̃tʀɛboʒaʀdɛ̃. **10.** ʒədvʀɛ mɑ̃nɔkype davɑ̃taʒ, **11.** mɛ ʒne paltɑ̃. **12.** ɛskəvuzave dymais? **13.** nõ, ʒnɑ̃nepɑ. **14.** dajœʀ, lete ɛtʀofʀɛ **15.** puʀkəl mais pɥis myʀiʀisi. **16.** ʒmɑ̃dutɛ œ̃pø. **17.** ʀəgaʀde sepwɑ, seaʀikovɛʀ eseʃu. **18.** ilpus amɛʀvɛj. **19.** wi, mɛ ilnagɛʀply sɛtane. **20.** ynbɔnplɥi fʀɛdybjɛ̃ amelegym. **21.** vøtyk(ə) nulezaʀozjõ? **22.** ʒkʀwakil vomjø(z)atɑ̃dʀ **23.** ʒyskaskilfas mwɛ̃ʃo.

CONVERSATION 36

IPA Transcription of Dialog

ynpaʀtid pɛʃ

1. si nuzaljõ(z)alapɛʃ dəmɛ̃matɛ̃? **2.** akwabõ? nunatʀapʀõ ʀjɛ̃. **3.** ʒnivɛpɑ puʀatʀape kɛlkəʃoz. **4.** puʀkwa ialevu alɔʀ? **5.** ʒivɛ paʀskə ʒɛmɛtʀ **6.** obɔʀdəlo, alõbʀədegʀɑ̃zaʀbʀ. **7.** ɛtvuʒamɛzale alapɛʃ ləmatɛ̃dbɔnœʀ? **8.** wi, ʒisɥizale kɛlkəfwa. **9.** nɛmevupɑ(z) ɛtʀɑ̃plɛnɛʀ? **10.** si. mɛ ʒənpʀɑ̃ ʒamɛdpwasõ. **11.** mwa nõply, mɛ slanfɛʀjɛ̃. **12.** silõnɑ̃pʀɑ̃, tɑ̃mjø, **13.** silõnɑ̃pʀɑ̃pɑ, tɑ̃pi. **14.** u vulevu(z)ale? **15.** ʒkɔnɛ(z)œ̃nɑ̃dʀwa sulvjøpõ, **16.** dəlotʀəkoted laʀivjɛʀ, **17.** u iljadɛpwasõ gʀɔkɔmsa! **18.** søk vumɑ̃ke? **19.** nəvumɔkepɑdmwa . . . **20.** akɛlœʀ vulevu paʀtiʀ? **21.** dəbɔnœʀ. ilfodʀak nunuləvjõ akatʀœʀ dymatɛ̃. **22.** mɛil nəfɛpɑ(z)ɑ̃kɔʀ ʒuʀ asɛtœʀla. **23.** ʒystəmɑ̃! nuvɛʀõlsɔlɛj sɔlve syʀlaʀivjɛʀ. **24.** dəkwa vuplɛɲevu? **25.** ʒənməplɛ̃pɑ. **26.** mɛ ʒɛm mjø dɔʀmiʀ dɑ̃mõli kədɔʀmiʀsyʀ lɛʀb — silepwasõn mɔʀdəpɑ.

CONVERSATION 37

IPA Transcription of Dialog

aʀive alagaʀ dəljõ

1. bõʒuʀ, ʒɑ̃. bõʒuʀ, ʀɔʒe. ʒsɥizœʀøz kəvuswaje dəʀtuʀ. **2.** nu(z)osi, nusɔmzɑ̃ʃɑ̃ted vuʀvwaʀ, maʀi. **3.** vunuzave mɑ̃ke boku, vusave. **4.** flatœʀ! **5.** sɛʒɑ̃tid ta paʀ dɛtʀ(ə) vny nuzatɑ̃dʀalagaʀ. **6.** ʒəmdəmɑ̃d sivuvuʀɑ̃dekõt kɔ ʒe fɛ puʀ vu œ̃ gʀɑ̃ sakʀifis. **7.** ʒədvɛ ʒwe otɛnis s(ə)matɛ̃. **8.** mɛ kɑ̃ ʒeapʀik vudəvje ʀəvniʀ oʒuʀdɥi, ʒɛdesided vɔniʀ vuzatɑ̃dʀisi. **9.** kɑ̃ atyʀsy ma depɛʃ? **10.** ilja apøpʀɛ ynœʀ. **11.** mɛtyɔʀɛdym diʀ lœʀɛgzakt dətõnaʀive. **12.** nunlasavjõpɑ numɛm. **13.** nunetjõpɑsyʀ datʀapeltʀɛ̃ də ɥitœʀedmi. **14.** ʒɑ̃, vɔtʀəkõsjɛʀʒ matelefɔne kœ̃ kablə puʀvu ɛtaʀivesmatɛ̃. **15.** o! ʒsɛskəsɛ. **16.** ɛlɛnfʀazɛʀdwataʀive sɛʒuʀsi. **17.** ɛlmɛ̃dik sɑ̃dut ləʒuʀd(ə) sõnaʀive. **18.** tjɛ̃, tjɛ̃! ki ɛ sɛt ɛlɛn? **19.** sɛtynʒœnameʀikɛn dəmezami kiɛtaktɥɛlmɑ̃ a lõdʀ. **20.** ɛlmadmɑ̃ded lɥisɛʀviʀdəgid apaʀi.

CONVERSATION 38

IPA Transcription of Dialog

alatɛʀas dœ̃kafe

1. asɛjõnu(z)alatɛʀas dəskafe. **2.** nupuʀõ vwaʀpɑse leʒɑ̃. **3.** kɛl ɛsmɔnymɑ̃ labɑ, obudlaʀy? **4.** vudəvʀije ləʀkɔnɛtʀ. sɛl pɑ̃teõ. **5.** o! ʒəmʀapɛl mɛ̃tnɑ̃. **6.** sɛlɑ̃dʀwa u lõnɑ̃tɛʀ legʀɑ̃zɔm, nɛspɑ? **7.** wi, kɛlkəzœ̃ dɑ̃tʀø. **8.** õtʀuvla nɔtamɑ̃ letõbodvɔltɛʀ ed viktɔʀygo. **9.** puʀkwa apɛltõ sɛtpaʀtidpaʀi l(ə) kaʀtjelatɛ̃? **10.** paʀskə sɛlkaʀtjedlynivɛʀsite, eklɔlatɛ̃ etetotʀəfwa la lɑ̃gdə lynivɛʀsite. **11.** u ɛ dõk lasɔʀbɔn? **12.** adøpɑ disi. **13.** nuziʀõ tutalœʀ, sivuvule. **14.** puʀkwa apɛltõ lynivɛʀsitedpaʀi la sɔʀbɔn? **15.** ʒely lɛksplikasjõ kɛlkəpaʀ, mɛ ʒən mɑ̃suvjɛ̃ply . . . **16.** sɛkotɑ̃d sɛ̃lwi, œ̃sɛʀtɛ̃ ʀɔbɛʀd(ə) sɔʀbõ afõde œ̃kɔlɛʒ puʀ lezetydjɑ̃d teɔlɔʒi. **17.** sə kɔlɛʒ, aple lasɔʀbɔn, ɛ dəvny lafakyltedclɛtʀə. **18.** tusezetydjɑ̃ õlɛʀ sɛʀjø e pʀeɔkype . . . **19.** iljadkwa. **20.** ilsõtɑ̃tʀɛ̃dpɑse lœʀzɛgzamɛ̃ e lezɛgzamɛ̃, ɑ̃fʀɑ̃s, nəsõpɑ fasil.

CONVERSATION 39

IPA Transcription of Dialog

lәlõdeke

1. kəʀgaʀd seʒɑ̃la, ləlõd lasɛn? **2.** ilzɛgzamin lezetalaʒ debukinist. **3.** kəvɑ̃d sebukinist? **4.** tutsɔʀtdəʃoz. **5.** lezœ̃vɑ̃d dəvjɛjzɛstɑ̃p, dotʀə detɛ̃bʀəpɔst, dotʀə dəvjɛj pjɛsdəmɔnɛ, mɛlaplypaʀ dɑ̃tʀø fõlkɔmɛʀs delivʀ(ə) dɔkɑzjõ. **6.** mõfʀɛʀ madmɑ̃ded lɥi ɑ̃vwaje detɛ̃bʀ. **7.** tʀavɛʀsõlaʀy. **8.** nupuʀõʒte œ̃kudœj syʀlezetalaʒ. **9.** savevu kɛltɛ̃bʀə vɔtʀ(ə) fʀɛʀ vøspʀɔkyʀe? **10.** wi, ʒedɑ̃mõsak ynlist kiladʀɛse. **11.** (o bukinist) avevu letɛ̃bʀɛ̃dike syʀsɛt list? **12.** vwajõzœ̃pø . . . maʀtinik dizɥisɑ̃katʀəvɛ̃sis; s(ə)gõtɑ̃piʀ, dizɥisɑ̃sɛ̃kɑ̃ttʀwɑ; senegal, diznœfsɑ̃tʀwɑ; ɛtseteʀa. **13.** wi, madmwazɛl. ʒkʀwa lezavwaʀ tus, sɔf letɛ̃bʀə dysgõtɑ̃piʀ, seʀi dizɥisɑ̃sɛ̃kɑ̃ttʀwɑ. **14.** il nəmɑ̃ʀɛst okœ̃. **15.** tɑ̃pi. **16.** vulevu kõsylte sɛtalbɔm? **17.** vuzitʀuvʀe pøtɛtʀ sɛʀtɛ̃ tɛ̃bʀ kivuzɛ̃teʀɛs. **18.** ʒənkɔnɛpɑ gʀɑ̃ʃoz otɛ̃bʀəpɔst. **19.** vunaveka ʃwazir leplyʒɔli. **20.** o nõ! iljakɛlkətɑ̃, ʒe ɑ̃vwaje plyzjœʀ tɛ̃bʀ amõfʀɛʀ. **21.** ʒavɛʃwazi leplyʒɔli. **22.** mɛ ilavɛ deʒa laplypaʀ dɑ̃tʀø, e ilmadik mõʃwan valɛʀjɛ̃.

CONVERSATION 40

IPA Transcription of Dialog

o tɥilʀi

1. mɛ̃tnɑ̃, ɑ̃tʀõ dɑ̃lʒaʀdɛ̃ detɥilʀi. **2.** kə pɑ̃sevudsəkwɛ̃d paʀi? **3.** ʒsɥizetɔned tʀuve tɑ̃dɛspɑs okœʀmɛm dəlavil. **4.** ʒnavɛ pɑ lamwɛ̃dʀided(ə) letɑ̃dyd laplasd(ə)lakõkɔʀd. **5.** mɛ, ditmwa, kɛlɛsgʀɑ̃batimɑ̃dvɑ̃nu? **6.** sɛl(ə)luvʀ, ɑ̃sjɛ̃palɛ ʀwajal. **7.** ɛskəsɛla kɛlmyzedy luvʀ? **8.** wi, lmyze ɔkyp laplygʀɑ̃d-paʀtid ledifis. **9.** il pɔsɛd dimɑ̃skɔlɛksjõ. **10.** e vwala laʀk də tʀiõf. **11.** dapʀɛ lefɔtɔgʀafik ʒevy, ʒəl kʀwajɛ plygʀɑ̃. **12.** sɛ laʀkdətʀiõf dykaʀuzɛl kəvuvwajela. **13.** lotʀ, selɥid letwal, ɛtobudlavny de ʃɑ̃zelize. **14.** sivuvuʀtuʀne, vupuʀelapɛʀsəvwaʀ labɑ . . . **15.** ʀ(ə)gaʀde sɛt pətitfij kiplœr, ʒɑ̃. **16.** ləvɑ̃ a ɑ̃mne sõbatoavwal omiljø dybasɛ̃. **17.** ɛskəvupuve lɛde? **18.** ʒɔʀɛ bo fɛʀ. **19.** l(ə)bato ɛtʀolwɛ̃ puʀkəʒpɥis latɛ̃dʀ. **20.** ləvɑ̃ finiʀa sɑ̃ dut paʀ ləʀamneobɔʀ. **21.** ʒe ɑ̃vidkœjiʀ yndəseflœʀ kɔmsuvniʀ dənɔtʀ(ə) pʀɔmnad. **22.** gaʀdevuzɑ̃ bjɛ̃. **23.** si œ̃naʒɑ̃dpɔlis vuvwajɛ, ilpuʀɛ bjɛ̃ vufɛʀ œ̃pʀɔsɛvɛʀbal.

CONVERSATION 41

IPA Transcription of Dialog

anɔtʀədam

1. nusɔm mɛ̃tnɑ̃ dɑ̃ lildəlasite. **2.** ɛskɔ̃napɛlpɑzosi sɛtil lildəfʀɑ̃s? **3.** ʒe pœʀ kə vun kɔ̃fɔ̃dje vozil, ɛlɛn. **4.** lildəfʀɑ̃s ɛ laʀeʒjɔ̃ otuʀd(ə)paʀi. **5.** lildəlasite ɛtynil omiljød lasɛn. **6.** ʒəʀkɔnɛ, adʀwat, letuʀ d(ə) nɔtʀədam. **7.** sinuvizitjɔ̃ nɔtʀədam? **8.** mɛwi. tʀavɛʀsɔ̃ laplas e ɑ̃tʀɔ̃ dɑ̃lakatedʀal. **9.** atɑ̃dekəʒpʀɛn ynfɔto.

(dɑ̃ nɔtʀədam)

10. kɔm lɛ̃teʀjœʀ ɛvast esilɑ̃sjø! **11.** ɔ̃nozapɛnpaʀle, mɛmavwabɑs. **12.** ʒvudʀɛbjɛ̃ asiste aynmɛs anɔtʀədam. **13.** sivuvule, nuʀvjɛ̃dʀɔ̃ dimɑ̃ʃpʀɔʃɛ̃. **14.** vupuʀezɑ̃tɑ̃dʀə legʀɑ̃dzɔʀg. **15.** ɛskɔ̃pømɔ̃te ɑ̃ o detuʀ? **16.** ʀjɛ̃d plyfasil. **17.** sɛtɛskalje ɑ̃kəlimasɔ̃ nuzikɔ̃dɥiʀa. **18.** ɑ̃naʀivɑ̃ ɑ̃ o, vupuʀepʀɑ̃dʀə dotʀəfɔto.

(ɑ̃ o dyndetuʀ dənɔtʀədam)

19. ʒsɥizesufle . . . **20.** mɛ kɛlpanɔʀama! ɔ̃vwapaʀi tutɑ̃tje. **21.** dəvɑ̃vu, vuzave la sɛ̃tʃapɛl, ləluvʀ elɛʃɑ̃zelize; syʀlaʀivgoʃ, ləkaʀtjelatɛ̃ e lasɔʀbɔn; esyrlaʀiv dʀwat, legʀɑ̃bulvaʀ emɔ̃maʀtʀ. **22.** ʒe ɑt dəvizite lekaʀtjedpaʀik(ə) ʒən kɔnɛpɑzɑ̃kɔʀ.

The Relation Between French Spelling and French Pronunciation

When students first begin to read French on their own, they sometimes seem to forget all they have learned about French pronunciation. They often even mispronounce words they have been using and pronouncing correctly for several weeks.

In order to combat this tendency, it is useful to explain what reading in a foreign language means (pp. xii–xiii, Introduction) and give the students information about diacritical marks and about the way the various combinations of vowels and consonants are pronounced. The following section contains the material we have found most effective. Useful as this information may be, however, rather than have students study the entire section at once, we try to introduce each item at a moment when it will actually clarify a difficulty which comes up in a reading exercise. For example, the moment at which the student will perhaps be most receptive to the statement that **-ien** is pronounced [jɛ̃] as in **bien, rien, le chien** is when he stumbles on the pronunciation of a form such as **Je viendrai.**

I. Diacritical Signs

The following typographical signs are used (*a*) to distinguish between two or more possible pronunciations of a letter, or (*b*) to distinguish between two words which are pronounced alike, and, except for the diacritical marks, are spelled alike. *In no case do these signs indicate that a syllable should be stressed.*

A. The acute accent (ʹ) (**accent aigu**) is used only on the letter **e: l'été, espérer.** The **é** is usually pronounced [e].

B. The grave accent (ˋ) (**accent grave**) is used mostly on **e** followed by a final **s** or **-re: très, près, après-midi; père, frère, j'espère, ils allèrent.** The **è** is always pronounced [ɛ].

This accent is also used on the **a** in the preposition **à**, *to*, to distinguish it from the third person singular of the present indicative of **avoir.** Likewise it is used on the **a** of the adverb **là,** *there*, to distinguish it from the article **la,** *the*, as well as on the **u** of the adverb **où,** *where*, to distinguish it from the conjunction **ou,** *or*.

C. The circumflex accent (ˆ) (**accent circonflexe**) is found on all the vowels (except the semi-vowel **y**): **âme, même, île, hôtel, sûr.** An **â** is usually pronounced [ɑ], **ê** [ɛ], **î** [i], **ô** [o], **û** [y]. It used to indicate a lengthening of the vowel (resulting from the fall of a consonant) but today this lengthening is observed only in the most conservative usage.

D. The cedilla (¸) (**cédille**) under **c** indicates that the letter is pronounced [s].

E. When a diaresis (¨) (**tréma**) is placed over the second of two vowels, it indicates that the vowel so marked begins a new syllable. **Noël, naïf.** Note, however, that the name **Saint-Saëns** is pronounced [sɛ̃ sɑ̃s].

II. Elision

When a vowel is dropped and replaced by an apostrophe before a word beginning with a vowel or mute **h,** elision (**élision**) is said to take place. You can't just assume that *any* final vowel is elided before all initial vowels. Elision takes place in the following cases:

A. When the article **le** or **la** is immediately followed by a noun or adjective beginning with a vowel sound, the **e** (or **a**) of the article is elided.

B. When **je, me, te, se, ce, le, la, ne, que** are immediately followed by a verb that begins with a vowel sound or the word **y** or **en,** the **e** is elided.

C. The **i** of **si** is elided when it is followed by **il, ils.** This vowel is not elided elsewhere: you write (and say) **si elle, si un homme, si on,** etc.

D. When **que, parce que, puisque, lorsque** are followed by a pronoun beginning with a vowel, the final **e** is elided: **parce qu'elle, lorsqu'il.**

Note that before the words **huit** and **onze, le** is not elided: **le huit** septembre, **le onze** mars.

Remember also that the demonstrative adjective **ce** is not elided but is replaced by the form **cet** before nouns beginning with a vowel sound.

III. Syllabication

In dividing French words into syllables, in so far as possible each syllable should begin with a consonant and end in a vowel.

A. When a single consonant stands between two vowels, the consonant goes with the vowel which follows it: **bu-reau, ta-bac, hô-tel, ga-rage, vou-lez.**

B. When a double consonant letter (**tt, dd, pp,** etc.) stands between two vowels:

(1) in most cases it represents a single sound and is pronounced with the following vowel: **donnez** [dɔ-ne], **allez** [a-le]. **addition** [a-di-sjõ], **intelligent** [ɛ̃tɛ-liʒɑ̃];

(2) in some cases it represents two consonants, both of which are pronounced with the following vowel: **accident** [a-ksi-dɑ̃], **suggérer** [sy-gʒe-ʀe].

C. When two or more different consonants stand between vowels:

(1) one consonant may go with the vowel that precedes and one with the one that follows: **mer-ci, par-lez, res-tau-rant, cul-ture;**

(2) two consonants may form a consonant cluster* and stand together at the beginning of the following syllable: **a-près, ta-bleau, pa-trie, é-crit;**

(3) one consonant may go with the preceding vowel and a consonant cluster* may stand together at the beginning of the next syllable: **mal-gré, ins-truit, ex-trême.**

The digraphs **ch, ph, th, gn** (each of which of course represents a single sound) always stand with the vowel that follows.

Repeat the following pairs of words and note especially the way the French words are divided: *American*, **A-mé-ri-cain;** *nationality*, **na-tio-na-li-té;** *profession*, **pro-fes-sion;** *democratic*, **dé-mo-cra-tique;** *Philadelphia*, **Phi-la-del-phie.**

Note that **n, m** behave one way when they are followed by a vowel (**i-nutile**) and another when they are not (**in-telligent, j'ai faim**), but in both cases the principle that syllables tend to begin with a consonant and end with a vowel is preserved: [i-ny-til], [ɛ̃-tɛ-li-ʒɑ̃], [ʒe fɛ̃].

* The following are the consonant clusters which occur most commonly: **bl, cl, fl, gl, pl; br, cr, dr, gr, pr, tr, vr.**

IV. Consonants

LETTER	PRONUNCIATION	
b	[b]	in practically all cases: une banane, le bébé.
	[p]	when followed by **t** or **s:** absurde, absent, absolument, obtenir.
		Silent when final: les soldats de plomb.
c	[k]	when followed by **a, o, u,** or **l, r:** le café, le corps, la curiosité, je crois.
	[s]	when followed by **e, i, y:** c'est, certainement, ici, la bicyclette.
	[k]	usually when final: avec, le sac.
		Silent in: le tabac, franc, blanc, le porc.
	[g]	in: second, secondaire, anecdote.
ç	[s]	Used only before **a, o, u:** le français, le garçon, j'ai reçu.
cc	[k]	except when followed by **e, i, y:** accorder.
	[ks]	when followed by **e, i, y:** accepter, accident.
ch	[ʃ]	usually: chercher, le chimiste, chez, Charles.
	[k]	sometimes: un orchestre, le chœur.
d	[d]	in practically all cases: dans, l'addition, madame, le sud.
		Usually silent when final: le pied, le nid, le hasard, le nord.
	[t]	in: tout de suite, le médecin, quand il . . .
f	[f]	in practically all cases: franc, le café.
	[f]	usually when final: le chef, neuf, le rosbif, un œuf.
		Silent in: les œufs, les bœufs, la clef.
	[v]	in: neuf heures, neuf ans.
g	[g]	when followed by **a, o, u,** or **l, r:** la gare, grand.
	[ʒ]	when followed by **e, i, y:** gentil, les gens, la girafe, le gymnase.
gg	[gʒ]	when followed by **e, i, y:** suggérer.
gn	[ɲ]	la campagne, la Bretagne, la vigne.
gu	[g]	in: la guerre, le guide.
	[gɥ]	in: aiguille.
	[gy]	in: aigu.
h		Always silent: l'homme, l'hôtel, les hors-d'œuvre.
j	[ʒ]	janvier, je déjeune.
k	[k]	le kilo, un biftek.
l	[l]	usually pronounced even when final: l'hôtel, le cheval.
		Silent in: gentil, le fusil, le fils [fis], le pouls [pu].
	[j]	when preceded by **ai** or **ei:** le travail, le soleil, vieil, etc.
ll	[j]	when preceded by **ai, ei, ui:** travailler, vieille.
	[j]	usually when preceded by **i:** la fille, gentille, juillet, la famille.
	[l]	in: ville, village, mille, tranquille, illustrer, etc.

LETTER	PRONUNCIATION	
m	[m]	When followed by a vowel letter: aimer, madame, calme. When not followed by a vowel letter, **m** causes the preceding vowel to be nasalized but is not otherwise pronounced: faim [fɛ̃], chambre [ʃɑ̃bʀ], ensemble [ɑ̃sɑ̃bl], important [ɛ̃pɔʀtɑ̃].
mm	[m]	l'homme, comment, femme, évidemment.
n	[n]	When followed by a vowel letter: nous, une, inutile. When not followed by a vowel letter, **n** nasalizes a preceding vowel but is not otherwise pronounced: bon [bõ], vingt [vɛ̃], enfant [ɑ̃fɑ̃], intelligent [ɛ̃teliʒɑ̃], la France [lafʀɑ̃s]. Silent in **-ent** verb endings.
nn	[n]	bonne, sonner, donnez, l'année, solennel.
p	[p]	in practically all cases: le papier, le départ, l'aptitude, le pneu, la psychologie, le psaume. Usually silent when final: trop, beaucoup. Silent in: le temps, compter, la sculpture, sept, etc.
q, qu	[k]	in practically all cases: qui, que, quel, le coq.
qu	[kw]	in: une aquarelle, un aquarium.
r	[ʀ]	in practically all cases: la rue, très, l'art, vers. Pronounced when final in: le fer, la mer, fier, cher, car, pour, l'hiver, etc. Silent in infinitive ending **-er,** and in: boucher, boulanger, charcutier, épicier, monsieur, léger, premier, volontiers, etc.
s	[s]	at the beginning of a word or when preceded or followed by a consonant: absent, sang, aspect, etc.
	[z]	when between vowels: la raison, la maison, les roses.
	[z]	when linked: vous‿avez. Usually silent when final: les, tables, lesquels.
	[s]	in: le fils, mars, le sens, tous (*pronoun*), omnibus, autobus, Reims, Saint-Saëns, etc.
sc	[sk]	when followed by **a, o, u,** or **l, r:** la sculpture, scolaire.
	[s]	when followed by **e, i, y:** la science, le scénario.
ss	[s]	assez, aussi, essayer.
t	[t]	at beginning of a syllable: le temps, l'été, l'amitié. Silent when final in verb forms (except in linking) and in most nouns and adjectives: le lit, élégant, différent, cent, vingt, tout, ils disent, il disait, il dit.
	[t]	in: l'est, l'ouest, net, la dot, Brest, tact, intact, exact.
th	[t]	le thé, le théâtre.
ti	[s]	in **-tion** ending (nation), and in: démocratie, initial, patience, etc.
v	[v]	in all cases: voulez-vous? avez-vous?

LETTER	PRONUNCIATION	
w	[v]	in: le wagon, Waterloo.
	[w]	in: le tramway, le sandwich.
x	[ks]	in: excellent, le luxe, l'index.
	[gz]	in: exact, exemple, examen.
	[s]	in: soixante; and in dix, six when final in a phrase.
	[z]	in: dix, six when linked: dix‿enfants. Silent in: dix, six, when followed by a word beginning with a pronounced consonant. dix francs; and in: paix, voix, etc.
y	[j]	in: les yeux, il y a, asseyez-vous.
z	[z]	le zéro, le gaz, zut! Silent in **-ez** verb ending and in: chez (except in linking).

V. Vowels

LETTER	PRONUNCIATION	
a, à	[a]	in most cases: la gare, l'accident, la table, à Paris.
	[ɑ]	in: pas, phrase, vase, etc.
â	[ɑ]	in most cases: âge, âme, pâle, château.
ai	[e]	when final: j'ai, j'irai.
	[ɛ]	except when final: j'avais, il avait, il fait, ils avaient.
	[ə]	in: nous faisons, je faisais, tu faisais, etc.
au	[o]	in most cases: au Canada, haut, il faut, chaud.
	[ɔ]	in: j'aurai, le restaurant, Paul.
ay	[ɛj]	in: essayer, payer, ayez.
	[ei]	in: le pays.
	[aj]	in: La Fayette.
è, ê	[ɛ]	je me lève, le père, la tête, vous êtes.
é	[e]	l'été, espérer, allé.
e	[ɛ]	when followed by two consonants or in final syllable when followed by a single pronounced consonant: rester, verte, avec, mettre; and in: il est.
	[e]	in final syllable when followed by silent **d, f, r, z:** pied, la clef, le boucher, allez; and in: et, and les, mes, etc.
	[ə]	in the words je, me, te, se, ce, le, de, ne, que; and before a single pronounced consonant: venir, demander, demain, cheval, parlement, comprenez. This [ə] is usually omitted in conversation if it is preceded by no more than one pronounced consonant in the phrase: seulement [sœlmɑ̃], la petite [laptit]. Silent in words of more than one syllable when final or when followed by silent **s** or **nt:** ville, robes, parle, parles, parlent.
eau	[o]	le bureau, l'eau, le veau.

LETTER	PRONUNCIATION	
ei	[ɛ]	la neige, la peine.
eu	[œ]	in most cases when followed in the same syllable by a pronounced consonant: neuf, leur, jeune, ils veulent;
	[ø]	when final of a syllable or when followed by the sound [z] or a silent final consonant: un peu, deux, il veut, les yeux, heureuse, jeudi, deuxième.
	[y]	in *passé simple*, imperfect subjunctive, and past participle of avoir: j'eus, etc.; il eût, etc.; il a eu, etc.
i	[i]	normally: ici, il finit.
	[j]	When followed by a vowel but not preceded by a consonant cluster: hier, papier, vieux, nation, question, banquier, janvier.
	[i-j]	When followed by a vowel and preceded by a consonant cluster: vous oubliez [vuzublije], il pria [il pri-ja], février [fevʀije].
o	[ɔ]	except when followed by a silent final consonant or the sound [z] or [sj]: notre, joli, l'école, objet, hors-d'œuvre, les pommes, la note, la dot, la robe.
	[o]	when followed by a silent final consonant or the sound [z] or [sj]: mot, dos, nos, gros, la rose, poser, motion.
ô	[o]	le nôtre, table d'hôte, ôter.
œu	[œ]	when followed in the same word by a pronounced consonant: la sœur, hors-d'œuvre, un œuf, le bœuf.
	[ø]	in the plural forms œufs [ø], bœufs [bø].
oi	[wa]	moi, une poire, la boîte, une fois.
	[wɑ]	trois, le mois, le bois, les pois, le roi, froid.
ou, où	[u]	nous, voulez-vous? toujours, où? ou.
oui	[wi]	Louis, oui.
oy	[waj]	loyer, soyons, voyons.
u	[y]	sur, plus, une, la rue, du café.
ua	[ɥa]	nuage.
ue	[ɥɛ]	actuel, actuellement.
ui	[ɥi]	puis, huit, je suis, la nuit, lui, le bruit, juillet.
uy	[yj]	gruyère.
	[ɥij]	fuyez, ennuyer, appuyer.
y	[i]	in: j'y vais, la bicyclette, Égypte, Yves, le système.

VI. Nasal Vowels

A. Generally speaking, when vowels are followed by **m, n,** the vowel is nasalized and the **m, n** are not pronounced unless they stand before a vowel-letter or a second **n** or **m.**

LETTER	PRONUNCIATION	
a	[ɑ̃]	quand, sans, grand, l'anglais, la chambre, allemand.
ae	[ɑ̃]	Caen, Saint-Saëns.
ai	[ɛ̃]	le pain, le bain, la faim, la main.
ao	[ɑ̃]	Laon, le paon.
e	[ɑ̃]	en, ensemble, le temps, le membre, la dent, vendre, emmener [ɑ̃mne], l'ennui, évident.
	[ɛ̃]	examen, européen, le citoyen.
i	[ɛ̃]	la fin, le vin, vingt, impossible.
ie	[jɛ̃]	bien, rien, le chien, ancien, il tient, vous viendrez, etc.
	[i]	in: ils étudient.
	[jɑ̃]	in: patience, orient, science.
o	[õ]	on, bon, non, sont, onze, l'oncle, le nom, le nombre, compter.
	[ə]	in: monsieur.
oi	[wɛ̃]	loin, moins, le coin, le point.
u	[œ̃]	un, chacun, lundi, le parfum.
	[ɔ]	in a few Latin words: album, postscriptum, maximum.
ui	[ɥɛ̃]	juin.

B. Vowels followed by **mm, nn** are usually not nasalized.

a	[a]	année, constamment, élégamment.
e	[ɛ]	ennemi, prennent, tiennent, viennent.
	[a]	évidemment, solennel, la femme.
o	[ɔ]	comme, comment, bonne, sonner, l'homme, nommer, le sommeil, Sorbonne, la monnaie.

I. Regular Verbs

118. *Formation of regular verbs from key forms.*

All the forms of regular verbs can be derived from the following key forms: the present infinitive, the present indicative, the past participle, and the *passé simple.* The following paragraphs contain an explanation of the way the various forms can be derived.

119. *Forms that can be derived from the infinitive.*

A. To form the future tense, add to the infinitive* the endings: **-ai, -as, -a, -ons, -ez, -ont.** Examples:

donner	je donner**ai**	*I shall give*
finir	je finir**ai**	*I shall finish*
vendre	je vendr**ai**	*I shall sell*

B. To form the present conditional, add to the infinitive* the endings: **-ais, -ais, -ait, -ions, -iez, -aient.** Examples:

donner	je donner**ais**	*I should* or *would give*
finir	je finir**ais**	*I should* or *would finish*
vendre	je vendr**ais**	*I should* or *would sell*

120. *Forms that can be derived from the present indicative.*†

A. To form *the present participle*, drop the **-ons** of the first person plural of the present indicative and add the ending **-ant.** Examples:

nous donnons	donn**ant**	*giving*
nous finissons	finiss**ant**	*finishing*
nous vendons	vend**ant**	*selling*

* For infinitives of the third conjugation, the **-e** of the **-re** ending is omitted. Ex.: je vendrai, je répondrai, etc.

† For the formation of the present indicative of regular verbs, see paragraph 14 (2); paragraph 33 (1); and paragraph 35 (1).

B. To form *the imperfect indicative*, drop the **-ons** of the first person plural of the present indicative and add the endings: **-als, -ais, -ait, -ions, -iez, -aient.** Examples:

nous donnons	je donn**ais**	*I was giving*, etc.
nous finissons	je finiss**ais**	*I was finishing*, etc.
nous vendons	je vend**ais**	*I was selling*, etc.

C. To form *the imperative*, use the following forms of the present indicative without the pronoun subject: the second person singular, the first person plural, and the second person plural. Examples:

tu donnes	**donne(s)***	*give*
tu finis	**finis**	*finish*
tu vends	**vends**	*sell*
nous donnons	**donnons**	*let's give*
nous finissons	**finissons**	*let's finish*
nous vendons	**vendons**	*let's sell*
vous donnez	**donnez**	*give*
vous finissez	**finissez**	*finish*
vous vendez	**vendez**	*sell*

D. To form *the present subjunctive* drop the **-ons** of the first person plural of the present indicative and add the endings: **-e, -es, -e, -ions, -iez, -ent.** Examples:

nous donnons	je donn**e**	*I give*†
nous finissons	je finiss**e**	*I finish*
nous vendons	je vend**e**	*I sell*

121. *Forms in which the past participle‡ is used.*

A. The past participle is used in conjunction with the different tenses of the auxiliary verb **avoir** (in a few cases **être,** see paragraph 32) to form the compound tenses of verbs.

(1) To form the **passé composé,** use the present tense of the auxiliary verb with the past participle of the verb. Examples:

j'ai donné	*I gave, I have given*
je suis arrivé	*I arrived, I have arrived*

* In the verbs of the first conjugation, the **s** of the second singular ending is used only when followed by the word **y** or **en.**

† The subjunctive forms are translated in several different ways, depending upon the context.

‡ For the formation of the past participle, see paragraphs 31 (C), 34 (3), 36 (2).

(2) To form *the pluperfect*, use the imperfect tense of the auxiliary verb with the past participle of the verb. Examples:

j'avais donné	*I had given*
j'étais arrivé	*I had arrived*

(3) To form *the past anterior* (a literary tense which is approximately equivalent to the pluperfect), use the **passé simple** of the auxiliary verb with the past participle of the verb. Examples:

j'eus donné	*I had given*
je fus arrivé	*I had arrived*

(4) To form *the future perfect*, use the future tense of the auxiliary verb with the past participle of the verb. Examples:

j'aurai donné	*I shall have given*
je serai arrivé	*I shall have arrived*

(5) To form *the conditional perfect*, use the present conditional of the auxiliary verb with the past participle of the verb. Examples:

j'aurais donné	*I should* or *would have given*
je serais arrivé	*I should* or *would have arrived*

(6) To form *the* **passé composé** *of the subjunctive*, use the present subjunctive of the auxiliary verb with the past participle of the verb. Examples:

j'aie donné	*I have given*, etc.
je sois arrivé	*I have arrived*, etc.

(7) To form *the pluperfect of the subjunctive*, use the imperfect subjunctive of the auxiliary verb with the past participle of the verb. Examples:

j'eusse donné	*I had given*, etc.
je fusse arrivé	*I had arrived*, etc.

(8) To form *the perfect infinitive*, use the present infinitive of the auxiliary verb and the past participle of the verb. Examples:

avoir donné	*to have given*
être arrivé	*to have arrived*

B. The past participle is used in conjunction with the different tenses of the auxiliary verb **être** to form the tenses of the passive voice of transitive verbs (i.e. of verbs normally conjugated with **avoir**). Examples:

PRESENT INDIC.	**je suis** flatté	*I am flattered*
IMPERFECT	**j'étais** flatté	*I was flattered*
FUTURE	**je serai** flatté	*I shall* or *will be flattered*
CONDITIONAL	**je serais** flatté	*I should* or *would be flattered*

PASSÉ COMPOSÉ	**j'ai été** flatté	*I was* or *have been flattered*
PLUPERFECT	**j'avais été** flatté	*I had been flattered*
PAST ANTERIOR	**j'eus été** flatté	*I had been flattered*

Although some of the forms of the passive voice look very complicated, they present no real difficulty either from the point of view of form or meaning. When broken down into their component parts and translated literally into English, they practically always make good sense *and good English.* Examples:

Il avait été tué.	*He*	*had*	*been*	*killed.*
Vous auriez été étonné.	*You*	*would have*	*been*	*surprised.*

The English passive voice is by no means always rendered in French by the passive voice. (See *use of* **faire** *with an infinitive* 93 (B).)

122. *Forms that can be derived from the* **passé simple.***

To form the imperfect subjunctive, drop the last letter of the first person singular of the **passé simple,** and add the endings: **-sse, -sses, -^t, -ssions, -ssiez, -ssent.**

PASSÉ SIMPLE		IMPERFECT SUBJ.
je donna**i**	*I gave*	je donn**asse**
je finis	*I finished*	je fin**isse**
je vendis	*I sold*	je vend**isse**

The vowel preceding the **t** of the third person singular of the imperfect subjunctive always has a circumflex accent. Ex.: donn**ât,** fin**ît,** vend**ît,** **eût,** **fût,** etc.

123. *Regular conjugations.*

A. Infinitive and tenses formed on it:

FUTURE

I	II	III
donner	**finir**	**vendre**
je donnerai	je finirai	je vendrai
tu donneras	tu finiras	tu vendras
il donnera	il finira	il vendra
nous donnerons	nous finirons	nous vendrons
vous donnerez	vous finirez	vous vendrez
ils donneront	ils finiront	ils vendront

* For the formation of the **passé simple,** see paragraph 70.

Conditional

donner	finir	vendre
je donnerais	je finirais	je vendrais
tu donnerais	tu finirais	tu vendrais
il donnerait	il finirait	il vendrait
nous donnerions	nous finirions	nous vendrions
vous donneriez	vous finiriez	vous vendriez
ils donneraient	ils finiraient	ils vendraient

B. Present indicative and tenses that can be formed from it:

Present Indicative

je donne	je finis	je vends
tu donnes	tu finis	tu vends
il donne	il finit	il vend
nous **donnons**	nous **finissons**	nous **vendons**
vous donnez	vous finissez	vous vendez
ils donnent	ils finissent	ils vendent

Imperative

donne(s)	finis	vends
donnons	finissons	vendons
donnez	finissez	vendez

Present Participle

donnant	finissant	vendant

Imperfect

je donnais	je finissais	je vendais
tu donnais	tu finissais	tu vendais
il donnait	il finissait	il vendait
nous donnions	nous finissions	nous vendions
vous donniez	vous finissiez	vous vendiez
ils donnaient	ils finissaient	ils vendaient

Present Subjunctive

je donne	je finisse	je vende
tu donnes	tu finisses	tu vendes
il donne	il finisse	il vende
nous donnions	nous finissions	nous vendions
vous donniez	vous finissiez	vous vendiez
ils donnent	ils finissent	ils vendent

C. Past participle and tenses in which past participle appears:

(1) Verbs conjugated with **avoir:**

	PAST PARTICIPLE	
donné	**fini**	**vendu**
	PASSÉ COMPOSÉ	
j'ai donné, etc.	j'ai fini, etc.	j'ai vendu, etc.
	PLUPERFECT	
j'avais donné, etc.	j'avais fini, etc.	j'avais vendu, etc.
	PAST ANTERIOR	
j'eus donné, etc.	j'eus fini, etc.	j'eus vendu, etc.
	FUTURE PERFECT	
j'aurai donné, etc.	j'aurai fini, etc.	j'aurai vendu, etc.
	CONDITIONAL PERFECT	
j'aurais donné, etc.	j'aurais fini, etc.	j'aurais vendu, etc.
	PASSÉ COMPOSÉ SUBJUNCTIVE	
j'aie donné, etc.	j'aie fini, etc.	j'aie vendu, etc.
	PLUPERFECT SUBJUNCTIVE	
j'eusse donné, etc.	j'eusse fini, etc.	j'eusse vendu, etc.
	PERFECT INFINITIVE	
avoir donné	avoir fini	avoir vendu
	PERFECT PARTICIPLE	
ayant donné	ayant fini	ayant vendu

(2) Verbs conjugated with **être:**

PAST PARTICIPLE	**arrivé** (*from* arriver)
PASSÉ COMPOSÉ	je suis arrivé(e), etc.
PLUPERFECT	j'étais arrivé(e), etc.
PAST ANTERIOR	je fus arrivé(e), etc.
FUTURE PERFECT	je serai arrivé(e), etc.
CONDITIONAL PERFECT	je serais arrivé(e), etc.
PASSÉ COMPOSÉ SUBJUNCTIVE	je sois arrivé(e), etc.
PLUPERFECT SUBJUNCTIVE	je fusse arrivé(e), etc.
PERFECT INFINITIVE	être arrivé(e)(s)
PERFECT PARTICIPLE	étant arrivé(e)(s)

D. Passé simple and imperfect subjunctive:

PASSÉ SIMPLE

je donnai	je finis	je vendis
tu donnas	tu finis	tu vendis
il donna	il finit	il vendit
nous donnâmes	nous finîmes	nous vendîmes
vous donnâtes	vous finîtes	vous vendîtes
ils donnèrent	ils finirent	ils vendirent

IMPERFECT SUBJUNCTIVE

je donnasse	je finisse	je vendisse
tu donnasses	tu finisses	tu vendisses
il donnât	il finît	il vendît
nous donnassions	nous finissions	nous vendissions
vous donnassiez	vous finissiez	vous vendissiez
ils donnassent	ils finissent	ils vendissent

124. *Verbs of the first conjugation that are regular except for a slight variation in their stem.*

A. Verbs whose stem vowel is a mute **e** (**acheter, appeler**) have two stems.

(1) Whenever in conjugation the mute **e** of the stem vowel is followed by a syllable containing a mute **e,** the **e** of the stem vowel is pronounced [ɛ]. This occurs in the following forms: the first, second, and third person singular and the third person plural of the present indicative and the present subjunctive **(e, -es, -e, -ent);** the second person singular of the imperative (**-e** or **-es**); and the six forms of both the future and conditional (**-erai,** etc., **-erais,** etc.).

(2) Whenever the mute **e** of the stem vowel is followed by a syllable containing any vowel other than a mute **e,** it is pronounced [ə] as in the infinitive. This phenomenon is reflected in the spelling as follows:

(*a*) In **acheter,** *to buy;* **lever,** *to raise;* **mener,** *to lead;* and a few other verbs, the stem vowel is written **è** when followed by a syllable containing a mute **e.** Ex.: PRESENT: **J'achète, tu achètes, il achète, nous achetons, vous achetez, ils achètent;** FUTURE: **j'achèterai,** etc.; CONDITIONAL: **j'achèterais,** etc.

(*b*) In **appeler,** *to call;* **jeter,** *to throw;* and a few other verbs ending in **-eler, -eter,** the final **l** or **t** of the stem is doubled when followed by a mute syllable. Ex.: PRESENT: **J'appelle, tu appelles, il appelle, nous appelons, vous appelez, ils appellent;** FUTURE: **j'appellerai,** etc.

B. Verbs whose stem vowel is **é:**

In **espérer,** *to hope;* **céder,** *to yield;* **préférer,** *to prefer* and a few other verbs whose stem vowel is **é,** the stem vowel is written **è** and pronounced [ɛ] in the present indicative (and present subjunctive) when followed by a mute syllable. Ex.: PRESENT: **J'espère, tu espères, il espère, nous espérons, vous espérez, ils espèrent.** (In the future and conditional, however, the stem vowel of these verbs is written **é.** Ex.: **J'espérerai.**)

C. Verbs ending in **-cer, -ger, -yer** show a slight variation in the spelling of the stem *but not in its pronunciation.*

(1) In **commencer, avancer,** etc., the final **c** of the stem is written **ç** whenever in conjugation it is followed by an **a** or **o.** Ex.: PRESENT: **Je commence, tu commences, il commence, nous commençons, vous commencez, ils commencent;** PRESENT PART.: **commençant;** IMPERFECT: **je commençais, tu commençais, il commençait, nous commencions, vous commenciez, ils commençaient;** PASSÉ SIMPLE: **je commençai,** etc.

(2) In **manger,** *to eat,* and other verbs ending in **-ger,** you write **ge** instead of **g** whenever the following vowel is **a** or **o.** Ex.: PRESENT: **je mange, tu manges, il mange, nous mangeons, vous mangez, ils mangent;** IMPERFECT: **je mangeais,** etc.; PASSÉ SIMPLE: **je mangeai,** etc.

(3) In **ennuyer,** *to bother,* and other verbs ending in **-oyer, -uyer,** you write **i** instead of **y** whenever the following letter is a mute **e.** Ex.: **il ennuie,** *but* **nous ennuyons.**

(4) In **payer,** *to pay,* and other verbs ending in **-ayer, -eyer,** you may write **y** throughout the verb, or, if you prefer, you may write **i** instead of **y** whenever the following letter is a mute **e.** Ex.: **Je paye** *or* **je paie,** *but* **nous payons.**

II. Auxiliary Verbs

125. *Conjugation of auxiliary verbs* **être** *and* **avoir.**

Simple tenses

INFINITIVE

être, *to be*	**avoir,** *to have*

PRESENT INDICATIVE

je suis, *I am*	j'ai, *I have*
tu es	tu as
il est	il a
nous sommes	nous avons
vous êtes	vous avez
ils sont	ils ont

IMPERFECT

j'étais, *I was*	j'avais, *I had*
tu étais	tu avais
il était	il avait
nous étions	nous avions
vous étiez	vous aviez
ils étaient	ils avaient

PASSÉ SIMPLE

je fus, *I was*	j'eus, *I had*
tu fus	tu eus
il fut	il eut
nous fûmes	nous eûmes
vous fûtes	vous eûtes
ils furent	ils eurent

FUTURE

je serai, *I shall* or *will be*	j'aurai, *I shall* or *will have*
tu seras	tu auras
il sera	il aura
nous serons	nous aurons
vous serez	vous aurez
ils seront	ils auront

être		**avoir**
	CONDITIONAL	
je serais, *I should* or *would be*		j'aurais, *I should* or *would have*
tu serais		tu aurais
il serait		il aurait
nous serions		nous aurions
vous seriez		vous auriez
ils seraient		ils auraient
	PRESENT SUBJUNCTIVE	
je sois, *I am*, etc.		j'aie, *I have*, etc.
tu sois		tu aies
il soit		il ait
nous soyons		nous ayons
vous soyez		vous ayez
ils soient		ils aient
	IMPERFECT SUBJUNCTIVE	
je fusse, *I was*, etc.		j'eusse, *I had*, etc.
tu fusses		tu eusses
il fût		il eût
nous fussions		nous eussions
vous fussiez		vous eussiez
ils fussent		ils eussent
	IMPERATIVE	
sois, *be*		aie, *have*
soyons		ayons
soyez		ayez
	PRESENT PARTICIPLE	
étant		ayant

Compound tenses

	PAST PARTICIPLE	
été		**eu**
	PASSÉ COMPOSÉ	
j'ai été, *I was*, *I have been*, etc.		j'ai eu, *I had*, *I have had*, etc.
	PLUPERFECT	
j'avais été, *I had been*, etc.		j'avais eu, *I had had*, etc.
	PAST ANTERIOR	
j'eus été, *I had been*, etc.		j'eus eu, *I had had*, etc.

FUTURE PERFECT

j'aurai été, *I shall have been*, etc.	j'aurai eu, *I shall have had*, etc.

CONDITIONAL PERFECT

j'aurais été, *I should* or *would have been*, etc.	j'aurais eu, *I should* or *would have had*, etc.

PASSÉ COMPOSÉ SUBJUNCTIVE

j'ai été, *I have been*, etc.	j'aie eu, *I have had*, etc.

PLUPERFECT SUBJUNCTIVE

j'eusse été, *I had been*, etc.	j'eusse eu, *I had had*, etc.

PERFECT INFINITIVE

avoir été, *to have been*	avoir eu, *to have had*

PERFECT PARTICIPLE

ayant été, *having been*	ayant eu, *having had*

III. Irregular Verbs

126. *Formation of irregular verbs.*

Although the rules for deriving the forms of regular verbs (see paragraphs 118–122) do not apply strictly to all irregular verbs, they do apply to a substantial proportion of their forms.

127. *Reference list of commonest irregular verbs.*

abattre	*see* battre	131
s'abstenir	*see* tenir	167
abstraire	*see* traire	167
accourir	*see* courir	137
accueillir	*see* cueillir	141
acquérir		128
admettre	*see* mettre	152
aller		129
apercevoir	*see* recevoir	161
apparaître	*see* connaître	135
appartenir	*see* tenir	167
apprendre	*see* prendre	160
assaillir	*see* cueillir	141
s'asseoir		130
astreindre	*see* craindre	138
atteindre	*see* craindre	138
avoir		125
battre		131
boire		132
bouillir	*see* dormir	144
combattre	*see* battre	131
commettre	*see* mettre	152

comprendre	*see* prendre	160
compromettre	*see* mettre	152
concevoir	*see* recevoir	161
conclure		133
conduire		134
connaître		135
conquérir	*see* acquérir	128
consentir	*see* dormir	144
construire	*see* conduire	134
contenir	*see* tenir	167
contraindre	*see* craindre	138
contredire	*see* dire	143
contrefaire	*see* faire	147
convaincre	*see* vaincre	169
convenir	*see* venir	171
coudre		136
courir		137
couvrir	*see* ouvrir	156
craindre		138
croire		139
croître		140
cueillir		141
se débattre	*see* battre	131
décevoir	*see* recevoir	161
découvrir	*see* ouvrir	156
décrire	*see* écrire	145
se dédire	*see* dire	143
déduire	*see* conduire	134
défaire	*see* faire	147
démentir	*see* dormir	144
dépeindre	*see* craindre	138
déplaire	*see* plaire	157
déteindre	*see* craindre	138
détenir	*see* tenir	167
détruire	*see* conduire	134
devenir	*see* venir	171
devoir		142
dire		143
discourir	*see* courir	137
disparaître	*see* connaître	135
distraire	*see* traire	168
dormir		144
écrire		145
élire	*see* lire	151
émettre	*see* mettre	152
émouvoir	*see* mouvoir	154
endormir	*see* dormir	144
s'endormir	*see* dormir	144
enfreindre	*see* craindre	138
s'enfuir	*see* fuir	149
entreprendre	*see* prendre	169
entretenir	*see* tenir	167
entrevoir	*see* voir	174
entr'ouvrir	*see* ouvrir	156
envoyer		146
éteindre	*see* craindre	138
être		125
exclure	*see* conclure	133
extraire	*see* traire	168
faire		147
falloir		148
feindre	*see* craindre	138
fuir		149
geindre	*see* craindre	138
haïr		150
inclure	*see* conclure	133
inscrire	*see* écrire	145
interdire	*see* dire	143
intervenir	*see* venir	171
introduire	*see* conduire	134
joindre	*see* craindre	138
lire		151
maintenir	*see* tenir	167
maudire	*see* dire	143
médire	*see* dire	143
mentir	*see* dormir	144
mettre		152
mourir		153
mouvoir		154
naître		155
obtenir	*see* tenir	167
offrir	*see* ouvrir	156
omettre	*see* mettre	152
ouvrir		156
paraître	*see* connaître	135
parcourir	*see* courir	137
partir	*see* dormir	144
parvenir	*see* venir	171

128. acquérir (*to acquire*).

Future
j'acquerrai, etc.; Cond. j'acquerrais, etc.

Present Indicative
j'acquiers, tu acquiers, il acquiert,
nous acquérons, vous acquérez, ils acquièrent.

Imperative
acquiers, acquérons, acquérez.

Pres. Part.
acquérant; Imperfect j'acquérais, etc.

Pres. Subj.
j'acquière, tu acquières, il acquière,
nous acquérions, vous acquériez, ils acquièrent.

Past Participle
acquis; Passé Composé j'ai acquis, etc.

Passé Simple
j'acquis, etc.; Imper. Subj. j'acquisse, etc.

129. aller (*to go*).

Future
j'irai, etc.; Cond. j'irais, etc.

Present Indicative
je vais, tu vas, il va,
nous allons, vous allez, ils vont.

Imperative
va(s), allons, allez.

Pres. Part.
allant; Imperfect j'allais, etc.

Pres. Subj.
j'aille, tu ailles, il aille,
nous allions, vous alliez, ils aillent.

Past Participle
allé; Passé Composé je suis allé, etc.

Passé Simple
j'allai, etc.; Imperf. Subj. j'allasse, etc.

130. s'asseoir (*to sit down*).

FUTURE
je m'assiérai, etc.; COND. je m'assiérais, etc.

PRESENT INDICATIVE
je m'assieds, tu t'assieds, il s'assied,
nous nous asseyons, vous vous asseyez, ils s'asseyent.

IMPERATIVE
assieds-toi, asseyons-nous, asseyez-vous.

PRES. PART.
s'asseyant;IMPERFECT je m'asseyais, etc.

PRES. SUBJ.
je m'asseye, tu t'asseyes, il s'asseye,
nous nous asseyions, vous vous asseyiez, ils s'asseyent.

PAST PARTICIPLE
assis; PASSÉ COMPOSÉ je me suis assis, etc.

PASSÉ SIMPLE
je m'assis, etc.; IMPERF. SUBJ. je m'assisse, etc.

Alternate form of **s'asseoir.**

FUTURE
je m'assoirai, etc. *or* je m'asseyerai, etc.

CONDITIONAL
je m'assoirais, etc. *or* je m'asseyerais, etc.

PRESENT INDICATIVE
je m'assois, tu t'assois, il s'assoit,
nous nous assoyons, vous vous assoyez, ils s'assoient.

PRES. PART.
s'assoyant; IMPERFECT je m'assoyais, etc.

PRES. SUBJ.
je m'assoie, tu t'assoie, il s'assoie,
nous nous assoyions, vous assoyiez, ils s'assoient.

asseoir, *to seat* is conjugated like **s'asseoir,** but it takes the auxiliary verb **avoir.**

131. battre (*to beat*)

All forms are regular except:

PRESENT INDICATIVE—je bats, tu bats, il bat, nous battons, vous battez, ils battent.

Like **battre: abattre,** *to fell, to beat down;* **combattre,** *to fight*, and **se débattre,** *to struggle.*

132. **boire** (*to drink*).

FUTURE and COND. regular.

PRESENT INDICATIVE
je bois, tu bois, il boit,
nous buvons, vous buvez, ils boivent.

IMPERATIVE
bois, buvons, buvez.

PRES. PART.
buvant; IMPERFECT je buvais, etc.

PRES. SUBJ.
je boive, tu boives, il boive,
nous buvions, vous buviez, ils boivent.

PAST PARTICIPLE
bu; PASSÉ COMPOSÉ j'ai bu, etc.

PASSÉ SIMPLE
je bus, etc.; IMPERF. SUBJ. je busse, etc.

133. **conclure** (*to conclude*).

FUTURE and COND. regular.

PRESENT INDICATIVE
je conclus, tu conclus, il conclut,
nous concluons, vous concluez, ils concluent.

IMPERATIVE
conclus, concluons, concluez.

PRES. PART.
concluant; IMPERFECT je concluais, etc.

PRES. SUBJ.
je conclue, etc.

PAST PARTICIPLE
conclu; PASSÉ COMPOSÉ j'ai conclu, etc.

PASSÉ SIMPLE
je conclus, etc.; IMPERF. SUBJ. je conclusse, etc.

Like **conclure: exclure,** *to exclude*, and **inclure,** *to include*, except that the past participle of the latter is **inclus.**

134. **conduire** (*to conduct, to drive*).

FUTURE and COND. regular.

PRESENT INDICATIVE
je conduis, tu conduis, il conduit,
nous conduisons, vous conduisez, ils conduisent.

IMPERATIVE
conduis, conduisons, conduisez.

PRES. PART.
conduisant; IMPERFECT je conduisais, etc.

PRES. SUBJ.
je conduise, etc.

PAST PARTICIPLE
conduit; PASSÉ COMPOSÉ j'ai conduit, etc.

PASSÉ SIMPLE
je conduisis, etc.; IMPERF. SUBJ. je conduisisse, etc.

Like **conduire: construire,** *to construct;* **déduire,** *to deduce;* **détruire,** *to destroy;* **introduire,** *to introduce;* **produire,** *to produce;* **reconduire,** *to lead back;* **réduire,** *to reduce;* **séduire,** *to seduce, to please;* **traduire,** *to translate;* etc.

135. **connaître** (*to know, to be acquainted with*).

FUTURE and COND. regular.

PRESENT INDICATIVE
je connais, tu connais, il connaît,
nous connaissons, vous connaissez, ils connaissent.

IMPERATIVE
connais, connaissons, connaissez.

PRES. PART.
connaissant; IMPERFECT je connaissais, etc.

PRES. SUBJ.
je connaisse, etc.

PAST PARTICIPLE
connu; PASSÉ COMPOSÉ j'ai connu, etc.

PASSÉ SIMPLE
je connus, etc.; IMPERF. SUBJ. je connusse, etc.

Like **connaître: apparaître,** *to appear;* **disparaître,** *to disappear;* **paraître,** *to appear;* **reconnaître,** *to recognize;* etc.

136. coudre (*to sew*).

FUTURE and COND. regular.

PRESENT INDICATIVE
je couds, tu couds, il coud,
nous cousons, vous cousez, ils cousent.

IMPERATIVE
couds, cousons, cousez.

PRES. PART.
cousant; IMPERFECT je cousais, etc.

PRES. SUBJ.
je couse, etc.

PAST PARTICIPLE
cousu; PASSÉ COMPOSÉ j'ai cousu, etc.

PASSÉ SIMPLE
je cousis, etc.; IMPERF. SUBJ. je cousisse, etc.

137. courir (*to run*).

FUTURE
je courrai, etc.; COND. je courrais, etc.

PRESENT INDICATIVE
je cours, tu cours, il court,
nous courons, vous courez, ils courent.

IMPERATIVE
cours, courons, courez.

PRES. PART.
courant; IMPERFECT je courais, etc.

PRES. SUBJ.
je coure, etc.

PAST PARTICIPLE
couru; PASSÉ COMPOSÉ j'ai couru, etc.

PASSÉ SIMPLE
je courus, etc.; IMPERF. SUBJ. je courusse, etc.

Like **courir: accourir,** *to hasten;* **discourir,** *to discourse;* **parcourir,** *to go over;* **secourir,** *to help;* etc.

138. craindre (*to fear*).

FUTURE and COND. regular.

PRESENT INDICATIVE

je crains, tu crains, il craint,
nous craignons, vous craignez, ils craignent.

IMPERATIVE

crains, craignons, craignez.

PRES. PART.

craignant; IMPERFECT je craignais, etc.

PRES. SUBJ.

je craigne, etc.

PAST PARTICIPLE

craint; PASSÉ COMPOSÉ j'ai craint, etc.

PASSÉ SIMPLE

je craignis, etc.; IMPERF. SUBJ. je craignisse, etc.

Like **craindre: astreindre,** *to compel;* **atteindre,** *to attain;* **contraindre,** *to compel;* **dépeindre,** *to depict;* **déteindre,** *to fade;* **enfreindre,** *to infringe;* **éteindre,** *to extinguish;* **feindre,** *to feign;* **geindre,** *to groan;* **joindre,** *to join;* **peindre,** *to paint;* **plaindre,** *to pity;* **se plaindre,** *to complain;* **rejoindre,** *to rejoin, to meet;* **restreindre,** *to restrain;* **teindre,** *to dye;* etc.

139. croire (*to believe*).

FUTURE and COND. regular.

PRESENT INDICATIVE

je crois, tu crois, il croit
nous croyons, vous croyez, ils croient.

IMPERATIVE

crois, croyons, croyez.

PRES. PART.

croyant; IMPERFECT je croyais, etc.

PRES. SUBJ.

je croie, tu croies, il croie,
nous croyions, vous croyiez, ils croient.

PAST PARTICIPLE

cru; PASSÉ COMPOSÉ j'ai cru, etc.

PASSÉ SIMPLE

je crus, etc.; IMPERF. SUBJ. je crusse, etc.

140. croître (*to grow*).

FUTURE and COND. regular.

PRESENT INDICATIVE
je croîs, tu croîs, il croît,
nous croissons, vous croissez, ils croissent.

IMPERATIVE
croîs, croissons, croissez.

PRES. PART.
croissant;IMPERFECT je croissais, etc.

PRES. SUBJ.
je croisse, etc.

PAST PARTICIPLE
crû; PASSÉ COMPOSÉ j'ai crû, etc.

PASSÉ SIMPLE
je crûs, etc.; IMPERF. SUBJ. je crusse, etc.

141. cueillir (*to pick up, to gather*).

FUTURE
je cueillerai, etc.; COND. je cueillerais, etc.

PRESENT INDICATIVE
je cueille, tu cueilles, il cueille,
nous cueillons, vous cueillez, ils cueillent.

IMPERATIVE
cueille(s), cueillons, cueillez.

PRES. PART.
cueillant; IMPERFECT je cueillais, etc.

PRES. SUBJ.
je cueille, etc.

PAST PARTICIPLE
cueilli; PASSÉ COMPOSÉ j'ai cueilli, etc.

PASSÉ SIMPLE
je cueillis, etc.; IMPERF. SUBJ. je cueillisse, etc.

Like **cueillir: accueillir,** *to welcome;* and **recueillir,** *to gather, to collect.*

Assaillir, *to assail* and **tressaillir,** *to start*, etc. are like **cueillir** except that the future and conditional are regular.

142. devoir (*must, etc.*).

FUTURE
je devrai, etc.; COND. je devrais, etc.

PRESENT INDICATIVE
je dois, tu dois, il doit,
nous devons, vous devez, ils doivent.

IMPERATIVE
——

PRES. PART.
devant; IMPERFECT je devais, etc.

PRES. SUBJ.
je doive, tu doives, il doive,
nous devions, vous deviez, ils doivent.

PAST PARTICIPLE
dû; PASSÉ COMPOSÉ j'ai dû, etc.

PASSÉ SIMPLE
je dus, etc.; IMPERF. SUBJ. je dusse, etc.

143. dire (*to say*).

FUTURE and COND. regular.

PRESENT INDICATIVE
je dis, tu dis, il dit,
nous disons, vous dites, ils disent.

IMPERATIVE
dis, disons, dites.

PRES. PART.
disant; IMPERFECT je disais, etc.

PRES. SUBJ.
je dise, etc.

PAST PARTICIPLE
dit; PASSÉ COMPOSÉ j'ai dit, etc.

PASSÉ SIMPLE
je dis, etc.; IMPERF. SUBJ. je disse, etc.

Like **dire: redire,** *to say again.*

The following verbs are like **dire** except that the 2nd person plural of the present indicative ends in **-disez: contredire,** *to contradict;* **se dédire,** *to retract;* **interdire,** *to prohibit;* **médire,** *to slander;* **prédire,** *to predict.*
Maudire, *to curse* is conjugated like **finir.**

144. dormir (*to sleep*).

FUTURE and COND. regular.

PRESENT INDICATIVE
je dors, tu dors, il dort,
nous dormons, vous dormez, ils dorment.

IMPERATIVE
dors, dormons, dormez.

PRES. PART.
dormant; IMPERFECT je dormais, etc.

PRES. SUBJ.
je dorme, etc.

PAST PARTICIPLE
dormi; PASSÉ COMPOSÉ j'ai dormi, etc.

PASSÉ SIMPLE
je dormis, etc.; IMPERF. SUBJ. je dormisse, etc.

Like **dormir: endormir,** *to put to sleep;* **s'endormir,** *to fall asleep;* etc.

The following verbs are conjugated like **dormir** but the present indicative of each is given in full:

bouillir, *to boil:* bous, bous, bout, bouillons, bouillez, bouillent.

mentir, *to lie*, and **démentir,** *to contradict:* mens, mens, ment, mentons, mentez, mentent.

partir, *to leave*, and **repartir,** *to leave again:* pars, pars, part, partons, partez, partent. (Conjugated with auxiliary **être.**)

se repentir, *to repent:* repens, repens, repent, repentons, repentez, repentent.

sentir, *to feel, to smell;* **consentir,** *to consent;* **pressentir,** *to have a presentiment;* **ressentir,** *to feel:* sens, sens, sent, sentons, sentez, sentent.

servir, *to serve;* **se servir de,** *to use:* sers, sers, sert, servons, servez, servent.

sortir, *to go out:* sors, sors, sort, sortons, sortez, sortent. (Conjugated with auxiliary **être.**)

145. écrire (*to write*).

FUTURE and COND. regular.

PRESENT INDICATIVE
j'écris, tu écris, il écrit,
nous écrivons, vous écrivez, ils écrivent.

IMPERATIVE
écris, écrivons, écrivez.

PRES. PART.
écrivant; IMPERFECT j'écrivais, etc.

PRES. SUBJ.
j'écrive, etc.

PAST PARTICIPLE
écrit; PASSÉ COMPOSÉ j'ai écrit, etc.

PASSÉ SIMPLE
j'écrivis, etc.; IMPERF. SUBJ. j'écrivisse, etc.

Like **écrire: décrire,** *to describe;* **inscrire,** *to inscribe;* **prescrire,** *to prescribe;* **proscrire,** *to proscribe;* **souscrire,** *to subscribe;* etc.

146. envoyer (*to send*).

FUTURE
j'enverrai, etc.; COND. j'enverrais, etc.

PRESENT INDICATIVE
j'envoie, tu envoies, il envoie,
nous envoyons, vous envoyez, ils envoient.

IMPERATIVE
envoie(s), envoyons, envoyez.

PRES. PART.
envoyant; IMPERFECT j'envoyais, etc.

PRES. SUBJ.
j'envoie, tu envoies, il envoie,
nous envoyions, vous envoyiez, ils envoient.

PAST PARTICIPLE
envoyé; PASSÉ COMPOSÉ j'ai envoyé, etc.

PASSÉ SIMPLE
j'envoyai, etc.; IMPERF. SUBJ. j'envoyasse, etc.

Like **envoyer: renvoyer,** *to send back, to send away.*

147. faire (*to do, to make*).

FUTURE
je ferai, etc.; COND. je ferais, etc.

PRESENT INDICATIVE
je fais, tu fais, il fait,
nous faisons, vous faites, ils font.

IMPERATIVE
fais, faisons, faites.

PRES. PART.
faisant; IMPERFECT je faisais, etc.

PRES. SUBJ.
je fasse, etc.

PAST PARTICIPLE
fait; PASSÉ COMPOSÉ j'ai fait, etc.

PASSÉ SIMPLE
je fis, etc., IMPERF. SUBJ. je fisse, etc.

Like **faire: contrefaire,** *to imitate;* **défaire,** *to undo;* **satisfaire,** *to satisfy;* etc.

148. falloir (*must, etc.*) [impersonal].

FUTURE
il faudra; COND. il faudrait.

PRESENT INDICATIVE
il faut.

IMPERATIVE
——

PRES. PART.
——; IMPERFECT il fallait.

PRES. SUBJ.
il faille.

PAST PARTICIPLE
fallu; PASSÉ COMPOSÉ il a fallu.

PASSÉ SIMPLE
il fallut; IMPERF. SUBJ. il fallût.

149. fuir (*to flee*).

FUTURE and COND. regular.

PRESENT INDICATIVE
je fuis, tu fuis, il fuit,
nous fuyons, vous fuyez, ils fuient.

IMPERATIVE
fuis, fuyons, fuyez.

PRES. PART.
fuyant; IMPERFECT je fuyais, etc.

PRES. SUBJ.
je fuie, tu fuies, il fuie,
nous fuyions, vous fuyiez, ils fuient.

PAST PARTICIPLE
fui; PASSÉ COMPOSÉ j'ai fui, etc.

PASSÉ SIMPLE
je fuis, etc.; IMPERF. SUBJ. je fuisse, etc.

Like **fuir: s'enfuir,** *to flee, to escape.*

150. *haïr (*to hate*).

FUTURE and COND. regular.

PRESENT INDICATIVE
je hais, tu hais, il hait,
nous haïssons, vous haïssez, ils haïssent.

IMPERATIVE
hais, haïssons, haïssez.

PRES. PART.
haïssant; IMPERFECT je haïssais, etc.

PRES. SUBJ.
je haïsse, etc.

PAST PARTICIPLE
haï; PASSÉ COMPOSÉ j'ai haï, etc.

PASSÉ SIMPLE
je haïs, tu haïs, il haït,
nous haïmes, vous haïtes, ils haïrent.

IMPERF. SUBJ. je haïsse, tu haïsses, il haït, etc.

* The **h** is aspirate in all the forms of **haïr.**

151. lire (*to read*).

FUTURE and COND. regular

PRESENT INDICATIVE
je lis, tu lis, il lit,
nous lisons, vous lisez, ils lisent.

IMPERATIVE
lis, lisons, lisez.

PRES. PART.
lisant; IMPERFECT je lisais, etc.

PRES. SUBJ.
je lise, etc.

PAST PARTICIPLE
lu; PASSÉ COMPOSÉ j'ai lu, etc.

PASSÉ SIMPLE
je lus, etc.; IMPERF. SUBJ. je lusse, etc.
Like **lire: élire,** *to elect.*

152. mettre (*to put*).

FUTURE and COND. regular.

PRESENT INDICATIVE
je mets, tu mets, il met,
nous mettons, vous mettez, ils mettent.

IMPERATIVE
mets, mettons, mettez.

PRES. PART.
mettant; IMPERFECT je mettais, etc.

PRES. SUBJ.
je mette, etc.

PAST PARTICIPLE
mis; PASSÉ COMPOSÉ j'ai mis, etc.

PASSÉ SIMPLE
je mis, etc.; IMPERF. SUBJ. je misse, etc.

Like **mettre: admettre,** *to admit;* **commettre,** *to commit;* **compromettre,** *to compromise;* **émettre,** *to put out, to emit;* **omettre,** *to omit;* **permettre,** *to permit;* **promettre,** *to promise;* **remettre,** *to put back, to hand to;* **soumettre,** *to submit;* **transmettre,** *to transmit;* etc.

153. **mourir** (*to die*).

FUTURE
je mourrai, etc.; COND. je mourrais, etc.

PRESENT INDICATIVE
je meurs, tu meurs, il meurt,
nous mourons, vous mourez, ils meurent.

IMPERATIVE
meurs, mourons, mourez.

PRES. PART.
mourant; IMPERFECT je mourais, etc.

PRES. SUBJ.
je meure, tu meures, il meure,
nous mourions, vous mouriez, ils meurent.

PAST PARTICIPLE
mort; PASSÉ COMPOSÉ je suis mort(e), etc.

PASSÉ SIMPLE
je mourus, etc.; IMPERF. SUBJ. je mourusse, etc.

154. **mouvoir** (*to move*).

FUTURE
je mouvrai, etc.; COND. je mouvrais, etc.

PRESENT INDICATIVE
je meus, tu meus, il meut,
nous mouvons, vous mouvez, ils meuvent.

IMPERATIVE
meus, mouvons, mouvez.

PRES. PART.
mouvant; IMPERFECT je mouvais, etc.

PRES. SUBJ.
je meuve, tu meuves, il meuve,
nous mouvions, vous mouviez, ils meuvent.

PAST PARTICIPLE
mû; PASSÉ COMPOSÉ j'ai mû, etc.

PASSÉ SIMPLE
je mus, etc.; IMPERF. SUBJ. je musse, etc.

Like **mouvoir: émouvoir,** *to stir;* **s'émouvoir,** *to be stirred;* etc., except that the past participle is **ému**—without the circumflex accent.

155. **naître** (*to be born*).

FUTURE and COND. regular.

PRESENT INDICATIVE
je nais, tu nais, il naît,
nous naissons, vous naissez, ils naissent.

IMPERATIVE
nais, naissons, naissez.

PRES. PART.
naissant; IMPERFECT je naissais, etc.

PRES. SUBJ.
je naisse, etc.

PAST PARTICIPLE
né; PASSÉ COMPOSÉ je suis né(e), etc.

PASSÉ SIMPLE
je naquis, etc.; IMPERF. SUBJ. je naquisse, etc.

Like **naître: renaître,** *to be reborn.*

156. **ouvrir** (*to open*).

FUTURE and COND. regular.

PRESENT INDICATIVE
j'ouvre, tu ouvres, il ouvre,
nous ouvrons, vous ouvrez, ils ouvrent.

IMPERATIVE
ouvre, ouvrons, ouvrez.

PRES. PART.
ouvrant; IMPERFECT j'ouvrais, etc.

PRES. SUBJ.
j'ouvre, etc.

PAST PARTICIPLE
ouvert; PASSÉ COMPOSÉ j'ai ouvert, etc.

PASSÉ SIMPLE
j'ouvris, etc.; IMPERF. SUBJ. j'ouvrisse, etc.

Like **ouvrir: couvrir,** *to cover;* **découvrir,** *to discover;* **entr'ouvrir,** *to open slightly;* **offrir,** *to offer, to give;* **souffrir,** *to suffer*, etc.

157. plaire (*to please*).

FUTURE and COND. regular.

PRESENT INDICATIVE
je plais, tu plais, il plaît,
nous plaisons, vous plaisez, ils plaisent.

IMPERATIVE
plais, plaisons, plaisez.

PRES. PART.
plaisant; IMPERFECT je plaisais, etc.

PRES. SUBJ.
je plaise, etc.

PAST PARTICIPLE
plu; PASSÉ COMPOSÉ j'ai plu, etc.

PASSÉ SIMPLE
je plus, etc.; IMPERF. SUBJ. je plusse, etc.

Like **plaire: déplaire,** *to displease.*

taire, *to say nothing about*, and **se taire,** *to be silent*, are conjugated like **plaire** except that the 3rd person singular of the present indicative is written without the circumflex accent.

158. pleuvoir (*to rain*) [impersonal].

FUTURE
il pleuvra; COND. il pleuvrait.

PRESENT INDICATIVE
il pleut.

PRES. PART.
pleuvant; IMPERFECT il pleuvait.

PRES. SUBJ.
il pleuve.

PAST PARTICIPLE
plu; PASSÉ COMPOSÉ il a plu.

PASSÉ SIMPLE
il plut; IMPERF. SUBJ. il plût.

159. pouvoir (*to be able, can, etc.*).

FUTURE
je pourrai, etc.; COND. je pourrais, etc.

PRESENT INDICATIVE
je peux (je puis), tu peux, il peut,
nous pouvons, vous pouvez, ils peuvent.

PRES. PART.
pouvant; IMPERFECT je pouvais, etc.

PRES. SUBJ.
je puisse, tu puisses, il puisse,
nous puissions, vous puissiez, ils puissent.

IMPERATIVE
—— —— ——

PAST PARTICIPLE
pu; PASSÉ COMPOSÉ j'ai pu, etc.

PASSÉ SIMPLE
je pus, etc.; IMPERF. SUBJ. je pusse, etc.

160. prendre (*to take*)

FUTURE and COND. regular.

PRESENT INDICATIVE
je prends, tu prends, il prend,
nous prenons, vous prenez, ils prennent.

IMPERATIVE
prends, prenons, prenez.

PRES. PART.
prenant; IMPERFECT je prenais, etc.

PRES. SUBJ.
je prenne, tu prennes, il prenne,
nous prenions, vous preniez, ils prennent.

PAST PARTICIPLE
pris; PASSÉ COMPOSÉ j'ai pris, etc.

PASSÉ SIMPLE
je pris, etc.; IMPERF. SUBJ. je prisse, etc.

Like **prendre: apprendre,** *to learn;* **comprendre,** *to understand;* **entreprendre,** *to undertake;* **reprendre,** *to take again*, etc.; **surprendre,** *to surprise;* etc.

161. **recevoir** (*to receive*).

FUTURE
je recevrai, etc.; COND. je recevrais, etc.

PRESENT INDICATIVE
je reçois, tu reçois, il reçoit,
nous recevons, vous recevez, ils reçoivent.

IMPERATIVE
reçois, recevons, recevez.

PRES. PART.
recevant; IMPERFECT je recevais, etc.

PRES. SUBJ.
je reçoive, tu reçoives, il reçoive,
nous recevions, vous receviez, ils reçoivent.

PAST PARTICIPLE
reçu; PASSÉ COMPOSÉ j'ai reçu, etc.

PASSÉ SIMPLE
je reçus, etc.; IMPERF. SUBJ. je reçusse, etc.

Like **recevoir: apercevoir,** *to catch a glimpse of;* **concevoir,** *to conceive;* **décevoir,** *to deceive;* **percevoir,** *to collect;* etc.

162. **résoudre** (*to resolve, to solve*).

FUTURE and COND. regular.

PRESENT INDICATIVE
je résous, tu résous, il résoud,
nous résolvons, vous résolvez, ils résolvent.

IMPERATIVE
résous, résolvons, résolvez.

PRES. PART.
résolvant; IMPERFECT je résolvais, etc.

PRES. SUBJ.
je résolve, etc.

PAST PARTICIPLE
résolu; PASSÉ COMPOSÉ j'ai résolu, etc.

PASSÉ SIMPLE
je résolus, etc.; IMPERF. SUBJ. je résolusse, etc.

163. rire (*to laugh*).

Future and Cond. regular.

Present Indicative
je ris, tu ris, il rit,
nous rions, vous riez, ils rient.

Imperative
ris, rions, riez.

Pres. Part.
riant; Imperfect je riais, etc.

Pres. Subj.
je rie, tu ries, il rie,
nous riions, vous riiez, ils rient.

Past Participle
ri; Passé Composé j'ai ri, etc.

Passé Simple
je ris, etc.; Imperf. Subj. je risse, etc.

Like **rire: sourire,** *to smile.*

164. savoir (*to know*).

Future
je saurai, etc.; Cond. je saurais, etc.

Present Indicative
je sais, tu sais, il sait,
nous savons, vous savez, ils savent.

Imperative
sache, sachons, sachez.

Pres. Part.
sachant; Imperfect je savais, etc.

Pres. Subj.
je sache, etc.

Past Participle
su; Passé Composé j'ai su, etc.

Passé Simple
je sus, etc.; Imperf. Subj. je susse, etc.

165. suffire (*to suffice, to be enough*).

FUTURE and COND. regular.

PRESENT INDICATIVE
je suffis, tu suffis, il suffit,
nous suffisons, vous suffisez, ils suffisent.

IMPERATIVE
suffis, suffisons, suffisez.

PRES. PART.
suffisant; IMPERFECT je suffisais, etc.

PRES. SUBJ.
je suffise, etc.

PAST PARTICIPLE
suffi; PASSÉ COMPOSÉ j'ai suffi, etc.

PASSÉ SIMPLE
je suffis, etc.; IMPERF. SUBJ. je suffisse, etc.

166. suivre (*to follow*).

FUTURE and COND. regular.

PRESENT INDICATIVE
je suis, tu suis, il suit,
nous suivons, vous suivez, ils suivent.

IMPERATIVE
suis, suivons, suivez.

PRES. PART.
suivant; IMPERFECT je suivais, etc.

PRES. SUBJ.
je suive, etc.

PAST PARTICIPLE
suivi; PASSÉ COMPOSÉ j'ai suivi, etc.

PASSÉ SIMPLE
je suivis, etc.; IMPERF. SUBJ. je suivisse, etc.

Like **suivre: poursuivre,** *to pursue*.

167. tenir (*to hold*).

FUTURE
je tiendrai, etc.; COND. je tiendrais, etc.

PRESENT INDICATIVE
je tiens, tu tiens, il tient,
nous tenons, vous tenez, ils tiennent.

IMPERATIVE
tiens, tenons, tenez.

PRES. PART.
tenant; IMPERFECT je tenais, etc.

PRES. SUBJ.
je tienne, tu tiennes, il tienne,
nous tenions, vous teniez, ils tiennent.

PAST PARTICIPLE
tenu; PASSÉ COMPOSÉ j'ai tenu, etc.

PASSÉ SIMPLE
je tins, tu tins, il tint,
nous tînmes, vous tîntes, ils tinrent. IMPERF. SUBJ. je tinsse, etc.

Like **tenir: s'abstenir,** *to abstain;* **appartenir,** *to belong;* **contenir,** *to contain;* **détenir,** *to detain;* **entretenir,** *to keep in good condition;* **maintenir,** *to maintain;* **obtenir,** *to obtain;* **retenir,** *to retain;* **soutenir,** *to sustain.*

168. traire (*to milk*).

FUTURE and COND. regular.

PRESENT INDICATIVE
je trais, tu trais, il trait,
nous trayons, vous trayez, ils traient.

IMPERATIVE
trais, trayons, trayez.

PRES. PART.
trayant; IMPERFECT je trayais, etc.

PRES. SUBJ.
je traie, tu traies, il traie,
nous trayions, vous trayiez, ils traient.

PAST PARTICIPLE
trait; PASSÉ COMPOSÉ j'ai trait, etc.

PASSÉ SIMPLE
——; IMPERF. SUBJ. ——.

Like **traire: abstraire,** *to abstract;* **distraire,** *to distract;* **extraire,** *to extract;* **soustraire,** *to subtract;* etc.

169. **vaincre** (*to conquer*).

FUTURE and COND. regular.

PRESENT INDICATIVE
je vaincs, tu vaincs, il vainc,
nous vainquons, vous vainquez, il vainquent.

IMPERATIVE
vaincs, vainquons, vainquez.

PRES. PART.
vainquant; IMPERFECT je vainquis, etc.

PRES. SUBJ.
je vainque, etc.

PAST PARTICIPLE
vaincu; PASSÉ COMPOSÉ j'ai vaincu, etc.

PASSÉ SIMPLE
je vainquis, etc.; IMPERF. SUBJ. je vainquisse, etc.

Like **vaincre: convaincre,** *to convince.*

170. **valoir** (*to be worth*).

FUTURE
je vaudrai, etc.; COND. je vaudrais, etc.

PRESENT INDICATIVE
je vaux, tu vaux, il vaut,
nous valons, vous valez, ils valent.

IMPERATIVE
vaux, valons, valez.

PRES. PART.
valant; IMPERFECT je valais, etc.

PRES. SUBJ.
je vaille, tu vailles, il vaille,
nous valions, vous valiez, ils vaillent.

PAST PARTICIPLE
valu; PASSÉ COMPOSÉ j'ai valu, etc.

PASSÉ SIMPLE
je valus, etc.; IMPERF. SUBJ. je valusse, etc.

171. venir (*to come*).

FUTURE
je viendrai, etc.; COND. je viendrais, etc.

PRESENT INDICATIVE
je viens, tu viens, il vient,
nous venons, vous venez, ils viennent.

IMPERATIVE
viens, venons, venez.

PRES. PART.
venant; IMPERFECT je venais, etc.

PRES. SUBJ.
je vienne, tu viennes, il vienne,
nous venions, vous veniez, ils viennent.

PAST PARTICIPLE
venu; PASSÉ COMPOSÉ je suis venu(e), etc.

PASSÉ SIMPLE
je vins, tu vins, il vint,
nous vînmes, vous vîntes, ils vinrent. IMPERF. SUBJ. je vinsse, etc.

Like **venir: convenir,** *to agree, to suit;* **devenir,** *to become;* **intervenir,** *to intervene;* **parvenir,** *to attain;* **prévenir,** *to warn,* etc.; **provenir,** *to come from;* **revenir,** *to come back;* **se souvenir,** *to remember;* etc.

172. vêtir (*to clothe*).

FUTURE and COND. regular.

PRESENT INDICATIVE
je vêts, tu vêts, il vêt,
nous vêtons, vous vêtez, ils vêtent.

IMPERATIVE
vêts, vêtons, vêtez.

PRES. PART.
vêtant; IMPERFECT je vêtais, etc.

PRES. SUBJ.
je vête, etc.

PAST PARTICIPLE
vêtu; PASSÉ COMPOSÉ j'ai vêtu, etc.

PASSÉ SIMPLE
je vêtis, etc.; IMPERF. SUBJ. je vêtisse, etc.

173. vivre (*to live*).

FUTURE and COND. regular.

PRESENT INDICATIVE
je vis, tu vis, il vit,
nous vivons, vous vivez, ils vivent.

IMPERATIVE
vis, vivons, vivez.

PRES. PART.
vivant; IMPERFECT je vivais, etc.

PRES. SUBJ.
je vive, etc.

PAST PARTICIPLE
vécu; PASSÉ COMPOSÉ j'ai vécu, etc.

PASSÉ SIMPLE
je vécus, etc.; IMPERF. SUBJ. je vécusse, etc.

174. voir (*to see*).

FUTURE
je verrai, etc.; COND. je verrais, etc.

PRESENT INDICATIVE
je vois, tu vois, il voit,
nous voyons, vous voyez, ils voient.

IMPERATIVE
vois, voyons, voyez.

PRES. PART.
voyant; IMPERFECT je voyais, etc.

PRES. SUBJ.
je voie, tu voies, il voie,
nous voyions, vous voyiez, ils voient.

PAST PARTICIPLE
vu; PASSÉ COMPOSÉ j'ai vu, etc.

PASSÉ SIMPLE
je vis, etc.; IMPERF. SUBJ. je visse, etc.

Like **voir: entrevoir,** *to catch sight of;* **revoir,** *to see again.*

prévoir is like **voir** except that the future and conditional are regular.

pourvoir is like **voir** except that the future and conditional are regular, the **passé simple** is **je pourvus,** etc., and the imperfect subjunctive **je pourvusse,** etc.

175. vouloir (*to want, to will*).

FUTURE
je voudrai, etc.; COND. je voudrais, etc.

PRESENT INDICATIVE
je veux, tu veux, il veut,
nous voulons, vous voulez, ils veulent.

IMPERATIVE
veux, voulons, voulez, *or*
veuille, veuillons, veuillez.

PRES. PART.
voulant; IMPERFECT je voulais, etc.

PRES. SUBJ.
je veuille, tu veuilles, il veuille,
nous voulions, vous vouliez, ils veuillent.

PAST PARTICIPLE
voulu; PASSÉ COMPOSÉ j'ai voulu, etc.

PASSÉ SIMPLE
je voulus, etc.; IMPERF. SUBJ. je voulusse, etc.

Common Units of Measurement

FRENCH-ENGLISH

1 centimètre	*.3937*	*of an inch* (less than half an inch)
1 mètre	*39.37*	*inches* (about 1 yard and 3 inches)
1 kilomètre **(1000 mètres)**	*.6213*	*of a mile* (about ⅝ of a mile)
1 gramme	*.03527*	*of an ounce*
100 grammes	*3.52*	*ounces* (a little less than ¼ of a pound)
500 grammes **(une livre)**	*17.63*	*ounces* (about 1.1 pounds)
1000 grammes **(un kilo)**	*35.27*	*ounces* (about 2.2 pounds)
1 litre	*1.0567*	*quarts* (a fraction over a quart, liquid)

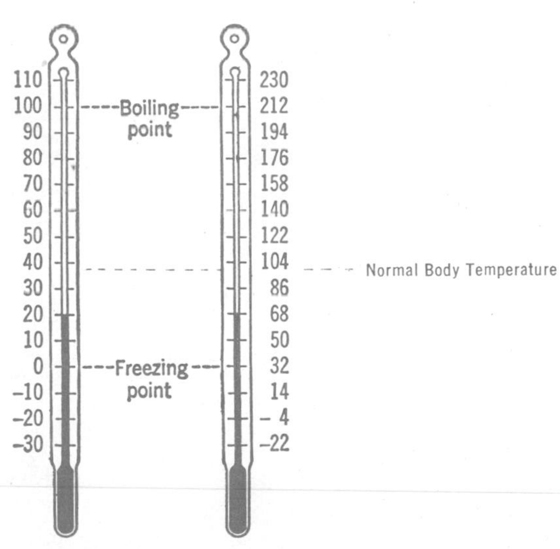

CENTIGRADE | FAHRENHEIT

Vocabularies

Abbreviations

abbr	abbreviation	*inf*	infinitive
adj	adjective	*interrog*	interrogative
adv	adverb	*m*	masculine
art	article	*n*	noun
* (asterisk)	aspirate *h*	*obj*	object
cond	conditional	*p part*	past participle
conj	conjunction	*p simple*	passé simple
conjug	conjugated	*pers*	person, personal
contr	contraction	*pl*	plural
dem	demonstrative	*poss*	possessive
dir obj	direct object	*pr*	present
f	feminine	*prep*	preposition
fut	future	*pron*	pronoun
imper	imperative	*rel*	relative
imperf	imperfect	*sg*	singular
ind	indicative	*subj*	subjunctive
indir obj	indirect object		

French-English

A

a: il a [ila] *pr ind 3rd sg of* **avoir**
à [a] at, to, in, into, for, by; **à jeudi** see you Thursday
abandonner [abɑ̃dɔne] to abandon; to give out
abord: d'abord [dabɔʀ] first, at first, first of all
absent [apsɑ̃] absent
absolument [apsɔlymɑ̃] absolutely
absurde [apsyʀd] absurd
accent [aksɑ̃] *m* accent
accepter [aksɛpte] to accept
accessible [aksɛsibl] accessible
accident [aksidɑ̃] *m* accident
accompagner [akõpaɲe] to accompany, go with, go along
accord: d'accord [dakɔʀ] in agreement (with); O.K.
accrocher [akʀɔʃe] to hook, to hang
achat [aʃa] *m* purchase
acheter [aʃte] to buy
actif, active [aktif, aktiv] active
actuel [aktɥɛl] present; **à l'heure actuelle** at the present time
actuellement [aktɥɛlmɑ̃] at present
addition [adisjõ] *f* bill
admirable [admiʀabl] admirable
admirablement [admiʀabləmɑ̃] admirably
admirer [admiʀe] to admire
adorer [adɔʀe] to be crazy about
adresse [adʀɛs] *f* address
adroit [adʀwa] skilful
aérien [aeʀjɛ̃], **aérienne** [aeʀjɛn] aerial
affirmativement [afiʀmativmɑ̃] affirmatively
Afrique [afʀik] *f* Africa; **l'Afrique du Nord** North Africa
âge [aʒ] *m* age; **quel âge avez-vous?** how old are you?; **d'un certain âge** elderly
agent [aʒɑ̃] *m* agent; **agent de police** policeman; **agent de change** stockbroker
agir: s'agir de [saʒiʀ də] *impers* to be a question of
agit: il s'agit de [ilsaʒidə] it is a question of
agréable [agʀeabl] pleasant
ai: j'ai [ʒe] *pr ind 1st sg of* **avoir**
aide [ɛd] *f* help
aider [ɛde] to help
aille: j'aille [ʒaj] *pr subj 1st sg of* **aller**
ailleurs [ajœʀ] elsewhere; **d'ailleurs** moreover, besides, anyway
aimable [ɛmabl] kind, nice
aimer [ɛme] to like, love; **aimer bien** to like, to be fond of; **aimer mieux** to prefer
ainsi [ɛ̃si] so, thus
air [ɛʀ] *m* air; **avoir l'air** to look, appear, seem; **en plein air** in the open
ait: il ait [ilɛ] *pr subj 3rd sg of* **avoir**
album [albɔm] *m* album
alla: il alla [ilala] *p simple 3rd sg of* **aller**
allais: j'allais [ʒalɛ] *imperf ind 1st sg of* **aller**
allé [ale] *p part of* **aller**
allée [ale] *f* walk, path
Allemagne [almaɲ] *f* Germany
allemand [almɑ̃] German
aller [ale] *m;* **aller et retour** round trip
aller [ale] to go; **aller bien** to feel well; **comment allez-vous?** how are you?; **ce chapeau vous va très bien** this hat is very becoming; **aller à pied** to walk; **aller chercher** to go get; **s'en aller** to go away; **comment ça va?** how are you?
allez: vous allez [vuzale] *pr ind 2nd pl of* **aller**
allumé [alyme] lighted
allusion [alyzjõ] *f* allusion
alors [alɔʀ] then
Alpes [alp] *f pl* Alps
américain [ameʀikɛ̃], **américaine** [ameʀikɛn] American (*takes a capital only when used as a noun referring to a person*)
Amérique [ameʀik] *f* America
ami [ami], **amie** [ami] friend
amusant [amyzɑ̃] amusing
amuser: s'amuser [samyze] to enjoy oneself
an [ɑ̃] *m* year; **tous les ans** every year; **le jour de l'An** New Year's day
ancien [ɑ̃sjɛ̃], **ancienne** [ɑ̃sjɛn] former, old
âne [ɑn] *m* donkey
anglais [ɑ̃glɛ], **anglaise** [ɑ̃glɛz] English (*takes a capital only when used as a noun referring to a person*)
Angleterre [ɑ̃glətɛʀ] *f* England
année [ane] *f* year

anniversaire [aniversɛʀ] *m* birthday
annoncer [anõse] to announce
antagoniste [ɑ̃tagɔnist] *m* opponent
antiquaire [ɑ̃tikɛʀ] *m* antique dealer
août [u] *m* August
apercevoir [apɛʀsəvwaʀ] to get a glimpse of
apparence [apaʀɑ̃s] *f* look
appartenir à [apaʀtəniʀa] to belong to (*conjug like* **tenir**)
appel [apɛl] *m* appeal
appeler [aple] to call, name; **s'appeler** to be called, be named; **comment vous appelez-vous?** what is your name?; **je m'appelle** my name is
appellation [apɛlasjõ] *f* name
appétit [apeti] *m* appetite
apporter [apɔʀte] to bring; **apportez-moi** bring me
apprendre [apʀɑ̃dʀ] to learn, to tell (*conjug like* **prendre**)
appris [apʀi] *p part of* **apprendre**
approcher: s'approcher [sapʀɔʃe] to come close to
après [apʀɛ] after; **d'après** according to
après-midi [apʀɛmidi] *m* afternoon; **l'après-midi** in the afternoon
arbre [aʀbʀ] *m* tree
arc [aʀk] *m* arch; **arc de triomphe** [aʀk dətʀiõf] arch of triumph; **arc en demi-cercle** [aʀk ɑ̃dmisɛʀkl] round arch
architecte [aʀʃitɛkt] *m* architect
architecture [aʀʃitɛktyʀ] *f* architecture
argent [aʀʒɑ̃] *m* money, silver
arme [aʀm] *f* weapon; **arme prohibée** concealed weapon
armée [aʀme] *f* army
arranger: s'arranger [saʀɑ̃ʒe] to fit in
arrêt [aʀɛ] *m* stop
arrêter: s'arrêter [saʀɛte] to stop
arrivée [aʀive] *f* arrival
arriver [aʀive] to arrive, come; to happen; **qu'est-ce qui lui est arrivé?** what happened to him (her)?
arrondissement [aʀõdismɑ̃] *m* administrative district in Paris
arroser [aʀoze] to water
art [aʀ] *m* art
article [aʀtikl] *m* article
artiste [aʀtist] *m* artist
ascenseur [asɑ̃sœʀ] *m* elevator
aspect [aspɛ] *m* aspect
asperge [aspɛʀʒ] *f* asparagus
aspirine [aspiʀin] *f* aspirin
assembler: s'assembler [sasɑ̃ble] to gather
asseoir: s'asseoir [saswaʀ] to sit down
asseyez-vous [asɛjevu] *imper 2nd pl of* **s'asseoir**
assez [ase] enough, rather, fairly
assis [asi] *p part of* **asseoir**
assistance [asistɑ̃s] *f* attendance, spectators
assister à [asiste a] to attend
assurer [asyʀe] to assure
Athènes [atɛn] Athens
Atlantique [atlɑ̃tik] *m* Atlantic
atteindre [atɛ̃dʀ] to reach, attain (*conjug like* **peindre**)
attendre [atɑ̃dʀ] to wait, wait for, await; **s'attendre à** to expect
attention [atɑ̃sjõ] *f* attention; **faire attention** to watch out
attentivement [atɑ̃tivmɑ̃] attentively
attirer [atiʀe] to attract
attraper [atʀape] to catch
au [o] *contr of* **à le**
auberge [obɛʀʒ] *f* inn
aucun [okœ̃], **aucune** [okyn] none; **ne . . . aucun** no . . .
aujourd'hui [oʒuʀdɥi] today; **d'aujourd'hui en huit** a week from today; **c'est aujourd'hui jeudi** today is Thursday
auparavant [opaʀavɑ̃] before
auquel [okɛl], **à laquelle** [alakɛl], **auxquels** [okɛl], **auxquelles** [okɛl] *prep* **à** + **lequel**, etc.
aurai: j'aurai [ʒɔʀe] *fut 1st sg of* **avoir**
aussi [osi] also, so, as, thus, therefore; **aussi . . . que** as . . . as
aussitôt [osito] immediately; **aussitôt que** as soon as
austère [ostɛʀ] severe
autant [otɑ̃] as much; **d'autant plus que** all the more so since
auteur [otœʀ] *m* author
auto [oto] *f* auto, car
autobus [otɔbys] *m* bus; **en autobus** on the bus, by bus
autocar [otɔkɑʀ] *m* tourist bus
automne [otɔn] *m* fall, autumn
automobile [otɔmɔbil] *f* auto, car
automobiliste [otɔmɔbilist] *m* motorist
autour de [otuʀdə] around

autre [otʀ] other
autrefois [otʀəfwa] formerly, once
avait: il avait [ilavɛ] *imperf ind 3rd sg of* **avoir; il y avait** there was, there were
avance: à l'avance [alavɑ̃s] in advance; **en avance** early
avant [avɑ̃] before
avantage [avɑ̃taʒ] *m* advantage
avec [avɛk] with
avenue [avny] *f* avenue
aveugle [avœgl] blind
avez: vous avez [vuzave] *pr ind 2nd pl of* **avoir**
avion [avjõ] *m* plane
avis [avi] *m* opinion, advice; **être de l'avis de quelqu'un** to agree with someone
avocat [avɔka] *m* lawyer
avoine [avwan] *f* oats
avoir [avwaʀ] to have; **avoir besoin de** to need; **avoir peur** to be afraid; **avoir froid** to be cold; **avoir mal à la gorge** to have a sore throat; **avoir l'air** to seem; **avoir lieu** to take place; **qu'est-ce que vous avez?** what is the matter with you?; **avoir envie de** to feel like; **avoir l'habitude de** to be used to; **avoir faim** to be hungry; **avoir soif** to be thirsty; **avoir l'intention de** to intend to; **avoir raison** to be right; **avoir tort** to be wrong; **il y a** there is, there are; **il y a dix ans** ten years ago; **avoir beau** to be in vain, be of no avail
avril [avʀil] *m* April
ayez: vous ayez [vuzɛje] *pr subj 2nd pl of* **avoir**

B

bagages [bagaʒ] *m pl* luggage
bain [bɛ̃] *m* bath; **salle de bains** *f* bathroom
bal [bal] *m* dance
Balzac [balzak] French novelist (1799-1850)
banane [banan] *f* banana
banlieue [bɑ̃ljø] *f* the outskirts, suburbs
banque [bɑ̃k] *f* bank
banquier [bɑ̃kje] *m* banker
barbe [baʀb]**: Quelle barbe! La barbe!** What a nuisance!
Barbizon [baʀbizõ] village near Fontainebleau, residence of famous French painters of the 19th century
barrage [baʀaʒ] *m* dam
bas [bɑ], **basse** [bɑs] low; **à voix basse** in a low voice
bassin [basɛ̃] *m* pool
Bastille: la Bastille [labastij] state prison, destroyed in 1789
bataille [bataj] *f* battle
bateau [bato] *m* boat
bâtiment [bɑtimɑ̃] *m* building
beau [bo], **bel** [bɛl], **belle** [bɛl], **beaux** [bo], **belles** [bɛl] beautiful, nice; **il fait beau** the weather is nice; **avoir beau** to be in vain, to be of no avail
beaucoup [boku] much, very much
Belgique [bɛlʒik] *f* Belgium
besoin [bəzwɛ̃] *m* need; **avoir besoin de** to need
betterave [bɛtʀav] *f* beet; **betterave à sucre** sugar beet
beurre [bœʀ] *m* butter
bicyclette [bisiklɛt] *f* bicycle
bien [bjɛ̃] *adv* well, indeed, very; **eh bien?** well?; *conj* **bien que** although; **bien** [bjɛ̃] *m* good; **cette promenade m'a fait beaucoup de bien** this walk did me a lot of good; many; **bien des statues** many statues
bientôt [bjɛ̃to] soon
bière [bjɛʀ] *f* beer
bifteck [biftɛk] *m* minute steak
billet [bijɛ] *m* ticket, banknote, bill; **billet aller et retour** roundtrip ticket
Bizet [bizɛ] French musician (1838-1875)
blanc [blɑ̃], **blanche** [blɑ̃ʃ] white
blé [ble] *m* wheat
blesser [blɛse] to wound
bleu [blø] blue
blond [blõ] blond
bœuf [bœf], *pl* **bœufs** [bø] *m* ox, beef
boire [bwaʀ] to drink
bois [bwɑ] *m* wood; **le Bois de Boulogne** park on the outskirts of Paris
bois: je bois [ʒəbwɑ] *pr ind 1st sg of* **boire**
boîte [bwat] *f* box
bon [bõ], **bonne** [bɔn] good; **de bonne heure** early; **la bonne route** the right road
bonbon [bõbõ] *m* candy
bondé [bõde] crowded
bonheur [bɔnœʀ] *m* happiness
bonjour [bõʒuʀ] *m* good morning, good afternoon, hello
bonne [bɔn] *f* maid
bonsoir [bõswaʀ] *m* good evening
bord [bɔʀ] *m* edge, side; **au bord de la mer** at the seashore

border [bɔRde] to line
botanique [bɔtanik] *f* botany
bouche [buʃ] *f* mouth; **faire venir l'eau à la bouche** to make one's mouth water
boucher [buʃe] *m* butcher
boucherie [buʃRi] *f* butcher's shop
boulangerie [bulɑ̃ʒRi] *f* bakery
boulevard [bulvaR] *m* boulevard
bouquet [bukɛ] *m* bouquet
bouquiniste [bukinist] *m* dealer in old books
bourguignon [buRgiɲõ] of Burgundy
Bourgogne [buRgɔɲ] *f* Burgundy
bout [bu] *m* end
bouteille [butɛ:j] *f* bottle
boutique [butik] *f* shop
brave [bRav] good, worthy
Bretagne [bRətaɲ] *f* Brittany
breton [bRətõ] from Brittany
bridge [bRidʒ] *m* bridge
brouillard [bRujaR] *m* mist
bruit [bRɥi] *m* noise
brûler [bRyle] to burn
brun [bRœ̃], **brune** [bRyn] brown
bu [by] *p part of* **boire**
buffet [byfɛ] *m* lunchroom (in a railroad station)
bureau [byRo] *m* office, desk
buvez: vous buvez [vubyve] *pr ind 2nd pl of* **boire**

C

c' *see* **ce**
ça [sa] (*contr of* **cela**) that; **c'est ça** that's it, that's right
câble [kablə] *m* cable
Caen [kɑ̃] city in Normandy
café [kafe] *m* coffee, café, pub
caisse [kɛs] *f* cashier's window
caissier [kɛsje], **caissière** [kɛsjɛR] cashier
Californie [kalifɔRni] *f* California
camion [kamjõ] *m* truck
campagne [kɑ̃paɲ] *f* country, countryside
Canada [kanada] *m* Canada
capitale [kapital] *f* capital
car [kaR] for, because
caractérisé [kaRakteRize] characterized
carnet [kaRnɛ] *m* notebook, booklet
carré [kaRe] *m* square
carte [kaRt] *f* card, menu, map; **jouer aux cartes** to play cards; **carte postale** *f* post card
carton [kaRtõ] *m* cardboard, cardboard box
cas [kɑ] *m* case; **en tout cas** at any rate
casser [kɑse] to break
casserole [kɑsRɔl] *f* saucepan
cathédrale [katedRal] *f* cathedral
cause [koz] *f* cause; **à cause de** because of
causer [koze] to chat
cave [kav] *f* cellar
ce [sə], **cet** [sɛt], **cette** [sɛt], **ces** [se] *adj* this, that; **cette écharpe-ci** this scarf; **cette écharpe-là** that scarf; **ce jour-là** that day; **ces jours-ci** some time soon
ce [sə] *pron* he, she, it, they, that; **ce qui, ce que** what
ceci [səsi] this
cela [sla] that
célèbre [selɛbR] well-known
celui [səlɥi], **celle** [sɛl], **ceux** [sø], **celles** [sɛl] the one; the ones; **celui-ci** this one; **celui-là** that one
cent [sɑ̃] a hundred
centigrade [sɑ̃tigRad] *m* centigrade
centime [sɑ̃tim] *m* one hundredth part of one franc
centre [sɑ̃tR] *m* center
cependant [səpɑ̃dɑ̃] however
cercle [sɛRkl] *m* circle; **arc en demi-cercle** round arch
certain [sɛRtɛ̃], **certaine** [sɛRtɛn] certain
certainement [sɛRtɛnmɑ̃] certainly
certes [sɛRt] certainly
Cézanne [sezan] French painter (1839-1906)
chacun [ʃakœ̃], **chacune** [ʃakyn] each, each one
chaise [ʃɛz] *f* chair
chaleur [ʃalœR] *f* heat
chambre [ʃɑ̃bR] *f* room
champ [ʃɑ̃] *m* field
champagne [ʃɑ̃paɲ] *m* champagne
champenois [ʃɑ̃pənwa] from Champagne
champignon [ʃɑ̃piɲõ] *m* mushroom
Champs-Élysées: les Champs-Élysées [leʃɑ̃zelize] avenue in Paris
chance [ʃɑ̃s] *f* luck; **avoir de la chance** to be lucky
changement [ʃɑ̃ʒmɑ̃] *m* change
changer [ʃɑ̃ʒe] to change; to change trains
chanter [ʃɑ̃te] to sing

Chantilly [ʃɑ̃tiji] town in the Île-de-France
chapeau [ʃapo] *m* hat
chapelle [ʃapɛl] *f* chapel
chaque [ʃak] each
charcuterie [ʃaʀkytʀi] *f* pork butcher shop
charmant [ʃaʀmɑ̃] charming
charme [ʃaʀm] *m* charm
chasse [ʃas] *f* hunting, hunting season
chasser [ʃase] to chase, to shoo out
chasseur [ʃasœʀ] *m* hunter
château [ʃɑto] *m* château, palace
chaud [ʃo] warm; **il fait chaud** it is warm; **j'ai chaud** I am warm
chauffage [ʃofɑʒ] *m* heating; **chauffage central** central heating
chauffeur [ʃofœʀ] *m* driver
chaussée [ʃose] *f* street, surface of a street
chaussette [ʃosɛt] *f* sock
chaussure [ʃosyʀ] *f* shoe
chemin [ʃmɛ̃] *m* road; **chemin de fer** *m* railroad
cheminée [ʃmine] *f* fireplace
chemise [ʃmiz] *f* shirt
chèque [ʃɛk] *m* check
cher [ʃɛʀ], **chère** [ʃɛʀ] expensive, dear
chercher [ʃɛʀʃe] to seek, look for; **aller chercher** to go for, go and get; **venir chercher** to come for
cheval [ʃval], *pl* **chevaux** [ʃvo] *m* horse
chevalier [ʃvalje] *m* knight
cheveu [ʃvø] *m* hair; **elle a les cheveux blonds** she has blond hair
chèvre [ʃɛvʀə] *f* goat
chez [ʃe] at the house of, at the shop of; **chez moi** at my house; **chez eux** at their house; **chez le coiffeur** at the barber's
chic [ʃik] stylish
chien [ʃjɛ̃] *m* dog
chiffre [ʃifʀ] *m* number
chimie [ʃimi] *f* chemistry
chimiste [ʃimist] *m* chemist
chocolat [ʃɔkɔla] *m* chocolate
choisir [ʃwaziʀ] to choose
choix [ʃwa] *m* choice
chose [ʃoz] *f* thing; **quelque chose** something; **autre chose** something else; **pas grand-chose** not much
chou [ʃu], *pl* **choux** [ʃu] *m* cabbage
ciel [sjɛl], *pl* **cieux** [sjø] *m* sky
cigare [sigaʀ] *m* cigar
cigarette [sigaʀɛt] *f* cigarette
cinéma [sinema] *m* movie
cinq [sɛ̃k] five
cinquantaine [sɛ̃kɑ̃tɛn] *f* about fifty
cinquante [sɛ̃kɑ̃t] fifty
cinquième [sɛ̃kjɛm] fifth
clair [klɛʀ] clear; light colored
clarinette [klaʀinɛt] *f* clarinet
classe [klɑs] *f* classroom
classer [klɑse] to classify
client [klijɑ̃] *m* client
clocher [klɔʃe] *m* steeple
cochon [kɔʃõ] *m* pig
cœur [kœʀ] *m* heart
coiffeur [kwafœʀ] *m* barber
coin [kwɛ̃] *m* corner, part of a town
colimaçon [kɔlimasõ]: **escalier en colimaçon** spiral staircase
collection [kɔlɛksjõ] *f* collection; **collection de timbres** stamp collection
collectionner [kɔlɛksjɔne] to collect
collectionneur [kɔlɛksjɔnœʀ] *m* collector
collège [kɔlɛʒ] *m* secondary school
colline [kɔlin] *f* hill
collision [kɔlizjõ] *f* collision
colonie [kɔlɔni] *f* colony
combien [kõbjɛ̃] how much, how many; **combien de temps** how long
Comédie-Française: la Comédie-Française [lakɔmedifʀɑ̃sɛz] theatre in Paris
commander [kɔmɑ̃de] to order
comme [kɔm] as, like; **comme d'habitude** as usual
commencement [kɔmɑ̃smɑ̃] *m* beginning
commencer [kɔmɑ̃se] to begin
comment [kɔmɑ̃] how; **comment allez-vous?** how are you?; **comment vous appelez-vous?** what is your name?; **comment cela?** how is that?
commerçant [kɔmɛʀsɑ̃] *m* merchant
commerce [kɔmɛʀs] *m* commerce, trade
commissaire de police [kɔmisɛʀdəpɔlis] *m* police lieutenant
commissariat de police [kɔmisaʀjadpɔlis] *m* police station
commode [kɔmɔd] *adj* convenient; *f noun* dresser
compagnie [kõpaɲi] *f* company
compartiment [kõpaʀtimɑ̃] *m* compartment
complet [kõplɛ], **complète** [kõplɛt] complete, full; **complet** [kõplɛ] *n m* man's suit

compliqué [kõplike] complicated
composer [kõpoze] to compose
comprendre [kõpʀɑ̃dʀ] to understand (*conjug like* **prendre**); **je comprends** I understand; **comprenez-vous?** do you understand?
compte [kõt]: **se rendre compte** to realize
compter [kõte] to count
comte [kõt] *m* count
concert [kõsɛʀ] *m* concert
concierge [kõsjɛʀʒ] *m or f* janitor, caretaker
Concorde: Place de la Concorde [kõkɔʀd] square in Paris
conditionnel [kõdisjɔnɛl] *m* conditional
conduire [kõdɥiʀ] to lead; to drive a car; to take (to a place)
confection [kõfɛksjõ] *f* **magasin de confection** ready made clothes
conférence [kõfeʀɑ̃s] *f* lecture
confiance [kõfjɑ̃s] *f* confidence
confondre [kõfõdʀ] to confuse
confortable [kõfɔʀtabl] comfortable
connais: je connais [ʒəkɔnɛ] *pr ind 1st sg of* **connaître**
connaissance [kɔnɛsɑ̃s] *f* acquaintance, consciousness; **faire la connaissance de** to meet, become acquainted with
connaissez: vous connaissez [vukɔnɛse] *pr ind 2nd pl of* **connaître**
connaître [kɔnɛtʀ] to know, be acquainted with
connu [kɔny] *p part of* **connaître**
conseil [kõsɛj] *m* advice
conseiller [kõsɛje] to advise
consentir [kõsɑ̃tiʀ] to consent (*conjug like* **sentir**)
conséquent: par conséquent [paʀkõsekɑ̃] therefore
construction [kõstʀyksjõ] *f* construction, building
construire [kõstʀɥiʀ] to build; **faire construire** to have built
consul [kõsyl] *m* consul
consulter [kõsylte] to consult, look at
contempler [kõtɑ̃ple] to look at
contenir [kõtniʀ] to contain
content [kõtɑ̃] glad
continuateur [kõtinɥatœʀ] *m* continuer, follower
continuer [kõtinɥe] to continue
contraire [kõtʀɛʀ] *adj* contrary; *n m* opposite; **au contraire** on the contrary, far from it
contre [kõtʀ] against; **par contre** on the other hand
convenable [kõvnabl] suitable
convenir [kõvniʀ] to suit, be appropriate (*conjug like* **venir**)
conversation [kõvɛʀsasjõ] *f* conversation
convient: il convient [ilkõvjɛ̃] *pr ind 3rd sg of* **convenir; cette chambre me convient** this room suits me very well
convocation [kõvɔkasjõ] *f* summons
cordonnier [kɔʀdɔɲe] *m* cobbler
Corot [kɔʀo] French painter (1796-1875)
corporel [kɔʀpɔʀɛl] *adj* of the body
corporellement [kɔʀpɔʀɛlmɑ̃] physically
correspondance [kɔʀɛspõdɑ̃s] *f* connection
corsaire [kɔʀsɛʀ] *m* corsair
Corse [kɔʀs] *f* Corsica
cosmopolite [kɔsmɔpolit] cosmopolitan
côté [kote] *m* side; **à côté de** near, beside; **de l'autre côté de** on the other side of
coucher: se coucher [skuʃe] to lie down, go to bed
couler [kule] to flow
couleur [kulœʀ] *f* color
coup: tout à coup [tutaku] suddenly
courant [kuʀɑ̃] current, common; **une expression courante** an everyday expression
courir [kuʀiʀ] to run
cours [kuʀ] *m* course; **au cours de** in the course of, during
course [kuʀs] *f* errand, race; **faire des courses** to do errands; **course de chevaux** horse race; **champ de courses** race track
court [kuʀ] short
cousin [kuzɛ̃], **cousine** [kuzin] cousin
couteau [kuto] *m* knife
coûter [kute] to cost
couture [kutyʀ] *f* dressmaking; **maison de couture** high fashion house
couturière [kutyʀjɛʀ] *f* dressmaker
couvert [kuvɛʀ] covered, cloudy
couverture [kuvɛʀtyʀ] *f* cover
couvrir [kuvʀiʀ] to cover (*conjug like* **ouvrir**)
craindre [kʀɛ̃dʀ] to fear (*conjug like* **plaindre**)
crains: je crains [ʒə kʀɛ̃] *pr ind 1st sg of* **craindre**
cravate [kʀavat] *f* tie, necktie
crème [kʀɛm] *f* cream

crémerie [kʀɛmʀi] *f* store for dairy products
croire [kʀwaʀ] to believe
crois: je crois [ʒəkʀwa] *pr ind 1st sg of* **croire**
croisade [kʀwazad] *f* crusade
croissant [kʀwasɑ̃] *m* crescent roll
croyez: vous croyez [vukʀwaje] *pr ind 2nd pl of* **croire**
cru [kʀy] *p part of* **croire**
cueillir [kœjiʀ] to pick
cuirassé [kɥiʀase] armored
cuisine [kɥizin] *f* food, cooking; kitchen
cuisinière [kɥizinjɛʀ] *f* woman cook
cuivre [kɥivʀ] *m* copper
curé [kyʀe] *m* priest
curiosité [kyʀjɔzite] *f* curiosity

D

d' *see* **de**
dame [dam] *f* lady
danger [dɑ̃ʒe] *m* danger
dangereux [dɑ̃ʒʀø], **dangereuse** [dɑ̃ʒʀøz] dangerous
dans [dɑ̃] in, into, on
date [dat] *f* date
dater de [datedə] to date from
Daumier [domje] French painter and etcher (1808-1879)
davantage [davɑ̃taʒ] more
de [də] of, from
debout [dəbu] standing
Debussy [dəbysi] French musician (1862-1918)
décembre [desɑ̃bʀ] *m* December
décider [deside] to decide
déclaration [deklaʀasjõ] *f* declaration
décoration [dekɔʀasjõ] *f* decoration
déçu [desy] disappointed
dedans [dədɑ̃] inside; **là-dedans** in there
dédier [dedje] to dedicate
déesse [deɛs] *f* goddess
défaire [defɛʀ] to undo (*conjug like* **faire**)
degré [dəgʀe] *m* degree
dehors [dəɔʀ] outside
déjà [deʒa] already, before
déjeuner [deʒœne] *m* lunch; **petit déjeuner** breakfast; **déjeuner** [deʒœne] to lunch, have lunch
delà: au delà [odla] beyond
délicieux [delisjø] delicious
demain [dəmɛ̃] tomorrow; **après-demain** day after tomorrow
demande [dəmɑ̃d] *f* request
demander [dəmɑ̃de] to ask; **se demander** to wonder
demeure [dəmœʀ] *f* house
demeurer [dəmœʀe] to live, reside; **où demeurez-vous?** where do you live?; **je demeure** I live
demi [dəmi] half; **onze heures et demie** half past eleven; **midi et demi** half past twelve; **une demi-heure** a half hour
démolir [demɔliʀ] to tear down
dent [dɑ̃] *f* tooth
dentiste [dɑ̃tist] *m* dentist
départ [depaʀ] *m* departure
dépêche [depɛʃ] *f* telegram
dépêcher: se dépêcher [sədepɛʃe] to hurry
dépenser [depɑ̃se] to spend
depuis [dəpɥi] since, for; **depuis quand? depuis combien de temps?** how long?; **j'attends depuis un quart d'heure** I have been waiting for a quarter of an hour
déranger [deʀɑ̃ʒe] to disturb, inconvenience
dernier [dɛʀnje], **dernière** [dɛʀnjɛʀ] last; **dimanche dernier** last Sunday
derrière [dɛʀjɛʀ] behind
des [de] (*contr of* **de les**) of the, from the, some, any
descendre [dɛsɑ̃dʀ] to go down, to take down
descriptif [deskʀiptif] descriptive
description [dɛskʀipsjõ] *f* description
désigner [deziɲe] to designate
désirer [deziʀe] to wish, desire
dessert [desɛʀ] *m* dessert
dessiner [desine] to draw, draw the plans of
dessous [dəsu] under; *n m* lower side; **au dessous de** below; **là-dessous** under that, under there
dessus [dəsy] on, upon; *n m* top side; **au-dessus de** above; **là-dessus** on that, thereon
destination [dɛstinasjõ] *f* destination
destiné [dɛstine] meant, intended
détail [detaj] *m* detail
détruit [detʀɥi] destroyed
deux [dø] two
deuxième [døzjɛm] second; **le deuxième (étage)** the third floor
devant [dəvɑ̃] before, in front of
devanture [dəvɑ̃tyʀ] *f* shop window

devenir [dəvniʀ] to become (*conjug like* **venir**); **qu'est-ce qu'il est devenu?** what has become of him?
devez: vous devez [vudve] (*pr ind 2nd pl of* **devoir**) you must, you are supposed to
deviez: vous deviez [vudəvje] (*imperf ind 2nd pl of* **devoir**) you were to
devoir [dəvwaʀ] to owe, must, be supposed to, ought to, etc.; **je dois** I must, I am supposed to; **je devais** I was supposed to; **j'ai dû** I must have, I had to; **je devrais** I should; **j'aurais dû** I should have
dévorer [devɔʀe] to devour
devriez: vous devriez [vudəvʀije](*pr condit 2nd pl of* **devoir**) you should, you ought to
dictée [dikte] *f* dictation
dieu [djø] *m* god
différent [difeʀɑ̃] different
difficile [difisil] difficult
difficulté [difikylte] *f* difficulty
dimanche [dimɑ̃ʃ] *m* Sunday; **le dimanche** on Sundays; **à dimanche** see you Sunday
dinde [dɛ̃d] *f* turkey
dîner [dine] *m* dinner; **dîner** [dine] to dine
diplomate [diplɔmat] *m* diplomat
dire [diʀ] to say, tell; **vouloir dire** to mean; **c'est-à-dire** that is to say
directement [diʀɛktəmɑ̃] directly
diriger: se diriger [sədiʀiʒe] to go toward
dis: je dis [ʒədi] *pr ind 1st sg of* **dire; se dire** to say to oneself
discuter [diskyte] to discuss
disent: ils disent [ildiz] *pr ind 3rd pl of* **dire**
disparaître [dispaʀɛtʀ] to disappear
dispos [dispo] fit, in good shape
disposer [dispoze] **(de)** to have at one's disposal
disposition [dispozisjõ] *m* disposal; **je suis à votre disposition** I am at your service
distance [distɑ̃s] *f* distance; **à quelle distance?** how far?
distraire [distʀɛʀ]: **se distraire** to relax and have a good time
dit: il dit [ildi] *pr ind 3rd sg of* **dire**
dites: vous dites [vudit] *pr ind 2nd pl of* **dire**
dix [dis] ten
dixième [dizjɛm] tenth
dix-huit [dizɥit] eighteen
dix-neuf [diznœf] nineteen
dix-neuvième [diznœvjɛm] nineteenth
dix-sept [dissɛt] seventeen
docteur [dɔktœʀ] *m* doctor; **le docteur Lambert** Dr. Lambert
documentaire [dɔkymɑ̃tɛʀ] documentary
dois: je dois [ʒədwɑ] (*pr ind 1st sg of* **devoir**) I must, I am supposed to
dollar [dɔlaʀ] *m* dollar
dominer [dɔmine] to overlook
dommage [dɔmaʒ] *m* **c'est dommage** it's too bad
donc [dõk] then, therefore; **et moi donc!** what about me!; **entrez donc** do come in
donner [dɔne] to give
dont [dõ] whose, of whom, of which
doré [dɔʀe] gilded
dormir [dɔʀmiʀ] to sleep
dort: il dort [ildɔʀ] *pr ind 3rd sg of* **dormir**
doute [dut] *m* doubt; **sans doute** no doubt, probably
douter to doubt; **se douter de** [sədutedə] to suspect
doux, douce [du, dus] sweet, soft
douzaine [duzɛn] *f* dozen; **une demi-douzaine** half a dozen; **vingt francs la douzaine** twenty francs a dozen
douze [duz] twelve
douzième [duzjɛm] twelfth
drapeau [dʀapo] *m* flag
dresser [dʀɛse] to draw up, make out
droit [dʀwɑ] straight, right; **tout droit** straight ahead; **à droite** to, on the right
drôle [dʀol] funny, queer
drugstore [dʀœgstɔʀ] *m* drugstore
du [dy] (*contr of* **de le**) of the, from the, some, any
dû [dy] *p part of* **devoir**
Dumas [dymɑ] French novelist (1803-1870)
duquel [dykɛl], **de laquelle** [dəlakɛl], **desquels** [dekɛl], **desquelles** [dekɛl] *rel pron; prep* **de + lequel,** etc.
dur [dyʀ] hard
durer [dyʀe] to last

E

eau [o] *f* water; **eau minérale** mineral water
échafaudage [eʃafodaʒ] *m* scaffolding
écharpe [eʃaʀp] *f* scarf
échelle [eʃɛl] *f* scale
école [ekɔl] *f* school

économie politique [ekɔnɔmi pɔlitik] *f* economics
Écosse [ekɔs] *f* Scotland
écouter [ekute] to listen
écrire [ekʀiʀ] to write
écris: j'écris [ʒekʀi] *pr ind 1st sg of* **écrire**
écrivain [ekʀivɛ̃] *m* writer
écrivez: vous écrivez [vuzekʀive] *pr ind 2nd pl of* **écrire**
édifice [edifis] *m* building
effet [efɛ] *m* effect; **en effet** indeed
effrayant [efʀɛjɑ̃] frightful
égal [egal] equal; **ça m'est égal** that's all the same to me
égaré [egaʀe] lost
église [egliz] *f* church
égyptien [eʒipsjɛ̃], **égyptienne** [eʒipsjɛn] Egyptian
Eiffel [ɛfɛl] French engineer (1832-1923)
électricité [elɛktʀisite] *f* electricity
élégance [elegɑ̃s] *f* elegance
élégant [elegɑ̃] graceful
élève [elɛv] *m or f* pupil
elle [ɛl] she, it
elles [ɛl] they
emmener [ɑ̃mne] to carry, take along
empêcher [ɑ̃pɛʃe] to prevent
empire [ɑ̃piʀ] *m* empire; **Second Empire** reign of Napoleon III (1852-1870)
emploi [ɑ̃plwa] *m* employment, use; **emploi du temps** *m* schedule
employé [ɑ̃plwaje] *m* employee
employer [ɑ̃plwaje] to employ, use
empoisonner [ɑ̃pwazɔne] to poison
emporter [ɑ̃pɔʀte] to take along, carry along
en [ɑ̃] *prep* in, into, at, to, by; **en** [ɑ̃] *pron* some, any, of it, of them
enchanté [ɑ̃ʃɑ̃te] delighted
encore [ɑ̃kɔʀ] yet, still, again; **pas encore** not yet
endormir: s'endormir [sɑ̃dɔʀmiʀ] to fall asleep
endroit [ɑ̃dʀwɑ] *m* place
énergie [enɛʀʒi] *f* energy
enfant [ɑ̃fɑ̃] *m or f* child
ennuyer [ɑ̃nɥije] to bother, worry
énorme [enɔʀm] enormous
enrichi [ɑ̃ʀiʃi] made wealthy
ensemble [ɑ̃sɑ̃bl] *n* whole, entirety; **vue d'ensemble** general view; *adv* together
ensuite [ɑ̃sɥit] then, afterwards
entendre [ɑ̃tɑ̃dʀ] to hear; **entendre parler de** to hear of; **entendre dire que** to hear that
entendu [ɑ̃tɑ̃dy] *p part of* **entendre; c'est entendu** agreed, all right
enterrer [ɑ̃tɛʀe] to bury
entier [ɑ̃tje], **entière** [ɑ̃tjɛʀ] entire, whole; **tout entier** entirely
entouré de [ɑ̃tuʀe də] surrounded with
entre [ɑ̃tʀ] between, among; **entre autres** among others
entrer [ɑ̃tʀe] to enter, go in
entr'ouvert [ɑ̃tʀuvɛʀ] partly open
enveloppe [ɑ̃vlɔp] *f* envelop
enverrai: j'enverrai [ʒɑ̃vɛʀe] *fut 1st sg of* **envoyer**
envie [ɑ̃vi] *f* envy, desire; **avoir envie de** to feel like
environ [ɑ̃viʀõ] about
envoie: j'envoie [ʒɑ̃vwa] *pr ind 1st sg of* **envoyer**
envoyer [ɑ̃vwaje] to send; **envoyer chercher** to send for; **faire envoyer** to have (something) sent
épais [epɛ] thick
épaule [epol] *f* shoulder
Épernay [epɛʀnɛ] town in Champagne
épicerie [episʀi] *f* grocery store
épidémie [epidemi] *f* epidemic
époque [epɔk] *f* period, time
escalier [ɛskalje] *m* stairway
espace [ɛspɑs] *m* space
Espagne [ɛspaɲ] *f* Spain
espagnol [ɛspaɲɔl] Spanish (*takes a capital only when used as a noun referring to a person*)
espalier [ɛspalje] *m* fruit tree trimmed and trained to grow against a wall or trellis
espèce [ɛspɛs] *f* kind, sort
espérer [ɛspeʀe] to hope; **je l'espère** I hope so
essayer [esɛje] to try, try on
essence [ɛsɑ̃s] *f* gasoline
essoufflé [esufle] out of breath
est: il est [ilɛ] *pr ind 3rd sg of* **être**
Est [ɛst] *m* East
estampe [ɛstɑ̃p] *f* print, engraving, etc.
et [e] and; **et cætera** [ɛtseteʀa] etc.
établi [etabli] established, settled
était: il était [iletɛ] *imperf ind 3rd sg of* **être**
étalage [etalaʒ] *m* display
États-Unis [etazyni] *m pl* United States

été [ete] *m* summer; **été** [ete] *p part of* **être**
éteindre [etɛ̃dʀ] to extinguish (*conjug like* **peindre**)
étendue [etɑ̃dy] *f* extent, size
êtes: vous êtes [vuzɛt] *pr ind 2nd pl of* **être**
étoffe [etɔf] *f* material
étoile [etwal] *f* star
étonnant [etɔnɑ̃] astonishing
étonné [etɔne] surprised
étonner: s'étonner [setɔne] to wonder at
étranger [etʀɑ̃ʒe], **étrangère** [etʀɑ̃ʒɛʀ] foreign; *n* foreigner; **à l'étranger** abroad
être [ɛtʀ] to be; **c'est** it is; **est-ce?** is it?; **est-ce que?** is it that?; **qu'est-ce que c'est que?** what is?; **c'est-à-dire** that is to say; **il est onze heures** it is eleven o'clock; **c'est aujourd'hui jeudi** today is Thursday; **être à** to belong to
étroit [etʀwa] narrow
étudiant [etydjɑ̃] *m*, **étudiante** [etydjɑ̃t] *f* student
étudier [etydje] to study
eu [y] *p part of* **avoir**
eurent; ils eurent [ilzyʀ] *p simple 3rd pl of* **avoir**
Europe [œʀɔp] *f* Europe
européen [œʀɔpeɛ̃], **européenne** [œʀɔpeɛn] European
eut: il eut [ily] *p simple 3rd sg of* **avoir: il y eut** there was, there were, there has been, there have been
eux [ø] they, them
évidemment [evidamɑ̃] evidently
exact [ɛgzakt] exact
examen [ɛgzamɛ̃] *m* examination
examiner [ɛ̃gzamine] to examine
excellent [ɛksɛlɑ̃] excellent
excursion [ɛkskyʀsjõ] *f* excursion
excuser: s'excuser [sɛkskyze] to apologize
exemple [ɛgzɑ̃pl] *m* example; **par exemple** for example
exercice [ɛgzɛʀsis] *m* exercise; **exercice d'application** drill
expérience [ɛkspeʀjɑ̃s] *f* experience
explication [ɛksplikasjõ] *f* explanation
expliquer [ɛksplike] to explain
exploiter [ɛksplwate] to make use of
express [ɛkspʀɛs] *m* fast train
expression [ɛkspʀɛsjõ] *f* expression
exprimer [ɛkspʀime] to express

F

fabriqué [fabʀike] made
façade [fasad] *f* front of a building
face [fas] *f* face; **en face de** opposite
fâché [fɑʃe] sorry, angry
facile [fasil] easy
facilement [fasilmɑ̃] easily
façon [fasõ] *f* way, manner
facteur [faktœʀ] *m* postman
facture [faktyʀ] *f* bill
Faculté [fakylte] *f* a Division of a University
faim [fɛ̃] *f* hunger; **avoir faim** to be hungry
faire [fɛʀ] to do, make; **faire une promenade** to take a walk; **faire du ski** to go skiing; **quoi faire?** what for?; **faire la connaissance de** to meet, become acquainted with; **faire venir** to have . . . come; **faire envoyer** to have . . . sent; **faire attention** to watch out; **quel temps fait-il?** what kind of weather is it?; **il fait beau** the weather is nice; **il fait du vent** it is windy; **il fait nuit** it is dark; **cela ne fait rien** it does not make any difference; **se faire un plaisir de** to be glad to; **faire bien de** to do well to; **faire penser** to remind
fais: je fais [ʒəfɛ] *pr ind 1st sg of* **faire**
faisait: il faisait [ilfəzɛ] *imperf ind 3rd sg of* **faire; il faisait beau** the weather was nice
fait [fɛ]: **tout à fait** quite, entirely
fait: il fait [ilfɛ] *pr ind 3rd sg of* **faire**
faites: vous faites [vufɛt] *pr ind 2nd pl of* **faire**
falloir [falwaʀ] *impers verb* to have to; **il faut** one must, it is necessary; **il fallait, il a fallu** it was necessary; **il faudra** it will be necessary
familial [familjal] of the family
famille [famij] *f* family; relatives
fasse: il fasse [ilfas] *pr subj 3rd sg of* **faire**
fatigue [fatig] *f* fatigue
fatigué [fatige] tired
faut: il faut [ilfo] *pr ind 3rd sg of* **falloir**
faute [fot] *f* fault
fauteuil [fotœj] *m* armchair
favori [favɔʀi], **favorite** [favɔʀit] favorite
femme [fam] *f* woman, wife
fenêtre [fənɛtʀ] *f* window
fer [fɛʀ] *m* iron; **chemin de fer** *m* railroad
ferai: je ferai [ʒəfʀe] *fut 1st sg of* **faire**
ferme [fɛʀm] *f* farm

fermenter [fɛʀmɑ̃te] to ferment
fermer [fɛʀme] to close
fertile [fɛʀtil] fertile
fête [fɛt] *f* celebration, holiday
feu [fø] *m* fire
feuille [fœj] *f* leaf
février [fevʀije] *m* February
fiancé, fiancée [fjɑ̃se] fiancé, fiancée
fièvre [fjɛvʀ] *f* fever
figure [figyʀ] *f* face
filet [filɛ] *m* fillet
fille [fij] *f* daughter; **jeune fille** girl; **petite fille** little girl
film [film] *m* film, movie
fin [fɛ̃] *f* end
finalement [finalmɑ̃] finally
finir [finiʀ] to finish
finissez: vous finissez [vufinise] *pr ind 2nd pl of* **finir**
fixer [fikse] to decide upon
flanc [flɑ̃] *m* side
flatteur [flatœʀ] *m* flatterer
fleur [flœʀ] *f* flower
fleuve [flœv] *m* larger river
Florence [flɔʀɑ̃s] Florence
foin [fwɛ̃] *m* hay
fois [fwa] *f* time; **la première fois** the first time; **plusieurs fois** several times; **à la fois** at the same time
foncé [fõse] dark colored; **bleu foncé** dark blue
fonctionnaire [fõksjɔnɛʀ] *m* government employee
fonder [fõde] to found
font: ils font [ilfõ] *pr ind 3rd pl of* **faire**
fontaine [fõtɛn] *f* fountain
Fontainebleau [fõtɛnblo] town in the Île-de-France
forcé [fɔʀse] forced
forêt [fɔʀɛ] *f* forest
forme [fɔʀm] *f* form
former [fɔʀme] to form
formidable [fɔʀmidabl] terrific
fort [fɔʀ] *adv* very
fortification [fɔʀtifikasjõ] *f* fortification
fourchette [fuʀʃɛt] *f* fork
fourgon [fuʀgõ] *m* baggage car
fragmentaire [fʀagmɑ̃tɛʀ] fragmentary
frais [fʀɛ], **fraîche** [fʀɛʃ] fresh, cool, cold
fraise [fʀɛz] *f* strawberry; **fraise des bois** wild strawberry
franc [fʀɑ̃] *m* franc
français [fʀɑ̃sɛ], **française** [fʀɑ̃sɛz] French (*takes a capital only when used as a noun referring to a person*)
France [fʀɑ̃s] *f* France
François Ier [fʀɑ̃swa pʀəmje] king of France (1494-1547)
fréquent [fʀekɑ̃] frequent
fréquenté [fʀekɑ̃te] popular (frequently visited)
frère [fʀɛʀ] *m* brother
frit [fʀi] fried; **pommes de terre frites** French fried potatoes
frites [fʀit] *f pl* French fried potatoes
froid [fʀwɑ] cold; **il fait froid** it is cold; **avoir froid** to be cold
fromage [fʀɔmɑʒ] *m* cheese
fruit [fʀɥi] *m* fruit
fumer [fyme] to smoke
furent: ils furent [ilfyʀ] *p simple 3rd pl of* **être**
fut: il fut [ilfy] *p simple 3rd sg of* **être**

G

gai [ge] gay
galerie [galʀi] *f* gallery, hall
gant [gɑ̃] *m* glove
garage [gaʀaʒ] *m* garage
garçon [gaʀsõ] *m* boy, waiter
garder [gaʀde] to keep; **se garder de** to be careful not to
gardien [gaʀdjɛ̃] *m* guard
gare [gaʀ] *f* station
gâteau [gato] *m* cake, pastry
gauche [goʃ] *f* left; **à gauche** to the left
Geneviève: sainte Geneviève [sɛ̃t ʒənvjɛv] patron saint of Paris
gens [ʒɑ̃] *f pl* people
gentil [ʒɑ̃ti], **gentille** [ʒɑ̃tij] nice
glace [glas] *f* ice, mirror; **la Galerie des Glaces** the Hall of Mirrors
glissant [glisɑ̃] slippery
glisser [glise] to slide
gorge [gɔʀʒ] *f* throat; **avoir mal à la gorge** to have a sore throat
gothique [gɔtik] Gothic
goût [gu] *m* taste
grand [gʀɑ̃] tall, large, great
grand-mère [gʀɑ̃mɛʀ] *f* grandmother
grappe [gʀap] *f* bunch (of grapes)

gras, grasse [gʀɑ, gʀɑs] fat
gratte-ciel [gʀatsjɛl] *m* skyscraper
grave [gʀav] serious
gravité [gʀavite] *f* gravity
gravure [gʀavyʀ] *f* etching
grec [gʀɛk] Greek
grille [gʀij] *f* iron gate
gris [gʀi] gray
gros [gʀo], **grosse** [gʀos] big
groupé [gʀupe] grouped
guère [gɛʀ]; **ne . . . guère** scarcely, hardly
guerre [gɛʀ] *f* war
guerrier [gɛʀje] *m* warrior
guichet [giʃɛ] *m* ticket window
guide [gid] *m* guide
guitare [gitaʀ] *f* guitar

H

(*Words beginning with an aspirate* **h** *are shown thus:* ***haricot**)
habile [abil] skillful
habilement [abilmɑ̃] skillfully
habiller [abije] to dress; **s'habiller** to get dressed
habite: il habite [ilabit] *pr ind 3rd sg of* **habiter**
habiter [abite] to live in
habitude [abityd] *f* habit, practice; **comme d'habitude** as usual; **avoir l'habitude de** to be used to
habituer: s'habituer à [sabitɥe a] to get used to
***haricot** [aʀiko] *m* bean
harmonie [aʀmɔni] *f* harmony
***harpe** [aʀp] *f* harp
***hasard** [azaʀ] *m* chance; **par hasard** by chance
***hâte** [ɑt] *f* haste; **avoir hâte de** to be eager to
***haut** [o] *m* top, upper part; **en haut de** at the top of; **là-haut** up there
herbe [ɛʀb] *f* grass
***héros** [eʀo] *m* hero
heure [œʀ] *f* hour, time; **quelle heure est-il?** what time is it?; **il est onze heures** it is eleven o'clock; **une demi-heure** a half hour; **à l'heure** on time; **de bonne heure** early; **tout à l'heure** in a while, a while ago; **à l'heure actuelle** at the present time
heureux [œʀø], **heureuse** [œʀøz] happy
hier [jɛʀ] *m* yesterday; **hier soir** last night
hippopotame [ipɔpɔtam] *m* hippopotamus
histoire [istwaʀ] *f* history, story; **l'histoire de France** French history
historique [istɔʀik] historical
hiver [ivɛʀ] *m* winter
homme [ɔm] *m* man; **jeune homme** boy, young man
honneur [ɔnœʀ] *m* honor
hôpital [ɔpital] *m* hospital
horaire [ɔʀɛʀ] *m* timetable
horloge [ɔʀlɔʒ] *f* clock
horloger [ɔʀlɔʒe] *m* jeweler
horriblement [ɔʀibləmɑ̃] terribly
***hors-d'œuvre** [ɔʀdœvʀ] *m* hors d'œuvres
hostilité [ɔstilite] *f* hostility
hôtel [otɛl] *m* hotel
hôtelier [otəlje] *m* hotel keeper
Hugo: Victor Hugo [viktɔʀygo] French writer (1802-1885)
***huit** [ɥit] eight; **huit jours** a week; **d'aujourd'hui en huit** a week from today
***huitième** [ɥitjɛm] eighth
humble [œ̃bl] humble
humide [ymid] humid
humidité [ymidite] *f* humidity

I

ici [isi] here
idée [ide] *f* idea
identifier [idɑ̃tifje] to identify
identité [idɑ̃tite] *f* identity; **carte d'identité** identification card
il [il] he, it
île [il] *f* island; **Île-de-France** the region around Paris; **l'île de la Cité** an island in the Seine, the heart of old Paris
illustration [ilystʀasjõ] *f* illustration
ils [il] they
image [imaʒ] *f* picture
imaginer [imaʒine] to imagine
immensité [imɑ̃site] *f* immensity
immeuble [imœbl] apartment house
impair [ɛ̃pɛʀ] odd (*of numbers*)
imparfait [ɛ̃paʀfɛ] imperfect
impassible [ɛ̃pasibl] impassive
imperméable [ɛ̃pɛʀmeabl] *m* raincoat
impétueux [ɛ̃petɥø] impetuous
impression [ɛ̃pʀɛsjõ] *f* impression
impressionné [ɛ̃pʀɛsjɔne] impressed

incident [ɛ̃sidɑ̃] *m* incident
indéfini [ɛ̃defini] indefinite
indépendance [ɛ̃depɑ̃dɑ̃s] *f* independence
indication [ɛ̃dikasjõ] *f* indication
indignation [ɛ̃diɲasjõ] *f* indignation
indiquer [ɛ̃dike] to indicate, tell
industriel [ɛ̃dystʀijɛl] *m* manufacturer
ingénieur [ɛ̃ʒenjœʀ] *m* engineer
injustice [ɛ̃ʒystis] *f* injustice
inquiet [ɛ̃kjɛ] worried
inscription [ɛ̃skʀipsjõ] *f* inscription
installer [ɛ̃stale] to set up; **s'installer** to settle
instant [ɛ̃stɑ̃] *m* instant; **un instant** for a moment
Institut [ɛ̃stity] *m* Institute
intelligent [ɛ̃teliʒɑ̃] intelligent
intention [ɛ̃tɑ̃sjõ] *f* intention; **avoir l'intention de** to intend to
intéressant [ɛ̃teʀɛsɑ̃] interesting, worth buying
intéresser [ɛ̃teʀɛse] to interest; **s'intéresser à** to be interested in
intérieur [ɛ̃teʀjœʀ] *m* inside; **à l'intérieur** inside
interrogatif [ɛ̃teʀɔgatif], **interrogative** [ɛ̃teʀɔgativ] interrogative
inventer [ɛ̃vɑ̃te] to invent
invention [ɛ̃vɑ̃sjõ] *f* invention
inversion [ɛ̃vɛʀsjõ] *f* inversion
invitation [ɛ̃vitasjõ] *f* invitation
inviter [ɛ̃vite] to invite
irai: j'irai [ʒiʀe] *fut 1st sg of* **aller**
irais: j'irais [ʒiʀɛ] *cond 1st sg of* **aller**
irlandais [iʀlɑ̃dɛ] Irish
ironique [iʀɔnik] ironical
Islande [islɑ̃d] *f* Iceland
Italie [itali] *f* Italy
italien [italjɛ̃], **italienne** [italjɛn] Italian (*takes a capital only when used as a noun referring to a person*)

J

j' *see* **je**
jaloux, jalouse [ʒalu, ʒaluz] jealous
jamais [ʒamɛ] never, ever; **ne . . . jamais** never
jambe [ʒɑ̃b] *f* leg
jambon [ʒɑ̃bõ] *m* ham
janvier [ʒɑ̃vje] *m* January
jardin [ʒaʀdɛ̃] *m* garden
jaune [ʒon] yellow
je [ʒə] I
Jeanne d'Arc [ʒɑndaʀk] Joan of Arc (1412-1431)
jeter [ʒəte] to throw, cast; **jeter un coup d'œil sur** to take a look at
jeudi [ʒødi] Thursday
jeune [ʒœn] young; **jeune fille** girl
Joconde: la Joconde [laʒɔkõd] the Mona Lisa
joindre [ʒwɛ̃dʀ] to join
joli [ʒɔli] pretty
joue [ʒu] *f* cheek
jouer [ʒwe] to play
jour [ʒuʀ] *m* day, daylight; **par jour** a day; **huit jours** a week; **quinze jours** two weeks; **tous les jours** every day; **ces jours-ci** some time soon; **il fait jour** it is daylight
journal [ʒuʀnal], **journaux** [ʒuʀno] *m* newspaper
journée [ʒuʀne] *f* day; **toute la journée** all day
juger [ʒyʒe] to judge
juillet [ʒɥijɛ] *m* July
juin [ʒɥɛ̃] *m* June
jumeaux [ʒymo] *m pl* twins
jus [ʒy] *m* juice
jusqu'à [ʒyska] until, up to, as far as; **jusque-là** that far, till then; **jusqu'à ce que** until
juste [ʒyst] exactly, just

K

kilo [kilo], **kilogramme** [kilɔgʀam] *m* kilo (2.2 lbs.)
kilomètre [kilɔmɛtʀ] *m* kilometer (about $\frac{5}{8}$ mile)
kiosque [kjɔsk] *m* stand, newsstand

L

l' *see* **le, la**
la [la] *art* the; *pron* her, it
là [la] there; **là-bas** over there; **là-haut** up there; **ce jour-là** that day
laboratoire [labɔʀatwaʀ] *m* laboratory
lac [lak] *m* lake
La Fayette [lafajɛt] French statesman (1757-1834)
laisser [lɛse] to let, leave
lait [lɛ] *m* milk
laitue [lɛty] *f* lettuce

lancer [lɑ̃se] to launch, to start, to throw
langue [lɑ̃g] *f* language
laquelle *see* **lequel**
lecture [lɛktyʀ] *f* reading
laver [lave] to wash
le [lə] *art* the; *pron* him, it
leçon [ləsõ] *f* lesson
légende [leʒɑ̃d] *f* legend
léger [leʒe] light
légume [legym] *m* vegetable
lendemain: le lendemain [ləlɑ̃dmɛ̃] the next day
Le Nôtre [lənotʀ] French landscape architect (1613-1700)
lequel [ləkɛl], **laquelle** [lakɛl], **lesquels** [lekɛl], **lesquelles** [lekɛl] *rel pron* which; who, whom; **lequel? laquelle? lesquels? lesquelles?** *interrog pron* which? which one? which ones?
les [le] *art* the; *pron* them
lettre [lɛtʀ] *f* letter; **papier à lettres** stationery
leur [lœʀ] *pers pron* to them, them; **leur** [lœʀ], **leurs** [lœʀ] *poss adj* their; **le leur, la leur, les leurs** *poss pron* theirs
lever: se lever [səlve] to get up, rise
lèvre [lɛvʀ] *f* lip
liberté [libɛʀte] *f* liberty
libraire [libʀɛʀ] *m* bookseller
librairie [libʀɛʀi] *f* bookstore
libre [libʀ] free
lieu [ljø] *m* place; **avoir lieu** to take place
ligne [liɲ] *f* line
lion [ljõ] *m* lion
lire [liʀ] to read
lis: je lis [ʒəli] *pr ind 1st sg of* **lire**
Lisbonne [lisbɔn] Lisbon
lisez: vous lisez [vulize] *pr ind 2nd pl of* **lire**
liste [list] *f* list
lit [li] *m* bed
litre [litʀ] *m* litre (1.0567 qts. liquid)
littérature [liteʀatyʀ] *f* literature
livre [livʀ] *m* book
livre [livʀ] *f* pound; **deux francs la livre** two francs a pound
loi [lwa] *f* law
loin [lwɛ̃] far
lointain [lwɛ̃tɛ̃], **lointaine** [lwɛ̃tɛn] distant
Londres [lõdʀ] London
long [lõ], **longue** [lõg] long; **le long de** along
longtemps [lõtɑ̃] a long time, long; **depuis longtemps** for a long time
lorsque [lɔʀsk] when
louer [lwe] to rent
Louis XIV [lwikatɔʀz] king of France (1638-1715)
loupe [lup] *f* magnifying-glass
lourd [luʀ] heavy
Louvre: le Louvre [ləluvʀ] former royal palace in Paris
loyer [lwaje] *m* rent
lu [ly] *p part of* **lire**
lugubre [lygybʀ] dismal, dreadful
lui [lɥi] him; to him, to her, to it
lundi [lœ̃di] *m* Monday
lune [lyn] *f* moon
lunettes [lynɛt] *f pl* glasses
luxe [lyks] *m* luxury
Luxembourg [lyksɑ̃buʀ]: **Jardin du Luxembourg** park in Paris
lycée [lise] *m* secondary school

M

M. *abbr of* **Monsieur**
ma *see* **mon**
madame [madam] *f* madam, Mrs.
mademoiselle [madmwazɛl] *f* Miss
magasin [magazɛ̃] *m* store
magnifique [maɲifik] magnificent, splendid
mai [mɛ] *m* May
maigre [mɛgʀ] skinny
main [mɛ̃] *f* hand
maintenant [mɛ̃tnɑ̃] now
maire [mɛʀ] *m* mayor
mais [mɛ] but; **mais oui** oh yes; **mais non** oh no
maïs [mais] *m* corn
maison [mɛzõ] *f* house, company; **à la maison** at home
majestueux [maʒɛstɥø], **majestueuse** [maʒɛstɥøz] majestic
mal [mal] *m* pain; **mal de tête** *m* headache; **avoir mal à la tête** to have a headache; **faire mal** to hurt; **mal** [mal] *adv* badly; **pas mal** all right
malade [malad] sick
maladie [maladi] *f* sickness
maladroit [maladʀwa] clumsy, awkward
malgré [malgʀe] in spite of
malheureusement [malœʀøzmɑ̃] unfortunately

malheureux [malœRø], **malheureuse** [malœRøz] unhappy
manger [mɑ̃ʒe] to eat
mannequin [mankɛ̃] *m* fashion model
manquer [mɑ̃ke] to miss; **mes parents me manquent** I miss my parents
Mansart *or* **Mansard** [mɑ̃saR] French architect (1646-1708)
mansarde [mɑ̃saRd] *f* garret
manteau [mɑ̃to] *m* coat, cloak
marchand [maRʃɑ̃] *m* merchant, dealer, shopkeeper
marché [maRʃe] *m* market; **à bon marché** cheap; **à meilleur marché** cheaper; **le Bon Marché** large department store in Paris
marcher [maRʃe] to walk
mardi [maRdi] *m* Tuesday
marguerite [maRgəRit] *f* daisy
mari [maRi] *m* husband
mariage [maRjaʒ] *m* marriage, wedding
marier: se marier [smaRje] to get married
marron [maRɔ̃] brown; **les yeux marron** brown eyes (*no agreement*)
marronnier [maRɔnje] *m* horse chestnut tree
mars [maRs] *m* March
Marseille [maRsɛj] city in southern France
Martinique [maRtinik] *f* Martinique
mathématiques [matematik] *f pl* mathematics
matin [matɛ̃] *m* morning; **le matin** in the morning; **tous les matins** every morning
mauvais [mɔvɛ] or [movɛ] bad, wrong; **la mauvaise route** the wrong road
me [mə] me, to me
mécontent [mekɔ̃tɑ̃] dissatisfied
médecin [metsɛ̃] *m* physician
médicament [medikamɑ̃] *m* medicine, drug
meilleur, meilleure, meilleurs, meilleures [mɛjœR] (*compar of* **bon**) better; **le meilleur, la meilleure, les meilleurs, les meilleures** (*superl of* **bon**) the best
Melun [məlœ̃] town in the Île-de-France
même [mɛm] *adv* even; **ne . . . même pas** not even; **tout de même** nevertheless, anyway; **au cœur même de Paris** in the very heart of Paris; **le même, la même, les mêmes** *adj and pron* the same
ménage [menaʒ] *m* housekeeping
ménager [menaʒe] to arrange
mener [məne] to lead
menu [məny] *m* menu
mer [mɛR] *f* sea
merci [mɛRsi] thank you
mercredi [mɛRkRədi] *m* Wednesday
mère [mɛR] *f* mother
merveille [mɛRvɛj]: **à merveille** marvelously
mes *see* **mon**
messe [mɛs] *f* mass
métallique [metalik] metallic
mètre [mɛtR] *m* meter (39.37 inches)
mettez: vous mettez [vumɛte] *pr ind 2nd pl of* **mettre**
mettre [mɛtR] to put, put on; **se mettre à** to begin; **mettre une lettre à la poste** to mail a letter
meuble [mœbl] *m* piece of furniture; **les meubles** furniture
meublé [mœble] furnished
Mexique [mɛksik] *m* Mexico
midi [midi] *m* noon; **après-midi** *m* afternoon
mien: le mien [ləmjɛ̃], **la mienne** [lamjɛn], **les miens** [lemjɛ̃], **les miennes** [lemjɛn] mine
mieux [mjø] *adv* (*compar of* **bien**) better; **aimer mieux** to prefer; **tant mieux** so much the better; **le mieux** (*superl of* **bien**) the best; **de son mieux** the best he could; **je vais le mieux du monde** I couldn't be better
milieu [miljø] *m* middle; **au milieu de** in the middle of, in the midst of
mille [mil] a thousand
Millet [milɛ] French painter (1815-1865)
million [miljɔ̃] *m* million
millionnaire [miljɔnɛR] *m* millionaire
mince [mɛ̃s] thin
ministère [ministɛR] *m* ministry
ministre [ministR] *m* Cabinet member
minuit [minɥi] *m* midnight
minute [minyt] *f* minute
mis [mi] *p part of* **mettre**
Mlle *abbr of* **Mademoiselle**
Mme *abbr of* **Madame**
mode [mɔd] *f* fashion; *pl* women's hats and other apparel
modiste [mɔdist] *f* milliner
moi [mwa] I, me, to me
moindre, moindres [mwɛ̃dR] lesser; **le moindre, la moindre, les moindres** the least, the slightest
moins [mwɛ̃] less; **moins . . . que** less . . . than; **à moins que** unless; **deux heures moins le**

quart a quarter of two; **du moins, au moins** at least
mois [mwɑ] *m* month; **au mois de décembre** in December
Molière [mɔljɛʀ] French playwright (1622-1673)
moment [mɔmɑ̃] *m* moment, time; **à ce moment-là** at that time; **au moment de** at the time of; **au moment où** at the time when
mon [mõ], **ma** [ma], **mes** [me] my
monde [mõd] *m* world, people; **tout le monde** everybody
mondial [mõdjal] world-wide
monnaie [mɔnɛ] *f* change; **porte-monnaie** *m* change purse
monotone [mɔnɔtɔn] monotonous
monsieur [məsjø] *m* Sir, Mr., gentleman
montagne [mõtaɲ] *f* mountain
Monte-Cristo [mõtekʀisto]: **Le Comte de Monte-Cristo** a novel by Dumas
monter [mõte] to go up
Montmartre [mõmaʀtʀ] a section of Paris
montre [mõtʀ] *f* watch; **montre-bracelet** wrist watch
montrer [mõtʀe] to show
Mont-Saint-Michel, le [mõ sɛ̃ miʃɛl] town built on a rock off the coast of Brittany, famous for its monastery
monument [mɔnymɑ̃] *m* monument
monumental [mɔnymɑ̃tal] monumental
moquer: se moquer de [səmɔke də] to laugh at, make fun of
mordre [mɔʀdʀə] to bite
mort [mɔʀ] *p part of* **mourir**
Moscou [mɔsku] Moscow
mot [mo] *m* word
mouchoir [muʃwaʀ] *m* handkerchief
mouillé [muje] wet
mourir [muʀiʀ] to die
mourut: il mourut [ilmuʀy] *p simple 3rd sg of* **mourir**
mousquetaire [muskətɛʀ] *m* musketeer; **Les Trois Mousquetaires** a novel by Dumas
mouton [mutõ] *m* sheep
mur [myʀ] *m* wall
mûrir [myʀiʀ] to ripen, mature
musclé [myskle] muscular
musée [myze] *m* museum
musique [myzik] *f* music
mutilé [mytile] mutilated

N

n' *see* **ne**
nager [naʒe] to swim
naître [nɛtʀ] to be born
Napoléon [napɔleõ] emperor of the French (1769-1821)
natal [natal] native
national [nasjɔnal] national
nationalité [nasjɔnalite] *f* nationality
naturellement [natyʀɛlmɑ̃] naturally
ne [nə] not; no; **ne . . . pas** not, no; **ne . . . plus** no more, no longer; **ne . . . que** only; **ne . . . ni . . . ni** neither . . . nor; **ne . . . guère** hardly, scarcely; **ne . . . personne** nobody; **ne . . . aucun(e)** none
né [ne] *p part of* **naître; je suis né à Philadelphie** I was born in Philadelphia
néanmoins [neɑ̃mwɛ̃] nevertheless
négatif [negatif], **négative** [negativ] negative
négativement [negativmɑ̃] negatively
négociant [negɔsjɑ̃] *m* wholesale merchant
neige [nɛʒ] *f* snow
neiger [nɛʒe] to snow; **il neige** it is snowing
nettoyer [nɛtwaje] to clean
neuf [nœf] nine
neuf [nœf], **neuve** [nœv] new
neuvième [nœvjɛm] ninth
ni [ni] neither, nor; **ne . . . ni . . . ni** neither . . . nor; **ni l'un ni l'autre** neither
nier [nije] to deny
noblesse [nɔblɛs] *f* nobility
Noël [nɔɛl] *m* Christmas
noir [nwaʀ] black
nom [nõ] *m* name
nombre [nõbʀ] *m* number
nombreux [nõbʀø], **nombreuse** [nõbʀøz] numerous
nommé [nɔme] named
non [nõ] no; **non plus** either
Nord [nɔʀ] *m* North
Normandie [nɔʀmɑ̃di] *f* Normandy
norvégien, norvégienne [nɔʀveʒjɛ̃, nɔʀveʒjɛn] Norwegian
notamment [nɔtamɑ̃] among others
notre [nɔtʀ], **nos** [no] *adj* our; **le nôtre** [lənotʀ], **la nôtre, les nôtres** *pron* ours
nous [nu] we, us, to us
nous-mêmes [numɛm] ourselves

nouveau [nuvo], **nouvel, nouvelle** [nuvɛl], **nouveaux, nouvelles** new; **de nouveau** again, once more; **La Nouvelle-Orléans** New Orleans
nouvelle [nuvɛl] *f* piece of news
novembre [nɔvɑ̃bʀ] *m* November
nuage [nɥaʒ] *m* cloud
nuit [nɥi] *f* night, darkness; **il fait nuit** it is dark
nul [nyl], **nulle** [nyl] no, no one; **nulle part** nowhere
numéro [nymeʀo] *m* number

O

obéir [ɔbeiʀ] to obey
obélisque [ɔbelisk] *m* obelisk
objet [ɔbʒɛ] *m* object
obligatoire [ɔbligatwaʀ] required
obliger [ɔbliʒe] to oblige; **noblesse oblige** rank imposes obligations
obscurité [ɔpskyʀite] *f* darkness
observatoire [ɔpsɛʀvatwaʀ] *m* observatory
occasion [ɔkazjõ] *f* occasion, bargain; **livre d'occasion** second-hand book
occupation [ɔkypasjõ] *f* occupation
occupé [ɔkype] busy
occuper: s'occuper de [sɔkype də] to take care of
octobre [ɔktɔbʀ] *m* October
oculiste [ɔkylist] *m* oculist
œil [œj], *pl* **yeux** [jø] *m* eye
œillet [œjɛ] *m* carnation
œuf [œf], *pl* **œufs** [ø] *m* egg
œuvre [œvʀ] *f* work
offrir [ɔfʀiʀ] to offer (*conjug like* **ouvrir**)
oie [wa] *f* goose
oiseau [wazo] *m* bird
olive [ɔliv] *f* olive
on [õ], **l'on** [lõ] one, they, someone
oncle [õkl] *m* uncle
ont: ils ont [ilzõ] *pr ind 3rd pl of* **avoir**
onze [õz] eleven
onzième [õzjɛm] eleventh
opéra [ɔpeʀa] *m* opera, opera house
opposé [ɔpoze] *m* opposite
orange [ɔʀɑ̃ʒ] *f* orange
ordinaire [ɔʀdinɛʀ] ordinary; **d'ordinaire** usually
ordre [ɔʀdʀ] *m* order
orgues [ɔʀg] *f pl* organ
ornement [ɔʀnəmɑ̃] *m* ornament
os [ɔs], *pl* **os** [o] *m* bone; **je suis mouillé jusqu'aux os** I am wet to the skin
oser [oze] to dare
ou [u] or
où (u) where, where?, in which, when; **d'où le nom** whence the name
oublier [ublije] to forget
oui [wi] yes
ours [uʀs] *m* bear
ouvert [uvɛʀ] *p part of* **ouvrir**
ouvrir [uvʀiʀ] to open

P

pain [pɛ̃] *m* bread
pair [pɛʀ]: **nombre pair** even number
paire [pɛʀ] *f* pair
paisible [pɛsibl] peaceful
paix [pɛ] *f* peace
palais [palɛ] *m* palace
panorama [panɔʀama] *m* sight, panorama
pantalon [pɑ̃talõ] *m* pants
Panthéon: le Panthéon [ləpɑ̃teõ] *m* monument in Paris
papier [papje] *m* paper; **papier à lettres** stationery
paquet [pakɛ] *m* package, pack
par [paʀ] by, through; **par jour** a day; **par ici** this way
paraître [paʀɛtʀ] to seem, to appear
parapet [paʀapɛ] *m* parapet, low wall as a railing
parapluie [paʀaplɥi] *m* umbrella
parc [paʀk] *m* park
parce que [paʀskə] because
pardessus [paʀdəsy] *m* overcoat, topcoat
pardon [paʀdõ] pardon me, excuse me
parent [paʀɑ̃] *m* parent, relative
parfaitement [paʀfɛtmɑ̃] perfectly
parfois [paʀfwa] sometimes
Paris [paʀi] *m* Paris
parisien [paʀizjɛ̃], **parisienne** [paʀizjɛ:n] Parisian (*takes a capital only when used as a noun referring to a person*)
parle: je parle [ʒəpaʀl] *pr ind 1st sg of* **parler**
parler [paʀle] to speak; **entendre parler de** to hear of

parlez: vous parlez [vupaʀle] *pr ind 2nd pl of* **parler**
parmi [paʀmi] among
part [paʀ] *f* share; **quelque part** somewhere; **nulle part** nowhere; **c'est gentil de votre part** it is nice of you
partager [paʀtaʒe] to divide
particulièrement [paʀtikyljɛʀmɑ̃] particularly
partie [paʀti] *f* part; **en partie** in part; **partie de pêche** fishing trip
partir [paʀtiʀ] to leave; **je pars** I leave, I am leaving
partout [paʀtu] everywhere
pas [pɑ] not; **ne . . . pas** not, no; **pas encore** not yet; **pas du tout** not at all
pas [pɑ] *m* step; **à deux pas d'ici** just a step from here
passant [pɑsɑ̃] *m* passer-by
passer [pɑse] to spend; to go by; **comme le temps passe!** how time flies!; **passer un examen** to take an examination; **se passer** [spɑse] to happen, take place; **passer par** to go through
Pasteur [pastœʀ] French scientist (1822-1895)
patiner [patine] to skate
pâtisserie [pɑtisʀi] *f* pastry, pastry shop
patrie [patri] *f* fatherland
patronne [patʀɔn] *f* patron saint
pauvre [povʀ] poor
payer [pɛje] to pay
pays [pei] *m* country
paysage [peizaʒ] *m* landscape
peau [po] *f* skin
pêche [pɛʃ] *f* fishing; **aller à la pêche** to go fishing
pêcheur [pɛʃœʀ] *m* fisherman
peindre [pɛ̃dʀ] to paint
peine [pɛn] *f* trouble; **ce n'est pas la peine** it is not worth while, don't bother; **à peine** scarcely, hardly
peint [pɛ̃] *p part of* **peindre**
peintre [pɛ̃tʀ] *m* painter
peinture [pɛ̃tyʀ] *f* painting
pendant [pɑ̃dɑ̃] during; **pendant que** as, while
pendre [pɑ̃dʀ] to hang
pendule [pɑ̃dyl] *f* clock
pénétrant [penetʀɑ̃] penetrating
pensée [pɑ̃se] *f* pansy
penser [pɑ̃se] to think, believe; **penser à** to think of; **penser de** to have an opinion about; **faire penser** to remind
penseur [pɑ̃sœʀ] *m* thinker; **le Penseur** a statue by Rodin
pension [pɑ̃sjɔ̃] *f* room and board
perdre [pɛʀdʀə] to lose
perdu [pɛʀdy] lost
père [pɛʀ] *m* father
permettre [pɛʀmɛtʀ] to allow
permission [pɛʀmisjɔ̃] *f* permission
personne [pɛʀsɔn] *f* person; no one, nobody; **ne . . . personne** no one
perspective [pɛʀspɛktiv] *f* perspective
petit [pəti] small, little; **petit déjeuner** breakfast
peu [pø] little; **un peu** a little; **à peu près** about; **racontez-nous un peu** just tell us
peur [pœʀ] *f* fear; **avoir peur de** to be afraid of; **avoir peur que** to be afraid that; **de peur que** for fear that
peut: il peut [ilpø] *pr ind 3rd sg of* **pouvoir**
peut-être [pøtɛtʀ] perhaps
pharmacie [faʀmasi] *f* drugstore
pharmacien [faʀmasjɛ̃] *m* druggist
Philadelphie [filadɛlfi] Philadelphia
photo [fɔto] *f* photograph, picture
photographie [fɔtɔgʀafi] *f* photograph, picture
phrase [fʀɑz] *f* sentence
piano [pjano] *m* piano
pièce [pjɛs] *f* coin; play; apiece; **dix francs (la) pièce** ten francs apiece; **pièce d'eau** ornamental pool
pied [pje] *m* foot; **aller à pied** to walk; **un pied de salade,** a head of lettuce
pierre [pjɛʀ] *f* stone
pigment [pigmɑ̃] *m* pigment
pique-nique [piknik] *m* picnic; **faire un pique-nique** to go on a picnic
pis [pi] worse; **tant pis** so much the worse, too bad
pistolet [pistɔlɛ] *m* pistol
pittoresque [pitɔʀɛsk] picturesque
pivoine [pivwan] *f* peony
place [plas] *f* square, space, room, seat; **il y a de la place** there is room; **à votre place** if I were you
placer [plase] to place
plafond [plafɔ̃] *m* ceiling
plage [plaʒ] *f* beach
plaignez: vous vous plaignez [vuvuplɛɲe] *pr ind 2nd pl of* **se plaindre**
plaindre: se plaindre [səplɛ̃dʀ] to complain

plaire [plɛʀ] to please; **s'il vous plaît** please; **est-ce que mon chapeau vous plaît?** do you like my hat?
plaisir [pleziʀ] *m* pleasure; **se faire un plaisir de** to be glad to
planter [plɑ̃te] to plant
plat *m* dish; **plat de viande** [pladvjɑ̃d] meat course, main course
plein [plɛ̃], **pleine** [plɛn] full; **en plein air** in the open
pleurer [plœʀe] to cry, weep
pleut: il pleut [ilplø] *pr ind 3rd sg of* **pleuvoir**
pleuvait: il pleuvait [ilplœvɛ] *imperf ind 3rd sg of* **pleuvoir**
pleuvoir [plœvwaʀ] to rain; **il pleut à verse** it is pouring
plu [ply] *p part of* **plaire** *and of* **pleuvoir**
pluie [plɥi] *f* rain
plume [plym] *f* feather, pen
plupart: la plupart [laplypaʀ] most, the greater part; **la plupart d'entre eux** most of them
pluriel [plyʀjɛl] *m* plural
plus [ply] more; **ne . . . plus** no more, no longer; **plus . . . que** more . . . than; **plus de** more than; **le plus grand** the tallest; **moi non plus** nor I either
plusieurs [plyzjœʀ] several
poche [pɔʃ] *f* pocket
poétique [pɔetik] poetic
point [pwɛ̃] *m* point; **point de vue** point of view
pointure [pwɛ̃tyʀ] *f* size
poire [pwaʀ] *f* pear
pois [pwɑ] *m* pea
poisson [pwasõ] *m* fish
police [pɔlis] *f* police; **agent de police** *m* policeman
politique [pɔlitik] political; **un homme politique** a statesman
pomme [pɔm] *f* apple; **pomme de terre** *f* potato
pont [põ] *m* bridge; **le Pont-Neuf** bridge in Paris
porc [pɔʀ] *m* pork, pig
port [pɔʀ] *m* port
porte [pɔʀt] *f* door, gate
portefeuille [pɔʀtəfœj] *m* pocketbook, billfold
porte-monnaie [pɔʀtəmɔnɛ] *m* change purse
porter [pɔʀte] to carry, wear, bear
portrait [pɔʀtʀɛ] *m* portrait
poser [poze] to set, lay, place; **poser une question** to ask a question
position [pɔzisjõ] *f* position
possession [pɔsɛsjõ] *f* possession
possible [pɔsibl] possible
poste [pɔst] *f* post, post office
potager [pɔtaʒe] *adj* vegetable
poulet [pulɛ] *m* chicken
pour [puʀ] to, for, in order to, so as to; **pour que** in order that, so that
pourquoi [puʀkwa] why; **pourquoi pas?** why not?
pourrai: je pourrai [ʒəpuʀe] *fut 1st sg of* **pouvoir**
pourtant [puʀtɑ̃] however
pousser [puse] to grow; **faire pousser** to grow (*transitive*)
pouvez: vous pouvez [vupuve] *pr ind 2nd pl of* **pouvoir**
pouvoir [puvwaʀ] to be able to, can, could, may, might
précédent [pʀesedɑ̃] preceding
préfecture [pʀefɛktyʀ] *f* office of a "préfet," administrator of a "département"
préférer [pʀefeʀe] to prefer
premier [pʀəmje], **première** [pʀəmjɛʀ] first; **le premier avril** the first of April; **premier** [pʀəmje] *m* second floor
prendre [pʀɑ̃dʀ] to take; **prendre quelque chose** to have something to eat or to drink
prends: je prends [ʒəpʀɑ̃] *pr ind 1st sg of* **prendre**
prenez: vous prenez [vupʀəne] *pr ind 2nd pl of* **prendre**
préoccupé [pʀeɔkype] worried
préparation [pʀepaʀasjõ] *f* preparation, making
près [pʀɛ] near, near by; **près de** near; **à peu près** about; **tout près** very close
présentation [pʀezɑ̃tasjõ] *f* presentation, introduction
présenter [pʀezɑ̃te] to introduce; **se présenter** to appear
président [pʀesidɑ̃] *m* president
presque [pʀɛskə] almost
pressé [pʀɛse]; **être pressé** to be in a hurry
prêt [pʀɛ] ready
prêter [pʀɛte] to lend

prévenir [pRevniR] to warn (*conjug like* **venir**)
prier [pRije] to pray; **Je vous en prie** You are welcome
principal [pRɛ̃sipal] principal
printemps [pRɛ̃tɑ̃] *m* spring; **au printemps** in the spring
pris [pRi] *p part of* **prendre**
prise [pRiz] *f* taking
Prisunic [pRizynik] *m* ten-cent store
prix [pRi] *m* price
procès-verbal [pRɔsɛvɛRbal] *m* police ticket
prochain [pRɔʃɛ̃], **prochaine** [pRɔʃɛn] next; **dimanche prochain** next Sunday; **la semaine prochaine** next week
procurer: se procurer [spRɔkyRe] to get
produit [pRɔdɥi] *m* product
professeur [pRɔfɛsœR] *m* professor
profession [pRɔfɛsjõ] *f* profession
profiter de [pRɔfite də] to take advantage of
progrès [pRɔgRɛ] *m* progress
prohibé [pRɔibe] forbidden; **arme prohibée** concealed weapon
projet [pRɔʒɛ] *m* plan
promenade [pRɔmnad] *f* walk, drive; **faire une promenade** to take a walk
promener: se promener [spRɔmne] to take a walk
promettre [pRɔmɛtR] to promise
pronom [pRɔnõ] *m* pronoun
proposer [pRɔpoze] to suggest
propre [pRɔpR] own
prospère [pRɔspɛR] prosperous
Provence [pRɔvɑ̃s] *f* province in south of France
province [pRɔvɛ̃s] *f* out of Paris (in the provinces)
provision [pRɔvizjõ] *f* supply; **provisions** provisions
psychologue [psikɔlɔg] *m* psychologist
put [py] *p part of* **pouvoir**
public [pyblik], **publique** [pyblik] public; **jardin public** public park
puis [pɥi] then; **et puis** and besides
puisque [pɥisk] since
puissent: ils puissent [ilpɥis] *pr subj 3rd pl of* **pouvoir**
pull-over [pylovɛR] *m* sweater
purement [pyRmɑ̃] purely
Pyrénées: les Pyrénées [lepiRene] *f pl* chain of mountains in southern France

Q

qu' *see* **que**
quai [ke] *m* platform, street along a river
qualité [kalite] *f* quality
quand [kɑ̃] when, when?; **depuis quand?** how long? since when?
quarante [kaRɑ̃t] forty
quart [kaR] *m* quarter; **onze heures et quart** a quarter past eleven; **onze heures moins le quart** a quarter to eleven
quartier [kaRtje] *m* quarter, part of a city
quatorze [katɔRz] fourteen
quatre [katR] four
quatre-vingt-dix [katRəvɛ̃dis] ninety
quatre-vingts [katRəvɛ̃] eighty
quatrième [katRijɛm] fourth
que [kə] *rel pron* whom, which; **ce que** [skə] that which, what; **que?** [kə]; **qu'est-ce qui?** [kɛski]; **qu'est-ce que?** [kɛskə] what?; **qu'est-ce que c'est que?** what is?; **que** *conj* that
quel? quelle? quels? quelles? [kɛl] *interrog adj* **what?; quel . . .!** what a . . .!
quelque, quelques [kɛlkə] some, a few; **quelque chose** something
quelquefois [kɛlkəfwa] sometimes
quelques-uns [kɛlkəzœ̃], **quelques-unes** [kɛlkəzyn] some, a few
quelqu'un [kɛlkœ̃] somebody, someone
question [kɛstjõ] *f* question
qui [ki] *rel pron* who, whom, which; **ce qui** [ski] what; **qui?** [ki] *interrog pron* who? whom?; **qui est-ce qui?** who?; **qui est-ce que?** whom?; **à qui est cette cravate?** whose tie is this?
quincaillerie [kɛ̃kajRi] *f* hardware store
quinze [kɛ̃z] fifteen; **Quinze-Vingts** [kɛ̃z vɛ̃] i.e. 300, name of a hospital in Paris
quinzième [kɛ̃zjɛm] fifteenth
quitter [kite] to leave
quoi [kwa] what, what?; **à quoi bon?** what is the use?; **il y a de quoi** there is reason for it; **il n y a pas de quoi** you are welcome

R

raconter [Rakõte] to tell, to narrate
rafraîchissant [RafRɛʃisɑ̃] cooling
raisin [Rɛzɛ̃] *m* grapes

raison [rɛzõ] *f* reason; **avoir raison** to be right
ramasser [ramɑse] to pick, pick up, gather
ramener [ramne] to bring back; to restore
rappeler [raple] to remind; **se rappeler** to remember
rapporter [rapɔrte] to take back, bring back
rare [rar] rare
rarement [rarmɑ̃] seldom
ravager [ravaʒe] to ravage
rayonner [rɛjɔne] to radiate
réalité [realite] *f* reality
recevoir [rəsəvwar] to receive
recevrai: je recevrai [ʒərəsəvre] *fut 1st sg of* **recevoir**
réciter [resite] to recite
recommander [rəkɔmɑ̃de] to recommend
reconnaissant [rəkɔnɛsɑ̃] grateful
reconnaître [rəkɔnɛtr] to recognize
reconstruire [rəkõstrɥir] to rebuild
reçu [rəsy] *p part of* **recevoir**
refus [rəfy] *m* refusal
refuser [rəfyze] to refuse
regarder [rəgarde] to look, look at
région [reʒjõ] *f* region
règle [rɛgl] *f* rule; **en règle** in order
règne [rɛɲ] *m* reign
regretter [rəgrɛte] to regret, be sorry for
Reims [rɛ̃s] Rheims, city in eastern France
reine [rɛn] *f* queen
rejoindre [rəʒwɛ̃dr] to meet, catch up with
relativement [rəlativmɑ̃] relatively
religieux [rəliʒjø] religious
remarquer [rəmarke] to notice, to observe
remède [rəmɛd] *m* remedy
remercier [rəmɛrsje] to thank
remettre [rəmɛtr] to put back
remplacer [rɑ̃plase] to replace
Renaissance [rənɛsɑ̃s] *f* Renaissance
rencontre [rɑ̃kõtr] *f* meeting; **aller, venir à la rencontre** to go to meet
rencontrer [rɑ̃kõtre] to meet
rendez-vous [rɑ̃devu] *m* appointment
rendre [rɑ̃dr] to render, give back; to make; **est-ce que cela vous rend triste?** does it make you sad?; **se rendre compte** to realize
rendu [rɑ̃dy] *p part of* **rendre**
renseignement [rɑ̃sɛɲmɑ̃] *m* information
renseigner [rɑ̃sɛɲe] to inform, give out information
réparation [reparasjõ] *f* repair
réparer [repare] to repair; **faire réparer** to have (something) repaired
repartir [rəpartir] to leave again, set out again
repas [rəpɑ] *m* meal
répéter [repete] to repeat
répondez: vous répondez [vurepõde] *pr ind 2nd pl of* **répondre**
répondre [repõdr] to answer
réponse [repõs] *f* answer
reposer: se reposer [sərpoze] to rest
représentation [rəprezɑ̃tasjõ] *f* performance
représenter [rəprezɑ̃te] to represent
réserver [rezɛrve] to reserve
résidence [rezidɑ̃s] *f* residence
résignation [reziɲasjõ] *f* resignation
responsable [rɛspõsabl] responsible
ressembler à [rəsɑ̃ble a] to resemble, look like
ressort [rəsɔr] *m* spring
restaurant [rɛstɔrɑ̃] *m* restaurant
reste [rɛst] *m* rest, remainder
rester [rɛste] to stay; to be left, remain; **il reste** there remains, there remain
rétabli [retabli] recovered
retard [rətar] *m* delay, lateness; **en retard** late
retour [rətur] *m* return; **aller et retour** round trip; **être de retour** to be back
retourner [rəturne] to go back; **se retourner** [sərturne] to turn around
retrouver [rətruve] to find again, meet
réussir à [reysir a] to succeed in
réveiller: se réveiller [sərevɛje] to wake up
réveillon [revɛjõ] *m* meal eaten on Christmas Eve at midnight
revenir [rəvnir] to return
révision [revizjõ] *f* review
revoir [rəvwar] to see again (*conjug like* **voir**); **au revoir** good-bye
Révolution, la [revɔlysjõ] the French Revolution
révolutionnaire [revɔlysjɔnɛr] revolutionary
revue [rəvy] *f* review, magazine
rhume [rym] *m* cold
riant [riɑ̃] *pres part of* **rire**
riche [riʃ] rich
rien [rjɛ̃] nothing; **ne . . . rien** nothing; **de rien** you are welcome; **rien d'intéressant** nothing interesting

rire [RiR] to laugh
risquer de [Riske də] to risk
rive [Riv] *f* bank; **la rive droite** the right bank of the Seine in Paris; **la rive gauche** the left bank
rivière [RivjɛR] *f* river, creek
robe [Rɔb] *f* dress
Rodin [Rɔdɛ̃] French sculptor (1840-1917)
roi [Rwa] *m* king
rôle [Rol] *m* rôle, part
roman [Rɔmɑ̃] *m* novel; **roman policier** detective story
roman [Rɔmɑ̃], **romane** [Rɔman] romanesque (architecture)
Rome [Rɔm] Rome
Ronsard [Rɔ̃saR] French poet (1524-1585)
rosbif [Rɔsbif] *m* roast beef
rose [Roz] rosy, pink
rose [Roz] *f* rose
rosier [Rozje] *m* rosebush
Rouen [Rwɑ̃] city in Normandy
rouge [Ruʒ] red
rouler [Rule] to roll along
route [Rut] *f* road; **en route** on the way; **la bonne route** the right road; **la mauvaise route** the wrong road
royal [Rwajal] royal
rue [Ry] *f* street
ruine [Rɥin] *f* ruin
russe [Rys] Russian (*takes a capital only when used as a noun referring to a person*)
Russie [Rysi] *f* Russia

S

s' *see* **si** *or* **se**
sa *see* **son**
sable [sabl] *m* sand
sac [sak] *m* bag
sacrifice [sakRifis] *m* sacrifice
sain et sauf [sɛ̃ e sof] safe and sound
saint [sɛ̃] saint, holy; **la Sainte-Chapelle** XIIIth century church in Paris; **Saint-Germain-des-Prés** [sɛ̃ʒɛRmɛ̃ dɛ pRe] section of Paris near the university and popular with students; **Saint-Malo** [sɛ̃ malo] old city on the coast of Brittany
sais: je sais [ʒəsɛ] *pr ind 1st sg of* **savoir**
saison [sɛzɔ̃] *f* season
sait: il sait [ilsɛ] *pr ind 3rd sg of* **savoir**
salade [salad] *f* salad; lettuce, etc.
salle [sal] *f* room; **salle à manger** dining room; **salle de bain** bathroom
salon [salɔ̃] *m* living room
samedi [samdi] *m* Saturday
sandwich [sɑ̃dwitʃ] *m* sandwich
sans [sɑ̃] without
satisfaction [satisfaksjɔ̃] *f* satisfaction
satisfait [satisfɛ] satisfied
sauf [sɔf] except
sauriez: vous sauriez [vusɔRje] *cond 2nd pl of* **savoir**
sauterie [sotRi] *f* small dance
sauvage [sovaʒ] wild
sauver [sove] to save
savez: vous savez [vusave] *pr ind 2nd pl of* **savoir**
savoir [savwaR] to know, know how
scène [sɛn] *f* scene
science [sjɑ̃s] *f* science
sculpture [skyltyR] *f* sculpture
se [sə] oneself, himself, herself, themselves; to oneself, etc.
second [səgɔ̃] second; **seconde** *f* second class
Seine [sɛn] *f* Seine
seize [sɛz] sixteen
selon [səlɔ̃] according to
semaine [səmɛn] *f* week; **la semaine prochaine** next week
sembler [sɑ̃ble] to seem
Sénégal [senegal] *m* Senegal
sentiment [sɑ̃timɑ̃] *m* sentiment
sentir [sɑ̃tiR] to smell; **se sentir** to feel
séparer [sɛpaRe] to separate
sept [sɛt] seven
septembre [sɛptɑ̃bR] *m* September
septième [sɛtjɛm] seventh
sépulture [sepyltyR] *f* burial
serai: je serai [ʒəsRe] *fut 1st sg of* **être**
série [seRi] *f* series
sérieux [seRjø], **sérieuse** [seRjøz] serious
serpent [sɛRpɑ̃] *m* snake
sert: il sert [ilsɛR] *pr ind 3rd sg of* **servir**
service [sɛRvis] *m* service; **à votre service** you are welcome
servir à [sɛRviR a] to serve, be of use; **se servir de** to use; **se servir** to help oneself; **servir de** to be used as
ses *see* **son**
seul, seule [sœl] alone, single

seulement [sœlmɑ̃] only, but
si [si] if, whether, so; **si** [si] yes; **mais si** oh yes
siècle [sjɛkl] *m* century; **au treizième siècle** in the thirteenth century
sien: le sien [ləsjɛ̃], **la sienne** [lasjɛn], **les siens** [lesjɛ̃], **les siennes** [lesjɛn] *poss pron* his, hers
silencieux [silɑ̃sjø], **silencieuse** [silɑ̃sjøz] silent
silhouette [silwɛt] *f* figure
simple [sɛ̃pl] simple
simplement [sɛ̃pləmɑ̃] simply, merely
singe [sɛ̃ʒ] *m* monkey
situé [sitɥe] situated
six [sis] six
sixième [sizjɛm] sixth
ski [ski] *m* ski; **faire du ski** to go skiing
société [sɔsjete] *f* society
sœur [sœʀ] *f* sister
soie [swa] *f* silk
soif [swaf] *f* thirst; **avoir soif** to be thirsty
soigner [swaɲe]: **se soigner** to take care of oneself
soir [swaʀ] *m* evening; **le soir** in the evening; **hier soir** last night
soirée [swaʀe] *f* evening
soit: il soit [ilswa] *pr subj 3rd sg of* **être**; **soit . . . soit** either . . . or
soixante [swasɑ̃t] sixty
soixante-dix [swasɑ̃tdis] seventy
sol [sɔl] *m* soil, ground
sole [sɔl] *f* a choice fish, which is different from the common flounder referred to in the expression "fillet of sole"
soleil [sɔlɛj] *m* sun, sunshine; **il fait du soleil** the sun is shining
sombre [sõbʀ] dark
somme [sɔm] *m* nap; **faire un somme** to take a nap
sommeil [sɔmɛj] *m* sleep
sommes: nous sommes [nusɔm] *pr ind 1st pl of* **être**
somptueux [sõptɥø], **somptueuse** [sõptɥøz] sumptuous
son [sõ], **sa** [sa], **ses** [se] *poss adj* his, her, its
sonner [sɔne] to ring
sont; ils sont [ilsõ] *pr ind 3rd pl of* **être**
Sorbon [sɔʀbõ] founder of the Sorbonne (1201-1274)
Sorbonne: la Sorbonne [lasɔʀbɔn] Division of Humanities of the University of Paris
sort [sɔʀ] *m* fate
sorte [sɔʀt] *f* sort, kind; **de sorte que** so that
sortie [sɔʀti] *f* exit, going out
sortir [sɔʀtiʀ] to go out
soufflé [sufle] *m* soufflé
souffrir [sufʀiʀ] to suffer (*conjug like* **ouvrir**)
souhaiter [swɛte] to wish
soulier [sulje] *m* shoe
souligné [suliɲe] underlined
soupe [sup] *f* soup
sourire [suʀiʀ] *m* smile
sous [su] under
souterrain [sutɛʀɛ̃] underground
souvenir [suvniʀ] *m* souvenir
souvenir: se souvenir [səsuvnir] to remember (*conjug like* **venir**)
souvent [suvɑ̃] often
soyez: vous soyez [vuswaje] *pr subj 2nd pl of* **être**
spécialement [spesjalmɑ̃] especially
spécialité [spesjalite] *f* specialty
spectacle [spɛktakl] *m* spectacle
spectateur [spɛktatœʀ] *m* spectator
spirituel [spiʀitɥɛl] spiritual
spirituellement [spiʀitɥɛlmɑ̃] mentally
splendeur [splɑ̃dœʀ] *f* splendor
statue [staty] *f* statue
style [stil] *m* style
substantif [sypstɑ̃tif] *m* noun
succéder [syksede] to follow, to be followed
sucre [sykʀ] *m* sugar
Sud [syd] *m* South
suédois [sɥedwa] Swedish
suffit: il suffit [il syfi] one only has to
suggérer [sygʒeʀe] to suggest
suis: je suis [ʒesɥi] *pr ind 1st sg of* **être; je suis** [ʒəsɥi] *pr ind 1st sg of* **suivre**
Suisse [sɥis] *f* Switzerland
suite [sɥit] *f* succession, continuation; **tout de suite** [tut sɥit] right away
suivant [sɥivɑ̃] following
suivre [sɥivʀ] to follow, to take (a course)
sujet [syʒɛ] *m* subject; **au sujet de** about
super-marché [sypɛʀmaʀʃe] *m* supermarket
supplémentaire [syplemɑ̃tɛʀ] supplementary
supportable [sypɔʀtabl] bearable, endurable
sur [syʀ] on, upon, about
sûr [syʀ] sure
sûrement [syʀmɑ̃] surely, certainly
surpris [syʀpʀi] surprised *p part of* **surprendre**

surprise [syRpRiz] *f* surprise
surtout [syRtu] above all
symboliser [sɛ̃bɔlize] to symbolize
symbolisme [sɛ̃bɔlism] *m* symbolism
symétrie [simetRi] *f* symmetry
sympathique [sɛ̃patik] friendly, congenial

T

tabac [taba] *m* tobacco
table [tabl] *f* table
tableau [tablo] *m* picture, painting
tailler [taje] to trim
tailleur [tajœR] *m* tailor
talent [talɑ̃] *m* talent
tandis que [tɑ̃di(s)kə] while
tant [tɑ̃] so much, so many; **tant mieux** so much the better
tante [tɑ̃t] *f* aunt
tapis [tapi] *m* rug
tapisserie [tapisRi] *f* tapestry
tard [taR] late; **plus tard** later; **au plus tard** at the latest
tasse [tas] *f* cup
taxi [taksi] *m* taxi
te [tə] to you, for you (*familiar*)
tel: un tel [œ̃tɛl], **une telle** [yntɛl], **de tels** [dətɛl], **de telles** [dətɛl] such a, such
téléphone [telefɔn] *m* telephone
téléphoner [telefɔne] to telephone
télévision [televizjõ] *f* television
témoin [temwɛ̃] *m* witness; **être témoin de** to witness
température [tɑ̃peRatyR] *f* temperature
temple [tɑ̃pl] *m* temple
temps [tɑ̃] *m* time, weather; **emploi du temps** *m* schedule; **quel temps fait-il?** how is the weather?; **à temps** on time; **combien de temps?** how long?; **avoir le temps de** to have time to; **au temps où** at the time when
tendre [tɑ̃dR] to hold out, to offer
tenez! [təne] here!
tenir [tənir] to hold, to keep; **tenir un petit café** to run a bistro
tennis [tɛnis] *m* tennis; **jouer au tennis** to play tennis
terminer [tɛRmine] to finish
terrasse [tɛRas] *f* terrace
terre [tɛR] *f* earth, ground
tête [tɛt] *f* head
texte [tɛkst] *m* text
thé [te] *m* tea
théâtre [teɑtR] *m* theatre
théologie [teɔlɔʒi] *f* theology
tien: le tien [lətjɛ̃], **la tienne** [latjɛn], **les tiens** [letjɛ̃], **les tiennes** [letjɛn] yours (*familiar*)
tiens! [tjɛ̃] well!
tient: il tient [iltjɛ̃] *pr ind 3rd sg of* **tenir**
timbre [tɛ̃bR] *m* stamp; **timbre-poste** postage stamp
tirer [tiRe] to pull
tiroir [tiRwaR] *m* drawer
titre [titR] *m* title
toi [twa] you (*familiar*)
toit [twa] *m* roof
tomate [tɔmat] *f* tomato
tombeau [tõbo] *m* monumental tomb
tomber [tõbe] to fall
ton [tõ), **ta** [ta], **tes** [te] your (*familiar*)
torche [tɔRʃ] *f* torch
tort [tɔR] *m* wrong; **avoir tort** to be wrong
tôt [to] soon; **plus tôt** sooner; **le plus tôt possible** as soon as possible
toucher [tuʃe] to touch; **toucher un chèque** to cash a check
toujours [tuʒuR] always, still
tour [tuR] *f* tower
touriste [tuRist] *m* tourist
tourner [tuRne] to turn
Tours [tuR] city in Touraine
tousser [tuse] to cough
tout [tu], **toute** [tut], **tous** [tu], **toutes** [tut] *adj* all, every; **toute la journée** all day; **tous les jours** every day; **tout le monde** everybody; **tout** [tu], **toute** [tut], **tous** [tus], **toutes** [tut] *pron* all, everybody, everything; **tout** [tu] *adv* all, quite, completely; **tout à fait** quite; **tout de suite** right away; **tout à l'heure** a while ago, in a while; **pas du tout** not at all; **tout de même** all the same; **rien du tout** nothing at all; **tout à coup** suddenly
trace [tRas] *f* trace
tracteur [tRaktœR] *m* tractor
tradition [tRadisjõ] *f* tradition
traditionnel [tRadisjɔnɛl] traditional
train [tRɛ̃] *m* train; **en train de** in the act of
tranquille [tRɑ̃kil] quiet; **soyez tranquille** don't worry
transformer [tRɑ̃sfɔRme] to transform
transposer [tRɑ̃spoze] to transpose

travail [tʀavaj] *m, pl* **travaux** [tʀavo] work
travailler [tʀavaje] to work
travers: à travers [atʀavɛʀ] through
traverser [tʀavɛʀse] to cross
treize [tʀɛz] thirteen
treizième [tʀɛzjɛm] thirteenth
trente [tʀɑ̃t] thirty
très [tʀɛ] very, very much
Trianon [tʀijanõ] *m* name of two small châteaux in the park of the Versailles palace
triste [tʀist] sad
Troglodyte [tʀɔglɔdit] *m* cave dweller
trois [tʀwɑ] three
troisième [tʀwɑzjɛm] third
tromper: se tromper [stʀõpe] to be mistaken, to miss (a road, etc.)
trop [tʀo] too, too much, too many
trou [tʀu] *m* hole
trouver [tʀuve] to find, think; **comment la trouvez-vous?** how do you like it?; **vous trouvez?** do you think so?; **se trouver** to be, be located
tu [ty] you (*familiar*)
tuer [tɥe] to kill
Tuileries: les Tuileries [letɥilʀi] park in Paris
tulipe [tylip] *f* tulip
Turquie [tyʀki] *f* Turkey

U

un [œ̃] *m* a, an; one; **l'un** one
une [yn] *f* a, an; one; **l'une** one
unique [ynik] unique
université [ynivɛʀsite] *f* University
uns: les uns [lezœ̃], **les unes** [lezyn] some; **les un(e)s . . . les autres** some . . . the others: **les un(e)s . . . d'autres** some . . . others
user [yze] to wear out
usine [yzin] *f* factory, plant
ustensile [ystɑ̃sil] *m* utensil
utile [ytil] useful; *nm* something useful

V

va: il va [ilva] *pr ind 3rd sg of* **aller**
vacances [vakɑ̃s] *f pl* vacation, holiday; **en vacances** on vacation
vache [vaʃ] *f* cow
vais: je vais [ʒəvɛ] *pr ind 1st sg of* **aller**
valeur [valœʀ] *f* value; **avoir de la valeur** to be valuable
valoir [valwaʀ] to be worth; **il vaut mieux** it is better, it is preferable
vaste [vast] vast
Vaugirard: rue de Vaugirard [ʀydvoʒiʀaʀ] street in Paris
vaut: il vaut [ilvo] *pr ind 3rd sg of* **valoir**
véhémence [veɛmɑ̃s]: **avec véhémence** violently
venant [vənɑ̃] *pr part of* **venir**
vend: il vend [ilvɑ̃] *pr ind 3rd sg of* **vendre**
vendanges [vɑ̃dɑ̃ʒ] *f pl* grape gathering
vendeur [vɑ̃dœʀ], **vendeuse** [vɑ̃døz] salesman, salesgirl
vendre [vɑ̃dʀ] to sell
vendredi [vɑ̃dʀədi] *m* Friday
venez: vous venez [vuvne] *pr ind 2nd pl of* **venir**
venir [vənir] to come; **faire venir** to have . . . come; **venir de** to have just; **il vient d'arriver** he has just come; **il venait d'arriver** he had just come
vent [vɑ̃] *m* wind; **il fait du vent** it is windy
véritablement [veʀitabləmɑ̃] really
verre [vɛʀ] *m* glass, lens
verrons: nous verrons [nuvɛʀõ] *fut 1st pl of* **voir**
vers [vɛʀ] towards, about; **vers deux heures** around two o'clock
Versailles [vɛʀsaj] city near Paris
verser [vɛʀse] to pour; **il pleut à verse** it is pouring
version [vɛʀsjõ] *f* version, account
veston [vɛstõ] *m* coat
veut: il veut [ilvø] *pr ind 3rd sg of* **vouloir**
veux: je veux [ʒəvø] *pr ind 1st sing of* **vouloir**
viande [vjɑ̃d] *f* meat
victime [viktim] *f* victim
vie [vi] *f* life
viens: je viens [ʒəvjɛ̃] *pr ind 1st sg of* **venir; je viens de** I have just . . .
vient: il vient [ilvjɛ̃] *pr ind 3rd sg of* **venir**
vieux [vjø] *m*, **vieil** [vjɛj] *m*, **vieille** [vjɛj] *f*, **vieux** [vjø] *m pl*, **vieilles** [vjɛj] *f pl* old; **mon vieux** pal, old man
vigne [viɲ] *f* vine, vineyard
vignoble [viɲɔbl] *m* vineyard
village [vilaʒ] *m* village
ville [vil] *f* city, town; **en ville** downtown
vin [vɛ̃] *m* wine
vingt [vɛ̃] twenty

violent [vjɔlɑ̃] violent
violette [vjɔlɛt] *f* violet
violon [vjɔlɔ̃] *m* violin
visite [vizit] *f* visit
visiter [vizite] to visit
visiteur [vizitœʀ] *m* visitor
vite [vit] fast
vitesse [vitɛs] *f* speed; **à toute vitesse** at great speed
vitrail [vitʀaj] *m*, **vitraux** [vitʀo] *pl* stained-glass window
vitrine [vitʀin] *f* show window
vivait: il vivait [ilvivɛ] *imperf ind 3rd sg of* **vivre**
vivant: de son vivant [də sɔ̃ vivɑ̃] when alive
vivre [vivʀ] to live
voici [vwasi] here is; **le voici, la voici** here it is, here he is, here she is
voie [vwa] *f* track
voile [vwal] *f* sail; **bateau à voile** *m* sail boat
voir [vwaʀ] to see; **voir venir** to see . . . coming
vois: je vois [ʒəvwa] *pr ind 1st sg of* **voir**
voisin [vwazɛ̃], **voisine** [vwazin] neighbor, neighboring; **voisin de** near
voisinage [vwazinaʒ] *m* neighborhood
voiture [vwatyʀ] *f* car
voix [vwa] *f* voice; **à voix basse** in a low voice
volant [vɔlɑ̃] *m* steering wheel
volcan [vɔlkɑ̃] *m* volcano
volet [vɔlɛ] *m* shutter
volontiers [vɔlɔ̃tje] willingly, gladly
Voltaire [vɔltɛʀ] French philosopher and writer (1694-1778)
vos *see* **votre**
votre [vɔtʀ], **vos** [vo] *poss adj* your
vôtre: le vôtre [ləvotʀ], **la vôtre** [lavotʀ], **les vôtres** [levotʀ] *poss pron* yours
voudrais: je voudrais [ʒəvudʀɛ] *cond 1st sg of* **vouloir**
voulez: vous voulez [vuvule] *pr ind 2nd pl of* **vouloir**
vouloir [vulwaʀ] to want, wish; to like; **vouloir bien** to be willing, be kind enough to; **je voudrais bien** I would like; **vouloir dire** to mean; **Que voulez-vous!** Well!
vous [vu] you, to you
voûte [vut] *f* arch
voyage [vwajaʒ] *m* trip
voyez: vous voyez [vuvwaje] *pr ind 2nd pl of* **voir**
voyons [vwajɔ̃] *imper 1st pl of* **voir**
vrai [vʀɛ] true
vraiment [vʀɛmɑ̃] truly, really
vu [vy] *p part of* **voir**
vue [vy] *f* view, sight; **point de vue** *m* point of view; **vue d'ensemble** general view

W

wagon [vagɔ̃] *m* car; **wagon-restaurant** diner
week-end [wikɛnd] *m* weekend

Y

y [i] to it, at it, to them, at them, there; **il y a** there is, there are; **y a-t-il?** is there? are there?; **il y avait** there was, there were; **il y a cinq ans** five years ago; **il y a un quart d'heure que j'attends** I have been waiting for fifteen minutes; **qu'est-ce qu'il y a?** what is the matter?
yeux [jø] *pl of* **œil; elle a les yeux bleus** she has blue eyes

Z

zéro [zeʀo] zero
zut! [zyt] confound it!

English-French

A

a un *m*, une *f*
able: to be able to pouvoir
about *prep* vers; *adv* à peu près, environ; *prep* au sujet de, à propos de; **about what time?** vers quelle heure?; **about one hundred** une centaine; **what about you?** et vous?; **how about going fishing?** si nous allions à la pêche?
above au-dessus de; **above all** surtout
abroad à l'étranger
absent absent
accent accent *m*
accept accepter
accident accident *m*
according to d'après
acquaintance connaissance *f;* **I made his acquaintance** j'ai fait sa connaissance
acquainted: to be acquainted with connaître
across en face de, de l'autre côté de
act: to act as servir de
active actif *m*, active *f*
actor, actress acteur, actrice
adjective adjectif *m*
admirable admirable
admire admirer
advantage avantage *m;* **to take advantage of** profiter de
advice conseil *m;* **to follow (an) advice** suivre un conseil
advise: to advise conseiller
affirmative affirmatif *m*, affirmative *f*
affirmatively affirmativement
afraid: to be afraid of avoir peur de; **I am afraid so** j'en ai peur
Africa Afrique *f;* **North Africa** l'Afrique du Nord
after après; **after having gone to Normandy, he went to Brittany** après être allé en Normandie, il est allé en Bretagne
afternoon après-midi *m;* **in the afternoon** l'après-midi
afterwards après, ensuite
again de nouveau, encore
age âge *m;* **how old are you?** quel âge avez-vous?
ago: five years ago il y a cinq ans; **a while ago** tout à l'heure; **some time ago** il y a quelque temps
agree être de l'avis de, être d'accord avec
agreeable agréable
agreed c'est entendu, entendu
ahead: straight ahead tout droit
air air *m;* **in the open air** en plein air
album album *m*
all tout, toute, tous, toutes; **is that all?** est-ce tout?; **not at all** pas du tout; **all of Paris** Paris tout entier; **all right** c'est entendu; **it is all right with me** cela m'est égal
allow permettre de
all right bon, bien, pas mal
almost presque
along le long de; **to go along** accompagner, suivre, venir
Alps Alpes *f pl*
already déjà
also aussi
although bien que, quoique
always toujours
am: I am je suis
America Amérique *f;* **South America** l'Amérique du Sud
American américain *m*, américaine *f*
among entre, parmi; **among others** entre autres
amusing amusant
an du, de la, de l', de, en; **not any** ne . . . pas de; **not any more** . . . ne . . . plus (de)
and et
angry fâché
announce annoncer
another un autre *m*, une autre *f*
answer réponse *f;* **to answer** répondre
any un *m*, une *f*
anyone quelqu'un; **not . . . anyone** ne . . . personne
anything quelque chose; **not . . . anything** ne . . . rien
anyway tout de même; d'ailleurs
apologize s'excuser de
appear: to appear se présenter

appetite appétit *m*
apple pomme *f*
appointment rendez-vous *m*
April avril *m*
arch arc *m;* **arch of triumph** arc de triomphe; **round arch** arc en demi-cercle
architect architecte *m*
are: they are ils sont; **there are** il y a; **you are** vous êtes; **are you?** êtes-vous?
armchair fauteuil *m*
army armée *f*
around vers, autour de; **around five o'clock** vers cinq heures; **around Paris** autour de Paris
arrival arrivée *f*
arrive arriver; **it arrives** il arrive
art art *m*
article article *m*
artist artiste *m*
as comme, pendant que; **as . . . as** aussi . . . que
ask demander, poser une question
asleep endormi; **to fall asleep** s'endormir
asparagus asperge *f*
aspect aspect *m*
aspirin aspirine *f*
astonish étonner
at à, chez; **at the** au, à la, à l', aux; **at Marie's** chez Marie; **at about six o'clock** vers six heures
Athens Athènes
Atlantic Atlantique
attain atteindre
attention attention *f*
attentively attentivement
attract attirer
August août *m*
aunt tante *f*
author auteur *m*
auto auto *f*
autumn automne *m*
avenue avenue *f*
await attendre
away: to go away partir, s'en aller; **right away** tout de suite; **to send away** renvoyer
awkward maladroit

B

back: to go back (home) rentrer; **to be back** être de retour
bad mauvais; **it is too bad** c'est dommage; **too bad** tant pis
badly mal
bag sac *m*
bakery boulangerie *f*
banana banane *f*
bank banque *f;* rive *f*
banker banquier *m*
barber coiffeur *m;* **to the barber's** chez le coiffeur
bath bain *m;* **bathroom** salle de bain *f*
battle bataille *f*
be: to be être; **how are you?** comment allez-vous?; **I am well** je vais bien; **he will be** il sera; **he would be** il serait; **there is, there are** il y a; **there was, there were** il y avait; **there will be** il y aura; **to be cold** avoir froid; **to be hungry** avoir faim; **to be right** avoir raison; **to be wrong** avoir tort; **to be (located)** se trouver; **to be (used) for** servir à; **I am to** je dois; **I was to** je devais
beach plage *f*
bean *haricot *m*
bear ours *m*
bear: to bear porter; supporter
beautiful beau, bel *m;* belle *f;* beaux *m pl;* belles *f pl*
because parce que; **because of** à cause de
become devenir
becoming: your hat is very becoming votre chapeau vous va très bien
bed lit; **to go to bed** se coucher; **to stay in bed** rester au lit
beef bœuf *m;* **roast beef** rosbif *m*
been été *p part of* être
beer bière *f*
beet betterave *f;* **sugar beet** betterave à sucre
before (*time*) avant, avant que; déjà; (*place*) devant
begin commencer, se mettre à
beginning commencement *m*
behind derrière
Belgium Belgique *f*
believe croire, penser
belong appartenir à, être à
beside à côté de
besides puis, d'ailleurs, en outre
best *adj* le meilleur, la meilleure, les meilleurs, les meilleures; *adv* le mieux; **the best he could** de son mieux

better *adj* meilleur, meilleure, meilleurs, meilleures; *adv* mieux; **I like spring better** j'aime mieux le printemps; **so much the better** tant mieux; **I am better** je vais mieux; **it is better to** il vaut mieux; **it would be better to** il vaudrait mieux
bicycle bicyclette *f;* **to bicycle** aller à bicyclette
big grand, gros; **that big** gros comme ça
bill addition *f;* facture *f;* **a fifty-franc bill** un billet de cinquante francs
billfold portefeuille *m*
bird oiseau *m*
birthday anniversaire *m*
bit: a bit un peu
bite: to bite mordre
black noir
blind aveugle
blond blond
blue bleu, bleue, bleus, bleues
board: room and board pension *f*
boat bateau *m*
bone os *m*
book livre *m;* **secondhand book dealer** bouquiniste *m;* **secondhand book** livre d'occasion
bookstore librairie *f*
born né; **to be born** naître
botany botanique *m*
bother: to bother ennuyer, déranger, se déranger
bottle bouteille *f*
bottom fond *m*
boulevard boulevard *m*
bouquet bouquet *m*
box boîte *f;* carton *m*
boy garçon, petit garçon, jeune homme *m*
bread pain *m*
break: to break casser
breakfast petit déjeuner *m*
breath souffle *m;* **to be out of breath** être essoufflé
bridge pont *m;* (*game*) bridge *m*
bring apporter; **bring me** apportez-moi; **to bring over** apporter; **to bring back** rapporter
Brittany Bretagne *f*
brother frère *m*
brown brun, marron; **she has brown eyes** elle a les yeux marron (*no agreement*)
brunette brune *f*
brush: to brush brosser
build: to build construire; **to have built** faire construire
building bâtiment *m*
burn: to burn brûler
bury enterrer
bus autobus *m;* autocar *m;* **on the bus** en autobus
busy occupé; **to be busy** être en train de (*followed by inf*)
but mais
butcher boucher *m;* **butcher shop** boucherie *f;* **pork butcher** charcutier *m;* **pork butcher's** charcuterie *f*
butter beurre *m*
buy: to buy acheter; **worth buying** intéressant
by par, de; *with pr part* en

C

cabbage chou *m*
Cabinet member ministre *m*
cable cable *m*
café café *m*
cake gâteau *m*
California Californie *f*
call: to call appeler; **to be called** s'appeler
can (pouvoir): **can you?** pouvez-vous?; **I can** je peux; **you can** vous pouvez, on peut
Canada Canada *m*
canal canal *m*
capital capitale *f*
car wagon (train) *m;* auto *f;* automobile *f;* voiture *f*
card carte *f;* **to play cards** jouer aux cartes
care soin *m;* **to take care of** s'occuper de; **to take care of oneself** se soigner
careful: to be careful faire attention; **to be careful not to** se garder de
caretaker concierge *m or f*
carnation œillet *m*
carpet tapis *m*
carry porter; **to carry away, to carry along** emmener, emporter
case cas *m;* **in any case** en tout cas; **in case of** en cas de
cash: to cash toucher (un chèque)
cashier caissier *m*, caissière *;* **cashier's window** caisse *f*
catch: to catch attraper; **to catch up with** rejoindre, rattraper

cathedral cathédrale *f*
ceiling plafond *m*
cellar cave *f*
center centre *m*
century siècle *m;* **in the fifteenth century** au quinzième siècle
certain certain
certainly certainement, volontiers
chair chaise *f*
champagne champagne *m*
chance occasion *f*, *hasard *m;* **by chance** par hasard; **to have a chance to** avoir l'occasion de
change monnaie *f* **change purse** portemonnaie *m;* **to change** changer; **to change trains** changer de train
characterized caractérisé
chase: to chase, to chase out chasser
château château *m*
cheap bon marché, à bon marché; **cheaper** (à) meilleur marché
check chèque *m*
cheek joue *f*
cheese fromage *m*
chemical *adj* chimique; **chemical engineer** ingénieur-chimiste *m*
chemistry chimie *f*
chicken poulet *m*
child enfant *m or f*
chocolate chocolat *m*
choose choisir
Christmas Noël *m;* **Christmas Day** le jour de Noël; **Christmas Eve midnight party** le réveillon
church église *f*
cigar cigare *m*
cigarette cigarette *f*
cinema cinéma *m*
city ville *f*
clarinet clarinette *f*
class classe *f*
classify classer
clean: to clean nettoyer
clock horloge *f*, pendule *f*
close fermer; **it closes** il ferme
cloud nuage *m*
coat (ladies') manteau *m;* (men's) veston *m*
cobbler cordonnier *m*
coffee café *m*
coin pièce *f*, pièce de monnaie *f*
cold (*illness*) rhume *m;* (*temperature*) froid; **it is cold** il fait froid; **I am cold** j'ai froid
collect: to collect ramasser; collectionner
collection collection *f;* **stamp collection** collection de timbres
college collège *m*
collide entrer en collision (avec)
colony colonie *f*
color couleur *f;* **what color?** de quelle couleur?
come venir, arriver; **he came** il est venu; **did he come?** est-il venu?; **to come back** revenir, rentrer; **to come in** entrer; **to come for, come to get** venir chercher; **to come along** venir avec, accompagner; **to have (someone) come** faire venir (quelqu'un)
comfortable confortable
compartment compartiment *m*
complain se plaindre de
complete complet *m*, complète *f*
compose composer
conditional conditionnel *m*
confidence confiance *f*
confound it! zut!
confuse confondre
connection correspondance *f*
consent: to consent consentir à
consul consul *m*
continue continuer à
contrary contraire *m;* **on the contrary** au contraire
conversation conversation *f*
cool frais *m*, fraîche *f*
cooling rafraîchissant
corn maïs *m*
corner coin *m*
cost: to cost coûter
cough: to cough tousser
could (pouvoir); **I could** je pouvais, j'ai pu, je pourrais; **I could have** j'aurais pu
count: to count compter
country campagne *f;* pays *m;* **in the country** à la campagne; **country house** maison de campagne
course cours *m;* **main course** plat de viande *m;* **of course** naturellement, mais oui, bien entendu; **in the course of** au cours de
cousin cousin *m*, cousine *f*
cover: to cover couvrir
cow vache *f*

crazy: to be crazy about adorer
cream crème *f*
creek rivière *f*
cross: to cross traverser
crowded bondé
crusade croisade *f*
cry: to cry pleurer
cup tasse *f*
customer client *m*, cliente *f*

D

dairy crémerie *f*
daisy marguerite *f*
damp humide
dance bal *m*
danger danger *m*
dangerous dangereux *m*, dangereuse *f*
dare: to dare oser
dark sombre; **it is dark** il fait nuit
darkness obscurité *f*
date date *f*, rendez-vous *m;* **to date from** dater de
day jour *m*, journée *f;* **per day, a day** par jour; **all day** toute la journée; **every day** tous les jours; **that day** ce jour-là; **the next day** le lendemain; **day after tomorrow** après-demain
daylight jour *m;* **it is daylight** il fait jour
dead mort
deal: a great deal, a good deal beaucoup; **a great deal of** beaucoup de; **a good rain would do a great deal for my vegetables** une bonne pluie ferait du bien à mes légumes; **to deal in** faire le commerce de
dealer marchand *m*, marchande *f;* **second-hand book dealer** bouquiniste *m;* **antique dealer** antiquaire *m*
December décembre *m*
decide décider, vouloir; **to decide upon** fixer
dedicate dédier
delay retard *m*
delicious délicieux, délicieuse
delighted enchanté
dentist dentiste *m*
departure départ *m*
descend: to descend descendre
desk bureau *m*
dessert dessert *m*
destroy détruire
detective story roman policier *m*
dictation dictée *f*
die: to die mourir; **he died** il est mort
difference différence *f;* **it doesn't make any difference** cela ne fait rien
different différent
difficult difficile
dine dîner; **dining room** salle à manger *f*
diner wagon-restaurant *m*
dinner dîner *m;* **to have dinner** dîner
directly directement
disappointed déçu
discuss discuter
display étalage *m*
distance distance *f*
do faire; **do you . . .?** est-ce que . . .?; **don't you? doesn't it?** n'est-ce pas?; **I did** j'ai fait; **I shall do** je ferai; **I should do** je ferais; **yes, you do** mais si; **how do you do?** comment allez-vous?; **to do again** refaire; **all you have to do . . .** vous n'avez qu'à; **don't do anything of the sort** gardez-vous en bien
doctor docteur *m*, médecin *m*
dog chien *m*
dollar dollar *m*
donkey âne *m*
door porte *f*
doubt doute *m;* **no doubt, doubtless** sans doute
doubt: to doubt douter
down en bas; **to go down** descendre; **downtown** en ville
dozen douzaine *f;* **five francs a dozen** cinq francs la douzaine
draw up dresser (une liste)
drawer tiroir *m*
dress robe *f;* **to dress** habiller; **to get dressed** s'habiller; **to be dressed** être habillé
dresser commode *f*
dressmaker couturière *f*
drink: to drink boire
drive: to drive conduire; **to drive a car** conduire
driver chauffeur *m*
drop: to drop laisser tomber
drugstore pharmacie *f*, drugstore *m*

E

each *adj* chaque; *pron* chacun, chacune; **each one** chacun, chacune; **ten francs each** dix francs (la) pièce

eager: to be eager to avoir *hâte de
early de bonne heure; en avance
easily facilement
East Est *m*
easy facile
eat manger
economics économie politique *f*
edge bord *m*
egg œuf *m*
Egyptian égyptien *m*, égyptienne *f*
eight *huit
eighteen dix-huit
eighth *huitième
eighty quatre-vingts
either: either . . . or soit . . . soit; **not . . . either** ne . . . non plus; **nor I either** (ni) moi non plus
elderly d'un certain âge
elevator ascenseur *m*
eleven onze
eleventh onzième
else: something else autre chose; **nothing else** rien d'autre
elsewhere ailleurs
emblem emblème *m*
empire empire *m*
employee employé *m;* **government employee** fonctionnaire *m*
end fin *f*, bout *m;* **at the end of the street** au bout de la rue; **to end** finir, terminer, achever
endurable supportable
engineer ingénieur *m;* **chemical engineer** ingénieur-chimiste *m*
England Angleterre *f*
English anglais *m*, anglaise *f*
enjoy: to enjoy aimer
enormous énorme, vaste
entire entier *m*, entière *f*
entirely tout à fait
envelope enveloppe *f*
epidemic épidémie *f*
equivalent équivalent
errand course *f;* **to do errands** faire des courses
Europe Europe *f*
European européen *m*, européenne *f*
even pair (*of numbers*)
even même
evening soir *m*, soirée *f;* **in the evening** le soir; **every evening** tous les soirs; **good evening** bonsoir
ever jamais
every chaque, tout; **every day** tous les jours; **every six months** tous les six mois
everyone chacun, tout le monde
everything tout
everywhere partout
exact exact
examination examen *m*
examine examiner
example exemple *m;* **for example** par exemple
excellent excellent
except sauf, excepté
exercise exercice *m*
exist exister
exit sortie *f*
expect attendre, s'attendre à
expensive cher *m*, chère *f*
explain expliquer
explanation explication *f*
express express *m*
extinguish éteindre
eye œil *m sg*, yeux *pl*

F

factory usine *f*
fall automne *m;* **in the fall** en automne; **to fall** tomber; **to fall asleep** s'endormir
family famille *f*
famous célèbre
far loin; **as far as** jusqu'à; **that far** jusque-là; **far from** loin de
farm ferme *f*
fast vite; **how fast?** à quelle vitesse?
fat gras *m*, grasse *f*
fate sort *m*
father père *m*
fault faute *f*
favorite favori *m*, favorite *f*
fear peur *f;* **for fear that** de peur que; **to fear** craindre, avoir peur de (que)
February février *m*
feel: to feel sentir, se sentir; **to feel like** avoir envie de
fertile fertile
fever fièvre *f*
few peu de, quelques; **a few** *pron* quelques-uns, quelques-unes
fiancé, fiancée fiancé *m*, fiancée *f*

field champ *m*
fifteen quinze
fifteenth quinzième
fifth cinquième
fifty cinquante; **about fifty** une cinquantaine
film film *m*
finally finalement; **he finally came** il a fini par venir
find: to find trouver, retrouver; **to find out** apprendre
fine beau; **it is fine weather** il fait beau
finish: to finish finir, terminer
fire feu *m*
first *adj* premier *m*, première *f; adv* d'abord
fish poisson *m;* **a fish story** une histoire de pêcheurs
fisherman pêcheur *m*
fishing pêche *f;* **to go fishing** aller à la pêche
five cinq
flatterer flatteur *m*
floor étage *m;* **the second floor** le premier (étage); **the third floor** le second (étage)
flow: to flow couler
flower fleur *f*
fly: to fly voler; **how time flies!** comme le temps passe!
follow suivre; succéder
following suivant
fond: to be fond of aimer
food (*cooking*) cuisine *f*
foot pied *m*
for pour; depuis; pendant; **I have been waiting for a quarter of an hour** j'attends depuis un quart d'heure
foreign étranger *m*, étrangère *f*
forget oublier de
fork fourchette *f*
form forme *f*
former ancien *m*, ancienne *f*
formerly autrefois
forty quarante
found fonder
fountain fontaine *f*
four quatre
fourteen quatorze
fourth quatrième
franc franc *m*
free libre
French français *m*, française *f*
Friday vendredi *m*
friend ami *m*, amie *f*
friendly aimable
frightful effrayant
from de, depuis, d'après; **from the** du, de la, de l', des
front: in front of devant
fruit fruit *m*
full plein, complet
fun: to make fun of se moquer de
funny drôle (de)
furnished meublé
furniture meubles *m pl;* **a piece of furniture** un meuble
further plus loin; **further on** plus loin
future futur *m*

G

gallery galerie *f;* **picture gallery** galerie de peinture
garage garage *m*
garden jardin *m*
garret mansarde *f*
gasoline essence *f*
gate porte *f*
gentleman monsieur *m*
get prendre, avoir, obtenir, recevoir, se procurer; **to get in, to get into** entrer, monter; **to get out** sortir; **to go to get** aller chercher; **to come to get** venir chercher; **to get to** arriver à; **to get up** se lever; **to get home** rentrer; **to get on** monter; **to get off** descendre; **to get used to** s'habituer à; **to get to the top** arriver en haut
gilded doré
girl jeune fille *f;* **little girl** petite fille; **girl friend** amie
give donner; **to give a ticket** faire un procès-verbal
glad content, heureux; **I'll be glad to** volontiers
gladly volontiers
glance: to glance at jeter un coup d'œil sur
glass verre *m;* **glasses** lunettes *f pl;* **magnifying glass** loupe *f*
glimpse: to get a glimpse apercevoir
glove gant *m*
go aller; **I go, I am going** je vais; **he goes, he is going** il va; **you go, you are going** vous allez; **I shall go** j'irai; **I should go** j'irais; **it is**

going to il va; **to go in** entrer; **to go out** sortir; **to go up** monter; **to go down** descendre; **to go to bed** se coucher; **to go along** venir avec, accompagner; **to go in for** aimer; **to go away** partir, s'en aller; **to go with** accompagner; **to go through** visiter
good bon; **good-looking** beau, joli; **it's no good** cela ne vaut rien; **good** bien *m*
good-bye au revoir
goose oie *f*
Gothic gothique
graceful élégant, gracieux
grandmother grand-mère *f*
grapes raisin *m sg*
grass herbe *f*
gray gris
greatly très, fort
Greek grec *m*, grecque *f*
green vert; **salad greens** salade *f*
grocer épicier *m*
grocery épicerie *f;* **grocery store** épicerie *f*
grow pousser
guard gardien *m*
guide guide *m*
guitar guitare *f*

H

habit habitude *f*
had eu *p part of* avoir
hair cheveu *m;* **she has blond hair** elle a les cheveux blonds
half demi *m*, demie *f;* **half past eleven** onze heures et demie; **a half hour** une demi-heure
hall galerie *f*
ham jambon *m*
hand main *f;* **secondhand book** livre d'occasion
handkerchief mouchoir *m*
happen arriver, se passer, avoir lieu
happiness bonheur *m*
happy heureux *m*, heureuse *f;* content
hard dur, difficile
hardly à peine, ne . . . guère
hardware store quincaillerie *f*
harmony harmonie *f*
harp harpe *f*
harvest moisson *f*
hat chapeau *m*
have avoir; **I have** j'ai; **I haven't** je n'ai pas; **have you?** avez-vous?; **to have to** devoir, il faut . . ., être obligé de, avoir besoin de; **I can have it sent to you** je peux vous le faire envoyer; **to have something to eat or drink** prendre quelque chose; **I have to** je dois; **I had to** j'ai dû; **all you have to do** vous n'avez qu'à
hay foin *m*
he il, lui, c'
head tête *f*
headache mal de tête *m;* **to have a headache** avoir mal à la tête; **a good headache** un bon mal de tête
hear entendre; **to hear of** entendre parler de, **to hear that** entendre dire que
heart cœur *m;* **in the very heart of Paris** au cœur même de Paris
heat chaleur *f*
heating chauffage *m*
hello bonjour
help: to help aider; **to help oneself** se servir
hen poule *f*
her *pers pron* la, lui, elle; *poss adj* son, sa, ses
here ici; **here is, here are** voici; **here it is** le (la) voici; **here they are** les voici; **here!** tenez!
hers le sien, la sienne, les siens, les siennes
him le, lui, **to him, for him** lui
hippopotamus hippopotame *m*
his *poss adj* son, sa, ses; *poss pron* le sien, la sienne, les siens, les siennes
historical historique
history histoire *f;* **French history** l'histoire de France
hold: to hold tenir; **to hold out** tendre
holiday fête *f;* **Christmas holidays** vacances de Noël
home maison *f;* **he is at home** il est chez lui; **to get home, to go home** rentrer
hope: to hope espérer; **I hope so** je l'espère
hors d'œuvres *hors-d'œuvre *m*
horse cheval *m sg*, chevaux *pl*
hospital hôpital *m*
hot chaud; **it is hot** il fait chaud
hotel hôtel *m*
hour heure *f;* **a half hour** une demi-heure
house maison *f;* **at our house** chez nous; **at their house** chez eux
housekeeping ménage *m*
how comment; **how much, how many** combien; **how much is it?** combien est-ce?; **how long** combien de temps

however pourtant, cependant
humble humble
humid humide
hundred cent; **about a hundred** une centaine
hungry: to be hungry avoir faim; **I am hungry** j'ai faim
hurry: to hurry se dépêcher; **to be in a hurry** être pressé
hurt: to hurt blesser, avoir mal à, faire mal à; **my legs are beginning to hurt** je commence à avoir mal aux jambes; **these shoes hurt my feet** ces chaussures me font mal aux pieds
husband mari *m*

I

I je, moi
idea idée *f*
identification identité *f*
if si, s'
imagine imaginer
immediately tout de suite
important important
impressed impressionné
impression impression *f*
in dans, en, à, de; **in Paris** à Paris; **in France** en France; **in Canada** au Canada; **in South America** dans l'Amérique du Sud; **in 1715** en 1715; **in the XVth century** au quinzième siècle; **in the month of October** au mois d'octobre; **in the spring** au printemps; **in the fall** en automne; **in winter** en hiver; **in the morning** le matin; **at 7:00 in the morning** à sept heures du matin; **in a half hour** dans une demi-heure; **in a week** dans huit jours; **in time** à temps; **in the country** à la campagne; **in the course of** au cours de
incident incident *m*
indeed en effet, bien
independence indépendance *f;* **Independence Day** le jour de la Déclaration de l'Indépendance
indicate indiquer
indignation indignation *f*
indirect indirect
inform renseigner
information renseignements *m pl*
injustice injustice *f*
inn hôtel *m*, auberge *f;* **innkeeper** hôtelier *m*
inside intérieur *m;* à l'intérieur; **to go inside** entrer
intelligent intelligent
intend to avoir l'intention de
interest: to interest intéresser
interesting intéressant
interior intérieur
interrogative interrogatif *m*, interrogative *f*
introduce présenter
invention invention *f*
invitation invitation *f*
invite inviter
Irish irlandais
ironical ironique
is est; **it is** c'est, il est, elle est; **is it?** est-ce? est-ce que c'est?; **there is** il y a; **is there?** y a-t-il?; **it is four o'clock** il est quatre heures; **it is cold** il fait froid
island île *f*
it *subj* il, elle, ce; **it is** c'est, il est, elle est; *dir obj* le, l', la; *ind obj* y; **of it** en
Italian italien *m*, italienne *f*
Italy Italie *f*
its son, sa, ses

J

January janvier *m*
jealous jaloux *m*, jalouse *f*
jeweler horloger *m*, bijoutier *m;* **at the jeweler's** chez l'horloger
judge: to judge juger
juice jus *m*
July juillet *m*
June juin *m*
just seulement, tout simplement; **to have just** venir de; **I have just finished** je viens de finir

K

keep: to keep garder, tenir, retenir; **to keep on** continuer à
keeper garde *m*, gardien *m;* **hotelkeeper** hôtelier *m*
kill: to kill tuer
kilo kilo *m;* **five francs a kilo** cinq francs le kilo
kilometer kilomètre *m*
kind espèce *f*, sorte *f*
king roi *m*

knife couteau *m*
knight chevalier *m*
know savoir, connaître; **I know** je sais, je connais; **do you know?** savez-vous? connaissez-vous?; **I shall know** je saurai; **I should know** je saurais; **to know how** savoir (*see Conversation 9*)
known connu, célèbre

L

laboratory laboratoire *m*
lack: to lack manquer
lady dame *f*
lake lac *m*
land terre *f*, pays *m*
landscape paysage *m*
language langue *f*
large grand, gros, vaste; **as large as that** gros comme ça
last dernier *m*, dernière *f;* **last week** la semaine dernière; **last night** hier soir; **last Saturday** samedi dernier; **to last** durer
late tard, en retard; **later** plus tard; **at the latest** au plus tard; **I shall finish late** je finirai tard; **do you think I'll be late?** croyez-vous que je sois en retard?
Latin latin
lead: to lead mener, conduire
leaf feuille *f*
learn apprendre
least: the least le moins, la moins, les moins
leave: to leave partir, s'en aller; quitter; laisser; **when are you leaving?** quand partez-vous?; **I am leaving tomorrow** je m'en vais demain; **we left Melun two hours ago** il y a deux heures que nous avons quitté Melun; **as you leave the village** à la sortie du village; **it is better to leave those you are not sure of** il vaut mieux laisser ceux dont vous n'êtes pas sûr
lecture conférence *f*
left gauche; **to the left** à gauche
left: I have not one of them left il ne m'en reste aucun
leg jambe *f*
legend légende *f*
lend prêter
lens verre *m*
less moins; **less . . . than** moins . . . que; (*numbers*) moins de; **more or less** plus ou moins; **she is less tall than her brother** elle est moins grande que son frère; **there were less than a hundred pupils** il y avait moins de cent élèves
lesson leçon *f*
let permettre, laisser
letter lettre *f*
lettuce laitue *f*, salade *f*
lie: to lie down se coucher
lieutenant lieutenant *m;* **police lieutenant** commissaire de police *m*
life vie *f*
like comme; **to like** aimer, aimer bien; **I like** j'aime; **do you like?** aimez-vous?; **do you like it?** est-ce qu'il vous plaît?; **how do you like it?** comment le (la) trouvez-vous?; **would you like to . . .?** voulez-vous bien . . .?; **I would like** je voudrais; **do you like my hat?** est-ce que mon chapeau vous plaît?
line ligne *f*
lion lion *m*
lip lèvre *f*
Lisbon Lisbonne
list liste *f*
listen: to listen écouter
literature littérature *f*
little *adj* petit; *adv* peu; **a little** un peu
live vivre; **to live at** demeurer, habiter
London Londres
long *adj* long *m*, longue *f; adv* longtemps; **no longer** ne . . . plus; **all day long** toute la journée; **how long?** combien de temps?; **for a long time** depuis longtemps, pendant longtemps
look regard *m*, coup d'œil *m;* **to take a look at** jeter un coup d'œil sur; **to look** regarder; avoir l'air; **it looks very well on you** il vous va très bien; **to look for** chercher; **good-looking** beau, joli; **to look like** ressembler à; **to look over** visiter; **to look at** regarder
lose: to lose perdre
lost perdu, égaré
lot: a lot of, lots of beaucoup de
Louis XIV Louis Quatorze
low bas *m*, basse *f*
luck chance *f;* **to be lucky** avoir de la chance; **tough luck!** vous n'avez pas de chance!; **what luck!** quelle chance! quelle veine!

lunch déjeuner *m;* **to have lunch** déjeuner; **lunchroom** buffet *m;* **to lunch** déjeuner

M

Madam madame *f*
magazine revue *f*
magnificence splendeur *f*
maid bonne *f;* **nursemaid** bonne *f*
mail: to mail mettre (une lettre) à la poste
main principal; **main course** plat de viande *m*
majestic majestueux *m*, majestueuse *f*
make faire; *followed by adj* rendre: **does that make you sad?** est-ce que cela vous rend triste?
man homme *m*
manufacturer industriel *m*
many beaucoup; **so many** tant; **too many** trop; **how many?** combien?
map carte *f*
March mars *m*
marriage mariage *m*
marry se marier; **to get married** se marier
marvelously à merveille
mass messe *f;* **midnight mass** la messe de minuit
material étoffe *f*
mathematics mathématiques *f pl*
matter: what is the matter? qu'est-ce qu'il y a?; **what is the matter with you?** qu'est-ce que vous avez?; **nothing is the matter with me** je n'ai rien
mature: to mature mûrir
May mai *m*
may (pouvoir): **I may** je peux, je pourrai; **may I?** est-ce que je peux?
mayor maire *m*
me me, moi
meal repas *m*
mean: to mean vouloir dire
meat viande *f*
medicine médicament *m*
meet: to meet rencontrer, rejoindre, faire la connaissance de; **I met him** j'ai fait sa connaissance; **to come to meet** venir attendre
mention: to mention parler de
menu carte *f*
merchant marchand *m*, marchande *f;* **wholesale merchant** négociant *m*
meter mètre *m;* **six francs a meter** six francs le mètre
Mexico Mexique *m*
middle milieu *m;* **in the middle of** au milieu de
midnight minuit *m*
midst milieu *m;* **in the midst of** au milieu de
might (pouvoir): **I might** je pourrais
milk lait *m*
milliner modiste *f*
million million *m*
millionaire millionnaire *m*
mind: if you don't mind si vous voulez
mine le mien, la mienne, les miens, les miennes; **it is mine** c'est à moi; **a friend of mine** un de mes amis
ministry ministère *m*
minute minute *f*
mirror glace *f*
Miss mademoiselle *f*
miss: to miss manquer; **to miss the road** se tromper de route
mistaken: to be mistaken se tromper
moment moment *m;* **a moment ago** tout à l'heure **at the moment when** au moment où; **at the moment of** au moment de
Mona Lisa la Joconde
Monday lundi *m*
money argent *m*
monkey singe *m*
month mois *m;* **per month, a month** par mois
monument monument *m*
monumental monumental
moon lune *f*
more plus, davantage; **not . . . any more** ne . . . plus; **more . . . than** plus . . . que; (*numbers*) plus de; **no more** ne . . . plus de; **more or less** plus ou moins; **more and more** de plus en plus; **some more** encore, d'autres; **he is more intelligent than his brother;** il est plus intelligent que son frère; **there were hardly more than a hundred pupils** il n'y avait guère plus de cent élèves; **you can take some more pictures** vous pourrez prendre d'autres photos; **all the more** d'autant plus
morning matin *m;* **good morning** bonjour; **every morning** tous les matins; **in the morning** le matin
most la plupart; **most of them** la plupart d'entre eux
mother mère *f*
mouth bouche *f*
movie film *m*, cinéma *m;* **movie house** cinéma *m*

Mr. Monsieur *m;* **Mr. Duval** M. Duval
much beaucoup; **very much** beaucoup; **so much** tant; **too much** trop; **how much?** combien?; **not much** pas beaucoup, pas grand-chose
museum musée *m*
mushroom champignon *m*
music musique *f*
musketeer mousquetaire *m*
must (devoir, falloir): **must I?** faut-il?; **I must** je dois, il faut que je . . .; **I must have** j'ai dû; **there must be** il doit y avoir
my mon, ma, mes

N

name nom *m;* **what is your name?** comment vous appelez-vous?; **my name is** je m'appelle; **to name** nommer; **to be named** s'appeler
named nommé
nap somme *m;* **to take a nap** faire un somme
narrow étroit
national national
nationality nationalité *f*
near près de; **near here, nearby** près d'ici
nearly presque
necessary nécessaire; **it is necessary** il faut que
need: to need avoir besoin de
negative négatif *m,* négative *f*
negatively négativement
neighbor voisin *m,* voisine *f*
neighboring voisin *m,* voisine *f*
neither ni l'un ni l'autre; **neither . . . nor** ne . . . ni . . . ni . . .
never jamais, ne . . . jamais
new nouveau *m,* nouvelle *f;* neuf *m,* neuve *f;* **New Orleans** La Nouvelle-Orléans
news nouvelles *f pl*
newspaper journal *m,* journaux *pl*
next prochain; **next Saturday** samedi prochain; **next week** la semaine prochaine; **the next day** le lendemain
next *adv* ensuite, puis
nice gentil *m,* gentille *f;* aimable; **it is nice of you** c'est gentil de votre part
night nuit *f;* **last night** hier soir; **tonight** ce soir; **at night** la nuit
nightfall nuit *f*
nine neuf
nineteen dix-neuf
nineteenth dix-neuvième
ninety quatre-vingt-dix
no non, ne . . . pas de; **no one** personne, ne . . . personne
nobility noblesse *f*
nobody personne, ne . . . personne
noise bruit *m*
none aucun *m,* aucune *f;* ne . . . aucun(e)
noon midi *m;* **at noon** à midi
nor ni; **neither . . . nor** ne . . . ni . . . ni . . .
Normandy Normandie *f*
North nord *m;* **North Africa** l'Afrique du Nord
Norwegian norvégien *m,* norvégienne *f*
not ne . . . pas; **not at all** pas du tout; **not much** pas beaucoup, pas grand-chose; **not one** aucun(e), ne . . . aucun(e)
note: to note noter
nothing rien, ne . . . rien; **nothing at all** rien du tout; **nothing interesting** rien d'intéressant; **nothing else** rien d'autre
noun nom *m*
novel roman *m*
November novembre *m*
now maintenant; actuellement
nowhere nulle part
number nombre *m;* **room No. 3** la chambre numéro trois
nurse, nursemaid bonne *f*

O

oats avoine *f*
obelisk obélisque *m*
obey obéir à
object objet *m*
observatory observatoire *m*
occasionally quelquefois
occupation occupation *f*
occupy occuper
o'clock heure *f;* **it is eleven o'clock** il est onze heures
October octobre *m*
oculist oculiste *m*
odd impair (*of numbers*)
of de; **of the** du, de la, de l', des; **of it, of them** en
offer: to offer offrir, tendre
office bureau *m*
often souvent
O.K. entendu

old vieux, vieil *m;* vieille *f;* vieux *m pl;* vieilles *f pl;* ancien, ancienne; **how old are you?** quel âge avez-vous? **old man** mon vieux
olive olive *f*
on sur, à, en, dans; **on the bus** dans l'autobus; **on the train** dans le train; **on time** à l'heure; **on Wednesday** mercredi; **on Christmas Day** le jour de Noël; **on arriving** en arrivant
once une fois, autrefois; **once a week** une fois par semaine
one un, une; *pers pron* on, l'on; *dem pron* **the one, the ones** celui, celle, ceux, celles; **this one** celui-ci, celle-ci; **that one** celui-là, celle-là; **not one** aucun(e), ne . . . aucun(e); **no one** personne, ne . . . personne; **I have one** j'en ai un(e); **here are some gray ones** en voici des gris
only *adj* seul; *adv* seulement, ne . . . que
open ouvert *adj and p part of* ouvrir; **to open** ouvrir; **it opens** il ouvre
opera opéra *m*
opposite opposé *m; adv* en face (de)
or ou; **either . . . or** soit . . . soit
orange orange *f*
order: in order to pour, afin de; **to order** commander
ordinarily d'habitude
organ orgues *f pl*
other autre; **some . . . others** les uns . . . d'autres; **the other one** l'autre
ought (devoir): **you ought to come** vous devriez venir; **you ought to have come** vous auriez dû venir
our notre *sg*, nos *pl*
ours le nôtre, la nôtre *sg*, les nôtres *pl*
ourselves nous-mêmes; **by ourselves** seuls
out: to go out sortir; **he is out** il est sorti
outside dehors, en dehors
over sur; **over there** là-bas
owe devoir
own propre; **they were victims of their own injustice** ils furent victimes de leurs propres injustices
ox bœuf *m*

P

package paquet *m*
pain mal *m*
paint: to paint peindre
painter peintre *m*
painting peinture *f*
pair paire *f*
pal mon vieux
palace palais *m*
pan: sauce pan casserole *f*
panorama panorama *m*
pansy pensée *f*
pants pantalon *m*
paper papier *m;* **newspaper** journal *m;* **writing paper** papier à lettres
pardon: to pardon pardonner; **pardon me** pardon
parent parent *m*
Parisian parisien, parisienne
park parc *m;* **public park** jardin public
part partie *f;* **part of town** quartier *m;* **to be a part of** faire partie de
particular particulier *m*, particulière *f;* **in particular** notamment
partly en partie
party soirée *f*
passer-by passant *m*
pasteboard (box) carton *m*
pastry pâtisserie *f*, gâteau *m*
patient malade *m or f;* client (d'un médecin) *m*
pay: to pay payer; **to pay for** payer
pea pois *m*
pear poire *f*
peony pivoine *f*
people gens *pl*, monde *m;* **too many people** trop de monde
per: 30 kilometers per hour 30 kilomètres à l'heure; **per month** par mois; **per dozen** la douzaine
perfectly parfaitement, tout à fait
performance représentation *f*
perhaps peut-être
period période *f;* époque *f*
perish mourir; **perish the thought!** ne m'en parlez pas!
permission permission *f*
person personne *f*
personal personnel *m*, personnelle *f*
pharmacist pharmacien *m*
photograph photographie *f*
piano piano *m*
pick: to pick cueillir, ramasser
picnic pique-nique *m*
picture photographie *f*, photo *f*, tableau *m;* **to take a picture** prendre une photo

picturesque pittoresque
piece pièce *f*, morceau *m;* **ten francs apiece** dix francs (la) pièce
pig porc *m*, cochon *m*
pink rose
pity: to pity plaindre
place endroit *m*, place *f;* **in your place** à votre place; **to take place** avoir lieu
plan: to plan avoir l'intention de; **to plan a garden** dessiner un jardin
plan projet *m*
plane avion *m*
plant: to plant planter
platform quai *m*
play pièce *f;* **to play** jouer; **to play tennis** jouer au tennis; **to play cards** jouer aux cartes; **to play the violin** jouer du violon
pleasant agréable; **the weather is pleasant** il fait bon
please s'il vous plaît; **to please** plaire à
plural pluriel *m*
pocket poche *f;* **pocketbook** portefeuille *m*
poem poème *m*, poésie *f*
point point *m;* **point of view** point de vue *m*
poison: to poison empoisonner
police police *f;* **police station** commissariat de police *m;* **police lieutenant** commissaire de police *m*
policeman agent de police *m*
pool bassin *m;* **ornamental pool** pièce d'eau *f*
poor pauvre
pork porc *m;* **pork butcher** charcutier *m;* **pork butcher's** charcuterie *f*
port port *m*
portrait portrait *m*
possible possible
post card carte postale *f*
postman facteur *m*
post office bureau de poste *m*, poste *f*
potato pomme de terre *f;* **French fried potatoes** pommes de terre frites, frites
pound livre *f;* **2 francs a pound** 2 francs la livre
pour verser; **it is pouring** il pleut à verse
practically à peu près
practice habitude *f*
preceding précédent
prefer préférer, aimer mieux
present *adj* présent, actuel; **at present** actuellement
president président *m*
pretty *adj* joli; *adv* assez; **pretty well** assez, assez bien
price prix *m*
priest curé *m*
print estampe *f*, gravure *f*
probably sans doute; **there is probably a train** il doit y avoir un train
profession profession *f*
professor professeur *m*
progress progrès *m*
promise promettre
pronoun pronom *m*
properly bien, comme il faut
provision provision *f*
pub petit café *m*
public public *m*, publique *f*
pull: to pull tirer; **to pull it in to the bank (shore) (edge)** l'amener au bord
pupil élève *m or f*
purchase achat *m*
purse bourse *f;* **change purse** porte-monnaie *m*
put mettre; **to put out** (to bother) déranger

Q

quality qualité *f*
quarter quart *m*, quartier *m;* **a quarter past eleven** onze heures et quart; **a quarter of two** deux heures moins le quart; **the Latin Quarter** le Quartier latin
queen reine *f*
question question *f;* **it is a question of** il s'agit de; **to be a question of** s'agir de
quiet tranquille
quite tout à fait

R

radiate rayonner
railroad chemin de fer *m;* **railroad station** gare *f*
rain pluie *f;* **to rain** pleuvoir; **it is raining** il pleut; **it was raining** il pleuvait; **it had rained** il avait plu
raincoat imperméable *m*
rare rare; **rarer and rarer** de plus en plus rare
rather plutôt, assez, un peu
ravage: to ravage ravager
reach: to reach atteindre
read: to read lire; **I have read** j'ai lu
ready prêt
realize se rendre compte de (que)

really vraiment, je vous assure; **really!** tiens!
reason raison *f;* **there is reason for it** il y a de quoi
rebuild reconstruire
receive recevoir; **I received** j'ai reçu
recognize reconnaître
red rouge
refusal refus *m*
refuse refuser
region région *f*
regret: to regret regretter de
reign règne *m*
relative parent *m*, parente *f*
relatively relativement
relax: to relax s'amuser
remedy remède *m*
remember se rappeler, se souvenir de
rent loyer *m;* **to rent** louer; **for rent** à louer
repair réparation *f;* **repair job** réparation; **to repair** réparer; **to have repaired** faire réparer
repeat répéter
replace remplacer
reply: to reply répondre à
represent représenter
request demande *f*
residence résidence *f*
responsible responsable
rest reste *m*, repos *m;* **to rest** se reposer
restaurant restaurant *m*
return: to return here revenir (ici); **to return (some place else)** retourner; **to return home** rentrer (à la maison)
review révision *f*, revue *f*
rich riche
ride promenade (à bicyclette, en auto) *f;* **to ride** aller en auto, à bicyclette
right droit (*opposite of* **left**), bon (*opposite of* **wrong**): **on, to the right** à droite; **the right road** la bonne route; **to be right** avoir raison; **that's right** justement; **all right** bon, entendu; **right to** jusqu'à; **right away** tout de suite
rise: to rise se lever
risk risque *m;* **to run the risk** risquer de
road route *f;* **the right road** la bonne route; **the wrong road** la mauvaise route; **country road** chemin *m*
roll croissant *m;* petit pain *m*
romanesque roman, romane
roof toit *m*
room chambre *f*, salle *f;* **room and board** pension *f;* **bathroom** salle de bain; **lunchroom** buffet *m;* **dining room** salle à manger; **living room** salon *m;* (*space*) place *f;* **there is room** il y a de la place
rose rose *f*
rosebush rosier *m*
rosy rose
royal royal
run: to run courir; **my watch doesn't run** ma montre ne marche pas; **to run a pub** tenir un café
Russia Russie *f*
Russian russe

S

sacrifice sacrifice *m*
sad triste
sail voile *f;* **sailboat** bateau à voile *m*
saint saint; **la Sainte-Chapelle** XIIIth century Gothic church in Paris
salad salade *f;* **salad greens** salade *f*
salesgirl vendeuse *f*
salesman vendeur *m*
same même; **the same** le même, la même, les mêmes; **that's all the same to me** cela m'est égal; **all the same** tout de même
sandwich sandwich *m*, sandwichs *pl*
Santa Claus le Père Noël
Saturday samedi *m;* **on Saturdays** le samedi
say dire; **they say** on dit; **how does one say?** comment dit-on?; **that is to say** c'est-à-dire; **to say to oneself** se dire
scarcely à peine, ne . . . guère
scarf écharpe *f*
schedule emploi du temps *m*
school école *f;* **secondary school** lycée *m;* collège *m;* **at school** à l'école
science science *f*
Scotland Écosse *f*
sea mer *f;* **seashore** le bord de la mer
season saison *f*
seat place *f*
second second, deuxième; **the second floor** le premier (étage); **second class** seconde *f;* deuxième (classe) *f*
secondary secondaire; **secondary school** lycée *m*, collège *m*
section section *f*
see: to see voir; **I see** je vois; **let's see** voyons;

you see vous voyez; **I saw** j'ai vu; **I'll see** je verrai; **see you Sunday** à dimanche
seem: to seem to avoir l'air de
seen vu *p part of* voir
selection choix *m*
sell vendre; **where do they sell newspapers?** où vend-on des journaux?
send envoyer; **to send for** envoyer chercher, faire venir; **to send away, send back** renvoyer
sentence phrase *f*
September septembre *m*
series série *f*
serious sérieux *m*, sérieuse *f;* grave
serve servir à
service service *m;* **I am at your service** je suis à votre disposition
set: to set mettre, poser; **to set out** partir
seven sept
seventeen dix-sept
seventeenth dix-septième
seventh septième
seventy soixante-dix
several plusieurs; **several times** plusieurs fois
shade ombre *f;* **in the shade** à l'ombre
she elle, ce
sheep mouton *m*
shirt chemise *f*
shoe chaussure *f*, soulier *m*
shoo: to shoo out chasser
shop magasin *m;* **tobacco shop** bureau de tabac *m;* **shop window** devanture *f;* **to shop** faire des courses
shopkeeper marchand *m*, marchande *f*
shore bord *m*, rive *f;* **seashore** le bord de la mer
short court
should (devoir): **you should** vous devriez; **you should have** vous auriez dû
shoulder épaule
show: to show montrer
sick malade
side côte *m*, bord *m;* **on the other side of** de l'autre côté de; **on the side of** au bord de; **the under side** le dessous
sidewalk trottoir *m;* **sidewalk café** la terrasse d'un café
significance signification *f;* **do you know the significance of . . .?** connaissez-vous?
silent silencieux *m*, silencieuse *f*
silk soie *f*
simple simple
since depuis, puisque
sing: to sing chanter
single seul; **not a single** ne . . . aucun
Sir Monsieur
sister sœur *f*
sit s'asseoir, être assis; **sit down** asseyez-vous; **to sit down at the table** se mettre à table
six six
sixteen seize
sixth sixième
sixty soixante
size étendue *f*, pointure *f*
skate: to skate patiner
ski: to ski faire du ski
skilful habile
skin peau *f;* **I am wet to the skin (to the bones)** je suis mouillé(e) jusqu'aux os
sky ciel *m*
skyscraper gratte-ciel *m*
sleep; to sleep dormir; **to fall asleep** s'endormir
slightest: the slightest le moindre, la moindre, les moindres
slippery glissant
small petit
smile sourire *m*
smoke: to smoke fumer
snake serpent *m*
snow neige *f;* **to snow** neiger
so aussi, si, ainsi; **so that** pour que; **so as to** pour
sock chaussette *f*
soil sol *m*
some du, de la, de l', des; *adj* quelque *sg*, quelques *pl; pron* en; quelques-uns, quelques-unes; les uns, les unes; **some of them** quelques-uns; **some . . . the others** les uns . . . les autres; **some . . . others** les uns . . . d'autres; **some more** encore, d'autres
someone quelqu'un
something quelque chose; **something good** quelque chose de bon; **something else** autre chose
sometimes quelquefois, parfois
somewhere quelque part
soon bientôt, tôt; **sooner** plus tôt; **as soon as possible** le plus tôt possible
sore: to have a sore throat avoir mal à la gorge

sorry fâché; **I am sorry** je regrette, je suis fâché
sort espèce *f*
soup soupe *f*
South sud *m*
souvenir souvenir *m*
space espace *m*
Spain Espagne *f*
Spanish espagnol
speak parler; **do you speak?** parlez-vous?; **I speak** je parle; **he speaks** il parle
speed vitesse *f*
spend passer; dépenser; **he spent three years in England** il a passé trois ans en Angleterre; **he spent his life building castles** il a passé sa vie à construire des palais
splendor splendeur *f*
spring printemps (saison) *m;* ressort (d'une montre) *m;* **in the spring** au printemps
square place *f*
stained-glass window vitrail *m*, vitraux *pl*
stair escalier *m*
staircase escalier *m;* **spiral staircase** escalier en colimaçon
stamp timbre *m;* **postage stamp** timbre-poste *m*
standing debout
star étoile *f*
start: to start commencer, se mettre à; **we started to work at 1:30** nous nous sommes mis à travailler à une heure et demie
station gare *f*
stay: to stay rester
steak: minute steak bifteck *m*
steering wheel volant *m*
step pas *m;* **steps** escalier *m;* **a step from here** à deux pas d'ici
still toujours, encore
stockbroker agent de change *m*
stop arrêt *m;* **to stop** arrêter, s'arrêter
store magasin *m*
story histoire *f*
straight droit; **straight ahead** tout droit
strawberry fraise *f;* **wild strawberry** fraise des bois *f*
street rue *f;* **surface of a street** chaussée *f*
structure bâtiment *m*
student étudiant *m*, étudiante *f*
study: to study étudier
style style *m*
succeed in réussir à
such un tel, une telle, de tels, de telles; **such a watch** une telle montre
suddenly tout à coup
suffer souffrir
sugar sucre *m*
suggest suggérer, proposer
suit complet *m;* **to suit** convenir à; **this room suits me perfectly** cette chambre me convient parfaitement
suitable convenable
summer été *m;* **in summer** en été
sun soleil *m*
Sunday dimanche *m;* **see you Sunday** à dimanche
supermarket super-marché *m*
suppose supposer; **suppose we take a few of them back home?** si nous en rapportions quelques-uns à la maison?; **I am supposed to** je dois
sure sûr
surely sûrement
surface surface *f;* **surface of a street** chaussée *f;* **the upper surface** le dessus
surprise surprise *f*
surprised surpris *p part of* surprendre
surround with entourer de
suspect: to suspect se douter de; **I suspected it** je m'en doutais
sweater pull-over *m*
Swedish suédois
sweet doux *m*, douce *f*
swim: to swim nager
Switzerland Suisse
symbolize symboliser

T

table table *f*
tailor tailleur *m*
take prendre, emporter, mener, conduire; **to take a walk** faire une promenade; **you take** vous prenez; **I took** j'ai pris; **to take place** avoir lieu; **to take along** emporter, emmener; **how long does it take?** combien de temps faut-il?; **to take an examination** passer un examen; **this road will take you to Fontainebleau** ce chemin vous mènera à Fontainebleau
taking prise *f*
talk: to talk parler; **to talk over** parler de

tall grand
tapestry tapisserie *f*
taste goût *m*
taxi taxi *m*
tea thé *m*
telegram dépêche *f*, télégramme *m*
telephone: to telephone téléphoner
television télévision *f*
tell dire; **to tell about** parler de
temperature température *f*
ten dix
tennis tennis *m;* **to play tennis** jouer au tennis
tenth dixième
terrific formidable
terrifically terriblement, horriblement
text texte *m*
thank remercier; **thank you** merci
that (those) *dem adj* ce, cet *m*, cette *f*, ces *pl;* ce . . .-là, cette . . .-là, ces . . .-là; **that** *dem pron* celui *m*, celle *f*, ceux *m pl*, celles *f pl;* cela; **that's it** c'est cela; **that** *rel pron* qui, que, lequel, laquelle, lesquels, lesquelles; **all that** tout ce qui, tout ce que; **that** *conj* que
the le, la, l', les
theater théâtre *m*
their *poss adj* leur *sg*, leurs *pl*
theirs *poss pron* le leur, la leur, les leurs
them les; leur; eux, elles; **of them** en
then alors, ensuite, puis; ainsi
theology théologie *f*
there là, y; **there is, there are** il y a; **is there? are there?** y a-t-il?; **thereon** là-dessus; **under there** là-dessous; **in there** là-dedans
these *dem adj* ces, ces . . .-ci; *dem pron* ceux-ci *m*, celles-ci *f*
they ils, elles; on
thick épais
thin mince
thing chose *f;* **many things** beaucoup de choses
think penser à, penser de, croire, trouver; **what do you think of Charles?** que pensez-vous de Charles?; **I think so** je crois que oui; **she thought it was very good** elle l'a trouvé très bon; **I thought that** je croyais que; **I rather thought so** je m'en doutais
thinker penseur *m*
third troisième
thirst soif *f;* **to be thirsty** avoir soif
thirteen treize
thirteenth treizième
thirty trente
this *dem adj* ce, cet *m*, cette *f;* ce . . .-ci, cet . . .-ci, cette . . .-ci; **this** *dem pron* celui *m*, celle *f;* celui-ci, celle-ci; ceci; **this one** celui-ci, celle-ci
those *dem adj* ces, ces . . .-là; *dem pron* ceux-là *m*, celles-là *f*
thousand mille
three trois
throat gorge *f*
Thursday jeudi *m*
ticket billet *m;* **ticket window** guichet *m;* **to give a ticket** faire un procès-verbal
tie cravate *f*
till jusqu'à; **till Sunday** à dimanche; **till then** jusque-là
time temps *m*, heure *f*, fois *f*, moment *m;* **what time is it?** quelle heure est-il?; **at what time?** à quelle heure?; **the first time** la première fois; **several times** plusieurs fois; **to have time to** avoir le temps de; **on time** à l'heure; **at that time** à ce moment-là, à cette époque; **to have a good time** s'amuser, s'amuser bien; **from time to time** de temps en temps; **in time** à temps; **at the time when** au moment où; **at the time of** au moment de; **some time soon** ces jours-ci; **some time ago** il y a quelque temps; **harvest time** le moment de la moisson
tired fatigué
to à, en, pour, chez, jusqu'à; **to the** au, à la, à l', aux; **it is ten minutes to four** il est quatre heures moins dix; **to the right** à droite; **to the top of** en haut de; **to, in the middle of** au milieu de; **I would go to Italy** j'irais en Italie; **to the United States** aux États-Unis; **to South America** dans l'Amérique du Sud; **to Versailles** à Versailles; **a round-trip ticket to Rheims** un billet aller et retour pour Reims; **to the Brown's** chez les Brown; **to our house** chez nous; **to the country** à la campagne; **I am wet to the skin (bones)** je suis mouillé jusqu'aux os; **they have been very nice to me** ils ont été très aimables pour moi; **how long does it take to go to Versailles?** combien de temps faut-il pour aller à Versailles?; **I'll be glad to** volontiers; **she is to arrive soon** elle doit arriver ces jours-ci

tobacco tabac *m;* **tobacco shop** bureau de tabac *m*
today aujourd'hui; **today is Friday** c'est aujourd'hui vendredi
together ensemble
tomato tomate *f*
tomb tombe *f*, (*monumental*) tombeau *m*
tomorrow demain; **day after tomorrow** après-demain
tonight ce soir
too trop, aussi
tooth dent *f;* **to have a toothache** avoir mal aux dents
top haut *m;* **at the top of** en *haut de; **from the top of** du *haut de
towards vers
tower tour *f;* **the Eiffel tower** la tour Eiffel
town ville *f;* **downtown** en ville
track voie *f*
train train *m;* **on the train** dans le train
travel: to travel voyager
tree arbre *m*
trim: to trim tailler
trip voyage *m;* **round trip** aller et retour; **to have a good trip** faire bon voyage; **to take a trip** faire un voyage
trouble peine *f;* **it is not worth the trouble** ce n'est pas la peine
truck camion *m*
true vrai
try: to try essayer (de); **to try on** essayer
Tuesday mardi *m*
tulip tulipe *f*
turkey dinde *f*
Turkey Turquie *f*
turn: to turn tourner; **to turn around** se retourner
twelfth douzième
twelve douze; **twelve o'clock (noon)** midi; **twelve o'clock (midnight)** minuit
twenty vingt
twenty-one vingt et un
twice deux fois
two deux

U

umbrella parapluie *m*
uncle oncle *m*
under sous, dessous; **under side** dessous *m;* **under there** là-dessous
understand comprendre; **do you understand?** comprenez-vous?; **I understand** je comprends
undo défaire
unhappy malheureux *m*, malheureuse *f*
United States États-Unis *m pl;* **in the United States** aux États-Unis
University université *f*
unless à moins que
until jusqu'à, jusqu'à ce que; **until tomorrow** à demain
up en haut; **up there** là-haut; **to go up** monter
upper: upper surface dessus *m*
use emploi *m;* **what's the use?** à quoi bon?; **there is no use trying** vous avez beau essayer; **to use** employer, se servir de; **to be used for** servir à; **used to** *expressed by imperf ind:* **I used to go** j'allais; **to be used to** avoir l'habitude de; **to get used to** s'habituer à
usual: as usual comme d'habitude
usually d'habitude, d'ordinaire

V

vacation vacances *f pl;* **on vacation** en vacances
vain: in vain avoir beau + *infin:* **you'll try in vain** vous aurez beau essayer
value valeur *f;* **to be valuable** avoir de la valeur
vegetable légume *m*
very très; **in the very heart of Paris** au cœur même de Paris
victim victime *f*
view vue *f;* **point of view** point de vue *m*
village village *m*
violet violette *f*
violent violent
violin violon *m*
visit visite *f;* **to visit** visiter (*things*), aller voir
voice voix *f;* **in a low voice** à voix basse

W

waiter garçon *m*
wake up se réveiller
waken se réveiller
walk promenade *f*, allée *f*
walk: to walk marcher, aller à pied, se promener
wall mur *m*
want: to want vouloir, avoir envie de; **I want**

je veux; **he wants** il veut; **do you want?** voulez-vous?
warm chaud; **it is warm** il fait chaud; **I am warm** j'ai chaud
warn prévenir; **I warn you** je vous préviens
was: I was j'étais, j'ai été; **I was born in Philadelphia** je suis né à Philadelphie
wash: to wash laver; **to wash one's hands** se laver les mains
watch montre *f;* **to watch out** faire attention à
water eau *f;* **to water** arroser
way moyen *m,* façon *f;* **this way** par ici; **on the way** en route; **it's a way of passing half an hour** c'est une façon de passer une demi-heure; **to lose one's way** s'égarer
wear porter; **to wear out** user
weather temps *m;* **how is the weather?** quel temps fait-il?; **the weather is fine** il fait beau
wedding mariage *m*
Wednesday mercredi *m*
week semaine *f;* **in a week** dans huit jours; **in two weeks** dans quinze jours; **last week** la semaine dernière; **a week from today** d'aujourd'hui en huit; **every week** tous les huit jours
weekend week-end *m*
welcome: you are welcome de rien, il n'y a pas de quoi, je vous en prie, à votre service
well bien, eh bien!, tiens!; **I am well** je vais bien
were: you were vous étiez, vous avez été; **where were you born?** où êtes-vous né?
wet mouillé; **I am wet to the skin (to the bones)** je suis mouillé jusqu'aux os
what? *interrog adj* quel? quelle? quels? quelles?; **what?** *interrog pron* que? qu'est-ce qui? qu'est-ce que? quoi?; **what is?** qu'est-ce que c'est que?; **what for?** pourquoi?; **what** *rel pron* ce qui, ce que; **what is . . .** ce que c'est que . . .
whatever: whatever you do will be in vain vous aurez beau faire
wheat blé *m*
when quand, lorsque; où
whence d'où
whenever quand, chaque fois que
where où
which? *interrog adj* quel? quelle? quels? quelles?; **which?** *interrog pron* lequel? laquelle? lesquels? lesquelles?; **which one?** lequel? laquelle?; **which ones?** lesquels? lesquelles?; **which** *rel pron* qui, que; lequel, laquelle, lesquels, lesquelles; **of which** dont; **in which** où
while tandis que, pendant que; **a while ago, in a while** tout à l'heure
white blanc *m,* blanche *f*
who? *interrog pron* qui? qui est-ce qui?; **who** *rel pron* qui; lequel, laquelle, lesquels, lesquelles
whom? *interrog pron* qui? qui est-ce que?; **whom** *rel pron* que; lequel, laquelle, lesquels, lesquelles, **of whom** dont, duquel; **to whom** à qui
whose? *interrog pron* à qui?; **whose gloves are these?** à qui sont ces gants?; **at whose house?** chez qui?; **whose** *rel pron* dont, de qui
why pourquoi; **why not?** pourquoi pas?
wife femme *f*
wild sauvage; **wild flower** fleur sauvage *f;* **wild strawberry** fraise des bois *f*
willing: I am willing je veux bien
wind vent *m;* **it is windy** il fait du vent
window fenêtre *f;* **ticket window** guichet *m;* **cashier's window** caisse *f;* **shop window** devanture *f;* **stained-glass window** vitrail *m,* vitraux *pl*
wine vin *m*
winter hiver *m;* **in winter** en hiver
wire dépêche *f,* télégramme *m*
wish: to wish souhaiter; **if you wish** si vous voulez
with avec
without sans
witness témoin *m;* **to witness** être témoin de
wonder: to wonder se demander
wood bois *m*
word mot *m*
work travail *m;* **to work** travailler
world monde *m*
worried préoccupé, inquiet
worry ennuyer; **don't worry** soyez tranquille
worse *adj* pire; *adv* pis; **so much the worse** tant pis
worth: to be worth valoir; **it is not worth while** ce n'est pas la peine; **worth buying** intéressant
wound: to wound blesser
write écrire

wrong: the wrong road la mauvaise route; **to be wrong** avoir tort; **something is wrong** il y a (vous avez) quelque chose

Y - Z

year an *m*, année *f;* **every year** tous les ans; **New Year's Day** le jour de l'an
yellow jaune
yes oui, si
yesterday hier
yet encore, déjà; **not yet** pas encore
you vous; tu, te, toi
young jeune
your votre *sg*, vos *pl;* ton, ta, tes
yours le vôtre, la vôtre, les vôtres; le tien, la tienne, les tiens, les tiennes; **is it yours?** est-ce à vous?; **a friend of yours** un de vos amis
zero zéro *m*

Index

PHOTOGRAPHS

P. 67 — Photographie Giraudon. Pp. 155, 226, 253 — François Vikar. Pp. 171, 204, 250 — Photo Yvon, © SPADEM 1968, French Reproduction Rights, Inc. P. 182 — Albert Monier. Pp. 213, 350 — French Embassy Press & Information Division. P. 290 — The Metropolitan Museum of Art, Rogers Fund, 1948. All other photographs by Helena Kolda.

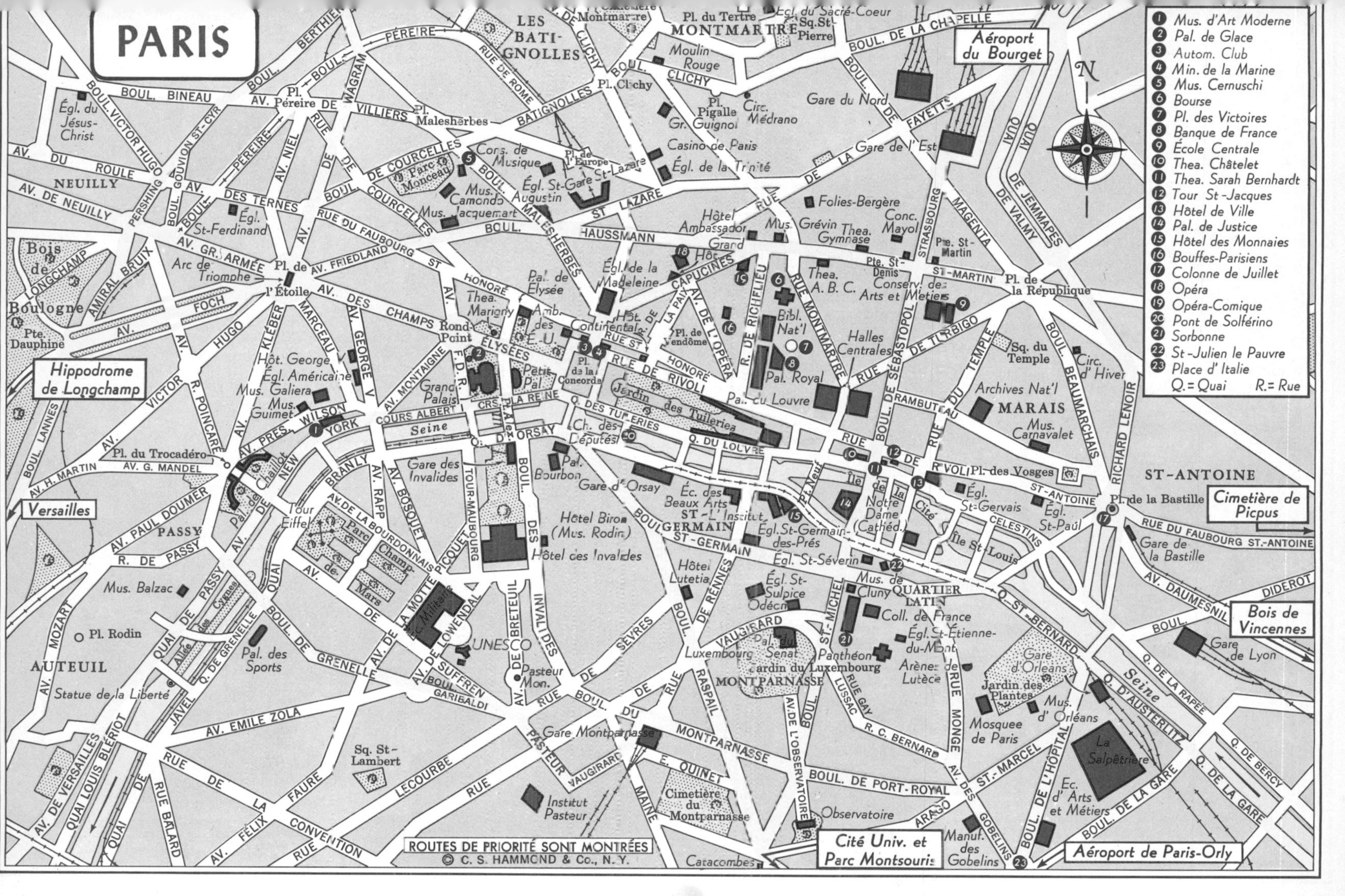

PARIS
1 Mus. d'Art Moderne
2 Pal. de Glace
3 Autom. Club
4 Min. de la Marine
5 Mus. Cernuschi
6 Bourse
7 Pl. des Victoires
8 Banque de France
9 École Centrale
10 Thea. Châtelet
11 Thea. Sarah Bernhardt
12 Tour St-Jacques
13 Hôtel de Ville
14 Pal. de Justice
15 Hôtel des Monnaies
16 Bouffes-Parisiens
17 Colonne de Juillet
18 Opéra
19 Opéra-Comique
20 Pont de Solférino
21 Sorbonne
22 St-Julien le Pauvre
23 Place d' Italie
Q.= Quai R.= Rue
N
Aéroport du Bourget
Hippodrome de Longchamp
Versailles
Cimetière de Picpus
Bois de Vincennes
Cité Univ. et Parc Montsouris
Aéroport de Paris-Orly
ROUTES DE PRIORITÉ SONT MONTRÉES
© C. S. HAMMOND & Co., N. Y.
LES BATIGNOLLES
MONTMARTRE
NEUILLY
PASSY
AUTEUIL
ST-GERMAIN
QUARTIER LATIN
MONTPARNASSE
MARAIS
ST-ANTOINE
Bois de Boulogne
Seine
Pl. du Tertre
Égl. du Sacré-Coeur
Sq. St-Pierre
Moulin Rouge
Pl. Clichy
Pl. Pigalle
Circ. Médrano
Gr. Guignol
Casino de Paris
Égl. de la Trinité
Gare du Nord
Gare de l'Est
Égl. du Jésus-Christ
Pl. Pereire
Pl. Malesherbes
Parc Monceau
Cons. de Musique
Pl. de l'Europe
Gare St-Lazare
Égl. St-Augustin
Mus. Camondo
Mus. Jacquemart
Égl. St-Ferdinand
Arc de Triomphe
Pl. de l'Étoile
Pte. Dauphine
Folies-Bergère
Conc. Mayol
Hôtel Ambassador
Mus. Grévin
Thea. Gymnase
Pte. St-Martin
Pte. St-Denis
Grand Hôt.
Égl. de la Madeleine
Pal. de Élysée
Thea. Marigny
Amb. des É.-U.
Rond Point
Hôt. Continental
Pl. de Vendôme
Thea. A. B. C.
Conserv. des Arts et Métiers
Pl. de la République
Bibl. Nat'l
Halles Centrales
Pal. Royal
Pal. du Louvre
Sq. du Temple
Circ. d'Hiver
Archives Nat'l
Mus. Carnavalet
Hôt. George V
Égl. Américaine
Mus. Galiera
Mus. Guimet
Grand Palais
Petit Pal.
Pl. de la Concorde
Jardin des Tuileries
Ch. des Députés
Pl. du Trocadéro
Pal. de Chaillot
Tour Eiffel
Parc du Champ de Mars
Gare des Invalides
Pal. Bourbon
Gare d'Orsay
Éc. des Beaux Arts
L'Institut
Île de la Cité
Notre Dame (Cathéd.)
Île St-Louis
Pl. des Vosges
Égl. St-Gervais
Égl. St-Paul
Pl. de la Bastille
Gare de la Bastille
Hôtel Biron (Mus. Rodin)
Hôtel des Invalides
Égl. St-Germain-des-Prés
Égl. St-Séverin
Hôtel Lutetia
Égl. St-Sulpice
Odéon
Mus. de Cluny
Coll. de France
Égl. St-Étienne-du-Mont
Panthéon
Arènes de Lutèce
Pal. du Luxembourg
Sénat
Jardin du Luxembourg
Gare d'Orléans
Jardin des Plantes
Mus. d'Orléans
Mosquee de Paris
Gare de Lyon
La Salpêtrière
Éc. d'Arts et Métiers
Manuf. des Gobelins
Observatoire
Catacombes
Cimetière du Montparnasse
Gare Montparnasse
Institut Pasteur
Sq. St-Lambert
Éc. Militaire
UNESCO
Pasteur Mon.
Mus. Balzac
Pl. Rodin
Pal. des Sports
Statue de la Liberté
Allée des Cygnes

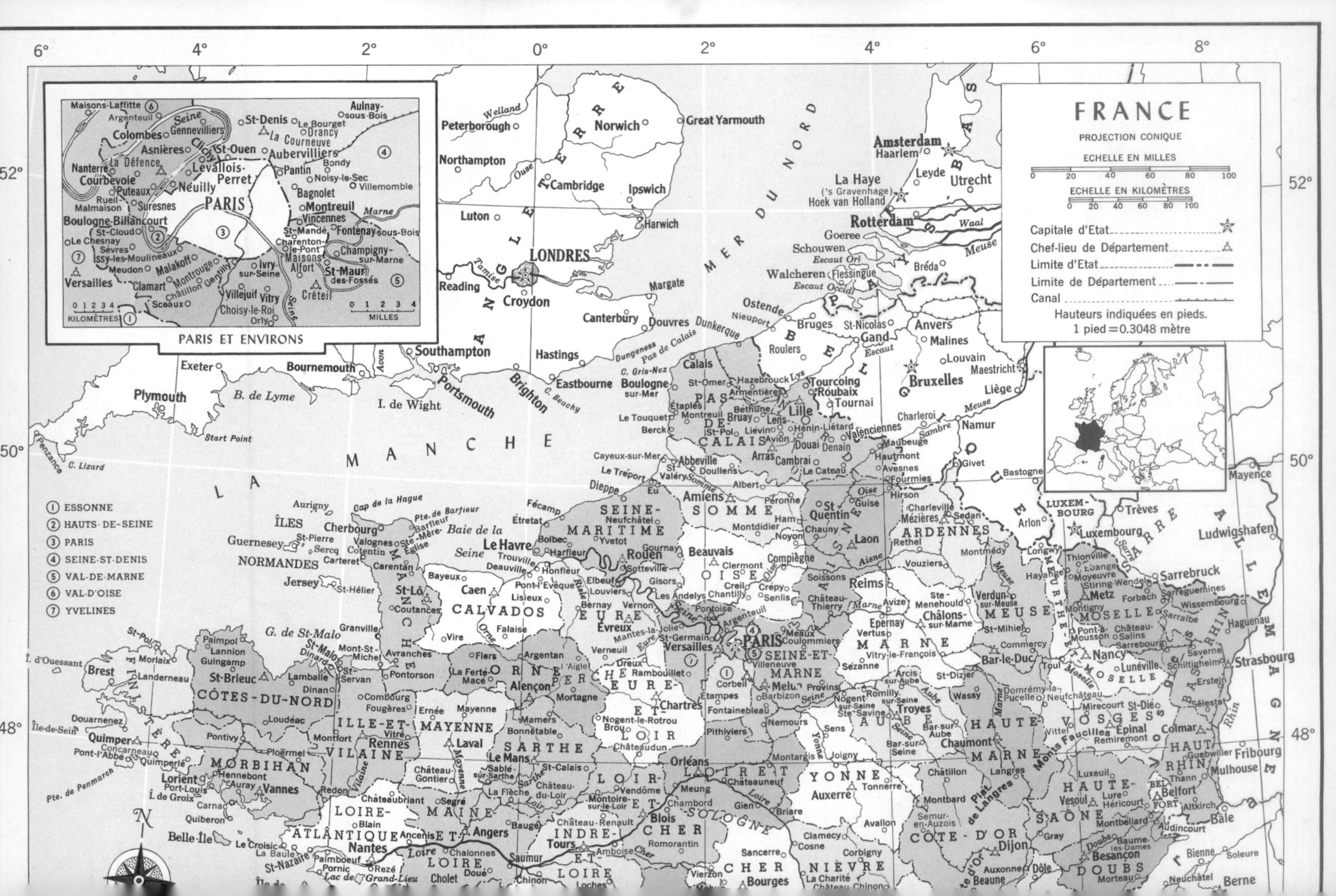

FRANCE
PROJECTION CONIQUE
ECHELLE EN MILLES
0 20 40 60 80 100
ECHELLE EN KILOMÈTRES
0 20 40 60 80 100
Capitale d'Etat
Chef-lieu de Département
Limite d'Etat
Limite de Département
Canal
Hauteurs indiquées en pieds.
1 pied = 0.3048 mètre
PARIS ET ENVIRONS
Maisons-Laffitte
Argenteuil
Colombes
Gennevilliers
Asnières
Clichy
St-Ouen
St-Denis
Le Bourget
Drancy
La Courneuve
Aubervilliers
Aulnay-sous-Bois
Nanterre
La Défence
Courbevoie
Levallois-Perret
Neuilly
Puteaux
Rueil-Malmaison
Suresnes
PARIS
Pantin
Bondy
Noisy-le-Sec
Villemomble
Bagnolet
Montreuil
Vincennes
Marne
Boulogne-Billancourt
St-Cloud
Le Chesnay
Sèvres
Issy-les-Moulineaux
Meudon
Malakoff
Montrouge
Gentilly
Châtillon
Clamart
Sceaux
Versailles
St-Mandé
Fontenay-sous-Bois
Charenton-le-Pont
Maisons-Alfort
Champigny-sur-Marne
St-Maur-des-Fossés
Ivry-sur-Seine
Villejuif
Vitry
Créteil
Choisy-le-Roi
Orly
Seine
0 1 2 3 4 KILOMÈTRES
0 1 2 3 4 MILLES
① ESSONNE
② HAUTS-DE-SEINE
③ PARIS
④ SEINE-ST-DENIS
⑤ VAL-DE-MARNE
⑥ VAL-D'OISE
⑦ YVELINES
ANGLETERRE
MER DU NORD
LA MANCHE
BELGIQUE
PAYS-BAS
ALLEMAGNE
SARRE
LUXEMBOURG
Peterborough
Welland
Norwich
Great Yarmouth
Northampton
Ouse
Cambridge
Ipswich
Luton
Harwich
LONDRES
Tamise
Reading
Croydon
Margate
Canterbury
Douvres
Southampton
Hastings
Exeter
Bournemouth
Portsmouth
Brighton
Eastbourne
Plymouth
B. de Lyme
I. de Wight
Start Point
Penzance
C. Lizard
Amsterdam
Haarlem
Leyde
Utrecht
La Haye
('s Gravenhage)
Hoek van Holland
Rotterdam
Waal
Meuse
Goeree
Schouwen
Escaut Or.
Walcheren
Flessingue
Escaut Occid.
Bréda
Ostende
Nieuport
Bruges
St-Nicolas
Anvers
Malines
Gand
Escaut
Roulers
Louvain
Bruxelles
Maestricht
Liège
Tourcoing
Roubaix
Tournai
Lille
Charleroi
Namur
Sambre
Dunkerque
Pas de Calais
Dungeness
C. Gris-Nez
Calais
Boulogne-sur-Mer
St-Omer
Hazebrouck
Armentières
Béthune
Bruay
Lens
Étaples
Montreuil
Le Touquet
Berck
St-Pol
Liévin
Hénin-Liétard
Valenciennes
Maubeuge
PAS-DE-CALAIS
Avion
Douai
Denain
Arras
Cambrai
Hautmont
Avesnes
Fourmies
Le Cateau
Givet
Bastogne
Mayence
Cayeux-sur-Mer
Abbeville
Doullens
Le Tréport
St-Valéry
Somme
Albert
Dieppe
Eu
Amiens
SOMME
Péronne
St-Quentin
Guise
Oise
Hirson
Charleville
Mézières
Sedan
Arlon
LUXEM-BOURG
Trèves
Luxembourg
Ludwigshafen
Fécamp
Étretat
SEINE-MARITIME
Neufchâtel
Ham
Montdidier
Noyon
Chauny
Laon
AISNE
ARDENNES
Rethel
Montmédy
Longwy
Thionville
Hayange
Moyeuvre
Stiring-Wendel
Sarrebruck
Sarreguemines
Wissembourg
Haguenau
Aurigny
Cap de la Hague
Pte. de Barfleur
Barfleur
ÎLES
NORMANDES
Guernesey
St-Pierre
Sercq
Jersey
St-Hélier
Cherbourg
Valognes
Ste-Mère-Église
Cotentin
Carteret
Carentan
Baie de la Seine
Le Havre
Bolbec
Harfleur
Yvetot
Rouen
Gournay
Beauvais
Trouville
Deauville
Honfleur
Sotteville
Clermont
OISE
Compiègne
Soissons
Reims
Bayeux
Caen
Pont-l'Évêque
Lisieux
Elbeuf
Louviers
Gisors
Les Andelys
Creil
Chantilly
Crépy
Senlis
Château-Thierry
Avize
Ste-Menehould
Verdun-sur-Meuse
Metz
Forbach
MOSELLE
Sarralbe
St-Lô
Coutances
CALVADOS
Falaise
Orne
Vire
Bernay
Vernon
EURE
Évreux
Mantes-la-Jolie
St-Germain
Pontoise
Argenteuil
Versailles
PARIS
Meaux
Coulommiers
Épernay
Vertus
MARNE
Châlons-sur-Marne
MEUSE
St-Mihiel
Commercy
Pont-à-Mousson
Château-Salins
Sarrebourg
Nancy
Lunéville
Saverne
Schiltigheim
Strasbourg
Erstein
G. de St-Malo
Granville
Mont-St-Michel
Avranches
Pontorson
Flers
Argentan
La Ferté-Macé
ORNE
Alençon
L'Aigle
Verneuil
Dreux
Rambouillet
SEINE-ET-MARNE
Villeneuve
Melun
Provins
Vitry-le-François
Sézanne
Bar-le-Duc
Toul
St-Dizier
Arcis-sur-Aube
MEURTHE-ET-MOSELLE
St-Pol
Paimpol
Lannion
Morlaix
Guingamp
St-Malo
Dinard
St-Servan
Lamballe
St-Brieuc
Dinan
CÔTES-DU-NORD
Combourg
Fougères
Ernée
Mayenne
Mortagne
EURE-ET-LOIR
Chartres
Corbeil
Étampes
Barbizon
Fontainebleau
Nogent-sur-Seine
Romilly-sur-Seine
Ste-Savine
Troyes
AUBE
Wassy
Domrémy-la-Pucelle
Neufchâteau
Mirecourt
St-Dié
VOSGES
Épinal
Sélestat
Colmar
Rhin
BAS-RHIN
Î. d'Ouessant
Brest
Landerneau
FINISTÈRE
Douarnenez
Île-de-Sein
Quimper
Concarneau
Quimperlé
Pont-l'Abbé
Pte. de Penmarch
Loudéac
Pontivy
Ploërmel
MORBIHAN
Lorient
Hennebont
Port-Louis
Auray
Vannes
Î. de Groix
Carnac
Quiberon
Belle-Île
ILLE-ET-VILAINE
Montfort
Rennes
Vitré
MAYENNE
Laval
Mamers
Bonnétable
SARTHE
Le Mans
Nogent-le-Rotrou
Brou
Châteaudun
LOIR-ET-CHER
Pithiviers
Nemours
Sens
Montargis
Joigny
YONNE
Auxerre
Tonnerre
Bar-sur-Aube
Bar-sur-Seine
Chaumont
HAUTE-MARNE
Langres
Vittel
Remiremont
Monts Faucilles
HAUT-RHIN
Guebwiller
Fribourg
Thann
Mulhouse
Redon
Vilaine
Château-Gontier
Sablé-sur-Sarthe
La Flèche
St-Calais
Château-du-Loir
Vendôme
Montoire-sur-le-Loir
LOIRET
Orléans
Meung
Châteauneuf
Gien
Briare
Loire
SOLOGNE
Châtillon
Montbard
Plat. de Langres
Luxeuil
HAUTE-SAÔNE
Vesoul
Lure
Héricourt
Belfort
Altkirch
Montbéliard
Audincourt
Bâle
Châteaubriant
Segré
LOIRE-ATLANTIQUE
Blain
Ancenis
MAINE-ET-LOIRE
Angers
Baugé
Chambord
Blois
Château-Renault
INDRE-ET-LOIRE
Tours
Amboise
Cher
Romorantin
Avallon
Semur-en-Auxois
CÔTE-D'OR
Dijon
Gray
Doubs
Baume-les-Dames
Besançon
Bienne
Soleure
Le Croisic
La Baule
St-Nazaire
Paimboeuf
Nantes
Pornic
Rezé
Lac de Grand-Lieu
Chalonnes
Saumur
Cholet
Doué
Chinon
Loches
Vierzon
CHER
Bourges
Sancerre
Cosne
Clamecy
Corbigny
NIÈVRE
La Charité
Château-Chinon
Beaune
Auxonne
Dôle
DOUBS
Morteau
Neuchâtel
Berne
6°
4°
2°
0°
2°
4°
6°
8°
52°
50°
48°

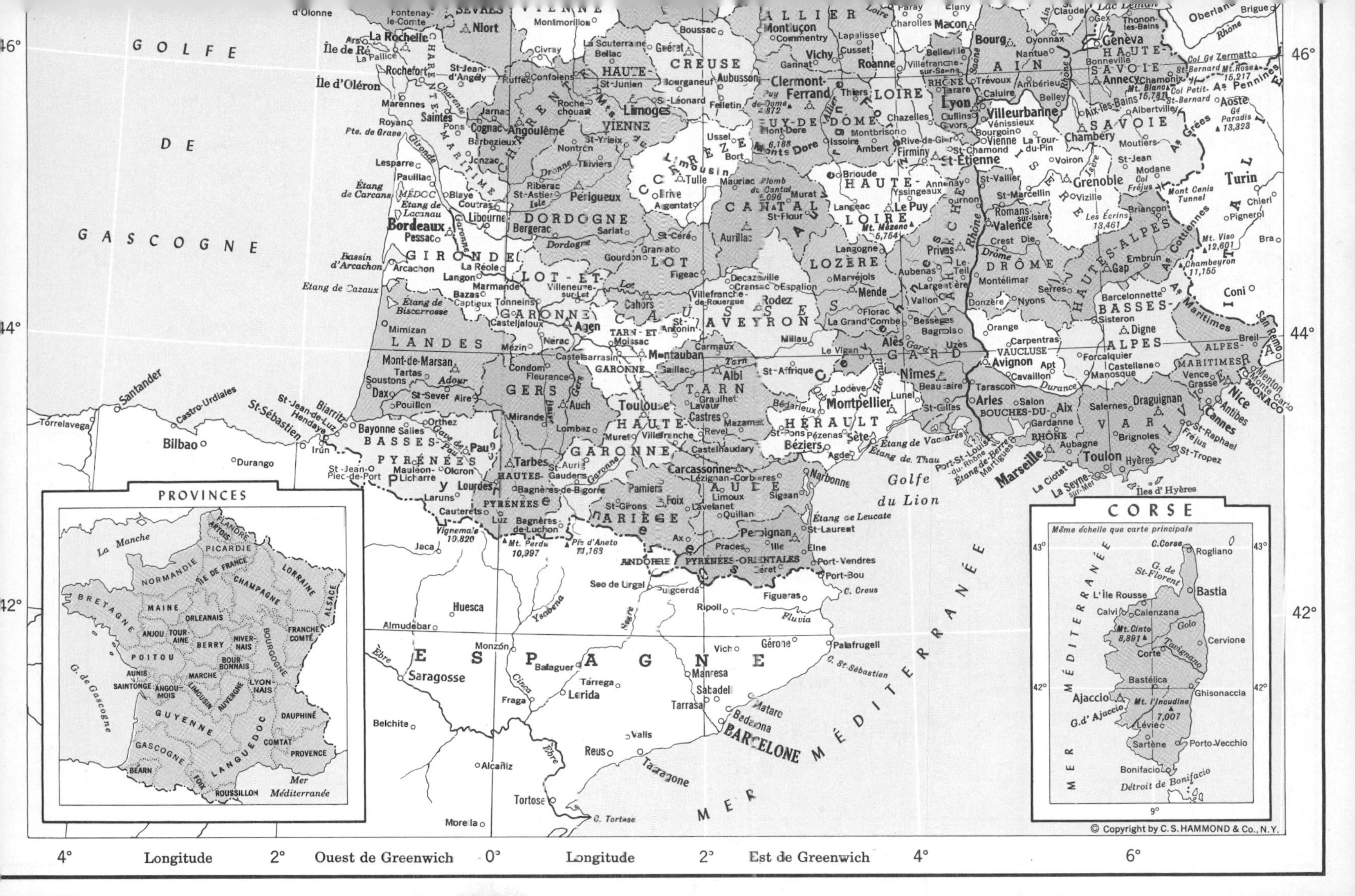

GOLFE DE GASCOGNE
Golfe du Lion
MER MÉDITERRANÉE
ESPAGNE
LANDES
GIRONDE
DORDOGNE
LOT-ET-GARONNE
GERS
BASSES-PYRÉNÉES
HAUTES-PYRÉNÉES
HAUTE-GARONNE
ARIÈGE
AUDE
PYRÉNÉES-ORIENTALES
TARN
TARN-ET-GARONNE
LOT
AVEYRON
CANTAL
LOZÈRE
HÉRAULT
GARD
HAUTE-LOIRE
PUY-DE-DÔME
CREUSE
HAUTE-VIENNE
CORRÈZE
CHARENTE
CHARENTE-MARITIME
ALLIER
LOIRE
RHÔNE
AIN
ISÈRE
DRÔME
ARDÈCHE
VAUCLUSE
BOUCHES-DU-RHÔNE
VAR
BASSES-ALPES
HAUTES-ALPES
ALPES-MARITIMES
SAVOIE
HAUTE-SAVOIE
MONACO
ANDORRE
Bordeaux
Toulouse
Marseille
Lyon
Montpellier
Nîmes
Avignon
Grenoble
Limoges
Clermont-Ferrand
Saint-Étienne
Toulon
Nice
Perpignan
Carcassonne
Pau
Bayonne
Biarritz
La Rochelle
Niort
Angoulême
Périgueux
Agen
Montauban
Albi
Rodez
Aurillac
Le Puy
Mende
Valence
Chambéry
Annecy
Geneva
Turin
Barcelone
Saragosse
Lérida
Huesca
Bilbao
Santander
Tortose
Mt. Perdu 10,997
Pic d'Aneto 11,163
Vignemale 10,820
Mt. Blanc 15,781
Mt. Viso 12,601
PROVINCES
FLANDRE
ARTOIS
PICARDIE
NORMANDIE
ÎLE DE FRANCE
CHAMPAGNE
LORRAINE
ALSACE
BRETAGNE
MAINE
ANJOU
TOURAINE
ORLÉANAIS
BERRY
NIVERNAIS
BOURGOGNE
FRANCHE-COMTÉ
POITOU
AUNIS
SAINTONGE
ANGOUMOIS
MARCHE
LIMOUSIN
BOURBONNAIS
AUVERGNE
LYONNAIS
DAUPHINÉ
GUYENNE
GASCOGNE
BÉARN
FOIX
LANGUEDOC
ROUSSILLON
COMTAT
PROVENCE
La Manche
G. de Gascogne
Mer Méditerranée
CORSE
Même échelle que carte principale
Bastia
Ajaccio
Corte
Bonifacio
Calvi
Porto-Vecchio
Mt. Cinto 8,891
Mt. l'Incudine 7,007
Détroit de Bonifacio
© Copyright by C.S.HAMMOND & Co., N.Y.
4° Longitude 2° Ouest de Greenwich 0° Longitude 2° Est de Greenwich 4° 6°

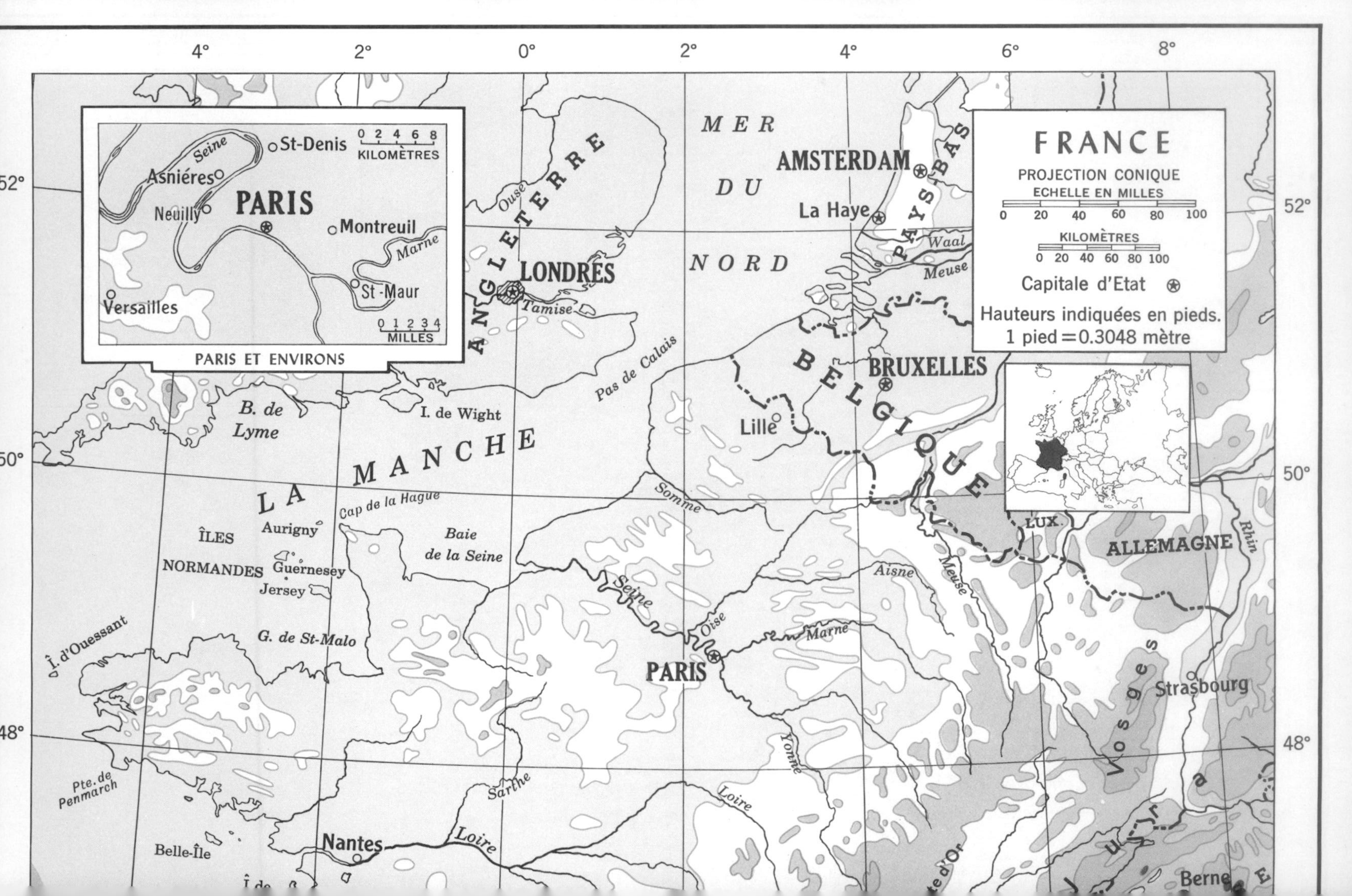
FRANCE
PROJECTION CONIQUE
ECHELLE EN MILLES
0 20 40 60 80 100
KILOMÈTRES
0 20 40 60 80 100
Capitale d'Etat
Hauteurs indiquées en pieds.
1 pied = 0.3048 mètre
PARIS ET ENVIRONS
PARIS
St-Denis
Asniéres
Neuilly
Montreuil
St-Maur
Versailles
Seine
Marne
0 2 4 6 8
KILOMÈTRES
0 1 2 3 4
MILLES
MER DU NORD
LA MANCHE
ANGLETERRE
LONDRES
Ouse
Tamise
Pas de Calais
I. de Wight
B. de Lyme
Cap de la Hague
Baie de la Seine
ÎLES NORMANDES
Aurigny
Guernesey
Jersey
G. de St-Malo
Î. d'Ouessant
Pte. de Penmarch
Belle-Île
Nantes
Loire
Sarthe
PARIS
Seine
Oise
Marne
Aisne
Yonne
Somme
Lille
BELGIQUE
BRUXELLES
PAYS BAS
AMSTERDAM
La Haye
Waal
Meuse
LUX.
ALLEMAGNE
Rhin
Strasbourg
Vosges
Jura
Berne
4°
2°
0°
2°
4°
6°
8°
52°
50°
48°

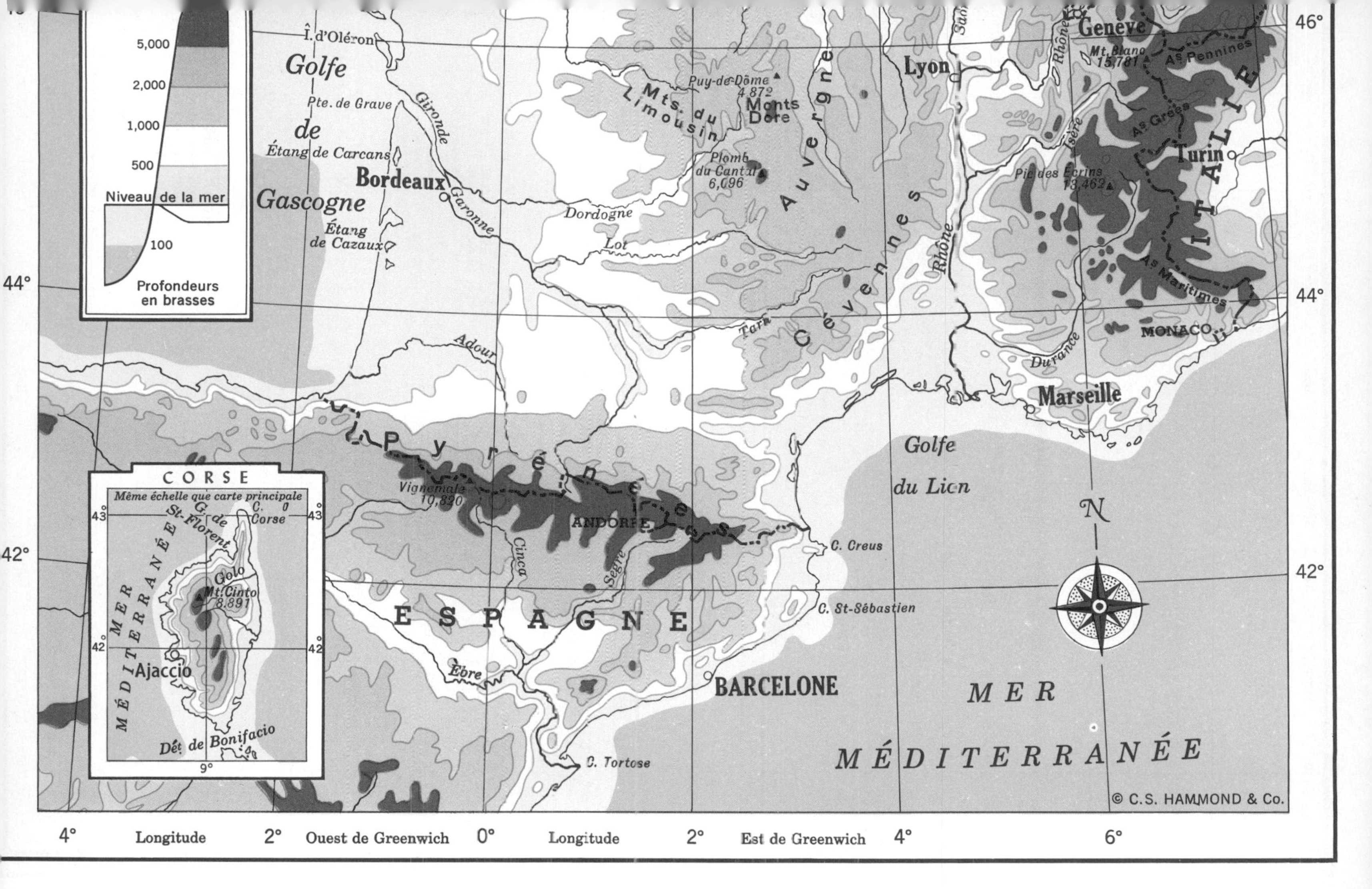

5,000
2,000
1,000
500
Niveau de la mer
100
Profondeurs en brasses
Î. d'Oléron
Golfe de Gascogne
Pte. de Grave
Gironde
Étang de Carcans
Bordeaux
Garonne
Étang de Cazaux
Dordogne
Lot
Adour
Mts. du Limousin
Puy-de-Dôme 4,872
Monts Dore
Plomb du Cantal 6,096
Auvergne
Cévennes
Tarn
Lyon
Rhône
Saône
Genève
Mt. Blanc 15,781
As. Pennines
As. Grées
Isère
Turin
ITALIE
Pic des Écrins 13,462
As. Maritimes
MONACO
Durance
Marseille
Pyrénées
Vignemale 10,820
ANDORRE
Cinca
Segre
C. Creus
Golfe du Lion
N
C. St-Sébastien
ESPAGNE
Èbre
BARCELONE
C. Tortose
MER MÉDITERRANÉE
CORSE
Même échelle que carte principale
G. de St-Florent
C. Corse
Golo
Mt. Cinto 8,891
Ajaccio
Dét. de Bonifacio
MER MÉDITERRANÉE
43°
42°
9°
46°
44°
42°
4°
Longitude
2°
Ouest de Greenwich
0°
Longitude
2°
Est de Greenwich
4°
6°

100°
120°
140°
160°
180°
160°
140°
120°
80°
60°
40°
0°
20°
40°
60°
OCÉAN GLACIAL
ARCTIQUE
N
I. Komsomolets
TERRE DU NORD
I. de la Révolution d'Octobre
I. Bolchevik
C. Tchélioushkine
IS. DE LA NOUVELLE SIBÉRIE
Is. DeLong
PÉN. DE TAÏMYR
MER DE LAPTEV
L. Taïmyr
Nordvik
Khatanga
Khatanga
Olenek
Léna
Iana
Indighirka
Kolyma
MER DE SIBÉRIE ORIENTALE
I. Wrangel
Is. Medveji
Verkhoïansk
Sredne-Kolymsk
PÉN. DES TCHOUKTCHIS
Cercle Polaire Arctique
Anadyr
Pte. Hope
Dét. de Bering
Barrow
Pte. Barrow
MER DE BEAUFORT
ÉTATS-UNIS
Ft-Yukon
Nome
Yukon
Fairbanks
ALASKA
Anchorage
I. St-Laurent
Dawson
Whitehorse
Mackenzie
Ile Borden
I. du Prce. Patrick
Lands End
I. Melville
Dét. de McClure
PÔLE MAG. NO
Dét. de Vico Melville
Ile de Banks
Golfe d'Amundsen
Ile Victoria
Grd. Lac de l'Ours
Grd. Lac de l'Esclave
UNION DES RÉPUBLIQUES
SOCIALISTES SOVIÉTIQUES
Toungouska Inférieure
Viliouï
Viliouisk
Iakoutsk
Olekminsk
Aldan
Oïmiakon
Guijiga
Okhotsk
Magadan
Toungouska Supérieure
Krasnoïarsk
L. Baïkal
Irkoutsk
Tchita
Oulan-Oude
Chilka
Amour
MER D'OKHOTSK
Nikolaïevsk
KAMCHATKA
Petropavlovsk-Kamtchatski
C. Lopatka
Komsomolsk
Khabarovsk
I. Sakhaline
IS. KOURILES
MER DE BERING
Is. Pribilof
Is. du Commandeur
Attu
ILES ALÉOUTIENNES
Golfe d'Alaska
I. Kodiak
I. du Prince de Galles
Sitka
Juneau
Prince Rupert
IS. DE LA REINE CHARLOTTE
I. Vancouver
Vancouver
Seattle
Portland
C. Mendocino
San Francisco
Los Angeles
Edmonton
Calgary
Saskatoon
Regina
L. Athabasca
Peace
Boise
Salt Lake City
Colorado
AMÉR
CAN
ÉTATS
MEXI
Oulan-Bator
MONGOLIE
Kéroulen
GOBI (Désert)
Kharbin
Tchang-tchouen
Vladivostok
Hokkaïdo
Pékin (Peiping)
Moukden
Pao-tou
MER DU JAPON
Tien-tsin
Dairen
Tsi-nan
CORÉE DU N.
Séoul
CORÉE DU S.
Hondo
JAPON
Tokyo
Yokohama
Nagoya
Osaka
Shikoku
Kyushu
Houang-ho
Lan-tcheou
CHINE
Nankin
Wou-han
Tcheng-tou
Tchoung-king
Yang-tsé-Kiang
Changhaï
MER JAUNE
MER DE CHINE OR.
Is. Ryu-kyu (Adm. E. U.)
Tchang-cha
Fou-tcheou
Koun-ming
Canton
Taï-peï
Taï-wan (Formose)
INDE
BIRMANIE
Hanoï
MACAO (Port.)
HONG KONG (Br.)
Haï-nan
Rangoun
THAÏLANDE
NORD VIET-NAM
SUD VIET-NAM
Bangkok
CAMB.
MER DE CHINE
Saigon
G. de Siam
MER
Luçon
Manille
RÉPUBLIQUE DES PHILIPPINES
Mindanao
FÉD. DE MALAISIE
BRUNEI (Br.)
SABAH
SARAWAK
SINGAPOUR
Sumatra
Bornéo
Célèbes
ILES DE LA SONDE
INDONÉSIE
Djakarta
Java
Is. Cocos (Austr.)
I. Christmas (Austr.)
Timor
MER D'ARAFURA
IR. OCC. (Adm. Indon.)
TERR. DE NLLE. GUINÉE
PAPUA
Nouvelle-Guinée
ARCH. BISMARCK (Austr.)
IS. SALOMON (Br.)
C. York
Darwin
Is. Bonin (Adm. E. U.)
IS. MARIANNES
Guam (E. U.)
ILES CAROLINES
Is. Palau
TERRITOIRE DES ILES DU PACIFIQUE:
(E. U.-Terr. sous tutelle)
I. Wake (E. U.)
IS. MARSHALL
IS. GILBERT (Br.)
Is. Santa Cruz (Br.)
OCÉAN PACIFIQUE
Is. Midway (E. U.)
Ligne du Changement de Date
ÉTATS-UNIS
IS. HAWAÏ
Honolulu
I. Hawaï
I. Johnston (E. U.)
I. Palmyra (E. U.)
I. Fanning (Br.)
I. Washington (Br.)
I. Christmas (E. U.-Br.)
I. Howland (E. U.)
I. Baker (E. U.)
I. Canton (E. U.-Br.)
I. Jarvis (E. U.)
IS. PHOENIX (E. U.-Br.)
I. Malden (E. U.-Br.)
I. Starbuck (E. U.-Br.)
IS. ELLICE (Br.)
I. Rotuma (Br.)
SAMOA OCC.
Tutuila (E. U.)
IS. FIJI (Br.)
IS. TONGA (Br.)
IS. COOK (N.Z.)
ILES DE LA SOCIÉTÉ (Br.)
Tahiti
Papeete
IS. AUSTRALES (Tubuai) (Fr.)
ILES MARQUISES (Fr.)
ARCHPEL DES TOUAMOTOU (Fr.)
I. Pitcairn (Br.)
I. Ducie (Br.)
I. de Pâques (Chili)
Tropique du Capric
Tropique du Cancer
I. Guadalupe (Mex.)
C. San Lucas
Guadalajara
Méxi
Is. Revilla Gigedo (Mex.)
I. Clipperton (Fr.)
Equateur
MER DE CORAIL
NLLES. HEBRIDES (Br. & Fr.)
Nouvelle-Calédonie
Is. Loyauté (Fr.)
Townsville
Port Hedland
Rockhampton
OCÉAN INDIEN
AUSTRALIE
Brisbane
Perth
Kalgoorlie
Fremantle
C. Leeuwin
Albany
Adélaïde
Murray
Newcastle
Sydney
Canberra
Melbourne
Dét. de Bass
Tasmanie
Hobart
MER DE TASMAN
I. Norfolk (Austr.)
I. Lord Howe (Austr.)
Is. Kermadec (N.Z.)
Cap Nord
Auckland
Ile du Nord
NOUVELLE-ZÉLANDE
Wellington
Ile du Sud
Christchurch
Dunedin
Is. Chatham (N.Z.)
I. Stewart
Is. Bounty (N.Z.)
Is. Auckland (N.Z.)
Is. Antipodes (N.Z.)
I. Campbell (N.Z.)
I. Macquarie (Austr.)
OCÉAN PACIFIQUE
MAPPEMONDE
PROJECTION DE MERCATOR
ÉCHELLE A L'EQUATEUR
MILLES
0 500 1000 1500 2000 2500
KILOMÈTRES
0 500 1000 1500 2000 2500
Capitales d' Etats
© C.S. HAMMOND & Co., Maplewood, N.J.
Territoire à langue française
Is. Balleny
I. Scott
Cercle Polaire Antarctique
ANTARCTIQUE
Longitude Est de Greenwich
Longitude Ouest de Greenwich
100°
120°
140°
160°
180°
160°
140°
120°

GROENLAND
(Dan.)
MER DU GROENLAND
MER DE BARENTS
MER DE NORVÈGE
SVALBARD
(SPITZBERG)
(Nor.)
ARCHIPEL FRANÇOIS JOSEPH
I. Graham Bell
I. Wilczek
Terre du Nord-Est
I. Edge
Spitzberg Occ.
I. de l'Ours
(Nor.)
I. Jan Mayen
(Nor.)
NOVAÏA ZEMLIA
MER DE KARA
MER DE LINCOLN
TERRE DE PEARY
TERRE DU ROI FRÉDÉRIC VIII
TERRE DU ROI CHRISTIAN IX
TERRE DU ROI FRÉDÉRIC VI
Bassin de Kane
Thule
Baie de Baffin
Upernavik
Godhavn
Détroit de Davis
Godthaab
Frederikshaab
Julianehaab
C. Farewell
C. Chidley
Angmagssalik
Reykjavik
ISLANDE
Détroit du Danemark
Bras Scoresby
Cercle Polaire Arctique
Is. Féroé
(Dan.)
Is. Shetland
Is. Orcades
Is. Hébrides
ROYAUME UNI
Glasgow
IRLANDE
Londres
PAYS-BAS
MER DU NORD
Copenhague
Berlin
Paris
La Manche
G. de Gascogne
C. Finisterre
FRANCE
ESPAGNE
PORTUGAL
Lisbonne
Madrid
Barcelone
Marseille
Milan
Rome
Vienne
Belgrade
Bucarest
Odessa
Athènes
Istanbul
Ankara
TURQUIE
CHYPRE
MER MÉDITERRANÉE
Sardaigne
Sicile
Crete
Gibraltar
Dét. de Gibraltar
C. St-Vincent
Alger
Tunis
Tripoli
Benghasi
Alexandrie
Le Caire
Rabat
Casablanca
MAROC
ALGÉRIE
LIBYE
TUNISIE
IFNI
SAHARA ESP.
El Aaiún
Is. CANARIES
(Esp.)
Madère
(Port.)
IS. AÇORES
(Port.)
C. Blanc
Nouakchott
MAURITANIE
MALI
NIGER
TCHAD
SAHARA
AFRIQUE
Dakar
SÉN.
GAMBIE
GUINÉE PORT.
SIERRA LEONE
Monrovia
LIBERIA
Abidjan
CÔTE D'IVOIRE
HAUTE VOLTA
GHANA
TOGO
Accra
Lagos
NIGERIA
Bamako
Niamey
Ft-Lamy
Khartoum
SOUDAN
ÉTHIOPIE
Addis Abeba
SOMALIE
Mogadiscio
KENYA
OUGANDA
Nairobi
CAMEROUN
Yaoundé
RÉP. CENTRAFR.
RIO MUNI
GABON
Golfe de Guinée
Brazzaville
Léopoldville
CONGO
Cabinda
(Ang.)
Loanda
Nova Lisboa
ANGOLA
ZAMBIA
Elisabethville
Tanganyika
TANZANIA
Dar-es Salam
Zanzibar
Salisbury
MOZAMBIQUE
Canal de Mozambique
SUD-OUEST AFRICAIN
Windhoek
Walvis Bay
PROT. DE BECH.
Pretoria
Johannesburg
Lourenco Marques
SWAZILD.
Durban
BASUTOLD.
AFRIQUE DU SUD
Cape Town
C. de Bonne Espérance
Port Elizabeth
(Prov. du Cap)
Orange
RÉP. MALGACHE
Tananarive
Madagascar
C. Ste-Marie
Is. Comores (Fr.)
SEYCHELLES
(Br.)
IS. MALDIVES
Is. Tchagos
Is. Rodrigues (I. Maurice)
I. Maurice (Br.)
I. de la Réunion (Fr.)
OCÉAN INDIEN
I. Amsterdam
(Fr.)
I. St-Paul
(Fr.)
Is. Prince Edouard
(S. Afr.)
Is. Crozet
(Fr.)
I. Kerguélen
(Fr.)
Is. McDonald
(Austr.)
I. Heard
(Austr.)
I. Bouvet
(Nor.)
NORVÈGE
SUÈDE
FINLANDE
G. de Botnie
Stockholm
Oslo
Helsinki
Tromsö
Is. Lofoten
C. Nord
Mourmansk
MER BLANCHE
Arkhangelsk
L. Onega
L. Ladoga
Leningrad
Tallinn
Riga
Vilnius
Minsk
Varsovie
POLOGNE
MER BALTIQUE
Moscou
Kalinin
Gorki
Kazan
Kiev
Kharkov
Voronej
Donetsk
Rostov
Volgograd
Saratov
Astrakhan
Tbilissi
Bakou
MER NOIRE
MER CASPIENNE
Perm
Sverdlovsk
Tcheliabinsk
Magnitogorsk
Oufa
Kouibychev
Rés. Kouibychev
UNION DES RÉPUBLIQUES SOCIALISTES SOVIÉTIQUES
EUROPE
ASIE
Omsk
Tomsk
Novo-Sibirsk
Semipalatinsk
Karaganda
L. Balkhach
MER D'ARAL
Alma-Ata
Tachkent
Douchanbe
Ouroumtchi
SINKIANG
CHINE
TIBET
Lhassa
Salekhard
Doudinka
Igarka
Ob
Ienisséi
Petchora
Dvina du Nord
Volga
Oural
Dniepr
Irtych
Syr
Amou
Tehran
IRAN
Bagdad
IRAK
SYRIE
LIB.
ISR.
JOR.
Bassora
KOWEIT
ARABIE SAOUDITE
Er Riad
La Mecque
MER ROUGE
Suez
RÉP. ARABE UNIE
ÉGYPTE
Mascate
Karachi
AFGHANISTAN
Kaboul
PAKISTAN
Rawalpindi
Delhi
New Delhi
Ahmadabad
NÉPAL
Gange
Calcutta
Bombay
INDE
Hyderabad
Bangalore
Madras
Golfe du Bengale
MER D'OMAN
Socotra
(Arabie du Sud)
ARABIE DU SUD
SOM. FR.
IS. LAQUEDIVES
(Inde)
C. Comorin
CEYLAN
Colombo
OCÉAN ATLANTIQUE
Tropique du Cancer
Tropique du Capricorne
Equateur
Is. Bermudes
(Br.)
IS. DU CAP VERT
(Port.)
I. Ascension
(Ste. Hélèna)
I. Ste-Hélèna
(Br.)
Tristan da Cunha
(Br.)
I. Gough
(Br.)
Georgie du Sud
(Br.)
IS. SANDWICH DU SUD
(Br.)
Is. Orcades du Sud
(Br.)
Is. Shetland du Sud
PÉN. ARCTIQUE
Cercle Polaire Antarctique
C. Batterbee
PÉN. DE RIISER-LARSEN
Longitude Ouest de Greenwich
Longitude Est de Greenwich
QUÉBEC
LABRADOR
Dét. de Belle-Isle
TERRE-NEUVE
St-Johns
C. Race
G. St-Laurent
St-Pierre et Miquelon (Fr.)
Halifax
Ottawa
Boston
New York
Philadelphie
Norfolk
C. Hatteras
BAHAMA (Br.)
RÉP. DOM.
PUERTO RICO (E. U.)
Guadeloupe (Fr.)
Martinique (Fr.)
ANT. NÉERLAND.
TRIN. & TOB.
Caracas
VENEZUELA
Georgetown
Paramaribo
Cayenne
GUY.
SUR.
G. FR.
Manaus
Belém
Amazone
Fortaleza
Natal
C. de São Roque
Recife
Salvador
AMÉRIQUE DU SUD
BRÉSIL
Brasília
La Paz
BOLIVIE
Sucre
São Paulo
Belo Horizonte
Rio de Janeiro
Santos
PARAGUAY
Asunción
Tucumán
Córdoba
Rosario
Pôrto Alegre
URUGUAY
Montevideo
Rio de la Plata
Buenos Aires
La Plata
Bahia Blanca
ARGENTINE
Rawson
Sta. Cruz
IS. FALKLAND (Br.)
Stanley
Terre de Feu
Cap Horn
Détroit de Drake
Dét. d'Hudson
60°
40°
20°
0°
80°

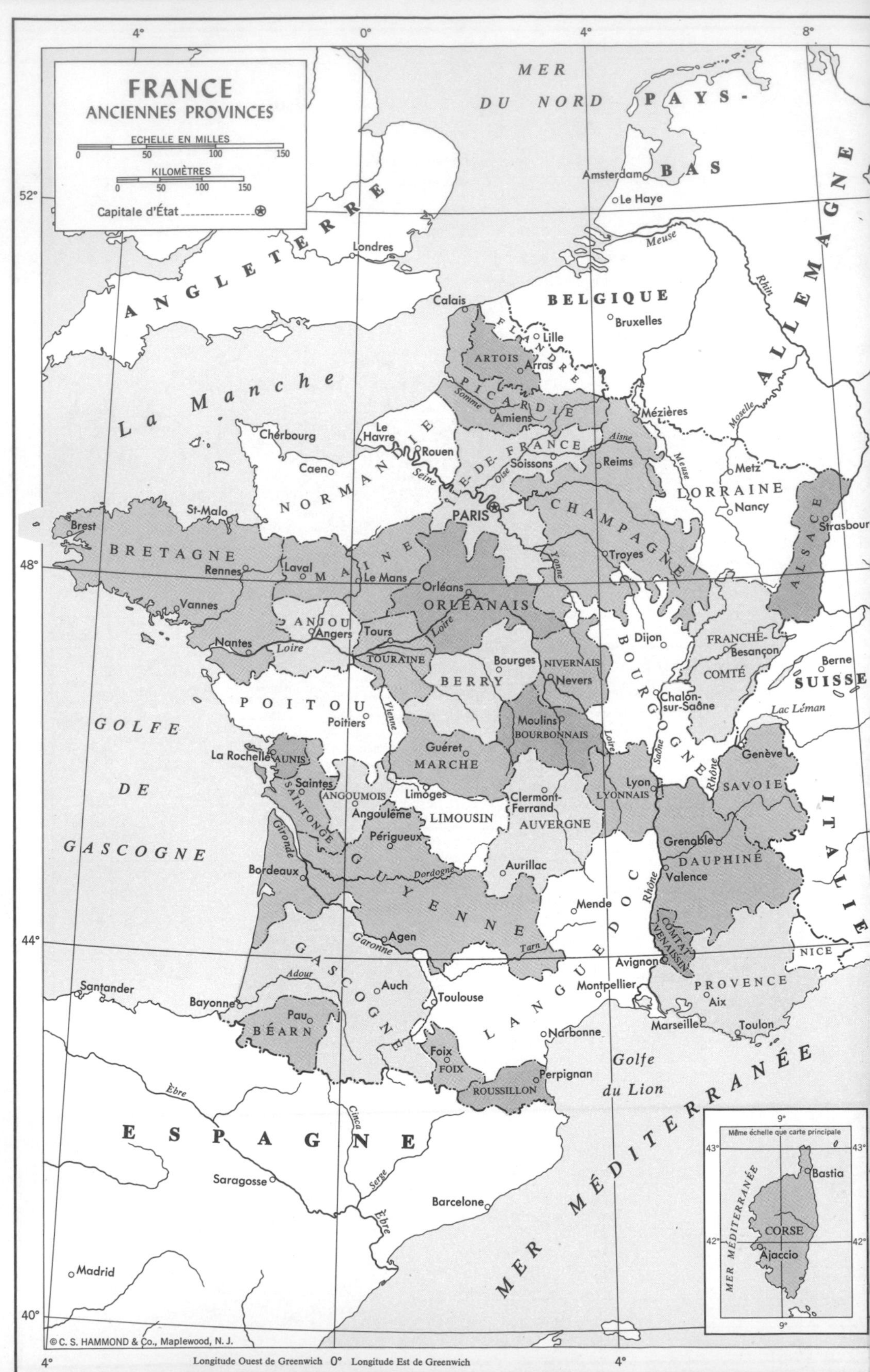

FRANCE
ANCIENNES PROVINCES
ECHELLE EN MILLES
KILOMÈTRES
Capitale d'État
MER DU NORD
PAYS-BAS
Amsterdam
Le Haye
ANGLETERRE
Londres
BELGIQUE
Bruxelles
ALLEMAGNE
Calais
FLANDRE
Lille
ARTOIS
Arras
PICARDIE
Amiens
La Manche
Cherbourg
Le Havre
Rouen
Caen
NORMANDIE
ILE-DE-FRANCE
Soissons
Reims
Mézières
Metz
LORRAINE
Nancy
ALSACE
Strasbourg
PARIS
CHAMPAGNE
Troyes
St-Malo
Brest
BRETAGNE
Rennes
Laval
MAINE
Le Mans
Orléans
ORLÉANAIS
Vannes
ANJOU
Angers
Tours
Nantes
TOURAINE
Bourges
BERRY
NIVERNAIS
Nevers
Dijon
BOURGOGNE
FRANCHE-COMTÉ
Besançon
Berne
SUISSE
Lac Léman
POITOU
Poitiers
Chalon-sur-Saône
Moulins
BOURBONNAIS
GOLFE DE GASCOGNE
La Rochelle
AUNIS
Guéret
MARCHE
Genève
SAVOIE
Saintes
SAINTONGE
ANGOUMOIS
Angoulême
Limoges
LIMOUSIN
Clermont-Ferrand
AUVERGNE
Lyon
LYONNAIS
ITALIE
Périgueux
Grenoble
DAUPHINÉ
Valence
Bordeaux
GUYENNE
Aurillac
Mende
LANGUEDOC
Agen
COMTAT VENAISSIN
NICE
Avignon
GASCOGNE
Auch
Toulouse
Montpellier
PROVENCE
Aix
Santander
Bayonne
Pau
BÉARN
Narbonne
Marseille
Toulon
Foix
FOIX
Perpignan
ROUSSILLON
Golfe du Lion
MER MÉDITERRANÉE
ESPAGNE
Saragosse
Barcelone
Madrid
Même échelle que carte principale
Bastia
CORSE
Ajaccio
Loire
Seine
Somme
Oise
Aisne
Meuse
Moselle
Rhin
Yonne
Vienne
Saône
Rhône
Gironde
Dordogne
Garonne
Tarn
Adour
Èbre
Cinca
Serge
Longitude Ouest de Greenwich 0° Longitude Est de Greenwich